Active Directory™ Programming

Gil Kirkpatrick

SAMS

A Division of Macmillan USA
201 W. 103rd St., Indianapolis, IN 46290.

Active Directory™ Programming
Copyright ©2000 by Sams Publishing

International Standard Book Number: 0-672-31587-4

Library of Congress Catalog Card Number: 98-89583

Printed in the United States of America

First Printing: April 2000

03   02   01   00   4   3   2   1

Trademarks

Warning and Disclaimer

ASSOCIATE PUBLISHER
Bradley Jones

EXECUTIVE EDITOR
Chris Webb

DEVELOPMENT EDITOR
Matthew Purcell

MANAGING EDITOR
Lisa Wilson

PROJECT EDITOR
Gayle Johnson

COPY EDITOR
Mike Henry

INDEXER
Cheryl Landes

PROOFREADER
Katherin Bidwell

TECHNICAL EDITOR
Greg Guntle

TEAM COORDINATOR
Meggo Barthlow

MEDIA DEVELOPER
Maggie Molloy

INTERIOR DESIGNER
Gary Adair

COVER DESIGNER
Aren Howell

COPY WRITER
Eric Borgert

LAYOUT TECHNICIAN
Darin Crone

Overview

Contents

Dedication

To Kiry, Molly, and Scott. And a player to be named later.

Acknowledgments

Putting together a book like *Active Directory Programming* is a big undertaking, and it doesn't get done by just one person. Probably 30 people, many of whom I have never met, have had their hands in this project at one point or another.

First, I have to thank the unknown person at Microsoft who pointed Macmillan USA in my direction when Macmillan was asking around for an Active Directory "expert" to write a book about programming for Active Directory. Whoever you are, thank you for thinking of me. Thanks also to Trina "T-Bone" Tobias, formerly Product Marketing Manager at NetPro, for making the connection and passing along the opportunity.

When I started this book at the end of 1998, I was NetPro's architect and lead engineer for Directory Analyzer for Active Directory, the first and only monitoring and troubleshooting product for Active Directory. Leading a large software project is a significant commitment, and by any conventional logic, I had no business taking on an outside project. But NetPro is an unconventional organization founded and run by unconventional people. Joanne Carthey, President, CEO, and Chief Defier of Convention at NetPro, has always pushed people to stretch their abilities and to take on the seemingly impossible. When I mentioned that I had the opportunity to write a book, Joanne winced but gave me her support and encouragement. Thank you, Joanne, for creating an organization that allows people to achieve things far beyond their expectations.

Many other NetPro people helped out on this book. Dana Wolf and Matt Celupica wrote a ton of sample code, which you will find on the enclosed CD-ROM. Thank you both for your midnight contributions. Clay Lyons, Webmaster extraordinaire at NetPro, created most of the illustrations in this book, all while juggling an over-full work and school schedule. You can check out his work at www.netpro.com and www.mightycreative.net. Rom Doerpholz and Rich Hoey recovered my machine more than a few times after the inevitable catastrophic failures—oh, the wonders of pre-Beta operating systems! Adele Revella, Christine McDermott, and Beth West also helped out tremendously on the marketing of this book, and I thank them all for their unsolicited (and uncompensated) efforts. Special thanks to Jim Cassidy for taking over as project lead on Directory

Analyzer and seeing it through to a successful completion. I also thank all the other NetPro people for their encouragement and support.

Many people at Microsoft also gave me encouragement and support. Margaret Johnson and Dave Thompson, Group Program Manager and General Manager, respectively, of the Server Products Group at Microsoft, were incredibly helpful in lining up people for me to work with at Microsoft. Ed Yoon and Steve Adler chased down the answers to my numerous questions. Stuart Kwan and Mark Brown spent the time to help me understand some of the thornier details of both DNS and Active Directory. Finally, I have to thank Dave Straube, lead developer of Active Directory (now semi-retired), for helping me understand the ins and outs of the Active Directory implementation. Without Dave's in-depth understanding and willingness to help out, neither this book nor Directory Analyzer would have been possible.

A veritable army of people at Macmillan USA helped get *Active Directory Programming* out the door. My heartfelt thanks go to Chris Webb and Matt Purcell for coaching me through my first book and for tolerating the innumerable delays. Matt teamed up with Gayle Johnson and Mike Henry to turn my tortured prose into something understandable. Greg Guntle was the technical editor for this book, and I am consistently amazed at the things he knows that I don't. Thanks also to Katie Robinson, Tina Perry, and Mandie Rowell for their formatting efforts.

I have to give special thanks to my parents for their continuous support and encouragement. My dad read one of the early chapters and promptly pronounced it "geek-speak," but that didn't stop both my mom and dad from cheering me on through the whole process. I love you both.

Finally, I have to thank Kiry, my wife, for her unfathomable patience, understanding, support, and encouragement. Working on this book kept me away from home almost every night and weekend for close to a year, leaving Kiry to manage the house, the children, friends, social commitments, and everything else that I studiously ignored in the name of "getting the book done." I am blessed to have you in my life, and I love you forever.

About the Author

Gil Kirkpatrick is Director of Engineering at NetPro. He recently was architect and lead engineer for Directory Analyzer for Active Directory, the first and only monitoring and troubleshooting tool for Active Directory.

Kirkpatrick's professional software experience dates back to 1976, when he started writing applications and software tools in DataBasic for the Pick operating system. Since then, he has had the good fortune to design and develop many different kinds of software, including embedded real-time systems, network protocols, compilers, distributed databases, and client/server applications. For the last eight years, he has focused on commercial enterprise-class directory-based applications and directory-management software.

Kirkpatrick lives in Fountain Hills, Arizona with Kiry, his wife, and their two children, Molly and Scott.

Foreword

To most readers, the Active Directory service of the Windows 2000 Server operating system is best known for its role in making Windows networks more scalable and easier to manage. What might be less well-known, however, is that the technologies that help Active Directory fulfill its primary mission also make it an ideal platform on which to develop and deploy applications that deliver significant total cost of ownership (TCO) savings.

To lower TCO, companies need applications that are more aware of the environment in which they are deployed, that can sense and adapt to changes, and that can share information about themselves with other applications. For example, client applications must be able to find resources such as printers and databases dynamically—regardless of where the resources happen to be running at the time. Applications must be able to store users' preferences in such a way that when users roam between locations, they have the same experiences regardless of the machine they use. Applications should use standards-based directory services to store, use, and share information about users, machines, application components, and infrastructure services. And applications must be able to sense the current role of the current user within the company and behave accordingly. Active Directory provides applications that have a platform for delivering all these capabilities.

Indeed, Active Directory enables applications to publish the names and locations of services they provide so that clients can locate and use services dynamically. Active Directory allows applications to take advantage of the multimaster replication technologies used by Active Directory to store copies of a user's profile automatically throughout the network. Active Directory also enables administrators to add new types of objects and to extend existing objects with new attributes, enabling Active Directory to be a consolidation point for reducing a company's number of directories. Finally, the Group Policy features of Active Directory enable administrators to define sets of applications, including specific configurations, that users should have available based on their location in the tree, the member domain, the site at which they are present, and the Windows 2000 security groups to which they belong.

Despite all these benefits of Active Directory-enabled applications, there is one downside: None occurs automatically. Each opportunity listed here requires that developers design and build their applications in specific ways that integrate with Active Directory. Fortunately, Microsoft has provided several powerful application programming interfaces to Active Directory. These include support for the industry-standard Lightweight Directory Access Protocol (LDAP) and the COM-based Active Directory Services Interface (ADSI).

Even more fortunate, Gil Kirkpatrick has written this valuable book that describes both how to use the APIs supported by Active Directory and how to think about key Active Directory paradigms. Understanding these paradigms is more important than it might seem. Standards-based directory services such as Active Directory organize data differently than databases, and features such as multimaster replication can have surprising side effects if they are not accounted for in an application's design. None of the paradigms is difficult to understand with practice and a book such as this. The knowledge you gain will almost certainly become more valuable over time as Windows 2000 and Active Directory proliferate. The Active Directory team at Microsoft appreciates Gil's hard work—and your interest in learning more about developing Active Directory-enabled applications!

Peter Houston
Lead Product Manager for Active Directory
Microsoft Corporation

Preface

Writing a book about Active Directory was about the last thing on my mind at the end of 1998. I was the architect and engineering lead for a new directory monitoring product for Active Directory at NetPro, I had two kids under the age of three (read: sleep deprivation), and each interim build of NT 5 I received from Microsoft was a new and frustrating adventure. I was your basic, busy, overstressed software guy. When someone at Microsoft suggested to Macmillan that I write this book, my first reaction was, "Oh, right—like I've got the time."

But as I thought about it, it was clear that 1) many developers were going to be writing applications using Active Directory, 2) the existing documentation from Microsoft was lacking (it has since improved a lot), and 3) this was an opportunity I couldn't pass up. I was in the unique position of having access to the development and program management team for Active Directory, and passing along what I was learning seemed like a great idea.

The goal of *Active Directory Programming* was to be the complete reference guide for C++ programmers writing Active Directory applications, and to be published before Windows 2000 shipped. As I started writing this book, I discovered that there was a lot more to Active Directory than I had experienced, much of it undocumented. The more questions I asked the folks at Microsoft, the more I discovered I didn't know. The chapters started getting longer and longer. I finally had to stop adding topics to the book so that I could get it to press by the time Windows 2000 was released to manufacturing. The result is, I think, a good introduction to Active Directory programming, and a fairly complete reference guide to the various Active Directory APIs. It is not, as I had originally hoped, the complete and final word on Active Directory programming for C++ programmers. Perhaps the next edition of *Active Directory Programming* will measure up to that goal.

Gil Kirkpatrick

Tell Us What You Think!

As the reader of this book, *you* are our most important critic and commentator. We value your opinion and want to know what we're doing right, what we could do better, what areas you'd like to see us publish in, and any other words of wisdom you're willing to pass our way.

As an associate publisher for Sams Publishing, I welcome your comments. You can fax, email, or write me directly to let me know what you did or didn't like about this book— as well as what we can do to make our books stronger.

Please note that I cannot help you with technical problems related to the topic of this book, and that due to the high volume of mail I receive, I might not be able to reply to every message.

When you write, please be sure to include this book's title and author as well as your name and phone or fax number. I will carefully review your comments and share them with the author and editors who worked on the book.

Fax: (317) 581-4770

Email: adv_prog@mcp.com

Mail: Bradley Jones
Associate Publisher
Sams Publishing
201 West 103rd Street
Indianapolis, IN 46290 USA

Introduction

If you're reading this introduction, I'll assume that you are either contemplating or have already started a programming project that will use Active Directory. If that is true, and you are programming in C or C++, you are my target reader, and frankly, you should just close this book and buy it. But if you don't want to take my word for it, read the remainder of the Introduction and flip through the rest of the book.

There has been a lot of noise about Active Directory over the last couple of years. Active Directory is at the heart of the "Digital Nervous System," Microsoft's vision of the computer network of the future. The Digital Nervous System can make organizations run faster and jump higher by improving communications with customers, speeding communications within the organization, and optimizing business processes. Even when you read past the marketing hype, it's a compelling vision, and it isn't just smoke and mirrors.

But what if your company isn't building a "Digital Nervous System"? What if you're just trying to make your homegrown factory-floor automation system work with Windows 2000? Or what if you're trying to make your Human Resources system easier to use so that the HR people don't have to enter the same employee information three different times? What if you're writing some tools to make it easier for your network administrators to find out who hasn't been changing their passwords frequently enough? What if you already have a network directory, but your company is deploying Windows 2000 and you need to synchronize the two directories? These are all applications that can benefit from using Active Directory.

In fact, there are several reasons why all your applications should integrate with Active Directory, even if you aren't buying into the whole Digital Nervous System vision:

- Integrating your applications with Active Directory can make them more secure and easier to use.
- Integrating your applications with Active Directory can make them easier to install and manage.
- Using Active Directory in your applications can make them easier to write and maintain.

Besides, everyone else is doing it, so why not you?

I have been working with Active Directory for the last couple of years, and I have become convinced that integrating your applications with Active Directory is a Good Thing. There is no reason for you to write another INI-file-parsing routine again. You don't have to lament the fact that your boss gets different user preference settings when she runs your application from home because you store the settings in the Registry. You also don't have to make your network administrator wander from PC to PC installing the latest upgrade to your application. Integrating your applications with Active Directory can solve these problems, and *Active Directory Programming* can show you how.

I hope you have as much fun with Active Directory as I've had.

How This Book Is Organized

Active Directory Programming is broken into five parts. Part I, "Active Directory Fundamentals," covers the basics of Active Directory, including terminology, the relationship between Active Directory and DNS, the Active Directory security model, and a road map to interesting bits of information contained in Active Directory.

Part II, "The Contents of Active Directory," describes the structure and contents of Active Directory. It lists the different kinds of objects you can find in the directory "out of the box" and describes their various attributes.

Part III, "Active Directory Services Interface," is a reference section for Active Directory Services Interfaces (ADSI). ADSI is Microsoft's preferred method for accessing Active Directory. ADSI is a COM-based API that exposes most of the facilities of Active Directory in a clean object-oriented form. If you haven't done any COM programming, don't worry. ADSI is quite simple to use after you get a couple of basic concepts down. Even though ADSI is object-oriented, you can still use it from C with some effort, although you might find the LDAP API a better alternative.

Part IV, "Lightweight Directory Access Protocol," is a reference section for Microsoft's implementation of the LDAP API. If you are a C programmer, or if you are writing code that you hope to use with other LDAP-compliant directories, the LDAP API is the way to go. Microsoft's implementation is generally compliant with the LDAP RFCs (some of the exceptions are noted in the text), so you can feel pretty good about writing cross-directory applications with Microsoft's LDAP library.

Part V consists of two appendixes for you to reference. Appendix A lists and briefly describes all the ADSI interfaces supported by Active Directory. Appendix B lists all the LDAP functions provided by the Microsoft LDAP client library.

The enclosed CD-ROM has a lot of sample code, both LDAP and ADSI, plus a couple of neat utilities that we wrote here at NetPro. There is also an LDAP class library that I put together to make it really easy to get your C++ programs working with Active Directory. I think the class library is easier to use than either ADSI or LDAP, but then again, I wrote it, so why wouldn't I think that? The CD-ROM also contains an appendix. Appendix C provides links to the various online resources for Active Directory and LDAP programming.

Active Directory Fundamentals

IN THIS PART

CHAPTER 1

An Introduction to Network Directories

This chapter explains the concept of network directories and why network directories are central to the current generation network operating systems (NOS). If you're an experienced directory programmer and just want to get on with the specifics of programming Active Directory, feel free to skip this chapter. But if you're new to directory programming, take the time to read this chapter; it will give you some context to help clarify some of the concepts discussed later in the book.

What's a Directory?

Before getting into the details of why directories are important and how they work, it would be useful to clear up what exactly a directory is.

Simple Directories

Fundamentally, a directory is a database that contains information needed for a network and its applications to run. Every network, even a simple one, has a directory of some sort or another, and usually it has several. For instance, in NetWare 3, user name and password information is stored in a database called the Bindery. In Windows NT 4, user security information is stored in the Security Accounts Manager (SAM) database. Even though these network operating systems aren't generally considered directory based, they both use simple directories to store user and network configuration information.

Application Directories

Network applications also have directories called (not surprisingly) application directories. These usually contain the names of the application's users, their passwords, and each individual's application configuration information.

Standalone Network Directories

As networks and network applications have grown in size and popularity, the administrative burden of maintaining all the different directories has grown substantially. In some environments, just providing network access to a new employee takes a three-page checklist and four or five hours of work by several administrators, just to add a user name, password, and some configuration information to the directories of each of thirty different systems. Wouldn't it be nice if all these systems shared the same directory? That's the idea behind network directories, or more commonly, just directories.

The adoption of directory standards such as X.500, the set of ISO standards for directories, and Lightweight Directory Access Protocol (LDAP), the Internet standard for directories, has created the possibility of a single directory service for all network and application needs.

But this is only a possibility. The key to a successful directory is not the directory itself, but how completely it integrates with all the network services and applications.

NOS-Integrated Directories

Back in 1983, Jim Allchin (yes, *that* Jim Allchin) and Anand Jaganathan at Banyan Systems realized that the key to reducing the cost of managing an enterprise network was to integrate a network directory with all the network services. Banyan's VINES NOS was revolutionary in that it integrated a distributed network directory service called StreetTalk with all the network services (login and authentication, file and print, email, 3270 emulation, and so on). VINES networks rapidly became popular for companies building large, enterprise-scale networks because the tight integration between the directory and the NOS resulted in a significantly easier-to-manage network. Today, a NOS-integrated directory is the foundation of all modern PC networks, and in particular, Active Directory is the foundation of Windows 2000 Server.

Global Directories

Some network visionaries have predicted that when corporations get their entire enterprise network working under the big integrated directory umbrella, they should then start connecting their directories to those of other corporations through the Internet, eventually creating a one true, all-encompassing Global Directory. The experts even go so far as to suggest that one day there will be one giant directory for the entire planet, containing everything from every Internet user's name and address to the thermostat setting for your directory-enabled house. Needless to say, this kind of a directory is a long way in the future. Nonetheless, a few years ago, Novell joined up with AT&T to build the precursor to such a directory, called AT&T NetWare Connect Services. More recently, Novell announced similar projects with other major telephone companies, including Nippon Telephone and Telegraph, Telstra (the Australian national phone company), Deutsche Telekom (the German phone company), and several others. To date, these initiatives haven't amounted to much, partly because the market isn't quite ready for it, and partly because building a truly global directory is quite a bit different from building an enterprise network directory. But the seeds are being sown.

1999—The Year of the Directory?

If you pay any attention at all to the PC networking industry, you will have noticed that network directories are one of the most talked-about topics in the business today (after the latest gossip about Microsoft and the Department of Justice, of course). The Great NOS War between Novell and Microsoft is being fought and directories are the primary weapons. Novell has based its entire business strategy on Novell Directory Services (NDS) and Microsoft, with its all-new-for-Windows 2000 Active Directory, has countered with its own equally heavy gun.

So, why is 1999 suddenly the "Year of the Directory"? Well, it isn't really. If you're old enough, you'll remember the industry press proclaiming 1986 as the "Year of the LAN." And then declaring 1987 as the "Year of the LAN." And then 1988 and 1989 as well. The industry migration from standalone PCs to corporate networks didn't happen in a single year; it was just too big a change. And so it is with directories.

The PC networking industry has been gradually moving toward directories since Banyan Systems released the first version of their VINES network operating system in 1986. When Banyan entered the market, the corporate PC network market was dominated by 3Com's LanManager, IBM's LanServer, and Novell's NetWare. Banyan never did gain much in the way of market share, at least when you looked at the number of servers they sold, but for a time Banyan practically owned the large enterprise network market. By 1988, Banyan VINES, though never a market leader, was acknowledged as having a five-year technological edge over the rest of the market. The primary reason? VINES's integrated directory, StreetTalk. And even though Banyan is not a significant player in the PC networking industry today, the so-called "Year of the Directory" really started back in 1986 when VINES 1 with StreetTalk first shipped.

Why Directories?

StreetTalk was the first commercially viable network directory. It provided VINES with several significant advantages over its nondirectory-enabled competition. Ultimately, all these advantages boiled down to reducing the costs of running a large enterprise network (referred to now as TCO, Total Cost of Ownership). This is still the primary reason for deploying network directories today.

Single Sign-on

The ability to log in to a network once, with a single user name and password, has been a goal of corporate network administrators since the first network-enabled applications hit the market in the early 1980s. Users had to (and in most cases today, still have to) log in to multiple applications every day. Not too long ago, a large public utility company determined that its employees each had to remember 12 user names and passwords, and were each spending almost 40 hours a year logging into network applications. 40 hours times 20,000 users, times a thousand bucks a week burdened cost, plus opportunity costs, plus—well, you can do the math. Single Sign-on is clearly a big factor in reducing net-work TCO, and directories are the fundamental mechanism for providing Single Sign-on.

Security

No matter how many security memos the company publishes, no matter how many times the company sends him to security class, the average user will either use the same name and password for every application (a bad idea) or write all those names and passwords down on little sticky notes and attach them to his PC's monitor (an even worse idea). This is a security hole of major proportions, and it drives network security auditors nuts because there's nothing they can really do about it.

When the company finally decides to fire an employee (maybe for gross security policy violations), the network administrator is saddled with the job of protecting the company's information assets and shutting down the now-disgruntled user's access to the network. In a large network, this can involve checking tens or hundreds of separate servers and applications. It's an error-prone process and is often left undone.

Both of these problems can be addressed with the Single Sign-on capability of a network directory. Because the user had only one login name and password to access all the network resources, the administrator needs only to disable a single account.

A network directory provides another security advantage. Every developer of network applications devises his own login and security mechanism. Generally these developers aren't security experts, and the application login mechanisms are, well, primitive. I've seen a network-based accounting package that stored the user name and password in clear text in a database file. If you knew where to look and how to dump the file (and many people did), you could gain complete access to the accounting system.

Today's network directories provide nearly unbreakable password security mechanisms using sophisticated public and private key authentication. And because the directory provides a single authentication mechanism for providing users access to all network resources, network applications can benefit from this enhanced security.

Device Identification and Location

Locating your files or your printer on your standalone PC is usually a pretty trivial exercise. Unless you are a supreme alpha geek, you only have one or two hard disks, and a single printer. But after you connect to a large enterprise network, you suddenly have hundreds, if not thousands, of server disk volumes and printers to choose from. How do you identify them? How do you access them?

A network directory provides a single catalog and look-up mechanism for locating the thousands of devices on a large enterprise network. The directory stores all the details needed to access the device, such as network address and configuration. Modern network directories also have an easy-to-use directory browser that lets you find devices by an understandable name such as Second Floor LaserJet or even by the device's characteristics—for instance, Find Me a Two-Sided Color Printer. Accessing a printer then becomes as simple as finding it in the browser and pushing the Connect button.

A directory also simplifies locating and accessing network services such as client/server databases, email services, print services, and fax servers. In a nondirectory environment, you have to identify these services by the name of the server they're running on or, even worse, by their network address. A network directory, on the other hand, provides a place to store such information in a way that users and administrators can identify and locate network services easily.

Location Independence

Along with providing an easy way to identify and locate network devices and services, network directories provide the benefit of location independence for them as well. Enterprise network administrators frequently move disk volumes from one server to another, or move database services from a busy server to one that might perform better. In a nondirectory environment, the administrator would have to go to each user's PC and change the configuration to refer to the new device or service location. But in a directory-based network, because users identify and access a network device or service by its directory name, the administrator simply changes the address and configuration data in the directory.

Global Address Book

Email has become a staple of corporate communications. Internal corporate email use has exploded over the last several years. Even my dad uses email regularly. But a large enterprise network might have tens or even hundreds of thousands of users. How do you find the email address for someone in the company you don't normally communicate with? You could call them on the phone and trade a half-dozen voice mail messages. Or you could look up her name in the corporate network directory. Because the directory already contains a record for the user (the user's name and password), adding an email address is pretty simple.

Simplified Administration

Providing a single repository for network management information is itself a great step in reducing the cost of administering a network. It removes the necessity of managing data in many different places with wildly different utilities. And having all the network management information in one place reduces the likelihood that the administrator will make a mistake.

Reliability

Network directories go a long way to making the network more reliable as well. Most directories today are *replicated*; that is, the directory data is actually kept on several different servers on the network. This reduces the possibility that a single server failure can prohibit users from logging in.

Quality of Service and the DEN Initiative

In May 1997, Microsoft and Cisco Systems (the leading network router manufacturer) announced the Directory Enabled Networks (DEN) Initiative. A cast of twenty-some other network equipment and software vendors ranging from DEC and Compaq to 3Com and Ascend joined them. The announcement described an industry-wide, open-standards initiative that would create a common directory format for network equipment configuration so that all network hardware administration could be done through the directory. One of the primary facilities to be so configured is Quality of Service (QoS), a relatively new buzzword in the networking world that provides different qualities of network service to different users and traffic types. For instance, your boss might get better network service for watching the video feed of the Dolphins-Patriots game than you would get trying to download a set of source files.

Directories—The Technical Challenge

There are several reasons why directories are a "good thing." But if directories are such a good thing, why doesn't everyone have one? One reason is that directories, particularly distributed directories, are hard to get right. This section discusses just why they're so difficult.

The Requirements for a Successful Directory

To be successful, an integrated network directory has to meet certain key requirements. There are five key requirements for an integrated network directory.

Scalability

Enterprise networks can be big, with tens of thousands of servers and hundreds of thousands of users working in hundreds of different locations. And they are getting bigger. For instance, Internet service providers (ISPs) need to build directories that support tens of millions of users, and Novell claims that NDS will support a *billion* directory objects. An integrated network directory has to scale both in how much information it can contain and in how geographically distributed it can be.

Reliability

Enterprise networks are mission-critical resources for corporations; in fact most companies would grind to a halt if their networks failed. If you are going to put all your network management eggs in one big directory-based basket, you had better make sure it is a very reliable basket.

Security

Because all network security is handled through the directory, it has to be very secure. A hole in the security scheme doesn't just expose a single application or server; it can expose the entire network to an attack.

Speed

An integrated network directory handles all the requests for login and authentication, checks all the access rights to network services, and processes directory browsing and lookup requests for the entire enterprise. Every single user on the network accesses the directory hundreds of times a day. Users just won't tolerate slow networks; the directory has to be fast, with the target being consistently subsecond access times.

Low Network Bandwidth Use

Network bandwidth is like disk space or desk space; it doesn't matter how much you have, you're always just *this close* to using it all up. Administrators can't afford to run a network that uses up too much of their precious bandwidth; consequently, the directory has to be very stingy in how much bandwidth it uses.

Integration

The key to a successful directory implementation is the integration of the directory with network services and applications. The directory has no value if applications and tools don't use it; and conversely, the more applications and tools integrate with the directory, the more valuable the directory becomes. All the network services have to work with the directory, and the directory has to support standard interfaces and protocols so that other applications can use it too.

The Solutions

Though these requirements can seem daunting, network directory designers have developed a few standard ways of meeting them. Both Novell's NDS and Microsoft's Active Directory use all these techniques in their directory implementations.

Partitioning

Building a directory database with potentially millions of names, while maintaining sub-second access times from anywhere on the network, is essentially impossible if you keep all the data in one place. Modern directories are *partitioned*, or split up into pieces, with each piece running on a separate server. This reduces the size of the database and spreads the processing load among several servers.

Replication and Synchronization

Large enterprise networks spread across tens or hundreds of locations are usually connected by slower network connections, ranging from 56 down to 9.6 Kb/sec. Even if the directory could respond instantaneously to lookup requests, the network couldn't get the lookup results back to the requestor fast enough. There are two solutions: 1) tear out all the slow links and replace them with faster ones, or 2) put copies of the directory at each site. If you're a network vendor, replication is the obvious choice. You won't go very far if you insist that your customers replace all their WAN links.

Replication, when properly designed and implemented, can also reduce the network bandwidth required by the directory. How? By moving replicas of the directory closer to the network users, directory traffic doesn't have to travel as far across the network.

Replication has an additional benefit: reliability. If one server fails, there is another server available with the same data. If the directory software is smart enough, even failures of multiple directory servers can be invisible to the network user.

Replication comes with a price though. You have to make sure that any change to a portion of the directory gets copied to all the replicas of that portion. This process of *synchronizing* the replicas requires extra processing from each server and uses extra network bandwidth.

Encryption

Security is a hot issue in the networking world, and network vendors compete for customers by promoting their security features. Modern directories employ some of the most sophisticated encryption and authentication algorithms available. NDS, for instance, uses RSA public/private key encryption, MD-2 message digests, nonces, and background authentications during the session. Active Directory uses Secure Sockets Layer (SSL) and MIT's Kerberos algorithm for authentication.

Integrated Services and Applications

Both Windows 2000 and NetWare 5 completely integrate their networking services with the directory. Login and authentication is done through the directory, access to network services is controlled through the directory, and network services such as WAN connections and file replication are all configured through the directory.

Both Novell and Microsoft also use the directory to configure desktop applications. Novell's ZENworks (which stands for Zero Effort Networks) lets network administrators deploy and configure desktop applications through the directory. Microsoft's Zero Administration Windows (ZAW) initiative does essentially the same thing. Both these products provide tighter integration of network services with the directory, reducing TCO and increasing the value of the directory.

By the time this book goes to print, both Novell and Microsoft will have integrated TCO email and collaboration applications (GroupWise from Novell and Exchange from Microsoft) with their respective directories as well.

Standard Protocols and APIs

Integrating the directory with the network's service is a big step in increasing the value of the directory. But most network users don't spend much time running network utilities. They run third-party applications. How do you get third-party developers to integrate their applications with your directory? Most developers aren't thrilled with the idea of tying their applications to a particular network vendor; they want to sell their applications to the broadest possible base of customers.

The obvious solution to this problem is to create an open directory standard, and it actually happened back in 1988. The International Standards Organization (ISO) and the Consultative Committee on International Telegraphy and Telephony (CCITT—but now it's the International Telecommunications Union, Telecommunications Standards Branch, or ITU-T) collaborated to create a standard for directory information formats and directory access protocols called X.500. As you might expect from the players involved, this was a big, big standard designed to satisfy every possible directory need. X.500 adoption was slow because of its size and complexity and also because it was defined on top of the unpopular OSI protocol stack.

Novell's NDS, which shipped in 1990, looked and smelled a lot like X.500, but it used a totally different directory access protocol running on top of Novell's IPX. Novell also provided a proprietary set of APIs developers had to use to access the directory. OK, to be fair there wasn't an API standard defined at the time that NDS shipped. In any case, the lack of a standard API severely limited the development of directory-aware applications.

In 1994, Wengyik Yeong, Steve Kille, and Tim Howes, at the University of Michigan (a big Banyan installation, by the way), decided to come up with a directory access protocol that provided "90 percent of the functionality of X.500 at 10 percent of the cost." This protocol became the Lightweight Directory Access Protocol, or LDAP for short. It was defined on top of TCP/IP and greatly simplified the task of communicating with an X.500-style server. LDAP became an Internet standard in July, 1993 as RFC 1487. Although LDAP is a protocol, the guys at Michigan also developed a simple C language API that was documented in RFC 1823. The API has not yet become an Internet standard, although it has become a de-facto standard in the industry because of its functionality and simplicity.

The development and rapid adoption of LDAP as a standard has opened the door for the development of directory-enabled applications. Third-party developers can now develop applications and legitimately expect them to run with different vendors' directories.

Extensible Schemas

Another feature that makes it easier to integrate applications and directories is a user-extensible schema. All directories have a schema, or formal description, of the kinds of things that can be stored in the directory. Many applications only need to access user names and such, and the standard schema works just fine for this. But there are a lot of applications that can benefit by storing their configuration or other application-specific data in the directory. The directory vendor can't possibly predict what kind of data application developers might want to store in the directory, so providing a way for the application developer to extend the schema makes a lot of sense. An extensible schema makes it possible for application developers to create applications that are highly integrated with the directory.

CHAPTER 2

An Introduction to Active Directory

Before we get into the nuts and bolts of Active Directory, it would be a good idea to briefly cover some of the features and facilities of Active Directory in Windows 2000. This chapter gives you an idea of the importance and scope of Active Directory. If you've already read the Microsoft white papers on Active Directory, you can skip to the next chapter.

Active Directory: The Directory for Windows 2000

Since the release of Windows NT Server 3.51, Microsoft has been steadily gaining network market share from the once-dominant Novell. But Microsoft has always had difficulties penetrating the enterprise network market. Banyan VINES and StreetTalk dominated the large PC network market for several years in the early 1990s, and recently Novell, with NetWare 4 and NetWare 5 and NDS, has started to take over that market segment. Microsoft Windows NT, although clearly superior to NetWare as an application server, has always had the reputation of being difficult and expensive to manage in large environments. With the release of Windows 2000 Server (the NOS formerly known as Windows NT 5), Microsoft is finally addressing the enterprise market with a directory-based NOS that promises to be deployable, scalable, and manageable in large enterprise environments.

Active Directory is distinguished by the key features discussed in the following sections.

Standards-Based

Microsoft made a very wise decision to base Active Directory completely on open standards. Microsoft has had a history of embracing standards and extending them with the hope of being able to control some market segment (witness C, C++, HTML, and Java). Microsoft hasn't done this (at least not obviously) with Active Directory, with the result that application developers can feel pretty comfortable about writing code that works with Active Directory as well as other standards-based directories. This is not to say that Active Directory is 100% compliant. There are some annoying incompatibilities here and there that you may run into, as described in the following sections. But for the most part, your existing LDAPv3 applications should work with, or be very close to working with, Active Directory.

Although I detail only LDAP and DNS as two of the standards that Active Directory relies on, Active Directory and Windows 2000 rely on several other standards, such as Dynamic Host Configuration Protocol (DHCP), TCP/IP, and Kerberos.

LDAP Protocol

Active Directory uses LDAPv3 as its native protocol through and through, and Microsoft's LDAP implementation adheres pretty closely to the standard. In general, existing LDAP applications should be able to connect to and work with Active Directory without any changes.

LDAP API

The Platform SDK for Windows 2000 includes an LDAP client library that follows the current draft standard C LDAP API reasonably well. Although the Microsoft Platform SDK contains most of the LDAP functions defined by the draft standard, there are a handful of inconsistencies. For instance, the draft standard generally uses signed integers for return types, whereas the Microsoft implementation consistently uses unsigned integers. The Microsoft LDAP API also does not provide any of the ASN.1 encoding and decoding functions, such as `ber_printf()` and `ber_scanf()`, which are part of the draft as well as part of other LDAP client libraries.

The Microsoft LDAP libraries provide both Unicode ("wide") and ANSI ("narrow") versions of the LDAP APIs. The Unicode functions are hidden behind macros, so from a programming perspective, you won't notice the difference.

Chapters 17 through 29 discuss the Microsoft LDAP APIs in detail.

DNS

Active Directory uses the Internet Domain Name System (DNS) as its server locator service. Active Directory depends on the presence of Dynamic DNS as specified in RFC 2136 to locate directory servers on the network. From a programming perspective, you don't need to know much about DNS, but when you need to understand exactly which domain controller your program is accessing, understanding the way Active Directory and DNS work together is crucial. Chapter 5, "Active Directory and DNS," describes how Active Directory uses DNS.

Scalable

Active Directory supports partitioning and replication so that administrators can design and deploy extremely large directories across highly distributed enterprise networks. The replication mechanism is very efficient in terms of bandwidth use, and you can even use SMTP (the Internet email protocol) as the replication transport for those hard-to-reach sites.

Secure

Active Directory uses Kerberos and Secure Sockets Layer (SSL) to create a highly secure directory environment.

Kerberos is a client-server authentication system developed at MIT. It uses private key encryption to efficiently authenticate network processes that want to obtain network resources—for instance, a file or a printer. Active Directory can integrate with other Kerberos servers on the network so that users authenticated by Active Directory can access other network services running on non-Windows 2000 servers.

Integrated and Integratable

All the core networking services provided with Windows 2000 Server are integrated with and managed through Active Directory: login and authentication, DNS configuration, RAS configuration, print service management, you name it. If it's a network service, it's managed through the directory. Microsoft is very close to shipping a version of Exchange Server that uses Active Directory as well.

Not only did Microsoft integrate Active Directory with all its own applications, Microsoft made it easy for third-party developers to integrate their applications with Active Directory.

ADSI

Microsoft has upgraded the Active Directory Services Interface to work with Active Directory, which previously worked only with Exchange, NDS, the Windows NT Security Accounts Manager database, and Microsoft's Site Server. ADSI is a COM-based API that exposes all the features of Active Directory while maintaining a clean object-oriented interface. Because it is COM-based, you can access Active Directory from C++, Visual Basic, Java, and Active Server Pages.

LDAP Protocol and APIs

As mentioned in the "Standards-Based" section, Active Directory also supports LDAP as a protocol and an API. Although ADSI provides different underlying "providers" to access different directory systems such as Novell Directory Services (NDS), the LDAP provider for ADSI does not work very well with other LDAP directories. LDAP will be the integration method of choice for developers who are building applications that must use different directory implementations.

Extensible Schema

Microsoft very cleverly chose to store the schema for Active Directory in Active Directory itself. Although this might seem a little confusing at first, it really simplifies your life because you can use the same directory access APIs to manipulate the schema. You don't have to learn a separate mechanism to add your applications configuration information to the directory.

The Active Directory schema is simply a collection of objects that define the allowed classes and attributes in the directory. The schema is extensible at runtime, so your applications can add new classes and attribute types to the directory without requiring the network administrator to shut down Active Directory. Chapter 9, "The Active Directory Schema," describes the Active Directory schema in some detail.

Backward-Compatible

Active Directory completely supports earlier Windows NT 4 servers and domains, as well as Windows NT 4, Windows 95, and Windows 98 clients.

When you upgrade existing Windows NT domains, Windows 2000 domain controllers running Active Directory replace Windows NT 3.51 and 4.0 primary domain controllers (PDCs). The Windows 2000 domain controllers support the existing Windows NT 3.51 and 4.0 security and authentication protocols, so existing clients and services don't need to be modified to work with the new domain controllers. The Windows 2000 domain controllers also assume responsibility for updating existing backup domain controllers (BDCs) with current user account and security information.

Integration with Windows 2000

As I mentioned in Chapter 1, "An Introduction to Network Directories," directories themselves aren't all that valuable; it's the integration of the NOS, administrative tools, and applications with the directory that makes networks easier to administer. Almost every aspect of Windows 2000 uses Active Directory in some way. Login and authentication use Active Directory. Most basic services, such as Remote Access Server (RAS), DNS, File Replication Service (FRS), and the indexing service, get their configuration from the directory. Although it is not true yet, eventually all Windows 2000 network service administration will be done through the directory.

Integration with Other Microsoft Products

Microsoft has not only completely integrated Windows 2000 with Active Directory, it is also in the process of integrating its BackOffice applications.

BackOffice 5.0, due out sometime after Windows 2000 ships in early 2000, will integrate all its components (SQL Server, Exchange, Systems Management Server, and Site Server, at the least) with Active Directory. This integration will further reduce administrative costs by uniting the different administrative tools and mechanisms under one directory umbrella.

Microsoft Exchange

The biggest application integration story for Active Directory is Exchange Server 6.0. Instead of using two separate directories, as did Windows NT 4 and Exchange Server 5.0, Exchange Server 6.0 will use Active Directory for its directory store. This means that there will be one common repository for directory information, one common security mechanism, one common replication mechanism, and a common set of administrative tools.

Zero Administration Windows and Active Directory

Zero Administration Windows (ZAW) is the name of a set of technologies that Microsoft is promoting to reduce the Total Cost of Ownership (TCO). ZAW is targeted specifically at reducing the cost of software installation and configuration on the desktop PC.

ZAW, via the Microsoft Installer (MSI) and other changes in the operating system, lets the administrator define in the directory which applications should be made available to which users on the network. The workstation component of ZAW will automatically make sure that those applications are installed (or available to be installed), no matter which machine the user logs in on. The workstation can check the directory for complete configuration information and automatically replace missing application files, fix improper Registry entries, and otherwise make it much easier for the network administrator to avoid having to touch the workstations on the network.

Integration with Other Directory Services

One of the neat things about Active Directory is the way it integrates with other LDAP-compliant directory services. The Active Directory administrator can "plug in" foreign directories at any convenient point in the directory tree. Active Directory will then automatically refer queries of that part of the tree to the foreign directory server. This is shown in Figure 2.1.

FIGURE 2.1

Integration of external directories with Active Directory.

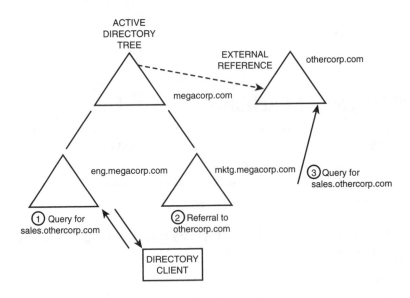

Active Directory Versus Windows NT 4 Domains

Active Directory is a big step up from NT domains. Even though the notion of domains still exists in Active Directory, the whole underlying directory model is different.

- The namespace supported by Windows NT 4 domains is flat, which is to say that a Windows NT 4 domain can contain users, but it can't contain subdomains. The Active Directory namespace is hierarchical. Figure 2.2 shows how the two kinds of namespaces differ.

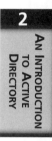

FIGURE 2.2

NT 4 domain namespace versus Active Directory namespace.

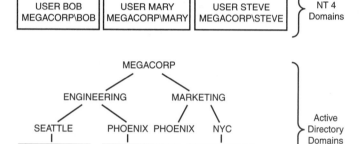

- Instead of one Primary Domain Controller (PDC) and zero or more Backup Domain Controllers (BDCs), Active Directory uses a multi-master scheme in which all domain controllers (DCs) are peers. Figure 2.3 shows how Windows 2000 domain controllers differ from Windows NT 4 domain controllers. Although there are some special operations that can only be performed on a single domain controller—for instance, modifications to the Active Directory schema—generally speaking, Windows 2000 domain controllers in the same domain are functionally identical from an Active Directory standpoint.

- In Windows NT 4, trust relationships between domains (the ability of one domain to use another domain for authentication) are one-way. Just because domain A trusts domain B, domain B doesn't necessarily trust domain A. In Active Directory, all trusts are inherently bidirectional. If domain A trusts domain B, domain B automatically trusts domain A. Figure 2.4 shows how trust relationships in Windows 2000 differ from those of Windows NT 4.

FIGURE 2.3

*NT 4 domain
controllers versus
Windows 2000
domain
controllers.*

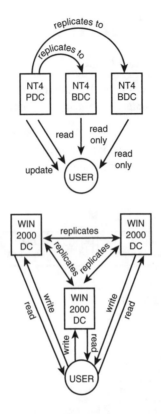

FIGURE 2.4

*One-way trusts in
NT 4 versus recip-
rocal trusts in
Active Directory.*

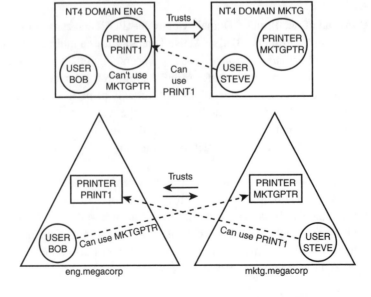

- Trust relationships between domains in Windows NT 4 are not transitive. If domain A trusts domain B, and domain B trusts domain C, domain A does not necessarily trust domain C. In Active Directory, trust relationships between domains are inherently transitive. If domain A trusts domain B, and domain B trusts domain C, domain A automatically trusts domain C. Figure 2.5 illustrates the difference between transitive and intransitive trust relationships.

FIGURE 2.5

Intransitive trusts in NT 4 versus transitive trusts in Active Directory.

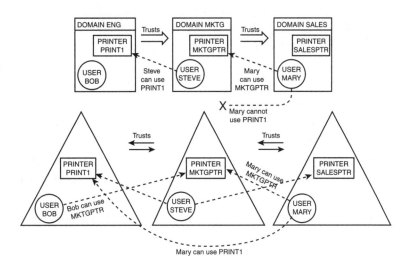

- Trust relationships between domains in Windows NT 4 must be defined manually. Trust relationships between domains in Active Directory are established and maintained automatically.

Active Directory Versus Novell Directory Services

Despite the marketing hype from both companies, Active Directory and Novell Directory Services are more alike than different. They are both fully integrated into the NOS. They are both enterprise-scalable. They both provide X.500-style hierarchical namespaces, and they are both accessible via ADSI and LDAP.

There are a few differences to keep in mind if you find yourself writing software for these two directories.

- Active Directory is tightly integrated with DNS. NDS doesn't use DNS at all. This primarily affects network administration, but it is worth keeping in mind.

- Active Directory uses LDAP as its wire protocol. NDS uses a protocol similar to the X.500 Directory Access Protocol (DAP) running over the NetWare Core Protocol (NCP). Recently, Novell added LDAP support to NDS, but the native protocol remains proprietary. The newly announced NDS Version 8 uses LDAP natively.

- Active Directory allows exactly one replica of a domain to reside on each domain controller. In Active Directory, domains serve as the unit of partitioning, so this limits the number of partitions a network administrator can place on a Windows 2000 domain controller to one. NDS allows you to host an essentially unlimited number of partitions on each directory server.

- Active Directory provides for integration with other LDAP-compliant directories. NDS does not, although this will change in NDS Version 8.

- Active Directory domains (partitions) act as a security boundary. NDS trees are homogenous with respect to security; there are no inherent security boundaries within the tree.

- The Active Directory schema is extensible at runtime. The NDS schema can be extended only by shutting down and restarting NDS. This might change in NDS Version 8.

- Active Directory only runs on Windows 2000. NDS runs on NetWare servers, Linux, Windows NT 4, and Solaris.

CHAPTER 3

The Components of Active Directory

This chapter describes the things that make up Active Directory, and it introduces a lot of new terminology that the rest of this book uses. It's very important that you understand the terms and concepts in this chapter before continuing through the rest of the book.

This chapter first describes the logical structure of Active Directory: what an object is, how objects are organized into domains, and how domains are organized into trees and forests.

The second part of this chapter describes the physical structure of Active Directory, including how domains are replicated on domain controllers and how domain controllers are organized into sites.

The Logical Structure of Active Directory

This section describes the logical structure of Active Directory, the components that make up this structure, and the ways these components relate to each other.

Active Directory Is a Collection of Objects

Active Directory is fundamentally a collection of *objects* (often called *entries*) that are stored in a database. An object, in this case, is not like a C++ object with fixed member variables and methods. A directory object is essentially a database record.

Usually, but not always, a directory object represents a real-world object or concept. For instance, there is an object in Active Directory that represents each user of the Windows 2000 network. There are objects in the directory that represent each computer and each server on the network as well.

Classes of Objects

Directory objects come in different types, or *classes*. The concept of class in Active Directory is analogous to the concept of class in object-oriented programming: A class defines a set of characteristics that all instances of the class share. Active Directory has more than 140 predefined classes, and you can add your own classes as well.

Attributes and Values

Each object has a set of *attributes* (sometimes called *properties*). An attribute is a named value contained by the object. For instance, a User object in Active Directory has attributes containing the user's first name, last name, and password (suitably encrypted, of course). One of these attributes is called `objectClass`. It contains the name of the class of which the object is an instance.

The object's class defines what attributes the object *must* contain. These *must-have* attributes are mandatory; Active Directory won't let you create an object without a value for all the must-have attributes for the object's class. For instance, each User object in Active Directory must have an attribute called `sAMAccountName`. This attribute contains the name of the user in a form usable by Windows NT 4 networks.

The object's class also defines what attributes the object *may* have. These attributes, sometimes called *may-have* attributes, are optional. You can create an object without values for its may-have attributes and then add values for them later.

It is not possible to have a `NULL` or empty value for an attribute. An attribute either exists and has a value, or it doesn't exist at all. This is an important concept to understand because it differs from the way C++ works. You can't just set an attribute to `NULL`; you have to remove it from the object entirely.

By the way, you'll notice that attribute names have the form *<lowercase letter>* *<Uppercase and lowercase letters>*, with no punctuation marks. This form is called the *LDAP display name* of the attribute, and it's the form you use when writing programs for the directory. Attributes also have a common name, which is usually formed from one or more words separated by hyphens. For instance, a User object has an attribute whose common name is `Street-Address` and whose LDAP display name is `street`. This book uses the LDAP display name exclusively.

Multivalued Attributes

The X.500 data model allows a single attribute to have one or more values. For instance, Active Directory defines an optional attribute, called `otherPhoneHome`, for a User object. This attribute contains other home phone numbers for the user. (I'm not sure what *other* refers to in this case.) This attribute is *multivalued,* meaning that it can contain one or more phone number values. You can think of it as a dynamically growing array of values that always contains at least one value.

Although there is no defined limit on how many values you can stick in a multivalued attribute, there are two important constraints:

- Values in a multivalued attribute must all be unique. You cannot store two identical values in a multivalued attribute.

- Values in a multivalued attribute are not ordered in any way. You may store the values in, for instance, alphabetical order, but when you retrieve them later, they might come back in some random order.

Attribute Syntax

In addition to each object being an instance of a single class, each attribute has a specific type. This type, or *syntax,* defines the kind of data an attribute can contain and how the data is stored in the directory. For instance, the `otherPhoneHome` attribute mentioned in the preceding section is a Unicode string. The `logonCount` attribute of a User object, which contains the number of times a user has logged in, is an Integer.

Active Directory defines 22 different attribute syntaxes, as listed in Table 3.1. These syntaxes are hard-wired; there is no mechanism for adding new syntaxes to Active Directory.

TABLE 3.1 ACTIVE DIRECTORY SYNTAXES

Syntax Name	Type of Data
DN	A string representing the distinguished name of an object.
OID	An object identifier (OID) as defined by the ITU. An OID is expressed as a string of integers separated by dots, such as `"1.3.12.7.22"`.
CaseExactString	A string of ASCII characters in which case is significant.
CaseIgnoreString	A string of ASCII characters in which case is not significant.
PrintableString	A string of printable ASCII characters.
NumericString	A string of ASCII digits 0 through 9.

continues

3

THE COMPONENTS
OF ACTIVE
DIRECTORY

TABLE 3.1 CONTINUED

Syntax Name	Type of Data
ORName	An X.400 email address.
AccessPointDN	An X.400 access point name.
Boolean	True or False.
Integer	A 32-bit signed integer.
Enumeration	One of a set of integral values. Active Directory handles this as an integer.
OctetString	An arbitrary string of bytes.
GeneralizedTime	The time and date, including 100ths of a second. A GeneralizedTime string has the format YYYYMMDDHHMMSS.ssZ, such as "20000201171515.0Z".
UTCTime	Another time and date representation, using a two-digit year with no seconds or fractions of a second. It has the format YYMMD-DHHMMSSZ, such as "991231091500Z".
DirectoryString	A case-insensitive Unicode string.
PresentationAddress	An OSI application address in string form.
DNWithString	A distinguished name combined with a string. The format of the value is S:<count>:<string>:<DN>. Used by Active Directory to link objects.
DNWithBinary	A distinguished name combined with a binary "blob" of data. The format of the value is B:<count>:<data>:<DN>. Used by Active Directory to link objects.
NTSecurityDescriptor	A Windows NT Security Descriptor structure.
INTEGER8	A 64-bit signed integer.
Sid	An NT security identifier.
ReplicaLink	A binary structure containing information about the state of a replication partner.

Note that even though you would expect integer and Boolean syntax values to be binary, the LDAPAPI handles these values as strings. For instance, the LDAPAPI represents the integer value 15 as a string "15". Boolean values are either "True" or "False".

The Active Directory Schema

All the information that describes the allowed structure and contents of the directory is called the *schema*. The schema defines what classes of objects may exist, what attributes may exist, which attributes each of the classes must and may have, and what classes of objects can contain other classes of objects.

The Active Directory schema is fully extensible. You can define your own classes and attributes (but not syntaxes). Active Directory keeps the schema information in a set of directory objects called the Schema naming context, which I describe later in this chapter. Chapter 9, "The Active Directory Schema," discusses the Active Directory schema in more detail.

The Directory Information Tree

One thing that makes LDAP directories like Active Directory quite a bit different from a typical database is the hierarchical organization of the objects in the directory.

Objects in Active Directory can contain zero or more subordinate objects, in much the same way a directory in the Windows NT file system can contain files. This capability to contain subordinate objects produces a hierarchical tree-like structure, just like a file system hierarchy. Figure 3.1 shows such a hierarchical structure.

FIGURE 3.1

A hierarchical structure.

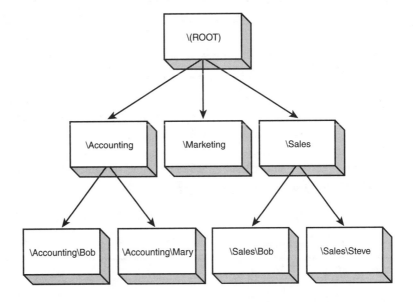

The file system analogy breaks down in one case, however. Objects in a file system can be either directories that contain subordinate files or files that contain data, but they can't be both. Directory objects, on the other hand, can contain data (attributes) *and* contain subordinate objects as well. For instance, a User object in Active Directory has name and phone number attributes, and it can contain subordinate objects, too. Note that the class of which an object is a member determines what kind of objects may contain it. These classes are called the object's *possible superiors*. Interestingly, the class does *not* define what kinds of objects an object may contain, except by the implication of all the class's possible superiors.

The collection of all the objects in the directory organized in a tree-like fashion is called the *directory information tree,* or *DIT*. The DIT is the logical structure made up of all the objects in the directory.

Identifying Directory Objects

As in any database system, the way you identify objects in the database is crucial to how you use the database and how the database works. In particular, there must be a way to uniquely identify each and every object in the database.

The X.500 data model defines two primary ways for identifying directory objects: the relative distinguished name (RDN) and the distinguished name (DN).

The Relative Distinguished Name

The *relative distinguished name* is comprised of one of the object's attributes, called its naming attribute. The RDN uniquely identifies each object *within its container*. Each class of object defines which attribute or attributes can act as the naming attribute, but for any instance of a class there is only one naming attribute.

For instance, the cn attribute (the Common-Name attribute) serves as the naming attribute for most classes of objects in Active Directory. So, within a given container, the cn attribute uniquely identifies a User object. If a User object has the string "Ed Harris" as the value of its cn attribute, the objects RDN would be expressed as "cn=Ed Harris". There could not be another User object in the same container with "Ed Harris" as the value of its cn attribute.

The possible naming attributes are shown in Table 3.2.

TABLE 3.2   RDN ATTRIBUTES

Attribute	Meaning
cn	Common name
l	Locality name
st	State or province name
o	Organization name
ou	Organizational unit name

Attribute	Meaning
c	Country name
street	Street address
dc	Domain component
uid	UserID

The RDN only identifies an object within a container. It is quite possible that there is another User object in another container with the RDN "cn=Ed Harris". To uniquely identify an object within the entire directory hierarchy, you have to use the distinguished name (DN) of the object.

The Distinguished Name

The DN of an object is simply the RDN of the object concatenated with the DN of its container. (Yes, it is a recursive definition, but trees *are* recursive, so that's not surprising.) Another way to look at it is that the DN of an object is a string containing the RDN of the object, the RDN of the object's container, the RDN of the container's container, and so on up to the root of the directory tree.

For instance, Ed Harris's user object in the Users container of the Engineering organizational unit of the megacorp.com domain would have the DN cn=Ed Harris, cn=Users,ou=Engineering,dc=megacorp,dc=com.

Figure 3.2 shows the distinction between relative distinguished names and distinguished names.

3

THE COMPONENTS
OF ACTIVE
DIRECTORY

FIGURE 3.2

Relative distinguished names and distinguished names.

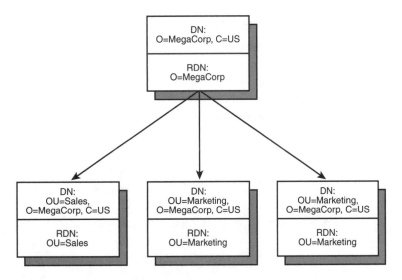

Distinguished Names and Domain Name System (DNS) Names

You'll notice that DNs don't look anything like the Internet-style DNS names you normally use, such as `www.megacorp.com`. This is largely because the X.500 standard was developed before the Internet became as pervasive as it is today. This might seem to be a big problem.

The domain component (DC) attribute type provides a clever way to associate X.500-style names with Internet-style DNS names. For instance, if your company has a DNS domain name of `engineering.megacorp.com`, it would have an X.500-style DN of `DC=engineering,DC=megacorp,DC=com`. A network user might have a DN like `CN=Bob, CN=Users,DC=Engineering,DC=MegaCorp,DC=com`. Basically, any DNS name can be mapped to an X.500 name using the DC attribute type. You will see why this is important in the section on how Active Directory integrates with DNS.

Other Object Identifiers

There are other ways to identify objects in Active Directory. For instance, each object in the directory has an attribute called `objectGUID` that contains a globally unique identifier, or GUID. Active Directory assigns this value when the object is created, and the `objectGUID` value stays with the object until the object is deleted from the directory, even if the object is moved or renamed.

User objects also have other names, such as the user principal name (which looks like the user's email address) and the Windows NT Security Identifier (SID). Chapter 10, "The Active Directory Domain Naming Context," discusses these in more detail.

Organizing the Directory Tree

The X.500 data model was designed to support extraordinarily large directories, potentially containing billions of objects representing each person on the planet. Dealing with a tree that large as a single structure is at least inconvenient (imagine how long the DNs would be!), if not impossible. The following sections describe the ways Active Directory breaks up the DIT into more manageable pieces.

Naming Contexts and Partitions

One way to address this issue is to use the divide-and-conquer rule and break the DIT into smaller subtrees. A subtree of the DIT, consisting of a single object and all objects in the tree subordinate to it is called a *naming context*. Naming contexts are arbitrary; you can pick any point in the tree and call it a naming context.

A naming context is just that: a context in which a name can be resolved. For instance, going back to the Ed Harris example, if we chose a naming context at `ou=Engineering,` `dc=megacorp,dc=com`, this defines a subtree in which the name `"cn=Ed Harris,` `cn=Users"` uniquely identifies the Ed Harris user object.

Active Directory Domains

The architects of Active Directory had a significant constraint on the design of the directory system. Windows 2000 and Active Directory had to completely support and integrate with earlier Windows NT 4.0 networks and their seemingly incompatible domain and security systems. The solution is at once clever and elegant.

Domains in Windows NT 4 networks serve two purposes: They act to define a scope security and management, and they act as a namespace in which you can resolve the names of users, computers, and other objects. This last point is strikingly similar to the notion of a naming context, and it points to the way the Microsoft architects addressed this design problem.

Active Directory defines a special kind of naming context called a *domain naming context* or *Active Directory domain* that provides a scope of security and administration as well as a namespace in which you can resolve the names of users, computers, and other resources. It provides the same sort of facilities as a Windows NT 4 domain, with enhancements such as a hierarchical structure and a fully extensible schema. You can also establish hierarchical relationships between Active Directory domains such that one domain can contain one or more subordinate domains. This makes it easier to build and organize large Active Directory DITs.

Domains as Security Boundaries

One thing to keep in mind when working with Active Directory domains: Domains form a security boundary. That means users in one domain do not (by default) have access to objects in another domain. Active Directory extends the Windows NT 4 trust mechanism to deal with this limitation.

With all the talk about how much better directories are for managing networks, you might think Active Directory had replaced the old NT 4–style domains. Not so at all.

> **NOTE**
>
> Domains aren't dead, they just smell funny.

The Root Domain, Domain Trees, and Forests

When you install Active Directory on your network, the very first thing you do is create a new domain. The first domain you create has special characteristics and is called the *root domain*. You can subsequently add new domains that are subordinate to the root domain so that you form a hierarchy of domains, or a *domain tree*. The name of a domain tree is the DN of its root domain. Figure 3.3 shows an Active Directory domain tree.

FIGURE 3.3

An Active Directory domain tree.

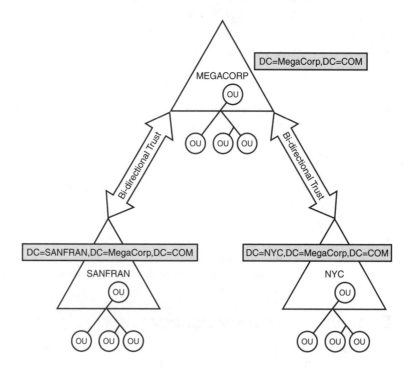

You can also add domains that will become the roots of their own domain trees. The collection of domain trees taken together is called an Active Directory *forest*. What else could you call it?

The Configuration and Schema Naming Contexts

I mentioned in the preceding section that the first domain you create in Active Directory, the root domain, has special characteristics. Specifically, the root domain contains two unique naming contexts called Configuration and Schema.

The Configuration naming context contains a set of objects that define the structure of Active Directory. There are objects that represent *domain controllers* (Windows 2000 servers that are running Active Directory), domains, trusts, replication schedules, and so forth. Chapter 8, "The Configuration Naming Context," describes the Configuration naming context in detail.

Subordinate to the Configuration naming context is the Schema naming context. The Schema naming context contains all the objects that define the Active Directory schema. Chapter 9 describes the Schema naming context.

The Domain Naming System and Active Directory Domains

The Domain Naming System (DNS) is the naming system used by the Internet. It is itself a directory, but it is oriented primarily toward mapping computer or host names to IP addresses.

DNS divides its hierarchical namespace into domains. (But don't confuse these with NT domains!) The DNS tree starts at an unnamed root, and the first-level domains are the familiar com, edu, mil, and so forth. These domains are managed by the Internet Assigned Numbers Authority (IANA). The next level of domains in DNS are typically Internet service provider (ISP) names, corporation names, and college and university names, and are managed by the entities that the names represent. Domain names below this level are generally departments or organizations within a company, or ISP customer names. Figure 3.4 shows a typical DNS domain hierarchy.

FIGURE 3.4

A DNS domain tree.

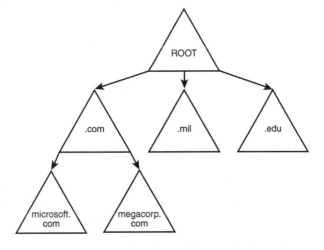

Active Directory integrates very tightly with DNS, but the relationship between the two can be very confusing.

Active Directory uses DNS for two purposes. First, Active Directory uses DNS to resolve server names to IP addresses so that it can establish communications with those servers. This is how DNS is normally used. Second (and here is the confusing part), Active Directory uses the DNS domain hierarchy to define the Active Directory domain hierarchy. Figure 3.5 helps clarify this.

FIGURE 3.5

The relationship between DNS and Active Directory domains.

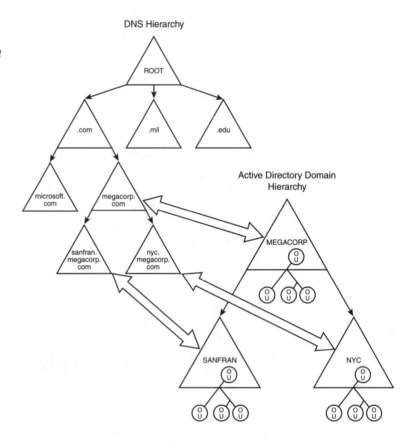

The important thing to keep in mind is that Active Directory and DNS are separate naming systems, and that Active Directory domains and DNS domains are completely different entities. Active Directory requires that its domains use the domain names and hierarchical relationships defined in DNS. I'll discuss the interaction between DNS and Active Directory in more detail later in this book.

The Physical Structure of Active Directory

So far in this chapter, I've only discussed the logical structure of Active Directory. Active Directory has a physical structure as well, and this structure is distinct from the logical structure. This section describes how Active Directory realizes its logical structure on the physical components of the network.

Domain Controllers

In Windows NT 4, user account and security information was maintained by a primary domain controller (PDC) and was replicated to one or more backup domain controllers (BDCs). In Windows 2000, all user account and security information resides in the Active Directory. A Windows 2000 server that maintains a portion of the directory is called a *domain controller*, or DC. A Windows 2000 DC provides the same sort of authentication and security services that PDCs and BDCs provided in Windows NT 4.

One important difference between Windows 2000 DCs and the PDCs and BDCs in Windows NT 4 is that there is no single master DC in Windows 2000. In Windows NT 4, you could make changes to a domain object only at the PDC. With Active Directory, you can make a change to a directory object at any domain controller, and Active Directory will make sure the change is properly replicated.

Partitions and Replicas

As I discussed earlier in the chapter, Active Directory domains are naming contexts that serve to break up the DIT into more manageable subtrees. These subtrees are called *naming contexts* when you are talking about resolving names in the directory (the logical view) and they are called *partitions* when you are talking about storing and replicating them.

When you actually store a copy of a naming context on a domain controller, the copy you store is called a *replica*. Even if you only have one copy of a partition, it is still a single replica.

Each Windows 2000 domain controller hosts exactly three replicas: a replica of the Configuration naming context, a replica of the Schema naming context, and a copy of the domain naming context of the domain of which the domain controller is a member. There are always exactly three replicas on a domain controller.

Global Catalogs

There is one exception to this rule, and that is when a domain controller is also a Global Catalog. A Global Catalog contains a partial read-only replica of all the domains in the forest. The Global Catalog is effectively a separate directory service running on a domain controller. You can search the entire forest by searching a single Global Catalog. The Schema defines which objects and which attributes of those objects appear in the Global Catalog.

Active Directory Replication

Although an in-depth discussion of Active Directory's replication mechanisms is beyond the scope of this book, there are a few things you should know:

- Active Directory partitions are *multimaster*. This means that, unlike with Windows NT 4 domains, you can modify an object in any replica of the partition, and Active Directory will ensure that the change eventually propagates to all the other domain controllers that host that partition.

- Active Directory is *loosely consistent*. This means that when you make a change to an object in the directory, there is no guarantee that all replicas of that object will be brought up-to-date any time soon. Even on a small network, a change on one domain controller might take 15 or 20 minutes to appear on all the domain controllers. On a large network, the change might take days to propagate to all the domain controllers.

- Active Directory replication is *transitive,* which means that it is not necessary for every domain controller in a domain to communicate with every other domain controller in the domain. If you make a change on domain controller A, it can replicate those changes to domain controller B, and then B can relay those changes to domain controller C. A does not have to communicate directly with C.

- Active Directory replicates attributes, not objects. If you change the otherHomePhone attribute of a user object, Active Directory will replicate that attribute and nothing else. This is very efficient, but it has a potentially annoying side effect because Active Directory replication is not transaction-oriented. If you make a change to two attributes in a User object on domain controller A—say, the otherHomePhone and the street attributes—it is quite possible that these changes will replicate to domain controller B at different times. This means that for some period of time, the User object on B might have the updated phone number but not the updated street address, or vice versa. Active Directory guarantees that the objects will be brought into sync eventually, however.

Active Directory Sites

Active Directory provides a way for the network administrator to divide the network into *sites*. A site is a portion of the network that is entirely connected by a high-speed LAN of 10Mbps or faster. Essentially, any group of computers that is connected via a single Ethernet network can be defined as a site.

The corollary of this is that Active Directory sites are connected to each other by something slower than 10Mbps Ethernet. This has some implications for the way replication happens. In particular, replication within a site happens more or less as required. If you change an object on domain controller A, A will notify domain controller B that it needs to synchronize with A. You can be pretty sure that a change will replicate to all the domain controllers within a site in quick order.

Between sites, however, replication follows a schedule defined by the administrator. For instance, the administrator might define the connection schedule between two sites as being available for replication traffic once a day at midnight. If that is the case, there is potentially a 24-hour lag between the time an update occurs on domain controller A and the time that domain controller Z in a different site sees the update. It's something to keep in mind when you write your Active Directory programs.

3

THE COMPONENTS OF ACTIVE DIRECTORY

CHAPTER 4

Active Directory Security

Not only does Active Directory centralize administrative and configuration information for the network, it centralizes network security data as well. Active Directory is the data store for most of the security information in a Windows 2000 network (pretty much everything except for file security, which Windows 2000 still keeps in the file system). Active Directory also extends the familiar Win32 security mechanism to all the objects in the directory.

Overview of Windows 2000 Security

This section is a brief overview of the Windows 2000 security system. It is not a complete description of how to manage and program Windows 2000 security—that would take another book. Instead, I'll just go through the basics so you can either refresh your memory or get sufficiently up to speed so that you can deal with the security issues in Active Directory.

The Features of Windows 2000 Security

Windows 2000 security touches almost every aspect of the operating system. Processes, threads, files, services, users, and domains all interact with some aspect of Windows 2000 security. Fortunately, they all share the same underlying mechanisms and data structures. This gives network administrators a common way to manage security, and it gives us programmers a lot fewer APIs to learn.

Manageable

Windows 2000 and Active Directory centralizes almost all the security system configuration information, such as usernames, passwords, and access rights. This makes it possible for network administrators to manage the security information for an entire enterprise.

Robust

By using standard security protocols such as Kerberos and standard encryption mechanisms such as DES, Windows 2000 provides a very secure computing environment. Coupled with the replication and redundancy provided by the directory, Windows 2000 security is both robust and reliable.

Backward-Compatible

Windows 2000 supports almost all aspects of Windows NT 4.0 network security. Windows NT 4.0 workstations and even Windows NT 4.0 Backup Domain Controllers (BDCs) can participate in the Windows 2000 security environment.

And, fortunately for developers, most of the earlier Windows NT security APIs work properly in the Windows 2000 environment.

Auditable

As part of its C2 compliance, Windows 2000 provides a complete set of auditing primitives that allow network security administrators to keep tabs on accesses to secure files and services.

The Components of Windows 2000 Security

This section reviews the components of Windows 2000 security.

Domains

A domain in Windows NT networking (including Windows 2000) is both a namespace and a security boundary. It is a namespace in that users, groups, and other security principals have unique names within a domain. You cannot have two user objects named JoeUser in the same domain, although you could have a JoeUser in one domain and a JoeUser in another domain.

A Windows NT domain is a security boundary in that access rights and privileges for a user apply only to objects within the same domain, and by default, a user in a domain can access only resources in that domain.

Domain Trusts

Limiting users' access to the resources in a single domain would be an impossible constraint for network administrators. To allow users in one domain to access resource in another, Windows NT networking supports the notion of interdomain trusts. An interdomain trust relationship allows users in one domain to be authenticated by and access resources in another domain. The domain that grants access is called the *trusting domain*; it trusts the users in the trusted domain to access its resources.

Security Principals

Anything in the system that uses securable resources is a *security principal*. Users, services, and computers are all security principals. All security principals have passwords that Windows 2000 uses to authenticate the security principal's identity.

The network administrator can give a security principal's access rights to objects in the system (see the section "Securable Objects"). When a security principal has rights to an object, that security principal is called a *trustee* of that object.

The network administrator can also assign privileges to security principals. These privileges are associated with the security principal (not with a secured object), and apply to any secured object the security principal accesses.

Groups

A *group* in Windows 2000 is a collection of security principals that share common security characteristics. For example, the Administrators group contains members who all have administrative access rights to system resources. Groups are security principals as well.

Using groups can reduce a system administrator's workload. Instead of setting up access rights for every single user individually, the administrator can define a group, set up access rights for that group, and add users as members to the group. The users will inherit the access rights of the group.

Securable Objects

Computer and network resources that security principals use, and to which Windows 2000 can control access, are called *securable objects*. Don't confuse securable objects with directory objects: Directory objects are a kind of securable object, and so are files, services, pipes, processes, threads, and the system Registry.

Every securable object has an owner—generally, the security principal that created the object. The owner of a secured object has certain inalienable rights that neither the administrator nor the system can give away.

4

ACTIVE
DIRECTORY
SECURITY

Note that processes and threads, although not security principals themselves, act on behalf of and with the access rights of a security principal.

Security Identifiers

Windows 2000 assigns a security identifier, or SID, to all security principals. A *SID* is a data structure that consists of a version number, a 48-bit top authority identifier, and one or more 32-bit subauthority identifiers. The subauthority identifiers (also called *relative identifiers* or *RIDs*) include identifiers for the server and the domain that created the SID. Taken together, the entire data structure constitutes a globally unique identifier (but it's not a GUID!) for a security principal. For all practical purposes, no two systems in the world will ever create the same SID. Figure 4.1 shows what a SID looks like.

FIGURE 4.1

A Windows 2000 security identifier.

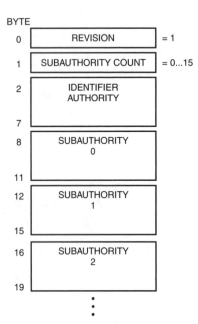

Windows 2000 creates and assigns a SID to each security principal when it creates the security principal. For instance, when you create a new user, Windows 2000 creates a new SID for the user and stores it with the user object in the directory.

If you move a user from one domain to another, a domain controller in the new domain assigns a new SID to the user object, and Windows 2000 saves the old SID in the user object in order to resolve old access rights. So, unlike GUIDs on directory objects, an object's SID can change during its lifetime.

Windows 2000 predefines RIDs for well-known users such as Administrator and Guest, as well as for well-known groups such as Admins, Users, and Computers. This lets the administrator define access rights not just in terms of specific security principals, but generically for groups of security principals. The next section describes this process in more detail.

When Windows 2000 displays a SID, it uses the following form:

> S-*<version>*-*<top authority>*-*<subauthority 1>*-*<subauthority 2>*-*<subauthority* n>...

For instance, the SID for one of my test users on our Windows 2000 network is S-1-5-21-484763869-789336058-1060284298-500.

S-1 indicates that this is a revision 1 SID. The 5 represents the NT top authority, 21 is a RID indicating that this SID was assigned by an NT domain controller, 484763869 is the RID for my domain, 789336058 is the RID for the domain controller that assigned the user RID, and 500 is the RID for the user. Other RIDs will have a similar structure.

Listing 4.1 shows a SID_IDENTIFIER_AUTHORITY and SID structures from WINNT.H.

LISTING 4.1 SID_IDENTIFIER_AUTHORITY AND SID STRUCTURES FROM WINNT.H

```
 1: typedef struct _SID_IDENTIFIER_AUTHORITY {
 2:    BYTE  Value[6];
 3: } SID_IDENTIFIER_AUTHORITY, *PSID_IDENTIFIER_AUTHORITY;
 4:
 5: typedef struct _SID {
 6:    BYTE  Revision;
 7:    BYTE  SubAuthorityCount;
 8:    SID_IDENTIFIER_AUTHORITY IdentifierAuthority;
 9:    DWORD SubAuthority[1];
10: } SID, *PISID;
```

4

ACTIVE DIRECTORY SECURITY

Well-Known Security Principals

The Windows 2000 security system defines several well-known RIDs. You can use them to define well-known entities within a domain by combining them with the domain SID. You can use the resulting well-known SID anywhere you use a regular SID. Table 4.1 lists the well-known RIDs in Windows 2000.

TABLE 4.1   WELL-KNOWN SECURITY PRINCIPALS FROM WINNT.H

Name	RID	Description
SECURITY_DIALUP_RID	0x00000001	Represents all dial-up users.
SECURITY_NETWORK_RID	0x00000002L	Represents all entities accessing the server over the network.
SECURITY_BATCH_RID	0x00000003L	Represents processes running in batch mode (noninteractive).
SECURITY_INTERACTIVE_RID	0x00000004L	Represents processes running interactively.
SECURITY_SERVICE_RID	0x00000006L	Represents all service processes.
SECURITY_ANONYMOUS_LOGON_RID	0x00000007L	Represents processes that are logged in anonymously.
SECURITY_PROXY_RID	0x00000008L	Unknown.
SECURITY_ENTERPRISE_ ➥CONTROLLERS_RID	0x00000009L	Represents all processes running on a domain controller.
SECURITY_PRINCIPAL_SELF_RID	0x0000000AL	Represents the SID of the security principal accessing the object. During an access check, the security system replaces this SID with the SID of the accessing process.
SECURITY_AUTHENTICATED_USER_RID	0x0000000BL	Represents any authenticated user.
SECURITY_RESTRICTED_CODE_RID	0x0000000CL	Unknown.
SECURITY_TERMINAL_SERVER_RID	0x0000000DL	Represents the Windows NT Terminal Server.
SECURITY_LOGON_IDS_RID	0x00000005L	Refers to processes associated with a given logon session.
SECURITY_LOCAL_SYSTEM_RID	0x00000012L	Represents the Local System service account.
SECURITY_NT_NON_UNIQUE	0x00000015L	Unknown.
SECURITY_BUILTIN_DOMAIN_RID	0x00000020L	Represents the domain to which the machine belongs.
DOMAIN_USER_RID_ADMIN	0x000001F4L	Represents any administrator of the domain of which the machine is a member.
DOMAIN_USER_RID_GUEST	0x000001F5L	Represents anyone logged in to the Guest account.
DOMAIN_USER_RID_KRBTGT	0x000001F6L	Represents any user with a Kerberos ticket-granting ticket.

Name	RID	Description
DOMAIN_GROUP_RID_ADMINS	0x00000200L	Represents the Admins group.
DOMAIN_GROUP_RID_USERS	0x00000201L	Represents the Users group.
DOMAIN_GROUP_RID_GUESTS	0x00000202L	Represents the Guests group.
DOMAIN_GROUP_RID_COMPUTERS	0x00000203L	Represents the Computers group.
DOMAIN_GROUP_RID_CONTROLLERS	0x00000204L	Represents the Domain Controllers group.
DOMAIN_GROUP_RID_CERT_ADMINS	0x00000205L	Represents the Certificate Admins group.
DOMAIN_GROUP_RID_SCHEMA_ADMINS	0x00000206L	Represents the Schema Admins group.
DOMAIN_GROUP_RID_ ➥ENTERPRISE_ADMINS	0x00000207L	Represents the Enterprise Admins group.

Win32 Security APIs for SIDs

Table 4.2 lists the Win32 APIs that are relevant to working with SIDs. You can find the details for these functions in the Microsoft online documentation at http://msdn.microsoft.com.

TABLE 4.2 WIN32 SECURITY APIS FOR SIDS

Name	Description
AllocateAndInitializeSID	Allocates and initializes a SID structure.
CopySid	Copies the contents of one SID to another.
EqualPrefixSid	Checks whether two SIDs are equal, not counting the last RID (that is, the two SIDs were issued by the same authority).
EqualSid	Checks whether two SIDs are equal.
FreeSid	Frees the memory associated with a SID created by AllocateAndInitializeSID.
GetLengthSid	Returns the length of a SID structure.
GetSidIdentifierAuthority	Returns the address of the SID_IDENTIFIER_AUTHORITY structure within a SID structure.
GetSidLengthRequired	Returns the number of bytes needed to store a SID with a specified number of subauthorities.
GetSidSubAuthority	Returns the address of a subauthority (RID) within a SID.

continues

4

ACTIVE DIRECTORY SECURITY

TABLE 4.2 CONTINUED

Name	Description
GetSidSubAuthorityCount	Returns the number of subauthorities (RIDs) within a SID.
InitializeSid	Initializes an already-allocated SID structure, given a top authority and the number of subauthorities.
IsValidSid	Returns TRUE if the specified SID is structurally valid (although not necessarily a real SID).
LookupAccountName	Returns the account name for a SID. This is equivalent to searching the directory for an object with a particular SID.
LookupAccountSID	Returns the SID given a valid account name. This is equivalent to reading the user, group, or computer object from the directory and getting its objectSID property.

Authentication

Authentication is the process of verifying the identity of a security principal. When you enter your username and password to log in to a network, you are asserting that you are that user. Windows 2000 uses the password you entered as a way of verifying that you are who you say you are.

Earlier versions of Windows NT used the NTLM (NT LAN Manager) protocol to pass your username and password to the domain controller for authentication. Windows 2000 uses the more modern (and robust) Kerberos Version 5 protocol to perform the same task.

The details of how Kerberos works are fascinating, but they're really beyond the scope of this book. If you would like to learn more about Kerberos, check out the Massachusetts Institute of Technology's Web site at http://web.mit.edu/kerberos/www or Microsoft's Web site at http://www.microsoft.com/security/resources/brundrett.asp.

Access Token

When a user (or any security principal, for that matter) logs in, the Local Security Authority (LSA) service on the domain controller verifies the user's identity by checking the user's password and then composing an *access token* for that user. The access token represents the user's roles and privileges within the security system. The access token contains the user's SID, the SIDs of all the groups the user is a member of, and a list of privileges that the user may have (see Figure 4.2). Whenever Windows 2000 creates a process on behalf of the user, the system ties the user's access token to that process. When the process attempts to perform some operation on a secured resource (such as Active Directory modifying an object in the directory), the Windows 2000 security system gets the access token from the process and uses it to determine whether the user is allowed to perform that operation.

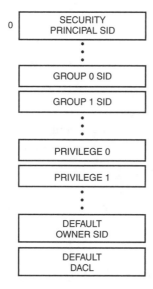

FIGURE 4.2
A Windows 2000 access token.

Win32 Security APIs for Access Tokens

Table 4.3 lists the Win32 APIs that specifically deal with access tokens. You can find the details for these functions in the Microsoft online documentation at `http://msdn.microsoft.com`.

TABLE 4.3 WIN32 APIs FOR ACCESS TOKENS

Name	Description
AdjustTokenGroups	Modifies the group information in an access token.
AdjustTokenPrivileges	Modifies the privileges information in an access token.
DuplicateToken	Creates an impersonation access token from an existing access token.
DuplicateTokenEx	Creates a primary or impersonation access token from an existing access token.
GetTokenInformation	Returns specific portions of an access token.
OpenProcessToken	Checks for appropriate access and returns a handle to a process's access token.
OpenThreadToken	Checks for appropriate access and returns a handle to a thread's access token.
SetThreadToken	Assigns an impersonation access token to the specified thread.
SetTokenInformation	Sets the owner, group, or default discretionary access control list of an access token.

4

ACTIVE DIRECTORY SECURITY

Impersonation

In a client/server environment, the server process typically services requests for many clients. The server process has its own identity in the security system, typically that of the LocalSystem account or of some special service account. The server process accesses securable objects on behalf of the client processes making the requests. Normally, the Windows 2000 security system would use the access token of the service to grant or deny access to securable objects, but this would create a giant security hole. Every client of the service would effectively have the access rights of the service, which is not a good idea.

The Windows 2000 security system uses a process called *impersonation,* where a thread of the server processes assumes the identity of the client making the request. In this way, the security system can grant access appropriate to the client making the request.

Secured Operations

Given the wide range of securable objects (files, processes, semaphores, directory objects, giraffes, aircraft carriers, and so forth), you might expect that there are more operations than just the usual read, write, and delete. And you would be right.

Each operation you can perform on a secured object requires the appropriate access right. Windows 2000 security divides the different types of access rights into three groups. *Standard access rights* are rights that apply to every kind of secured object (and to the security descriptor of the secured object). For instance, the delete operation applies to all secured objects. *Specific access rights* are rights that apply only to a particular kind of object. For instance, a file has specific rights for reading, writing, and executing. A Windows 2000 service has access rights for starting and stopping the service. *Generic access rights* are rights for operations that apply to all secured objects, but have different meanings depending on the kind of object.

You can also extend the Windows 2000 security system with user-defined secured operations. See the later section "Extending Windows 2000 Security with Private Object Security."

Access Masks

Windows 2000 security uses a 32-bit mask to represent the kinds of operations a user wants to perform on a secured object; each bit represents a different kind of operation. When a process attempts to perform an operation, it presents an access mask to the security system.

Windows 2000 reserves separate portions of the access mask to represent different kinds of operations. Figure 4.3 shows the different parts of the access mask.

FIGURE 4.3

A Windows 2000 access mask.

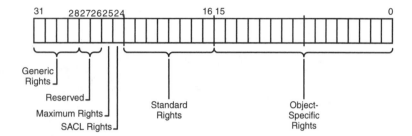

Security Descriptor

A Windows 2000 security descriptor is a data structure that contains all the information needed to determine what operations a user (or other security principal) may perform on a secured object. Every secured object has a security descriptor attached to it in some way.

Each security descriptor contains the following pieces of data:

- The SID of the owner of the secured object—If a process presents an access token containing this SID, the process will be granted owner privileges to the secured object.
- The SID of the primary group of the secured object—This is only used for POSIX compatibility, but otherwise is not particularly interesting.
- A set of control flags that provides additional information about the security descriptor.
- A discretionary access control list that defines which users may perform which operations on the secured object.
- A system access control list that determines which operations by which users will generate security audit messages.

Active Directory stores security descriptors for a directory object as an attribute of the object itself called nTSecurityDescriptor. Every object in the directory has an nTSecurityDescriptor attribute. Figure 4.4 illustrates a Windows 2000 Security Descriptor.

> **NOTE**
>
> Although each object in the directory has an nTSecurityDescriptor attribute, you can't access this attribute by using the LDAP functions in the usual way. You must use an extended search function—either ldap_search_ext() or ldap_search_ext_s()—and specify the security descriptor server control as "1.2.840.113556.1.4.801". If you do not use an extended LDAP search, Active Directory will not return the nTSecurityDescriptor attribute.
>
> If you use ADSI to access an object's security descriptor, use the IADsSecurityDescriptor interface. ADSI uses the extended LDAP search automatically.

FIGURE 4.4

A Windows 2000 security descriptor.

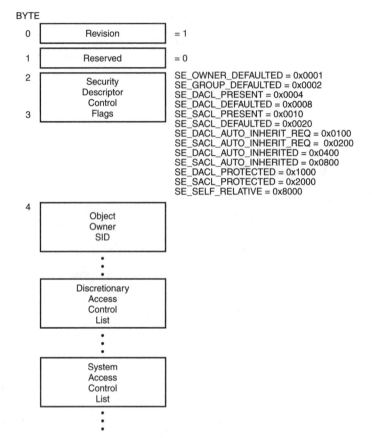

BYTE

0	Revision — = 1
1	Reserved — = 0
2	Security Descriptor Control
3	Flags

SE_OWNER_DEFAULTED = 0x0001
SE_GROUP_DEFAULTED = 0x0002
SE_DACL_PRESENT = 0x0004
SE_DACL_DEFAULTED = 0x0008
SE_SACL_PRESENT = 0x0010
SE_SACL_DEFAULTED = 0x0020
SE_DACL_AUTO_INHERIT_REQ = 0x0100
SE_SACL_AUTO_INHERIT_REQ = 0x0200
SE_DACL_AUTO_INHERITED = 0x0400
SE_SACL_AUTO_INHERITED = 0x0800
SE_DACL_PROTECTED = 0x1000
SE_SACL_PROTECTED = 0x2000
SE_SELF_RELATIVE = 0x8000

4

Object
Owner
SID

Discretionary
Access
Control
List

System
Access
Control
List

Absolute and Self-Relative Security Descriptors

Windows 2000 can store a security descriptor in memory in two different forms. The first form is called *absolute* format. In this case, the security descriptor structure, the SIDs, the system access control list (SACL), and the discretionary access control list (DACL) are not contiguous in memory. The absolute security descriptor structure contains pointers that refer to the other parts of the security descriptor, such as the owner SID and the access control lists. This is the simplest format to use when you are creating a security descriptor from scratch. Listing 4.2 shows the SECURITY_DESCRIPTOR structure definition that you would normally use to access a security descriptor in absolute format.

LISTING 4.2 ABSOLUTE SECURITY DESCRIPTOR STRUCTURE IN WINNT.H

```
1: typedef struct _SECURITY_DESCRIPTOR {
2:    BYTE  Revision;    // SD revision; currently 1
```

```
3:      BYTE  Sbz1;          // unused; always 0
4:      SECURITY_DESCRIPTOR_CONTROL Control;    // SD control flags
5:      PSID Owner;          // Pointer to SID of owner
6:      PSID Group;          // Pointer to SID of group
7:      PACL Sacl;           // Pointer to SACL
8:      PACL Dacl;           // Pointer to DACL
9:      } SECURITY_DESCRIPTOR, *PISECURITY_DESCRIPTOR;
```

The second way Windows 2000 stores a security descriptor in memory is the *self-relative* format. A self-relative security descriptor occupies a single block of contiguous memory. Instead of containing pointers to the various parts of the security descriptor, the self-relative security descriptor structure contains DWORD byte offsets from the beginning of the security descriptor. This is the form you would use if you wanted to read or write the security descriptor from a file. Listing 4.3 shows the SECURITY_DESCRIPTOR_RELATIVE structure that you would use to access a security descriptor in relative format.

LISTING 4.3   SELF-RELATIVE SECURITY DESCRIPTOR STRUCTURE IN WINNT.H

```
1: typedef struct _SECURITY_DESCRIPTOR_RELATIVE {
2:      BYTE  Revision;     // version of security descriptor
3:      BYTE  Sbz1;      // always zero
4:      SECURITY_DESCRIPTOR_CONTROL Control;    // SD control flags
5:      DWORD Owner;     // offset of owner SID from start of SD
6:      DWORD Group;     // offset of group SID from start of SD
7:      DWORD Sacl;      // offset of SACL from start of SD
8:      DWORD Dacl;      // offset of DACL from start of SD
9:      } SECURITY_DESCRIPTOR_RELATIVE, *PISECURITY_DESCRIPTOR_RELATIVE;
```

Security Descriptor Control Flags

Each security descriptor has a 16-bit word that contains a set of control flags that provide additional information about the security descriptor. Table 4.4 describes these flags.

TABLE 4.4   SECURITY DESCRIPTOR CONTROL FLAGS FROM IADS.H

Flag	Value	Description
ADS_SD_CONTROL_SE_GROUP_DEFAULTED	0x0002	The owner field of the security descriptor is not necessarily the creator. Instead, it was created by a default mechanism.

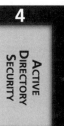

continues

TABLE 4.4 CONTINUED

Flag	Value	Description
ADS_SD_CONTROL_SE_DACL_PRESENT	0x0004	The security descriptor contains a discretionary access control list. If this flag is not set, the DACL is NULL (as opposed to empty), and Windows 2000 will grant all access rights to everyone.
ADS_SD_CONTROL_SE_DACL_DEFAULTED	0x0008	The DACL of the security descriptor was defaulted from the creator's access token.
ADS_SD_CONTROL_SE_SACL_PRESENT	0x0010	The security descriptor contains a system access control list. If this flag is not set, the SACL is NULL, and no security auditing will occur.
ADS_SD_CONTROL_SE_SACL_DEFAULTED	0x0020	The SACL was created as a result of a default mechanism.
ADS_SD_CONTROL_SE_DACL_ ➥AUTO_INHERIT_REQ	0x0100	The object must inherit (inheritance required) its DACL from its parent.
ADS_SD_CONTROL_SE_SACL_ ➥AUTO_INHERIT_REQ	0x0200	The object must inherit (inheritance required) its SACL from its parent.
ADS_SD_CONTROL_SE_DACL_ ➥AUTO_INHERITED	0x0400	The DACL for this security descriptor was created by inheriting access control entries from parent objects.
ADS_SD_CONTROL_SE_SACL_ ➥AUTO_INHERITED	0x0800	The SACL for this security descriptor was created by inheriting access control entries from parent objects.
ADS_SD_CONTROL_SE_DACL_PROTECTED	0x1000	The DACL in the security descriptor cannot be altered by inheritable access control entries in parent objects.

Flag	Value	Description
ADS_SD_CONTROL_SE_SACL_PROTECTED	0x2000	The SACL in the security descriptor cannot be altered by inheritable access control entries in parent objects.
ADS_SD_CONTROL_SE_SELF_RELATIVE	0x8000	The security descriptor is stored in self-relative format. If this bit is not set, the security descriptor is stored in absolute format.

Win32 Security APIs for Security Descriptors

Table 4.5 lists the Win32 APIs that specifically deal with security descriptors. You can find the details for these functions in the Microsoft online documentation at `http://msdn.microsoft.com`.

TABLE 4.5 WIN32 APIs FOR SECURITY DESCRIPTORS

Name	Description
ConvertToAutoInheritPrivateObjectSecurity	Resolves the noninherited security descriptors of a parent and child object so that the child's security descriptor can be rewritten as an inherited security descriptor.
GetSecurityDescriptorControl	Returns the control flags from the specified security descriptor.
GetSecurityDescriptorDacl	Gets a pointer to the discretionary access control list of the specified security descriptor.
GetSecurityDescriptorGroup	Retrieves the SID of the primary group of the security descriptor.
GetSecurityDescriptorLength	Gets the total size in bytes of all the elements of the specified security descriptor. This is the amount of contiguous memory needed to store the security descriptor in self-relative format.

4

ACTIVE
DIRECTORY
SECURITY

continues

TABLE 4.5 CONTINUED

Name	*Description*
GetSecurityDescriptorOwner	Returns a pointer to the owner SID of the specified security descriptor.
GetSecurityDescriptorSacl	Returns a pointer to the system access control list of the specified security descriptor.
InitializeSecurityDescriptor	Initializes a security descriptor, given a pointer to a SECURITY_DESCRIPTOR structure and a security descriptor version number.
IsValidSecurityDescriptor	Determines whether the specified security descriptor is structurally correct.
MakeAbsoluteSD	Creates an absolute format copy of a self-relative format security descriptor. This is the API you would use to pull out the various pieces of a security descriptor to manipulate them. This function will also return the sizes of the various portions of the security descriptor.
MakeAbsoluteSD2	Creates an absolute format copy of a self-relative format security descriptor.
MakeSelfRelativeSD	Creates a self-relative copy of an absolute format security descriptor. This is the API you would use before writing the security descriptor to disk, for instance.
SetSecurityDescriptorControl	Sets the control flags of the specified security descriptor to the value given.
SetSecurityDescriptorDacl	Sets the discretionary access control list of the specified security descriptor.
SetSecurityDescriptorGroup	Sets the primary group entry of a security descriptor.
SetSecurityDescriptorOwner	Sets the owner SID of the specified security descriptor.
SetSecurityDescriptorSacl	Sets the system access control list of the specified security descriptor.

Discretionary Access Control List

The Discretionary Access Control List (DACL) contains a list of access control entries. Each access control entry contains the SID of a security principal and an access mask that defines the operations that principal may (or may not) perform.

System Access Control List

The System Access Control List (SACL) looks just like a DACL. It is a list of access control entries, in which each access control entry specifies a SID and an access mask (see Figure 4.5).

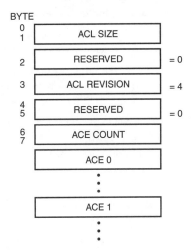

The Windows 2000 security system doesn't use the SACL to determine which users can perform which operations; the security system uses the SACL to determine which operations performed by which users will appear in the security audit log. Table 4.6 lists the functions you use to work with DACLs and SACLs.

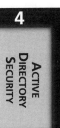

NOTE

Only security administrators can modify the SACL of an object.

TABLE 4.6 WIN32 APIs FOR ACCESS CONTROL LISTS

Name	Description
AddAccessAllowedAce	Creates and adds an access allowed ACE to the end of the specified discretionary access control list.
AddAccessAllowedAceEx	Creates and adds an access allowed ACE to the end of specified discretionary access control list and lets you specify the ACE flags for the new ACE.
AddAccessAllowedObjectAce	Creates and adds an access allowed object ACE to the end of the specified discretionary access control list. You specify the object GUID, inherited object GUID, and ACE flags for the new ACE.
AddAccessDeniedAce	Creates and adds an access denied ACE to the end of the specified discretionary access control list.
AddAccessDeniedAceEx	Creates and adds an access denied ACE to the end of the specified discretionary access control list and lets you specify the ACE flags for the new ACE.
AddAccessDeniedObjectAce	Creates and adds an access denied object ACE to the end of the specified discretionary access control list. You specify the object GUID, inherited object GUID, and ACE flags for the new ACE.
AddAce	Adds a list of ACEs to the specified access control list at the specified position in the list.
AddAuditAccessAce	Creates and adds a system audit access ACE to the end of the specified security access control list.
AddAuditAccessAceEx	Creates and adds a system audit access ACE to the end of the specified security access control list and lets you specify the ACE flags for the new ACE.
AddAuditAccessObjectAce	Creates and adds an system audit object ACE to the end of the specified system access control list. You specify the object GUID, inherited object GUID, and ACE flags for the new ACE.
DeleteAce	Deletes the ACE at the specified position in the access control list.
FindFirstFreeAce	Returns a pointer to the first free byte in the specified access control list.
GetAce	Returns a pointer to the ACE at the specified position in the access control list.
GetAclInformation	Returns the requested information (either version or size) from the specified access control list.

Name	Description
InitializeAcl	Initializes an access control list structure.
IsValidAcl	Returns TRUE if the specified access control list (either discretionary or system) is structurally valid.
SetAclInformation	Sets the revision number of the access control list to the value specified.

Access Control Entry

Four kinds of access control entries (ACEs) can appear in a discretionary access control list:

- The SID of a security principal
- An access control entry type indicating which kind of ACE it is
- An access mask that describes the operations the security principal may or may not perform
- A set of flags that indicates how the ACE can be inherited by other secured objects

Two of the four ACE types come straight from earlier versions of Windows NT. These ACEs use the same structure, which is shown in Figure 4.6. Windows 2000 adds two new types of ACEs, the access allowed object ACE and the access denied object ACE, which are specific to objects in the directory.

FIGURE 4.6

A Windows 2000 access control entry.

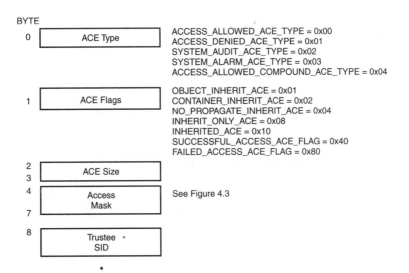

The access allowed object ACE and the access denied object ACE share the same structure, which is shown in Figure 4.7.

FIGURE 4.7

A Windows 2000 access control entry.

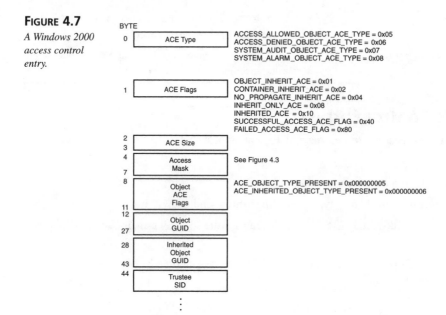

The access allowed object ACE allows the security principal to perform the operations indicated in the access mask on the secured object.

The access denied object ACE prohibits the security principal from performing the operations indicated in the access mask.

The access allowed object ACE can appear only on a directory object, not on other securable objects such as files or semaphores. The access allowed object ACE allows the security principal to perform the operations in the access mask on a specific attribute or set of attributes of the directory object that holds the security descriptor. A variant of the access allowed object ACE grants an extended access right to the security principal. (You'll read more about extended access rights later.)

The access denied object ACE works the same way as the access allowed object ACE, except that it prohibits the security principal from performing the operations in the access mask on the specific attributes or set of attributes of the directory object.

Access Mask Flags

Table 4.7 describes all the possible flags you can use in the access mask of an access control entry.

TABLE 4.7 ACCESS MASK FLAGS DEFINED IN ADS_RIGHTS_ENUM IN IADS.H

Mask	Value	Description
ADS_RIGHT_DELETE	0x10000	Gives the right to delete the object.
ADS_RIGHT_READ_CONTROL	0x20000	Gives the right to read the control flags from the security descriptor.
ADS_RIGHT_WRITE_DAC	0x40000	Gives the right to modify the discretionary access control list.
ADS_RIGHT_WRITE_OWNER	0x80000	Gives the right to assign ownership of the object to self, though not to another user. The user must already appear in the ACL for the object.
ADS_RIGHT_SYNCHRONIZE	0x100000	Gives the right to use object for synchronization. Applies to synchronization objects such as semaphores and mutexes, not to directory objects.
ADS_RIGHT_ACCESS_SYSTEM_SECURITY	0x1000000	Gives read and write access to the objects security access control list.
ADS_RIGHT_GENERIC_READ	0x80000000	Gives the right to read the object, read the object's discretionary access control list, and read all the object's attributes. Also gives the right to read this object's children in the directory tree.

continues

4

ACTIVE DIRECTORY SECURITY

TABLE 4.7 CONTINUED

Mask	Value	Description
ADS_RIGHT_GENERIC_WRITE	0x40000000	Gives the right to add or modify all the attributes of the object and modify the object's discretionary access control list. This also gives the right to delete the object.
ADS_RIGHT_GENERIC_EXECUTE	0x20000000	Gives the right to enumerate the child objects of this object in the directory.
ADS_RIGHT_GENERIC_ALL	0x10000000	Gives the right to read and write all the object's attributes, and all the attributes of child objects. Also gives the right to add and delete child objects of this object, and to invoke operations that require an extended right.
ADS_RIGHT_DS_CREATE_CHILD	0x00000001	Gives the right to create a child object of this object. To grant the right to only create child objects of a particular class, make this an object access control entry and set the GUID in the ACE to the schemaIDGUID of the class of object the user can create. If no GUID is specified, the user can create child objects of any class.
ADS_RIGHT_DS_DELETE_CHILD	0x00000002	Gives the right to delete child objects of this object. To restrict this right to the ability to only delete child objects of a particular class, make this an object access control entry and specify the schemaIDGUID of the class that can be deleted.
ADS_RIGHT_ACTRL_DS_LIST	0x00000004	Gives the right to enumerate the child objects of this object. Equivalent to ADS_RIGHT_ GENERIC_EXECUTE for directory objects.

Mask	Value	Description
ADS_RIGHT_DS_SELF	0x00000008	Gives the right to modify the group membership of a group object.
ADS_RIGHT_DS_READ_PROP	0x00000010	Gives the right to read this object's attributes. To restrict read access to a single property or property set, make this an object access control entry and specify the schemaIDGUID of the attribute, or the attributeSecurityGUID shared by a group of attributes.
ADS_RIGHT_DS_WRITE_PROP	0x00000020	Gives the right to modify this object's attributes. To restrict read access to a single property or property set, make this an object access control entry and specify the schemaIDGUID of the attribute, or the attributeSecurityGUID shared by a group of attributes.
ADS_RIGHT_DS_DELETE_TREE	0x00000040	Gives the right to delete all the children of this object. Overrides any delete restrictions on the child objects.
ADS_RIGHT_DS_LIST_OBJECT	0x00000080	Gives the right to retrieve this object as part of an enumeration. If this right is not granted, the user will not see this object in the directory.
ADS_RIGHT_DS_CONTROL_ACCESS	0x00000100	Gives the right to perform operations that require an extended access right. To specify a specific extended access right, make this an object access control entry and set the object GUID to the GUID of the extended right you are granting. If no GUID is specified, the user can perform any operation requiring an extended right.

4

ACTIVE
DIRECTORY
SECURITY

There are two Win32 security APIs that deal explicitly with access masks. Table 4.8 describes them.

TABLE 4.8 WIN32 APIS FOR ACCESS MASKS

Name	Description
AreAllAccessesGranted	Returns TRUE if all the specified access rights bits are set in the given access mask.
AreAnyAccessesGranted	Returns TRUE if any of the specified access rights bits are set in the given access mask.

The flags listed in Table 4.9 define the possible types of Access Control Entries you can create. Any given ACE can be only one of these types.

TABLE 4.9 FLAGS THAT DEFINE THE TYPE OF ACCESS CONTROL ENTRY

Mask	Value	Description
ADS_ACETYPE_ACCESS_ALLOWED	0x00	Specifies an Access Allowed ACE. It grants the rights in the access mask to the trustee.
ADS_ACETYPE_ACCESS_DENIED	0x01	Specifies an Access Denied ACE. It denies the rights in the access mask to the trustee.
ADS_ACETYPE_SYSTEM_AUDIT	0x02	Specifies an Audit ACE. It generates security audit messages when the trustee performs the operations specified in the access mask. You can modify this behavior to generate a message only when the operation succeeds or fails by specifying the appropriate ACE flag.
ADS_ACETYPE_ACCESS_ALLOWED_OBJECT	0x05	Specifies an Access Allowed Object ACE. Grants the rights in the access mask to the trustee for the specific attribute or group of attributes given by the object GUID.
ADS_ACETYPE_ACCESS_DENIED_OBJECT	0x06	Specifies an Access Denied Object ACE. It denies the rights in the access mask to the trustee for the specific attribute or group of attributes given by the object GUID.

Mask	Value	Description
ADS_ACETYPE_SYSTEM_AUDIT_OBJECT	0x07	Specifies an Audit Object ACE. It generates security audit messages when the trustee performs the operations specified in the access mask. You can modify this behavior to generate a message only when the operation succeeds or fails by specifying the appropriate ACE flag.

Associated with each ACE is a set of flags that define how (or if) an Access Control Entry will be inherited. Table 4.10 describes each of these flags.

TABLE 4.10   ACE FLAGS DEFINED IN ADS_ACEFLAG_ENUM

Type	Value	Description
ADS_ACEFLAG_INHERIT_ACE	0x02	Indicates that all subordinate objects will inherit this access control entry unless specifically inhibited by the ADS_SD_CONTROL_SE_DACL_ PROTECTED or ADS_SD_CONTROL_ SE_SACL_PROTECTED security descriptor control flags.
ADS_ACEFLAG_NO_PROPAGATE_ ➥INHERIT_ACE	0x04	Indicates that only the immediate children of this object will inherit this access control entry unless specifically inhibited by the ADS_SD_CONTROL_ SE_DACL_ PROTECTED or ADS_SD_CONTROL_ SE_ SACL_PROTECTED security descriptor control flags. Note that you must specify this in conjunction with ADS_ACEFLAG_INHERIT_ACE to have any effect.
ADS_ACEFLAG_INHERIT_ONLY_ACE	0x08	Indicates that this access control entry does not apply to the current object; it applies only to subordinate objects that inherit it. Note that you must specify this in conjunction with ADS_ACEFLAG_INHERIT_ACE to have any effect.

continues

4

ACTIVE
DIRECTORY
SECURITY

TABLE 4.10   CONTINUED

Type	Value	Description
ADS_ACEFLAG_INHERITED_ACE	0x10	Indicates this flag is automatically set by the system to indicate that this ACE was inherited.
ADS_ACEFLAG_SUCCESSFUL_ACCESS	0x40	Indicates that the security system should generate a security audit message if the operation specified in the access mask is successful. This flag is meaningful only if the ACE type is either ADS_ACETYPE_SYSTEM_AUDIT or ADS_ACETYPE_SYSTEM_AUDIT_OBJECT.
ADS_ACEFLAG_FAILED_ACCESS	0x80	Indicates that the security system should generate a security audit message if the operation specified in the access mask is unsuccessful. This flag is meaningful only if the ACE type is either ADS_ACETYPE_SYSTEM_AUDIT or ADS_ACETYPE_SYSTEM_AUDIT_OBJECT.

Empty DACLs and NULL DACLs

There is a big, big difference between a discretionary access list that is missing (the ADS_SD_CONTROL_SE_DACL_PRESENT flag in the security descriptor control word is 0) and a discretionary access list that has no access control entries. A NULL DACL indicates that there is no security associated with the object; therefore, all security principals have the right to perform any operation on the object.

An empty DACL, on the other hand, indicates that the object does have security associated with it, and that because no rights have been granted to anyone, no one has access to the object (although the owner still has access to the DACL itself).

Default Access Rights

When you create a securable object, you can generally specify the access control list you want to give it in the API function that created it.

If you do not specify an access control list when you create a securable object, Windows 2000 will create one for you at no charge.

Windows 2000 first determines whether there is a parent object for the object you've created—for instance, a directory for a file or a parent key for a Registry entry. Windows 2000 uses the inheritable access rights from that object to create the default security descriptor for the new object.

If there are no inheritable rights for the default security descriptor, Windows 2000 uses the default DACL from the access token of the thread creating the object.

If there is no default DACL in the access token, Windows 2000 does not create a DACL for the security descriptor, thereby granting all access to the object for all users.

Evaluating Access Rights

When a thread of some client process tries to access a securable object, the thread passes an access rights mask to the Windows 2000 security system. The access rights mask contains all the access rights the thread needs to obtain. Windows 2000 uses the access token of the thread (which contains the identity, group membership, and privileges of the user) against the discretionary access control list of the securable object.

> **NOTE**
>
> When a client makes a directory request, a thread of the Directory Service Agent (part of the LSASS process on the domain controller), not the client process, actually accesses the objects in the directory. Because the Directory Service Agent (DSA) threads impersonate the identity of the requesting client, Windows 2000 will properly evaluate the access rights.

4

ACTIVE DIRECTORY SECURITY

If the object does not have a discretionary access control list, Windows 2000 grants access to the object.

If the object has a discretionary access control list, the Windows 2000 security system evaluates the access control entries of the DACL in the order they exist in the SID. The security system continues checking access control entries until it 1) finds access control entries that grant all the rights requested in the access rights mask (access granted); 2) finds an access control entry that denies one or more of the requested rights (access denied); or 3) runs out of access control entries (access denied).

The order of access control entries in the access control list is critical. It is quite possible for an object to have conflicting access rights in its discretionary access control list. For instance, the list could contain an ACE denying all access to dial-up users, followed by an ACE granting access to all administrators. If an administrator attempted to access the object over a dial-up connection, the system would deny access, which is probably not what was intended.

Microsoft defines a "preferred order" of access control entries in a discretionary access control list to minimize unexpected behavior and security holes. The rules are as follows:

- Put noninherited ACEs in a group in front of any inherited ACEs. This prevents inherited rights from taking precedence over noninherited rights.

Within the groups of inherited and noninherited ACEs, order the ACEs as follows:

- Access denied ACEs for the object
- Access denied ACEs for properties or property sets
- Access allowed ACEs for the object
- Access allowed ACEs for properties or property sets

Windows 2000 Security and Active Directory

In earlier versions of Windows NT networking, each domain controller maintained a copy of the security accounts manager (SAM) database for the domain. The SAM database contained all the users and group definitions and the corresponding SIDs and privileges. The local security authority (LSA) process was responsible for authenticating all users attempting to access securable objects in the system.

In Windows 2000, Active Directory serves as the store for all security information. In fact, the directory service agent (DSA) is actually a set of threads that are part of the LSA on each domain controller. Active Directory is an integral part of the Windows 2000 security system.

Active Directory also stores most of the network and service configuration information for the entire enterprise; this information must be protected too. Active Directory uses the same Windows 2000 security mechanisms to protect the objects in the directory.

Domain Controllers and the Local Security Authority

Every domain controller in a Windows 2000 network has a replica of the domain's directory naming context. The domain naming context contains directory objects for all security principals in the domain, including users, groups, services, computers, and others.

The LSA on each domain controller processes logon requests. Because the user object contains the encrypted version of the user's password, the LSA can determine whether the user provided the correct password. Because the directory contains all the group membership information, the LSA can issue access tokens to processes that provide the proper credentials.

The LSA process (the program is LSASS.EXE) actually runs Active Directory; there is no separate directory service per se. The LSASS is the only process that can access the Active Directory database. You can't shut down LSASS, and if it crashes for some reason, Windows 2000 will shut the server down as well. So the directory is pretty secure—at least from direct access.

Active Directory Domains

Ideally, a global directory such as Active Directory would eliminate the need for domains. After all, why break the tree into arbitrary security boundaries? But for many reasons, not the least of which is backward compatibility with "classic NT" (Windows NT 3.5x and 4.x) networks, Active Directory implements domains.

There is one significant difference between Active Directory domains and classic NT domains. You can create a hierarchy of domains in Active Directory, with one domain effectively containing one or more subordinate domains. But this hierarchical relationship is really just one of namespaces. The security relationship between domains in Active Directory remains essentially the same as with classic NT domains.

Domain Trusts

Active Directory also supports the classic Windows NT notion of domain trusts. But in this area, Active Directory has really enhanced what classic NT provided.

In classic NT, trust relationships were one-way. In other words, just because the engineering domain trusted the users in the accounting domain, the accounting domain did not necessarily trust the users in the engineering domain. Although one-way trusts are a good thing from a security standpoint, they made the lives of network administrators pretty difficult.

Trusts between two Active Directory domains in the same forest are always two-way trusts. This means that users in both domains can access the resources in the other. The improved group and access rights mechanisms in Active Directory prevent this from being a security problem.

Active Directory domain trusts are also transitive. If the engineering domain trusts the accounting domain, and the accounting domain trusts the sales domain, the engineering domain also trusts the sales domain. This is another simplification for administrators.

Taken together, two-way trusts and transitive trusts knit the domain tree together almost seamlessly. In fact, a network administrator can pretty much ignore Active Directory domain trusts altogether—at least the trusts between domains in the same forest. Active Directory automatically creates trusts between parent and child domains, and also

4

ACTIVE
DIRECTORY
SECURITY

between the roots of domain trees in the same forest. Because the trusts are all two-way and transitive, every domain in the forest trusts every other domain in the forest.

Figure 4.8 shows how trusts are automatically generated in Active Directory.

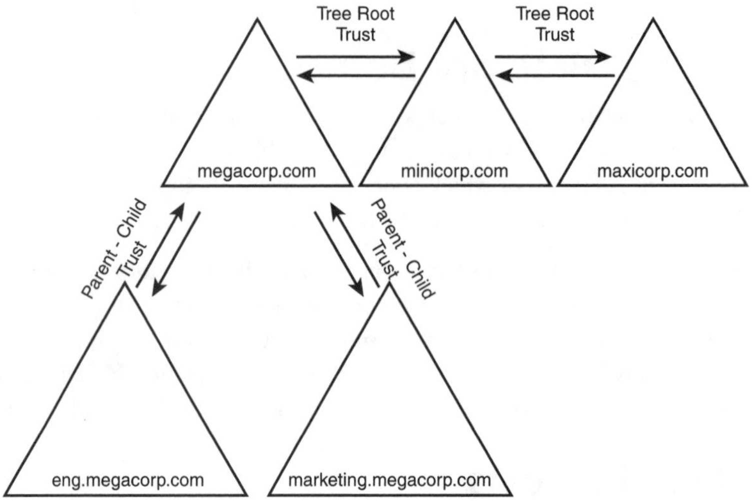

FIGURE 4.8
Trust relationships in an Active Directory forest.

Access Rights Inheritance

Active Directory organizes its directory objects as a tree, with objects containing other objects. This tree structure provides another way to simplify the administration of access rights in the directory: inheritance. Inheritance of access rights lets administrators define access rights on container objects that will then trickle down to the objects the containers contain.

> **NOTE**
>
> Access rights do not propagate between domains. In other words, an object in a subordinate domain will not inherit any access rights from the parent domain.

Making Access Rights Inheritable

You can control the inheritance of access rights on an access control entry level. In other words, you can control which ACEs a child object will inherit from its parent's DACL and SACL. There are four ways to control the way an ACE is inherited:

- To make an ACE inheritable, simply set the `ADS_ACEFLAG_INHERIT_ACE` flag for the ACE. All subordinate objects will then inherit the ACE.

- To make an ACE inheritable by only the immediate children of an object, in addition to the `ADS_ACEFLAG_INHERIT_ACE` flag, also set the `ADS_ACEFLAG_NO_PROPAGATE_INHERIT_ACE` flag in the parent ACE. The immediate children of the object will inherit the ACE, but their children will not.

- To make an ACE apply only to the objects that inherit it (and not to the object the ACE is attached to), in addition to the `ADS_ACEFLAG_INHERIT_ACE` flag, also set the `ADS_ACEFLAG_INERHIT_ONLY_ACE` flag.

- If you want to cause only immediate children to inherit an ACE, and not have the ACE apply to the object it is attached to, set the `ADS_ACEFLAG_INHERIT_ACE` flag, the `ADS_ACEFLAG_INERHIT_ONLY_ACE` flag, and the `ADS_ACEFLAG_NO_PROPAGATE_INHERIT_ACE` flag.

> **NOTE**
>
> Regardless of the kind of inheritance you want to use, you must always set the `ADS_ACEFLAG_INHERIT_ACE` flag in the ACE.

Preventing Inheritance of Access Rights

You can also prevent an object from inheriting access rights from its parent. This is useful if you want to ensure that no one can gain access to a child object, even if he obtains access to the parent. For instance, if you stored salary information in the directory in an object under the user object, anyone who could gain access to the user object and modify its access control list could then gain access to the subordinate salary object.

To prevent the inheritance of access rights, set the `ADS_SD_CONTROL_SE_DACL_PROTECTED` flag on the security descriptor of the child object. This will prevent inheritance of any access rights by the child object. Set the `ADS_SD_CONTROL_SE_SACL_PROTECTED` flag in the child's security descriptor if you want to prevent the inheritance of any of the ACEs in the system access control list.

Default Access Rights

When you create a secured object, Windows 2000 has a mechanism for creating a default security descriptor if you do not specify any access rights for the new object. The rules for creating a default discretionary access control list or system access control list for a new Active Directory object are somewhat different than the usual scheme. This process describes how Active Directory creates a default DACL; the same process applies to the creation of a default SACL.

1. When you create the object, if you specify a value for the `nTSecurityDescriptor` attribute, Active Directory will use the DACL you specified and add any inheritable ACEs from the `nTSecurityDescriptor` attribute of the containing (parent) object. If you set the `ADS_SD_CONTROL_SE_DACL_PROTECTED` flag in the security descriptor control flags, Active Directory will not add any inheritable ACEs.

2. If you don't specify a value for the `nTSecurityDescriptor` attribute, the security system will copy the inheritable access control entries from the DACL of the containing object into the DACL of the created object.

3. If there are no inheritable access control entries in the DACL of the containing object, Active Directory will use the DACL from the `defaultSecurityDescriptor` attribute from the `classSchema` object for the class of the created object.

4. If the `defaultSecurityDescriptor` attribute in the `classSchema` object does not have a DACL, Active Directory uses the default DACL from the client's access token.

5. If the access token has no default DACL, Active Directory creates the object with no DACL, which provides full access to the object for all users.

Default Owner

If you do not set the owner and primary group elements in the security descriptor for your new object, or if you don't specify a `nTSecurityDescriptor` at all, Active Directory will set default owner and primary group values for you.

Active Directory uses the SID from the access token as the owner of the new object; if you create it, you own it. The only exception to this is that Active Directory will set the owner to the Administrators group if the creator of the new object is a member of that group. This behavior makes more sense than you might think. It means that any administrator is the effective owner of any objects an administrator creates.

> **NOTE**
>
> Even though it creates a default primary group, Active Directory does not use the Primary Group element of an object's security descriptor.

Property and Property Group Access Rights

Normally, Windows access control lists determine the access rights for an object such as a file, a process, or a directory object. In Windows 2000, Active Directory provides a way for you to set the access rights on a specific attribute or group of attributes in an object. This gives the administrator the ability to, for instance, allow users to change the phone number attribute of their user object, but not the manager attribute.

You assign access rights to a property by adding an access allowed object ACE to the ACL for the object. In addition to specifying the SID of the security principal that will be granted access and the access mask that describes what access will be granted, the access allowed object ACE contains the GUID of the attribute's schema entry. This is how the security system knows what attribute the access mask applies to.

You use the access allowed object ACE to set access rights for a group of attributes, too. In this case, instead of specifying the GUID that identifies an attribute, you specify the GUID that identifies a group of attributes.

To create the group of attributes you want to assign access rights to, you must generate a GUID for the attributes to share, and then set the `attributeSecurityGUID` attribute of the `attributeSchema` object for that attribute. The Windows 2000 security system will apply the access rights in the ACE to all attributes of the object that share the GUID specified in the ACE.

Extending Windows 2000 Security with Private Object Security

Windows 2000 defines security over a wide range of objects and operations. But what if you create your own network service that provides new operations? For instance, let's say you've created a new network calendar service. Users can schedule meetings and can put meetings on other users' calendars, subject to appropriate access rights. How can you leverage Windows 2000 security for your service? Windows 2000 doesn't know about the "Add Meeting" operation, so how can you define an access control entry that grants or denies this access?

The answers are extended access rights and the private object security APIs. The Windows 2000 security system lets you define new application operations such as "Add Meeting" by adding a `controlAccessRight` object to the Extended-Rights container in the Configuration naming context. The private object security APIs give you access to the access rights inheritance and access rights evaluation mechanisms so that your service can evaluate access rights the same way Windows 2000 does.

4

ACTIVE
DIRECTORY
SECURITY

The `controlAccessRight` Object

Each `controlAccessRight` object defines a new secured operation. The name of the object is not important, although you should select a name that reflects the nature of the operation. For instance, Add-Meeting would be a good name for our calendar service.

In addition to the `objectGUID` that Active Directory automatically assigns to any new object, we have to assign a unique GUID that we can use to identify the operation in an object access control entry. This GUID goes in the `rightsGuid` attribute of the `controlAccessRight` object.

> **NOTE**
>
> The `rightsGuid` attribute is a Unicode string syntax attribute. You have to convert the `rightsGuid` value to a string before storing it by calling `StringFromGUID2()` and then removing the curly braces from either end of the string. The string you store should look something like this:
>
> `f0f8ffab-1191-11d0-a060-00aa006c33ed`

Next, we have to tell the security system what kinds of objects our new access right pertains to. In the case of our imaginary calendar service, this would be a Calendar object that we have added to the schema. To associate the Calendar object with the Add-Meeting access right, we set the `appliesTo` attribute of the Add-Meeting object to the `schemaIDGuid` of the Calendar `schemaClass` object. The `appliesTo` attribute is multivalued, so if we wanted to use the Add-Meeting right for, say, a Meeting-Room object, we would add the `schemaIDGuid` of the Meeting-Room object to the `appliesTo` attribute as well.

Setting Up the Access Control Entry

Like other directory objects, our Calendar object has an `nTSecurityDescriptor` attribute that defines the access rights for that object. The next step is to add an access control entry to provide Add-Meeting access to everyone in the Management group.

To add an ACE with a user-defined access right, create a access allowed object ACE and specify the SID (from the `objectSID` attribute) of the Management group. Instead of setting the object GUID in the ACE to the `schemaIDGuid` of a schema class, set it to the `rightsGuid` of the user-defined access right object. When Active Directory looks up the GUID in the directory, it will see that the GUID is a user-defined access right instead of an object class, and do the right thing.

Checking for User-Defined Access Rights

Active Directory can't automatically check that a calendar user has the Add-Meeting right when the user attempts to add a meeting object. As far as Active Directory is concerned, the user is simply adding an object. It is up to us as authors of the calendar service to explicitly evaluate the access rights when we add the meeting. To check a user-defined access right, use the `AccessCheckByType()` and `AccessCheckByTypeResultList()` functions to check for the `rightsGUID` of the user-defined access rights object.

Windows 2000 provides several functions to help with this, as shown in Table 4.11.

TABLE 4.11   WIN32 APIS FOR PRIVATE CHECKING ACCESS RIGHTS

Name	*Description*
`AccessCheck`	Checks whether the specified security descriptor will grant the desired rights.
`AccessCheckAndAuditAlarm`	Checks whether the specified security descriptor will grant the desired access rights, and generates a security log entry if the SACL so indicates.
`AccessCheckByType`	Checks whether the specified security descriptor will grant the desired access rights. You can specify a list of child object types as well, and this API will tell you whether you have the desired access to all of them.
`AccessCheckByTypeAndAuditAlarm`	Checks whether the specified security descriptor will grant the desired access rights. You can specify a list of child object types as well, and this API will tell you whether you have the desired access to all of them. If the SACL indicates, this API will generate a security log entry as well.
`AccessCheckByTypeResultList`	Same as `AccessCheckByType`. In addition, this call returns the granted access rights broken out by class of subordinate object.
`AccessCheckByType` ➥`ResultListAndAuditAlarm`	Same as `AccessCheckByTypeResultList`. In addition, this API will generate a security log entry if the SACL so indicates.

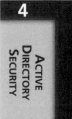

4

ACTIVE
DIRECTORY
SECURITY

Security Descriptors as Strings

There's a new feature in the Win32 security APIs that I find very intriguing. The Security Descriptor Description Language (SDDL) is a "little language" designed solely for the purpose of expressing security descriptors in almost human-readable form. I'm not sure why Microsoft added this functionality; it might have been because the LDAP standard strongly encourages vendors to provide a string format for all attribute syntaxes. Whatever the reason, SDDL provides a very convenient mechanism for converting complex security descriptor structures into easy-to-manage strings.

Getting Security Descriptors from the Directory

The `defaultSecurityDescriptor` attribute of the `classSchema` object contains the default security descriptor for objects of that class. Active Directory stores this security descriptor as an SDDL string.

Converting Between SDDL String and Security Descriptors

Windows NT security descriptors are fairly complicated structures that are inconvenient to manipulate, even with the myriad of APIs supplied in Win32. Windows 2000 provides four new APIs that help by converting security descriptors to and from a string format called Security Descriptor Description Language, or SDDL. The four SDDL functions are described in Table 4.12.

TABLE 4.12 WIN32 APIS FOR CONVERTING SECURITY DESCRIPTORS TO AND FROM STRINGS

Name	Description
`ConvertStringSecurity` `➥DescriptorToSecurity` `➥Descriptor`	Converts an SDDL string into a `SECURITY_DESCRIPTOR` structure.
`ConvertSecurityDescriptor` `➥ToStringSecurityDescriptor`	Converts a `SECURITY_DESCRIPTOR` structure into an SDDL string.
`ConvertStringSidToSid`	Converts a Security ID (SID) expressed as a SDDL string into a SID structure.
`ConvertSidToStringSid`	Converts a SID structure to an SDDL string.

SDDL Syntax

Just to give you a flavor of SDDL, here is the `defaultSecurityDescriptor` attribute from the ACS-Policy `attributeSchema` object in the default Active Directory schema.

```
D:(A;;RPWPCRCCDCLCLOLORCWOWDSDDTDTSW;;;DA)
➡(A;;RPWPCRCCDCLCLORCWOWDSDDTSW;;;SY)(A;;RPLCLORC;;;AU)
```

Now you see what I meant by "almost human-readable."

Actually, the SDDL syntax is straightforward. The `D:` indicates that the DACL follows. The strings of characters in parentheses are representations of the access control entries. The `A` in each parenthesized group indicates the entry is an access allowed ACE. The long string of letters indicates the kinds of access rights granted by the ACE. In the case of the last ACE, it includes `ADS_RIGHT_DS_READ_PROP`, `ADS_RIGHT_ACTRL_DS_LIST`, `ADS_RIGHT_DS_LIST_OBJECT`, and `ADS_RIGHT_READ_CONTROL`.

Here's the Backus Naur description of SDDL:

```
security-descriptor = [O: <owner-SID>][G: <group-SID>][D: <dacl>]
➡[S: <sacl>]
<owner-SID> = <sid>
<group-SID> = <sid>
<dacl> = <dacl-flags><dacl-ace>*
<dacl-flags> = DACL_FLAG // see table 4.13
<dacl-ace> = <ace-type>;<ace-flags>;<ace-rights>;[<object-guid>];
➡[<inherit-object-guid>];[<trustee-SID>]
<ace-type> = ACE_TYPE // see table 4.14
<ace-flags = ACE_FLAG* // see table 4.15
<ace-rights = ACE_RIGHT* // see table 4.16
<object-guid> = GUID
<inherit-object-guid> = GUID
<trustee-SID> = SID
```

> `DACL_FLAG` is one of the strings listed in Table 4.13.
>
> `ACE_TYPE` is one of the strings listed in Table 4.14.
>
> `ACE_FLAG` is one or more of the strings listed in Table 4.15.
>
> `ACE_RIGHT` is one or more of the strings listed in Table 4.16.
>
> `GUID` is a 128-bit globally unique identifier expressed in the form generated by the `GuidToString()` function, minus the braces.
>
> `SID` is a variable-length security identifier expressed in the following string form:
>
> S-*<revision>*-*<top authority>*-*<RID 1>*-*<RID 2>*-...
>
> An example is `S-1-0-0`.

Table 4.13 lists the possible string values for the `DACL_FLAG` portion of an SDDL string. One or more of these strings might appear.

TABLE 4.13 POSSIBLE DACL_FLAG VALUES IN SDDL

String	Description
P	The ADS_SD_CONTROL_SE_DACL_PROTECTED is set in the flags field of the DACL.
AI	The ADS_SD_CONTROL_SE_DACL_AUTO_INHERIT_REQ flag is set for the DACL.
AR	The ADS_SD_CONTROL_SE_DACL_AUTO_INHERITED flag is set for the DACL.

Table 4.14 lists the possible string values for the ACE type in SDDL. Each ACE must have exactly one ACE type string.

TABLE 4.14 POSSIBLE ACE_TYPE VALUES IN SDDL

String	Description
A	The ACE type is ADS_ACETYPE_ACCESS_ALLOWED.
D	The ACE type is ADS_ACETYPE_ACCESS_DENIED.
OA	The ACE type is ADS_ACETYPE_ACCESS_ALLOWED_OBJECT.
OD	The ACE type is ADS_ACETYPE_ACCESS_DENIED_OBJECT.
AU	The ACE type is ADS_ACETYPE_SYSTEM_AUDIT.
AL	The ACE type is ADS_ACETYPE_SYSTEM_ALARM (not supported).
OU	The ACE type is ADS_ACETYPE_SYSTEM_AUDIT_OBJECT.
OL	The ACE type is ADS_ACETYPE_SYSTEM_ALARM_OBJECT (not supported).

Table 4.15 lists the possible string values for the ACE flags in SDDL. Each ACE may have one or more of these strings.

TABLE 4.15 POSSIBLE ACE_FLAG VALUES IN SDDL

String	Description
CI	The ADS_ACEFLAG_CONTAINER_INHERIT_ACE flag is set.
OI	The ADS_ACEFLAG_OBJECT_INHERIT_ACE flag is set.
NP	The ADS_ACEFLAG_OBJECT_ACCESS_ALLOWED_ACE flag is set.
IO	The ADS_ACEFLAG_INHERIT_ONLY_ACE flag is set.
ID	The ADS_ACEFLAG_INHERITED_ACE flag is set.
SA	The ADS_ACEFLAG_SUCCESSFUL_ACCESS_ACE flag is set.
FA	The ADS_ACEFLAG_FAILED_ACCESS_ACE flag is set.

The strings listed in Table 4.16 show the possible values for the access rights defined by an ACE. Each ACE may have one or more of these strings.

> **NOTE**
>
> Table 4.16 lists the rights that apply to Active Directory objects; SDDL defines other rights codes for files and Registry access rights.

TABLE 4.16   POSSIBLE ACE_RIGHT VALUES IN SDDL

String	Description
GA	The ADS_RIGHT_GENERIC_ALL rights flag is set.
GR	The ADS_RIGHT_GENERIC_READ rights flag is set.
GW	The ADS_RIGHT_GENERIC_WRITE rights flag is set.
GX	The ADS_RIGHT_GENERIC_EXECUTE rights flag is set.
RC	The ADS_RIGHT_READ_CONTROL rights flag is set.
SD	The ADS_RIGHT_DELETE rights flag is set.
WD	The ADS_RIGHT_WRITE_DAC rights flag is set.
WO	The ADS_RIGHT_WRITE_OWNER rights flag is set.
RP	The ADS_RIGHT_DS_READ_PROP rights flag is set.
WP	The ADS_RIGHT_DS_WRITE_PROP rights flag is set.
CC	The ADS_RIGHT_DS_CREATE_CHILD rights flag is set.
DC	The ADS_RIGHT_DS_DELETE_CHILD rights flag is set.
LC	The ADS_RIGHT_ACTRL_DS_LIST rights flag is set.
SW	The ADS_RIGHT_DS_SELF rights flag is set.
LO	The ADS_RIGHT_DS_LIST_OBJECT rights flag is set.
DT	The ADS_RIGHT_DS_DELETE_TREE rights flag is set.
CR	The ADS_RIGHT_DS_CONTROL_ACCESS rights flag is set.

4

ACTIVE DIRECTORY SECURITY

> **NOTE**
>
> The ACE_RIGHT string can be a hex string representing the flags in the access rights integer, such as "0x1234abcd", or it can be a list of one or more of the ACE_RIGHT strings named in the table.

Programming Active Directory Security

Programming Active Directory security really isn't much different than programming security for any other Windows 2000 facility. The security mechanisms in Active Directory are essentially the same as for the rest of the operating system, with the few extensions we've discussed.

Active Directory Security Attributes

Each object in Active Directory can have an attribute named nTSecurityDescriptor. This attribute contains the security descriptor for the object.

nTSecurityDecsriptor

Although the individual attributes of an object do not have a security descriptor, you can specify access rights for individual attributes or groups of attributes by using the object access allowed or object access denied access control entries as covered earlier in this chapter.

defaultSecurityDescriptor

The Active Directory schema defines a default security descriptor in the classSchema object. The defaultSecurityDescriptor attribute contains the security descriptor to use if none was specified when the object was created, and none of the containing object's access control entries were inheritable.

objectSID

Each security principal object, such as users and groups, has a SID that uniquely identifies it to the Windows 2000 security system. The SID is always in the objectSID attribute of the security principal object.

schemaIDGuid

When you refer to an Active Directory attribute in an object access allowed ACE or an object access denied ACE, you use the schemaIDGuid attribute defined in the attributeSchema object for the attribute.

When you refer to an Active Directory class in an object access allowed ACE or an object access denied ACE, you use the schemaIDGuid attribute defined in the classSchema object for the class.

Active Directory Security and LDAP

Because Active Directory security information is kept in directory attributes, you just use the regular LDAP APIs to access it, but with a twist. By default, LDAP doesn't return the nTSecurityDescriptor attribute when you request it as part of an LDAP search. To get the nTSecurityDescriptor attribute for an object, you must use the LDAP ldap_search_ext() or ldap_search_ext_s() function and specify the Security Descriptor control (OID 1.2.840.113556.1.4.801). The sample programs in Chapter 22, "Extending LDAP Searches," show you how to do this.

You can also obtain the defaultSecurityDescriptor attribute for a classSchema object. This is the security descriptor that Active Directory will assign to a new object if you do not specify explicit rights and there are no rights for the new object to inherit. The defaultSecurityDescriptor attribute is a Unicode string attribute, and the security descriptor it contains is in SDDL format.

Active Directory Security and ADSI

ADSI can retrieve security descriptors as SDDL strings the same way that LDAP can. (ADSI uses LDAP to access Active Directory, so this is not surprising.) You simply use the IDirectoryObject, IADsProperty, and IADsPropertyValue interfaces to get to the security descriptor as a string.

But ADSI goes one step further and provides the ADSI interfaces IADsSecurity Descriptor, IADsAccessControlList, and IADsAccessControlEntry to provide a simpler object-oriented approach to the Active Directory object's security descriptor. These aren't Active Directory interfaces per se, so I don't cover them in this book.

4

ACTIVE
DIRECTORY
SECURITY

CHAPTER 5

Active Directory and DNS

Long before there were global directories, X.500, and LDAP, there was DNS. DNS (short for Domain Name System) has been the directory of the Internet since 1984, when the IETF released RFCs 882 and 883. It has grown to handle millions of domain names and hundreds of millions of accesses every day. DNS is definitely the mother of all directories, at least in terms of size and scope.

Why bring up DNS in a book about Active Directory? Well, Active Directory has a very close relationship with DNS—so close that if DNS doesn't work, neither does Active Directory. Although understanding DNS isn't strictly necessary to use Active Directory, it never hurts to know how your tools work.

This chapter gives a brief overview of DNS and describes in some detail the way Active Directory uses DNS. If you want to understand how Active Directory works, read on. If all you want to know is how to get data in and out of Active Directory, you can skip this chapter.

The Origins of DNS and DNS Basics

During the early days of the ARPAnet (the precursor of the Internet), computer administrators kept track of computer names and addresses manually. Periodically, someone at the Network Information Center (NIC) at Stanford University would email a text file called *hosts* to all other system administrators on the network. The hosts file contained the names and addresses of all the computers ("hosts") on the network. Life was good.

When the number of hosts on the ARPAnet began to explode in the early 1980s, this scheme started to break down. No one could keep up with all the new hosts appearing on the network. No one could make sure the host names were unique. No one could keep the host name-to-address mappings current. Life was bad.

The gods of the ARPAnet wanted a new scheme for managing host name-to-address mappings that would scale up as the network grew and that would allow the delegation of the administration of the namespace.

Enter DNS. Paul Mockapetris, then at the University of Southern California, designed a new naming system called the Domain Name System, or DNS. The design of DNS applied the techniques of partitioning, distribution, and replication to make the management of tens of thousands of host names more, well, manageable. This design, with relatively minor extensions, has supported the unimaginable growth of the Internet to this day.

DNS Domains

Like Active Directory, DNS is a client/server naming system. The DNS namespace is organized hierarchically into domains (not to be confused with Windows NT domains). As with Active Directory names, DNS names within a DNS domain must be unique.

Figure 5.1 shows the organization of DNS domains.

FIGURE 5.1
DNS domain hierarchy.

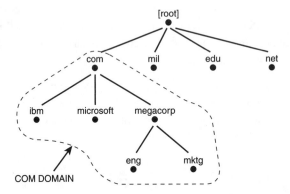

Part of the beauty of the design of DNS is that it allows the NIC (later the InterNIC) to delegate management responsibility for portions of the namespace to other organizations. (This has now been delegated to private organizations.) This delegation forms a natural partitioning of the namespace into domains. The InterNIC manages the top-level domains, such as .edu and .com, and delegates the responsibility for subdomains, such as netpro.com and berkeley.edu, to the appropriate organizations. These organizations can further partition their domains into subdomains and delegate responsibility for the subdomains to their own internal groups.

DNS Zones

A DNS domain is a subtree of the namespace that starts at a domain node and extends all the way down to the bottom of the tree. It includes all the names in the subtree.

A DNS zone, on the other hand, is a subtree of the namespace that starts at a domain node and extends all the way down to the point that has been delegated to another authority.

For example, the .edu domain is divided up into subdomains, one subdomain per school. This creates subdomains such as berkeley.edu, tufts.edu, and so on. These schools further delegate the responsibility for their trees to departments in the schools such as cs.berkeley.edu (the Computer Science department) or astro.berkeley.edu (the Astronomy department).

The berkeley.edu domain contains all the names in all the departments at University of California at Berkeley. The berkeley.edu zone only contains those names that aren't delegated to subordinate domains. In fact, the berkeley.edu zone might have no names in it at all; they might all be delegated to other subdomains. Figure 5.2 shows the difference between domains and zones.

FIGURE 5.2

DNS zones.

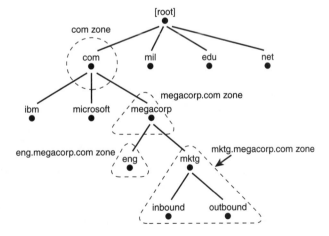

Host Names

The basic purpose of DNS is to translate computer names, or *host names*, into IP addresses. DNS does other things too, but DNS's primary purpose is to turn names into numbers.

DNS host names are the familiar Internet .com-type names that you use whenever you browse the Web. To create a fully qualified host name, you start with the computer name, append a dot and the name of the lowest level domain the host is part of, followed by another dot and the next higher domain, and so on, up to the root of the DNS namespace. For instance, engserver.engineering.megacorp.com is a fully qualified host name.

Name Servers

The computers that provide the DNS naming service are called *name servers*. Each name server has responsibility for one or more DNS zones. These name servers are called *authoritative* for that zone. They have the last word as to the names and address for that part of namespace.

Name servers traditionally keep their DNS information in a file called a *zone file*. A zone file is an ASCII text file that contains the names and addresses for all the hosts in the zone. Zone files also contain delegation information so that the name server can properly refer requests for subordinate names to the proper authoritative name server. Name servers typically read the zone file when they start up and then keep the name information in memory for fast access.

Windows 2000 DNS servers also have the option to store their zone information in Active Directory objects (more on this at the end of the chapter).

Primary and Secondary DNS Servers

DNS name servers can replicate their zone information to other name servers. The server that maintains the master copy of the zone file is called the *primary server*. The network administrator can also set up multiple secondary name servers that get all their zone file information from the primary server or from another secondary server.

Both primary and secondary name servers are considered authoritative for their zones.

DNS Records

A DNS name server breaks up its zone information into different kinds of *resource records*, typically one record per line in the zone file.

There are many different kinds, or *classes,* of resource records. The most common records are the Start of Authority record, the Address record, the Canonical Name record, and the Name Service record. The Start of Authority (SOA) record defines the zone a name server is responsible for. The Address (A) record contains host name and address information. The Canonical Name (CNAME) record defines aliases for host names, and the Name Server (NS) record defines the name server to which a subdomain is delegated. There are many other kinds of records that define mail services and provide other kinds of information.

There is one other record that is particularly interesting in the context of Active Directory: the Service (SRV) Record. Each SRV record names a network service and provides the host name of a server that can provide that service. We'll cover why this is important to Active Directory a little later in this chapter.

Name Resolution

DNS name resolution comes in two flavors: recursive and nonrecursive. In recursive name resolution, the queried server starts the search at the root DNS server and follows referrals until it encounters a name server that is the authoritative name server for the zone it is querying. The queried server must return an answer or an indication that the requested name or its domain does not exist. This is the kind of query a DNS resolver makes of its DNS server.

In a nonrecursive query, the queried server can return a referral to a name server that is "closer" to the one the client is looking for. DNS servers typically make nonrecursive queries of each other.

Updating DNS

Traditionally, DNS has been a read-only system. The DNS protocol did not provide for updating the namespace. The only way an administrator could update the namespace was to stop the DNS service, edit the zone file, and restart the service.

RFC 2136 defines a new variant of the DNS protocol, called Dynamic DNS (DDNS), which extends the DNS protocol to allow updating zone files. DDNS continues to distinguish between primary and secondary name servers for a zone, but it adds a new wrinkle

called a "primary master" name server. The primary master is the only name server in the zone that can update the zone files. Although having only one name server to process updates is a limitation, it avoids the problem of resolving multiple updates from different servers.

The DNS service in Windows 2000 supports Dynamic DNS.

Why DNS?

After this admittedly brief introduction to DNS, you might be wondering why Microsoft is even bothering with DNS. Isn't DNS just a simple name-resolution system? And doesn't Active Directory do the same thing (only better)? Well, sort of.

First, DNS is an Internet standard. DNS is *the* naming system of the Internet. Microsoft realizes the importance of having its systems integrate seamlessly with the Internet. So, using DNS makes sense from that perspective.

There's a technical reason for using DNS as well. One of the thornier problems of implementing a global directory is the discovery problem. To be specific, how does a directory client find an appropriate directory server to communicate with? If you keep all the name and address information in the directory, how does a client get to the directory to start with? It's a chicken-and-egg kind of problem.

There are several possible solutions. You can configure the workstation explicitly to communicate with a particular directory server (inflexible and an administrative nightmare). Or, you can have the workstation broadcast for a directory server (nondeterministic and doesn't scale well). Or, you can use another existing naming system like DNS to find the directory server you want. This is the tack that Microsoft took.

Active Directory and DNS

Active Directory integrates with DNS for three purposes. First, DNS domains form the framework of the Active Directory domain structure. Second, Active Directory clients use DNS to locate Active Directory domain controllers. Finally, Microsoft's DNS service optionally uses Active Directory for data storage and replication.

How DNS Defines the Active Directory Domain Structure

Active Directory uses DNS domains to form the framework of the Active Directory domain structure. Every Active Directory domain must have a corresponding DNS domain.

I'll admit that when I first encountered this requirement, I thought it was a hack. But after working with Active Directory for more than a year, I've come to realize that using DNS is a very natural way to define the domain structure, and it makes integration with the Internet a given. That's not to say that it didn't take me a while to understand how Active Directory actually worked with DNS. Having two semi-integrated systems with their own idea of what a domain is a source of much confusion.

To avoid the confusion, just remember that the DNS domain tree and the Active Directory domain tree are completely separate naming systems. They reference each other internally, but they are separate and distinct systems (see Figure 5.3).

FIGURE 5.3

DNS domains and Active Directory domains.

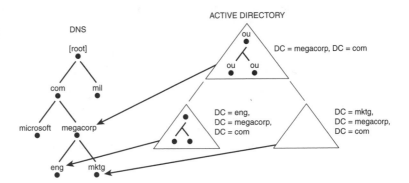

Locating Domain Controllers with DNS

By using DNS, Microsoft solves two server location problems in Active Directory. First, Microsoft made DNS the mechanism used by client workstations to find an appropriate domain controller on the network. Second, Microsoft used DNS as the way domain controllers find each other on the network.

To accomplish these two related tasks, Microsoft used a fairly new addition to the DNS standard: the Service Locator, or SRV record.

Active Directory SRV Records in DNS

The SRV record names a network service that is provided by a host computer. The specific kind of service is arbitrary; the SRV record simply maps a service name to a host name (and, therefore, to an IP port number). This is exactly what an Active Directory client needs to connect to a domain controller.

When a Windows 2000 workstation boots up, it can't authenticate to just any domain controller. The workstation needs a domain controller that is in the same domain as the workstation, preferably one in the same site—that is, one that is connected by a high-speed network. When a user logs in to the workstation, the logon process needs a global catalog to verify the user's group membership, which should also be in the same site as the workstation.

So, instead of just publishing in DNS that a particular server is a domain controller, Active Directory domain controllers publish several SRV records that indicate the domain controller's characteristics. Here is an example of a SRV record created by a domain controller:

```
ldap._tcp.chicago._sites.megacorp.com. 600 IN SRV 0 100 389
➥SERVER1.sales.megacorp.com.
```

First, notice that the service name is a set of names separated by dots. Even though these look like domain names, they aren't. The form of the service name in a SRV resource record is `<service name>.<protocol>.<domain name>`.

- The first part of the name, `ldap`, indicates that this server provides a LDAP service. In this case, it is an Active Directory domain controller.

- The `_tcp` part is the protocol field, and this one indicates that the host provides the LDAP service over the TCP protocol.

- `chicago._sites.megacorp.com` is sort of a virtual domain name. The clever thing here is that this is not a real domain name—just the `megacorp.com` part is. The `chicago._sites` portion of the name provides a way for DNS to categorize the SRV records for domain controllers.

- `600` is the DNS time-to-live field. It indicates how long this record can be held by a caching DNS server.

- `IN` indicates the class of DNS record. It indicates the kind of network this record applies to. `IN` stands for Internet and is probably the only network class you will see in practice.

- `0` indicates the priority for this record. The priority and the next field, weight, give a DNS client a way to select from multiple SRV records for the same service.

- `100` is the weight.

- `389` is the IP port number the service listens to on the host.

- `SERVER1.sales.megacorp.com` is the DNS name of the host computer that provides the LDAP service.

Creating a virtual domain name like this provides an interesting capability. The service names form a hierarchy within the domain, not unlike containers in the directory form a hierarchy within an Active Directory domain. The hierarchy looks like this. (I've left out the additional SRV record data, such as time-to-live, priority, weight, and so forth.)

Listing 5.1 contains the names from a DNS zone file taken from an Active Directory domain controller that was running DNS as well.

LISTING 5.1   A DNS ZONE FILE SRV RESOURCE RECORD NAMES

```
 1: megacorp.com
 2:    _sites
 3:       chicago
 4:          _tcp
 5:             _ldap      SERVER1.sales.megacorp.com
 6:             _ldap      SERVER2.sales.megacorp.com
 7:             _kerberos     SERVER1.sales.megacorp.com
 8:       boston
 9:          _tcp
10:             _ldap      NEWSERVER.mktg.megacorp.com
11:             _kerberos      NEWSERVER.mktg.megacorp.com
12:    _msdcs
13:       dc
14:          chicago
15:             _tcp
16:                _ldap      SERVER1.sales.megacorp.com
17:                _ldap      SERVER2.sales.megacorp.com
18:                _kerberos      SERVER1.sales.megacorp.com
19:          boston
20:             _tcp
21:                _ldap      NEWSERVER.mktg.megacorp.com
22:                _kerberos      NEWSERVER.mktg.megacorp.com
23:       gc
24:          chicago
25:             _tcp
26:                _ldap      SERVER1.sales.megacorp.com
27:          boston
28:             _tcp
29:                _ldap      NEWSERVER.mktg.megacorp.com
30:       _pdc
31:          _tcp
32:             _ldap      NEWSERVER.mktg.megacorp.com
33:       domains
34:          f72e6e66-0a5f-11d3-9952-00609779521e
35:             _tcp
36:                _ldap      SERVER1.sales.megacorp.com
37:          f72e6e67-0a5f-11d3-9952-00609779521e
38:             _tcp
39:                _ldap      NEWSERVER.mktg.megacorp.com
```

Listing 5.1 shows the SRV record names from a DNS zone file for the zone megacorp.com. By default, you can find this file in the \winnt\system32\dns directory of the DNS name server; the name of the file will be *<zone name>*.dns. For instance, this file was named megacorp.com.dns. Note that I've truncated each line after the name and indented it to show the hierarchical relationship of the names.

Line 1 contains the name of the zone this file corresponds to.

Lines 2, 3, and 4 form the first "virtual domain" named chicago._sites.megacorp.com. It is not really a domain, but a container used to organize the DNS names. The leading underscore in _sites makes it impossible to confuse it with a legitimate domain name because underscores are not legal characters for domain names.

Line 4 gives the protocol field, which in this case is TCP.

Lines 5 and 6 contain the service record (SRV) entries for the LDAP service over TCP in the chicago site. You could take either of these host names and open an LDAP connection to them. Line 7 contains an SRV record for a Kerberos service in the chicago site.

Line 12 contains the top of the _msdcs container. It is analogous to the _sites container, except that it breaks the type of domain controller into _dc, _gc, and _pdc containers so that you can locate a particular type of domain controller in a specific site. It also has a container called domains that contains entries that map the GUIDs of Active Directory domains to the correct domain name. Active Directory uses this to find domain controllers when the domain containing them has been renamed.

The next section describes how Active Directory clients use this hierarchy to find an appropriate domain controller.

How Windows 2000 Workstations Locate a Domain Controller

A Windows 2000 workstation looks for an appropriate domain controller when it boots up. Generally, a workstation uses the domain controller it connected to during the previous boot-up.

If that domain controller is unavailable or is otherwise unsuitable, the workstation then tries to find a domain controller in its domain in the same site as the workstation. It does this by querying DNS for SRV records matching _ldap._tcp.<site name>.dc._msdcs.<domain name>, where the values for <site name> and <domain name> come from the workstation Registry.

DNS will return zero or more host names. If there is more than one host name, the workstation will issue an LDAP ping (a short LDAP search using UDP) in parallel to each of the returned hosts in the weighted random order specified by RFC 2052.

If there are no domain controllers in the site, or none of them responds properly to the LDAP ping, the workstation will query DNS again, looking for SRV records matching `_ldap._tcp.dc._msdcs.<domain name>`. The workstation will use the same pinging scheme as before. The responding domain controllers will reply to the ping request with the site the workstation belongs in, based on the workstation's subnet. The workstation will then try to contact another domain controller in that site using the previous algorithm.

You can take advantage of the domain controller SRV resource records in your own applications by using the `DsGetDcName()` API function (described in Chapter 18, "Connecting to Active Directory with LDAP"). `DsGetDcName()` uses the DNS SRV resource records to locate domain controllers based on the parameters you specify.

Active Directory: Integrated DNS Servers

Not only does Active Directory use DNS for defining domains and finding domain controllers, Microsoft's DNS service (optionally) actually uses Active Directory as well.

The network administrator can configure a Microsoft DNS service to store its zone file information not in a text file, but in Active Directory objects instead. Why would you want to do this? There are three main reasons: faster updates, more sophisticated replication, and multimaster updates.

Simplified Updates

Normally, DNS keeps its zone file data in a simple text file. This is convenient for the administrator because it's easy to read and the administrator can use any suitable text editor to edit the zone file. But now that DNS supports updates via the DNS protocol, DNS has to update the text file. This isn't particularly easy or efficient. Storing the zone information in Active Directory makes updates much simpler.

Replication

DNS has its own replication protocol that transfers zone file information from a zone's primary master server to its other primary and secondary servers. This replication process is efficient and straightforward, but you have to configure it manually at each DNS server. This is further complicated by the fact that DNS doesn't have any notion of sites, or fast or slow WAN links, or link schedules. Devising an efficient replication scheme in DNS is problematic.

Active Directory's replication mechanism takes into account link speed and link schedules, and it can even replicate data between two domain controllers that are never connected directly to each other by virtue of its transitive replication scheme. Using Active Directory-integrated DNS lets the administrator configure the network topology once, and both Active Directory and DNS will take advantage of it.

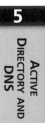

Multimaster Updates

Another thing that Active Directory integration provides to DNS is a more robust handling of updates from multiple servers. DNS servers can handle updates to zone information, but they have to pass them to the primary master server to have the updates applied. This can be problematic, particularly if the primary master is down or is otherwise unavailable. DNS can't apply the update in this case.

Active Directory can handle updates submitted to any domain controller. When DNS is integrated with Active Directory, DNS submits its zone updates directly to Active Directory. The Active Directory replication process takes care of updating the local database and making sure the changes are replicated to the other domain controllers in the domain. Because there is no master domain controller, there is no single point of failure.

Finding DNS Zone Information in Active Directory and Where It Is Stored

DNS stores its zone file information in Active Directory objects; consequently, you can read them (or write them) using the usual Active Directory programming interfaces: ADSI and LDAP.

Active Directory-integrated DNS servers store their resource records in the Active Directory container `CN=MicrosoftDNS,CN=System,<first domain DN>`. For instance, if the first domain you created in your Active Directory was `megacorp.com`, Active Directory-integrated DNS servers would put the zone file information in `CN=MicrosoftDNS,CN=System,DC=megacorp,DC=com`.

The DNS servers create a `dnsZone` object in the MicrosoftDNS container for each Active Directory-integrated zone. Each `dnsZone` object contains one or more `dnsNode` objects, which represent the resources records that make up the DNS zone. The following sections describe these two kinds of Active Directory objects.

The `dnsZone` Object

Microsoft DNS creates a `dnsZone` object for each DNS zone that is marked as Active Directory integrated. DNS creates these records in the `DC=<domain name>,CN=MicrosoftDNS,CN=System,DC=<root domain name>` container. For instance, if the root domain were `megacorp.com`, the distinguished name of the `dnsZone` object for the `engineering.megacorp.com` zone would be

`DC=engineering.megacorp.com,CN=MicrosoftDNS,CN=System,DC=megacorp,DC=com`

The `dnsNode` Object

Each `dnsZone` object is a container, and it contains a single `dnsNode` object for each resource record in the DNS zone. The relative distinguished name of the `dnsRecord` object is the same as the resource record name, so a typical `dnsNode` distinguished name would be

```
CN=_ldap.tcp,DC=engineering.megacorp.com,CN=MicrosoftDNS,CN=System,
➥DC=megacorp,DC=com
```

Each `dnsNode` object has a multivalued octet-string (binary) attribute called `dnsRecord`. This attribute contains the resource information, such as time-to-live, weight, priority, and host name or IP address. Unfortunately, the exact format of this attribute isn't documented. However, if you have a pressing desire to make some use of these attributes, reverse-engineering them by comparing them to the resource records in DNS shouldn't be too hard.

The Contents of Active Directory

IN THIS PART

CHAPTER 6

Active Directory Operational Attributes

Each Active Directory domain controller maintains a set of information that describes the state and the configuration of the domain controller itself.

RFC 2251 specifies that every LDAPv3 server must provide information about itself and its status through a group of attributes that can be accessed via a special LDAP search. These attributes are called *operational attributes* because they contain information specific to the operation of the LDAP server. Each Active Directory domain controller maintains a set of operational attributes.

These attributes are not part of an actual LDAP object, even though you can access them as if they were. The operational attributes are actually maintained in memory by the domain controller, and returned to any client requesting them via a special LDAP search operation.

RootDSE

If these attributes aren't part of an actual LDAP object, how do you request them in a search? It's simple but not particularly obvious. Instead of extending the API and the protocol with a special operation to retrieve the operational attributes, the designers of LDAP chose to create a special-case distinguished name known as the *Root Directory Services Entry* or *RootDSE*. You retrieve the attributes of the RootDSE by specifying an empty string for the search name, `"objectClass=*"` for the search attributes, and a search scope of `LDAP_SCOPE_BASE`. In effect, you are reading the attributes of the object that has no name. Listing 6.1 shows how you perform this search operation.

LISTING 6.1   USING `ldap_search_s()` TO READ THE ROOTDSE

```
LDAPMessage* pmsgResult = NULL;
int nErr = ldap_search_s(
    psLdap,                // LDAP connection
    "",                    // empty container name means RootDSE
    LDAP_SCOPE_BASE,       // search scope
    "objectClass=*",       // search criteria
    NULL,                  // return all attributes
    (ULONG)false,          // not attrs only
    &pmsgResult );         // the result structure

LDAPMessage* pmsgObject = ldap_first_entry(psLdap, pmsgResult);
if(nErr == 0 && pmsgObject != NULL)
{
    char* pszAttrName;
    BerElement* psberAttrValue;

    for( pszAttrName = ldap_first_attribute( psLdap, pmsgObject,
    ➥&psberAttrValue);
        pszAttrName != NULL;
        pszAttrName = ldap_next_attribute(psLdap, pmsgObject,
        ➥psberAttrValue ) )
    {
        // get attribute pszAttrName values using
    }
}
```

What kind of things can you find in the operational attributes of an Active Directory domain controller? The rest of this chapter covers the attributes found in the Active Directory rootDSE entry, as well as operational attributes associated with other directory objects.

configurationNamingContext

The `configurationNamingContext` operational attribute holds the fully distinguished name. The Configuration naming context is a special naming context that contains LDAP objects describing how the Active Directory is deployed and configured throughout the enterprise. The Active Directory creates the Configuration naming context when you promote the first domain controller in the enterprise, and it appears as a subordinate naming context to the first domain you created. See Chapter 8, "The Configuration Naming Context," for more information about the contents of the Configuration naming context.

If you write any code that needs access to the Configuration naming context, the value of the `configurationNamingContext` attribute gives the container name to start your searches with.

currentTime

The `currentTime` operational attribute contains the current time as the Active Directory DSA sees it. It is a single-valued attribute of the form:

`YYYYMMDDhhmmss.tZ`

YYYY is the year, MM is the month number with `01` indicating January, DD is the day number of the month, hh is the hour in twenty-four-hour format, mm is the number of minutes past the hour, and ss is the number of seconds. The t indicates the number of milliseconds, but this is always `0` on Active Directory domain controllers. The Z indicates the time zone. On Active Directory domain controllers, the time zone is always the letter Z indicating Greenwich mean time, or Zulu time.

defaultNamingContext

The `defaultNamingContext` operational attribute contains the distinguished name of the default naming context for this domain controller. In the first release of Windows 2000, this is always equal to the domain that the domain controller is a member of. This is a very convenient way to search the domain naming context for any domain controller you might connect to. Just use the value of `defaultNamingContext` as the base for your search operation.

dnsHostName

Every domain controller must have a DNS host name; Active Directory relies on DNS to locate domain controllers. The `dnsHostName` operational attribute contains the DNS host name of the domain controller. See Chapter 5, "Active Directory and DNS," for more information about how Active Directory uses DNS to locate domain controllers.

dsServiceName

The `dsServiceName` operational attribute contains the fully distinguished name of the directory entry that holds the configuration information for the DSA on this domain controller. An example is

```
CN=NTDS Settings,CN=ACCTGSRVR,CN=Servers,CN=New-York,CN=Sites,
➡CN=Configuration,DC=megacorp,DC=com
```

The `Settings` object that `dsServiceName` refers to is of `objectClass nTDSDSA`, and it is always in the site container for the site that contains the domain controller.

The Settings object has attributes that determine whether the domain controller has master copies of any of its naming contexts. The Settings object is also a container, and it contains nTDSConnection objects that define where this domain controller replicates from.

You might wonder why the DSA configuration information isn't located with the Computer object in the domain's Domain Controllers container. Because the configuration information is shared between all domain controllers, Active Directory has to put the Settings object in the Configuration naming context so that it will be replicated to all domain controllers in the enterprise.

highestCommittedUSN

The highestCommittedUSN operational attribute contains the highest Update Sequence Number (USN) that this domain controller has processed. It is a large (64-bit) integer that the domain controller uses to determine what attributes it should replicate from other domain controllers.

ldapServiceName

The ldapServiceName operational attribute contains the service principal name (SPN) of the domain controller. This name is used by domain controllers when they authenticate with each other.

An example of an ldapServiceName is

```
acctg.megacorp.com:LITHIUM$@ACCTG.MEGACORP.COM
```

namingContexts

An Active Directory domain controller maintains replicas of one or more naming contexts. The namingContexts operational attribute is multivalued, with each value being the distinguished name of one of the naming contexts replicated on this server.

rootDomainNamingContext

The very first domain you create on a Windows 2000 network is different from subsequent domains, even those domains that form the roots of other trees. In particular, it contains the Configuration and Schema naming contexts. This special domain is called the root domain naming context.

The rootDomainNamingContext operational attribute contains the fully distinguished name of the root domain naming context for the enterprise.

schemaNamingContext

The Schema naming context describes the form of all the objects Active Directory can contain. It contains objects that describe all of the classes of objects, all the properties the classes contain, and how the classes inherit properties from each other. Every domain controller in the enterprise has a copy of the Schema naming context. See Chapter 9, "The Active Directory Schema," for more information about the Active Directory schema. Active Directory automatically creates the Schema naming context when you promote the very first domain controller in your enterprise.

The schemaNamingContext operational attribute contains a single value that is the distinguished name of the Schema naming context. When you write a program to access the schema, this is the distinguished name that you use to start all of your searches for schema information.

serverName

The serverName operational attribute contains the distinguished name of the domain controller. This is usually of the following form:

```
CN=ACCTSRVR,CN=Servers,CN=New-York,CN=Sites,CN=Configuration,
DC=megacorp,DC=com
```

The distinguished name in the serverName operational attribute refers to the computer object in the Domain Controllers container in the domain. This computer object is the security principal for the domain controller; this is not the same object referred to by the dSServiceName operational attribute. The dSServiceName operational attribute refers to the Domain Controllers configuration object in the Sites container.

subschemaSubentry

The subschemaSubentry operational attribute specifies the distinguished name of an object in the directory that contains a description of the directory's schema. This value is typically something like this:

```
CN=Aggregate,CN=Schema,CN=Configuration,DC=megacorp,DC=com
```

The Aggregate object is of objectClass Subschema. It contains five attributes of interest: attributeTypes, dITContentRules, extendedAttributeInfo, extendedClassInfo, and objectClasses. Chapter 9 describes the Aggregate object in detail.

supportedControl

The LDAP specification provides for extending the capabilities of an LDAP server while staying within the LDAP standard. These extensions are called LDAP controls. Each LDAP control has an OID that uniquely identifies it.

The `supportedControl` attribute is a multivalued list of object IDs (OIDs), each one identifying an LDAP extension supported by the domain controller.

> **TIP**
>
> Always check the `supportedControl` attribute before using an LDAP extension supported by a domain controller. This will help make your code more portable to other LDAP environments and to later versions of Active Directory.

Appendix A, "ADSI Interfaces for Active Directory," lists the controls supported by Active Directory domain controllers in Windows 2000.

supportedLDAPPolicies

`supportedLDAPPolicies` is a multivalued string attribute that contains the names of the configuration parameters found in the `lDAPAdminLimits` attribute of the `Query Policy` object for the directory service. `lDAPAdminLimits` contains operational limits for the directory service agent. For example, one of the `supportedLDAPPolicies` values is `MaxQueryDuration`. The `MaxQueryDuration` parameter limits the amount of time any directory query can take. Chapter 8 discusses the `lDAPAdminLimits` attribute in more detail.

supportedLDAPVersion

The `supportedLDAPVersion` attribute contains a list of the LDAP protocol versions a domain controller supports. It is a multivalued attribute, and contains each major version number as a string. In Windows 2000, domain controllers all contain 2 and 3 as the values of `supportedLDAPVersion`, indicating that they support LDAPv2 and LDAPv3 protocols.

This attribute is useful if you expect to run your LDAP code with different (non–Active Directory) LDAP servers, or with different versions of Active Directory. You should check that the server you connect to supports the LDAPv3 protocol.

> **TIP**
>
> If you are chasing a referral from an Active Directory domain controller, check the `supportedLDAPVersion` attribute on the new server. Active Directory can refer you to other, non–Active Directory LDAP servers.

supportedSASLMechanisms

The Simple Authentication and Security Layer (SASL) is a protocol that allows applications to negotiate which authentication mechanism they will use when establishing a connection. LDAP supports SASL through the `ldap_sasl_bind()` and `ldap_sasl_bind_s()` functions.

The `supportedSASLMechanisms` attribute is a multivalued attribute that contains the names of the authentication mechanisms supported by the server. Windows 2000 domain controllers all support GSSAPI (Generic Security Services API) and GSS-SPNEGO (Simple and Protected GSS API Negotiation) as the only SASL mechanisms.

If there are no supported SASL mechanisms (never the case with Active Directory domain controllers), the `supportedSASLMechanisms` attribute will not be present.

Operational Attributes on Active Directory Objects

Active Directory maintains several other operational attributes on objects in the directory. These attributes don't really exist in the directory; Active Directory synthesizes them for you when you explicitly request them.

allowedAttributes

`allowedAttributes` is a multivalued string attribute that contains the LDAP display name of every attribute defined in the schema for this object. It doesn't include attributes the object might have by virtue of inheritance or inclusion.

allowedAttributesEffective

`allowedAttributesEffective` is a multivalued string attribute that contains the LDAP display name of every attribute defined in the schema for this object, including attributes the object might have by virtue of inheritance or inclusion.

Reading this attribute is the easiest way to find out what the allowed objects are for a given object. The only other ways to determine the allowed attributes for a class are to read the subschema entry and parse the `objectClasses` attributes or to read all the `classSchema` objects in the Schema container and compute the effective attribute list yourself.

allowedChildClasses

allowedChildClasses is a multivalued string attribute that contains the LDAP display names of all the classes of objects the class is allowed to contain, not counting those it has via inheritance. Active Directory calculates the allowedChildClasses attribute by finding all the classSchema objects that name the class of this object in their possSuperiors and systemPossSuperiors attributes. This doesn't contain the complete list of classes the object can contain.

allowedChildClassesEffective

allowedChildClassesEffective is a multivalued string attribute that contains the LDAP display name of all the classes of objects the object is allowed to contain. Active Directory generates this attribute from the possSuperiors and systemPossSuperiors attributes of the classSchema objects in the schema and from the classSchema objects the object inherits from.

Reading this attribute is the easiest way to determine if a given object can be a container or not. It is much faster than searching for any subordinate objects.

canonicalName

The canonicalName attribute contains the Microsoft canonical name of the object. The canonical name looks a lot like a UNIX file path. It starts with the name of the domain the object is in, followed by any containers separated by forward slashes—for instance,

```
Engineering.megacorp.com/Configuration/Schema/MSMQ-Dependent-Client-
➥Services
```

> **NOTE**
>
> Canonical names are Microsoft-specific. You can use them when specifying object names with ADSI, but not with LDAP.

createTimeStamp

The createTimeStamp attribute contains the time and date the object was created, in the following format:

```
YYYYMMDDhhmmss.tZ
```

YYYY is the year, MM is the month number (with 01 indicating January), DD is the day number of the month, hh is the hour in twenty-four-hour format, mm is the number of minutes past the hour, and ss is the number of seconds. The t indicates the number of milliseconds, but this is always 0 on Active Directory domain controllers. The Z indicates the time zone. On Active Directory domain controllers, the time zone is always the letter Z, indicating Greenwich mean time, or Zulu time.

dITContentRules

dITContentRules is an operational attribute and is part of the Aggregate object in the Schema container. It contains the structural rules for the directory—specifically what attributes each class of object must and can contain and the auxiliary classes each class includes attributes from. Chapter 9 discusses the Aggregate object in detail.

extendedAttributeInfo

The extendedAttributeInfo operational attribute is also contained only by the Aggregate object in the Schema container. The extendedAttributeInfo attribute contains additional information for each attribute in the schema, beyond that contained in the attributeTypes attribute. Chapter 9 discusses the Aggregate object in more detail.

extendedClassInfo

The extendedClassInfo operational attribute is also contained only by the Aggregate object in the Schema container. The extendedClassInfo attribute contains additional information for each class in the schema, beyond that contained in the objectClasses attribute. Chapter 9 discusses the Aggregate object in more detail.

modifyTimeStamp

The modifyTimeStamp attribute contains the time and date the object was last modified, in the same format as createTimeStamp, described earlier.

objectClasses

objectClasses is another operational attribute that is only contained by the Aggregate object in the Schema container. The objectClasses attribute contains a value for each class defined in the schema. Each value contains the OID of the class, the name of the class, and the must-have and can-have attributes for the class. Chapter 9 discusses the Aggregate object in more detail.

sDRightsEffective

sDRightsEffective is a single-valued integer attribute that contains the effective rights for the current user—that is, the user reading the operational attribute. Chapter 4, "Active Directory Security," discusses access rights and security in more detail.

CHAPTER 7

The Active Directory Domain Structure

Active Directory is the primary mechanism for organizing and administering Windows 2000 networks. The directory contains the information that describes essentially all of the resources on the network. Active Directory represents every printer, every server, every client workstation, and every network user with an object in the directory. Active Directory also contains all the security information that defines which users may access what resource on the network.

Active Directory is fundamentally an X.500/LDAP-style directory. However, in order to achieve backward compatibility with Windows NT 3.x and Windows NT 4.0 networks, and to better integrate with intranets and the Internet, Microsoft has enhanced (some might say "corrupted") the conventional LDAP directory structure with two other naming systems. Active Directory incorporates some of the structures and technology of the old NT domain system. This combination, although confusing, greatly enhances Active Directory's utility and its ability to integrate with older NT networks and the Internet.

LDAP Directory Hierarchy

The LDAP data model (which is based on the X.500 data model) defines a directory as a hierarchical collection of named objects. An LDAP directory has a single root, and each object in the directory is either a container object (meaning that it logically contains other objects) or a leaf object. Because of this container relationship, a LDAP directory forms a hierarchical, tree-like structure, not unlike a computer file system structure.

Container Objects

Any object in a LDAP directory can be a container, although the directory schema may restrict this. (See Chapter 9, "The Active Directory Schema," for more details.) Container objects can contain leaf objects or other container objects. Returning to the file system analogy, LDAP container objects are like file system directories.

Each child object contained by a container object must have a unique name within the container—again, just like in a computer file system. LDAP does not allow multiple objects with the same name in a container.

Leaf Objects

Objects in a LDAP directory that do not contain other objects are called *leaf objects*. Leaf objects form the bottom of the directory tree. In the file system analogy, leaf objects are like files. The file system analogy breaks down in one respect: A leaf object can become a container object simply by adding a child object (assuming the schema allows it). Most file systems don't let you turn a file into a directory just by adding another file to it!

Hierarchical Object Names

The hierarchical structure is reflected in the way LDAP names the directory objects. Every object in the directory has a naming attribute. This attribute serves as the object's name within its container. For instance, the cn (common name) attribute is the naming attribute for user objects, and the dc (domain component) attribute is the naming attribute for domains.

In LDAP, the name of an object in its container (its relative distinguished name) is expressed as `<naming attribute name>"="<naming attribute value>`. For instance, if a user object has a common name attribute of `"Kate Donlon"`, its relative distinguished name would be `"cn=Kate Donlon"`.

The fully qualified name of an object in an LDAP directory (its distinguished name) is the concatenation of its relative distinguished name and the distinguished name of its container. So, if the container `"DC=mktg,DC=megacorp,DC=com"` contained the object `"cn=Kate Donlon"`, Kate's distinguished name would be

`"cn=Kate Donlon,DC=mktg,DC=megacorp,DC=com"`

Figure 7.1 shows the hierarchical structure of the objects in an LDAP directory.

Figure 7.1

The hierarchical directory structure.

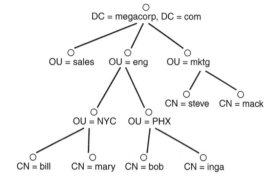

Naming Contexts

When working with large tree structures such as LDAP directories, it is often useful to break the tree into subtrees for searching or management. X.500 and LDAP define a *naming context* as a contiguous subtree of the directory that contains at least one entry. A naming context always starts with a single entry and includes all subordinate entries that are not a part of another naming context. Naming contexts cannot overlap, so any given object is contained within a single naming context. Figure 7.2 shows how you can break a directory tree into naming contexts.

Figure 7.2

Naming contexts.

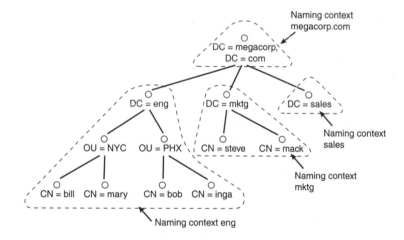

The name of a naming context is the same as the name of the naming context's topmost object. Naming contexts provide a way of breaking the logical hierarchy into distinct subtrees.

7

THE ACTIVE
DIRECTORY DOMAIN
STRUCTURE

Partitions and Replicas

When you divide a directory tree into naming contexts for the purpose of storage or replication, the naming contexts are called *partitions*. Each copy of a partition stored on a server (even if there is only one copy) is called a *replica*.

Generally speaking, partitions are the same as naming contexts, and you can use the terms interchangeably.

Windows NT Domains

One of the early requirements for Windows 2000 (then Windows NT 5) was compatibility and interoperability with Windows NT 4.0 networks. Windows NT 4.0 domains (called *downlevel domains* in the Microsoft literature) define a security context for authentication and evaluation of access rights. Windows NT 4.0 performs all security identification and evaluation in the context of a domain.

Downlevel domains are not hierarchical data structures; they form a "flat" namespace that contains all the objects in the domain.

How do you make the hierarchical namespace of a Windows 2000 directory interoperate with the flat namespace of a Windows NT 4.0 domain?

Active Directory Domains

The solution to this problem isn't obvious (at least not to me). Microsoft ingeniously designed into the directory the notion of a domain. A *domain* in Active Directory is a naming context that forms a security boundary within the directory. All access rights and security identification in Windows 2000 are done in the context of an Active Directory domain.

In Active Directory, domains are also partitions. This means that a domain forms a naming context that is stored in its entirety on a domain controller and is replicated to other domain controllers that have replicas of that domain.

To continue with the hierarchical nature of the directory, Active Directory provides for hierarchical domains, so that one domain can contain other, subordinate domains. This would seem to be a problem for downlevel domains, because they do not support hierarchical domains. To address this problem, each Windows 2000 domain has a Windows NT 4.0–style name in addition to its distinguished name in Active Directory. Downlevel domain controllers and workstations use this "flat" name when referring to Windows 2000 domains.

Domain Trusts

Previous Windows NT domain systems also defined the notion of domain trusts. A *trust* in Windows NT 4.0 is a logical link between domains that allows the security principals (for instance, users) in one domain to access the resources in another domain. Windows 2000 implements the notion of domain trusts as well; however, Active Directory domains have transitive, bidirectional trusts where, by default, domains trust all other domains in the forest. Trust relationships in Windows NT 4.0, on the other hand, are one-way.

Figure 7.3 shows how Active Directory domains relate to each other.

FIGURE 7.3

Active Directory domains.

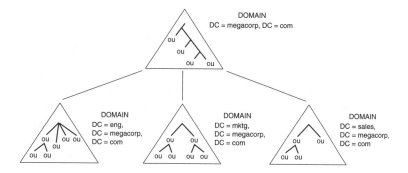

DNS Domains

In addition to incorporating the notion of Windows NT–style domains, Microsoft also integrated the Internet's Domain Name System (DNS) with Active Directory.

DNS provides a hierarchical namespace as X.500/LDAP directories do, although the naming convention in DNS is quite different. DNS names are the familiar `sales.megacorp.com`-style names you use when browsing the Web.

DNS also defines the notion of domains as a contiguous subtree of the namespace, but don't confuse DNS domains with Active Directory domains. They are completely separate and different concepts.

Active Directory uses DNS for two purposes. First, Active Directory uses DNS as a locator to find domain controllers and their IP addresses. Second, the DNS domain hierarchy defines the Active Directory domain hierarchy. Each Active Directory domain corresponds to a DNS domain, and the hierarchical relationship of Active Directory domains follows that defined by DNS. Figure 7.4 illustrates this.

FIGURE 7.4

*DNS domains and
Active Directory
domains.*

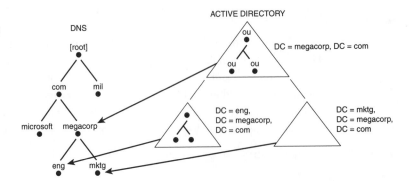

Active Directory Trees and Forests

When you create the first Active Directory domain on your network, you define the top
of your first domain tree. The first domain you create on your network is special in a
couple of ways that I'll describe later. When you create additional domains on your network, you have a choice. You can make them subordinate to an existing domain, in
which case you are extending your domain tree, or you can make them the top of a new
domain tree. In this case, you are adding a new tree to the system. A collection of distinct domain trees is called a *forest,* or sometimes, the *enterprise.* All the domains in the
forest share a common configuration and directory schema.

The Root Domain

The very first domain you created on your network has special characteristics in Active
Directory. It is not only the root of the first domain tree, it contains the Configuration
and Schema naming contexts.

The Configuration naming context contains the configuration for all of the domain controllers on the network. The Configuration naming context also contains the definitions
of Active Directory sites, replication topology, and link schedules. The Configuration
naming context also contains the Schema naming context.

The Schema naming context is subordinate to the Configuration naming context. It contains the definitions of all the classes of objects that can exist in the directory, along with
rules that describe what objects may contain other objects, and which attributes a given
class of object must or may contain. The Configuration and Schema naming contexts
replicate to every domain controller in the forest.

Domain Controllers and Replicas

Active Directory spreads the workload of the directory across multiple domain controllers. There are one or more domain controllers in each domain in Active Directory.

Each domain controller in a domain maintains replicas of three naming contexts. First, the domain controller has a replica of the domain naming context. The domain naming context contains objects that represent users, computers, and services that are part of the domain.

The second replica is a replica of the Configuration naming context. Every domain controller in the forest has a replica of the Configuration naming context. The Configuration naming context is subordinate to the first domain created in the forest.

Finally, each domain controller in the enterprise has a replica of the Schema naming context, which is subordinate to the Configuration naming context.

Sites

Active Directory provides a way for administrators to organize domain controllers into sites. A site, in this case, is an area of high-speed network connectivity. Active Directory uses the site information to improve the performance of directory replication and to make sure that Active Directory clients communicate by default with domain controllers that are physically nearby.

The organization of domain controllers into sites is independent from the organization of domain controllers into domains. A single domain can have domain controllers in several sites. Likewise, a single site can contain domain controllers from several different domains.

Figure 7.5 shows how domain controllers can be organized into sites.

FIGURE 7.5

Domain controllers and sites.

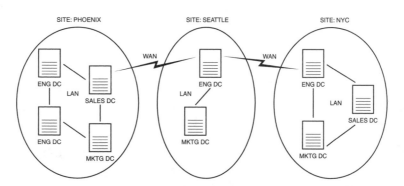

CHAPTER 8

The Configuration Naming Context

The Configuration naming context is the one-stop-shop for all the configuration for Active Directory. The Configuration naming context contains entries for all the domain controllers in the system, entries for all the domains in the system, an entry for each site defined by the administrator, the replication topology and schedules, and so on. If you're looking for interesting information about Active Directory, you'll find it somewhere in the Configuration naming context.

Active Directory creates the Configuration naming context automatically when you create the first domain for the system. The Configuration naming context is subordinate to the first domain (sometimes called the root domain) you created in the enterprise. For instance, if the first domain you created in Active Directory was named `DC=MegaCorp,DC=com`, the distinguished name of the Configuration naming context would be `CN=Configuration,DC=MegaCorp,DC=com`.

Because the Configuration naming context contains all the information about the structure of Active Directory, Active Directory automatically replicates the Configuration naming context to each domain controller in the enterprise. Keeping the Configuration naming context consistent across all the domain controllers in the enterprise is crucial to the proper operation of Active Directory.

A Quick Tour of the Configuration Naming Context

The next section goes through the more interesting bits of the Configuration naming context and describes what you can find there.

A note of caution: If you want to change the objects in the Configuration naming context, use the administrative utilities that come with Windows 2000. Active Directory depends on the contents of the Configuration naming context to operate properly, and if you incorrectly modify or delete objects in the Configuration naming context, you can break Active Directory, possibly beyond repair.

The Configuration Container Object

The Configuration naming context object contains several attributes that control replication and define the structure of the Configuration naming context. The following sections describe the most important of these attributes.

Several of the attributes of the Configuration naming context object (`repsUpToDateVector`, `repsFrom`, and `repsTo`) are different in each replica of the Configuration naming context; they are not replicated between servers.

replUpToDateVector

The `replUpToDateVector` attribute is an array of binary structures, one structure per replication partner. Each structure represents the objects that have been replicated from that replication partner.

Each structure in the array contains three Update Sequence Numbers (USNs). Each USN is a 64-bit integer.

- The Object Update High Water Mark is the last USN that the replication neighbor considered to replicate to this server. The replication neighbor passed this USN to this server during the last replication sequence.

- The Object Create High Water Mark is the USN of the last new object that was replicated from the replication neighbor. The replication neighbor passed this USN to this server during the last replication sequence.

- The Property Update High Water Mark is the highest USN of a modified property from the replication partner that this domain controller has successfully processed.

Microsoft has not made the structure of this attribute public, so I can't describe it in any more detail than this.

repsFrom

The `repsFrom` attribute contains replication topology information for this replica of the Configuration naming context. The `repsFrom` attribute is created by the Knowledge Consistency Checker process based on the administrator-configured information in the `nTDSSettings` object for the server. There is one value in the `repsFrom` attribute for each domain controller this replica replicates from.

The `repsFrom` attribute has octet string syntax. (It's actually a C language structure stored unaltered in the directory.) It contains the GUID of the server this server replicates from, the time that replication from that server last succeeded, the number of consecutive failures replicating from that server, the error code of the last replication failure, and the replication schedule for that server. Unfortunately, Microsoft has not made the structure of this attribute public, so I can't say anything more specific about it.

repsTo

The `repsTo` attribute contains replication topology information for this replica of the Configuration naming context. The `repsFrom` attribute is created by the Knowledge Consistency Checker process based on the administrator-configured information in the `nTDSSettings` object for the server. `repsTo` is a multivalued attribute, and each value represents another domain controller that this domain controller notifies when there is a change in the Configuration naming context.

The `repsTo` attribute is an octet string. (It contains another C language structure.) It contains the name and GUID of the domain controller to be notified in the case of any Configuration naming context changes, as well as some flags that govern how replication works. Microsoft has not made the structure of this attribute public either.

subRefs

The `subRefs` attribute of the Configuration container object is a list of the subordinate naming contexts of the Configuration naming context. By default there is only one: the Schema naming context.

wellKnownObjects

The `wellKnownObjects` attribute has OR-Name syntax, and contains the links to two hidden containers in the Configuration naming context: `CN=Deleted Objects` and `CN=LostAndFound`. Active Directory uses the `wellKnownObjects` attribute to find important objects in the directory, even if someone moves or renames them.

DisplaySpecifiers

Active Directory supports the notion of associating user interface components (property pages, dialog boxes, icons, and such) with classes of objects in the directory. Windows 2000 uses these user interface components in the Microsoft Management Console (MMC) and in the Windows 2000 Shell. Associating object classes with user interface components gives Active Directory developers the unique ability to integrate a new directory class seamlessly into the operating system's native tools.

To make this work, you have to build your user interface as a set of Component Object Model (COM) components. The MMC and the shell look in the directory to find the interface GUIDs for the COM components that correspond to a class, and voilà—instant integrated user interface.

Programming MMC snap-ins is a bit outside the scope of this book, so I won't discuss it much here. In any case, Microsoft's documentation treats it pretty thoroughly.

The `DisplaySpecifiers` container in the Configuration container contains the objects that associate user interface components with directory object classes. The `DisplaySpecifiers` container contains one container for the locales the server supports. The name of each locale container is the Locale ID (LCID)—for instance, Windows 2000 domain controllers for the US English market have a container called `409`.

Each object in the locale container is of class `displaySpecifier`. Each `displaySpecifier` object has a distinguished name comprised of the class name, a hyphen, and the word *Display*—for instance, `CN=siteLink-Display,CN=409,CN=DisplaySpecifiers,` `CN=Configuration,DC=MegaCorp,DC=com`. It is important for you to use this convention when you add your own display specifiers because that is how the MMC and the shell will find your `displaySpecifier` object.

`displaySpecifier` objects have the following interesting attributes.

treatAsLeaf

`treatAsLeaf` is a single-valued Boolean attribute that indicates to directory browsers such as MMC or the Windows shell not to look for objects below this object in the hierarchy. That is not to say that the object isn't a container, but for the purposes of the user interface component, the object doesn't contain any additional objects.

contextMenu

The `contextMenu` attribute is a multivalued `DirectoryString` that contains information that links the class to a right-click menu. The format of each value is *<order number>*, *<CLSID GUID>*—for instance, `1,{08eb4fa6-6ffd-11d1-b0e0-00c04fd8dca6}`.

The MMC and the Windows shell use the `<order number>` value to sort multiple context menus. Note that the *CLSID* is expressed as it is in the Registry: as a hyphenated string within braces. You can use the Windows COM function `StringFromCLSID()` or `StringFromCLSID()` to create the *CLSID* string.

classDisplayName

`classDisplayName` is single-valued `DirectoryString` that contains the class name as MMC and the Windows shell should display it. MMC and the Windows shell will used the `lDAPDisplayName` for the class if you don't specify the `classDisplayName`.

attributeDisplayNames

`attributeDisplayNames` is a multivalued attribute that contains an value for each attribute that the class may contain. Each value has the form `<attribute name>,<name to display>`—for instance, primaryInternationalISDNNumber,International ISDN Number. `<attribute name>` is the `lDAPDisplayName` of the attribute, and `<name to display>` is the string that MMC and the Windows shell use to display that attribute. If there is no value for a particular attribute, MMC and Windows shell default to using the `lDAPDisplayName`.

adminContextMenu

`adminContextMenu` is a multivalued `DirectoryString` attribute that contains the order number and CLSID GUID for a context menu that the MMC administrative snap-ins display when the administrator right-clicks on an object of the display specifier's class. The format of each value is the same as that of `contextMenu`.

adminPropertyPages

This multivalued attribute contains a value for each property page to display when an administrator selects an object of this class. Only the administrative MMC snap-ins will display these pages. Each value of `adminPropertyPages` has the following format: `<order number>,<CLSID GUID>`—for example, {6dfe6488-a212-11d0-bcd5-00c04fd8d5b6}.

MMC and the shell use the `<order number>` value to determine the order to display multiple property pages for an object. `<CLSID GUID>` is the CLSID of the snap-in property page.

createDialog

The `createDialog` attribute of the `displaySpecifier` object is a single-valued `DirectoryString` that defines the dialog box to run when a user selects New for a particular class of object. The `createDialog` attribute just contains the CLSID string as formatted by `StringFromCLSID()` or `StringFromGUID2()`—for instance, {E62F8206-B71C-11D1-808D-00A024C48131}.

iconPath

The `iconPath` is a multivalued `DirectoryString` attribute that contains the path to the icon file that MMC and the Windows shell use when they display an object of the particular class. There are two possible forms for the `iconPath` attribute.

The first form, `<state>,<icon file name>`, specifies an .ico file that contains the icon for the class. `<state>` is an integer, where 0 indicates the closed state of the icon, 1 indicates the open state of the icon, and 2 indicates the icon's disabled state. You can specify other state values between 2 and 15 and use these icons for your own purposes.

The second form of the `iconPath` attribute is `<state>,<DLL file name>,<resource ID>`. `<state>` has the same meaning as in the first form, `<DLL file name>` is the name of a resource DLL file, and `<resource ID>` is the numeric resource ID of the desired icon in the DLL.

creationWizard

The `creationWizard` attribute specifies the CLSID of a wizard-type user interface component that walks the user through the steps of creating an object of this class. The `creationWizard` attribute is single valued, and contains a single CLSID GUID, expressed in the form of `StringFromCLSID()` or `StringFromGUID2()`—for instance, `,{D6D8C25A-4E83-11d2-8424-00C04FA372D4}`.

creationWizardExt

Microsoft provides several object-creation wizards for specific classes of objects in Active Directory, and Microsoft has also provided you the ability to extend those wizards with your own pages.

The `creationWizardExt` attribute specifies extensions to an existing object creation wizard. `creationWizardExt` is a multivalued `DirectoryString` attribute, with each value specifying another extension page to add. The format of each value is `<order number>,<CLSID GUID>`, where `<order number>` indicates where in the sequence of property pages the MMC or Windows shell should insert this page. `0` indicates the page should be inserted at the beginning. `<CLSID GUID>` is the CLSID of the wizard page to add, in the form given by `StringFromGUID2()` and `StringFromCLSID()`.

shellContextMenu

The `shellContextMenu` attribute is a multivalued `DirectoryString` attribute that contains an order number and CLSID GUID. `shellContextMenu` identifies a menu that the MMC or the Windows shell will invoke when a user right-clicks in an object of the corresponding class. The format of each value of the attribute is `<order number>,<CLSID GUID>`, where *<order number>* determines the order in which the MMC or Windows shell will display the context menu, and *<CLSID GUID>* is the CLSID that identifies the menu, in the format created by `StringFromCLSID()` or `StringFromGUID2()`. An example is `1,{08eb4fa6-6ffd-11d1-b0e0-00c04fd8dca6}`.

shellPropertyPages

The `shellPropertyPages` attribute is a multivalued `DirectoryString` attribute that identifies the property pages the Windows shell will display when a user selects an object of the corresponding class. The format of each value of the `shellPropertyPages` attribute is *<order number>,<CLSID GUID>*, where *<order number>* is a integer that determines the order in which the Windows shell will display the property pages, and *<CLSID GUID>* is the CLSID of the property page in the format produced by `StringFromCLSID()` or `StringFromGUID2()`. An example is `2,{dde2c5e9-c8ae-11d0-bcdb-00c04fd8d5b6}`.

ExtendedRights

The `ExtendedRights` container in the Configuration naming context contains `controlAccessRights` objects that define extended access rights for use by applications implementing their own access rights scheme. Refer to Chapter 4, "Active Directory Security," for more information about how these extended rights work.

Each `controlAccessRights` object contains the attributes discussed in the following sections.

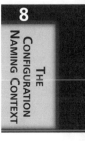

displayName

The `displayName` attribute is a single-valued `DirectoryString` string that contains the name of the extended right as it should be displayed by the administration utilities.

rightsGuid

The `rightsGuid` attribute is a single-valued `DirectoryString` attribute containing the string representation of the GUID to store in security descriptors containing this extended right. See Chapter 4 for more information about extended rights.

The GUID is stored in the form returned from `StringFromGUID2()`, with the leading and trailing curly braces removed—for instance, `"f0f8ffab-1191-11d0-a060-00aa006c33ed"`.

appliesTo

The `appliesTo` attribute is a multivalued attribute containing the `schemaIDGUID` of the classes to which this extended right applies. Each value is a `DirectoryString` containing the `schemaIDGUID` in the format as returned by `StringFromGUID2()`, with the curly braces removed—for instance, `"bf967a9c-0de6-11d0-a285-00aa003049e2"`.

LostAndFoundConfig

Active Directory uses the LostAndFoundConfig container to store orphaned objects it received during the replication process. Each partition (or naming context) in the system has a LostAndFound container; the LostAndFound container for the Configuration naming context is just named differently.

An *orphaned object* is one whose parent container doesn't exist. A directory object can become orphaned this way:

> A user connected to domain controller A deletes container X from the directory.
>
> Simultaneously, another user connected to domain controller B modifies an object Y contained by container X.

When the replication of the modification of object Y appears on domain controller A, there is no container to put the modified object in. Instead of throwing the object away, Active Directory puts the object in the LostAndFound (or in the case of the Configuration naming context, LostAndFoundConfig) container.

Partitions

The Partitions container in the Configuration naming context contains a cross-reference entry (objectClass=crossRef) for each naming context in the system. It also contains entries that represent external naming contexts (naming contexts that reside in other Active Directory forests, or in other non-Microsoft directories).

The relative distinguished name for each crossRef object is the NetBIOS name of the domain, so if there were a domain called Engineering in the MegaCorp forest, the distinguished name for the crossRef object would be CN=ENGINEERING,CN=Partitions, CN=Configuration,DC=MegaCorp,DC=com.

dNSRoot

The dNSRoot attribute of the crossRef object for a naming context contains the DNS domain name that corresponds to the naming context. This is the DNS name you would use to query DNS for the domain controllers for a particular domain. The dNSRoot attribute is a DirectoryString.

nCName

The nCName is the full distinguished name for the naming context. This is the name you would use to find the domainDNS object for the domain.

nETBIOSName

The nETBIOSName attribute contains the NetBIOS name for the naming context. It is always the same as the relative distinguished name of the crossRef object.

rootTrust

Every naming context is either a tree root or a subordinate naming context. If the naming context is a tree root, the rootTrust attribute contains the distinguished name of the root domain (the first domain created) of the enterprise. The rootTrust attribute has distinguished name syntax.

trustParent

Every naming context is either a tree root or a subordinate naming context. If the naming context is a subordinate naming context, the trustParent attribute contains the distinguished name of the parent naming context. The trustParent attribute has distinguished name syntax.

Schema

The Schema container in the Configuration naming context is actually the root of a new naming context, the Schema naming context. The Schema naming context contains the definitions of the classes and attributes Active Directory allows you to create. Chapter 9, "The Active Directory Schema," discusses the contents of the Schema naming context.

The Schema naming context is also replicated on every domain controller, just like the Configuration naming context.

Note that even though the Schema naming context is subordinate to the Configuration naming context, Schema is not contained within the Configuration naming context. Schema and Configuration have their own separate (though equivalent) replication schedules and topology.

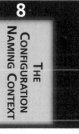

Services

The Services container in the Configuration naming context contains enterprise-wide configuration information for network services. By default, the Services container just contains information for Microsoft Windows 2000 services, but you can certainly put your own service configuration here if you want.

By convention, each type of service has its own container. For instance, the RRAS container contains configuration information for Microsoft's Routing and Remote Access Service.

One object in the Services container is particularly interesting. The object with distinguished name CN=Default Query Policy,CN=Query-Policies,CN=Directory Service, CN=Windows NT in the Services container contains default configuration information for each directory services agent in the enterprise.

The multivalued DirectoryString attribute lDAPAdminLimits contains various default configuration parameters for the directory service agents throughout the enterprise. The configuration parameters look like environment strings; they are composed of a parameter name and a value, separated by an equal sign.

Note that this object is the default query policy for the enterprise. You can create additional query policies and place them in the Query-Policies container. You can then assign the query policy to one or more domain controllers by setting the queryPolicyObject attribute of the nTDSSettings object for the domain controller to the distinguished name of the query policy object. The distinguished name for the nTDSSettings object for the server MEGACORP1 would be CN=NTDS Settings,CN=MEGACORP1,CN=Servers, CN=Chicago,CN=Sites,CN=Configuration,DC=MegaCorp,DC=com.

MaxPageSize

The MaxPageSize parameter determines the largest value you can use for the page size parameter in a paged LDAP search. (See Chapter 21, "Advanced Searching with LDAP," for more about paged searches.) The page size parameter determines how many entries the DSA will pass back for each page of search results. The default value is 1000.

MaxActiveQueries

The MaxActiveQueries parameter defines the maximum number of outstanding directory queries the DSA will support. Decreasing this number will allow fewer concurrent search operations and will decrease the maximum load directory searches will place on the server. Increasing the MaxActiveQueries parameter will allow more concurrent searches, but will increase the total load that searches will place on the server.

The default value for MaxActiveQueries is 20.

InitRecvTimeout

The InitRecvTimeout parameter determines the number of seconds the DSA will wait for a response to an RPC issued to another DSA before failing with a timeout error.

The default value is 120 seconds, which means that the DSA will wait two minutes before timing out a receive operation.

MaxConnections

The MaxConnections parameter sets the maximum number of TCP connections the DSA will support at one time. Each ADSI or LDAP bind operation uses one connection, and the connection will stay in use until the connecting client process unbinds the connection by calling ldap_unbind, until the client process terminates, or until the DSA times out the connection because it has become idle for too long. If a client attempts to establish a connection when the maximum number of connections is already in use, the DSA will deny the connection.

The default value for the MaxConnections parameter is 5000.

MaxConnIdleTime

The MaxConnIdleTime parameter determines how long a connection between a directory client and the DSA must be idle before the DSA will reuse the connection.

Idle connections don't create much of a problem for the DSA other than they use a little memory. They also count toward the MaxConnections value, so if the number of active connections on your domain controller is consistently bumping up against the MaxConnections value, decreasing the MaxConnIdleTime will help by disconnecting unused connections sooner.

The default value for the MaxConnIdleTime parameter is 900 seconds.

MaxNotificationsPerConn

The MaxNotificationsPerConn parameter defines how many notification searches the DSA will allow per connection.

A notification search provides a mechanism by which a directory client can register for changes to a particular object or container. When a change to the object or container occurs, the DSA will notify the client by sending an asynchronous search result.

Each outstanding notification search uses some amount of memory on the DSA. Each notification search also generates additional network traffic (assuming the clients are not running on the domain controller) whenever a directory object that has outstanding notifications changes.

The default value for MaxNotificationsPerConn is 5.

MaxQueryDuration

The MaxQueryDuration parameter sets the limit on the amount of clock time the DSA will spend on any given search. If your directory search takes longer than the MaxQueryDurationValue, the DSA will terminate the search prematurely and return the partial results, if any. The `MaxQueryDuration` parameter applies to each page in a paged search operation.

The default value for the `MaxQueryDuration` parameter is 120 seconds.

MaxResultSetSize

The `MaxResultSetSize` parameter defines the maximum number of bytes the DSA will return in response to a single search operation, or in the case of a paged search, the maximum number of bytes the DSA will return in a single search page.

Setting the `MaxResultSetSize` parameter higher will make it easier to do large subtree searches and retrieve all the attributes for each object returned by the search. On the downside, this will increase the amount of network traffic a search will be able to generate.

The default value for the `MaxResultSetSize` is 262144 bytes.

MaxTempTableSize

The Active Directory DSA builds a temporary table when you perform a search with sorting. The `MaxTempTableSize` parameter defines how large this table can be.

The default value for the `MaxTempTableSize` parameter is 10000 entries.

MaxPoolThreads

The Active Directory DSA is a highly threaded application. It maintains a pool of available threads (created but idle) that it can assign to process incoming directory requests. The `MaxPoolThreads` parameter defines how many threads the DSA will create for the pool.

Setting this number will allow more simultaneous search operations, but will also allow the DSA to use more of the available CPU resources.

The default value for the `MaxPoolThreads` parameter is 4.

Sites

The `Sites` container contains all the information that describes the physical deployment of Active Directory in the enterprise. The Sites container contains objects that represent the physical sites in the enterprise, the domain controllers in each site, and the replication topology between servers within a site and between servers in different sites.

Inter-Site Transports

The Inter-Site Transports container contains the Site Link and Site Link Bridge objects that define how Active Directory replicates data between sites.

There are two subcontainers in Inter-Site Transports. The first, IP, contains the Site Link and Site Link Bridge objects that the administrator has defined for the IP protocol. The Active Directory installation process defines one initial Site Link object called DEFAULTIPSITELINK.

The second subcontainer in the Inter-Site Transports container is named SMTP. It contains Site Link and Site Link Bridge objects for those sites that perform directory replication via the Simple Message Transport Protocol (SMTP). Sites that use SMTP use email to communicate their replication information.

Site Containers

There is one subcontainer in the Sites container for each site the administrator defines. The relative distinguished name of this subcontainer is the name of the site itself. For instance, the distinguished name of the Chicago site would be CN=Chicago,CN=Sites, CN=Configuration,DC=MegaCorp,DC=com.

The Servers container within the site container—for instance, CN=Servers,CN=Chicago, CN=Sites,CN=Configuration,DC=MegaCorp,DC=com—contains a container object for each server in that site. The name of this container is the NetBIOS name of the server, such as CN=MEGACORP1,CN=Servers,CN=Chicago,CN=Sites,CN=Configuration, DC=MegaCorp,DC=com.

The server object in the CN=Servers,CN=<site name> container is *not* the same object as the computer object representing the server in the CN=Domain Controllers, DC=<domain name> container, although they represent the same physical server.

The server object in CN=Servers,CN=<site name> container contains the DSA configuration information that Active Directory replicates to every domain controller in the enterprise (because it is part of the Configuration naming context). It contains the distinguished name attribute serverReference that contains the name of the computer object in the CN=Domain Controllers,CN=<domain name> container.

The computer object in the CN=Domain Controllers,DC=<domain name> is the security principal that represents the domain controller. It exists only on those domain controllers that are part of the domain <domain name>.

The server object in the CN=Servers,CN=<site name> container is itself a container. It contains yet another container (how many levels deep are we now? six?) named NTDS Settings. This nTDSDSA object has several interesting attributes.

The options attribute of the nTDSDSA object, if present and equal to 1, indicates that this DSA is also a global catalog.

The `hasMasterNCs` attribute is a multivalued attribute, each value containing the distinguished name of the naming context this server has a full writable copy of. There should always be three values: one for the Configuration naming context, one for the Schema naming contest, and one for the domain naming context for the domain the domain controller is a member of.

The `hasPartialReplicaNCs` is a multivalued attribute that contains the names of the partial replicas this domain controller maintains. This attribute is only present on global catalog servers. The `hasPartialReplicaNCs` attribute only contains the names of the naming contexts that the domain controller does not have a full writable copy of. On a global catalog server, the combination of the `hasPartialReplicaNCs` attribute and the `hasMasterNCs` attributes should name every naming context in the enterprise.

The `queryPolicyObject` attribute contains the distinguished name of the Active Directory `queryPolicy` object that this domain controller uses. If you create a new `queryPolicy` object in the `CN=Query-Policies,CN=Directory Service,CN=Windows NT,CN=Services, CN=Configuration,DC=megaCorp,DC=com` container, you assign that policy to a domain controller by setting its distinguished name in the `queryPolicyObject` attribute of the `nTDSDSA` object for the domain controller.

WellKnownSecurityPrincipals

The `WellKnownSecurityPrincipals` container contains a set of `foreignSecurityPrincipal` objects. Each `foreignSecurityPrincipal` object represents a predefined security principal in Windows 2000. Some examples of well-known security principals are Dialup, which refers to processes connected via modem; Interactive, which refers to processes that interact with the user through the screen and keyboard; and Authenticated users, which refers to any user. The Windows 2000 security subsystem associates each process with zero or more of these objects when the system creates the process's access token. In effect, Windows 2000 treats these well-known security principals as groups, and dynamically assigns processes to the appropriate group memberships.

CHAPTER 9

The Active Directory Schema

Active Directory, like most other directories, is primarily a database. And like any good database system, Active Directory has a set of rules that determine what kind of data can appear in the database. These rules are represented in the Active Directory schema.

The first part of this chapter describes the Active Directory schema and how it is stored in the directory. The last part of the chapter shows you how to access the contents of the schema, and how to extend the schema to accommodate new classes and attributes.

Introduction to the Active Directory Schema

Instead of hard-coding the schema information in the directory service code, or perhaps storing it in a special file, Microsoft elected to store the Active Directory schema in the directory itself. This design decision has several consequences.

First, it makes it easy to modify and extend the schema simply by adding objects to the directory; there is no special set of APIs and associated code.

Second, storing the schema in the directory takes advantage of the already-existing replication mechanism to make sure the schema ends up on all the domain controllers in the enterprise.

Finally, storing the schema in the directory lets the system use the existing security mechanisms built into the directory to control access to the schema.

The Active Directory schema is stored in its own naming context called (not surprisingly) Schema. The Schema naming context is subordinate to the Configuration naming context. Hence, the full distinguished name for the Schema naming context would be, for example, CN=Schema,CN=Configuration,DC=eng,DC=megacorp,DC=com, where eng.megacorp.com is the name of the first domain created in the Active Directory enterprise.

The Active Directory schema primarily defines two things: the kinds of attributes that may be stored in the directory, and the classes of objects that may be stored in the directory. The schema contains two classes of objects to do this. Objects of class attributeSchema define the allowed attributes, and objects of class classSchema define the allowed classes. Later sections in this chapter will describe these in more detail.

Note that the Schema naming context does not have any subcontainers. The entire Active Directory schema appears directly in the Schema naming context. You cannot add any objects to the Schema naming context (including container objects) other than classSchema and attributeSchema objects.

Class Definitions

Every object in Active Directory is a member of a specific class. Each class defines what attributes objects of that class may (or must) contain, what classes of objects can contain objects of this class, and the default security settings that newly created objects of that class will have.

Each class in Active Directory is defined by a single object in the Schema container; these class definition objects have a relative distinguished name that is the name of the class, and they are of class classSchema. For instance, the class definition for User objects is kept in the classSchema object CN=User,CN=Schema,CN=Configuration, DC=MegaCorp,DC=com.

When you first bring up a domain controller, the Active Directory schema contains definitions for more than 140 different classes. These classes define objects ranging from fundamental network management objects, such as users and domains, to more obscure objects such as pKIEnrollmentService. (PKI refers to Public Key Infrastructure.) Pretty much every kind of useful Windows 2000 network configuration data appears somewhere in the directory.

This next section describes the contents of classSchema objects and how to define the kinds of objects you can create in the directory.

Three Kinds of Class Definitions

There are three fundamental kinds of classes you can define in Active Directory. The integer attribute of `classSchema` named `objectClassCategory` defines what kind of class the `classSchema` object defines. `classSchema` objects that define structural classes have an `objectClassCategory` of `1`, `classSchema` objects that define abstract classes have an `objectClassCategory` of `2`, and `classSchema` objects that define auxiliary classes have an `objectClassCategory` value of `3`. There is a fourth `objectClassCategory` value of `0` that Active Directory uses for legacy classes defined before the 1994 X.500 specification. These are called 88-Class or Type 88 classes, referring to the 1988 X.500 specification that they comply with. You should always specify an `objectClassCategory` of `1`, `2`, or `3` when creating your own classes.

The following sections describe these three kinds of classes in more detail.

Abstract Classes

Abstract classes exist in the Active Directory schema so that other class definitions can inherit the abstract class's characteristics. You cannot create instances of abstract classes in the directory, but abstract classes can inherit from other abstract classes. In this way, abstract classes are similar to abstract classes in C++.

Abstract classes make sense when you want to model a "kind-of" relationship in the directory. For instance, Active Directory contains an abstract class called `organizationalPerson`. If you want to create objects to represent different kinds of persons in the directory, you could create classes such as `departmentManager` and `outsideVendor` that inherit all the characteristics of `organizationalPerson`. If you search the directory for objects of class `organizationalPerson`, the search will return `departmentManagers` and `outsideVendors` because they are both kinds-of `organizationalPersons`. The section "Inheritance in the Active Directory Schema" explains this relationship in more detail.

There are 14 abstract classes in the initial Active Directory schema. They include classes such as `domain`, `device`, and `organizationalPerson`.

Unless you are planning on making significant additions to the Active Directory schema, there isn't a good reason for you to create abstract classes.

Auxiliary Classes

Auxiliary classes are similar to abstract classes in that you cannot create instances of auxiliary classes in the directory. You can include the characteristics of auxiliary classes in other classes you create. I use the word *include* instead of *inherit* because a class that refers to an auxiliary class is not a kind-of that auxiliary class. It simply includes some of the auxiliary class's characteristics. The section "Inheritance in the Active Directory Schema" explains this relationship in more detail.

9

THE ACTIVE
DIRECTORY
SCHEMA

Auxiliary classes make particular sense when you consider that the inheritance model in Active Directory is single inheritance. For instance, `mailRecipient` is an auxiliary class in Active Directory. Many different classes of objects should contain mail recipient attributes. For instance, users need mail recipient attributes, but so do automated tech support services that run on a Web server. But it doesn't make sense to define a single-inheritance hierarchy where a user class and a service class end up inheriting from each other.

You can think of including an auxiliary class as being similar to inheriting from multiple interface classes in C++, or perhaps like including header files in your source code.

There are four auxiliary classes defined in the initial Active Directory schema. They are `mailRecipient`, `securityPrincipal`, and `samDomainBase`.

Structural Classes

Structural classes are the meat of the schema. Structural classes define the objects that actually appear in the directory.

Structural classes can inherit from either an abstract class or another structural class, and they can include the attributes of multiple auxiliary classes.

The majority of the classes in the base Active Directory schema are structural classes. They include classes such as `user`, `server`, and `printQueue`.

Identifying the Class

Each `classSchema` object has four mandatory attributes that identify the class it defines. The relative distinguished name of the `classSchema` object is the name of the class. For instance, `Application-Settings` is the name of the class defined by the `classSchema` object `CN=Application-Settings,CN=Schema,CN=Configuration,DC=megaCorp,DC=com`. By definition, the relative distinguished name is unique within the Schema container, and because all the schema objects appear in the Schema container, the relative distinguished name uniquely names the class.

By convention, class names start with a capital letter, and individual words in the name are separated by hyphens. But in general, you will see class names with an initial lower-case letter, and individual words after the first starting with capital letters. For instance, instead of `Application-Settings`, you will see `applicationSettings`. This is the LDAP display name, and it too must be unique among all the objects in the schema. The `ldapDisplayName` attribute of `classSchema` contains the LDAP display name.

The `governsID` attribute of `classSchema` contains the third identifier for the class.

governsID contains an ITU Object Identifier (OID) string that, theoretically at least, uniquely identifies the class among all directory schemas in the world. When you add a class to the Active Directory schema, you must assign the class a unique OID. The section "Obtaining OIDs for Schema Extensions" describes how you can go about doing this.

The schemaIDGUID attribute contains a 128-bit globally unique identifier (GUID) for the class. Every object in the Active Directory schema has a unique GUID.

Defining the Attributes of a Class

Ignoring inheritance and inclusion, four attributes of the classschema object define the attributes that instances of the class can contain.

The mustContain attribute contains the names of the attributes that instances of the class must contain. You cannot create an instance without values defined for each of these attributes, and you can't remove any of these attributes after the object has been created.

The mayContain attribute contains the names of the attributes that instances may contain. You don't have to have values for any of these values, but you can if you want.

The systemMustContain attribute behaves the same way as the mayContain attribute, with one important difference: You cannot change the systemMustContain attribute in the schema. You can change the mustContain attribute (if you have the appropriate privileges), but Active Directory will never let you change the systemMustContain attribute. This is one way that Microsoft can ensure that customers don't modify their schema so much that the Microsoft products themselves can't run.

As you might guess, there is also a systemMayContain attribute of the classSchema object. This attribute contains a list of names of attributes that instances may contain. You cannot change the value of this attribute.

Defining Containment Relationships

In Active Directory, any object can be a container. The Active Directory schema defines which classes of objects may be contained by which other classes. The classSchema attribute possSuperiors contains the names of the classes that are allowed to contain instances of this class. The systemPossSuperiors attribute does the same thing; however, you cannot change the value of systemPossSuperiors in the schema.

If you want to define a class whose instances cannot be containers, derive your class from the abstract class leaf.

Similarly, if you want your class to be able to contain most things, including other containers, derive your class from the class `container`.

One problem with this scheme for defining the classes that can contain other classes is that it is quite difficult to determine whether a given class is a container or not. If you wanted to find out if an instance of the `user` class could be a container, you would effectively have to search the entire schema and find whether any class had a `possSuperiors` (or `systemPossSuperiors`) attribute that contained the `user` class name. It's even somewhat worse than that because you have to handle the inheritance of these attributes from parent classes.

Thankfully, Active Directory synthesizes an attribute for every directory object called `allowedChildClasses`. This multivalued property contains the names of all the classes this class is allowed to contain. Note that this is an attribute of each object, not an attribute of the `classSchema` object.

Inheritance in the Active Directory Schema

In addition to the four attributes mentioned in the preceding section, there are two mechanisms you can use to define the attributes a class may contain. I touched on them earlier. They are inheritance and inclusion.

Inheritance

Active Directory supports a single-inheritance model. This means that any given class must inherit from exactly one other class. The `subClassOf` attribute contains the LDAP display name of the class this class inherits from. Every class must inherit from an existing class; in the case where you don't really want a class to inherit from anything, you can inherit from the abstract class `top`. This class has only four `mustContain` attributes: `objectClass`, `instanceType`, `nTSecurityDescriptor`, and `objectCategory`. (It does, however, have a bunch of `mayContain` attributes, which is a little surprising.)

When a class inherits from another existing class, several things happen:

- When you create an instance of the derived class, Active Directory will automatically set the `objectClass` attribute to contain the names of all the classes that this class inherits from, all the way up to the class `top`. For instance, if you defined a class `programmer` that inherits from class `user` (which inherits from `organizationalPerson`, which inherits from `person`, which inherits from `top`), the `objectClass` attribute of each `programmer` object would contain `programmer`, `user`, `organizationalPerson`, `person`, and `top`.

- The derived class inherits the `mayContain`, `mustContain`, `systemMayContain`, and `systemMustContain` attributes from the parent class. The values for these attributes in the parent class are effectively (not actually) merged into the `mayContain`, mustContain, systemMayContain, and systemMustContain attributes of the derived class. When you create an instance of the derived class, it must have values defined for all the attributes named in its mustContain and systemMustContain attributes, as well as all those named in all the parent classes.

- The derived class inherits the possSuperiors and systemPossSuperiors attributes from the parent class. The values for these attributes from the parent class are effectively merged with those of the derived class. This means that the derived class can be contained by any objects named in its possSuperiors and systemPossSuperiors attributes, and it can be contained by anything named in the possSuperiors and systemPossSuperiors attributes of its parent classes.

Inclusion

You can include attributes in your class from other classes through another mechanism called *inclusion*. You name the classes whose attributes you want to include in the auxiliaryClass and systemAuxiliaryClass attributes. The effect is similar to inheritance, but with a couple of important differences.

- Your class will include the attributes named in the mayHave, mustHave, systemMayHave, and systemMustHave attributes of the included class, just as with the inheritance case.

- The objectClass attribute of instances of your class will be unchanged by the inclusion process. Including attributes from an auxiliary class does not affect the class inheritance hierarchy.

- The possSuperiors and systemPossSuperiors attributes in your class will also be unaffected. Including attributes from an auxiliary class does not affect the container status of your class.

Defining Class Security

In Active Directory, you can set access rights on individual attributes of objects. This gives you an incredibly fine-grained level of access control, but you can see that managing individual access rights on all the attributes in the system would be a nightmare.

Active Directory simplifies this problem by providing for default security settings for new objects. The classSchema object contains an attribute named defaultSecurityDescriptor. It is a single-valued attribute of the nTSecurityDescriptor syntax. Active Directory uses the value of this attribute to initialize the nTSecurityDescriptor attribute of each new instance of the class. Chapter 4, "Active Directory Security," describes how the nTSecurityDescriptor attribute governs access rights to the object.

The classSchema Attributes

Table 9.1 shows all the attributes that make up a classSchema object.

9

THE ACTIVE
DIRECTORY
SCHEMA

TABLE 9.1 classSchema ATTRIBUTES

Attribute Name	Required?	Multivalued?	Description
auxiliaryClass	No	Yes	The LDAP display names of the classes that this class includes attribute definitions from.
classDisplayName	No	Yes	The localized string containing the name of the class as it should be displayed by applications.
cn	Yes	No	The common name of the class. It defaults to the RDN if not specified.
defaultHidingValue	No		A Boolean value that is True if new instances of this class will have their showInAdvancedViewOnly set to True so that they will not be displayed in the Active Directory administrative tools by default.
defaultObjectCategory	Yes	No	The single-valued category of this class. It defaults to the class itself if not specified.
defaultSecurityDescriptor	No	No	The security descriptor assigned to new instances of this class.
governsID	Yes	No	The unique ITU OID that identifies the class.
isDefunct	No	No	A Boolean value that is True if the class has been removed. You may not create instances of a class when it is marked as defunct.
ldapDisplayName	No	No	The LDAP-style name of this class. This is the name used when referring to the class via LDAP.

Attribute Name	Required?	Multivalued?	Description
mayContain	No	Yes	The LDAP display names of the attributes instances of this class may contain. It is multi-valued.
mustContain	No	Yes	The LDAP display names of the attributes that instances of this class must have values for.
objectClassCategory	Yes	No	An integer indicating that this class is structural (1), abstract (2), or auxiliary (3). 0 indicates a legacy class, and should not be used.
possSuperiors	No	Yes	The LDAP display names of the class that can contain instances of this class. It is multivalued.
RDNAttID	No	No	The name of the attribute that is used when composing the relative distinguished name of objects of this class. It defaults to cn if not specified.
schemaFlagsEx	No	No	An integer containing several bit flags that further define characteristics of the class. These flags are defined by the ADS_SYSTEMFLAG_ ENUM enumeration in iads.h.
schemaIDGUID	Yes	No	The GUID that uniquely identifies this class. It is generated automatically if not specified.
subClassOf	Yes	No	The ldapDisplayName of the class that this class inherits from.

9

THE ACTIVE
DIRECTORY
SCHEMA

continues

TABLE 9.1   CONTINUED

Attribute Name	Required?	Multivalued?	Description
systemAuxiliaryClass	No	No	The LDAP display names of the auxiliary classes that this class includes. After the `classSchema` object has been created, you may not change this attribute.
systemMayContain	No	Yes	The LDAP display names of the attributes that this class may contain. It is multivalued. After the `classSchema` object has been created, you may not change this value.
systemMustContain	No	No	The LDAP display names of the attributes that instances of this class must have values for. After the `classSchema` object has been created, you may not change this attribute.
systemOnly	No	No	A Boolean attribute that if set to `True` indicates that instances of this class may only be modified by Active Directory itself. By default this value is `False`.
systemPossSuperiors	No	Yes	The LDAP display names of the classes that can contain instances of this class. It is multivalued. After the `classSchema` object has been created, you may not change this value.

Attribute Definitions

As with classes, Active Directory also stores attribute definitions in the Schema naming context. Each attribute in Active Directory is defined by an `attributeSchema` object in the Schema container. The relative distinguished name of the `attributeSchema` object is the name of the attribute it defines.

The attributeSchema object defines what values an attribute is allowed to take. It determines whether the attribute has numeric or string values, whether it is single-valued or multivalued, and how large the attribute value can be.

There are 854 attributeSchema objects in the base Active Directory schema.

> **NOTE**
>
> One thing that surprised me when I first looked at Active Directory was the fact that the attribute definitions are global to all classes. That is to say, if there are two classes that have an attribute named description, there is single attributeSchema object that defines that attribute. If the description for a user is 32 characters long, the description for all objects that have a description attribute is 32 characters long. This isn't a problem, but it was certainly surprising to me.

Identifying the Attribute

Each attributeSchema object in the Schema container defines an attribute in Active Directory. The relative distinguished name of the attributeSchema object is the name of the attribute it defines. The naming convention for attributes is the same as that for classes. The relative distinguished name has initial capital letters, and hyphens separate individual words in the name. Because all the attributeSchema objects are in the Schema container, attribute names are guaranteed to be unique across the system.

Attributes also have an ldapDisplayName attribute. This attribute contains the display-format name of the object, just as with classSchema objects. The ldapDisplayName attribute must also be unique across all objects in the Schema container (attributeSchema and classSchema objects as well). This implies that not only can two attributes not have the same ldapDisplayName, but that an attribute cannot have the same ldapDisplayName as any class.

Attributes, like classes, also have an ITU object identifier (OID) that uniquely identifies the attribute definition across all directory schemas in the world. When you create a new attribute, you must specify a unique OID string in the attributeID attribute of the attributeSchema object.

The cn attribute of the attributeSchema object contains the common name of the attribute. The cn attribute is mandatory, but if you don't specify it when you create a new attribute, Active Directory will default its value to the relative distinguished name of the attributeSyntax object.

Defining the Attribute's Type

Fundamentally, a schemaAttribute object defines the types of values the attribute may have. There are several attributes of the attributeSchema object that define the allowable values.

First, the attributeSyntax attribute contains the OID of the attribute's type, or *syntax*. There are 18 predefined attribute syntaxes in Active Directory. These are essentially hard-coded into the directory service software, and there is no way to add or modify these syntaxes. See the section "Attribute Syntax" to learn more about attribute syntaxes.

The oMSyntax and oMObjectClass attributes define the attribute's syntax in a form defined by the Open Group's XDS directory protocol. oMSyntax is an integer-valued attribute, but the values are closely associated with the values of the attributeSyntax attribute. Each Active Directory syntax has a corresponding oMSyntax value, and they must match up. The oMObjectClass attribute contains an ASN-1 encoded binary string that identifies the XDS object class this attribute corresponds to. oMObjectClass is only defined when the value of the oMSyntax attribute is 127. The section "Attribute Syntax" explains this in more detail.

rangeLower and rangeUpper are integer-valued attributes that provide a limited way of modifying the normally hard-coded syntaxes. In the case of string-valued syntaxes such as Unicode String or Case-Insensitive String, rangeLower and rangeUpper define the minimum and maximum lengths of the attribute's value, respectively. In the case of integer-valued syntaxes such as Integer or Large Integer, rangeLower and rangeUpper define the minimum and maximum values allowed.

The extendedCharsAllowed attribute is a Boolean value that indicates non-ASCII characters are allowed in a normally ASCII-only string. As of Windows 2000 Release Candidate 1, it does not appear that this attribute is in use.

The isSingleValued attribute of the attributeSchema object determines whether or not the attribute can be multivalued. If isSingleValued is True, the attribute can contain only a single value. False indicates that the attribute can be multivalued.

Indexing and the Global Catalog

There are two important ways Active Directory improves the performance of directory queries. The first is by creating database indexes for attributes that are frequently specified in a search criteria. The second is by creating global catalogs that eliminate the need for queries to chase referrals to other domain controllers. Both of these mechanisms are controlled through the attributeSchema object.

Directory administrators can determine which attributes will be indexed by setting the low-order bit of the searchFlags attribute. Table 9.2 shows the meanings of the different bits of the searchFlags attribute. Likewise, the administrator can reduce the amount of disk space used by directory indexes by setting the low-order bit of the searchFlags attribute to 0.

TABLE 9.2   POSSIBLE VALUES OF THE searchFlags ATTRIBUTE

Bit Mask Value	Description
0x01	Indexes only the attribute value.
0x02	Indexes the container and attribute values together.
0x04	Use this attribute in the Ambiguous Name Resolution index so that it can be searched with the LDAP partial-match search filter. Must be used with 0x01 as well.
0x08	Keep this attribute in the tombstone object after the object has been deleted.

NOTE

The Schema naming context is replicated to every domain controller in the enterprise, and consequently, all domain controllers share the same schema information. This means that all domain controllers will index the same attributes. There is no way to have only some domain controllers index an attribute.

Active Directory global catalogs contain partial replicas of all the naming contexts in the enterprise. This is how they can service some directory searches without referring the search to another domain controller. The directory administrator can determine which attributes will be replicated to the global catalogs by setting the isMemberOfPartialAttributeSet attribute to True. Setting this attribute to True will cause Active Directory to replicate all instances of the attribute to all the global catalogs in the enterprise.

NOTE

The Schema naming context is replicated to every domain controller in the enterprise, and consequently, all domain controllers share the same schema information. This means that Active Directory will replicate the same attributes to all global catalogs in the system. There is no way to specify that an attribute be replicated to some global catalogs but not others.

9

**THE ACTIVE
DIRECTORY
SCHEMA**

Linked Attributes

Active Directory supports the notion of linking one object in the directory to another. Active Directory accomplishes this by creating a forward link attribute that contains the DN of the linked-to object, and a backward link attribute in the linked-to object that refers to the linked-from object.

To provide for such a link between class A and class B, you have to create a forward link attribute in class A and a backward link attribute in class B.

The forward link attribute in class A must have the following characteristics:

- It must have a syntax of distinguished name, OR name, or Distname-Address (see Table 9.4 for descriptions of these syntax values).
- The linkID attribute of the attributeSchema object must be a unique, even nonzero, value.
- The attribute can be single-valued (which creates a one-to-many relationship between class A and class B) or multivalued (which creates a many-to-many relationship between class A and class B).

The backward link attribute must have the following characteristics:

- It must have a syntax of Distinguished Name.
- The linkID attribute must have the value of the forward link attribute's linkID attribute plus 1.
- It must be multivalued.

Other Administrative Attributes

Several attributes of the attributeSchema class control the way Active Directory handles an attribute.

The systemOnly attribute is a Boolean value that, when set to True, indicates that only Active Directory can create or modify instances of this attribute. Attributes that Active Directory uses to control replication, such as dSCorePropagationData and uSNChanged, are system-only attributes.

schemaFlagsEx is an integer that contains flags that determine whether the attribute is replicated and whether the attribute is constructed. Some attributes are not replicated because they represent information about the replication process itself.

Table 9.3 summarizes the attributeSchema attributes.

TABLE 9.3 attributeSchema ATTRIBUTES

Attribute Name	Required?	Multivalued?	Description
attributeID	Yes	No	The ITU OID string that uniquely identifies the attribute.
attributeSecurityGUID	No	No	An optional 128-bit GUID that identifies this attribute for the purposes of establishing access controls.
attributeSyntax	Yes	No	The OID of the Active Directory syntax that defines the values this attribute may have.
classDisplayName	No	Yes	Contains the localized representation of the class's name.
cn	Yes	No	The common name of the attribute. It is a single-valued string.
extendedCharsAllowed	No	No	A Boolean value that, when set to True, indicates that the attribute may contain extended characters.
isDefunct	No	No	A Boolean value that, when set to True, indicates that this attribute is no longer part of the schema, and no objects may be created that contain this attribute.
isEphemeral	No	No	Indicates that the attribute is constructed on demand by Active Directory.
isMemberOfPartial ➥AttributeSet	No	No	A Boolean value that, when set to True, indicates that this attribute will be stored in global catalog servers.
isSingleValued	Yes	No	A Boolean value that, when set to False, indicates whether this attribute can have multiple values. If True, the attribute may contain only a single value.

9

**THE ACTIVE
DIRECTORY
SCHEMA**

continues

TABLE 9.3 CONTINUED

Attribute Name	Required?	Multivalued?	Description
ldapDisplayName	Yes	No	A single-valued string containing the LDAP-format display name of the attribute. It must be unique among all objects in the Schema container.
linkID	No	Yes	An integer that is shared between the two attributes that make up a linked attribute pair. This value must be unique across all linked attribute pairs in the schema.
MAPIID	No	Yes	An integer that contains the Mail Application Programming Interface (MAPI) display ID for this attribute.
oMObjectClass	No	No	The ASN-1 encoded octet string that defines the XDS object class for this attribute. It is only used when oMSyntax is equal to 127.
oMSyntax	Yes	No	An integer value that identifies the type of this attribute using the scheme defined by the Open group's XDS directory service API.
rangeLower	No	No	An integer that defines the minimum value or minimum length of this attribute. If this attribute is string-valued, rangeLower defines the minimum length of the value. If the attribute is integer-valued, rangeLower defines the minimum value of the attribute.

Attribute Name	Required?	Multivalued?	Description
rangeUpper	No	No	An integer that defines the maximum value or maximum length of this attribute. If this attribute is string-valued, rangeUpper defines the maximum length of the value. If the attribute is integer-valued, rangeUpper defines the maximum value of the attribute.
schemaFlagsEx	No	No	A single-valued integer that contains flags describing this attribute. See ADS_SYSTEMFLAG_ENUM in iads.h.
schemaIDGUID	Yes	No	The 128-bit globally unique identifier for this attribute.
searchFlags	No	No	An integer whose low-order bit determines whether or not this attribute will be indexed. A low-order bit of 1 indicates that the attribute will be indexed; 0 indicates that it will not be indexed.
systemOnly	No	No	A Boolean value that, if set to True, indicates that only Active Directory can create or modify instances of this attribute.

Attribute Syntax

Every attribute defined in the Active Directory schema has a single syntax, or data type, that defines the values the attribute can contain. Each syntax has an OID that identifies it uniquely. Some of these syntaxes, such as the Distinguished Name syntax and the Case-Sensitive String syntax are defined by X.500. Other syntaxes, such as the Security Descriptor syntax and the SID syntax, are defined by Microsoft.

Although you can define new attributes in the schema that use the various syntaxes, the set of syntaxes you can choose from is fixed by Active Directory. The remainder of this section describes the various syntaxes that attributes can use in the Active Directory schema.

The Undefined Syntax

The Undefined syntax is essentially a placeholder. No attribute defined in the schema uses this syntax, and Active Directory will not let you add an attribute definition to the schema that uses this syntax.

The DN Syntax

Attributes defined with the DN (/) Distinguished Name syntax can contain the distinguished names of objects in the directory. Active Directory maintains an internal link between a Distinguished Name attribute and the object it refers to. If the object's distinguished name changes, either because it was renamed or it was moved to another container, Active Directory will automatically update the attribute's value.

The OID Syntax

Attributes that have OID syntax can contain a dotted-decimal ASN.1-style object identifier.

The CaseExactString Syntax

This syntax defines values consisting of valid ASCII characters. Active Directory performs case-sensitive comparison and sorting of attributes that use this syntax.

> **CAUTION**
>
> Current Microsoft documentation indicates that even though this syntax limits strings to the ASCII character set, Active Directory does not enforce this limitation. Therefore, it is possible to store values that contain non-ASCII characters in attributes that have this syntax.

The CaseIgnoreString Syntax

This syntax defines values consisting of valid ASCII characters. Active Directory ignores case when comparing and sorting attributes that use this syntax.

> **CAUTION**
>
> Current Microsoft documentation indicates that even though this syntax limits strings to the ASCII character set, Active Directory does not enforce this limitation. Therefore, it is possible to store values that contain non-ASCII characters in attributes that have this syntax.

The `IA5String` Syntax

The `IA5String` syntax defines string values that are composed of only printable characters.

> **CAUTION**
>
> Current Microsoft documentation indicates that even though this syntax limits strings to the ASCII character set, Active Directory does not enforce this limitation. Therefore, it is possible to store values that contain non-ASCII characters in attributes that have this syntax.

The `NumericString` Syntax

The `NumericString` syntax defines values that are composed of the numeric characters 0 through 9 and -.

> **CAUTION**
>
> Current Microsoft documentation indicates that even though this syntax limits strings to the ASCII numeric characters, Active Directory does not enforce this limitation. Therefore, it is possible to store values that contain nonnumeric characters in attributes that have this syntax.

The `ORName` Syntax

Attributes with the `ORName` syntax can contain X.400 email addresses.

The `Boolean` Syntax

Attributes that use the `Boolean` syntax can be either true or false, or, more precisely, `"True"` or `"False"` because LDAP returns these values as strings.

The `Integer` Syntax

Attributes with `Integer` syntax can contain a 32-bit integer.

The `OctetString` Syntax

The `OctetString` syntax defines values composed of an arbitrary number of bytes with no particular encoding. This is the syntax you should use if you need to store some arbitrary data structures in the directory.

> **NOTE**
>
> When you use LDAP to access attributes that use the OctetString syntax, you must use `LDAP_BERVAL` structures to contain the attribute values.

The `GeneralizedTime` Syntax

Attributes that use the `GeneralizedTime` syntax can contain a time and date value. LDAP represents the time as `YYYYMMDDHHMMSS.0Z`, where `YYYY` is the four-digit year, `MM` is the two-digit month with `01` representing January, and `DD` is the two-digit day of the month from `01` to `31`. The time portion is in 24-hour format, with `HH` representing the two-digit hours past midnight, `MM` the number of minutes, and `SS` the number of seconds. The value always ends in a decimal point followed by the number of 100-nanosecond ticks past the second. The value after the decimal point is always `0`. Active Directory converts all times to UTC time, so you will have to adjust any time values using the local time zone information.

> **NOTE**
>
> There are several time-valued attributes in Active Directory that are not stored as `GeneralizedTime` syntax values. For instance, the `creationTime` attribute of a domain is stored as a `DSTIME` (64-bit integer). It contains the time as the number of seconds since January 1, 1601. Note that this is similar to the Windows 2000 `FILETIME` structure, which expresses the time as 100-nanosecond ticks since January 1, 1601. You can scale the `DSTIME` value by multiplying it by 10,000 and then using the `FileTimeToSystemTime()` function to convert it to MM/DD/YY format.

The `DirectoryString` Syntax

Attributes that use the Unicode String syntax can contain arbitrary directory strings.

The `PresentationAddress` Syntax

The OSI network model defines a presentation address for OSI Application Entities (services) to address each other. This syntax defines the string representation of these addresses.

The `DNWithString` Syntax

This syntax allows you to store a text string along with the distinguished name of some object in the directory. Active Directory keeps the distinguished name portion of the value up to date even if the object is moved or renamed. The format of values with this syntax is `S:<byte count>:<string value>:<distinguished name>`.

> `<byte count>` is the number of bytes in `<string value>`.
>
> `<string value>` is the string value to store.
>
> `<distinguished name>` is the DN to store. It must refer to an existing object in the directory.

The `NTSecurityDescriptor` Syntax

This syntax defines attributes that contain Windows NT–style security descriptors. They are stored as octet strings in the directory.

The `INTEGER8` Syntax

The `INTEGER8` syntax represents 64-bit integer values. It behaves just like the Integer syntax.

The `DNWithBinary` Syntax

This syntax allows you to store a binary "blob" of data along with the distinguished name of some object in the directory. Active Directory keeps the distinguished name portion of the value up to date even if the object is moved or renamed. The format of values with this syntax is `B:<byte count>:<binary value in hex>:<distinguished name>`.

> `<byte count>` is the number of characters in `<binary value in hex>`.
>
> `<binary value in hex>` is the string representation of the binary data, with each byte of the value represented as two hex digits.
>
> `<distinguished name>` is the DN to store. It must refer to an existing object in the directory.

Usually you would store a GUID representing the object as the binary data, but you are not required to do so.

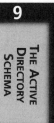

9

THE ACTIVE
DIRECTORY
SCHEMA

The `Sid` Syntax

The `Sid` syntax accommodates Windows NT–style security identifiers (SIDs). The directory stores them as octet strings.

Table 9.4 lists the attribute syntaxes supported by Active Directory.

TABLE 9.4   ATTRIBUTE SYNTAXES SUPPORTED BY ACTIVE DIRECTORY

Syntax	*OID*	*ASN 1 Encoded OID*	*OM Syntax*	*Represented as String?*	*Description*
Undefined	2.5.5.0	\x550500	0	No	Invalid syntax.
DN	2.5.5.1	\x550501	127	Yes	Distinguished name of an object in the directory.
OID	2.5.5.2	\x550502	6	Yes	ITU OID string.
CaseExactString	2.5.5.3	\x550503	27	Yes	IA5 string where case is significant in comparisons.
CaseIgnoreString	2.5.5.4	\x550504	20	Yes	IA5 string where case is not significant in comparisons.
IA5String	2.5.5.5	\x550505	22	Yes	String constraining IA5-printable characters.
NumericString	2.5.5.6	\x550506	18	Yes	IA5 string of digits, including . and -.
ORName	2.5.5.7	\x550507	127	Yes	An X.400 email address.
Boolean	2.5.5.8	\x550508	1	Yes	Boolean "True" or "False".
Integer	2.5.5.9	\x550509	2	Yes	32-bit integer.
Enumeration	2.5.5.9	\x550509	10	Yes	One of a set of integers.
Octet String	2.5.5.10	\x55050A	4	No	A string of arbitrary bytes.
ReplicaLink	2.5.5.10	\x55050A	127	No	A binary structure containing information about replication partners.

Syntax	OID	ASN 1 Encoded OID	OM Syntax	Represented as String?	Description
GeneralizedTime	2.5.5.11	\x55050B	24	Yes	The time and date, including 100ths of a second. A `GeneralizedTime` string has the format YYYYMMDDHH-MMSS.ssZ. An example is `"20000 201171515.0Z"`.
UTCTime	2.5.5.11	\x55050B	23	Yes	Another time and date representation that has a two-digit year with no seconds or fractions of a second. It has the format YYMMDD-HHMMSSZ. An example is `"991231091500Z"`.
DirectoryString	2.5.5.12	\x55050C	64	Yes	A case-insensitive Unicode string.
Presentation ➥Address	2.5.5.13	\x55050D	127	Yes	OSI application address in string form.
AccessPointDN	2.5.5.14	\x55050E	127	Yes	An X.400 access point name.
DNWithString	2.5.5.14	\x55050E	127	Yes	A string combined with a distinguished name. The format of the value is `S:<byte count>:<string>:<DN>`. Used by Active Directory to link objects.
NTSecurity ➥Descriptor	2.5.5.15	\x55050F	66	No	A Windows NT security descriptor.
INTEGER8	2.5.5.16	\x550510	65	Yes	A 64-bit integer.

9

continues

TABLE 9.4 CONTINUED

Syntax	OID	ASN 1 Encoded OID	OM Syntax	Represented as String?	Description
DNWithBinary	2.5.5.17	\x550511	127	Yes	A binary "blob" combined with a distinguished name. The format of the value is B:\<byte count\>:\<data\>: \<DN\>. Used by Active Directory to link objects.
Sid	2.5.5.17	\x550511	4	No	A Windows NT security identifier.

The Aggregate Object

Active Directory keeps a summary of the schema in a special object on each domain controller. This object, called the subschema subentry, is defined by RFC 2252, and it contains five attributes that describe the attributes and classes in the schema.

To find the subschema subentry, you first need to get the subschemaSubentry attribute from the rootDSE. This attribute contains the distinguished name of the subschema subentry object. In Windows 2000, the distinguished name of the subschema subentry is always CN=Aggregate,CN=Schema,CN=Configuration,DC=\<root domain\>.

attributeTypes

The attributeTypes attribute of the subschema subentry object contains one value for each attribute defined in the schema. Each value is a string with the following format:

```
( <attr OID> NAME '<attr name>' SYNTAX '<syntax OID>' <options> )
```

> \<attr OID\> is the ITU object identifier for that attribute (found in the attributeID attribute of the schema object).

> \<attr name\> is the LDAP display name of the attribute, as contained by the ldapDisplayName attribute.

`<syntax OID>` is the ITU object identifier for the attribute's syntax.

`<options>` is zero or more of the following:

SINGLE-VALUE indicates the attribute cannot have multiple values. This comes from the `isSingleValued` attribute.

NO-USER-MODIFICATION indicates the value can be modified only by the system. This comes from the `systemOnly` attribute of the `attributeSchema` object.

An example of an `attributeTypes` value is

```
( 1.2.840.113556.1.2.16 NAME 'nCName' SYNTAX
➥'1.3.6.1.4.1.1466.115.121.1.12' SINGLE-VALUE NO-USER-MODIFICATION )
```

objectClasses

The `objectClasses` attribute of the subschema subentry object contains one value for each class defined in the schema. Each value is a string with the following format:

```
( <class OID> NAME '<class name>' [ OBSOLETE ]
➥SUP <parent class> <object class category> MUST ( <must have attrs> )
➥MAY ( <may have attrs> ) )
```

`<class OID>` is the ITU object identifier for the class. It comes from the `classSchema` object's `governsID` attribute.

`<class name>` is the LDAP display name of the class, taken from the `lDAPDisplayName` attribute.

OBSOLETE, if present, indicates that the class has been disabled.

`<parent class>` is the LDAP display name of the class this class inherits from. This comes from the `subClassOf` attribute.

`<object class category>` is one of STRUCTURAL, ABSTRACT, or AUXILIARY

`<must have attrs>` is a list of the LDAP display names of the attributes this class must have. A dollar sign separates the attribute names. This list does not include the attributes that are inherited or included from other classes.

`<may have attrs>` is a list of the LDAP display names of the attributes this class may have. A dollar sign separates the attribute names. This list does not include the attributes that are inherited or included from other classes.

9

THE ACTIVE DIRECTORY SCHEMA

An example of an `objectClasses` value is

```
( 1.2.840.113556.1.5.147 NAME 'siteLink' SUP top STRUCTURAL
➥MUST (siteList ) MAY (cost $ schedule $ options $ replInterval ) )
```

dITContentRules

The `dITContentRules` attribute is defined by both X.500 and RFC 2252. However, RFC 2252 makes its use optional, and Microsoft does not implement this attribute completely.

The `dITContentRules` attribute has a value for each class. It defines which attributes the class may and must have, as well as the class's auxiliary classes.

The Active Directory implementation includes only the auxiliary class list, and even this seems incomplete.

The attribute contains one value for each class. Each value is a string with the following format:

```
( <class OID> NAME '<class name>' AUX ( <auxiliary classes> ) MUST
➥(<must-have attributes> ) MAY (<may-have attributes>) NOT
➥(<must-not-have attributes>)
```

> `<class OID>` is the ITU OID string for the class.
>
> `<class name>` is the LDAP display name for the class.
>
> `<auxiliary classes>` is a dollar-sign-separated list of auxiliary classes included by the class named in `<class name>`.
>
> `<must-have attributes>` is a dollar-sign-separated list of attributes that instances of this class must have.
>
> `<may-have attributes>` is a dollar-sign-separated list of attributes that instances of this class may have.
>
> `<must-not-have attributes>` is a dollar-sign-separated list of attributes that instance of this class must not have.

The following is an example of a `dITContentRule` entry:

```
( 1.2.840.113556.1.5.15 NAME 'contact' AUX ( mailRecipient ) )
```

extendedAttributeInfo

The `extendedAttributeInfo` attribute of the subschema subentry object contains additional information about attributes in the schema. This attribute is not defined by RFC 2252, so it appears to be a Microsoft extension.

The `extendedAttributeInfo` attribute contains one value for each attribute in the schema. Each value is a string with the following format:

```
( <attribute OID> NAME '<attribute name>' RANGE-LOWER '<low value>'
➥RANGE-UPPER '<high value>' PROPERTY-GUID '<GUID string>'
➥PROPERTY-SET-GUID '<Property Set GUID string>' )
```

> `<attribute OID>` is the ITU object identifier for the attribute in the schema.

> `<attribute name>` is the LDAP display name of the attribute. It comes from the `lDAPDisplayName` attribute of the `attributeSchema` object.

> `<low value>` is a number indicating the low range for the attribute. If the attribute is numeric, it is the lowest value the number may have. If the attribute is a string, it is the shortest length the string may have.

> `<high value>` is a number indicating the high range for the attribute. If the attribute is numeric, it is the highest value the number may have. If the attribute is a string, it is the longest length the string may have.

> `<GUID string>` is a string of 32 hex digits that represents the GUID of the attribute definition. This comes from the `schemaIDGUID` property.

> `<Property Set GUID string>` is a string of 32 hex digits that represents the `attributeSecurityGUID` attribute.

The following is an example of an `extendedAttributeInfo` value:

```
( 1.2.840.113556.1.2.146 NAME 'company' RANGE-LOWER '1'
➥RANGE-UPPER '64' PROPERTY-GUID '88FFF8F09111D011A06000AA006C33ED'
➥PROPERTY-SET-GUID '54018DE4F8BCD111870200C04FB96050' )
```

extendedClassInfo

The `extendedClassInfo` attribute of the subschema subentry object contains a value for the class in the schema. Each value contains additional information about class, beyond that defined in RFC 2252. Each value has this form:

```
( <class OID> NAME '<class name>' CLASS-GUID '<GUID string>' )
```

> `<class OID>` is the ITU object identifier for the class. It comes from the `classSchema` object's `governsID` attribute.

<class name> is the LDAP display name of the class, taken from the lDAPDisplayName attribute.

<GUID string> is a string of 32 hex digits that represent the value of the schemaIDGUID attribute of the classSchema object.

The following is an example of an extendedClassInfo value:

```
( 1.2.840.113556.1.5.147 NAME 'siteLink' CLASS-GUID
➥'DE2C0CD55189D111AEBC0000F80367C1' )
```

Investigating the Schema

Because the schema is just a collection of directory objects, you can inspect the schema by using the usual directory access functions. Both ADSI and LDAP provide search functions that let you access the schema.

In general you will need to know the name of the Schema naming context before you start searching for objects in the schema. The easiest way to find the name of the Schema naming context is to query the rootDSE of the domain controller and retrieve the attribute named schemaNamingContext. It contains the full distinguished name of the Schema naming context.

Be sure that you have at least read access to the Schema naming context. An easy way to do this is to put yourself in the SchemaAdministrators group.

Using LDAP to Search the Schema

If you want to use the LDAP API to search the schema, you can use any of the ldap_search...() functions to read schema objects. Specify the Schema naming context as the search base and use LDAP_SCOPE_ONELEVEL as the search scope. You can start out with a search filter of "objectClass=attributeSchema" to find attribute definitions objects, or "objectClass=classSchema" to find class definition objects. For instance:

```
// Assume pLdap and pszSchemaNC have been set
int nErr = ldap_search_s(
        psLdap,                 // LDAP session
        pszSchemaNC,            // search base
        LDAP_SCOPE_ONELEVEL,    // search scope
        "objectClass=classSchema"    // search filter
        false,                  // attribute names only?
        NULL                    // attrs to get
);
```

This LDAP search would retrieve all the class definition objects from the schema.

Using ADSI to Search the Schema

You can use ADSI to access the schema instead of LDAP. In addition to accessing schema objects using the basic ADSI interfaces such as IADs, IADsSearch, IADsContainer, and IADsObject, ADSI provides a specialized set of interfaces that provide limited access to what Microsoft calls the abstract schema. The abstract schema is really just the Aggregate object described earlier.

Generally, it is easier to manipulate the schema using the basic ADSI interfaces such as IADs, IADsObject, and IADsSearch. See Chapter 15, "Accessing the Active Directory Schema with ADSI," for examples of how to do this.

Manipulating the Schema

Microsoft has made it pretty simple to extend the Active Directory schema by adding new classes and attributes. But just because it's easy to do doesn't mean you should do it. Most directory administrators are (perhaps justifiably) paranoid about modifying such a central and critical piece of their network.

So perhaps the first thing you need to do when you want to extend the schema is see whether there is a way you can do what you need without extending the schema. Ask yourself, "Can I store my data outside of the directory? Can I use an existing class?"

Given that you have to extend the schema, you need to keep in mind the following things:

- Schema changes are replicated to every domain controller in the enterprise. This can generate a lot of network traffic. It also can generate a significant amount of overhead on each domain controller as it unloads and reloads its schema cache.

- Schema changes can't be undone. Because the schema is so fundamental to the operation of Active Directory, after you make a change to the schema, it's there forever. Active Directory assumes that if you've added a new class to the schema, there are probably instances of the class on some domain controller somewhere. Instead of going through the trauma of trying to clean up these objects when you delete a class definition, Active Directory just doesn't let you delete the class definition.

- You must obtain valid OIDs for the new classes and attributes you add to the schema. Active Directory relies (in fact, insists) on the fact that the OIDs for all objects in the Schema are unique.

Finding the Schema FSMO Master

Active Directory is a multimaster directory. This means that, as a rule, you can update the directory from any domain controller in the system without needing to prevent other

domain controllers from processing updates. However, there are a handful of directory operations that must be guaranteed to occur in one place at a time. For instance, if you were to rename the FOO domain to BAR on one domain controller while, simultaneously, someone else was renaming the FOO domain to BAZ, Active Directory would have a difficult time resolving the change.

To prevent this kind of update conflict, Microsoft invented the Flexible Single-Master Operation, or FSMO. An FSMO is conceptually a token that is owned by one domain controller at a time. When a domain controller needs to perform a restricted operation such as renaming a domain, it first checks to see that it has the token for domain renaming. If the domain controller does have the token, it performs the operation; if it doesn't have the token, it will reject the operation. The administrator must make sure the correct domain controller has the token before initiating a restricted operation.

> **NOTE**
>
> In earlier versions of Windows 2000, FSMO actually stood for Floating Single-Master Operation. If a domain controller attempted to perform a restricted operation such as modifying the schema, it would automatically request the token from the domain controller that had it. Microsoft changed this automatic facility to a manual one (and changed the name along with it) early in the Beta 3 version of Windows 2000.

The FSMO for schema operations is located in the fSMORoleOwner attribute of the Schema naming context object. This attribute contains the distinguished name of the server that currently holds the Schema FSMO. This is the domain controller that can update the schema.

So, when your program isn't connected to the domain controller that can update the Schema (the Schema Master), what do you do? There are basically three choices:

- Punt. Tell the administrator to use the Schema Management utility to make your domain controller the Schema Master and try running your program again.

- Connect to the Schema Master. The fSMORoleOwner attribute contains the DN of the domain controller that can update the schema, so connecting to it is not particularly difficult. This might be a problem if that domain controller is located on the other end of a slow WAN connection.

- Make your domain controller become the Schema Master. This is fairly straightforward to do if you have authenticated with an appropriately privileged user name. To move the FSMO token to the server you are connected to, use LDAP to write any value to the becomeSchemaMaster attribute of rootDSE. becomeSchemaMaster is an operational attribute. It doesn't really exist as an attribute; instead, it serves as a mechanism for making the domain controller obtain the Schema FSMO token from the domain controller that currently has it.

Listing 9.1 shows you how to get the DNS hostname of the Schema Master so that you can connect to it directly. I've left out some of the error checking to make the program a little more readable. Chapters 17 through 20 discuss the LDAP functions I used in this example.

LISTING 9.1 FINDING THE SCHEMA MASTER WITH LDAP

```
1:   #include <windows.h>
2:   #include <winldap.h>
3:   #include <iostream.h>
4:
5:   int main( int argc, char** argv )
6:   {
7:       LDAP* psLdap = ldap_init( NULL, LDAP_PORT );
8:       if( psLdap != NULL )
9:       {
10:          ULONG uErr = ldap_bind_s( psLdap, NULL, NULL,
        ➥LDAP_AUTH_NEGOTIATE );
11:          if( uErr == LDAP_SUCCESS )
12:          {
13:              // set LDAP API version
14:              int nVersion = LDAP_VERSION3;
15:              ldap_set_option( psLdap, LDAP_OPT_VERSION, &nVersion );
16:
17:              // DN of search base
18:              char szSchemaDN[ 1024 ] = "";
19:
20:              LDAPMessage* psMsg = NULL;
21:
22:              // Get rootDSE attr defaultNamingContext
23:              uErr = ldap_search_s(
24:                  psLdap,
25:                  NULL,
26:                  LDAP_SCOPE_BASE,
27:                  "objectClass=*",
28:                  NULL,
29:                  false,
30:                  &psMsg
31:              );
32:              if( uErr == LDAP_SUCCESS )
33:              {
34:                  char** ppszDomain = ldap_get_values( psLdap,
                ➥ldap_first_entry( psLdap, psMsg),
                ➥"schemaNamingContext" );
```

9

THE ACTIVE
DIRECTORY
SCHEMA

continues

LISTING 9.1 CONTINUED

```
35:                    if( ppszDomain != NULL )
36:                    {
37:                        strcat( szSchemaDN, ppszDomain[ 0 ] );
38:                    }
39:                    ldap_msgfree( psMsg );
40:                }
41:
42:            // szSchemaDN contains the DN of the schema naming context.
43:            // Get the fSMORoleOwner attribute from the NC object
44:
45:            char* apszAttrs[] = { "fSMORoleOwner", NULL };
46:
47:            uErr = ldap_search_s(
48:                psLdap,
49:                szSchemaDN,
50:                LDAP_SCOPE_BASE,
51:                "objectClass=*",
52:                apszAttrs,
53:                false,
54:                &psMsg
55:            );
56:
57:            char szSettingsDN[ 1024 ] = "";
58:
59:            if( uErr == LDAP_SUCCESS )
60:            {
61:                LDAPMessage* psEntry = ldap_first_entry( psLdap,
                    ➥psMsg );
62:                if( psEntry != NULL )
63:                {
64:                    char** ppszValues = ldap_get_values( psLdap,
                        ➥psMsg, "fSMORoleOwner" );
65:                    if( ppszValues != NULL )
66:                    {
67:                        strcpy( szSettingsDN, ppszValues[ 0 ] );
68:                    }
69:                }
70:                ldap_msgfree( psMsg );
71:            }
72:
73:            // szSettingsDN has the name of the Settings object for
74:            // the role owner DC. Need to trim off the RDN to get the
75:            // DN of the server itself and then get its host name
76:
77:            char* pszTrim = strchr( szSettingsDN, ',' );
78:            if( pszTrim != NULL )
79:            {
80:                strcpy( szSettingsDN, pszTrim + 1 );
81:            }
```

```
82:
83:                    // Now get the DC entry
84:                    char* apszSettingsAttrs[] = { "dNSHostName", NULL };
85:
86:               uErr = ldap_search_s(
87:                    psLdap,
88:                    szSettingsDN,
89:                    LDAP_SCOPE_BASE,
90:                    "objectClass=*",
91:                    apszSettingsAttrs,
92:                    false,
93:                    &psMsg
94:               );
95:
96:               char szHostDN[ 1024 ] = "";
97:
98:               if( uErr == LDAP_SUCCESS )
99:               {
100:                  LDAPMessage* psEntry = ldap_first_entry( psLdap,
                     ➥psMsg );
101:                  if( psEntry != NULL )
102:                  {
103:                       char** ppszValues = ldap_get_values( psLdap,
                          ➥psEntry, "dNSHostName" );
104:                       if( ppszValues != NULL )
105:                       {
106:                            cout << "The host name of the Schema master
                               ➥is " << ppszValues[ 0 ] << endl;
107:                       }
108:                  }
109:                  ldap_msgfree( psMsg );
110:               }
111:          }
112:
113:          ldap_unbind( psLdap );
114:     }
115:
116:     return 0;
117: }
```

9

The program in Listing 9.1 creates an LDAP session with the default domain controller at line 7 by calling ldap_init(). It then authenticates to the domain controller using ldap_bind_s() at line 10. The program sets the LDAP protocol to LDAPv3 at line 15 by calling ldap_set_option().

The call to ldap_search_s() at line 23 gets the full distinguished name of the Schema naming context in the variable szSchemaDN.

The program then uses this name to read the Schema naming context object at line 47 and get the value of the fSMORoleOwner attribute at line 67. This is the distinguished name of the nTDSSettings object that is contained by the domain controller object.

The code at lines 77–81 trims off the relative distinguished name of the settings object to get the distinguished name of the domain controller object itself.

The program then reads the domain controller object at line 86 and retrieves the dNSHostName attribute at line 103. This is the DNS hostname of the Schema Master.

Making Sure the Schema Can Be Changed

By default, Active Directory domain controllers are configured with a software interlock that disables all changes to the schema. This is one way Microsoft hopes to keep directory administrators from shooting themselves in the foot.

This software interlock is actually a registry key located at HKEY_LOCAL_MACHINE\System\Current Control Set\Services\NTDS\Parameters in the Registry of the domain controller. You must set the DWORD value Schema Update Allowed to 1 to enable Schema updates on the domain controller. To set this value, you can use REGEDIT.EXE, you can use the WIN32 registry APIs, or you can use the Schema MMC snap-in. If you use the MMC Snap-in, you must do the following:

1. Right-click Active Directory Schema.
2. Select Change Operations Master.
3. Check the box labeled The Schema May Be Modified on This Server.

> **NOTE**
>
> Only the Schema Master needs the Schema Update Allowed registry value set. The other domain controllers will properly replicate the schema changes from the Schema Master.

Obtaining OIDs for Schema Extensions

There are two ways for you to obtain OIDs to use with your schema extensions.

The first, and probably best, way is to register with the Internet Assigned Number Authority (IANA) and receive a unique private enterprise identifier. This identifier (it's just a number) represents a subtree in the global ITU object identifier tree. You will be responsible for allocating OIDs anywhere within this subtree. If your organization does not already have a private enterprise number assigned by IANA, you can obtain one at `http:\\www.iana.org`. Select Application Forms from the IANA home page, and select Private Enterprise Numbers (SNMP) from the Application Forms page. This will present you with a Web form to fill out. You will need to supply some contact information, including an address, phone number, and email address. A few days after you submit the form, you will receive your own PEN via email. Use it in good health.

The second scheme for generating OIDs is to use the Microsoft OIDGEN.EXE utility that will ship as part of the Windows 2000 Resource Kit. This utility uses an algorithm similar to that used by GUIDGEN.EXE to generate a unique OID that is part of the Microsoft subtree. This OID and the subtree below it becomes your own personal part of the SMI identified tree.

> **NOTE**
>
> The OIDGEN.EXE utility was not available at the time of this writing.

> **TIP**
>
> It's very easy to lose track of what numbers in your SMI subtree you've used. Organize your tree and use a spreadsheet to keep track of your OIDs.
>
> For instance, at NetPro, we've divided our 1.3.6.1.4.1.1593 tree into subtrees for different products and directory platforms. 1.3.6.1.4.1.1593.3 is for products, ...1593.4 is for directory platforms, ...1593.4.1 is Novell's NDS, ...1593.4.2 is for Microsoft Active Directory, and so on. We have one person who is responsible for allocating numbers to particular projects; he keeps all this information in an Excel spreadsheet.

Why Your Schema Changes Don't Show Up

You will find that after you update the schema, your changes do not appear in the schema for several minutes. There are two things that are going on that prevent your updates from being visible immediately.

Updating the Schema Cache

Active Directory accesses the schema constantly, at least once for each directory request. To make performance acceptable, Active Directory loads a copy of the schema into memory when it starts up. When you make a change to the schema, Active Directory keeps the current copy of the schema cache so that currently executing operations can continue unaffected. It then concurrently starts building a new version of the schema cache from the current values of the objects in the Schema container. When all the pending operations are complete, Active Directory replaces the old schema cache with the new one. This process can take several minutes to complete. During this time, your schema changes will not be visible.

Replication Latency

Active Directory keeps a replica of the Schema naming context on every domain controller in the enterprise. Depending on the size and complexity of your network, replicating your schema changes to all the domain controllers might take minutes, hours, or even days if some communication links are unavailable. During this time, any programs that require the schema changes will be unable to run until the schema replicates to the domain controller the program is running on.

Sample Schema Manipulation Programs

The next sections contain several simple programs that show how to modify the schema. Some are written using ADSI and some using the LDAP C interface. The sample programs show you how to

- Find and connect to the current Schema Master domain controller
- Make the current domain controller the Schema Master
- Add a new class to the schema
- Add a new attribute to the schema
- Disable a class in the schema

Obtaining the Schema FSMO

This short sample program in Listing 9.2 shows you how to use LDAP to make the domain controller you are connected to obtain the FSMO token.

Listing 9.2 Obtaining the Schema FSMO

```
1:    #include <windows.h>
2:    #include <winldap.h>
3:    #include <iostream.h>
4:
5:    int main( int argc, char** argv )
6:    {
7:        LDAP* psLdap = ldap_init( NULL, LDAP_PORT );
```

```
8:       if( psLdap != NULL )
9:       {
10:        ULONG uErr = ldap_bind_s( psLdap, NULL, NULL,
          ➥LDAP_AUTH_NEGOTIATE );
11:         if( uErr == LDAP_SUCCESS )
12:         {
13:             // set LDAP API version
14:             int nVersion = LDAP_VERSION3;
15:             ldap_set_option( psLdap, LDAP_OPT_VERSION, &nVersion );
16:
17:             // Define array of values to be assigned to
                // becomeSchemaMaster
18:             char* becomeMasterVal[] =
19:             {
20:                 "TRUE",
21:                 NULL
22:             };
23:
24:             //Initialize the LDAPMod Structure
25:             LDAPMod becomeSchemaMasterMod;
26:
27:             becomeSchemaMasterMod.mod_op = LDAP_MOD_ADD;
28:             becomeSchemaMasterMod.mod_type = "becomeSchemaMaster";
29:             becomeSchemaMasterMod.mod_vals.modv_strvals =
          ➥becomeMasterVal;
30:
31:             LDAPMod* attribsToAdd[] =
32:             {
33:                 &becomeSchemaMasterMod,
34:                 NULL
35:             };
36:
37:             uErr = ldap_modify_s( psLdap, NULL, attribsToAdd );
38:             if( uErr == LDAP_SUCCESS )
39:             {
40:                 cout << "Successfully reassigned the Schema FSMO"
          ➥<< endl;
41:             }
42:             else
43:             {
44:                 cout << "Failed to reassign the Schema FSMO: "
          ➥<< ldap_err2string( uErr ) << endl;
45:             }
46:         }
47:
48:         ldap_unbind( psLdap );
49:     }
50:
51:     return 0;
52: }
```

9

**THE ACTIVE
DIRECTORY
SCHEMA**

The program in Listing 9.2 initializes an LDAP session with `ldap_init()` at line 7 and authenticates it using `ldap_bind_s()` at line 10.

The program then initializes an array of values for the operational attribute to be set. The array contains the single value `"TRUE"`.

Starting at line 25, the program initializes an `LDAPMod` structure that indicates the attribute to be modified.

The program then calls `ldap_modify_s()` to set the operational attribute `becomeSchemaMaster` to force the currently connected domain controller to obtain the Schema FSMO.

Adding a New Class to the Schema

Adding a new class to the Active Directory Schema is fairly straightforward because the directory defaults so many attributes for you. To create a new class, you only need to come up with a name for the class, an OID to identify the class, and the names of the attributes your class will contain. That's about it; Active Directory defaults the rest of the attributes for you.

> **CAUTION**
>
> Don't use the OID values from the sample programs on your own schema. You must obtain your own OIDs from IANA or by using OIDGEN.EXE.

Adding a New Attribute to the Schema

Adding a new attribute to the schema is about as simple as adding a new class. You have to come up with values for `lDAPDisplayName`, `attributeID` (the unique OID for the attribute), `attributeSyntax`, and `oMSyntax`. The only tricky part is that you must make sure that the value of `oMSyntax` corresponds to the `attributeSyntax`. Refer to Table 9.3 for the appropriate values for `oMSyntax`.

Listing 9.3 adds a new attribute named `foo` and a new class named `bar` to the schema using ADSI.

> **CAUTION**
>
> Don't use the OID values from the sample programs on your own schema. You must obtain your own OIDs from IANA or by using OIDGEN.EXE.

Listing 9.3 Adding a Class and an Attribute to the Schema

```
1:   #include <windows.h>
2:   #include <activeds.h>
3:   #include <comutil.h>
4:   #include <comdef.h>
5:   #include <iostream.h>
6:
7:   HRESULT BindToSchemaNC( IUnknown** piUnknown );
8:
9:   int main(int argc, char* argv[])
10:  {
11:      HRESULT hr = CoInitialize( NULL );
12:
13:      if( SUCCEEDED( hr ) )
14:      {
15:          IUnknown* piunkSchema = NULL;
16:
17:          hr = BindToSchemaNC( &piunkSchema );
18:          if( SUCCEEDED( hr ) )
19:          {
20:              IADsContainer* piSchema = NULL;
21:
22:              hr = piunkSchema->QueryInterface( IID_IADsContainer,
              ( void** )&piSchema );
23:              if( SUCCEEDED( hr ) )
24:              {
25:                  IDispatch* piDisp = NULL;
26:
27:                  hr = piSchema->Create( L"attributeSchema", L"CN=Foo",
              &piDisp );
28:                  if( SUCCEEDED( hr ) )
29:                  {
30:                      IADs* piIADsAttr = NULL;
31:
32:                      hr = piDisp->QueryInterface( IID_IADs,
              ( void** )&piIADsAttr );
33:                      if( SUCCEEDED( hr ) )
34:                      {
35:                          hr = piIADsAttr->Put( L"objectClass",
              _variant_t( L"attributeSchema" ) );
36:                          hr = piIADsAttr->Put( L"lDAPDisplayName",
              _variant_t( L"foo" ) );
37:                          hr = piIADsAttr->Put( L"attributeID",
              _variant_t
              ( L"1.3.6.1.4.1.1593.4.2.1.1.2.29" ) );
38:                          hr = piIADsAttr->Put( L"attributeSyntax",
              _variant_t( L"2.5.5.5" ) );
39:                          hr = piIADsAttr->Put( L"oMSyntax",
              _variant_t( "22" ) );
```

continues

9

The Active Directory Schema

LISTING 9.3   CONTINUED

```
40:
41:                        hr = piIADsAttr->SetInfo();
42:                        if( ! SUCCEEDED( hr ) )
43:                        {
44:                            cout << "Error " << hr << " adding
                             ➥attribute to Schema" << endl;
45:                        }
46:
47:                        piIADsAttr->Release();
48:
49:                    }
50:
51:                    piDisp->Release();
52:                }
53:
54:            hr = piSchema->Create( L"classSchema", L"CN=Baz",
                ➥&piDisp );
55:            if( SUCCEEDED( hr ) )
56:            {
57:                IADs* piIADsClass = NULL;
58:
59:                hr = piDisp->QueryInterface( IID_IADs,
                    ➥( void** )&piIADsClass );
60:                if( SUCCEEDED( hr ) )
61:                {
62:                    hr = piIADsClass->Put( L"objectClass",
                        ➥_variant_t( L"classSchema" ) );
63:                    hr = piIADsClass->Put( L"lDAPDisplayName",
                        ➥_variant_t( L"baz" ) );
64:                    hr = piIADsClass->Put( L"governsID",
                        ➥_variant_t
                        ➥( L"1.3.6.1.4.1.1593.4.2.1.1.2.31" ) );
65:                    hr = piIADsClass->Put( L"subClassOf",
                        ➥_variant_t( L"top" ) );
66:                    hr = piIADsClass->Put( L"mayContain",
                        ➥_variant_t( L"foo" ) );
67:
68:                    hr = piIADsClass->SetInfo();
69:                    if( ! SUCCEEDED( hr ) )
70:                    {
71:                        cout << "Error " << hr
                            ➥<< " adding class to Schema" << endl;
72:                    }
73:
74:                    piIADsClass->Release();
75:
76:                }
77:
78:                piDisp->Release();
```

```
79:                  }
80:
81:
82:                  piSchema->Release();
83:              }
84:
85:              piunkSchema->Release();
86:          }
87:
88:          ( void )CoUninitialize();
89:      }
90:
91:      return 0;
92:  }
93:
94:
95:  HRESULT BindToSchemaNC( IUnknown** piUnknown )
96:  {
97:      IADs* piRootDSE = NULL;
98:
99:      HRESULT hr = ADsGetObject( L"LDAP://rootDSE", IID_IADs,
      ➥( void** )&piRootDSE );
100:     if( SUCCEEDED( hr ) )
101:     {
102:         _variant_t varSchemaNC;
103:         _bstr_t strSchemaNC;
104:
105:         hr = piRootDSE->Get( L"schemaNamingContext", &varSchemaNC );
106:         if( SUCCEEDED( hr ) )
107:         {
108:             strSchemaNC = varSchemaNC;
109:
110:             // Get the schema NC object
111:             IADs* piSchema = NULL;
112:
113:             hr = ADsGetObject( _bstr_t( "LDAP://" )
             ➥+ strSchemaNC, IID_IADs, ( void** )&piSchema );
114:             if( SUCCEEDED( hr ) )
115:             {
116:                 _variant_t varFSMORoleOwner;
117:
118:                 // get the dn of the schema master nTDSSettings object
119:                 hr = piSchema->Get( L"fSMORoleOwner",
                 ➥&varFSMORoleOwner );
120:                 if( SUCCEEDED( hr ) )
121:                 {
122:                     IDirectoryObject* piDCSettings;
123:
124:                     hr = ADsGetObject( _bstr_t( "LDAP://" )
                     ➥+ _bstr_t( varFSMORoleOwner ),
```

continues

LISTING 9.3   CONTINUED

```
                         ➥IID_IDirectoryObject,
                         ➥( void** )&piDCSettings );
125:          if( SUCCEEDED( hr ) )
126:          {
127:              ADS_OBJECT_INFO* psInfo = NULL;
128:
129:              // Get the DN of the parent of the
                  // nTDSSettings object
130:              hr = piDCSettings->GetObjectInformation
                  ➥( &psInfo );
131:              if( SUCCEEDED( hr ) )
132:              {
133:                  IADs* piDC = NULL;
134:
135:                  hr = ADsGetObject( psInfo->pszParentDN,
                      ➥IID_IADs, ( void** )&piDC );
136:                  if( SUCCEEDED( hr ) )
137:                  {
138:                      _variant_t varServerDN;
139:
140:                      // Get the DN of the actual schema
141:                      ( void )piDC->Get( L"serverReference",
                          ➥&varServerDN );
142:
143:                      IADs* piSchemaMaster = NULL;
144:
145:                      hr = ADsGetObject( _bstr_t(
                          ➥"LDAP://" )+ _bstr_t( varServerDN ),
                          ➥IID_IADs,
                          ➥( void** )&piSchemaMaster );
146:                      if( SUCCEEDED( hr ) )
147:                      {
148:                          _variant_t varHostName;
149:
150:                          // Get the host name of the
                              // schema master
151:                          hr = piSchemaMaster->Get
                              ➥( L"dNSHostName",
                              ➥&varHostName );
152:                          if( SUCCEEDED( hr ) )
153:                          {
154:                          // Compose the ADsPath of the
                              // Schema NC
155:                              _bstr_t strSchemaMasterPath =
                                  ➥_bstr_t( "LDAP://" ) +
                                  ➥_bstr_t( varHostName ) + _
                                  ➥_bstr_t( "/" ) + strSchemaNC;
```

```
156:
157:                                    hr = ADsGetObject(
                                   ➥strSchemaMasterPath,
                                   ➥IID_IUnknown,
                                   ➥( void** )piUnknown );
158:                                }
159:
160:                            piSchemaMaster->Release();
161:                        }
162:
163:
164:                        piDC->Release();
165:                    }
166:
167:                    FreeADsMem( psInfo );
168:
169:                }
170:
171:                piDCSettings->Release();
172:            }
173:        }
174:
175:        piSchema->Release();
176:    }
177:
178:        piRootDSE->Release();
179:    }
180:   }
181:
182:   return hr;
183: }
```

The code in Listing 9.3 initializes the COM subsystem at line 11 by calling
CoInitialize() and then calls BindToSchema() to bind to the Schema naming context.

At line 27, after binding to the Schema naming context, the program creates a new
attribute by defining the objectClass, lDAPDisplayName, attributeID,
attributeSyntax, and oMSyntax attributes of a new attributeSchema object.

At line 54, the program creates a new classSchema object by defining the objectClass,
lDAPDisplayName, governsID, subClassOf, and mayContain attributes.

BindToSchema starts at line 95. It first binds to the rootDSE to get the distinguished name
of the Schema naming context. It then gets the fSMORoleOwner from the Schema naming
context object. This is the name of the nTDSSettings object that is contained by the
domain controller object we actually want.

At line 130, the program uses the GetObjectInformation() function to get the name of the parent object of the nTDSSettings object, which the program then uses to read the DC object.

At line 141, the program gets the serverReference object, which is the DN of the actual domain controller security principal. It then composes an ADSI path to the DC object and gets the dNSHostName attribute from it. BindToSchema then binds to the Schema naming context on the server that is the Schema Master.

Disabling a Class in the Schema

Active Directory does not allow you to remove class objects from the schema; you can only disable them. After you have disabled a class, Active Directory will not allow you to create any more instances of that class. Existing objects of that class will remain unaffected in the directory.

To disable a class, you simply set the Boolean value isDefunct to True in the classSchema object for the class.

You can re-enable the class by setting the isDefunct value back to False.

The program in Listing 9.4 disables the bar class by setting its isDefunct attribute to True.

> **NOTE**
>
> The sample program in Listing 9.4 assumes that the default server you connect to is the Schema Master. You should always include code to make sure you connect to the Schema Master, as demonstrated in Listings 9.1 and 9.2.

LISTING 9.4 DISABLING A CLASS IN THE SCHEMA

```
1:    #include <windows.h>
2:    #include <winldap.h>
3:    #include <iostream.h>
4:
5:    int main( int argc, char** argv )
6:    {
7:        LDAP* psLdap = ldap_init( NULL, LDAP_PORT );
8:        if( psLdap != NULL )
9:        {
10:           ULONG uErr = ldap_bind_s( psLdap, NULL, NULL,
          ➥LDAP_AUTH_NEGOTIATE );
11:           if( uErr == LDAP_SUCCESS )
12:           {
13:               // set LDAP API version
```

```
14:                int nVersion = LDAP_VERSION3;
15:                ldap_set_option( psLdap, LDAP_OPT_VERSION, &nVersion );
16:
17:                // DN of search base
18:                char szClassDN[ 1024 ] = "CN=bar,";
19:
20:                LDAPMessage* psMsg = NULL;
21:
22:                // Get rootDSE attr defaultNamingContext
23:                uErr = ldap_search_s(
24:                    psLdap,
25:                    NULL,
26:                    LDAP_SCOPE_BASE,
27:                    "objectClass=*",
28:                    NULL,
29:                    false,
30:                    &psMsg
31:                );
32:
33:                if( uErr == LDAP_SUCCESS )
34:                {
35:                    char** ppszDomain = ldap_get_values( psLdap, psMsg,
                   ➥"schemaNamingContext" );
36:                    if( ppszDomain != NULL )
37:                    {
38:                        strcat( szClassDN, ppszDomain[ 0 ] );
39:                    }
40:                    ldap_msgfree( psMsg );
41:                }
42:                char* isDefunctVal[] =
43:                {
44:                    "TRUE",
45:                    NULL
46:                };
47:
48:                LDAPMod isDefunctMod =
49:                {
50:                    LDAP_MOD_REPLACE,
51:                    "isDefunct",
52:                    isDefunctVal
53:                };
54:
55:                LDAPMod* mods[] =
56:                {
57:                    &isDefunctMod,
58:                    NULL
59:                };
60:
61:                // modify the class object
62:                uErr = ldap_modify_s( psLdap, szClassDN, mods );
63:
```

9

THE ACTIVE
DIRECTORY
SCHEMA

continues

LISTING 9.4   CONTINUED

```
64:                if( uErr == LDAP_SUCCESS )
65:                {
66:                    cout << "Disabled the schema entry" << endl;
67:                }
68:                else
69:                {
70:                    cout << "Failed to disable the schema entry - error
                       ➥0x"<< hex << uErr << endl;
71:                }
72:            }
73:
74:            ldap_unbind( psLdap );
75:        }
76:
77:        return 0;
78:    }
```

The program in Listing 9.4 initializes an LDAP session with `ldap_init()` and authenticates it with `ldap_bind_s()` at lines 7 and 10, respectively.

At line 15, the program sets the LDAPv3 protocol option for the LDAP session.

Lines 18–41 construct the distinguished name of the `classSchema` object for the class `bar` by concatenating the string `"CN=bar"` and the distinguished name of the Schema naming context from the `rootDSE`.

The program sets up the attribute values and `LDAPMod` structure at lines 48–59 and then modifies the schema at line 61 by calling `ldap_modify_s()`.

The program closes the LDAP session with `ldap_unbind()` at line 74.

Disabling an Attribute in the Schema

Disabling attributes in the schema works exactly the same way as disabling classes. You simply set the `isDefunct` attribute to `True`. Active Directory will then prohibit you from creating or modifying any instances of the defunct attribute.

> **NOTE**
>
> Remember that attribute definitions are shared by classes in the schema. You probably do *not* want to disable all the attributes used by a class, because some other classes might be using them.

The code to disable an attribute is exactly the same as the code to disable a class. Refer to Listing 9.4 for an example.

CHAPTER 10

The Active Directory Domain Naming Context

The third naming context on every Active Directory domain controller is the naming context for the domain of which the server is a member. This chapter describes the contents of the domain naming context.

Active Directory Domains

Unlike Novell Directory Services (NDS), Active Directory domain controllers can host only a single domain naming context; NDS supports multiple partitions, which are roughly equivalent to domains, on a single directory server. In fact, this is not a limitation of Active Directory, per se. Active Directory already handles three naming contexts on a single server (Configuration, Schema, and the domain naming context), so handling more naming contexts would not be a problem. However, the rest of Windows 2000, much of which comes from Windows NT 4.0, assumes a single domain on a server. Consequently, there is only one domain naming context on a domain controller. This is not likely to change any time soon.

Recall from Chapter 3, "The Components of Active Directory," that each Active Directory domain corresponds to an existing DNS domain. When you create a new domain in Windows 2000, you must name the DNS domain to which the new domain corresponds. The new Active Directory domain will have the same name as the DNS domain. For instance, if you create a new domain that corresponds to the DNS domain marketing.megacorp.com, the Active Directory domain's name will be MARKETING. The distinguished name for the Active Directory domain will be `DC=Marketing,DC=MegaCorp,DC=com`.

In addition to specifying a DNS domain when you create a new Windows 2000 domain, you also specify whether the new domain will be the root of a new domain tree, or whether it will be subordinate to an existing domain. Your choice determines the position of your new domain in the forest as well as the domain's distinguished name.

Active Directory then creates a new directory naming context for your domain and populates it with default objects. The following sections describe the more interesting objects you'll find in an Active Directory domain naming context.

The Builtins Container

The Builtins container contains the default groups every Windows 2000 domain comes with. You can also add groups to the Builtins container (although then it wouldn't be a built-in group, would it?).

There are two kinds of groups in Windows 2000. A security group is a set of users who share the privileges granted to the group. An email group has no security or access rights associated with it. It acts strictly as a mailing list.

Windows 2000 groups have inherited the perpetually confusing notion of local and global groups from Windows NT 3.5x and 4.x. This is really unfortunate, but it is understandable because of the requirement that Windows 2000 be backward compatible with Windows NT 4.x domains.

Local Groups

Windows 2000 local groups are not visible outside the domain they are part of. Local groups can contain users from the same domain. Local groups can also contain global groups from the same or other domains. When the domain is in native Windows 2000 mode (there are no downlevel domain controllers in the domain), local groups can also contain other local groups and Windows 2000 universal groups.

Global Groups

Global groups are visible to other domains. Global groups can contain only users from the same domain, and they cannot contain any other groups, unless the domain is in a native Windows 2000 mode. If the domain is a native-mode domain, a global group can contain other global groups from the same domain.

Universal Groups

Windows 2000 groups are what groups really should be, but you can only create universal groups in a Windows 2000–native mode domain (no downlevel domain controllers).

A universal group can contain user objects from any domain in the enterprise. Universal groups can also contain global groups from any domain, and other universal groups defined in any domain.

Each object in the Builtins container is of class group. Each group object represents a particular group in the domain. Each group has the attributes discussed in the following sections.

Attributes of Group Objects

There are two must-have attributes of a group object: the groupType (indicating what type of group it is) and member, a multivalued attribute containing the names of the members of the group. (Actually, member isn't strictly speaking a must-have attribute; you can create a group with no members.)

groupType

groupType is an integer that contains a set of flags indicating the type of group this object represents. The ADS_GROUP_TYPE_ENUM enumeration in IADS.H contains the bit definitions. Table 10.1 lists the possible values of the groupType attribute.

TABLE 10.1 POSSIBLE VALUES FOR THE groupType ATTRIBUTE

Name	Value	Description
ADS_GROUP_TYPE_GLOBAL_GROUP	0x02	Indicates this group is global to the enterprise.
ADS_GROUP_TYPE_DOMAIN_LOCAL_GROUP	0x04	Indicates this group is local to its domain.
ADS_GROUP_TYPE_UNIVERSAL_GROUP	0x08	Indicates this group is a universal group that can be used in any domain in the enterprise.
ADS_GROUP_TYPE_SECURITY_ENABLED	0x80000000	Indicates this is a security group and not a mail group.

member

member is a multivalued, distinguished name attribute that contains the distinguished names of the members of the group. Depending on the type of group, the distinguished name can refer to a user or another group object.

sAMAccountName

The sAMAccountName is the name of the group formatted appropriately for the Windows NT 4.0 SAM database. This is the version of the name that downlevel BDCs use.

10

THE DOMAIN
NAMING CONTEXT

sAMAccountType

This attribute contains a set of flags that describe the type of the account. They correspond to the groupType flags but use constants defined for Windows NT 4.0 domains.

The Computers Container

The Computers container in a domain contains a computer object for every workstation that is a member of the domain. Objects for domain controllers don't appear in the Computers container; they appear in their own container in the root of the domain called (not surprisingly) Domain Controllers.

Computer Attributes Inherited from the User Class

The computer object class inherits from the user object class, so each computer object can potentially contain all the attributes a user object can. Most of these attributes apply only to users. For instance, it doesn't really make sense to talk about a computer's surname. Some of the attributes a computer object inherits from the user class are quite important. In particular, the following attributes from the user class are useful to know.

accountExpires

The accountExpires attribute is a large integer that contains the time and date the computer account will expire, expressed as a DSTIME. A DSTIME is the number of seconds since January 1, 1601.

TIP

You can convert a DSTIME to a Win32 FILETIME by multiplying the DSTIME by 10000. You can then convert the FILETIME value to a SYSTEMTIME structure containing the year, month, and day, and so on by using the Win32 FileTimeToSystemTime() function.

CAUTION

The early versions of the Microsoft documentation describe this value as the number of seconds since January 1, 1970. That is incorrect.

lastLogon

The lastLogon attribute is a single-valued large integer that contains the DSTIME corresponding to the time the computer last successfully logged in using this domain controller. The value is stored as a DSTIME, and it is not replicated between domain controllers in the domain. A DSTIME is the number of seconds since January 1, 1601.

> **TIP**
>
> You can convert a DSTIME to a Win32 FILETIME by multiplying the DSTIME by 10000. You can then convert the FILETIME value to a SYSTEMTIME structure containing the year, month, and day, and so on by using the Win32 FileTimeToSystemTime() function.

> **CAUTION**
>
> The early versions of the Microsoft documentation describe this value as the number of seconds since January 1, 1970. That is incorrect.

logonCount

The logonCount is a single-valued integer that contains the number of times the user has successfully logged in using this domain controller. Active Directory does not replicate the logonCount attribute.

objectSID

objectSID is a SID-syntax attribute that contains the unique security identifier assigned to the computer by the Windows 2000 security system. The objectSID is what the security system uses to identify the computer login account.

The objectSID is comprised of the domain's unique identifier plus a relatively unique identifier (RID) assigned by the domain controller when the computer object is created.

Chapter 4, "Active Directory Security," contains more details about SIDs, RIDs, and the Windows 2000 security system.

pwdLastSet

Periodically, the Windows 2000 security system changes the password for each computer login account. The pwdLastSet attribute is a single-valued, large integer attribute containing the DSTIME value of the last time the security system changed the password on this account. A DSTIME is expressed as the number of seconds since January 1, 1601.

10

THE DOMAIN NAMING CONTEXT

sAMAccountName

The sAMAccountName attribute contains the name of the computer's login account. The name follows the rules of downlevel SAM names: up to 20 characters, uppercase, with no spaces. Windows 2000 appends a $ character to the NetBIOS name of the computer to form the sAMAccount name.

sAMAccountType

The sAMAccountType attribute is a single-valued integer that indicates the type of account this is. It uses a set of flags compatible with downlevel domain controllers.

Other Attributes of the Computer Object

The computer object itself can contain another twenty or so different attributes beyond the ones inherited from the user class. Most are not documented, and I haven't been able to deduce how they are used. Some of the ones that I have been able to figure out are discussed in the following sections.

dNSHostName

This is a single-valued DirectoryString attribute containing the DNS name of the computer. The DNS name for the computer is generally *<computer name>*.*<domain DNS name>*. For instance, if your computer is named FRED and it is in the engineering.megacorp.com domain, the DNS name of the computer would be fred.engineering.megacorp.com.

operatingSystem

The operatingSystem attribute is a single-valued DirectoryString attribute containing a text description of the primary operating system running on the computer. For Windows 2000 workstations, this attribute contains the string "Windows 2000 Professional". For Windows NT 4.0 workstations, the operatingSystem attribute contains the string "Windows NT".

operatingSystemHotfix

The operatingSystemHotfix attribute is a single-valued DirectoryString attribute containing the name of the hotfix or patch that was last applied to this computer. It does not have any value for Windows NT 4.0 workstations, and there haven't been any Windows 2000 hotfixes yet, so I don't know what this string will look like.

operatingSystemVersion

The operatingSystemVersion is a single-valued DirectoryString attribute containing the currently running version of the operating system on this computer. For Windows 2000 workstations, the string looks something like this: `"5.0 (2072)"`, where `2072` is the build number of the operating system. For Windows NT 4.0 workstations, the string is `"4.0"`.

servicePrincipalName

The `servicePrincipalName` attribute is a multivalued `DirectoryString` attribute containing a service principal name for each published service running on the computer. Generally, each computer will have a service principal name of `HOST/fred.engineering.megacorp.com`. It might also have service principal names for other services, such as `FTP/fred.engineering.megacorp.com` and `TELNET/ fred.engineering.megacorp.com`. Clients and other services use the service principal names to locate and perform mutual authentication with the services that publish the service principal names.

The ForeignSecurityPrincipals Container

Whenever you create a domain in Windows 2000, the operating system automatically creates a container in the domain named ForeignSecurityPrincipals. The ForeignSecurityPrincipals container contains objects of class `foreignSecurityPrincipal`.

The `foreignSecurityPrincipal` Object

Active Directory creates a `foreignSecurityPrincipal` object whenever it creates a reference to a security principal outside of the tree. For instance, if you create a local group called Friends in the domain engineering.megacorp.com, and then add the user `CN=Bob Kelly,DC=othercorp,DC=com` to that group, Active Directory will create a `foreignSecurityPrincipal` object in the ForeignSecurityPrincipals container. The relative distinguished name of each `foreignSecurityPrincipal` object is the string representation of the foreign object's Security ID (SID). Each `foreignSecurityPrincipal` object can also contain two attributes.

objectSID

The `objectSID` attribute of the `foreignSecurityPrincipal` is a single-valued SID-syntax attribute that contains the SID of the foreign security principal.

foreignIdentifier

The `foreignIdentifier` attribute of the `foreignSecurityPrincipal` object is a single-valued octet string containing an identifier for the foreign security principal. This might be the distinguished name of the foreign object if it is part of an LDAP or X.500 directory, or it might be the user principal name of an object in a Kerberos realm.

The Infrastructure Object

The infrastructure object in the Domain container has one purpose in life: to identify the domain controller in the domain that runs the interdomain daemon process. This process periodically checks each reference to an object in an external domain and makes sure that object still exists.

For instance, if you had a group in the Engineering domain that contained the distinguished name of a user object in the Marketing domain, it is possible that an administrator could rename or delete the Marketing user object. Because the domains form the boundaries of the replication process (there is no replication between domains), the Engineering list would have a stale entry for the Marketing user. The interdomain daemon process periodically goes through all the external domain references in the domain and fixes them up if necessary.

Because this process is relatively expensive, and because having more than one domain controller run the interdomain daemon process could create inconsistencies in the directory, Active Directory uses a FSMO to make sure only one domain controller in the domain runs the interdomain daemon.

CAUTION

FSMO consistency across all domain controllers in the domain is critical to proper operation of the directory. Don't try to manipulate the `fSMORoleOwner` attribute directly. Instead, if you must change the current FSMO value (for instance, if the domain controller holding the FSMO has been removed from the system), use the NTDSUTIL utility program to change the current FSMO holder.

The LostAndFound Container

Every domain in the enterprise has a container named LostAndFound. (The Configuration naming context has an equivalent container named LostAndFoundConfig.) The Active Directory replication mechanism puts "orphaned" objects it encounters during replication in the LostAndFound container so that an administrator can recover the object if necessary.

Orphaned objects appear when the incoming replication process refers to an object whose container has already been deleted. For instance, suppose the administrator in Chicago connects to his local server and deletes the EngineeringInterns container under the Users container in the Engineering domain. After all, school is back in and all the interns are gone. At the same time, the administrator in Boston connects to her local domain controller and changes the phone number for one of her interns. The intern is only going to school part time, and will continue working during the school year.

Now suppose that the modification of the intern user object replicates to the Chicago domain controller before the deletion of the EngineeringInterns container replicates to the Boston domain controller. The Chicago domain controller won't be able to process the update to the intern's phone number, because not only doesn't the object exist anymore, neither does the container the object belongs in. Instead of just throwing the update away, the Chicago domain controller will place the data for the intern user object in the LostAndFound container, using the object's GUID as its relative distinguished name.

You can list the items in the LostAndFound container using a normal LDAP or ADSI search. The presence of many entries in the LostAndFound container might indicate a replication problem in the domain.

The System Container

The System container plays host to a hodgepodge of other containers and attributes. Some containers, such as File Replication Service, IP Security, and MicrosoftDNS, contain configuration information for specific services. The trustedDomain objects in the System container represent trust links between this domain and other domains both within and outside of the tree.

The following sections describe some of the objects and containers you will find in the System container.

trustedDomain Objects

The System container contains a trustedDomain object for each trust relationship this domain has with other domains. The trustedDomain object contains attributes that name the trusted (or trusting) domain, the type of the trust relationship, and the direction of the trust relationship. Active Directory creates the appropriate trustedDomain objects automatically whenever you add a new Windows 2000 domain. However, the administrator has to manually create trust links with downlevel domains or Kerberos realms.

The relative distinguished name of a trustedDomain object is the DNS name (Windows 2000) or NetBIOS name (Windows NT 4) of the domain with which the trust relationship exists. Each trustedDomain object contains the attributes discussed in the following sections.

flatName

The flatName attribute has DirectoryString syntax and contains the Windows NT 3.5x/4.x-style domain name of the trust partner. For instance, if the trust partner domain's DNS name is marketing.megacorp.com, the flatName attribute would be MARKETING.

trustAttributes

trustAttributes is an integer-valued attribute that contains a set of bit values that define characteristics of the trust. These flags are defined in the NTSecAPI.h header file in the Windows 2000 Platform SDK. Some of the bit values are listed in Table 10.2.

TABLE 10.2 POSSIBLE VALUES FOR THE trustAttributes ATTRIBUTE

Name	Value	Description
TRUST_ATTRIBUTE_NON_TRANSITIVE	0x00000001	The trust relationship is not transitive.
TRUST_ATTRIBUTE_UPLEVEL_ONLY	0x00000002	The trust relationship is with another Windows 2000 domain.
TRUST_ATTRIBUTE_TREE_PARENT	0x00400000	The trust relationship is with a superior domain in the tree.
TRUST_ATTRIBUTE_TREE_ROOT	0x00800000	The trust relationship is between two domain-tree root domains.

trustDirection

The trustDirection attribute contains an integer that indicates in which direction the trust relationship goes. The possible values for the trustDirection attribute are given in Table 10.3.

TABLE 10.3 POSSIBLE VALUES FOR THE trustDirection ATTRIBUTE

Name	Value	Description
TRUST_DIRECTION_DISABLED	0x00000000	The trust link is disabled.
TRUST_DIRECTION_INBOUND	0x00000001	This domain is trusted by the domain named by this object.
TRUST_DIRECTION_OUTBOUND	0x00000002	This domain trusts the domain named by this object.
TRUST_DIRECTION_BIDIRECTIONAL	0x00000003	The domains mutually trust each other.

trustPartner

The `trustPartner` attribute contains the DNS name of the trust partner domain. It is a `DirectoryString` syntax.

trustType

The `trustType` attribute is an integer that indicates what kind of entity the `trustParent` is. Table 10.4 describes the possible values for the `trustType` attribute.

TABLE 10.4   POSSIBLE VALUES FOR THE `trustType` ATTRIBUTE

Name	*Value*	*Type*
TRUST_TYPE_DOWNLEVEL	0x00000001	The trust relationship is with a Windows NT 3.5x or Windows NT 4.x domain.
TRUST_TYPE_UPLEVEL	0x00000002	The trust relationship is with a Windows 2000 domain.
TRUST_TYPE_MIT	0x00000003	The trust relationship is with an MIT Kerberos realm.
TRUST_TYPE_DCE	0x00000004	The trust relationship is with a DCE realm.

The `RIDManager$` Object

The `RIDManager$` object holds the Flexible Single Master Operation (FSMO) token for the RID allocation process. A single domain controller in each domain allocates pools of Relative Identifiers (RIDs) to the other domain controllers in the domain. The `RIDManager$` object contains a reference to this particular domain controller.

There are two interesting attributes in the `RIDManager$` object.

fSMORoleOwner

The `fSMORoleOwner` attribute is a single-valued DN attribute that contains the distinguished name of the domain controller that has the responsibility for allocating pools of RIDs to the other domain controllers in the domain.

CAUTION

FSMO consistency across all domain controllers in the domain is critical to proper operation of the directory. Don't try to manipulate the `fSMORoleOwner` attribute directly. Instead, if you must change the current FSMO value (for instance, if the domain controller holding the FSMO has been removed from the system), use the NTDSUTIL utility program to change the current FSMO holder.

10

THE DOMAIN
NAMING CONTEXT

rIDAvailablePool

The `rIDAvailablePool` attribute contains the current RID allocation for the domain. The `rIDAvailablePool` attribute is a 64-bit integer. The low 32 bits of the attribute represent the low end of the RID range for this domain. The high 32 bits of the attribute represent the high end of the RID pool for the domain.

Each domain controller keeps its current RID allocation in a `rIDSet` object contained in the server object. We'll look at the `rIDSet` object further on in this chapter.

The CN=System,CN=Policies Container and Group Policy Objects

A significant network management enhancement in Windows 2000 is the integration of Windows 2000 group policies into the directory. A *group policy* is a set of system and software configuration standards that apply to group of computers and users.

The goal of a group policy is to simplify the network administrator's life by automating (and restricting) the configuration of network PCs and applications.

Windows 2000 stores group policy information in two places: in `groupPolicyContainer` objects in the directory, and in group policy objects stored in files in the SYSVOL file share on each domain controller. The group policy containers in the directory contain references to the group policy files in the SYSVOL.

Each time an administrator creates a group policy, Windows 2000 creates a new `groupPolicyContainer` object for the policy. The relative distinguished name of the `groupPolicyContainer` object is a GUID, and the object contains an attribute that refers to the SYSVOL file that contains the group policy settings. The `groupPolicyContainer` objects in the directory server as identifiers for the group policy objects in the SYSVOL.

A Windows 2000 administrator can associate one or more `groupPolicyContainer` objects with sites, domains, and organizational units (OUs) in the directory. These group policies then apply to the users and computers that are members of those sites, domains, and OUs.

The Windows 2000 Platform SDK provides a set of APIs for manipulating group policy objects (both the directory objects and the group policy files). If you need to write programs that access or manipulate group policies, you should definitely use the APIs, as opposed to dealing with the directory objects directly.

The Users Container

The Users container in the domain contains the (what else?) user objects for those users who are members of the domain. The Users container also contains machine logon accounts, domain accounts, and some other predefined groups. Network administrators will probably put new users and groups in the Users container as well.

The Active Directory user object has more attributes than any other class in the schema; there are at least 50 attributes, not even counting the ones it inherits from the organizationalPerson class, which number another 40 or so. When you add up all the attributes from the parent classes and auxiliary classes, you end up with more than 200 attributes that you can set for a user object.

Most of the attributes aren't terribly interesting; for instance, there are eight different flavors of telephone number. This section just covers the interesting ones.

In fact, out of the more than 200 attributes a user object might have, only seven of them are required, and Active Directory will assign default values to all but two of them. You can create a new user object in Active Directory by specifying only the objectClass as user, and the sAMAccountName, which should be a valid downlevel account name, which means all uppercase letters, numbers, and no spaces.

Listing 10.1 is a quick sample program that shows how to easy it is to add a user using the LDAP library supplied on the CD-ROM.

LISTING 10.1 SAMPLE PROGRAM FOR ADDING A USER OBJECT

```
1:   #include <windows.h>
2:   #include <winldap.h>
3:   #include <iostream.h>
4:
5:   int main( int argc, char** argv )
6:   {
7:       LDAP* psLdap = ldap_init( NULL, LDAP_PORT );
8:       if( psLdap != NULL )
9:       {
10:          ULONG uErr = ldap_bind_s( psLdap, NULL, NULL,
          ➡LDAP_AUTH_NEGOTIATE );
11:          if( uErr == LDAP_SUCCESS )
12:          {
13:              // set LDAP API version
14:              int nVersion = LDAP_VERSION3;
15:              ldap_set_option( psLdap, LDAP_OPT_VERSION, &nVersion );
16:
```

continues

10

THE DOMAIN NAMING CONTEXT

LISTING 10.1 CONTINUED

```
17:                // turn off referrals chasing
18:                int nChaseReferrals = 0;
19:               ldap_set_option( psLdap, LDAP_OPT_REFERRALS,
           ➥&nChaseReferrals );
20:
21:                // DN of new container
22:                char szNewDN[ 1024 ] = "CN=NewUser,CN=Users,";
23:
24:                LDAPMessage* psMsg = NULL;
25:
26:                // Get rootDSE attr defaultNamingContext
27:                uErr = ldap_search_s(
28:                    psLdap,
29:                    NULL,
30:                    LDAP_SCOPE_BASE,
31:                    "objectClass=*",
32:                    NULL,
33:                    false,
34:                    &psMsg
35:                );
36:                if( uErr == LDAP_SUCCESS )
37:                {
38:                    char** ppszDomain = ldap_get_values( psLdap,
           ➥"defaultNamingContext" );
           ➥ldap_first_entry(psLdap,psMsg),
39:                    if( ppszDomain != NULL )
40:                    {
41:                        strcat( szNewDN, ppszDomain[ 0 ] );
42:                    }
43:                    ldap_msgfree( psMsg );
44:                }
45:
46:                // values for the objectClass attr
47:                char* apszObjectClassVals[] =
48:                {
49:                    "user", // a single value for the objectClass attr
50:                    NULL
51:                };
52:
53:                // operation for the objectClass attr
54:                LDAPMod sAddObjectClass =
55:                {
56:                    LDAP_MOD_ADD, // the operation
57:                    "objectClass", // the name of the attribute
58:                    apszObjectClassVals // pointer to array of values
59:                };
60:
61:                // values for the cn attr
62:                char* apszSAMVals[] =
63:                {
```

```
64:                    "NEWUSER", // a single value sAMAccountName attribute
65:                    NULL
66:                };
67:
68:                // operation for the cn attr
69:                LDAPMod sAddSAM =
70:                {
71:                    LDAP_MOD_ADD, // the operation
72:                    "sAMAccountName",  // the name of the attribute
73:                    apszSAMVals
74:                };
75:
76:                // list of attributes to add
77:                LDAPMod* asAttrsToAdd[] =
78:                {
79:                    &sAddObjectClass,
80:                    &sAddSAM,
81:                    NULL
82:                };
83:
84:                // add the new container
85:                uErr = ldap_add_s( psLdap, szNewDN, asAttrsToAdd );
86:
87:                cout << "Error is " << uErr << endl;
88:            }
89:
90:        ldap_unbind( psLdap );
91:    }
92:
93:    return 0;
94: }
```

If you run this program and subsequently try to log in using the NewUser name, you'll find the account has been disabled. If you don't specify any value for the userAccountControl attribute, Active Directory will default the value to 0x00000222, which indicates the account is a normal account, a password is not required, and the account is disabled.

You can modify the code to include adding a value for userAccountControl by adding another attribute definition before the call to the ldap_add_s() operation. See Chapter 25, "Adding Active Directory Objects with LDAP," for information on how to do this.

The following are the more interesting attributes of an Active Directory user object.

User Identification Attributes

Of the hundreds of attributes a user object might have, about a half-dozen serve to identify the user in one fashion or another. These attributes are cn (common name), userPrincipalName, canonicalName, sAMAccountName, objectGUID, and objectSID. The following sections describe these user-identification attributes in more detail.

cn

This is the common name for the user object. It is a single-valued DirectoryString attribute that Active Directory defaults to the relative distinguished name of the user object. The cn attribute is indexed and stored in the global catalog, so it is a good name to use when logging in.

userPrincipalName

The userPrincipalName (UPN) is an Internet–email-style name, such as bob@engineering. megacorp.com. RFC 822 defines the format of user principal names. Microsoft's documentation describes the UPN as the preferred login name. It is also indexed and stored in the global catalog. userPrincipalName is not a mandatory attribute.

canonicalName

The canonicalName is a multivalued DirectoryString attribute that contains the user's name in yet another format: *<domain DNS name>/<container name>/<user name>*—for instance, engineering.megacorp.com/users/bob. You can also use this name to log in.

sAMAccountName

The sAMAccountName attribute contains the name of the user's login account. The name should follow the rules of downlevel SAM names: up to 20 characters, uppercase, with no spaces.

objectGUID

The objectGUID is the only truly unique identifier for a user. It is a 16-byte binary attribute that Active Directory initializes when you create the user object. For what it's worth, you can actually log in using a GUID!

objectSID

The objectSID attribute is a SID-syntax attribute that contains the unique security identifier assigned to the user by the Windows 2000 security system. The objectSID is what the security system uses to identify the user.

The objectSID is comprised of the domain's unique identifier plus a relatively unique identifier (RID) assigned by the domain controller when the user object is created.

Chapter 4 contains more details about SIDs, RIDs, and the Windows 2000 security system.

Security Attributes

Many of the attributes of a user object are part of the security information the Windows 2000 Security system uses to control the user's access to system resources. These four security-related attributes are nTSecurityDescriptor, altSecurityIdentities, memberOf, and sIDHistory. The following sections describe these security attributes.

nTSecurityDescriptor

The nTSecurityDescriptor has NTSecurityDescriptor syntax, and it contains the Access Control List (ACL) for the user object. The ACL determines which users can perform which operations on the user object. Chapter 4 describes Windows NT security descriptors and the API functions you can use to manipulate them.

altSecurityIdentities

The altSecurityIdentities attribute is a multivalued DirectoryString that contains additional Kerberos account names or X.509 certificates that can be used as part of the Simple Authentication and Security Layer (SASL) authentication process. Chapter 4 discusses Kerberos and the authentication process in more detail.

memberOf

The memberOf attribute is a multivalued operational attribute that contains the distinguished names of the groups this user is a member of. Active Directory automatically keeps this attribute up-to-date whenever you add a user object to a group.

> **NOTE**
>
> When you read the memberOf attribute from a domain controller, it contains only those groups the user is a member of that are in the user's domain. It doesn't contain the names of groups the user is a member of that are outside of the domain.
>
> If you read the memberOf attribute from a global catalog, however, it will have the complete list of groups the user is a member of.

> **NOTE**
>
> Active Directory does not return operational attributes like memberOf by default during directory searches. You must specify the attribute named explicitly in the search operation to retrieve its value.

10

THE DOMAIN NAMING CONTEXT

sIDHistory

The `sIDHistory` attribute is a multivalued SID attribute that contains all the previous SIDs this user object has been assigned. Normally, Active Directory assigns a SID to a user object only when it is created. However, if the administrator moves a user object from one domain to another, the Windows 2000 security system will assign a new SID to the user object that corresponds to the user's new domain. Active Directory places the old SID in the `sIDHistory` attribute. The user will acquire the rights implied by all the SIDs in the user object's `sIDHistory` attribute. Keeping the previous values of the user's SIDs this way lets the security system continue to grant the user the access rights he had before the administrator moved the user object.

Login Attributes

Several of the attributes of the user object are intended to control or monitor the user login process. Some of these attributes, for instance, `logonHours` and `logonWorkstation`, restrict the places and times the user may log in to the network. Other attributes such as `badPwdCount` and `badPasswordTime` record the number of failed login attempts by a user in order to prevent unauthorized users from logging in by trying a bunch of different passwords. The following sections describe the attributes of the user object that participate in the login process.

accountExpires

The `accountExpires` attribute is a large integer that contains the time and date the account will expire, expressed as a DSTIME. A DSTIME is the number of seconds since January 1, 1601.

> ### TIP
>
> You can convert a DSTIME to a Win32 FILETIME by multiplying the DSTIME by 10000. You can then convert the FILETIME value to a SYSTEMTIME structure containing the year, month, and day, and so on by using the Win32 `FileTimeToSystemTime()` function.

> ### CAUTION
>
> The early versions of the Microsoft documentation describe this value as the number of seconds since January 1, 1970. That is incorrect.

badPasswordTime

The `badPasswordTime` attribute contains the last time and date the user attempted to log in to this domain controller with an invalid password. Active Directory does not replicate the `badPasswordTime` attribute, so it is different on each replica of the domain.

The `badPasswordTime` attribute is a single-valued DSTIME value stored as a large integer. A DSTIME is the number of seconds since January 1, 1601.

> **TIP**
>
> You can convert a DSTIME to a Win32 FILETIME by multiplying the DSTIME by 10000. You can then convert the FILETIME value to a SYSTEMTIME structure containing the year, month, and day, and so on by using the Win32 `FileTimeToSystemTime()` function.

> **CAUTION**
>
> The early versions of the Microsoft documentation describe this value as the number of seconds since January 1, 1970. That is incorrect.

badPwdCount

The `badPwdCount` attribute is a single-valued integer attribute that contains the number of times the user has tried to log in using an invalid password. Active Directory does not replicate this attribute, so it is different on each replica of the domain.

lastLogoff

The `lastLogoff` attribute contains the time and date of the time the user last logged off stored as a DSTIME value. The `lastLogoff` attribute is a single-valued large integer. A DSTIME is the number of seconds since January 1, 1601. Active Directory does not replicate this attribute to other domain controllers in the domain.

> **TIP**
>
> You can convert a DSTIME to a Win32 FILETIME by multiplying the DSTIME by 10000. You can then convert the FILETIME value to a SYSTEMTIME structure containing the year, month, and day, and so on by using the Win32 `FileTimeToSystemTime()` function.

CAUTION

The early versions of the Microsoft documentation describe this value as the number of seconds since January 1, 1970. That is incorrect.

lastLogon

The `lastLogon` attribute is a single-valued large integer that contains the DSTIME corresponding to the time the user last successfully logged in using this domain controller. The value is stored as a DSTIME, and it is not replicated between domain controllers in the domain. A DSTIME is the number of seconds since January 1, 1601.

TIP

You can convert a DSTIME to a Win32 FILETIME by multiplying the DSTIME by 10000. You can then convert the FILETIME value to a SYSTEMTIME structure containing the year, month, and day, and so on by using the Win32 `FileTimeToSystemTime()` function.

CAUTION

The early versions of the Microsoft documentation describe this value as the number of seconds since January 1, 1970. That is incorrect.

logonCount

`logonCount` is a single-valued integer that contains the number of times the user has successfully logged in using this domain controller. Active Directory does not replicate the `logonCount` attribute.

logonHours

`logonHours` is an single-valued octet-string attribute that contains the hours during which the user may log in. The login schedule is stored as a 21-byte login bitmap, with each bit representing an hour of the week (7 days per week times 24 hours a day divided by 8 bits per byte = 21 bytes). The schedule starts at midnight on Sunday, so the bit representing 8:00 a.m. on Monday would be the first bit of the fifth byte of the attribute, or expressed as a C expression, `attr[ 4 ] & 0x80`.

lmPwdHistory

The lmPwdHistory attribute contains the password history of this account in the form required by LAN Manager clients and Windows 95 and Windows 98 workstations. Windows 2000 and Windows NT do not use this attribute. The system uses this attribute to ensure that users do not reuse passwords more often than the administrator has allowed.

> **NOTE**
>
> You cannot change the password history attribute directly, nor can you deduce the passwords the attribute contains.

ntPwdHistory

The ntPwdHistory attribute contains the password history of this account in the form used by Windows 2000 and Windows NT workstations. The system uses this attribute to ensure that users do not reuse passwords more often than the administrator has allowed.

> **NOTE**
>
> You cannot change the password history attribute directly, nor can you deduce the passwords the attribute contains.

pwdLastSet

The pwdLastSet attribute is a single-valued large integer attribute containing the DSTIME value of the last time the administrator or user changed the password on this account. A DSTIME is the number of seconds since January 1, 1601.

unicodePwd

unicodePwd contains the encrypted version of the users' password. unicodePwd is encrypted and you cannot read or modify the attribute directly. You can use the ADSI functions IADsUser::ChangePassword() and IADSUser::SetPassword() to change the password.

userAccountControl

The userAccountControl attribute is an single-valued integer that contains various flags that describe characteristics of the account. iads.h contains the definitions for these flags in the ADS_USER_FLAG enumeration. You can also find these flags without the ADS prefix in lmaccess.h. Table 10.5 lists the possible values for the userAccountControl attribute.

TABLE 10.5   POSSIBLE VALUES FOR THE userAccountControl ATTRIBUTE

Flag	*Description*
ADS_UF_SCRIPT	If this bit is set, the account will execute a login script upon successful authentication.
ADS_UF_ACCOUNTDISABLE	If this bit is set, the account is disabled and will not allow logins.
ADS_UF_HOMEDIR_REQUIRED	If set, indicates that a home directory must be configured for this user.
ADS_UF_LOCKOUT	If this bit is set, it indicates that the account is currently locked out because there were too many failed login attempts.
ADS_UF_PASSWD_NOTREQD	This flag indicates that a password is not required for this account.
ADS_UF_PASSWD_CANT_CHANGE	If set, this flag indicates that the user may not change the password.
ADS_UF_ENCRYPTED_TEXT_PASSWORD_ALLOWED	If this bit is set, Active Directory will store the plain-text password in the directory using simple text encryption.
ADS_UF_TEMP_DUPLICATE_ACCOUNT	This indicates the account is a temporary duplicate of an account in another domain.
ADS_UF_NORMAL_ACCOUNT	This flag indicates the account is a normal user account, not a domain trust account or machine account.
ADS_UF_INTERDOMAIN_TRUST_ACCOUNT	This flag indicates the account is a domain trust account.
ADS_UF_WORKSTATION_TRUST_ACCOUNT	This flag indicates the account is a workstation account.
ADS_UF_SERVER_TRUST_ACCOUNT	This flag indicates the account is a trust account for a domain server.
ADS_UF_DONT_EXPIRE_PASSWD	If set, this flag indicates the account password will not expire.
ADS_UF_MNS_LOGON_ACCOUNT	Unknown.
ADS_UF_SMARTCARD_REQUIRED	If this flag is set, the user can only log in using a smart card.
ADS_UF_TRUSTED_FOR_DELEGATION	If this flag is set, a service running under this account can impersonate a client.
ADS_UF_NOT_DELEGATED	This flag indicates that the rights of this account may not be delegated to another account.

userWorkstations

The `userWorkstations` attribute is a `DirectoryString` containing a comma-separated list of the NetBIOS names of the machines this user may log in from.

System Service Attributes

There are many attributes of the user object that configure various services the user can use. These are just a few of them.

aCSPolicyName

The `aCSPolicyName` attribute is a single-valued `DirectoryString` that contains the filename of the Admission Control Services (ACS) policy file that applies to this user. ACS is part of the Quality of Service (QoS) infrastructure in Windows 2000. ACS helps determine how much network bandwidth the system should grant to a particular user or application.

profilePath

The `profilePath` attribute is a single-valued `DirectoryString` that contains the Universal Naming Convention (UNC) path of the user's login profile.

scriptPath

The `scriptPath` attribute is a single-valued `DirectoryString` that contains the Universal Naming Convention (UNC) path of the user's login script.

The Domain Controllers Container

The Domain Controllers container contains an object of class computer for each domain controller in the domain. The computer objects in the Domain Controllers container are the actual security principals for the domain controller; they contain the SID for the domain controller.

Note that the class computer inherits from the user class. This might seem bizarre at first: Why would a computer need a home address or telephone number? But computers access network resources, so they need to authenticate with the domain and receive an access token before they can use any securable resources. From the point of view of the Windows 2000 security system, computers look pretty much like users.

Some of the attributes of a computer object in the Domain Controllers container that we haven't already covered are discussed in the following sections.

10

THE DOMAIN NAMING CONTEXT

dNSHostName

This single-valued `DirectoryString` contains the DNS host name of the domain controller.

operatingSystem

The `operatingSystem` attribute is a single-valued `DirectoryString` that contains the text description of the current version of the operating system running on the domain controller. An example is `"Windows 2000 Server"`.

operatingSystemHotfix

The `operatingSystemHotfix` attribute contains the name of the latest hotfix to be applied to this domain controller. It is a single-valued `DirectoryString`.

operatingSystemServicePack

The `operatingSystemServicePack` attribute contains the name of the latest service pack to be successfully applied to this domain controller. It is a single-valued `DirectoryString`.

operatingSystemVersion

The `operatingSystemVersion` attribute is a single-valued `DirectoryString` that contains the version of the operating system running on the domain controller in the form *<major>.<minor> (<build number>)*. An example is `5.0 (2031)`.

rIDSetReferences

The `rIDSetReferences` attribute is a multivalued DN that contains the names of the `rIDSet` objects that govern the RID allocation on this domain controller. Currently, each domain controller has a single `rIDSetReference` value, and it is always in an object contained by the domain controller.

The `rIDSet` object contains the information that defines the next relative identifier (RID) the domain controller will allocate. Four attributes govern the allocation of RIDs, and each is covered in the following sections.

rIDAllocationPool

The `rIDAllocationPool` is a single-valued large integer that contains the RID pool range last allocated to this domain controller. The low-order word of the attribute contains the low end of the RID range. The high-order word of the attribute contains the last RID the domain controller can allocate.

rIDNextRID

The `rIDNextRID` attribute contains the next RID value the domain controller will allocate. It is a single-valued integer attribute. When the `rIDNextRID` value gets within 80% of the high end of the range (as defined by the `rIDAllocationPool` attribute), the domain controller will contact the RID FSMO role owner, and request another range of RIDs.

rIDPreviousAllocationPool

The `rIDPreviousAllocationPool` is a single-valued large integer that contains the last version of the `rIDAllocationPool` attribute, before the domain controller requested a new range from the RID FSMO role owner.

serverReferenceBL

`serverReferenceBL` is a single-valued DN attribute that refers back to the server object at `CN=<server name>,CN=Servers,CN=<Site name>,CN=Sites,CN=Configuration, <first domain>`. The server object in the Domain Controllers container is the security principal for the domain controller. The object in the Sites container contains configuration information for the domain controller that must be replicated to all domain controllers in the enterprise.

servicePrincipalName

The `servicePrincipalName` attribute is a multivalued `DirectoryString`, with each value containing the service principal name for a service located on the domain controller. An example of a service principal name is `SMPTSVC/engserver.engineering.megacorp.com`.

Active Directory
Services Interface

PART

III

IN THIS PART

CHAPTER 11

ADSI Fundamentals

Active Directory Services Interface (ADSI) is a directory-independent interface to network directories. According to Microsoft, ADSI is the preferred method for accessing Active Directory. If you want to write a single piece of code that will run against a variety of directory service providers, ADSI is the ticket.

This chapter is an overview of and an introduction to ADSI. The following sections discuss when it is appropriate to use ADSI versus LDAP to program your Active Directory applications. This chapter also presents an overview of COM programming guidelines. Finally, several sample applications are presented that provide an overview of basic ADSI programming techniques using C++.

Introduction to Active Directory Services Interface

The Active Directory Services Interface is a set of Component Object Model (COM) APIs that provides a common programming interface to multiple directories. ADSI is the Microsoft-recommended mechanism for accessing Active Directory.

> **NOTE**
>
> Component Object Model (COM) is a language-independent, object-oriented facility that provides a common way for application programs to access shared software components.

Multiple Client Platforms

Because ADSI is based on COM, you can use ADSI with any programming language that supports COM. These include Microsoft Visual Basic, Java, C, C++, and VBScript. Some implementations of Perl and Python support access to ADSI as well.

Using an interpreted language such as Perl or VBScript in conjunction with ADSI is an ideal way to build "quick-and-dirty" directory administration utilities.

Multiple Directory Providers

ADSI not only supports access from multiple programming languages, but it also provides access to multiple directories. ADSI 2.5, the current shipping version, comes with service providers that provide access to the Windows NT Security Accounts Manager (SAM), Novell Directory Services (NDS), LDAPv3-compliant directories such as Active Directory, and Novell NetWare 3.x server binderies (the NetWare 3.x equivalent of the Windows NT SAM).

Figure 11.1 shows how the ADSI architecture supports multiple languages and multiple directories.

FIGURE 11.1

The ADSI architecture.

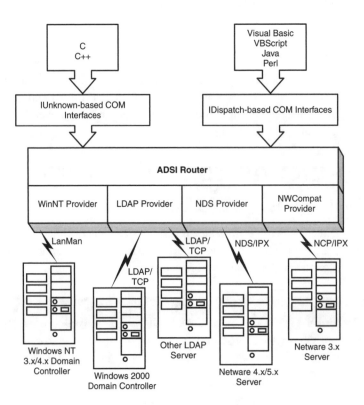

ADSI or LDAP?

One of the first questions you will face when tasked with writing software for Active Directory is "Which interface do I use?" Active Directory supports both ADSI and Lightweight Directory Access Protocol (LDAP) API interfaces. In fact, under the covers, ADSI uses the LDAP API to communicate with Active Directory. Here are some guidelines for making your choice.

Platform

The first thing to consider when choosing between ADSI and LDAP is the operating system platform your program will run on.

Win32

If your software will run on a 32-bit Windows platform, you can use either ADSI or LDAP. If your code will run on Windows 95, Windows 98, or Windows NT 3.51 or 4.x, you must make sure you have installed the latest service packs that provide access to Active Directory. The service packs haven't been finalized at this point, so check Microsoft's Web site for the latest information.

Win16

If your software will run on Windows 3.x, ADSI is not an option, so you'll have to use LDAP. I'm not aware of any LDAP client libraries available for Win16, although there might be one. Another possibility is to port the LDAP client library from the Open LDAP Project to the Win16 environment.

UNIX

If your software will run on some variant of UNIX, you'll have to use LDAP.

There may be an alternative, however. There are at least two third-party COM-on-UNIX vendors (Mainsoft and Bristol Technologies) that might provide ADSI functionality on UNIX. I don't have any experience with either of these products, so you'll have to check them out yourself.

Others

If your software is running on something that is not Windows and not UNIX (which doesn't leave much), your only choice is to use LDAP to access Active Directory. There is an LDAP client implementation publicly available from the Open LDAP Project that works with the GNU compiler gcc. If the GNU tools support your platform, the Open LDAP client will probably work for you.

Language

The next major area to consider when evaluating the ADSI versus LDAP decision is the programming language you will use.

Visual Basic and VBScript

If you are using Visual Basic or VBScript, you have to use ADSI. There is no convenient interface between VB and LDAP, although with some effort you could write one. But your interface wouldn't be nearly as slick as the integration between VB and ADSI, so you would be wasting your time.

Java

This one can be a little sticky. If you are using Microsoft's Java running on Windows, use ADSI. It's well integrated and it works. If you are using someone else's Java implementation on Windows, you will need to find out whether it supports access to COM components. If the Java implementation supports COM access, you can access ADSI.

C

If you are writing in C, you can use either ADSI or LDAP. LDAP is a C-language API and is pretty easy to use. ADSI is COM-based, and its use from C is, at best, tedious. I recommend using the LDAP interface to Active Directory from C programs.

C++

If you are using C++, you have a choice. The LDAP API is a C-language API, so you can use it easily from C++. ADSI, being COM-based, also works well from C++. Both LDAP and ADSI are legitimate choices for writing Active Directory programs in C++. So which should you use?

Forgive me while I inject some of my own personal preferences into this discussion.

ADSI is a relatively clean, object-oriented interface to Active Directory. It mostly hides the underlying details of the directory from your program, and the COM programming paradigm fits neatly into the C++ language. Even so, I find ADSI programming in C++ complicated and error prone. It seems that I always have to make four function calls to do one thing, and each of those calls returns an error code. This makes for wordy code and more complicated control flow than I think is necessary. Also, reference counting in COM has to be the most popular source of COM programming problems—it is for me, anyway. And don't even start with me about VARIANTs and BSTRs.

Part of my concern is due, I'm sure, to my relative inexperience in COM programming, but in looking at Microsoft's sample ADSI programs, I get the idea that you have to write a lot of code for not much functionality.

That being said, the LDAP APIs have their own idiosyncrasies, including error-prone memory management and excessive wordiness. Unless you're a long-time C programmer (like me), the LDAP APIs will seem primitive, bizarre, and not at all object-oriented.

My favorite solution for C++ is an LDAP class library (included on the CD-ROM in the back of this book) I wrote using the Standard Template Library. This LDAP class library hides the complexity of the LDAP APIs quite well and reduces to the bare minimum the amount of code necessary to accomplish a given directory function. It's pretty easy to learn; a couple of interns here at NetPro picked it up and were writing useful directory programs within an hour, with no documentation. I wrote it, so why shouldn't it be my favorite?

Putting aside my personal preferences, I have to say that if you're comfortable writing COM programs in C++, use ADSI. It's what Microsoft recommends and supports, and it is certainly where Microsoft is going to invest its development effort going forward. If you're new to COM and ADSI, and you want to get something running quickly, try using the LDAP class library on the CD-ROM. Appendix B, "Microsoft Windows 2000 LDAP Functions," describes the LDAP class library.

Portability Between Directories

Theoretically, you can use ADSI to write programs that access different directories—in particular, the Microsoft Active Directory, the NDS, the Novell NetWare 3.x Bindery, and the legacy Windows NT SAM database.

Also theoretically, you can use ADSI to write programs that access any LDAP-compliant directory, such as Netscape, the University of Michigan's SLAPD, or Microsoft's own Site Server.

Practice falls a little short of the theory, however. ADSI works great for Active Directory and Site Server, which is not surprising because they are Microsoft products. ADSI works pretty well for writing NDS programs, too. But don't expect any but the simplest program to work with more than one kind of directory.

The problem lies in the implementation of the ADSI providers, the layer of code that translates ADSI requests to the appropriate native directory API calls. None of the four providers (LDAP, NDS, WINNT, and NWCOMPAT) implements all the defined ADSI interfaces, and several interfaces are implemented by only one of the providers. Even worse, some of the interfaces are implemented incompletely (for instance, the IADsContainer interface is only partially implemented by the LDAP provider).

Unless you limit your program to using only those interfaces and functions that are actually implemented by multiple providers, your program will not work with different directories.

There also appears to be some difficulty using ADSI to access generic LDAP servers such as Netscape Directory Server. Because LDAPv3 implementations still vary in their specifics, and because the schemas used by different LDAP directories are not at all the same, using the ADSI LDAP provider with non-Microsoft directories is a hit-or-miss deal. If you elect to use the ADSI LDAP provider to access a non-Microsoft LDAP directory such as Netscape, you should limit yourself to the IDirectoryObject and IDirectorySearch interfaces, and leave some time in the project for working out the kinks in the ADSI-to-directory interface.

Other Considerations

You should take into account some other issues when deciding between ADSI and LDAP.

First, Microsoft definitely encourages developers to use ADSI. As I mentioned before, ADSI is where Microsoft puts most of its time and attention.

Second, ADSI can insulate you from changes in the directory implementation in a way that LDAP cannot. For instance, if Microsoft decides to move the Schema container out of the Configuration naming context and put it somewhere else, Microsoft will probably make the change invisible to ADSI programs. LDAP programs that access the Schema container, on the other hand, will require some rework.

Finally, Microsoft might choose to embed extra semantics within ADSI that will not be available to the LDAP interface. For instance, there will certainly be an ADSI function to perform the proper encoding to change a user's password so that the cleartext password doesn't go over the network. This facility likely won't be available to LDAP programs.

Component Object Model (COM) Basics

The Component Object Model (COM) is a sophisticated and highly evolved specification for building reusable software components. COM technology underlies OLE (Object Linking and Embedding) and ActiveX, as well as all the currently fashionable acronyms such as DAO (Data Access Objects), RDO (Remote Data Objects), ADO (ActiveX Data Objects), and OLEDB. If you get the idea that every piece of software Microsoft writes has something to do with COM, you're pretty close to the truth.

COM is the latest stage of a software technology evolution that began with the Clipboard in Windows 3.0. What started out as a way for one program to communicate with another has evolved into a scheme for embedding Excel spreadsheets in Word documents, building user interface widgets for Visual Basic, and providing simple mechanisms for accessing different kinds of databases. COM is pervasive in Windows 2000. Almost every aspect of Windows 2000, outside of the kernel, relies on COM in some fashion or other.

I Know Don Box, and I'm No Don Box

Let me start off by warning you: I'm not a COM programming expert. I've written enough COM code to get myself into trouble, but if you really want to understand COM, you should read Don Box's book *Essential COM*. Reading Don's book is the best way to gain understanding of how and why COM works the way it does.

My goal in this section is to give you enough background in COM so that programming with ADSI makes sense and doesn't leave you with a big "Why am I doing this?" mystery. There is much more to learn about COM programming than you will get from this section.

What Is COM?

COM is a binary specification that describes how applications and COM components interact. COM also includes a set of services used by those applications and COM components.

COM is, at least nominally, an open standard, although as yet it is used widely only on Microsoft Windows platforms. The Windows-centricity of COM is changing, however. There are UNIX implementations of COM from Digital (now Compaq) and Software AG. Many CORBA (Common Object Request Broker) vendors are supplying COM interfaces for their products. COM is not just for Windows anymore.

Why COM?

The purpose of COM is to make it possible to develop and deploy software *components*, which are reusable pieces of software that implement some related set of functions. Although object-oriented programming languages are supposed to be the panacea to software reuse problems, programming languages address only the development side of the problems. You are still faced with the problems of how to package a component, how to discover the components available on a system, how to access the functions a component provides, and how to upgrade the component through its lifecycle.

COM addresses all these issues and is language-independent to boot.

What's the Big Idea?

There are a lot of big ideas behind COM, but they all revolve around the following theme:

> To make components reusable, you must separate interface from implementation.

After you get your head around this idea, everything else in COM starts to make sense.

Aren't interfaces already separate from implementation in C++? After all, the interface is in the header file and the implementation is in the cpp file, right? No! When you use a class declaration from a C++ header file in your application, the compiler has intimate knowledge about the size and layout of the object declared in the header file, and the compiler builds that knowledge into the generated code for your application. For instance, if you change that class declaration by adding a member variable, you must rebuild all the programs that use that class, *even if you keep the class interface the same*. In C++ classes, interfaces are most definitely *not* separate from their implementations.

The Components of COM

To become comfortable using COM, you have to become familiar with the components (pun intended) of COM programming, primarily COM interfaces, COM objects, reference counting, and the IUnknown interface.

Because this is not a tutorial on COM, but merely an introduction so that you can write ADSI programs, I'm leaving out a lot of important COM concepts, such as apartments, marshalling, and the Interface Definition Language (IDL). You can learn more about those in books devoted to COM programming.

COM Interfaces

In keeping with the philosophy that the interface must be separate from the implementation, it makes sense that the primary thing you must deal with in COM programming is an *interface*.

A COM interface is, at its simplest, a set of related functions by which you can communicate with a COM object. Every COM object provides at least one interface. If the object doesn't have at least one interface, how could you ever use it? In particular, every COM object has at least the IUnknown interface. IUnknown is the minimal set of functions a COM object can support and still be considered a COM object. The IUnknown interface contains three functions: QueryInterface(), AddRef(), and Release(). I'll discuss each of these functions later in the chapter.

In C++, COM interfaces are implemented by pointers to abstract C++ classes—that is, classes with no data members and whose member functions are all pure virtual. The C++ class declaration describing a COM interface has no information whatsoever regarding the implementation of the COM object, which enforces the separation of the interface to the object from the implementation of the object.

COM Objects

A COM *object* is essentially a collection of COM interfaces. This is different from the traditional definition of an object that usually goes something like "some data and a set of functions to act on the data." It's important to realize that the data associated with an object is really part of that object's implementation, and therefore must be hidden behind the object's interfaces. This leaves you with, well, a collection of interfaces.

No C++ language construct implements a COM object per se, at least not from the component user's perspective, so from the COM client's perspective, COM objects exist only conceptually. All you get are interfaces.

Reference Counting

Reference counting is one of the nasty corners of COM programming that I wish didn't exist, but nonetheless, there it is.

COM objects don't exist in the client program's universe, only interfaces to COM objects. The COM objects themselves live somewhere in DLLs or in services that implement the COM objects. The only connection a client program has to a COM object is through the object's interfaces, which is the whole idea.

A client program will often obtain several separate interface pointers to a COM object, and as with any situation in which there are multiple outstanding references to an object, the issue comes up of when it is safe to delete the object.

The solution in COM is reference counting. Every COM object maintains a reference count of the number of outstanding interfaces to that object held by client programs. COM provides two functions, AddRef() and Release(), for manipulating the reference count.

When you obtain an interface to a COM object (more on how to do that later), the object automatically increments its reference count. When your program is done with an interface, it is up to the program to call `Release()` on that interface. This decrements the reference count and gives the object a way to know when it can destroy itself.

When your program makes a copy of an interface pointer—for instance, when one of your functions returns an interface pointer to its caller—it is up to the function returning the pointer to call `AddRef()` to increment the reference count. It is up to the calling function to call `Release()` when it is done with the pointer or the pointer goes out of scope.

When your program overwrites a variable containing an interface pointer, your program must call `Release()` on the interface pointer before it is overwritten. Overwriting an interface pointer effectively destroys it, so your program has to let the object know that the interface is no longer in use.

Although the rules for handling interface pointers are simple, mishandling interface pointers is probably the single most common COM programming error.

Here are the basic rules for `AddRef()` and `Release()`:

- When you make a copy of an interface pointer, call `AddRef()`.
- When you destroy a copy of an interface pointer, call `Release()`.

The version of COM that comes with Windows 2000 and the Visual C++ 6.0 compiler provides a way to define "smart pointers," which are class wrappers for reference-counted interface pointers. You can use the `_COM_SMARTPTR_TYPEDEF` preprocessor macro to define a smart pointer for any kind of COM interface pointer. Using smart pointers to handle COM interface pointers reduces the number of common programming errors associated with `AddRef()` and `Release()`, but it doesn't eliminate all the possible ways you can misuse those two functions.

Two Kinds of COM Interfaces

COM defines two kinds of interfaces. The first kind, designed for compiled languages such as C, C++, and Visual Basic (yes, VB is compiled...sort of), is often called the vtable interface because it is implemented via C++ virtual function tables, or vtables. The vtable interface is the most efficient way to invoke a function on a COM interface because doing so simply involves dereferencing a pointer and calling the function it points to. It is also quite convenient to use the vtable interface from C++ programs.

The second kind of interface is designed for interpreted languages such as Active Server Pages (ASP) and VBScript. It is called the `IDispatch` interface, and it is named after the COM interface that provides the member function dispatching service for a COM object.

Because an interpreted language has no compilation step, the language interpreter has no information about a COM interface and its functions other than the name of the interface and the names of the functions the program is trying to invoke. The interpreter must take the text representations of the interface name and the function name, find the appropriate function to call, package the arguments for the call, and finally invoke the member function. It sounds slow, and it is. But it is the only way to provide access to COM components from interpreted languages.

COM objects can support vtable interfaces, `IDispatch` interfaces, or both. In the latter case, the objects are called dual-interface objects. ADSI objects, for instance, are all dual-interface.

Interface Identifiers (IIDs)

COM interfaces must be uniquely identifiable. Relying on a semi-meaningful, developer-defined name such as `IFooBar` to identify an interface is not workable because there is nothing to prevent two different component developers from implementing two different interfaces that use the same name.

The solution to this problem is the GUID, or Globally Unique Identifier. A GUID is a 128-bit, guaranteed-to-be-unique-everywhere number that you can generate by making a simple API call. Every time you generate a GUID, you get a different number. When you print out a GUID, or when you see one in the Registry, it usually looks something like this:

```
{fd8256d0-fd15-11ce-abc4-02608c9e7553}
```

The brackets and hyphenation are not significant; GUIDs are, for all intents and purposes, 128-bit blobs.

When used to identify COM interfaces, GUIDs are called Interface Identifiers, or IIDs. Every COM interface (and, therefore, every ADSI interface) is identified by a GUID. When you want to get an interface to an object from COM, you call a COM function such as `QueryInterface()` and supply the IID of the interface you want.

The main ADSI header file, iads.h, contains the IIDs for all the ADSI interfaces. In general, you can simply treat IIDs as named constants.

Class Identifiers (CLSIDs)

COM also uses GUIDs to identify COM classes. Generally, when you want to create a new instance of a COM class, you call one of the COM factory functions, such as `CoCreateInstance()` or `CoCreateInstanceEx()`. To specify the kind of object you want to create, you pass the GUID that identifies the object's class to the function.

When you are writing ADSI programs, you don't have to worry about CLSIDs or calling `CoCreateInstance()`. When you get an interface to an existing directory object, the class of the ADSI object is implied by the class of directory object you are referring to. When you create a new directory object through ADSI, the class of the object is implied by the function you use to create the object, or you explicitly specify the class of the directory object.

Obtaining Interface Pointers

There are several ways to get interface pointers to COM objects. Primarily, you use `CoCreateInstance()` or `CoCreateInstanceEx()` to create the object and return an interface pointer, or you use the function `QueryInterface()` to obtain a different kind of interface pointer from an existing interface pointer. In both cases, you specify the IID of the interface you want.

In ADSI, you don't call `CoCreateInstance()` or `CoCreateInstanceEx()` to get an interface to a directory object. Instead, you use one of the ADSI binding functions, either `IADsOpenDSObject::OpenDSObject()` or the helper function `AdsOpenObject()`. These functions accept the distinguished name of a directory entry and an IID, and return the appropriate interface pointer to the directory object by setting the objectClass attribute.

I'll show how this works later in this chapter.

COM Data Types for ADSI

COM programs (and, therefore, ADSI programs) use a mixture of conventional C++ datatypes (such as `ints` and `longs`) and unconventional data types (such as `VARIANT`s) for storing data values with types determined at runtime, and `BSTR`s for storing strings.

Table 11.1 lists the COM datatypes used with ADSI. COM supports other datatypes as well, but these are the ones you will run into while using ADSI.

TABLE 11.1 COM DATATYPES USED WITH ADSI

C++ Type	Enum	Description
boolean	VT_BOOL	Boolean (True or False)
unsigned char	VT_UI1	Single byte
unsigned short	VT_UI2	Unsigned 16-bit integer
unsigned long	VT_UI4	Unsigned 32-bit integer
unsigned __int64	VT_UI8	Unsigned 64-bit integer
short	VT_I2	16-bit signed integer
long	VT_I4	32-bit signed integer

C++ Type	*Enum*	*Description*
_ _int64	VT_I8	64-bit signed integer
int	VT_INT	32-bit signed integer
unsigned int	VT_UINT	32-bit unsigned integer
float	VT_R4	32-bit floating point
double	VT_R8	64-bit floating point
CURRENCY	VT_CY	Currency value
DATE	VT_DATE	Date and time value
IUnknown*	VT_UNKNOWN	IUnknown interface pointer
BSTR	VT_BSTR	Basic length-preceded string
IDispatch*	VT_DISPATCH	IDispatch* interface pointer
VARIANT	VT_VARIANT	Data type determined at runtime

The first 12 data types are native C/C++ types, and they behave the way you expect.

The CURRENCY data type corresponds to Visual Basic's Currency type, and represents a monetary quantity. ADSI does not use the CURRENCY data type.

The DATE data type contains a representation of a calendar year, month, and day, and possibly the time of day as well.

IUnknown* is a pointer to an IUnknown interface.

A BSTR (it stands for Basic STRing) is the standard COM string data type. BSTRs contain a variable-length Unicode value, and instead of using a NULL to mark the end of the string as do C++ strings, BSTRs precede the string data with a 16-bit length field. This means two things to you as a C++ programmer: One, BSTRs can contain a NULL character within them; and two, BSTRs are incompatible with all C and C++ string functions. Although these are pretty severe annoyances, Microsoft Visual C++ provides a built-in class called _bstr_t to make your life a little easier.

IDispatch* is a pointer to an IDispatch interface. All ADSI objects have an IDispatch interface.

A VARIANT can contain any of the standard COM data types. You have to query a VARIANT variable to see what type of data it currently contains, and then cast the value appropriately. VARIANTs are a big slap in the face of type-safety, but they are necessary to support typeless languages such as Visual Basic, VBScript, and so forth.

The Canonical COM Program

A typical COM program does five things: initialize the COM subsystem, create a COM object, get an interface pointer to the object, invoke one or more functions on the interface pointer, and clean up the COM subsystem. Pretty straightforward, and the code to do this is pretty straightforward, too. Listing 11.1 is an example of a canonical COM program that demonstrates these five steps.

LISTING 11.1   A CANONICAL COM PROGRAM

```
 1: #include <windows.h>
 2: #include <ifoo.h>
 3:
 4: int main( int argc, char** argv )
 5: {
 6:     HRESULT hr = CoInitialize( NULL );
 7:     if( SUCCEEDED( hr ) )
 8:     {
 9:         IBar* piBar = NULL;     // Pointer to IBar interface
10
11:         // Create a Foo COM object and get an IBar interface to it
12:
13:         hr = CoCreateInstance(
14:             CLSID_Foo,              // Class of object to create
15:             NULL,                   // No container
16:             CLSCTX_INPROC_SERVER,   // Server is in-process
17:             IID_IBar,               // Get the Bar interface
18:             ( void** )&piBar        // Interface pointer
19:         );
20:
21:         if( SUCCEEDED( hr ) )
22:         {
23:             // Invoke the Baz() function on the IBar interface
24:
25:             hr = piBar->Baz();
26:
27:             piFoo->Release();  // Release the IFoo interface
28:         }
29:
30:         CoUninitialize();
31:     }
32:
33:     return hr;
34: }
```

At line 6, the program initializes the COM subsystem by calling CoInitialize(). If the call succeeds, the program calls CoCreateInstance() to create a mythical Foo COM object and get an IBar interface pointer to the new object.

The program then invokes the Baz() function on the IBar interface pointer, releases the IBar interface pointer, and wraps up by calling CoUninitialize().

There are several notable things about this simple COM program. First, almost all COM functions return an error code that is declared as an HRESULT, which is a 32-bit unsigned integer. An HRESULT is not a simple integer error code, however. COM uses several of the bits to indicate the kind of error that occurred. That's why, at lines 7 and 21, the program uses the SUCCEEDED macro to determine whether the APIs succeeded or failed.

Table 11.2 shows how COM uses the various bits in an HRESULT.

TABLE 11.2 HRESULT BIT ENCODINGS

Bit	Meaning
31	Error severity; 1 = failure, 0 = success
30	Reserved; part of facility code
29	Reserved; part of facility code
28	Reserved; part of facility code
27	Reserved; part of facility code
26–16	Facility code indicating which facility generated the error
15–0	Error code indicating the particular error

Table 11.3 shows the macros provided by VC++ to assist in working with HRESULTs.

TABLE 11.3 MACROS FOR HANDLING COM ERROR CODES

Macro	Function
SUCCEEDED(hr)	Returns True if the error code indicates that the function completed properly.
FAILED(hr)	Returns True if the error code indicates that the function failed.
IS_ERROR(hr)	Returns True if the severity indicates a failure. Essentially the same as FAILED().
HRESULT_CODE(hr)	Returns the error code portion of the HRESULT.
HRESULT_FACILITY(hr)	Returns the facility code portion of the HRESULT.
HRESULT_SEVERITY(hr)	Returns the severity bit of the HRESULT.

Getting Started with ADSI

This section shows you how to get your first ADSI program up and running. It will show you how to get your machine set up with the proper SDKs and what compiler and linker options to use. Finally, you'll walk through the code for a simple program that gets and prints a user's name.

Setting Up Your Machine

The first thing you need to get is the ADSI version 2.5 SDK from the Microsoft MSDN Web site. The ADSI SDK is part of the all-encompassing Microsoft Platform SDK. The Platform SDK includes almost everything you need to develop any kind of Windows 2000 application, including the Kitchen Sink 2.0 SDK. The Platform SDK is huge (over 600MB), and you can find it at `http://www.microsoft.com/downloads`. Search for the Platform SDK product, and select the platform appropriate for your development PC— for instance, Windows 2000.

Downloading and Starting the Platform SDK Setup Wizard

When you download the Platform SDK from the Microsoft Web site, you will download the SDK Setup Wizard program psdk-x86.exe, which is about 700KB. This program will prompt you for the components of the platform SDK you want to install. The SDK Setup Wizard will download only those components you select. Figure 11.2 shows the opening dialog for the SDK Setup Wizard.

FIGURE 11.2

The Windows 2000 Platform SDK Setup Wizard.

Completing the Platform SDK Setup Wizard

After you get past the initial startup dialog, the Platform SDK Setup Wizard will

- Prompt you to accept the license agreement

- Confirm your username and organization name
- Prompt you to select Typical or Custom installation

If you have the disk space, about 700MB, select "Typical." This will install all the ADSI and LDAP components, the up-to-date COM headers and libraries, the documentation, and nearly everything else you will need to write software for Windows 2000.

If you don't have the disk space, select "Custom." You will have the opportunity to choose the Platform SDK components to install.

Selecting Individual Platform SDK Components

If you select a Custom installation, you must select the components of the Platform SDK you want to install. You will see a dialog that looks like the one shown in Figure 11.3.

FIGURE 11.3

The Windows 2000 Platform SDK Setup Custom Installation screen.

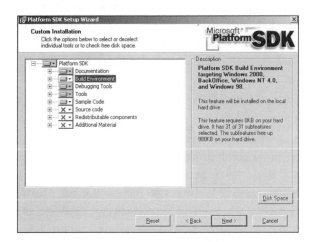

To write programs that access Active Directory using ADSI and LDAP, you must expand the Build Environment entry in the list and select Active Directory Services Interface Headers and Libs and COM Headers and Libs.

If you want the ADSI and LDAP documentation (highly recommended), you must expand the Documentation entry. Then expand the Networking section underneath it and select Active Directory.

You can then deselect the other components of the Platform SDK.

Setting Up Visual Studio for ADSI Programming

You must configure Visual Studio properly so that it can locate the ADSI include files and libraries. You can set up Visual Studio by modifying your INCLUDE and LIB environment variables, by modifying your project's preprocessor and linker settings, or by modifying Visual Studio's directory lists under the Tools menu.

Whichever method you choose, be sure that the Platform SDK include and lib directories occur in the list *before* the Visual Studio include and lib directories. Otherwise, you will use the older ADSI and LDAP files supplied with Visual Studio, and your programs will fail to run properly.

The "Hello, World" ADSI Program

Before we get into the details of ADSI functions and interfaces, I would like to go through the steps of getting a trivial "Hello, world" type of program compiled and running. It's a good way to make sure your network, domain controller, and development environment are set up properly, and it is easier to dive into a new programming environment if you have some working code to look at. I assume that you have already installed Visual C++ 6.0 and ADSI 2.5.

Note that you must explicitly link in ACTIVEDS.LIB and ADSIID.LIB to each of your ADSI programs. You may also need to link in COMSUPP.LIB if you use the COM object helper classes described later in this chapter. Make sure that you use the libraries from the ADSI installation and not those from the Visual C++ installation. The ADSI libraries that ship with Visual C++ 6.0 are out of date.

Our trivial ADSI program has to perform five steps. We'll cover those steps in more detail later, but for now, these short descriptions should suffice:

1. Initialize the COM subsystem by calling `CoInitialize()`.
2. Bind (connect) to an object in Active Directory. We'll cover binding in more detail in Chapter 12, "Basic Active Directory ADSI Interfaces."
3. Obtain an interface pointer to the Active Directory object. There are a couple of ways to do this, all of which are covered in Chapter 12.
4. Invoke a method on the interface. More than 30 ADSI interfaces work with Active Directory. They are covered in detail in the following chapters.
5. Clean up.

Initialize (and Then Clean Up) the COM Subsystem

Before you do anything in an ADSI program, you must initialize the COM subsystem. A single call to `CoInitialize()` will do the trick. Listing 11.2 shows how to initialize and clean up the COM subsystem.

LISTING 11.2 INITIALIZING THE COM SUBSYSTEM

```
1: #include <windows.h>
2: #include <activeds.h>
3:
4: int main( int argc, char** argv )
5: {
6:     HRESULT hr = CoInitialize( NULL );
7:     if( SUCCEEDED( hr ) )
8:     {
```

```
 9:        // ADSI code goes here
10:
11:        CoUninitialize();
12:    }
13:
14:    return hr;
15: }
```

Notice the call to `CoUninitialize()` in line 11. Every time you successfully call `CoInitialize()`, you must call `CoUninitialize()` to clean up the COM subsystem before your program exits.

That's all there is to getting COM (and ADSI) ready to go.

Bind to a Directory Object and Get an Interface Pointer

The next step is to connect to Active Directory. This action is called *binding*. When you use ADSI, you always bind to a specific object in the directory; you don't just create a connection to the directory server. I'll cover binding completely in the next chapter.

To keep things simple, we'll bind to the `rootDSE` object on a domain controller. The `rootDSE` object is not really an object at all; it is a collection of attributes that describe the state of the directory service on the domain controller. It contains, for instance, the LDAP versions the directory supports, the names of all the naming contexts present on the server, and so forth. As an added bonus, you don't have to have any particular access rights to read the `rootDSE` attributes.

For Listing 11.3, we'll use the `ADsGetObject()` function to bind to the `rootDSE` of a server in our domain. There are other ways of binding to an object in the directory that I'll describe in a different section.

LISTING 11.3   SAMPLE PROGRAM TO GET AN ADSI INTERFACE

```
 1: #include <windows.h>
 2: #include <activeds.h>
 3:
 4: int main( int argc, char** argv )
 5: {
 6:    HRESULT hr = CoInitialize( NULL );
 7:    if( SUCCEEDED( hr ) )
 8:    {
 9:        IADs* piIADs = NULL;
10:
11:        hr = ADsGetObject(
12:            L"LDAP://rootDSE",
13:            IID_IADs,
```

continues

LISTING **11.3**   CONTINUED

```
14:                 ( void** )&piIADs
15:           );
16:
17:           if( SUCCEEDED( hr ) )
18:           {
19:                 // Do something with the IADs interface
20:                 piIADs->Release();
21:           }
22:
23:           ( void )CoUninitialize();
24:       }
25:
26:       return hr;
27: }
```

CAUTION

If you are not running Windows 2000 on your workstation, the sample code as written will not work. The sample uses *serverless* binding (binding without specifying a specific domain controller) to pick a domain controller to connect to. Windows NT 4.0 doesn't have the capability to perform serverless binding.

To make the sample work on NT 4.0, change the call to ADsGetObject() to include the server name, as follows:

```
hr = AdsGetObject( L"LDAP://<host name>/rootDSE", IID_IADs,
                   (void**)piRootDSE );
```

where *<host name>* is the DNS host name of the Windows 2000 domain controller you would like to connect to—for instance, engserver.megacorp.com.

Listing 11.3 initializes the COM subsystem as before, by using CoInitialize(). It then gets an IADs interface pointer to the directory's rootDSE object by calling AdsGetObject() and specifying rootDSE as the object to bind to, and IID_IADs as the ADSI interface to retrieve. If the program successfully obtains the interface pointer, the program releases the interface, and calls CoUninitialize().

A couple of notes regarding the bind string argument passed to AdsGetObject(): First, the bind string, generally called the ADsPath, has a specific syntax that includes the name of the ADSI provider to use. In this case, the program invokes the LDAP ADSI provider by specifying "LDAP://" as the first part of the bind string. The second part of the bind string (the "rootDSE" part) indicates the object to bind to. I'll discuss ADsPaths in more detail in Chapter 12.

The second parameter passed to AdsGetObject() is the interface identifier (IID) for the IADs interface. The IADs interface supplies generic directory object functions for operations such as getting and setting directory attributes. All objects in the directory support the IADs interface.

Invoke an ADSI Method

So far, the sample programs haven't really done anything useful, other than prove that you can connect to a domain controller. Listing 11.4 goes through the same steps as before and then invokes one of the functions that make up the IADs interface.

LISTING 11.4 SAMPLE PROGRAM THAT USES AN ADSI INTERFACE FUNCTION

```
 1: #include <windows.h>
 2: #include <activeds.h>
 3: #include <comutil.h>
 4: #include <stdio.h>
 5:
 6: int main( int argc, char** argv )
 7: {
 8:    HRESULT hr = CoInitialize( NULL );
 9:    if( SUCCEEDED( hr ) )
10:    {
11:        IADs* piIADs = NULL;
12:
13:        hr = ADsGetObject(
14:            L"LDAP://rootDSE",
15:            IID_IADs,
16:            ( void** )&piIADs
17:        );
18:
19:        if( SUCCEEDED( hr ) )
20:        {
21:            _variant_t varDefaultNamingContext;
22:
23:            hr = piIADs->Get( _bstr_t( "defaultNamingContext" ),
24:                    &varDefaultNamingContext );
25:            if( SUCCEEDED( hr ) )
26:            {
27:                _bstr_t strDefaultNamingContext =
28:                    varDefaultNamingContext;
29:                printf( "%s\n",
30:                    ( const char* )strDefaultNamingContext );
31:            }
32:
33:            piIADs->Release();
34:        }
35:
```

continues

LISTING 11.4 CONTINUED

```
36:          ( void )CoUninitialize();
37:     }
38:
39:     return hr;
40: }
```

There are several new things in Listing 11.4. First, I've added some include files at the top—specifically, comutil.h, which has the class definitions for _bstr_t and _variant_t. The program needs stdio.h for the `printf()` function prototype.

This program starts the same way the preceding one did: by calling `CoInitialize` and `AdsGetObject()` to bind to `rootDSE` and get an interface pointer.

If the call to `ADsGetObject()` succeeds, the program declares the variable `varDefaultNamingContext` as a _variant_t. _variant_t is a class that wraps the basic COM VARIANT data type. You should definitely use _variant_t instead of VARIANT in your ADSI programs; _variant_t simplifies your COM programming life dramatically.

At line 23, the program calls the `Get()` function on the IADs interface. The `Get()` function retrieves a specific directory attribute as a VARIANT.

If the `Get()` function succeeds, the program converts the _variant_t to a BSTR at line 27. _bstr_t is another COM data type wrapper that encapsulates the BSTR data type.

Finally, at line 29, the program prints the attribute it retrieved from `rootDSE`; specifically, it prints the default naming context for the domain controller.

Special COM Data Classes

COM functions frequently use two data types that exist primarily to support interpreted languages such as Visual Basic and VBScript. The BSTR data type is a length-preceded, wide-character string with no NUL terminator. This maps directly to the Visual Basic string implementation. The VARIANT data type is a C union that can contain any one of the COM data types. The VARIANT data type supports the typelessness of interpreted languages.

The C++ language doesn't handle either of these data types very elegantly. BSTRs are completely different from C or C++ strings in that they have a length word and no NUL terminator. Using VARIANTs in C or C++ requires extra work on the part of the programmer to ensure proper memory management as well as some degree of type safety.

Microsoft has supplied two C++ classes that really simplify using BSTRs and VARIANTs: the _bstr_t class and the _variant_t class. I use these classes in all the sample code in this chapter, and I recommend that you use them as well. Along with these two wrapper classes, Microsoft has also supplied the _com_error class, which is a wrapper for COM error codes.

The declarations for both of these classes are in comutil.h, which is part of the Visual Studio 6.0 distribution, and not part of the Platform SDK. You must include comutil.h in any program that uses _bstr_t or _variant_t.

The code for these three classes is in the library comsupp.lib, which is also part of the Visual Studio 6.0 package. If you use _bstr_t or _variant_t, you must add this library to your project as well.

One deficiency with _variant_t is that it does not support the SAFEARRAY COM data type. ADSI sometimes uses SAFEARRAYs to handle multivalued attributes, so you can't use _variant_t in all cases. *C'est la vie.*

Because _bstr_t and _variant_t don't relate directly to Active Directory programming, I won't describe them in detail here. You should consult the Microsoft documentation for the specifics of using _bstr_t and _variant_t.

A Note on Exceptions with _bstr_t and _variant_t

Both the _bstr_t and _variant_t classes throw _com_error exceptions. You must be sure to use try/catch blocks around code that makes use of either of these two classes. For instance:

```
 1: #include <comutil.h>
 2:
 3: int main(int argc, char* argv[])
 4: {
 5:   HRESULT hr = CoInitialize( NULL );
 6:
 7:   if( SUCCEEDED( hr ) )
 8:   {
 9:     try
10:     {
11:         // Code that uses _variant_t and _bstr_t here
12:     }
13:
14:     catch( const _com_error& e )
15:     {
16:         HRESULT hr = e.Error();
17:         printf( "Exception %x\n", hr );
18:         printf( "Description: %s\n", ( const char* )e.Description() );
19:     }
20:
21:     ( void )CoUninitialize();
22:   }
23:
24:   return 0;
25: }
```

The `_bstr_t` Class

The `_bstr_t` class is a wrapper for the BSTR data type. It provides automatic memory management of the BSTR buffer, conversions to and from NUL-terminated ANSI and Unicode strings, and a host of constructors and comparison operations. The `_bstr_t` class also provides some useful operator overloads for string concatenation.

The `_variant_t` Class

The `_variant_t` class is a wrapper for the VARIANT type. It provides functions that keep track of the type of the VARIANT, convert the VARIANT to and from other COM types, and constructors to build VARIANTs from other COM types as well. It eliminates the need for using VariantClear() every time you declare a VARIANT variable.

The `_com_error` Class

The `_com_error` class encapsulates two aspects of COM error handling. First, the `_com_error` class has functions for accessing the actual HRESULT error code that might be generated by invoking a COM function. The `_com_error` class also provides access to another COM interface, called IErrorInfo. Some COM objects provide this interface so that not only can you get the HRESULT error code, you can also get the error description, help file and help context, and the source of the error by invoking functions on the IErrorInfo interface.

Binding to Active Directory Objects

The first thing every ADSI program must do (after initializing the COM infrastructure by calling CoInitialize()) is establish a connection with an Active Directory domain controller. There are two ways to do this, which I will describe in the following sections.

ADsPaths

Whenever you bind to a directory object by using ADSI, you must specify the ADSI provider, the server, and the object in the directory you want to bind to. You identify the object using a string called an ADsPath.

The ADsPath syntax lets you specify three things: the ADSI provider name, the server whose directory you want to access, and the distinguished name of the object you want to bind to. The following sections describe the ADsPath syntax in more detail.

ADSI 2.5 ships with four Microsoft-developed ADSI providers. Because we are dealing with only Active Directory in this book, I will discuss only ADSI objects and interfaces that are supported by the LDAP ADSI provider.

ADsPath Syntax

The general form of an `ADsPath` is as follows:

```
<provider name> "://" [<host name> "/"] <object name>
```

    <provider name> is one of the strings listed in Table 11.4.

TABLE 11.4 ADSI PROVIDER NAMES

Provider Name	Description
LDAP	Specifies the Active Directory LDAP provider connected to an Active Directory domain controller.
GC	Specifies the Active Directory LDAP provider connected to an Active Directory global catalog server.
WinNT	Specifies a Windows NT 4.x domain controller.
NDS	Specifies a Novell NetWare Directory Services server.
NWCompat	Specifies a Novell NetWare 3.x server.

> **NOTE**
>
> LDAP and GC actually specify the same Active Directory LDAP provider. The GC specifier tells the LDAP provider to connect to the domain controller using the Active Directory global catalog port number 3268 (or 3269 for an encrypted connection).

    <host name> is the DNS or NetBIOS-style name of the server to connect to. If you omit *<host name>*, ADSI will attempt to find an appropriate domain controller to connect to.

    <object name> is the fully qualified distinguished name of the object in the directory you want to bind to. When your program first binds to the directory, you will generally specify the string `"rootDSE"` to bind to the `rootDSE` entry of the directory. You can then get the name of the appropriate naming contexts from `rootDSE` to search the directory. The following section shows how to do this.

Here are some examples of valid ADsPaths:

The following ADsPath would establish an LDAP connection with the server engserver.megacorp.com and read the user object CN=Steve Calderon,CN=Users, DC=support,DC=megacorp,DC=com.

```
LPWSTR pszPath = L"LDAP://engserver.megacorp.com/CN=Steve Calderon,
➥CN=Users,DC=support,DC=megacorp,DC=com";
```

The next ADsPath connects to the domain controller whose IP address is 208.192.211.112 and reads the user object CN=Dana Wolf,CN=Users,DC=engineering, DC=megacorp,DC=com.

```
LPWSTR pszPath = L"LDAP://208.192.211.112/
➥CN=Dana Wolf,CN=Users,DC=engineering,DC=megacorp,DC=com";
```

The following ADsPath is the same as the first one, except that it binds to the global catalog running on the same domain controller.

```
LPWSTR pszPath = L"GC://engserver.megacorp.com/CN=Steve Calderon,
➥CN=Users,DC=support,DC=megacorp,DC=com";
```

Serverless Binding with ADSI

One problem with the kinds of ADsPaths I've shown you so far is that they require you to specify a server in some way, either by naming the server or by giving its IP address. This is problematic because your application probably can't assume a fixed specific server name. You will have to prompt the user for a server name or otherwise discover the server to which you can bind.

A good way to make your programs independent of a specific server or domain is to bind to the directory using *serverless binding*. Instead of providing a domain controller host name in the ADsPath (and therefore needing to know the host name of an appropriate domain controller), serverless binding lets you tell ADSI to find an "appropriate" domain controller to connect to. If you use serverless binding, you won't have to save host names in the Registry or in an .ini file, and you won't have to prompt your users for a server name they might not know.

By default, when you use serverless binding, ADSI will find a domain controller in the same site and domain as the user running the program. This is ideal for most programs in which you want to access the Active Directory domain of the user running the program.

This first ADsPath uses serverless binding to connect to a domain controller in the current user's domain, and to get the rootDSE properties from that domain controller.

```
LPWSTR pszPath = L"LDAP://rootDSE";
```

The next ADsPath uses serverless binding to connect to the global catalog in the site and forest of the currently logged-in user. This is the string you would use to initiate a

catalog search across all domains in the enterprise. A later sample program shows how to do this.

```
LPWSTR pszPath = L"GC://rootDSE";
```

Binding to a Directory Object by GUID

In some cases, you want to make sure you can bind to a directory object even if its name has been changed. For instance, if your program keeps configuration data in a specific container in the root domain naming context, what happens to your program if someone renames the container? The solution to that problem is to bind to the configuration container by using the GUID of the container itself. Normally, ADSI expects the distinguished name of the object you want to bind to. If you want to bind to an object by using its GUID, you have to use a special form of the ADsPath. The following line of code shows what that looks like:

```
LPWSTR pszPath = L"LDAP://engserver.engineering.megacorp.com/
➥<GUID=67e2ef75f0ad3119952006O9779521e>";
```

The string of characters following <GUID= is the string representation of the GUID of the object you want to bind to. This is the format that the get_GUID() function of the IADs ADSI interface returns. You can also use the ADsEncodeBinaryData() function with a GUID structure to produce the same format.

What Happens When You Bind to a Directory Object?

When you bind to a directory object using ADSI, several important things happen "underneath the covers" to establish a connection with a domain controller.

First, the ADSI LDAP provider tries to locate an appropriate domain controller for you to connect to. If you specify a domain controller in the ADsPath, ADSI will use that host name and then query DNS to get the host address.

If you use serverless binding, ADSI will locate an appropriate domain controller for you to use by calling the function DsGetDcNames(), which also makes one or more queries to DNS to get a host name and address. Chapter 16, "Other Active Directory API Functions," discusses DsGetDcNames() in more detail.

Next, ADSI will establish a TCP connection with the domain controller on the standard LDAP port 389 or, if you specified a global catalog connection, on port 3268. If you specified encryption when making the connection (see the following section), ADSI will use port 636 for an encrypted domain controller connection or 3269 for an encrypted global catalog connection.

After the TCP connection is established, ADSI will create an LDAP session with the server and authenticate to the directory using the credentials you specified.

When the LDAP connection is set up, the ADSI LDAP provider tries to read the object you specified in the ADsPath. If the object does not exist, the bind operation fails. If the object does exist, the ADSI LDAP provider reads the entire directory object, and based on the objectClass attribute of the object, creates a local COM object that exposes the appropriate interfaces for that object class.

You can see from this sequence of events that binding to an object in the directory, although straightforward, can be a lengthy process, particularly if you do it over a slow link. To speed up this process, you can use a process called fast binding, described in the next section.

Fast Binding with ADSI

To make the binding process faster, the ADSI LDAP provider supports a process called fast binding. Fast binding eliminates some of the steps in the normal binding process, but also gives up some functionality. Specifically, the ADSI LDAP provider will not the object you are binding to. That means the traffic from the client to the server is limited to the LDAP session setup, which usually requires anywhere from one to three packets.

The downside is that because the ADSI LDAP provider does not read the object from the directory, the provider does not know what class of object it is (or if it even exists); therefore, it cannot provide the appropriate interfaces for the object. Instead, when you use fast binding to bind to a directory object, ADSI will provide only the basic directory object interfaces supported by all classes of directory objects: IADs, IADsContainer, IDirectoryObject, IDirectorySearch, IADsPropertyList, IADsObjectOptions, and IADsDeleteOps.

> ### CAUTION
>
> Before you use fast binding, be sure the object you want to bind to already exists. If the object does not exist, the bind call will succeed, but all subsequent access to the object's interfaces will fail.

You can either invoke fast binding by specifying the ADS FAST BIND flag with either the ADsOpenObject() or IADsOpenDSObject::OpenDSObject() functions.

Binding with the Helper Functions ADsGetObject()

The simplest way to bind to an object in Active Directory, and probably the way you will use most frequently, is by using the ADsGetObject() function. ADsGetObject() is not a

COM function per se; it is not part of an interface to any COM object. It is a helper function that can return a COM interface pointer to the object that you specify in the ADsPath.

```
HRESULT AdsGetObject( LPWSTR pszPathName, REFIID riid, VOID** ppInterface )
```

pszPathName is a pointer to a NUL-terminated wide-character string containing the ADSI path of the provider, server, and object to bind to. See the section on ADsPaths for more details.

riid is the IID of the interface you want to retrieve. This should be one of the constants names in adsiid.h—for instance, IID_IADs.

ppInterface is the address of the interface pointer ADsGetObject will set upon successful return. You must cast this value to a void** to match the prototype of AdsGetObject.

CAUTION

Be sure to pass the address of the interface pointer you want to set, *not* the interface pointer itself. Because you must cast this parameter explicitly, the compiler will not help you if you make this mistake, and your program will GPF at runtime.

Returns: ADsGetObject() returns an ADSI or COM error code. Check the result with one of the COM error macros described earlier.

Listing 11.5 shows how to bind to rootDSE using serverless binding and ADsGetObject().

LISTING 11.5 SERVERLESS BINDING USING ADsGetObject

```
1: #include <windows.h>
2: #include <activeds.h>
3: #include <comutil.h>
4: #include <stdio.h>
5: #include <shlobj.h>
6:
7: int main(int argc, char* argv[])
8: {
9:    HRESULT hr = CoInitialize( NULL );
10:
```

continues

LISTING 11.5   CONTINUED

```
11:    if( SUCCEEDED( hr ) )
12:    {
13:       IADs* piIADs = NULL;
14:
15:       hr = ADsGetObject(
16:               L"LDAP://rootDSE",
17:               IID_IADs,
18:               ( void** )&piIADs
19:            );
20:
21:       if( SUCCEEDED( hr ) )
22:       {
23:          // do things with the interface pointer here
24:
25:          piIADs->Release();
26:       }
27:
28:       ( void )CoUninitialize();
29:    }
30:
31:    return 0;
32: }
```

Listing 11.5 starts in line 9 by calling `CoInitialize()` to initialize the COM infrastructure.

At line 13, the program declares an interface pointer that will be set by calling `ADsGetObject()`. In this case, I used an `IADs` interface pointer, but you could use any ADSI interface pointer supported by LDAP and the object you are binding to.

The program calls `ADsGetObject()` at line 15, specifying the serverless `ADsPath` for `rootDSE`. This will cause ADSI to locate a domain controller in the domain of the user running the program. Note that the address of the interface `&piIADs` is cast to `void**`.

The program checks the return value from `AdsGetObject()` by using the `SUCCEEDED()` macro; if the call was successful, the program releases the interface by calling `Release()` at line 25.

At line 28, the program cleans up the COM subsystem by calling `CoUninitialize()`.

Listing 11.6 contains a program that shows how to bind to an object using its GUID. This program gets the domain naming context from the `rootDSE` entry, reads the domain object from the directory to get its GUID, and then uses that GUID to bind to the same domain object.

LISTING 11.6 USING ADsGetObject TO BIND TO AN OBJECT BY GUID

```
 1: #include <windows.h>
 2: #include <activeds.h>
 3: #include <comutil.h>
 4: #include <stdio.h>
 5: #include <shlobj.h>
 6:
 7: int main(int argc, char* argv[])
 8: {
 9:   HRESULT hr = CoInitialize( NULL );
10:   if( SUCCEEDED( hr ) )
11:   {
12:     IADs* piIADs = NULL;
13:
14:     // First get the rootDSE
15:     hr = ADsGetObject( L"LDAP://rootDSE", IID_IADs,
16:                        ( void** )&piIADs );
17:     if( SUCCEEDED( hr ) )
18:     {
19:       _variant_t varNC;
20:
21:       // Now get the domain naming context from rootDSE
22:       hr = piIADs->Get( L"defaultNamingContext", &varNC );
23:       if( SUCCEEDED( hr ) )
24:       {
25:         piIADs->Release();
26:
27:         // Bind to the domain NC object
28:         _bstr_t strNCPath = _bstr_t( L"LDAP://" ) +
29:                             ( _bstr_t )varNC;
30:
31:         hr = ADsGetObject( strNCPath, IID_IADs,
32:                            ( void** )&piIADs );
33:         if( SUCCEEDED( hr ) )
34:         {
35:           BSTR strGuid;
36:
37:           // Get the GUID of the domain NC object
38:           hr = piIADs->get_GUID( &strGuid );
39:           if( SUCCEEDED( hr ) )
40:           {
41:             piIADs->Release();
42:
43:             // Create the <GUID=xxx> ADsPath
44:             _bstr_t strGuidPath = _
45:             _bstr_t( "LDAP://<GUID=" ) + strGuid + _bstr_t( ">" );
46:
47:             // Bind to the domain NC using the GUID
48:             IADs* piDomainNC = NULL;
49:
```

continues

LISTING 11.6   CONTINUED

```
50:                    hr = ADsGetObject( strGuidPath, IID_IADs,
51:                         ( void** )&piDomainNC );
52:                    if( SUCCEEDED( hr ) )
53:                    {
54:                        // do something with piDomainNC
55:                        piDomainNC->Release();
56:                    }
57:                }
58:            }
59:        }
60:    }
61:
62:    ( void )CoUninitialize();
63: }
64:
65:    return 0;
66: }
```

This program is quite a bit longer than the one in Listing 11.5, but it uses the same functions in a slightly different way.

At line 15, the program binds to the rootDSE using serverless binding. This will get the rootDSE from a domain controller in the same domain as the current user.

The program then gets the defaultNamingContext attribute at line 22. This is the distinguished name of the domain object for the domain of which the domain controller is a member.

At line 28, the program composes the ADsPath for the domain object by concatenating the string "LDAP://" with the distinguished name of the domain. Note that because it uses serverless binding, this call might actually end up going to a different domain controller in the same domain.

The program then gets the GUID of the domain object at line 38 by calling the get_GUID() function in the IADs interface. get_GUID() returns the objectGUID attribute as a BSTR, not as a binary blob, which makes things easier when we compose the ADsPath using the GUID.

At line 44, the program composes the ADsPath using the domain object's GUID by concatenating the string "LDAP://<GUID=" with the GUID string returned in line 35 from the get_GUID() call. It then binds to the domain object again, this time using the domain object's GUID at line 50.

Binding with the Helper Functions
`ADsOpenObject()`

The `ADsOpenObject()` function is another non-COM helper function. `ADsOpenObject()` works essentially the same way as `ADsGetObject()`, except that it accepts three additional arguments for specifying user name, password, and authentication options. Use `ADsOpenObject` if you need to authenticate using as a user other than the one currently logged in, or if you need to specify additional authentication options.

```
HRESULT ADSOpenObject( LPWSTR pszPathName,
                       LPWSTR pszUserName,
                       LPWSTR pszPassword,
                       DWORD dwAuthentication,
                       REFIID riid,
                       VOID** ppInterface )
```

`pszPathName` is a pointer to a NUL-terminated wide-character string containing the ADSI path of the provider, server, and object to bind to. See the section on `ADsPaths` for more details.

`pszUserName` is pointer to a NUL-terminated wide-character string containing the login name of the user to authenticate as. This can be the user principal name of the user (for instance, `"jimc@netpro.com"`), the Windows NT4–style domain name and user name of the user (for instance, `"engineering\jimc"`), or the distinguished name of the user (for instance, `"cn=jimc,cn=Users,dc=engineering,dc=megacorp,dc=com"`). If you pass a NULL for the user name, ADSI will authenticate using the credentials of the currently logged-in user.

`pszPassword` is a pointer to a NUL-terminated wide-character string containing the password for the user name given by `pszUserName`. If `pszUserName` is NULL, `pszPassword` should be NULL, too.

`dwAuthentication` is a bit mask indicating the authentication mechanism to use when binding to the directory. You must pass one of the values named in the `ADS_AUTHENTICATION_ENUM` enumeration definition contained in iads.h. Table 11.5 lists the possible values for `dwAuthentication`.

TABLE 11.5 ADSI AUTHENTICATION VALUES

Provider Name	Value	Description
ADS_SECURE_AUTHENTICATION	0x01	Requests that ADSI authenticate the client before granting access. When binding to Active Directory using the LDAP provider, ADSI uses the Kerberos service to authenticate to the directory.
ADS_USE_ENCRYPTION	0x02	Requests that ADSI encrypt all network traffic between the client and the server. When using the LDAP provider, this will always result in using Secure Sockets Layer (SSL) encryption. Active Directory must have already been configured to use a Public Key Infrastructure (PKI) Certificate Authority before you can use this option.
ADS_USE_SSL	0x02	Same as ADS_USE_ENCRYPTION.
ADS_READONLY_SERVER	0x04	Tells ADSI that a read-only server is acceptable for a connection. Because all Active Directory domain controllers are read-write, this flag has no meaning with the LDAP provider.
ADS_PROMPT_CREDENTIALS	0x08	Requests that ADSI use the provider-supplied dialog box to obtain the user name and password to use for binding.

> **NOTE**
>
> The ADSI LDAP provider will prompt for credentials only if it cannot authenticate using the user name and password specified in the parameter list. If you specify NULL for the user name and password, the ADSI LDAP provider will authenticate using the current login credentials. So, the only way to force the LDAP provide to always prompt for a user name and password is to pass in a bogus user name and password.

11

Provider Name	*Value*	*Description*

> **NOTE**
>
> The ADSI LDAP provider in Windows 2000 RC1 did not properly implement the `ADS_PROMPT_CREDENTIALS` flag, and would never prompt for a user name and password. This may be fixed before Windows 2000 actually ships.

Provider Name	Value	Description
`ADS_NO_AUTHENTICATION`	`0x10`	Requests that ADSI create an unauthenticated anonymous connection with the domain controller.

> **NOTE**
>
> If you use `ADS_NO_AUTHENTICATION`, you will be able to access the `rootDSE` for the directory, but access to the rest of the directory tree will be limited to whatever access is granted to the Everyone well-known security principal.

Provider Name	Value	Description
`ADS_FAST_BIND`	`0x20`	Requests that ADSI use fast binding. See the "Fast Binding with ADSI" section for more details on fast binding.
`ADS_USE_SIGNING`	`0x40`	Requests that ADSI include a message digest with each message sent to ensure that the data sent between client and sever is not corrupted. Generally speaking, if you use the LDAP provider over TCP, you don't need to use this facility because TCP is quite reliable.
`ADS_USE_SEALING`	`0x80`	Requests that ADSI use Kerberos to encrypt each LDAP request and response message. If you specify this option, the ADSI LDAP provider will also enable `ADS_USE_SIGNING`. You must be logged in to a Windows 2000 domain, or a domain trusted by a Windows 2000 domain, to use this option.

riid is the interface identifier of the interface you want to retrieve. This should be one of the constant's names in adsiid.h—for instance, IID_IADs.

ppInterface is the address of the interface pointer ADsOpenObject will set upon successful return. You must cast this value to a void** to match the prototype of AdsOpenObject.

CAUTION

Be sure to pass the address of the interface pointer you want to set, *not* the interface pointer itself. Because you must cast this parameter explicitly, the compiler will not help you if you make this mistake, and your program will GPF at runtime.

Returns: ADsOpenObject() returns an ADSI or COM error code. Check the result with one of the COM error macros described earlier in this chapter.

The program in Listing 11.7 shows how to use ADsOpenObject to bind to the rootDSE of a specific server using a specific user name and password.

LISTING 11.7 USING ADsOpenObject()

```
 1: #include <windows.h>
 2: #include <activeds.h>
 3: #include <comutil.h>
 4: #include <stdio.h>
 5: #include <shlobj.h>
 6:
 7: int main(int argc, char* argv[])
 8: {
 9:   HRESULT hr = CoInitialize( NULL );
10:
11:   if( SUCCEEDED( hr ) )
12:   {
13:     IADs* piRootDSE = NULL;
14:
15:     hr = ADsOpenObject(
16:         L"LDAP://engserver.engineering.megacorp.com/rootDSE",
17:         L"Administrator",
18:         L"xyzzy",
19:         ADS_SECURE_AUTHENTICATION,
20:         IID_IADs,
21:         (void**)&piRootDSE
22:     );
23:
```

```
24:    if( SUCCEEDED( hr ) )
25:    {
26:        // do things with the piRootDSE interface pointer here
27:
28:        piRootDSE->Release();
29:    }
30:
31:    ( void )CoUninitialize();
32:    }
33:
34:    return 0;
35: }
```

Listing 11.7 initializes the COM subsystem in the usual way at line 9.

The program then calls ADsOpenObject at line 15, specifying the server
engserver.engineering.megacorp.com and rootDSE in the ADsPath argument. The
program also provides the user name ("Administrator") and the password ("xyzzy").

Finally, the program releases the interface pointer at line 28 and uninitializes the COM
subsystem at line 31.

Binding with the
IADsOpenDSObject::OpenDSObject() Function

The last way to bind to a directory object in Active Directory is to use the
IADsOpenDSObject interface. Given that IADsOpenDSObject::OpenDSObject() does the
same thing as the helper function ADsOpenObject(), there isn't a very compelling reason
to use the IADsOpenDSObject interface. It exists primarily to support Visual Basic.

Outside of the usual IUnknown and IDispatch functions, the IADsOpenDSObject interface
has only one member function: OpenDSObject(). The calling sequence for
OpenDSObject() is the same as that for ADsOpenObject(). It lets you specify an ADsPath
indicating the ADSI provider, server, and object you want to bind with, as well as a user
name, password, and authentication option flags. See Table 11.6 for more details.

TABLE 11.6 THE IADsOpenDSObject INTERFACE

Function Name	Description
QueryInterface()	IUnknown interface.
AddRef()	IUnknown interface.
Release()	IUnknown interface.

continues

TABLE 11.6 CONTINUED

Function Name	Description
GetTypeInfoCount()	IDispatch interface.
GetTypeInfo()	IDispatch interface.
GetIDsOfNames()	IDispatch interface.
Invoke()	IDispatch interface.
OpenDSObject()	Binds to the specified object using the ADsPath, user name, password, and authentication options provided. Creates an IDispatch interface pointer for the object specified.

How do you go about getting an interface pointer to an IADsOpenDSObject object? Well, the CLSID for IADsOpenDSObject isn't exposed, so you can use CoCreateInstance(). The only obvious way to get an interface pointer is to call ADsGetObject() or ADsOpenObject().

```
HRESULT IADsOpenDSObject::OpenDSObject( BSTR strADsPath,
                                        BSTR strUserName,
                                        BSTR strPassword,
                                        LONG lAuthenticationOptions,
                                        IDispatch** ppiDispatch )
```

strADsPath is a BSTR containing the ADsPath of the provider, server, and object to bind to. See the section "ADsPaths" for more details.

strUserName is a BSTR containing the login name of the user to authenticate as. This can be the user principal name of the user (for example, "jimc@netpro.com"), the Windows NT4–style domain name and user name of the user (for example, "engineering\jimc") or the distinguished name of the user (for example, "cn=jimc,cn=Users,dc=engineering,dc=megacorp,dc=com"). If you pass a NULL for the user name, ADSI will authenticate using the credentials of the currently logged-in user.

strPassword is a BSTR containing the password for the user name given by pszUserName. If pszUserName is NULL, pszPassword should be NULL, too.

lAuthenticationOptions is a bit mask indicating the authentication mechanism to use when binding to the directory. You must pass one of the values named in the ADS_AUTHENTICATION_ENUM enumeration definition contained in iads.h. Table 11.5 contains the possible values for lAuthentication.

ppiDispatch is the address of an IDispatch pointer that the function will set. This will be the IDispatch pointer for the object specified by strPathName. You can call QueryInterface() using the returned pointer to obtain other interfaces to the directory object.

Returns: `IADsOpenDSObject::OpenDSObject()` returns an ADSI or COM error code. Check the result with one of the COM error macros described earlier in this chapter.

Listing 11.8 shows how you can use the `IADsOpenDSObject` interface to bind to an Active Directory object. The program gets an `IADsOpenDSObject` interface pointer by calling `ADsGetObject()`, and then binds to the `rootDSE` by invoking the `IADsOpenDSObject::OpenDSObject()` function.

LISTING 11.8 BINDING USING `IADsOpenDSObject::OpenDSObject()`

```
1: #include <windows.h>
2: #include <activeds.h>
3: #include <comutil.h>
4: #include <stdio.h>
5: #include <shlobj.h>
6:
7: int main(int argc, char* argv[])
8: {
9:   HRESULT hr = CoInitialize( NULL );
10:
11:   if( SUCCEEDED( hr ) )
12:   {
13:     _bstr_t strRootDSEPath( "LDAP://rootDSE" );
14:     IADsOpenDSObject *piOpenObject = NULL;
15:
16:     hr = ADsGetObject( L"LDAP:", IID_IADsOpenDSObject,
17:                        ( void** )&piOpenObject );
18:     if( SUCCEEDED( hr ) )
19:     {
20:       IDispatch *piDispatch = NULL;
21:       hr = piOpenObject->OpenDSObject(
22:           strRootDSEPath,
23:           NULL,
24:           NULL,
25:           ADS_SECURE_AUTHENTICATION,
26:           &piDispatch
27:       );
28:
29:       if( SUCCEEDED( hr ) )
30:       {
31:         IADs* piADs = NULL;
32:         hr = piDispatch->QueryInterface( IID_IADs,
33:                   ( void** )&piADs );
34:         if( SUCCEEDED( hr ) )
35:         {
36:           // do something with piADs
37:
38:           piADs->Release();
39:         }
```

continues

LISTING 11.8 CONTINUED

```
40:
41:            piDispatch->Release();
42:          }
43:        }
44:
45:      CoUninitialize();
46:    }
47:
48:    return 0;
49: }
```

Listing 11.8 starts the same as the previous programs by initializing the COM subsystem by calling CoIntitialize() at line 9.

The program then calls ADsGetObject() at line 16 to get a pointer to an IADsOpenDSObject interface. Note that the ADsPath is "LDAP:" with no additional path information.

At line 21, the program calls the OpenDSObject() function of the IADsOpenDSObject interface. The program passes in the rootDSE ADsPath so that the program will bind to the rootDSE entry of a domain controller in the domain of the current user. OpenDSObject() returns an IDispatch pointer.

At line 32, the program calls QueryInterface() on the IDispatch pointer returned by OpenDSObject() so that it can get an IADs interface pointer to the rootDSE.

The program wraps up by releasing the interface pointers and shutting down the COM subsystem by calling CoUninitialize().

CHAPTER 12

Basic Active Directory ADSI Interfaces

This chapter covers all the basic directory object interfaces—that is, the interfaces that allow you to write programs that handle generic directory objects. These interfaces treat directory objects the same, without concern for their particular directory object classes. Other interfaces I'll cover in later chapters are targeted to specific classes of objects, such as the IADsUser interface.

This chapter covers the IADs and IADirectoryObject interfaces for handling individual directory objects, the IADsContainer interface for enumerating objects in directory containers, and the IADsPropertyList, IADsPropertyValue, and IADsPropertyValue2 interfaces for handling the attributes of objects. Toward the end of the chapter, I'll cover the IADsObjectOptions and IADsDeleteOps utility interfaces.

If you master the interfaces described in this chapter, you'll be able to write almost any program you want for Active Directory using ADSI. The other interfaces simplify the access to some classes of directory objects, but you can, in fact, do everything you need to by using the interfaces described here.

The ADSI Directory Object Interfaces

The following sections describe the ADSI interfaces that apply to all Active Directory objects. These interfaces, called the directory object interfaces, work with every object in Active Directory, regardless of class. No matter which object you get from the directory, you can use these interfaces.

The most popular interface is probably the IADs interface. It provides functions for getting and setting the directory object's attributes, getting the object's GUID as a BSTR, and getting the object's ADsPath. It includes a property cache, described later in this chapter, that simplifies getting and setting attributes.

Because every object in Active Directory has the potential to be a container, you can get an IADsContainer interface to any directory object. The IADsContainer interface provides functions for enumerating the contents of a directory container object.

The IADsPropertyList interface provides functions that access the directory object's attributes and values, as well as functions to enumerate the attributes of the directory object. The IADsPropertyValue and IADsPropertyValue2 interfaces provide functions that manipulate the individual values of an attribute according to their directory syntax.

The IDirectoryObject interface is a simplified version of the IADs interface. The IDirectoryObject interface provides similar functionality as IADs, but with a little more fine-grained control and without the complexity of the property cache.

The IADsDeleteOps interface provides a way to delete directory objects and entire directory subtrees, and the IADsObjectOptions interface provides a way to alter the way some of the LDAP functions underlying ADSI behave.

The IADs Interface

The IADs interface provides an automation-based interface (IDispatch) for accessing Active Directory objects. It provides functions for loading the IADs property cache (see the next section), for getting and setting attributes in the property cache, and for retrieving other information about each directory object, such as getting the object's GUID and distinguished name. Table 12.1, shown in a moment, lists the functions that make up the IADs interface.

When you manipulate Active Directory objects using the IADs interface, you do not manipulate the directory objects directly. Instead, you manipulate an in-memory copy of the object's attributes called the property cache. This has some important consequences, as I will describe.

What Is the Property Cache?

The *property cache* is an in-memory table of attribute names and values. Each object from which you obtain an IADs interface pointer has a property cache.

Typically, you load the property cache from the domain controller after you get the object's interface pointer. Your application then accesses the properties in the property cache without going over the network. Finally, if your program has modified any properties, it then flushes the changed properties back to the domain controller.

Loading the Property Cache

After you obtain an IADs interface pointer to a directory object, calling the IADS::Get() function causes ADSI to load the entire property cache from the directory. You can also explicitly load the property cache by calling the IADS::GetInfo() or IADS::GetInfoEx() functions. Curiously, calling the IADs:get GUID() function also loads the property cache, though the other get...() functions do not.

When the property cache is loaded, all subsequent calls to the Get() function operate against the values in the property cache and do not contact the directory. If you need to refresh the values in the property cache for some reason, you can simply call GetInfo() or GetInfoEx() again.

It is often a much better idea to use GetInfoEx() instead of GetInfo(), as I explain in a later section.

Accessing Attributes in the Property Cache

After you have loaded the property cache—either implicitly by calling Get() or explicitly by calling GetInfo()—you can access the attributes using the IADs::Get() and IADs::Put() functions. These functions get and set attribute values in the property cache.

12

BASIC ACTIVE DIRECTORY INTERFACES

ADSI provides four other interfaces for dealing with the properties in the property cache: IADsPropertyList, IADsPropertyEntry, IADsPropertyValue, and IADsPropertyValue2. I discuss all these interfaces later in this chapter.

Updating the Directory with the Property Cache

After your program has modified attribute values in the property cache, you must flush the changes back to the directory service; otherwise, your changes will never be stored in the directory. You use the IADs::PutInfo() function to flush the property cache back to the domain controller.

The Property Cache and Network Traffic

The intent of the property cache is to reduce network traffic, and it's a good idea. But if you use the IADs interface in the simple and obvious way, you will actually *increase* network traffic, not decrease it.

Why? Simple. By default, when you load the property cache by using IADs::GetInfo() or any of the get_...() functions, ADSI retrieves *all* the attributes of the object. Objects in Active Directory can have tens or hundreds of attributes. If your application needs to access only a couple attributes, which is the usual case, you will waste a lot of network bandwidth retrieving a lot of attributes you don't need.

The solution to this problem is easy. When you load the property cache, use the IADs::GetInfoEx() function instead of GetInfo() or one of the get_...() functions. GetInfoEx() lets you name the attributes you want to retrieve, thereby substantially reducing the network traffic you would create using the GetInfo() function.

Enough about the property cache. Table 12.1 describes the functions that make up the IADs interface.

TABLE 12.1 THE IADs INTERFACE

Function Name	Description
QueryInterface()	IUnknown interface.
AddRef()	IUnknown interface.
Release()	IUnknown interface.
GetTypeInfoCount()	IDispatch interface.
GetTypeInfo()	IDispatch interface.
GetIDsOfNames()	IDispatch interface.

Function Name	Description
Invoke()	IDispatch interface.
get_Name()	Retrieves the relative distinguished name of the object.
get_Class()	Retrieves the class name of the object from the object's objectClass attribute.
get_GUID()	Retrieves the GUID of the object from the object's objectGUID attribute. The returned GUID is formatted as a 32-character string containing two hex characters for each byte of the GUID. You can use this form of the GUID to bind to the object.
get_AdsPath()	Retrieves the ADsPath of the object, including the provider name and server name, if one was specified in the ADsPath used to bind to the object.
get_Parent()	Retrieves the GUID of the object containing this object, in the same form as provided by the get_GUID function. You can use this value to compose an ADsPath string to bind to the parent object by GUID.
get_Schema()	Retrieves the ADsPath of the classSchema object in the Active Directory schema that corresponds to the class of this object. You can use this path to bind to the classSchema object.
GetInfo()	Loads or reloads the property cache with all the attributes for this object.
SetInfo()	Flushes any changes in the property cache back to the directory server.
Get()	Retrieves an attribute from the property cache as a VARIANT.
Put()	Stores an attribute in the property cache.
GetEx()	Gets an attribute from the property cache as an array of VARIANTs to simplify handling of multivalued attributes.
PutEx()	Sets an attribute in the property cache with an array of VARIANTs, one element of the array per value.
GetInfoEx()	Loads or reloads the property cache from the directory—as GetInfo() does—and allows you to specify which attributes you want to retrieve from the directory. You can reduce network traffic by retrieving only the attributes you need. This is the only way to retrieve the operational attributes of an object that would normally not be retrieved with GetInfo().

Using IADs::Get() to Get a Single-Valued Attribute

The first sample program, shown in Listing 12.1, shows how to bind to the rootDSE of a specific server, retrieve a couple of attribute values, and print them. The program uses the IADs::Get() function to retrieve the attribute values.

HRESULT IADs::Get(BSTR strAttributeName, VARIANT* pvarAttribute)

strAttributeName is a BSTR containing the name of the attribute to retrieve from the property cache. If the property cache has not been loaded, IADs::Get() will load all the directory object's attributes into the cache.

pvarAttribute is the address of a VARIANT that will be set to the value of the attribute.

Returns: An ADSI or COM error code. Check the result with one of the COM error macros described in Chapter 11, "ADSI Fundamentals."

LISTING 12.1   USING THE IADs INTERFACE TO RETRIEVE rootDSE ATTRIBUTES

```
 1: #include <windows.h>
 2: #include <activeds.h>
 3: #include <comutil.h>
 4: #include <stdio.h>
 5:
 6: int main(int argc, char* argv[])
 7: {
 8:   HRESULT hr = CoInitialize( NULL );
 9:
10:   if( SUCCEEDED( hr ) )
11:   {
12:     IADs* piIADs = NULL;
13:
14:     hr = ADsGetObject(
15:         L"LDAP://rootDSE",
16:         IID_IADs,
17:         ( void** )&piIADs
18:     );
19:
20:     if( SUCCEEDED( hr ) )
21:     {
22:       _variant_t varDefaultNamingContext;
23:
24:       hr = piIADs->Get( L"defaultNamingContext",
25:           &varDefaultNamingContext );
25:       if( SUCCEEDED( hr ) )
26:       {
27:         _bstr_t strDefaultNamingContext = varDefaultNamingContext;
28:         printf( "defaultNamingContext is: %s\n",
29:                 ( const char* )strDefaultNamingContext );
```

```
30:        }
31:
32:        _variant_t varHostName;
33:        hr = piIADs->Get( L"dNSHostName", &varHostName );
34:        if( SUCCEEDED( hr ) )
35:        {
36:          _bstr_t strHostName = varHostName;
37:          printf( "hostName is: %s\n", ( const char* )strHostName );
38:        }
39:
40:        piIADs->Release();
41:      }
42:
43:      ( void )CoUninitialize();
44:    }
45:
46:    return 0;
46: }
```

After initializing the COM subsystem at line 8, the program binds to the `rootDSE` of `engserver.engineering.megacorp.com` by using the `ADsGetObject()` helper function.

If the bind succeeds, the program retrieves the default naming context attribute of the domain controller's `rootDSE` at line 24, (thereby loading the property cache) and prints the value of the default naming context at line 28. Note that the `IADs::Get()` function retrieves all attributes as `VARIANT`s. You have to then convert the `VARIANT` to an appropriate type to use it. In this case, because we know that the default naming context attribute is a string, we convert the `_variant_t` variable to a `_bstr_t` variable and then use the `const char*` conversion operation of `_bstr_t` to print the value.

At line 33, the program gets another attribute from `rootDSE`, this time the `dNSHostName` attribute. It does this in exactly the same way as it did the default naming context.

At line 40, the program releases the interface pointer and wraps up the COM subsystem at line 43.

Using `IADs::Get()` to Get a Multivalued Attribute

Getting a single-valued attribute is pretty easy; handling a multivalued attribute is a little more complicated. Actually, *getting* the multivalued attribute is still easy: You just use the `IADs::Get()` function as in the earlier example. The additional difficulty comes when you have to use the COM `SafeArray` functions to access the elements of the array.

The program in Listing 12.2 shows how to retrieve the multivalued attribute `namingContexts` from the `rootDSE` of a domain controller. The `namingContexts` attribute contains one value for each naming context maintained by the server. Nonglobal catalog domain controllers always have three values: one for the Schema naming context, one for the Configuration naming context, and one for the domain naming context.

LISTING 12.2   USING THE IADs INTERFACE TO RETRIEVE A MULTIVALUED ATTRIBUTE

```
 1: #include <windows.h>
 2: #include <activeds.h>
 3: #include <comutil.h>
 4: #include <stdio.h>
 5:
 6: int main(int argc, char* argv[])
 7: {
 8:   HRESULT hr = CoInitialize( NULL );
 9:
10:   if( SUCCEEDED( hr ) )
11:   {
12:     IADs* piIADs = NULL;
13:
14:     hr = ADsGetObject(
15:         L"LDAP://engserver.engineering.megacorp.com/rootDSE",
16:         IID_IADs,
17:         ( void** )&piIADs
18:         );
19:
20:     if( SUCCEEDED( hr ) )
21:     {
22:       _variant_t varNCs;
23:
24:       // get the namingContexts attribute
25:       hr = piIADs->Get( L"namingContexts", &varNCs );
26:
27:       // make sure we got an array
28:       if( SUCCEEDED( hr ) && V_ISARRAY( &varNCs ) )
29:       {
30:         // turn it into a COM SAFEARRAY
31:         SAFEARRAY* aNCs = V_ARRAY( &varNCs );
32:         if( aNCs != NULL )
33:         {
34:           long lLBound = 0;
35:           long lUBound = 0;
36:
37:           // Get the range of the array
38:           ( void )SafeArrayGetLBound( aNCs, 1, &lLBound );
39:           ( void )SafeArrayGetUBound( aNCs, 1, &lUBound );
40:
41:           // for each element
42:           for( long lIndex = lLBound; lIndex <= lUBound; lIndex++)
43:           {
44:             _variant_t varNC;
45:
46:             hr = SafeArrayGetElement( aNCs, &lIndex, &varNC );
```

```
47:                 if( SUCCEEDED( hr ) )
48:                 {
49:                   printf( "namingContext(%d) is: %s\n", lIndex,
50:                           ( const char* )_bstr_t( varNC ) );
51:                 }
52:               }
53:             }
54:           }
55:         piIADs->Release();
56:       }
57:
58:       ( void )CoUninitialize();
59:     }
60:
61:   return 0;
62: }
```

The program in Listing 12.2 starts in the usual way, and uses `ADsGetObject()` to bind to the `rootDSE` of a domain controller in the current user's domain at line 14.

At line 25, the program gets the `namingContexts` attribute as a `VARIANT`. Because there are always three values in this attribute, `varNCs` will be a `VT_ARRAY`.

At line 31, the program gets a `SAFEARRAY` pointer from the `_variant_t` `varNCs`. The only way to manipulate `VARIANT` arrays returned from ADSI is through the `SafeArray` APIs.

The program gets the bounds of the array of naming contexts at lines 38 and 39. These give the lowest array index and highest array index of the entries in the array.

The program then iterates through the values of the `SAFEARRAY`, starting at line 42. Note that the terminating condition is `lIndex <= lUBound` instead of the usual `lIndex < lUBound` you use for C++ arrays. This is due to the fact that `lUBound` is the index of the last valid array entry, not the size of the array.

At line 46, the program gets the element as a `_variant_t`, and at line 49, it converts the `_variant_t` to `_bstr_t` and then to `const char*` so that `printf` can print the naming context string.

At line 55, the program releases the interface pointer to `rootDSE` and then calls `CoUninitialize()` at line 58.

Using `IADs::GetEx()` to Get a Multivalued Attribute

The `IADs::GetEx()` function is the same as the `IADs::Get()` function except for one significant difference: It returns the attribute as an array of `VARIANT`s instead of as a single `VARIANT` that might or might not be an array.

This has one important consequence. It means that when you get an attribute using IADs::GetEx(), no matter whether it is single-valued or multivalued, you must treat the attribute as multivalued. If the attribute has only a single value, GetEx() will return a VARIANT array with one entry in it, and the lower and upper bounds of the VARIANT array will both be 0.

```
HRESULT IADs::GetEx( BSTR strAttributeName, VARIANT* pvarAttributes )
```

strAttributeName is a BSTR containing the name of the attribute to retrieve from the property cache. If the property cache has not been loaded, IADs::Get() will load all the directory object's attributes into the cache.

pvarAttributes is the address of a VARIANT that will be set to a VARIANT array of VARIANTs, one entry in the array for each value of the attribute. If the attribute has a single value, the VARIANT array will contain one entry.

Returns: An ADSI or COM error code. Check the result with one of the COM error macros described in Chapter 11.

The program in Listing 12.3 shows how to use IADs::GetEx() to retrieve both a single-valued attribute and a multivalued attribute from rootDSE. Note that the code to handle single-valued and multivalued attributes is the same. You treat a single-valued attribute as a multivalued attribute with only one value.

LISTING 12.3   USING THE IADs::GetEx FUNCTION TO RETRIEVE SINGLE-VALUED AND MULTIVALUED ATTRIBUTES

```
 1: #include <windows.h>
 2: #include <activeds.h>
 3: #include <comutil.h>
 4: #include <stdio.h>
 5:
 6: int main(int argc, char* argv[])
 7: {
 8:   HRESULT hr = CoInitialize( NULL );
 9:
10:   if( SUCCEEDED( hr ) )
11:   {
12:     IADs* piIADs = NULL;
13:     SAFEARRAY* aNCs;
14:     long lLBound = 0;
15:     long lUBound = 0;
16:     _variant_t varNCs;
17:     _variant_t varNC;
18:
19:     hr = ADsOpenObject(
20:       L"LDAP://rootDSE",
21:       NULL,
22:       NULL,
23:       ADS_SECURE_AUTHENTICATION,
```

```
24:        IID_IADs,
25:        ( void** )&piIADs
26:      );
27:
28:    if( SUCCEEDED( hr ) )
29:    {
30:      printf( "Using GetEx() to get defaultNamingContext\n" );
31:      hr = piIADs->GetEx( L"defaultNamingContext", &varNCs );
32:      if( SUCCEEDED( hr ) && V_ISARRAY( &varNCs ) )
33:      {
34:        aNCs = V_ARRAY( &varNCs );
35:        if( aNCs != NULL )
36:        {
37:          ( void )SafeArrayGetLBound( aNCs, 1, &lLBound );
38:          ( void )SafeArrayGetUBound( aNCs, 1, &lUBound );
39:
40:          for( long lIndex = lLBound; lIndex <= lUBound;
41:               lIndex++ )
42:          {
43:            hr = SafeArrayGetElement( aNCs, &lIndex, &varNC );
44:            if( SUCCEEDED( hr ) )
45:            {
46:              printf( "namingContext(%d) is: %s\n",
47:                      lIndex, ( const char* ) _bstr_t( varNC ) );
48:            }
49:          }
50:        }
51:      }
52:
53:      printf( "Using GetEx() to get namingContexts\n" );
54:      hr = piIADs->Get( L"namingContexts", &varNCs );
55:      if( SUCCEEDED( hr ) && V_ISARRAY( &varNCs ) )
56:      {
57:        aNCs = V_ARRAY( &varNCs );
58:        if( aNCs != NULL )
59:        {
60:          ( void )SafeArrayGetLBound( aNCs, 1, &lLBound );
61:          ( void )SafeArrayGetUBound( aNCs, 1, &lUBound );
62:
63:          for( long lIndex = lLBound; lIndex <= lUBound;
64:               lIndex++ )
65:          {
66:            hr = SafeArrayGetElement( aNCs, &lIndex, &varNC );
67:            if( SUCCEEDED( hr ) )
68:            {
69:              printf( "namingContext(%d) is: %s\n",
70:                      lIndex, ( const char* ) _bstr_t( varNC ) );
71:            }
72:          }
73:        }
74:      }
```

12

**BASIC ACTIVE
DIRECTORY
INTERFACES**

continues

LISTING 12.3   CONTINUED

```
75:        piIADs->Release();
76:    }
77:
78:    ( void )CoUninitialize();
79:  }
80:
81:  return 0;
82: }
```

At line 19, the program in Listing 12.3 calls `ADsOpenObject` to get an `IADs` interface pointer to the `rootDSE` of a domain controller in the current user's domain.

At line 31, the program calls the `GetEx()` function to get the values of the `defaultNamingContext` attribute of the `rootDSE`. This is a single-valued attribute. The program checks to make sure it got a valid `VARIANT` array at line 32.

The program gets the lower and upper bounds of the `VARIANT` array at line 37. In this case, because `defaultNamingContext` is a single-valued attribute, both array bounds will be `0`.

The program then gets the single array value at line 43. At line 46, it converts the `_variant_t` value to a `_bstr_t`, and prints the single default naming context value. The `for` loop at line 40 will execute only one iteration because the attribute is single-valued.

Next, the program repeats the same sequence of code, only this time it calls `IADs::GetEx()` to get the multivalued `namingContexts` attribute from the `rootDSE`.

After verifying the attribute at line 55, the program then gets the array bounds for the `VARIANT` array at lines 60 and 61 and iterates through the multiple values starting at line 63.

For each of the three values in the attribute, the program calls `SafeArrayGetElement()` to get the `VARIANT` array entry as a `_variant_t`, converts the value to a `_bstr_t` and then prints the value at line 69.

The program releases the `rootDSE` interface pointer at line 75 and shuts down the COM subsystem at line 78.

Using `IADs::GetInfoEx()` to Retrieve Selected Attributes from the Server

One of the bad characteristics of the preceding three sample programs is that they all use either the `IADs::Get()` or the `IADs::GetEx()` function to retrieve the attribute values of rootDSE. As I discussed in the section about the `IADs` property cache, when you use the

Get() or GetEx() function, ADSI will load *all* the attributes of the current object. In the case of rootDSE, this isn't a big deal because rootDSE only has between 20 and 30 attributes. The difference between reading one or two attributes and reading all the attributes of rootDSE is not significant. If you were getting a large user object from the directory and you just needed the first and last names, the difference between reading the two attributes you need and all the attributes of the user object can be substantial.

To solve this problem, instead of relying on the IADs::Get() or IADs::GetEx() function to load the property cache, you can use the IADs::GetInfoEx() function to load only those properties you want.

```
HRESULT IADs::GetInfoEx( VARIANT varPropertyNames, LONG lMustBeZero )
```

> varPropertyNames is a VARIANT array of BSTRs, each containing the name of an attribute to load into the property cache.

> lMustBeZero is reserved for later use and must be set to 0.

Returns: An ADSI or COM error code. Check the result with one of the COM error macros described in Chapter 11.

The program in Listing 12.4 shows how you can use GetInfoEx() to load selected attributes into the property cache. Although the sample program uses the default domain object, you can use GetInfoEx() to load the selected attributes of any object in the directory.

12

BASIC ACTIVE DIRECTORY INTERFACES

LISTING 12.4 USING THE IADs::GetInfoEx FUNCTION TO LOAD SELECTED rootDSE ATTRIBUTES

```
 1: #include <windows.h>
 2: #include <activeds.h>
 3: #include <comutil.h>
 4: #include <stdio.h>
 5:
 6: int main(int argc, char* argv[])
 7: {
 8:     HRESULT hr = CoInitialize( NULL );
 9:
10:     if( SUCCEEDED( hr ) )
11:     {
12:         IADs* piIADs = NULL;
13:
14:         hr = ADsOpenObject(
15:             L"LDAP://rootDSE",
16:             NULL,
17:             NULL,
18:             ADS_SECURE_AUTHENTICATION,
```

continues

LISTING 12.4   CONTINUED

```
19:            IID_IADs,
20:            ( void** )&piIADs
21:        ); // search rootDSE to get selected attrs, bind
22:
23:        if( SUCCEEDED( hr ) )
24:        {
25:            _variant_t varDomainNC;
26:
27:            // Get the defaultNamingContext attr from rootDSE
28:            hr = piIADs->Get( L"defaultNamingContext",
                ➥&varDomainNC );
29:            if( SUCCEEDED( hr ) )
30:            {
31:                piIADs->Release();
32:
33:                // Bind to the domain NC of the domain controller
34:                hr = ADsGetObject(
35:                    _bstr_t( "LDAP://" ) + _bstr_t( varDomainNC ),
36:                    IID_IADs,
37:                    ( void** )&piIADs
38:                ); // bind, search, and get objectClass attr
39:
40:                if( SUCCEEDED( hr ) )
41:                {
42:                    wchar_t* apszAttrNames[] = { L"name" };
43:                    _variant_t varAttrNames;
44:
45:                    hr = ADsBuildVarArrayStr( apszAttrNames, 1,
                        ➥&varAttrNames );
46:                    if( SUCCEEDED( hr ) )
47:                    {
48:                        // Load the property cache with the single
                            // property "name". Search and get name
49:                        // attr, search and get all attrs, search
                            // aggregate object
50:                        hr = piIADs->GetInfoEx( varAttrNames, 0 );
51:
52:                        if( SUCCEEDED( hr ) )
53:                        {
54:                            // Dump the property cache
55:                            // (should be only one item)
56:                            IADsPropertyList* piPropertyList = NULL;
57:                            hr = piIADs->QueryInterface(
                                ➥IID_IADsPropertyList, ( void** )
                                ➥&piPropertyList );
58:                            if( SUCCEEDED( hr ) )
59:                            {
60:                                long lCount = 0;
61:
```

```
62:                              // get the count of entries in
                                 // the property cache
63:                              ( void )piPropertyList->
                              ➥get_PropertyCount( &lCount );
64:                              for( int nProp = 0; nProp <
                              ➥lCount; nProp++ )
65:                              {
66:                                  _variant_t varAttr;
67:                                  ( void )piPropertyList->
                                  ➥Next( &varAttr );
68:
69:                                  IADsPropertyEntry* piEntry =
                                  ➥NULL;
70:
71:                                  // get an IADsPropertyEntry
72:                                  // interface for the property
73:                                  hr = (( IDispatch* )varAttr)->
                                  ➥QueryInterface( IID
                                  ➥_IADsPropertyEntry,
                                  ➥( void** )&piEntry );
74:                                  if( SUCCEEDED( hr ) )
75:                                  {
76:                                      BSTR strAttrName;
77:
78:                                      piEntry->get_Name
                                      ➥( &strAttrName );
79:                                      printf( "%s\n",
                                      ➥( const char* )_bstr_t
                                      ➥( strAttrName ) );
80:
81:                                      piEntry->Release();
82:                                  }
83:                              }
84:
85:                              piPropertyList->Release();
86:                          }
87:
88:                          // Get the short name of the domain NC,
                             // no additional traffic
89:                          _variant_t varName;
90:                          hr = piIADs->Get( L"name", &varName );
91:                          if( SUCCEEDED( hr ) )
92:                          {
93:                              printf( "NC name is: %s\n",
                              ➥( const char* )
                              ➥_bstr_t( varName ) );
94:                          }
95:                      }
96:                  }
97:              }
98:
```

continues

LISTING 12.4   CONTINUED

```
 99:                    piIADs->Release();
100:                }
101:            }
102:
103:            ( void )CoUninitialize();
104:        }
105:
106:        return 0;
107: }
```

The program in Listing 12.4 starts by calling CoInitialize() at line 8 and ADsOpenObject() for the rootDSE at line 14. The program then retrieves the defaultNamingContext attribute from the rootDSE. At line 34, the program binds to the domain naming context object using ADsGetObject().

Next the program creates a VARIANT array of strings using the ADsBuildVarArrayStr() function. This array contains the name of a single attribute, "name".

The program then calls GetInfoEx() at line 50, passing the VARIANT array of attribute names. If this succeeds, the program prints the entire contents of the property cache using the IADsPropertyList interface. There will be only one entry in the property cache, corresponding to the "name" attribute.

At line 90, the program calls the Get() function to retrieve the value of the "name" attribute. This call to Get() will not generate any additional network traffic, because the "name" attribute is already in the property cache.

The program then releases all the interface pointers, and it closes up shop by calling CoUninitialize() at line 103.

> **CAUTION**
>
> GetInfoEx() is not implemented for rootDSE.

Note that Listing 12.4 uses the ADSI helper function ADsBuildVarArrayStr(). This function creates a VARIANT array of BSTRs from a C++ array of Unicode strings. ADsBuildVarArrayStr() greatly simplifies the task of building a VARIANT array.

```
HRESULT ADsBuildVarArrayStr( LPWSTR* ppszStrings, DWORD dwStringCount,
                        ➥VARIANT* pvarArray )
```

ppszStrings is the address of an array of NUL-terminated Unicode strings that will be added to the VARIANT array.

dwStringCount is the number of entries in the ppszStrings array.

pvarArray is the address of a VARIANT in which the array will be constructed.

Returns: A COM error code indicating success or failure. Check the result using one of the COM error code macros described in Chapter 11.

Using IADs::Put() to Change a Single-Valued Attribute

When you need to change an attribute in the property cache, you use the IADs::Put() function. Put() takes an attribute name and a VARIANT containing the new value of the attribute, and updates the attribute in the property cache. When you want to update the directory object, you have to call IADs::SetInfo().

The IADs::Put() function allows you to replace only the entire attribute; it does not provide for appending new values to the existing attribute or for removing existing values. To manipulate the values in an attribute, you have to use the IADs::PutEx() function, which I describe in the next section.

The program in Listing 12.5 shows how to change a single attribute of a user object—in this case, the givenName attribute that contains the user's first name.

LISTING 12.5 USING THE IADs::Put() FUNCTION TO CHANGE A SINGLE-VALUED ATTRIBUTE

```
 1: #include <windows.h>
 2: #include <activeds.h>
 3: #include <comutil.h>
 4: #include <stdio.h>
 5:
 6: int main(int argc, char* argv[])
 7: {
 8:   HRESULT hr = CoInitialize( NULL );
 9:
10:   if( SUCCEEDED( hr ) )
11:   {
12:     IADs* piIADs = NULL;
13:
14:     hr = ADsGetObject( L"LDAP://rootDSE", IID_IADs,
15:         ( void** )&piIADs );
16:     if( SUCCEEDED( hr ) )
17:     {
18:       _variant_t varDomainNC;
19:
20:       hr = piIADs->Get( L"defaultNamingContext", &varDomainNC );
```

continues

12

BASIC ACTIVE
DIRECTORY
INTERFACES

LISTING 12.5 CONTINUED

```
21:        if( SUCCEEDED( hr ) )
22:        {
23:          piIADs->Release();
24:
25:          // Bind to the Administrator user in the domain NC
26:          hr = ADsGetObject( _bstr_t( "LDAP://" ) +
27:                             _bstr_t( L"CN=Administrator,CN=Users," ) +
28:                             _bstr_t( varDomainNC ),
29:                             IID_IADs,
30:                             ( void** )&piIADs
31:                  );
32:
33:          if( SUCCEEDED( hr ) )
34:          {
35:            // Change the givenName attribute of the Administrator
36:            hr = piIADs->Put( L"givenName",
37:                              _variant_t( L"First name" ) );
38:            if( SUCCEEDED( hr ) )
39:            {
40:              // Flush changes to the directory
41:              piIADs->SetInfo();
42:            }
43:          }
44:        }
45:
46:        piIADs->Release();
47:      }
48:
49:      ( void )CoUninitialize();
50:    }
51:
52:    return 0;
53: }
```

The program in Listing 12.5 starts out in the usual way by getting the
defaultNamingContext attribute from the rootDSE of a domain controller in the current
user's domain.

At line 26, the program composes the distinguished name of the Administrator in the
domain and then binds to the user object, retrieving an IADs interface pointer in the
process.

At line 36, the program sets the givenName attribute of the Administrator's user object
to "First name". The Put() function changes only the attribute value in the property
cache.

The program calls SetInfo() to flush the change to the directory at line 41.

Finally, the program releases the interface pointer to the user object at line 46 and calls `CoUninitialize()` at line 49 to shut down the COM subsystem.

Using `IADs::Put()` to Change a Multivalued Attribute

You can use the `IADs::Put()` function to update a multivalued attribute as well. Instead of passing a single `VARIANT` value as the second parameter to `IADs::Put()`, you should pass a `VARIANT` array of values. You can build the array using `ADsBuildVarArrayStr()` as we did in the earlier example.

One thing to note about using `IADs::Put()` to save multivalued attributes: All you can do is overwrite the entire attribute. `IADs::Put()` does not provide a way to remove values from or append values to an attribute. If you want to manipulate the values of the attribute directly, you must either get and set the individual elements of the `VARIANT` array by using the `SafeArray...()` functions and then using `IADs::Put()`, or you can use the `IADs::PutEx()` function (described in the next section) to manipulate the individual values in the property cache. One more thing to note: If you want to remove an entire attribute from a directory object, you must use `IADs::PutEx()`. You can't just replace the attribute with an empty array by using `IADs::Put()`.

12

BASIC ACTIVE DIRECTORY INTERFACES

> **CAUTION**
>
> The LDAP object model does not allow a multivalued attribute to contain more than one instance of a given value. For instance, a multivalued integer directory attribute could contain the values 1, 7, and 10, but it could not contain the values 1, 7, and 1.
>
> If you attempt to add or modify an attribute such that it will contain duplicate values, the operation will fail and no modification will occur.

The following code snippet shows how you can use the `IADs::Put()` function to update a multivalued attribute. In this case, the code updates the `accountNameHistory` attribute of the `Administrator` user in the `megacorp.com` domain. This code overwrites the existing value of the `accountNameHistory` attribute with the new values `"name1"` and `"name2"`.

```
1: IADs* piIADs = NULL;
2:
3: hr = ADsGetObject(
4:        L"CN=Administrator,CN=Users,DC=megacorp,DC=com",
5:        IID_IADs, ( void** )&piIADs );
6: if( SUCCEEDED( hr ) )
7: {
```

```
 8:    _variant_t varNames;
 9:    LPWSTR apszNames[] = { L"name1", L"name2" };
10:
11:    ( void )ADsBuildVarArrayStr( apszNames,
12:            sizeof( apszNames ) / sizeof( apszNames[ 0 ] ),
13:            &varNames );
14:    hr = piIADs->Put( L"accountNameHistory", varNames );
15:    if( SUCCEEDED( hr ) )
16:    {
17:      hr = piIADs->SetInfo();
18:    }
19:
20:    piIADs->Release();
21: }
```

A Note on Constraint Violation Errors from `IADs::SetInfo()`

A common error to get from the `IADs::SetInfo()` function is `0x8007202F`, which indicates a constraint violation. A *constraint violation* is an error that occurs because you attempted to violate some structure rule in the directory. Active Directory will return this error if you attempt to store multiple values in an attribute defined as being single-valued. (`isSingleValued` is `TRUE` in the `attributeSchema` object.) You will also get this error if you try to create an object in a container that is not allowed to contain that class of object. A host of other conditions can also lead to a constraint violation error.

If you get a constraint violation error from `IADs::SetInfo()`, make sure you are not violating any structural rules by checking all the attributes you are trying to update.

Using `IADs::PutEx()` to Append to a Multivalued Attribute

Normally, you don't want to completely overwrite a multivalued attribute with a whole set of new values. You usually want to add new values to an existing multivalued attribute or remove or modify existing values of a multivalued attribute. You can perform these tasks with the `IADs::PutEx()` function.

The `IADs::PutEx()` gives you fine-grained control over the values in a multivalued attribute. `IADs::PutEx()` lets you append new values to an existing attribute, remove individual values from an existing attribute, and replace the entire attribute with a new set of values. You can also use `IADs::PutEx()` to delete the entire attribute from the directory object.

```
HRESULT IADs::PutEx( LONG lControlCode, BSTR strAttributeName,
                     ➥VARIANT varValue )
```

lControlCode is a value from the ADS_PROPERTY_OPERATION_ENUM enumeration, described in Table 12.2.

strAttributeName is the name of the attribute in the property cache to modify.varValue is a VARIANT array of the values to append to the attribute (ADS_PROPERTY_APPEND), the values to remove from the attribute (ADS_PROPERTY_DELETE), or the new values of the entire attribute (ADS_PROPERTY_UPDATE).

TABLE 12.2   THE ADS_PROPERTY_OPERATION_ENUM ENUMERATION

Name	*Value*	*Description*
ADS_PROPERTY_CLEAR	1	Deletes the named attribute entirely from the property cache.
ADS_PROPERTY_UPDATE	2	Replaces the named attribute in the property cache with the given value or creates a new attribute in the property cache if one does not exist.
ADS_PROPERTY_APPEND	3	Appends the given value to the existing attribute in the property cache or creates a new attribute in the property cache if one does not exist.
ADS_PROPERTY_DELETE	4	Removes the given value from the attribute in the property cache if the value already exists.

The sample program in Listing 12.6 shows how you can use IADs::PutEx() to append new values to an existing attribute (or create a new attribute if it does not already exist). This sample program adds two new names to the accountNameHistory attribute of the Administrator user object.

LISTING 12.6   USING THE IADs::PutEx() FUNCTION TO APPEND A VALUE TO A MULTIVALUED ATTRIBUTE

```
1: #include <windows.h>
2: #include <activeds.h>
3: #include <comutil.h>
4: #include <stdio.h>
5:
6: int main(int argc, char* argv[])
7: {
8:   HRESULT hr = CoInitialize( NULL );
9:
10:   if( SUCCEEDED( hr ) )
11:   {
```

continues

12

BASIC ACTIVE
DIRECTORY
INTERFACES

LISTING 12.6 CONTINUED

```
12:     IADs* piIADs = NULL;
13:
14:     hr = ADsGetObject( L"LDAP://rootDSE", IID_IADs,
15:                      ( void** )&piIADs );
16:     if( SUCCEEDED( hr ) )
17:     {
18:       _variant_t varDomainNC;
19:
20:       hr = piIADs->Get( L"defaultNamingContext", &varDomainNC );
21:       if( SUCCEEDED( hr ) )
22:       {
23:         piIADs->Release();
24:
25:         // Bind to the Administrator user in the domain NC
26:         hr = ADsGetObject( _bstr_t( "LDAP://" ) +
27:                 _bstr_t( L"CN=Administrator,CN=Users," ) +
28:                 _bstr_t( varDomainNC ), IID_IADs,
29:                 ( void** )&piIADs
30:                 );
31:
32:         if( SUCCEEDED( hr ) )
33:         {
34:           LPWSTR apszNewNames[] =
35:             { L"another name", L"yet another name" };
36:           _variant_t varNames;
37:
38:           ADsBuildVarArrayStr( apszNewNames,
39:             sizeof( apszNewNames ) / sizeof( apszNewNames[ 0 ] ),
40:             &varNames );
41:
42:           hr = piIADs->PutEx( ADS_PROPERTY_APPEND,
43:                   L"accountNameHistory", varNames );
44:           if( SUCCEEDED( hr ) )
45:           {
46:             hr = piIADs->SetInfo();
47:             if( ! SUCCEEDED( hr ) )
48:             {
49:               printf( "Error %s from SetInfo()\n", hr );
50:             }
51:           }
52:         }
53:       }
54:
55:       piIADs->Release();
56:     }
57:
58:     ( void )CoUninitialize();
59:   }
60:
61:   return 0;
62: }
```

The program in Listing 12.6 starts the same way as the preceding program does—by getting the domain naming context name from the rootDSE (lines 14–20) and then composing the Administrator's `ADsPath` and binding to the Administrator's user object at line 26.

At line 34, the program declares an array of wide-character strings containing the new names to add to the Administrator's `accountNameHistory` attribute.

The program creates a `VARIANT` array from the `apszNewNames` array at line 38 by calling `ADsBuildVarArrayStr()`.

At line 42, the program calls `IADs::PutEx()` to append the two new values to the `accountNameHistory` attribute. At line 46, the program updates the directory from the property cache. If there is an error updating the directory, the program prints the error at line 49.

The program then releases the interface pointer at line 55 and shuts down the COM subsystem at line 58.

Using `IADs::PutEx()` to Remove Values from a Multivalued Attribute

You can also use the `IADs::PutEx()` function to remove values from an existing attribute. In this case, you create a `VARIANT` array containing the values you want to delete and pass `ADS_PROPERTY_DELETE` for the control code parameter to `IADs::PutEx()`.

> **NOTE**
>
> If you use the `IADs::PutEx()` function with the `ADS_PROPERTY_DELETE` control code to delete all the values of an attribute, ADSI will remove the entire attribute from the directory object when you call `IADs::SetInfo()`.

The sample program in Listing 12.7 shows how to use `IADSs::PutEx()` to delete individual values from an existing attribute. The program removes the value `"another name"` from the `accountNameHistory` attribute of the `Administrator` user object.

LISTING 12.7 USING THE `IADs::PutEx()` FUNCTION TO REMOVE A VALUE FROM A MULTIVALUED ATTRIBUTE

```
1: #include <windows.h>
2: #include <activeds.h>
3: #include <comutil.h>
```

continues

LISTING 12.7 CONTINUED

```c
 4: #include <stdio.h>
 5:
 6: int main(int argc, char* argv[])
 7: {
 8:   HRESULT hr = CoInitialize( NULL );
 9:
10:   if( SUCCEEDED( hr ) )
11:   {
12:     IADs* piIADs = NULL;
13:
14:     hr = ADsGetObject( L"LDAP://rootDSE",
15:             IID_IADs, ( void** )&piIADs );
16:     if( SUCCEEDED( hr ) )
17:     {
18:       _variant_t varDomainNC;
19:
20:       hr = piIADs->Get( L"defaultNamingContext", &varDomainNC );
21:       if( SUCCEEDED( hr ) )
22:       {
23:         piIADs->Release();
24:
25:         // Bind to the Administrator user in the domain NC
26:         hr = ADsGetObject( _bstr_t( "LDAP://" ) + _
27:               _bstr_t( L"CN=Administrator,CN=Users," ) + _
28:               _bstr_t( varDomainNC ),
29:               IID_IADs,
30:               ( void** )&piIADs
31:             );
32:
33:         if( SUCCEEDED( hr ) )
34:         {
35:           LPWSTR apszDelNames[] = { L"another name" };
36:           _variant_t varDelNames;
37:
38:           ADsBuildVarArrayStr( apszDelNames,
39:             sizeof( apszDelNames ) / sizeof( apszDelNames[ 0 ] ),
40:             &varDelNames );
41:
42:           hr = piIADs->PutEx( ADS_PROPERTY_DELETE,
43:                 L"accountNameHistory", varDelNames );
44:           if( SUCCEEDED( hr ) )
45:           {
46:             hr = piIADs->SetInfo();
47:             if( ! SUCCEEDED( hr ) )
48:             {
49:               printf( "Error %s from SetInfo()\n", hr );
50:             }
51:           }
52:         }
```

```
53:        }
54:
55:        piIADs->Release();
56:    }
57:
58:    ( void )CoUninitialize();
59: }
60:
61:    return 0;
62: }
```

The program in Listing 12.7 is essentially identical to the preceding sample program. It gets the domain naming context name from the rootDSE and binds to the Administrator user object at line 26.

At line 35, the program declares an array of name values to delete. In this case, the array contains only one element.

At line 38, the sample program builds a VARIANT array of BSTRs from the array declared at line 33, and the program then calls IADs::PutEx with the ADS_PROPERTY_DELETE control code at line 42.

The program commits the changes to the directory at line 46 by calling IADs::SetInfo(), and finishes up by releasing the interface pointer at line 55 and shutting down the COM subsystem at line 58.

Using IADs::PutEx() to Delete an Entire Attribute

The last capability of the IADs:PutEx() function I'll describe here is the ability to remove an entire attribute from an object. To remove an entire attribute, you have to call IADs::PutEx() with the ADS_PROPERTY_CLEAR control code. In this case, you do not need to specify any particular value for the varValue parameter; an empty VARIANT will do just fine.

The program in Listing 12.8 uses the IADs::PutEx() function and the ADS_PROPERTY_CLEAR control code to delete the accountNameHistory attribute of the Administrator user object.

LISTING 12.8 USING THE IADs::PutEx() FUNCTION TO REMOVE AN ATTRIBUTE

```
1: #include <windows.h>
2: #include <activeds.h>
3: #include <comutil.h>
4: #include <stdio.h>
5:
```

continues

LISTING 12.8   CONTINUED

```
 6: int main(int argc, char* argv[])
 7: {
 8:   HRESULT hr = CoInitialize( NULL );
 9:
10:   if( SUCCEEDED( hr ) )
11:   {
12:     IADs* piIADs = NULL;
13:
14:     hr = ADsGetObject( L"LDAP://rootDSE", IID_IADs,
15:           ( void** )&piIADs );
16:     if( SUCCEEDED( hr ) )
17:     {
18:       _variant_t varDomainNC;
19:
20:       hr = piIADs->Get( L"defaultNamingContext", &varDomainNC );
21:       if( SUCCEEDED( hr ) )
22:       {
23:         piIADs->Release();
24:
25:         // Bind to the Administrator user in the domain NC
26:         hr = ADsGetObject( _bstr_t( "LDAP://" ) + _
27:               _bstr_t( L"CN=Administrator,CN=Users," ) + _
28:               _bstr_t( varDomainNC ),
29:               IID_IADs,
30:               ( void** )&piIADs
31:             );
32:
33:         if( SUCCEEDED( hr ) )
34:         {
35:           _variant_t varDummy;
36:
37:           hr = piIADs->PutEx( ADS_PROPERTY_CLEAR,
38:                 L"accountNameHistory", varDummy );
39:           if( SUCCEEDED( hr ) )
40:           {
41:             hr = piIADs->SetInfo();
42:             if( ! SUCCEEDED( hr ) )
43:             {
44:               printf( "Error %s from SetInfo()\n", hr );
45:             }
46:           }
47:         }
48:       }
49:
50:       piIADs->Release();
51:     }
52:
53:     ( void )CoUninitialize();
```

```
54:    }
55:
56:    return 0;
57: }
```

The program in Listing 12.8 is again very similar to the programs in Listings 12.6 and 12.7. It binds to the `rootDSE` at line 14 to get the domain naming context and then binds to the `Administrator` user object in that domain at line 26.

At line 35, the program declares an empty `VARIANT` to pass to `IADs::PutEx()`. At line 37, the program calls `IADs::PutEx()` using the `ADS_PROPERTY_CLEAR` control code and the dummy `VARIANT`.

The program commits the change to the directory at line 41, releases the interface pointer at line 50, and shuts down the COM subsystem at line 53.

The `IADsPropertyList` Interface

The `IADsPropertyList` interface provides a way for you to treat a directory object as an arbitrary collection of attributes. This is particularly useful when you are writing a program such as a directory browser where you won't know *a priori* the names of all the attributes an object has.

The `IADsPropertyList` is an automation (`IDispatch`) interface that provides functions to count the number of properties an object has and to enumerate through the properties of an object.

The `IADsPropertyList` interface shares the property cache with the `IADs` interface, so changes you make with `IADs::Put()` (for instance) will be visible to the `IADsPropertyList` interface.

Several functions in the `IADsPropertyList` interface—for instance, `Item()`, `GetPropertyItem()`, and `PutPropertyItem()`—let you refer to a property in the property cache by attribute name or by index value in the cache.

In general, the functions in the `IADsPropertyList` interface return `VARIANT`s that contain `IDispatch` pointers to `IADsPropertyEntry` objects. The `IADsPropertyEntry` interface provides functions for inspecting the name of an attribute and all its values. I discuss the `IADsPropertyEntry` interface later in this chapter.

Because the `IADsPropertyList` interface deals only with the property cache, you must be sure to call the `IADs::SetInfo()` function after you make any changes to the attribute values in the property cache.

Table 12.3 details the IADsPropertyList interface.

TABLE 12.3 THE IADsPropertyList INTERFACE

Function Name	Description
QueryInterface()	IUnknown interface.
AddRef()	IUnknown interface.
Release()	IUnknown interface.
GetTypeInfoCount()	IDispatch interface.
GetTypeInfo()	IDispatch interface.
GetIDsOfNames()	IDispatch interface.
Invoke()	IDispatch interface.
get_PropertyCount()	Returns the number of properties in this object's property cache.
Next()	Retrieves the next property in the property cache as a VARIANT.
Skip()	Skips over the next property in the property cache.
Reset()	Resets the enumeration of properties so that a subsequent call to Next() will retrieve the first property in the property cache.
Item()	Retrieves a property from the property cache by attribute name or by index number in the cache.
GetPropertyItem()	Retrieves a property from the property cache by attribute name.
PutPropertyItem()	Stores a property entry in the property cache.
ResetPropertyItem()	Removes a property entry from the property cache.
PurgePropertyList()	Clears out the entire property cache.

Enumerating an Object's Attributes

The sample program shown in Listing 12.9 demonstrates how to get the rootDSE entry from the directory and display all its attributes, without knowing ahead of time what attributes it actually has. The program uses the IADsPropertyList interface to enumerate all the properties of rootDSE.

The program uses two methods to enumerate the attributes of rootDSE. First, it uses the IADsPropertyList::Next() function to walk through all the entries in the list. After the program has enumerated the attributes of rootDSE in this way, it gets the count of attributes in rootDSE and references them by using the IADsPropertyList::Item() function with a numeric index.

The sample program then uses IADsPropertyList::Item() with an attribute name (instead of a number) to retrieve the defaultNamingContext attribute. This shows how you can specify an entry in the property cache either by its index number or its attribute name.

The function DisplayAttr() at the end of the sample program uses the IADsPropertyEntry and IADsPropertyValue interfaces to get the individual values of each attribute and print them. I describe these interfaces later in this chapter.

LISTING 12.9 USING THE IADsPropertyList INTERFACE TO DISPLAY THE ATTRIBUTES OF rootDSE

```
 1: #include <windows.h>
 2: #include <activeds.h>
 3: #include <comutil.h>
 4: #include <stdio.h>
 5:
 6: void DisplayAttr( _variant_t& varAttr );
 7:
 8: int main(int argc, char* argv[])
 9: {
10:   HRESULT hr = CoInitialize( NULL );
11:
12:   if( SUCCEEDED( hr ) )
13:   {
14:     IADs* piRootDSE = NULL;
15:
16:     hr = ADsGetObject( L"LDAP://rootDSE",
17:             IID_IADs, ( void** )&piRootDSE );
18:     if( SUCCEEDED( hr ) )
19:     {
20:       piRootDSE->GetInfo();
21:
22:       IADsPropertyList* piPropList = NULL;
23:
24:       // Get the property list interface for rootDSE
25:       hr = piRootDSE->QueryInterface( IID_IADsPropertyList,
26:             ( void** )&piPropList );
27:       if( SUCCEEDED( hr ) )
28:       {
29:         // Enumerate the attributes in the property cache
30:         // using  Next()
31:         _variant_t varAttr;
32:         while( piPropList->Next( &varAttr ) == S_OK )
33:         {
34:           DisplayAttr( varAttr );
35:         }
36:
37:         long lCount;
38:
```

continues

LISTING 12.9   CONTINUED

```
39:            // Enumerate the attributes in the property cache by
40:            // number using the Item() function
41:            hr = piPropList->get_PropertyCount( &lCount );
42:            if( SUCCEEDED( hr ) )
43:            {
44:              for( int nAttr = 0; nAttr < lCount; nAttr++ )
45:              {
46:                hr = piPropList->Item( _variant_t( ( long )nAttr ),
47:                      &varAttr );
48:                if( SUCCEEDED( hr ) )
49:                {
50:                  DisplayAttr( varAttr );
51:                }
52:              }
53:            }
54:
55:            // Get an attribute from the property cache by name using
56:            // the Item() function
57:            hr =
58:              piPropList->Item(_variant_t(L"defaultNamingContext"),
59:                &varAttr );
60:            if( SUCCEEDED( hr ) )
61:            {
62:              DisplayAttr( varAttr );
63:            }
64:
65:            piPropList->Release();
66:          }
67:
68:          piRootDSE->Release();
69:        }
70:
71:      ( void )CoUninitialize();
72:    }
73:
74:    return 0;
75: }
76:
77: void DisplayAttr( _variant_t& varAttr )
78: {
79:    IADsPropertyEntry* piEntry = NULL;
80:
81:    HRESULT hr = (( IDispatch* )varAttr)->QueryInterface(
82:                  IID_IADsPropertyEntry, ( void** )&piEntry );
83:    if( SUCCEEDED( hr ) )
84:    {
85:      BSTR strAttrName;
86:
87:      piEntry->get_Name( &strAttrName );
88:
89:      printf( "%s\n", ( const char* )_bstr_t( strAttrName ) );
```

```
90:
91:     _variant_t varValues;
92:
93:     // Get the entry values as a VARIANT array
94:     piEntry->get_Values( &varValues );
95:
96:     // Make a SAFEARRAY from the values
97:     SAFEARRAY* aVals = V_ARRAY( &varValues );
98:     if( aVals != NULL )
99:     {
100:      long lLBound = 0;
101:      long lUBound = 0;
102:
103:      // Get the range of the array
104:      ( void )SafeArrayGetLBound( aVals, 1, &lLBound );
105:      ( void )SafeArrayGetUBound( aVals, 1, &lUBound );
106:
107:      // For each entry in the array
108:      for( long lIndex = lLBound; lIndex <= lUBound; lIndex++ )
109:      {
110:        _variant_t varVal;
111:
112:        // varVal is another IDispatch pointer that we
113:        // can change to a IADsPropertyValue
114:        hr = SafeArrayGetElement( aVals, &lIndex, &varVal );
115:        if( SUCCEEDED( hr ) )
116:        {
117:          IADsPropertyValue* piPropValue;
118:
119:          // Get the IADsPropertyValue interface pointer
120:          hr = (( IDispatch* )varVal)->QueryInterface(
121:                  IID_IADsPropertyValue, ( void** )&piPropValue );
122:          if( SUCCEEDED( hr ) )
123:          {
124:            BSTR strValue;
125:
126:            // print the string
127:            hr = piPropValue->get_CaseIgnoreString( &strValue );
128:            if( SUCCEEDED( hr ) )
129:            {
130:              printf( "\t%s\n",
131:                ( const char* ) _bstr_t( strValue ) );
132:            }
133:            piPropValue->Release();
134:          }
135:        }
136:      }
137:    }
138:
139:    piEntry->Release();
140:  }
141: }
```

12

BASIC ACTIVE
DIRECTORY
INTERFACES

The sample program in Listing 12.9 starts by binding to the rootDSE of a domain controller in the currently logged-in user's domain at line 16.

At line 20, the program loads the property cache for rootDSE by calling GetInfo().

At line 25, the program gets an IADsPropertyList interface to rootDSE.

At lines 32–35, the program uses the IADsPropertyList::Next() function to iterate through the list of attributes in rootDSE. For each attribute, the program calls the DisplayAttr() function.

The program gets the count of attributes in the cache at line 41. With the for loop starting at line 44, the program enumerates all the attributes in the cache by referring to them by index using the IADsPropertyList::Item() function.

At line 58, the sample program uses the IADsPropertyList::Item() function again, but this time instead of using a numeric index, it refers to the attribute by name.

The function DisplayAttr() starts at line 77. It accepts a VARIANT containing an IDispatch interface pointer to a property cache entry.

At line 81, DisplayAttr() gets an IADsPropertyEntry interface to the property entry and then calls get_Name() to retrieve the name of the attribute contained in that entry.

At line 97, DisplayAttrs() converts the returned VARIANT into a SAFEARRAY. It gets the upper and lower bounds of the array at lines 104 and 105. This array contains one entry for each attribute value in the property cache entry.

The for loop that starts at line 108 iterates through all the values in the SAFEARRAY. The call to SafeArrayGetElement() returns the array element as a VARIANT.

At line 120, DisplayAttrs() gets an IADsPropertyValue interface pointer to a particular value. It gets the value as a case-insensitive string at line 127.

DisplayAttrs() finally prints the individual value at line 130, after which DisplayAttrs() releases its interface pointers and returns to the main routine.

The program releases its interface pointers and otherwise cleans up starting at line 65.

The **IADsPropertyEntry** Interface

Each attribute of a directory object is represented by a property cache entry. Each property cache entry has an attribute name, a type, a control code indicating what operation to execute when ADSI updates the directory from the cache, and multiple values containing the values of the directory attribute. You use the IADsPropertyEntry interface to manipulate property cache entries. Table 12.4 describes the IADsPropertyEntry interface.

TABLE 12.4 THE IADsPropertyEntry INTERFACE

Function Name	*Description*
QueryInterface()	IUnknown interface.
AddRef()	IUnknown interface.
Release()	IUnknown interface.
GetTypeInfoCount()	IDispatch interface.
GetTypeInfo()	IDispatch interface.
GetIDsOfNames()	IDispatch interface.
Invoke()	IDispatch interface.
get_Name()	Retrieves the attribute name of this property cache entry.
put_Name()	Changes the attribute name of this property cache entry.
get_ADsType()	Retrieves the ADsType of this property cache entry.
put_ADsType()	Changes the ADsType of this property cache entry.
get_ControlCode()	Retrieves the control code of this property cache entry. The control code is one of the values in the ADS_PROPERTY_OPERATION_ENUM enumeration described in Table 12.2.
put_ControlCode()	Changes the control code of this property cache entry. The new value is one of the values in the ADS_PROPERTY_OPERATION_ENUM enumeration described in Table 12.2.
get_Values()	Retrieves the values of the property cache entry as a VARIANT array.
put_Values()	Stores the VARIANT array in the property cache entry, replacing the existing set of values.

12

BASIC ACTIVE
DIRECTORY
INTERFACES

The sample program in Listing 12.9 shows how to get an IADsPropertyEntry interface pointer from the IADsPropertyList interface, and how to invoke the IADsPropertyEntry::get_Name() and IADsPropertyEntry::get_Values() functions.

The IADsPropertyValue Interface

The sample program in Listing 12.9 shows how to get an IADsPropertyValue interface pointer from the IADsPropertyEntry interface. It also shows how to invoke the IADsPropertyEntry::get_CaseIgnoreString() function to get an attribute value.

Table 12.5 provides a detailed list of the IADsPropertyValue interface.

TABLE 12.5 THE `IADsPropertyValue` INTERFACE

Function Name	*Description*
QueryInterface()	IUnknown interface.
AddRef()	IUnknown interface.
Release()	IUnknown interface.
GetTypeInfoCount()	IDispatch interface.
GetTypeInfo()	IDispatch interface.
GetIDsOfNames()	IDispatch interface.
Invoke()	IDispatch interface.
Clear()	IDispatch interface.
get_ADsType()	Gets the ADSTYPE of the value.
put_ADsType()	Sets the ADSTYPE of the value.
get_DNString()	Gets the value as a distinguished name string.
put_DNString()	Sets the value from a distinguished name string.
get_CaseExactString()	Gets the value as a case-sensitive Unicode string.
put_CaseExactString()	Sets the value from a case-sensitive Unicode string.
get_CaseIgnoreString()	Gets the value as a case-insensitive Unicode string.
put_CaseIgnoreString()	Sets the value from a case-insensitive Unicode string.
get_PrintableString()	Gets the value as a string containing printable Unicode characters.
put_PrintableString()	Sets the value from a string containing printable Unicode characters.
get_NumericString()	Gets the value as a string containing numeric characters.
put_NumericString()	Sets the value from a string containing numeric Unicode characters.
get_Boolean()	Gets the value as a Boolean. 1 = TRUE and 0 = FALSE.
put_Boolean()	Sets the value from a Boolean.
get_Integer()	Gets the value as a 32-bit integer.
put_Integer()	Sets the value from a 32-bit integer.
get_OctetString()	Gets the value as an arbitrary collection of bytes.
put_OctetString()	Sets the value from an arbitrary collection of bytes.
get_SecurityDescriptor()	Gets the value as a Windows NT security descriptor.
put_SecurityDescriptor()	Sets the value from a Windows NT security descriptor.
get_LargeInteger()	Gets the value as a 64-bit integer.
put_LargeInteger()	Sets the value from a 64-bit integer.
get_UTCTime()	Gets the value as a SYSTEMTIME structure.
put_UTCTime()	Sets the value from a SYSTEMTIME structure.

The `IADsPropertyValue2` Interface

The `IADsPropertyValue2` interface is an alternative form of the `IADsPropertyValue` interface. Instead of providing separate `get_...()` and `set_...()` functions for each possible data type, `IADsPropertyValue2` provides one function to get the value and one function to set the value. Each function accepts an `ADSTYPE` value to indicate the type of the value.

Table 12.6 provides a detailed list of the `IADsPropertyValue2` interface.

TABLE 12.6 THE `IADsPropertyValue2` INTERFACE

Function Name	Description
`QueryInterface()`	IUnknown interface.
`AddRef()`	IUnknown interface.
`Release()`	IUnknown interface.
`GetTypeInfoCount()`	IDispatch interface.
`GetTypeInfo()`	IDispatch interface.
`GetIDsOfNames()`	IDispatch interface.
`Invoke()`	IDispatch interface.
`GetObjectProperty()`	Retrieves the attribute value as a particular type.
`PutObjectProperty()`	Stores the attribute value as a particular type.

The `IDirectoryObject` Interface

The `IDirectoryObject` interface provides the same sorts of services as the `IADs` interface, but without the benefit (or complexity, depending on your point of view) of the property cache. `IDirectoryObject` is an IUnknown-type (nonautomation) interface, so it does not have the additional `IDispatch` interface functions.

`IDirectoryObject` also does not use the COM `VARIANT` and `BSTR` types to contain directory object attributes. Instead, `IDirectoryObject` uses a structure called `ADSTYPE` that is very similar to a `VARIANT`. I describe this structure a little later in this section.

The `IDirectoryObject` interface provides functions for getting and setting the attributes of an object, and for creating and deleting directory objects. Table 12.7 lists the functions that make up the `IDirectoryObject` interface.

TABLE 12.7 THE IDirectoryObject INTERFACE

Function Name	*Description*
QueryInterface()	IUnknown interface.
AddRef()	IUnknown interface.
Release()	IUnknown interface.
GetObjectInformation()	Retrieves an ADS_OBJECT_INFO structure for the object containing the relative distinguished name of the object, the distinguished names of the object, the object's parent, the classSchema object, and the lDAPDisplayName of the object's class.
GetObjectAttributes()	Retrieves one or more attributes of the object.
SetObjectAttributes()	Sets new values for one or more attributes of the object.
CreateDSObject()	Creates a new object in the directory.
DeleteDSObject()	Deletes an object from the directory.

You can see that the IDirectoryObject interface is quite a bit simpler than the IADs interface described in the preceding section, but IDirectoryObject encompasses the same functionality.

> **CAUTION**
>
> The rootDSE does not support the IDirectoryObject interface. You must use the IADs interface when you access rootDSE.

Attributes and Values Using **IDirectoryObject**

When you get or set attributes using the IDirectoryObject interface, instead of using VARIANTs and BSTRs as with the IADs interface, you use the ADSVALUE data type. ADSVALUE is a structure that can contain an attribute value of any allowed directory type. Its definition is similar to that of a VARIANT, except that it is limited to the data types that Active Directory attributes can take on. The ADSVALUE structure contains a type tag indicating the type of value the structure contains, and a union of all the possible data types. The structure definition looks like this (it's taken from iads.h):

```
typedef struct _adsvalue
    {
    ADSTYPE dwType;
    union
        {
```

```
        ADS_DN_STRING DNString;
        ADS_CASE_EXACT_STRING CaseExactString;
        ADS_CASE_IGNORE_STRING CaseIgnoreString;
        ADS_PRINTABLE_STRING PrintableString;
        ADS_NUMERIC_STRING NumericString;
        ADS_BOOLEAN Boolean;
        ADS_INTEGER Integer;
        ADS_OCTET_STRING OctetString;
        ADS_UTC_TIME UTCTime;
        ADS_LARGE_INTEGER LargeInteger;
        ADS_OBJECT_CLASS ClassName;
        ADS_PROV_SPECIFIC ProviderSpecific;
        PADS_CASEIGNORE_LIST pCaseIgnoreList;
        PADS_OCTET_LIST pOctetList;
        PADS_PATH pPath;
        PADS_POSTALADDRESS pPostalAddress;
        ADS_TIMESTAMP Timestamp;
        ADS_BACKLINK BackLink;
        PADS_TYPEDNAME pTypedName;
        ADS_HOLD Hold;
        PADS_NETADDRESS pNetAddress;
        PADS_REPLICAPOINTER pReplicaPointer;
        PADS_FAXNUMBER pFaxNumber;
        ADS_EMAIL Email;
        ADS_NT_SECURITY_DESCRIPTOR SecurityDescriptor;
        };
    }   ADSVALUE;
```

The possible values for the dwType field of the ADSVALUE structure are given by the ADSTYPE enumeration. Table 12.8 lists the possible values and their meanings.

TABLE 12.8 POSSIBLE VALUES OF ADSTYPE

Name	*C++ Type*	*Description*
ADSTYPE_DN_STRING	LPWSTR	Distinguished name.
ADSTYPE_CASE_EXACT_STRING	LPWSTR	Unicode string. Case is significant.
ADSTYPE_CASE_IGNORE_STRING	LPWSTR	Unicode string. Case is not significant.
ADSTYPE_PRINTABLE_STRING	LPWSTR	Unicode string containing only printable characters.
ADSTYPE_NUMERIC_STRING	LPWSTR	Unicode string containing only numeric characters.
ADSTYPE_BOOLEAN	DWORD	Boolean value. 1 = TRUE and 0 = FALSE.

continues

TABLE 12.8 CONTINUED

Name	C++ Type	Description
ADSTYPE_INTEGER	DWORD	Unsigned 32-bit integer.
ADSTYPE_OCTET_STRING	struct	Arbitrary string of bytes.
ADSTYPE_UTC_TIME	SYSTEMTIME	Structure containing year, month, day, hour, minute, and second information.
ADSTYPE_LARGE_INTEGER	_int64	63-bit integer.
ADSTYPE_PROV_SPECIFIC	struct	Arbitrary collection of bytes.
ADSTYPE_OBJECT_CLASS	LPWSTR	Unicode string containing the name of an object class.
ADSTYPE_CASEIGNORE_LIST	struct	Linked list of Unicode strings.
ADSTYPE_OCTET_LIST	struct	Arbitrary collection of bytes.
ADSTYPE_PATH	LPWSTR	Unicode string containing an ADsPath.
ADSTYPE_POSTALADDRESS	struct	Structure containing six Unicode X.400 email addresses.
ADSTYPE_TIMESTAMP	struct	64-bit timestamp.
ADSTYPE_BACKLINK	struct	ID and name of another directory object.
ADSTYPE_TYPEDNAME	struct	Not used by Active Directory.
ADSTYPE_HOLD	struct	Not used by Active Directory.
ADSTYPE_NETADDRESS	struct	Network address.
ADSTYPE_REPLICAPOINTER	struct	Structure representing the replica of a naming context on some directory server.
ADSTYPE_FAXNUMBER	struct	Fax telephone number and associated configuration information.
ADSTYPE_EMAIL	struct	Email address.
ADSTYPE_NT_SECURITY_DESCRIPTOR	struct	Windows NT security descriptor.

The ADS_ATTR_INFO Structure

The IDirectoryObject::GetObjectAttributes() and
IDirectoryObject::SetObjectAttributes() functions both use the ADS_ATTR_INFO

structure to represent attribute values. The GetObjectAttributes() function returns an array of ADS_ATTR_INFO structures containing attributes retrieved from the directory. When you call SetObjectAttributes(), you must pass in an array of ADS_ATTR_INFO structure describing how you want to update the object in the directory.

The ADS_ATTR_INFO structure contains a pointer to an array of ADSVALUE structures that contain one or more attribute values. The IDirectoryObject functions don't distinguish between single-valued and multivalued attributes. IDirectoryObject treats all attributes as multivalued; single-valued attributes are treated as multivalued attributes with only one value.

The structure definition for ADS_ATTR_INFO (as defined in iads.h) follows:

```
typedef struct _ads_attr_info
    {
    LPWSTR pszAttrName;      // name of the attribute
    DWORD dwControlCode;     // used to indicate update or delete
    ADSTYPE dwADsType;       // type of value
    PADSVALUE pADsValues;    // pointer to array of ADSVALUE structures
    DWORD dwNumValues;       // number of values in the array
    } ADS_ATTR_INFO;
```

Table 12.9 describes the various fields of the ADS_ATTR_INFO structure.

TABLE 12.9   THE ADS_ATTR_INFO STRUCTURE

Name	C++ Type	Description
pszAttrName	LPWSTR	Unicode string containing the name of the attribute.
dwControlCode	DWORD	Flags indicating how SetObjectAttributes() should update the directory object with the attribute. Not used by GetObjectAttributes().
dwADsType	ADSTYPE	Indicates the type of value.
pADsValues	ADSVALUE*	Pointer to array of ADSVALUE structures containing the attribute's values.
dwNumValues	DWORD	Number of array elements in pADsValues.

The dwControlCode element of the ADS_ATTR_INFO structure indicates how SetObjectAttributes() should process the update operation. Table 12.10 shows the possible values and their meanings.

12

BASIC ACTIVE DIRECTORY INTERFACES

TABLE 12.10   dwControlCode FLAG VALUES

Name	Value	Description
ADS_ATTR_CLEAR	1	Causes the attribute named in the ADS_ATTR_INFO structure to be deleted.
ADS_ATTR_UPDATE	2	Causes the existing value of the attribute to be replaced by the values contained in the ADS_ATTR_INFO structure.
ADS_ATTR_APPEND	3	Causes the values contained in the ADS_ATTR_INFO structure to be appended to the attribute in the directory.
ADS_ATTR_DELETE	4	Causes the values contained in the ADS_ATTR_INFO structure to be removed from the attribute in the directory.

CAUTION

The LDAP object model does not allow a multivalued attribute to contain more than one instance of a given value. For instance, a multivalued integer directory attribute could contain the values 1, 7, and 10, but it could not contain the values 1, 7, and 1.

If you attempt to add or modify an attribute such that it will contain duplicate values, the operation will fail, and no modification will occur.

Retrieving Attributes Using IDirectoryObject::GetObjectAttributes()

The IDirectoryObject::GetObjectAttributes() function returns an array of ADS_ATTR_INFO structures to contain the attribute values you requested. The pszAttrName element points to a NUL-terminated string containing the name of the returned attribute.

```
HRESULT IDirectoryObject::GetObjectAttributes(
➥LPWSTR apszAttrNames[], DWORD dwNameCount,
➥ADS_ATTR_INFO** ppsAttrInfo,  DWORD* pdwAttrCount )
```

apszAttrNames is an array of NUL-terminated wide character strings containing the names of the attributes to return.

dwNameCount is a DWORD containing the number of attribute names in apszAttrNames.

ppsAttrInfo is the address of a pointer to an ADS_ATTR_INFO structure. Upon successful return, it is set to point to an array of ADS_ATTR_INFO structures. You should free the memory associated with this array by passing *ppsAttrInfo to ADsMemFree().

pdwAttrCount is the address of a DWORD that is set to the number of returned entries in the ppsAttrInfo array.

Returns: An ADSI or COM error code. Check the result with one of the COM error macros described in Chapter 11.

The first sample program using IDirectoryObject (refer to Listing 12.8) shows how to get a single-valued attribute and a multivalued attribute from the domain naming context object. The program in Listing 12.10 uses the IDirectoryObject::GetObjectAttributes() function to get two attributes from the domain naming context object. GetObjectAttributes() returns an array of ADS_ATTR_INFO structures, which are described later. The program simply walks through the returned ADS_ATTR_INFO structures and displays the attribute values they contain.

LISTING 12.10   USING THE IDirectoryObject::GetObjectAttributes FUNCTION TO RETRIEVE SINGLE-VALUED AND MULTIVALUED ATTRIBUTES

```
 1: #include <windows.h>
 2: #include <activeds.h>
 3: #include <comutil.h>
 4: #include <stdio.h>
 5:
 6: int main(int argc, char* argv[])
 7: {
 8:   HRESULT hr = CoInitialize( NULL );
 9:
10:   if( SUCCEEDED( hr ) )
11:   {
12:     IADs* piIADs = NULL;
13:     _variant_t varNC;
14:
15:     // Bind to rootDSE
16:     hr = ADsGetObject( L"LDAP://rootDSE", IID_IADs,
17:                        ( void** )&piIADs );
18:     if( SUCCEEDED( hr ) )
19:     {
20:       // Get the default naming context from rootDSE
21:       hr = piIADs->Get( L"defaultNamingContext", &varNC );
22:       if( SUCCEEDED( hr ) )
23:       {
24:         IDirectoryObject* piIDO = NULL;
25:
```

continues

LISTING 12.10 CONTINUED

```
26:            // Get an IDirectoryObject interface to the
27:            // domain NC object
28:            hr = ADsGetObject( _bstr_t( "LDAP://" ) +
29:                               _bstr_t( varNC ),
30:                               IID_IDirectoryObject,
31:                               ( void** )&piIDO
32:                             );
33:
34:        if( SUCCEEDED( hr ) )
35:        {
36:            // Get the name attribute using GetObjectAttributes
37:            LPWSTR apszAttrNames[] = { L"name", L"masteredBy" };
38:            DWORD dwAttrsReturned = 0;
39:            ADS_ATTR_INFO* ppsAttrInfo = NULL;
40:
41:            hr = piIDO->GetObjectAttributes( apszAttrNames,
42:            sizeof( apszAttrNames ) / sizeof( apszAttrNames[ 0 ] ),
43:                        &ppsAttrInfo,
44:                        &dwAttrsReturned );
45:
46:            if( SUCCEEDED( hr ) )
47:            {
48:              for( int nAttr = 0; nAttr < ( int )dwAttrsReturned;
49:                        nAttr++ )
50:              {
51:                for( int nValue = 0;
52:                  nValue < ( int )ppsAttrInfo[ nAttr ].dwNumValues;
53:                  nValue++ )
54:                {
55:                  printf( "%S (%d): %S\n",
56:        ppsAttrInfo[ nAttr ].pszAttrName, nValue,
57:        ppsAttrInfo[ nAttr ].pADsValues[ nValue ].CaseIgnoreString );
58:                }
59:              }
60:
61:              FreeADsMem( ppsAttrInfo );
62:            }
63:
64:          piIDO->Release();
65:        }
66:      }
67:
68:      piIADs->Release();
69:    }
70:
71:    ( void )CoUninitialize();
72:  }
73:
74:  return 0;
75: }
```

At line 16, the program in Listing 12.10 gets an IADs interface pointer to the rootDSE of a domain controller in the domain of the current user. The program uses an IADs interface because the rootDSE does not provide an IDirectoryObject interface.

The program gets the domain naming context at line 21 and binds to the domain NC object by calling ADsGetObject() at line 28. It retrieves an IDirectoryObject interface to the domain object.

At line 37, the program creates an array of NUL-terminated wide character strings containing the names of the attributes it will retrieve—in this case, "name" and "masteredBy".

At line 41, the program calls the GetObjectAttributes() function.

The for loop starting at line 48 iterates through the one or more attributes returned by the GetObjectAttributes() call. Each of these attributes may have one or more values.

The for loop starting at line 51 iterates through the values of each attribute and prints each value. Note that the program assumes that the strings are of type CaseIgnoreString. Normally, you should check the type of each attribute before you try to do anything with it.

At line 61, the program frees the ADS_ATTR_INFO array returned by the GetObjectAttributes() call.

Finally, the program releases the interface pointers at lines 64 and 68 and wraps up the COM subsystem at line 71.

The IADsContainer Interface

The IADsContainer interface provides a mechanism for you to enumerate the elements in a directory container and to move objects from one container to another. Although you can also use the IADsDirectorySearch interface to enumerate items in a container, the IADsContainer interface is simpler to use. Table 12.11 describes the IADsContainer interface.

TABLE 12.11 THE IADsContainer INTERFACE

Function Name	Description
QueryInterface()	IUnknown interface.
AddRef()	IUnknown interface.
Release()	IUnknown interface.
GetTypeInfoCount()	IDispatch interface.

continues

12

BASIC ACTIVE
DIRECTORY
INTERFACES

TABLE 12.11 CONTINUED

Function Name	Description
GetTypeInfo()	IDispatch interface.
GetIDsOfNames()	IDispatch interface.
Invoke()	IDispatch interface.
get_Count()	Not implemented by the ADSI LDAP provider.
get__NewEnum()	Creates a new enumerator for the container. Note that the function name contains two underscore (_) characters.
get_Filter()	Retrieves the current filter for the container. The filter specifies the classes of objects to return during iteration.
put_Filter()	Sets a new filter for the container. The filter specifies the classes of objects to return during iteration.
get_Hints()	Retrieves the current hints for the container. The hints specify which attributes of each object should be returned during iteration.
put_Hints()	Sets the current hints for the container. The hints specify which attributes of each object should be returned during iteration.
GetObject()	Retrieves an interface on the object in the container whose name you specify.
Create()	Creates a new object of the class you specify in the container, and returns an IDispatch interface to it.
Delete()	Deletes the object whose name you specify from the container.
CopyHere()	Copies an object within the container.
MoveHere()	Moves (renames) an object within the container.

The get__NewEnum() function returns an IUnknown interface pointer to a new IEnumVARIANT object. Table 12.12 describes the IEnumVARIANT interface.

TABLE 12.12 THE IEnumVARIANT INTERFACE

Function Name	Description
QueryInterface()	IUnknown interface.
AddRef()	IUnknown interface.
Release()	IUnknown interface.
GetTypeInfoCount()	IDispatch interface.
GetTypeInfo()	IDispatch interface.
GetIDsOfNames()	IDispatch interface.

Function Name	Description
Invoke()	IDispatch interface.
Next()	Retrieves the next object in the container.
Skip()	Skips the next object in the container.
Reset()	Resets the iterator to the beginning of the container.
Clone()	Creates a new enumerator that has the same settings as this one.

Simplify Container Iteration Using the Enumerator Helper Functions

Enumerating the directory objects in a container using the IADsContainer and IEnumVARIANT interfaces is straightforward, but it requires a lot of code. The basic sequence of events is as follows:

1. Bind to the container object using ADsGetObject() or ADsOpenObject().

2. Get a new enumerator with get_ _NewEnum().

3. Query the interface pointer returned from get_ _NewEnum() to get a IEnumVARIANT interface pointer.

4. Call the IEnumVARIANT::Next() function repeatedly to get an IDispatch interface to the contained objects.

5. Call QueryInterface to get an IADs interface to the enumerated object.

This is, as my friend Jesse likes to describe it, "a lot of finger aerobics."

Microsoft provides three helper functions to reduce the amount of code you have to write when you want to enumerate the directory objects in a container. ADsBuildEnumerator() creates an enumerator and returns an IEnumVARIANT interface pointer to it. ADsEnumerateNext() retrieves the next set of entries in the container. ADsFreeEnumerator releases the interface pointers created by ADsBuildEnumerator. You can reduce the number of lines of code you must write to enumerate a container by using these helper functions.

```
HRESULT ADsBuildEnumerator( IADsContainer* piContainer,
                    ➡IEnumVARIANT** ppiEnumerator )
```

piContainer is an IADsContainer* interface pointer to the container object you want to enumerate.

ppiEnumerator is the address of the IEnumVARIANT pointer to set to the new enumerator.

12

BASIC ACTIVE DIRECTORY INTERFACES

Returns: An ADSI or COM error code. Check the result with one of the COM error macros described in Chapter 11.

```
HRESULT ADsEnumerateNext( IEnumVARIANT* piEnumerator,
➥ULONG uCountRequested, VARIANT* pvarEntries,
➥ULONG* puCountReturned )
```

piEnumerator is an IEnumVARIANT interface pointer to iterate.

uCountRequested is the number of entries you want to retrieve at one time.

pvarEntries is the address of a VARIANT that the function will set to contain the returned pointers to contained objects.

puCountReturned is the address of a ULONG variable to set to the actual number of entries returned in pvarEntries.

Returns: S_OK if it successfully retrieved one or more entries, or a 1 if it did not.

CAUTION

Do not test the return value of ADsEnumerateNext() using the SUCCEEDED() macro. ADsEnumerateNext returns either S_OK or a 1. The SUCCEEDED() macro evaluates to TRUE for both these values. Instead, you should test the return value of ADsEnumerateNext() explicitly with S_OK.

```
HRESULT ADsFreeEnumerator( IEnumVARIANT* piEnumerator )
```

piEnumerator is a pointer to an IEnumVARIANT interface that was created with ADsBuildEnumerator.

Using `IADsContainer` to Enumerate Objects in a Container

The program in Listing 12.11 shows how to enumerate the objects in a container using the ADSI enumerator helper functions. This sample gets the domain naming context from rootDSE, binds to the Users container in the domain NC, and enumerates all the objects in the Users container.

The sample program uses the three enumerator helper functions ADsBuildEnumerator(), ADsEnumerateNext(), and ADsFreeEnumerator().

LISTING 12.11 USING THE ADSI CONTAINER ENUMERATION HELPER FUNCTIONS

```
1: #include <windows.h>
2: #include <activeds.h>
3: #include <comutil.h>
4: #include <stdio.h>
```

```
 5: #include <oaidl.h>
 6:
 7: int main(int argc, char* argv[])
 8: {
 9:   HRESULT hr = CoInitialize( NULL );
10:
11:   if( SUCCEEDED( hr ) )
12:   {
13:     IADs* piIADs = NULL;
14:
15:     // Get rootDSE
16:     hr = ADsGetObject( L"LDAP://rootDSE", IID_IADs,
17:                        ( void** )&piIADs );
18:     if( SUCCEEDED( hr ) )
19:     {
20:       // Get the domain NC
21:       _variant_t varDefaultNamingContext;
22:       hr = piIADs->Get( L"defaultNamingContext",
23:                         &varDefaultNamingContext );
24:       if( SUCCEEDED( hr ) )
25:       {
26:         // Compose the DN of the User container in the domain
27:         _bstr_t strUserPath = _bstr_t( "LDAP://CN=Users," ) +
28:                               _bstr_t( varDefaultNamingContext );
29:         IADsContainer* piContainer = NULL;
30:
31:         hr = ADsGetObject( strUserPath, IID_IADsContainer,
32:                            ( void** )&piContainer );
33:         if( SUCCEEDED( hr ) )
34:         {
35:           IEnumVARIANT* piEnum;
36:
37:           // Create an enumerator on the User container
38:           hr = ADsBuildEnumerator( piContainer, &piEnum );
39:           if( SUCCEEDED( hr ) )
40:           {
41:             ULONG ulCount;
42:             _variant_t varEntry;
43:
44:             // Enumerate the entries
45:             while( ADsEnumerateNext( piEnum, 1, &varEntry,
46:                    &ulCount ) == S_OK && ulCount == 1 )
47:             {
48:               IADs* piEntry = NULL;
49:
50:               // Get an IADs interface to the child object
51:               hr = (( IDispatch* )varEntry)->QueryInterface(
52:                    IID_IADs, ( void** )&piEntry );
53:               if( SUCCEEDED( hr ) )
54:               {
```

continues

LISTING 12.11 CONTINUED

```
55:                BSTR strName;
56:
57:                piEntry->get_Name( &strName );
58:                printf( "%S\n", strName );
59:
60:                piEntry->Release();
61:            }
62:
63:            (( IDispatch* )varEntry)->Release();
64:        }
65:
66:        piEnum->Release();
67:      }
68:
69:        piContainer->Release();
70:      }
71:    }
72:  }
73:
74:  CoUninitialize();
75:  }
76:
77:  return 0;
78: }
```

The sample program in Listing 12.11 gets the domain naming context from rootDSE at line 22, and binds to the Users container in the domain at line 31.

At line 38, the program calls ADsBuildEnumerator to create an IEnumVARIANT interface to the Users container.

For each entry returned by ADsEnumerateNext(), the loop starting at line 45 casts the _variant_t to an IDispatch pointer and then calls QueryInterface to get an IADs interface pointer to the object.

At line 57, the program calls IADs::get_Name() to get the relative distinguished name from the IADs interface pointer and then prints the name.

The loop terminates if ADsEnumerateNext() returns anything other than S_OK or if it doesn't return exactly one entry.

Using IADsContainer Filters and Hints to Limit an Enumeration

Two problems with using the IADsContainer and IEnumVARIANT interfaces are that they return all the entries in a container and they return all the attributes of each entry.

Sometimes that is what you want to do, but more often you want to look at only certain objects in the container and certain attributes of those objects.

The `IADsContainer` interface supports two mechanisms for reducing the amount of data returned during an enumeration. The first, called a *container filter,* lets you specify one or more classes of objects you want to retrieve during the enumeration. For instance, if you want to skip the group objects in the Users container and retrieve only the user objects, you set the container filter to contain the entry `"user"`. The `IADsContainer::put_Filter()` function lets you set the filter, and the `IADsContainer::get_Filter()` function lets you retrieve the current filter.

The second mechanism for reducing the amount of data returned by the enumeration is called a *container hint.* A container hint is very similar to a container filter, except that you specify the names of the attributes you want returned for each object in the enumeration. The `IADsContainer` interface provides the `IADsContainer::put_Hints()` to set the list of attributes to retrieve and the `IADsContainer::get_Hints()` function to get the current list of attributes to be retrieved.

One particular thing to note about filters and hints: You must set the filter and hints *before* you create the enumerator. When you create the enumerator for the container, ADSI grabs the current settings for the filter and hints and copies them into the enumerator. Changing the filter or hints does not affect the behavior of existing enumerators.

The sample program in Listing 12.12 is identical to the preceding program, except that it creates a container filter to limit the enumeration to user objects, and it sets the hints to only return the common name (`cn`) and surname (`sn`) attributes.

```
HRESULT IADsContainer::put_Filter( VARIANT varClassNames )
```

> `varClassNames` is a `VARIANT` array containing one or more class names that indicate the classes of objects the enumerator should return.

Returns: An ADSI or COM error code. Check the result with one of the COM error macros described in Chapter 11.

```
HRESULT IADsContainer::put_Hints( VARIANT varAttrNames )
```

> `varAttrNames` is a `VARIANT` array containing one or more attribute names that indicate the attributes the enumerator should return for each returned object.

Returns: An ADSI or COM error code. Check the result with one of the COM error macros described in Chapter 11.

The sample program shown in Listing 12.12 demonstrates using `put_Filter` and `put_Hints`.

LISTING 12.12 USING THE IADsContainer FILTERS AND HINTS

```
 1: #include <windows.h>
 2: #include <activeds.h>
 3: #include <comutil.h>
 4: #include <stdio.h>
 5: #include <oaidl.h>
 6:
 7: int main(int argc, char* argv[])
 8: {
 9:   HRESULT hr = CoInitialize( NULL );
10:
11:   if( SUCCEEDED( hr ) )
12:   {
13:     IADs* piIADs = NULL;
14:
15:     // Get rootDSE
16:     hr = ADsGetObject( L"LDAP://rootDSE", IID_IADs,
17:                        ( void** )&piIADs );
18:     if( SUCCEEDED( hr ) )
19:     {
20:       // Get the domain NC
21:       _variant_t varDefaultNamingContext;
22:       hr = piIADs->Get( L"defaultNamingContext",
23:                         &varDefaultNamingContext );
24:       if( SUCCEEDED( hr ) )
25:       {
26:         // Compose the DN of the User container in the domain
27:         _bstr_t strPath = _bstr_t( "LDAP://CN=Users," ) +
28:                           _bstr_t( varDefaultNamingContext );
29:         IADsContainer* piContainer = NULL;
30:
31:         hr = ADsGetObject( strPath, IID_IADsContainer,
32:                            ( void** )&piContainer );
33:         if( SUCCEEDED( hr ) )
34:         {
35:           IEnumVARIANT* piEnum;
36:
37:           // Set filter
38:           LPWSTR apszClassNames[] = { L"user" };
39:           _variant_t varClassNames;
40:           ADsBuildVarArrayStr( apszClassNames,
41:           sizeof( apszClassNames ) / sizeof( apszClassNames[ 0 ] ),
42:                               &varClassNames );
43:           hr = piContainer->put_Filter( varClassNames );
44:
45:           // Set hints
46:           LPWSTR apszAttrNames[] = { L"sn", L"cn" };
47:           _variant_t varAttrNames;
48:           ADsBuildVarArrayStr( apszAttrNames,
49:           sizeof( apszAttrNames ) / sizeof( apszAttrNames[ 0 ] ),
```

```
50:                             &varAttrNames );
51:            hr = piContainer->put_Hints( varAttrNames );
52:
53:            // Create an enumerator on the User container
54:            hr = ADsBuildEnumerator( piContainer, &piEnum );
55:            if( SUCCEEDED( hr ) )
56:            {
57:              ULONG ulCount;
58:              _variant_t varEntry;
59:
60:              // Enumerate the entries
61:              while( ( hr = ADsEnumerateNext( piEnum, 1, &varEntry,
62:                    &ulCount ) == S_OK ) && ulCount == 1 )
63:              {
64:                IADs* piEntry = NULL;
65:
66:                // Get an IADs interface to the child object
67:                hr = (( IDispatch* )varEntry)->QueryInterface(
68:                        IID_IADs, ( void** )&piEntry );
69:                if( SUCCEEDED( hr ) )
70:                {
71:                  _variant_t varCN;
72:                  _variant_t varSN;
73:
74:                  piEntry->Get( L"cn", &varCN );
75:                  piEntry->Get( L"sn", &varSN );
76:
77:                  printf( "cn: %s sn: %s\n",
78:                    ( const char* )_bstr_t( varCN ),
79:                    ( const char* )_bstr_t( varSN ) );
80:
81:                  piEntry->Release();
82:                }
83:
84:                (( IDispatch* )varEntry)->Release();
85:              }
86:
87:              piEnum->Release();
88:            }
89:
90:            piContainer->Release();
91:          }
92:        }
93:      }
94:
95:      ( void )CoUninitialize();
96:    }
97:
98:    return 0;
99: }
```

The program in Listing 12.12 starts in the usual way by getting the domain naming context from the `rootDSE` and binding the Users container in that domain at line 31.

At line 43, the program sets the filter for the container so that subsequent enumerators will return only objects of class `"user"`. Note that the `IADsContainer::put_Filter()` function requires a `VARIANT` array of class names, not just a scalar `VARIANT`.

At line 51, the program sets the filter for the container so that enumerators will return only the common name (`cn`) and surname (`sn`) attributes. Note that, like `put_Filter()`, the `IADsContainer::put_Hints()` function requires a `VARIANT` array of attribute names.

The program creates the enumerator for the Users container at line 54 and enters a loop to enumerate the objects in the Users container at line 61.

For each returned user object, the program gets the `cn` and `sn` attributes at lines 74 and 75 and prints them at line 77.

The program finally releases the interface pointers and cleans up the COM subsystem in the usual way starting at line 87.

Using `IADsContainer` to Create an Object

The `IADsContainer` interface provides a really simple way to create a new object in the container to which it refers: the `IADsContainer::Create()` function.

```
IADsContainer::Create( BSTR strClassName, BSTR strName,
                    ➦IDispatch* ppiDispatch )
```

> `strClassName` is the name of the class of the object you want to create—for instance, `"user"` or `"group"`.
>
> `strName` is the relative distinguished name of the object you want to create. It must not already exist in the container in which you are creating the object.
>
> `ppiDispatch` is the address of an `IDispatch` interface pointer to set to refer to the new object.

Returns: An ADSI or COM error code. Check the result with one of the COM error macros described in Chapter 11.

`IADsContainer::Create()` does not actually create the object in the directory. It simply creates a new object locally in memory, and assigns it an empty property cache. It is up to you to populate the property cache with all the attributes the object requires, as determined by its class.

When you call `SetInfo()` using the new object's interface pointer, the ADSI LDAP provider writes the new object to the directory.

Listing 12.13 creates a new user object in the Users container of the domain of the currently logged-in user.

LISTING 12.13 USING THE IADsContainer::Create() FUNCTION TO CREATE A NEW USER

```
 1: #include <windows.h>
 2: #include <activeds.h>
 3: #include <comutil.h>
 4: #include <stdio.h>
 5: #include <oaidl.h>
 6:
 7: int main(int argc, char* argv[])
 8: {
 9:   HRESULT hr = CoInitialize( NULL );
10:
11:   if( SUCCEEDED( hr ) )
12:   {
13:     IADs* piIADs = NULL;
14:
15:     // Get rootDSE
16:     hr = ADsGetObject( L"LDAP://rootDSE", IID_IADs,
17:                        ( void** )&piIADs );
18:     if( SUCCEEDED( hr ) )
19:     {
20:       // Get the domain NC
21:       _variant_t varDefaultNamingContext;
22:       hr = piIADs->Get( L"defaultNamingContext",
23:                         &varDefaultNamingContext );
24:       if( SUCCEEDED( hr ) )
25:       {
26:         // Compose the DN of the User container in the domain
27:         _bstr_t strPath = _bstr_t( "LDAP://CN=Users," ) +
28:                           _bstr_t( varDefaultNamingContext );
29:         IADsContainer* piContainer = NULL;
30:
31:         // Get the interface to the Users container
32:         hr = ADsGetObject( strPath, IID_IADsContainer,
33:                            ( void** )&piContainer );
34:         if( SUCCEEDED( hr ) )
35:         {
36:           IDispatch* piDispatch = NULL;
37:
38:           hr = piContainer->Create( L"user", L"New User",
39:                                     &piDispatch );
40:           if( SUCCEEDED( hr ) )
41:           {
42:             IADs* piIADs = NULL;
43:             hr = piDispatch->QueryInterface( IID_IADs,
```

continues

12

BASIC ACTIVE
DIRECTORY
INTERFACES

Listing 12.13   CONTINUED

```
44:                                        ( void** )&piIADs );
45:
46:            if( SUCCEEDED( hr ) )
47:            {
48:                hr = piIADs->Put( L"cn",
49:                        _variant_t( _bstr_t( "CN=NewUser" ) ) );
50:                hr = piIADs->Put( L"sAMAccountName",
51:                        _variant_t( _bstr_t( "NEWUSER" ) ) );
52:                hr = piIADs->Put( L"userAccountControl",
53:                        _variant_t( ( long )ADS_UF_NORMAL_ACCOUNT ) );
54:
55:                hr = piIADs->SetInfo();
56:                if( ! SUCCEEDED( hr ) )
57:                {
58:                    printf( "Error %x adding user\n", hr );
59:                }
60:
61:                piIADs->Release();
62:            }
63:
64:            piDispatch->Release();
65:        }
66:
67:        piContainer->Release();
68:        }
69:    }
70:    }
71:
72:    ( void )CoUninitialize();
73:    }
74:
75:    return 0;
76: }
```

The program in Listing 12.13 starts in the usual way by getting the domain naming context from the rootDSE of a domain controller in the currently logged-in user's domain at line 16.

The program gets an IADsContainer interface to the Users container at line 32.

At line 38, the program creates a new object locally named "New User". It then sets (in the property cache) the cn and userAccountControl attributes of the new user object.

At line 55, the program adds the object to the directory by calling SetInfo.

The program then releases all the interface pointers and calls CoUninitialize() at line 72.

Using `IADsContainer` to Delete an Object

Deleting an object from the directory using the `IADsContainer` interface is even easier than creating one. The `IADsContainer::Delete()` function takes the class and relative distinguished name of the object in the container to delete and then deletes the object immediately from the directory.

`IADsContainer::Delete()` does not modify the property cache of the deleted object; it simply deletes the object from the directory. There is a potential problem with this behavior. If you have one or more interface pointers outstanding to an object that you then delete from the directory, all the interface pointers will remain pointing to a valid local copy of the object in your program's address space, even though the object itself no longer exists. If you happen to call `SetInfo()` or `SetInfoEx()` on one of the interfaces later, you will get an error because the object no longer exists in the directory.

The `IADsContainer::Delete()` function can delete only a single object, and it cannot delete an object that still contains other objects. You can also use the `IADsDeleteOps` interface to delete objects, and the `IADsDeleteOps::DeleteObject()` function lets you delete an entire directory subtree.

```
HRESULT IADsContainer::Delete( BSTR strClassName, BSTR strObjectName )
```

> `strClassName` is the name of the class of the object to delete.
>
> `strObjectName` is the relative distinguished name of the object in the container to delete.

Returns: `IADsContainer::Delete()` returns an ADSI or COM error code. Check the result with one of the COM error macros described in Chapter 11.

The sample program in Listing 12.14 deletes the user object named New User created by the preceding sample program.

LISTING 12.14   USING THE `IADsContainer::Delete()` FUNCTION TO DELETE A USER OBJECT

```
 1: #include <windows.h>
 2: #include <activeds.h>
 3: #include <comutil.h>
 4: #include <stdio.h>
 5: #include <oaidl.h>
 6:
 7: int main(int argc, char* argv[])
 8: {
 9:   HRESULT hr = CoInitialize( NULL );
10:
```

continues

12

BASIC ACTIVE DIRECTORY INTERFACES

LISTING 12.14   CONTINUED

```
11:    if( SUCCEEDED( hr ) )
12:    {
13:      IADs* piIADs = NULL;
14:
15:      // Get rootDSE
16:      hr = ADsGetObject( L"LDAP://rootDSE", IID_IADs,
17:                         ( void** )&piIADs );
18:      if( SUCCEEDED( hr ) )
19:      {
20:        // Get the domain NC
21:        _variant_t varDefaultNamingContext;
22:        hr = piIADs->Get( L"defaultNamingContext",
23:                          &varDefaultNamingContext );
24:        if( SUCCEEDED( hr ) )
25:        {
26:          // Compose the DN of the User container in the domain
27:          _bstr_t strPath = _bstr_t( "LDAP://CN=Users," ) +
28:                            _bstr_t( varDefaultNamingContext );
29:          IADsContainer* piContainer = NULL;
30:
31:          // Get the interface to the Users container
32:          hr = ADsGetObject( strPath, IID_IADsContainer,
33:                             ( void** )&piContainer );
34:          if( SUCCEEDED( hr ) )
35:          {
36:            hr = piContainer->Delete( L"user", L"New User" );
37:            if( ! SUCCEEDED( hr ) )
38:            {
39:              printf( "Error %x deleting user\n", hr );
40:            }
41:            piContainer->Release();
42:          }
43:        }
44:
45:        piIADs->Release();
46:      }
47:
48:      ( void )CoUninitialize();
49:    }
50:
51:    return 0;
52: }
```

The program in Listing 12.14 starts by getting the domain naming context from the
rootDSE of a domain controller in the currently logged-in user's domain.

At line 27, the program composes the name of the Users container using the name of the
domain obtained from rootDSE.

At line 32, the program binds to the Users container and gets an `IADsContainer` interface pointer to the Users container.

At line 36, the program calls `IADsContainer::Delete()` to delete the user object named `"New User"`.

The program releases the interface pointers at lines 41 and 45, and shuts down the COM subsystem by calling `CoUninitialize()` at line 48.

Using `IADsContainer` to Copy or Rename an Object

The last two functions in the `IADsContainer` interface I will cover are `IADsContainer::CopyHere()` and `IADsContainer::MoveHere()`. The `CopyHere()` function copies an existing object from anywhere within the current domain to the container. The `MoveHere()` function is the same as the `CopyHere()` function, except that it deletes the source object after it has copied it to the container. Both `IADsContainer::CopyHere()` and `IADsContainer::MoveHere()` accept an `ADsPath` as their first parameter. This is the path of the source object to be copied or moved into the container. The second parameter is the relative distinguished name of the new object within the container. Both functions return an IADs interface pointer.

```
HRESULT IADsContainer::CopyHere( BSTR strADsPath, BSTR strNewName,
                       ➥IADs** ppiIADs )
```

> `strADsPath` is the `ADsPath` of the object to be copied.
>
> `strNewName` is the relative distinguished name of the new object in the container. You can set this parameter to `NULL` and the copied object will retain its original relative distinguished name.
>
> `ppiIADs` is the address of an `IADs` interface pointer to set to refer to the new object.

Returns: An ADSI or COM error code. Check the result with one of the COM error macros described in Chapter 11.

```
HRESULT IADsContainer::MoveHere( BSTR strADsPath, BSTR strNewName,
                       ➥IADs** ppiIADs )
```

> `strADsPath` is the `ADsPath` of the object to be moved.
>
> `strNewName` is the relative distinguished name of the new object in the container. You can set this parameter to `NULL` and the copied object will retain its original relative distinguished name.
>
> `ppiIADs` is the address of an `IADs` interface pointer to set to refer to the new object.

Returns: An ADSI or COM error code. Check the result with one of the COM error macros described in Chapter 11.

12

BASIC ACTIVE DIRECTORY INTERFACES

The sample program in Listing 12.15 moves a user object from the container
OU=Marketing to the Users container within the same domain.

LISTING 12.15   USING THE IADsContainer::MoveHere() FUNCTION TO MOVE A
USER OBJECT

```
 1: #include <windows.h>
 2: #include <activeds.h>
 3: #include <comutil.h>
 4: #include <stdio.h>
 5:
 6: int main(int argc, char* argv[])
 7: {
 8:   HRESULT hr = CoInitialize( NULL );
 9:
10:   if( SUCCEEDED( hr ) )
11:   {
12:     IADs* piIADs = NULL;
13:
14:     // Get rootDSE
15:     hr = ADsGetObject( L"LDAP://rootDSE", IID_IADs,
16:                        ( void** )&piIADs );
17:     if( SUCCEEDED( hr ) )
18:     {
19:       // Get the domain NC
20:       _variant_t varDefaultNamingContext;
21:       hr = piIADs->Get( L"defaultNamingContext",
22:                         &varDefaultNamingContext );
23:       if( SUCCEEDED( hr ) )
24:       {
25:         // Compose the DN of the User container in the domain
26:         _bstr_t strPath = _bstr_t( "LDAP://CN=Users," ) +
27:                           _bstr_t( varDefaultNamingContext );
28:         IADsContainer* piContainer = NULL;
29:
30:         hr = ADsGetObject( strPath, IID_IADsContainer,
31:                            ( void** )&piContainer );
32:         if( SUCCEEDED( hr ) )
33:         {
34:           _bstr_t strSourcePath =
35:             _bstr_t( L"LDAP://CN=New User,OU=Marketing," ) +
36:             _bstr_t( varDefaultNamingContext );
37:           IDispatch* piIDispatch = NULL;
38:
39:           hr = piContainer->MoveHere( strSourcePath, NULL,
40:                                       &piIDispatch );
41:           if( SUCCEEDED( hr ) )
42:           {
43:             printf( "Move was successful\n" );
44:             piIDispatch->Release();
45:           }
```

```
46:
47:              piContainer->Release();
48:          }
49:       }
50:    }
51:
52:    ( void )CoUninitialize();
53: }
54:
55:    return 0;
56: }
```

The sample program in Listing 12.15 gets the domain naming context name from the rootDSE at line 21 and then creates the ADsPath for the Users container at line 26.

At line 30, the program binds to the Users container and creates the ADsPath for the source object at line 34.

The program calls the IADsContainer::MoveHere() function at line 39, which moves the "New User" object from the OU=Marketing to the Users container.

The program releases the interface pointers at lines 44 and 47 and calls CoUninitialize() at line 52.

The IADsContainer::CopyHere() function accepts the same parameters as IADsContainer::MoveHere(), and you use it in exactly the same way.

The **IADsDeleteOps** Interface

The IADsDeleteOps interface provides a single function that lets you delete an object from the directory. All objects in the directory support the IADsDeleteOps interface.

Table 12.13 details the IADsDeleteOps interface.

TABLE 12.13   THE IADsDeleteOps INTERFACE

Function Name	Description
QueryInterface()	IUnknown interface.
AddRef()	IUnknown interface.
Release()	IUnknown interface.
GetTypeInfoCount()	IDispatch interface.
GetTypeInfo()	IDispatch interface.
GetIDsOfNames()	IDispatch interface.
Invoke()	IDispatch interface.
DeleteObject()	Deletes the current object and any objects it contains.

Here is the syntax for IADsDeleteOps::DeleteObject:

HRESULT IADsDeleteOps::DeleteObject(long lMustBeZero)

lMustBeZero is a long that is reserved for later use. You must initialize it to 0.

Returns: An ADSI or COM error code. Check the result with one of the COM error macros described in Chapter 11.

The sample program in Listing 12.16 deletes the container OU=Marketing in the current domain, along with any objects it contains.

LISTING 12.16 USING THE IADsDeleteOps::DeleteObject() FUNCTION TO DELETE AN ORGANIZATIONAL UNIT

```
1: #include <windows.h>
2: #include <activeds.h>
3: #include <comutil.h>
4: #include <stdio.h>
5:
6: int main(int argc, char* argv[])
7: {
8:   HRESULT hr = CoInitialize( NULL );
9:
10:   if( SUCCEEDED( hr ) )
11:   {
12:     IADs* piIADs = NULL;
13:
14:     // Get rootDSE
15:     hr = ADsGetObject( L"LDAP://rootDSE", IID_IADs,
16:                        ( void** )&piIADs );
17:     if( SUCCEEDED( hr ) )
18:     {
19:       // Get the domain NC
20:       _variant_t varDefaultNamingContext;
21:       hr = piIADs->Get( L"defaultNamingContext",
22:                         &varDefaultNamingContext );
23:       if( SUCCEEDED( hr ) )
24:       {
25:         // Compose the DN of the Marketing OU container
26:         // in the domain
27:         _bstr_t strPath = _bstr_t( "LDAP://OU=Marketing," ) +
28:                           _bstr_t( varDefaultNamingContext );
29:         IADsDeleteOps* piDelOps = NULL;
30:
31:         hr = ADsGetObject( strPath, IID_IADsDeleteOps,
32:                            ( void** )&piDelOps );
33:         if( SUCCEEDED( hr ) )
34:         {
35:           hr = piDelOps->DeleteObject( 0 );
```

```
36:
37:             piDelOps->Release();
38:         }
39:      }
40:
41:      piIADs->Release();
42:   }
43:
44:   ( void )CoUninitialize();
45: }
46:
47:   return 0;
48: }
```

The sample program in Listing 12.16 gets the domain naming context from the rootDSE at line 15 and gets the default naming context at line 21.

At line 31, the program gets an IADsDeleteOps interface to the OU=Marketing container.

At line 35, the program deletes the entire OU, along with any objects it might contain.

The program releases its interface pointers and shuts down the COM subsystem starting at line 37.

12

BASIC ACTIVE
DIRECTORY
INTERFACES

CHAPTER 13

Searching Active Directory with ADSI

If you're writing directory-based programs, chances are that ninety percent of the code you write will be routines that search the directory. ADSI provides a single interface for performing directory searches called IDirectorySearch. This chapter shows how to search Active Directory using IDirectorySearch.

If you are already familiar with LDAP searches, the first part of this chapter will be old hat; you should skip to the description of the IDirectorySearch interface. If searching a directory using LDAP is new to you, read the entire chapter, as well as Chapters 20 and 21, regarding searching Active Directory with LDAP.

Introduction to Searching with ADSI

The IDirectorySearch interface provides a peculiar mix of search models. IDirectorySearch is based on LDAP, and so has several characteristics, such as search scope and search filters, that are straight from the LDAP search APIs.

ADSI is also the underlying database provider for Microsoft's ActiveX Data Objects (ADO), which implements a sort of relational database abstraction over any arbitrary data source. The IDirectorySearch interface therefore provides a row/column interface that makes Active Directory look similar to a relational database.

The combination of the hierarchical LDAP search model and the ADO relational search model makes for a workable, if not concise, search interface.

When you initiate an Active Directory search using the `IDirectorySearch` interface, you specify three key parameters:

- The base of the search (the starting location of the search in the directory)
- The search filter (which objects you want to retrieve)
- The attribute list (which attributes of the objects passing the filter you want to retrieve)

You can also set several other search parameters, such as the scope of the search and whether or not the search should chase referrals that you can set using the `IDirectorySearch` search preferences mechanism. I describe search preferences later in this chapter.

The following sections describe these three concepts in more detail.

Specifying a Search Base

All Active Directory objects support the `IDirectorySearch` interface. When you obtain an `IDirectorySearch` interface to an existing Active Directory object, that object becomes the *search base* for the search operation. The search operation will start at the search base and can potentially include the entire directory subtree beneath the base, as determined by the search scope (described in the next section).

It's a good strategy to pick a search base as low (that is, far from the root) in the directory tree as possible to reduce the size of the namespace ADSI will have to search. For instance, if you are searching for user objects and all the user objects are in the Users container of the domain naming context, start your search in the Users container, not at the root of the domain naming context.

Search Filter

Generally speaking, you do not want to retrieve all the directory objects beneath the search base; you only want a few selected objects. The `IDirectoryObject` interface provides a powerful mechanism for specifying search criteria called a *search filter*. The `IDirectorySearch` search filter (actually, it's the LDAP search filter; `IDirectorySearch` simply passes the filter to the ADSI LDAP provider) lets you specify attribute values that an object must match before `IDirectorySearch` will return that object as part of the search results. You can build complex search filters using Boolean AND, OR, and NOT operators as well. A typical `IDirectorySearch` search filter looks something like this:

```
(&(objectClass=user)(cn=Steve))
```

This filter would select all objects in the search scope that are of class user (the objectClass attribute is equal to user) and have a common name attribute equal to Steve.

Chapter 21, "Advanced Searching with LDAP," provides a complete description of the LDAP search filter syntax.

Specifying Attributes to Return

After you have specified the search base and search filter, the last thing you must specify for an IDirectorySearch operation is the list of attributes you want returned from the server. The IDirectorySearch interface accepts an array of attribute names to return. IDirectorySearch will return only those attributes for each object (assuming the object has values for those attributes) that passes the search filter.

It is a good strategy to retrieve only the attributes your application needs. Retrieving only a few attributes for each object that passes your search filter can substantially reduce network traffic.

Objects as Rows

Unlike the LDAP interface, which treats search results as a sequence of directory entries, the IDirectorySearch interface treats search results as a sequence of *rows* in a table, where each row contains the attributes of a single directory object. This is analogous to the way a relational database handles searches. The IDirectorySearch interface provides functions for retrieving the first row of the result set, retrieving the next row of the result set, and for retrieving the previous row of the result set.

Attributes as Columns

In keeping with the relational database–like interface, DirectorySearch does not present the attributes of the result set as attributes, but as columns in a table. IDirectorySearch provides functions for enumerating the names of the result table columns and for retrieving a given column of the current row.

The IDirectorySearch Interface

This section describes the IDirectorySearch interface in more detail. Table 13.1 lists the functions that make up the interface. Subsequent sections show how to use these functions to search Active Directory.

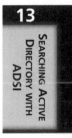

13

SEARCHING ACTIVE
DIRECTORY WITH
ADSI

TABLE 13.1 THE IDirectorySearch INTERFACE

Function Name	*Description*
QueryInterface()	IUnknown interface.
AddRef()	IUnknown interface.
Release()	IUnknown interface.
SetSearchPreference()	Sets one or more search preferences for this search.
ExecuteSearch()	Establishes the search criteria and allocates a search handle to use with subsequent functions.
AbandonSearch()	Terminates a search before it is complete.
GetFirstRow()	Returns the first object meeting the search criteria.
GetNextRow()	Returns the next object meeting the search criteria.
GetPreviousRow()	Returns the previous object meeting the search criteria.
GetNextColName()	Returns the next attribute of the current row.
GetColumn()	Returns a specific column's data item from the current row.
FreeColumn()	Frees the memory associated with the specified attribute.
CloseSearchHandle()	Terminates the search.

Starting and Ending a Search with IDirectorySearch

To start a search using the IDirectorySearch interface, you have to do three things: get an interface pointer to the directory object that will serve as the base of the search, define the search filter, and provide a list of attributes to retrieve.

You then call the IDirectorySearch::ExecuteSearch() function to start the search. IDirectorySearch::ExecuteSearch() returns a search handle that you must use when you retrieve the search results.

The first thing you must do to use the IDirectorySearch interface is obtain an IDirectorySearch interface pointer to the directory object that will serve as the base of your search. The easiest way to get an interface pointer is to call either ADsGetObject() or ADsOpenObject(), passing the constant IID_IDirectorySearch as the interface identifier. For instance, Listing 13.1 shows how to get an IDirectorySearch interface to the root of the domain naming context.

LISTING 13.1 GETTING AN IDirectorySearch INTERFACE

```
IADs* pIADs = NULL;

hr = ADsGetObject( L"LDAP://rootDSE", IID_IADs, ( void** )&piIADs );
if( SUCCEEDED( hr ) )
{
    _variant_t varDefaultNamingContext;
    _bstr_t strDefaultNamingContext;

    hr = piIADs->Get( L"defaultNamingContext", &varDefaultNamingContext );
    if( SUCCEEDED( hr ) )
    {
        IDirectorySearch* piSearch = NULL;

        hr = ADsGetObject( _bstr_t( "LDAP://" ) +
                            _bstr_t( varDefaultNamingContext ),
                            IID_IDirectorySearch,
                            ( void** )&piSearch
                          );
        if( SUCCEEDED( hr ) )
        {
            // do the search here
            piSearch->Release();
        }
    }
}
```

The first call to `ADsGetObject()` retrieves the attributes of `rootDSE`. The code uses the `defaultNamingContext` attribute to form the `ADsPath` of the second `ADsGetObject` call.

The second call to `ADsGetObject()` specifies `IID_IDirectorySearch` to get an `IDirectorySearch` interface pointer to the domain naming context. If you use this interface pointer to start a search, the search will start at the root of the domain naming context.

When you call `IDirectorySearch::ExecuteSearch()`, you must pass in an LDAP search filter string that specifies the particular directory objects you want to retrieve. Chapter 21 describes the LDAP search filter syntax in detail. The following is the function definition for `IDirectorySearch::ExecuteSearch()`:

```
HRESULT IDirectorySearch::ExecuteSearch( LPWSTR pszSearchFilter,
                                         LPWSTR apszAttributeNames[],
                                         DWORD dwAttributeCount,
                                         ADS_SEARCH_HANDLE* phSearch )
```

`pszSearchFilter` is the LDAP search filter to use in the search. To indicate that you want to retrieve all objects, use `L"objectClass=*"`.

apszAttributeNames is the address of an array of NUL-terminated strings containing the LDAP display names of the attributes you want the search to return. If you want the search to return all attributes, specify NULL for this parameter, and -1 for the dwAttributeCount parameter.

dwAttributeCount is the count of the number of entries in the apszAttributeNames array. If you want the search to return all attributes, specify -1 for the this parameter and NULL for the apszAttributeNames parameter.

phSearch is the address of an ADS_SEARCH_HANDLE that ExecuteSearch will set. You must use this handle to retrieve the search results. You must also pass this handle to IDirectorySearch::CloseSearchHandle() after the search is complete to free the resources associated with the search.

Returns: IDirectorySearch::ExecuteSearch() returns an ADSI or COM error code. Check the result with one of the COM error macros described in Chapter 11, "ADSI Fundamentals."

Listing 13.2 shows a typical search of all user objects in the Users container.

LISTING 13.2 SEARCHING FOR USERS

```
IADs* pIADs = NULL;

hr = ADsGetObject( L"LDAP://rootDSE", IID_IADs, ( void** )&piIADs );
if( SUCCEEDED( hr ) )
{
    _variant_t varDefaultNamingContext;
    _bstr_t strDefaultNamingContext;

    hr = piIADs->Get( L"defaultNamingContext", &varDefaultNamingContext );
    if( SUCCEEDED( hr ) )
    {
        IDirectorySearch* piSearch = NULL;

        hr = ADsGetObject( _bstr_t( "LDAP://CN=Users," ) +
                           _bstr_t( varDefaultNamingContext ),
                           IID_IDirectorySearch,
                           ( void** )&piSearch
                         );
        if( SUCCEEDED( hr ) )
        {
            ADS_SEARCH_HANDLE hSearch;

            hr = piSearch->ExecuteSearch(
                L"objectClass=user",    // search filter
                NULL,           // array of attribute names
                -1,             // number of elements in attr names array
                &hSearch        // returned search handle
```

```
            );

            if( SUCCEEDED( hr ) )
            {
                // Process search results here
                ( void )piSearch->CloseSearchHandle( hSearch );
            }

            piSearch->Release();
        }
    }
}
```

The call to IDirectorySearch::ExecuteSearch() initializes the search, although the search process does not actually start on the server until you call IDirectorySearch::GetFirstRow().

After processing the search results, you must pass the handle returned from the IDirectorySearch::ExecuteSearch() to IDirectorySearch::CloseSearchHandle(), as shown in the code snippet. The next section discusses the IDirectorySearch::CloseSearchHandle() function.

Terminating a Search with IDirectorySearch::CloseSearchHandle()

The ADSI LDAP provider allocates several in-memory data structures to handle the results returned by the search process. After you have processed the search results, you must pass the search handle to IDirectorySearch::CloseSearchHandle() to free up the resources associated with the search.

HRESULT IDirectorySearch::CloseSearchHandle(ADS_SEARCH_HANDLE hSearch)

> hSearch is a search handle returned by a call to IDirectorySearch::ExecuteSearch()

Returns: IDirectorySearch::CloseSearchHandle() returns an ADSI or COM error code. Check the result with one of the COM error macros described in Chapter 11.

The preceding code snippet shows how to clean up after a search by calling CloseSearchHandle().

> **NOTE**
>
> `IDirectorySearch::CloseSearchHandle()` cleans up resources allocated by the ADSI LDAP provider on your behalf. If you perform an asynchronous search or a paged search (discussed in the section "Extended Searches Using Search Preferences"), you must first call `IDirectorySearch::AbandonSearch()` to free up resources allocated on the server.

Retrieving Objects with `IDirectorySearch::GetNextRow()`

So far, I've shown you how to start a search and finish a search; I haven't explained how to get the search results. This section shows how to get the rows of the result table.

The `IDirectorySearch` interface provides three functions that access the rows of the result table: `GetFirstRow()`, `GetNextRow()`, and `GetPreviousRow()`. But, in fact, you need only one of those functions: `GetNextRow()`. I'll leave the discussion of `GetFirstRow()` and `GetPreviousRow()` until the later section "Extended Searches Using Search Preferences."

The first time you call `IDirectorySearch::GetNextRow()` after initializing a search with `IDirectorySearch::ExecuteSearch()`, the ADSI LDAP provider passes the search information to the server and waits for the search results to return from the server. When the results come back to the client, the ADSI LDAP provider sets the current row to the first entry in the result set.

```
HRESULT IDirectorySearch::GetNextRow( ADS_SEARCH_HANDLE hSearch )
```

> `hSearch` is a search handle returned by a call to `IDirectorySearch::ExecuteSearch()`.

Returns: `IDirectorySearch::GetNextRow()` returns an ADSI or COM error code. When you have exhausted the returned results, `GetNextRow()` returns `S_ADS_NOMORE_ROWS`.

> **CAUTION**
>
> The `S_ADS_NOMORE_ROWS` error code does not have the severity flag set, so the `SUCCEEDED()` macro evaluates to `TRUE`. This means that you can't simply test for `SUCCEEDED() == FALSE` to see when there are no more rows in the result set. Instead, you have to explicitly compare the result to `S_ADS_NOMORE_ROWS`.

The following code snippet shows the typical way to go through the results of a search using `IdirectorySearch`.

```
// Initialize the search and call IdirectorySearch
// piSearch is the IdirectorySearch interface pointer
// hSearch is the search handle

HRESULT hr = piSearch->GetNextRow( hSearch );
if( SUCCEEDED( hr ) && hr != S_ADS_NOMORE_ROWS )
{
    do
    {
        // process result row here

        hr = piSearch->GetNextRow( hSearch );
    }
    while( SUCCEEDED( hr ) && hr != S_ADS_NOMORE_ROWS );
}
```

Another, more concise way to do the same thing (and my personal preference) is to use a `for` loop, as follows:

```
// Initialize the search and call IDirectorySearch
// piSearch is the IDirectorySearch interface pointer
// hSearch is the search handle

for( hr = piSearch->GetNextRow( hSearch );
   SUCCEEDED( hr ) && hr != S_ADS_NOMORE_ROWS;
   hr = piSearch->GetNextRow( hSearch ) )
{
    // process search results here
}
```

You can also use the `IDirectorySearch::GetFirstRow()` function to accomplish the same thing:

```
// Initialize the search and call IDirectorySearch
// piSearch is the IDirectorySearch interface pointer
// hSearch is the search handle

for( hr = piSearch->GetFirstRow( hSearch );
   SUCCEEDED( hr ) && hr != S_ADS_NOMORE_ROWS;
   hr = piSearch->GetNextRow( hSearch ) )
{
    // process search results here
}
```

Retrieving Attributes with IDirectorySearch::GetNextCol() and IDirectorySearch::GetColumn()

Now that you can retrieve the rows from the result table, how do you actually get to the attribute values? The IDirectorySearch interface returns the attributes of the selected objects as columns in the result table. There are two functions you can use to get the column information from the result table.

If you know the names of the attributes you want to retrieve—for instance, if you specifically requested some specific attributes in ExecuteSearch()—you can use the GetColumn() function to retrieve the value (or values) of the attribute for each row of the result table. The GetColumn function accepts the search handle and the name of the column (actually the lDAPDisplayName of the attribute) and returns an ADS_SEARCH_COLUMN structure. The ADS_SEARCH_COLUMN structure contains the values of the requested attribute for the current row in the result table.

```
HRESULT IDirectorySearch::GetColumn( ADS_SEARCH_HANDLE hSearch,
                                     LPWSTR pszColumnName,
                                     ADS_SEARCH_COLUMN* psColumnInfo )
```

hSearch is the handle to the search operation returned from IDirectorySearch::ExecuteSearch().

pszColumnName is a NUL-terminated wide-character string containing the name of the column (the attribute name) you want to retrieve.

psColumnInfo is the address of an ADS_SEARCH_COLUMN structure that will be set to contain the values for the column you requested. It is the caller's responsibility to allocate memory for the ADS_SEARCH_COLUMN structure, and GetColumn() will allocate additional memory to contain the values of the requested attribute. You must free the memory associated with the attribute values by calling IDirectorySearch:FreeColumn().

The ADS_SEARCH_COLUMN structure contains the name of the column, the ADSTYPE of the attribute, and an array of ADSVALUE structures containing one or more values of the attribute for the current row of the result table. The elements of the ADS_SEARCH_COLUMN structure are show in Table 13.2.

TABLE 13.2 ELEMENTS OF THE ADS_SEARCH_COLUMN STRUCTURE

Field Name	Type	Description
pszAttrName	LPWSTR	The name of the column or attribute as a NUL-terminated wide-character string.
dwADsType	ADSTYPE	The type of the attribute. This value is taken from the ADSTYPEENUM enumeration in iads.h.
pADsValues	PADSVALUE	The address of the array of values of this attribute for the current row in the result table.
dwNumValues	DWORD	The number of entries in the pADsValues array.
hReserved	HANDLE	Unused and reserved for later use.

The following code shows how to retrieve a specific column of a result table row:

```
// Initialize the search and call IDirectorySearch
// piSearch is the IDirectorySearch interface pointer
// hSearch is the search handle

for( hr = piSearch->GetFirstRow( hSearch );
SUCCEEDED( hr ) && hr != S_ADS_NOMORE_ROWS;
hr = piSearch->GetNextRow( hSearch ) )
{
    ADS_SEARCH_COLUMN sColumn;

    hr = piSearch->GetColumn( hSearch, L"cn", &sColumn );
    if( SUCCEEDED( hr ) )
    {
        // print the common name value (there can be only one)
        printf( "cn: %S\n", sColumn.pADsValues[ 0 ].CaseIgnoreString );
        ( void )piSearch->FreeColumn( sColumn );
    }
}
```

If you don't know the names of the attributes—for instance, if you specified NULL for the list of attributes to return in the call to IDirectorySearch::ExecuteSearch()— the IDirectorySearch interface gives you a way to enumerate the returned column with the IDirectorySearch::GetNextColumnName() function.

You pass the address of an LPWSTR value, and GetNextColumnName() will set the value to the name of the next attribute in the result table. You have to free the memory associated with the string by passing the LPWSTR value to ADsFreeMem() after you are done with the column.

```
HRESULT IDirectorySearch::GetNextColumnName( ADS_SEARCH_HANDLE hSearch,
                                             LPWSTR* ppszAttributeName )
```

hSearch is the handle to the search operation returned from
IDirectorySearch::ExecuteSearch().

ppszAttributeName is the address of a pointer that GetNextColumnName() will set
to point to a NUL-terminated, wide-character string containing the name of the
next column in the result row. You must free the memory allocated by
GetNextColumnName() by passing this value to ADsMemFree() when you are done
with the column name.

Returns: IDirectorySearch::GetNextColumnName() returns an ADSI or COM error
code. When you have exhausted the returned attributes for the current row,
GetNextColumnName() returns S_ADS_NOMORE_COLUMNS and it sets *ppszAttributeName
to NULL.

Listing 13.3 shows how to enumerate all the columns for each row in a result set.

LISTING 13.3   ENUMERATING A RESULT SET

```
// Initialize the search and call IDirectorySearch
// piSearch is the IDirectorySearch interface pointer
// hSearch is the search handle

for( hr = piSearch->GetFirstRow( hSearch );
SUCCEEDED( hr ) && hr != S_ADS_NOMORE_ROWS;
hr = piSearch->GetNextRow( hSearch ) )
{
    ADS_SEARCH_COLUMN sColumn;

    hr = piSearch->GetColumn( hSearch, L"cn", &sColumn );
    if( SUCCEEDED( hr ) )
    {
        LPWSTR pszAttrName = NULL;

        for( hr = piSearch->GetNextColumnName( &pszAttrName );
        SUCCEEDED( hr ) && hr != S_ADS_NOMORE_COLUMNS;
        hr = piSearch->GetNextColumnName( &pszAttrName ) )
        {
            ADS_SEARCH_COLUMN sColumn;

            hr = piSearch->GetColumn( hSearch, pszAttrName, &sColumn );
            if( SUCCEEDED( hr ) )
            {
                // print the name and CaseIgnoreString value(s)
                // of the attribute
```

```
            for( int nValue = 0; nValue < sColumn.dwNumValues;
            ➥nValue++ )
            {
                printf( "%S(%d): %S\n", sColumn.pszAttrName, nValue,
                        sColumn.pADsValues[ nValue ].CaseIgnoreString
                        ➥);
            }

            // Free the memory associated with the column
            ( void )piSearch->FreeColumn( sColumn );
        }

        ( void )ADsFreeMem( pszAttrName );
    }
  }
}
```

A Simple Search Using `IDirectorySearch`

Listing 13.4 demonstrates how to use the `IDirectorySearch` interface to list the first name and last name of all the user objects in the Users container of the domain naming context. The sample program sets the search base at the Users container and uses the search filter `"objectClass=user"` to find all user objects anywhere in or below the Users container. For each user it finds, the program gets the `distinguishedName`, common name (`cn`) and surname (`sn`) attributes and then prints them.

LISTING 13.4 LISTING FIRST AND LAST NAMES

```
 1: #include <windows.h>
 2: #include <activeds.h>
 3: #include <comutil.h>
 4: #include <stdio.h>
 5:
 6: int main(int argc, char* argv[])
 7: {
 8:     HRESULT hr = CoInitialize( NULL );
 9:
10:     if( SUCCEEDED( hr ) )
11:     {
12:         IADs* piIADs = NULL;
13:
14:         // Get rootDSE
15:         hr = ADsGetObject( L"LDAP://rootDSE", IID_IADs,
16:                             ( void** )&piIADs );
17:         if( SUCCEEDED( hr ) )
18:         {
```

continues

LISTING 13.4 CONTINUED

```
19:                 _variant_t varDefaultNamingContext;
20:                 _bstr_t strDefaultNamingContext;
21:
22:                 // Get the domain naming context
23:                 hr = piIADs->Get( L"defaultNamingContext",
24:                                   &varDefaultNamingContext );
25:                 if( SUCCEEDED( hr ) )
26:                 {
27:                     IDirectorySearch* piSearch = NULL;
28:
29:                     // bind to the Users container and get an
30:                     // IDirectorySearch interface
31:                     hr = ADsGetObject( _bstr_t( "LDAP://CN=Users," ) +
32:                                        _bstr_t( varDefaultNamingContext ),
33:                                        IID_IDirectorySearch,
                                           ( void** )&piSearch );
34:                     if( SUCCEEDED( hr ) )
35:                     {
36:                         // Retrieve these attributes for each user object
37:                         LPWSTR apszAttrNames[] =
38:                             { L"distinguishedName", L"cn", L"sn" };
39:                         ADS_SEARCH_HANDLE hSearch = NULL;
40:
41:                         // Initialize the search for user objects
42:                         piSearch->ExecuteSearch(
43:                             L"objectClass=user",
44:                             apszAttrNames,
45:                 sizeof( apszAttrNames ) / sizeof( apszAttrNames[ 0 ] ),
46:                             &hSearch
47:                         );
48:
49:                         // Get each row from the result table
50:                         for( hr = piSearch->GetFirstRow( hSearch );
51:                              SUCCEEDED( hr ) && hr != S_ADS_NOMORE_ROWS;
52:                              hr = piSearch->GetNextRow( hSearch ) )
53:                         {
54:                             ADS_SEARCH_COLUMN sColumn;
55:
56:                             // Get the DN column
57:                             hr = piSearch->GetColumn( hSearch,
58:                                     L"distinguishedName", &sColumn );
59:                             if( SUCCEEDED( hr ) )
60:                             {
61:                                 printf( "dn: %S\n",
62:                                     sColumn.pADsValues[ 0 ].CaseIgnoreString );
63:                                 piSearch->FreeColumn( &sColumn );
64:                             }
```

```
65:
66:                          // Get the common name (cn) column
67:                          hr = piSearch->GetColumn( hSearch,
68:                                                    L"cn", &sColumn );
69:                          if( SUCCEEDED( hr ) )
70:                          {
71:                              printf( "cn: %S\n",
72:                                sColumn.pADsValues[ 0 ].CaseIgnoreString );
73:                              piSearch->FreeColumn( &sColumn );
74:                          }
75:
76:                          // Get the surname (sn) column
77:                          hr = piSearch->GetColumn( hSearch,
78:                                                    L"sn", &sColumn );
79:                          if( SUCCEEDED( hr ) )
80:                          {
81:                              printf( "sn: %S\n",
82:                                sColumn.pADsValues[ 0 ].CaseIgnoreString );
83:                              piSearch->FreeColumn( &sColumn );
84:                          }
85:
86:                          printf( "\n" );
87:                      }
88:
89:                      piSearch->Release();
90:                  }
91:              }
92:
93:              piIADs->Release();
94:          }
95:
96:          ( void )CoUninitialize();
97:      }
98:
99:      return 0;
100: }
```

Listing 13.4 starts by binding to the rootDSE for a domain controller in the current users domain at line 15.

The program then gets the name of the domain naming context at line 23 and binds to the Users container in the domain naming context at line 31. The program obtains an IDirectorySearch interface to the Users container.

At line 37, the program declares the list of attributes to retrieve for each user object found in the search. The list includes the distinguishedName, cn, and sn attributes. Note that distinguishedName is an operational attribute and is not retrieved by default.

At line 42, the program calls `IDirectorySearch::ExecuteSearch()` to initialize the search. It uses the search filter `"objectClass=user"` to obtain all user objects in the Users container.

The program retrieves the rows of the result table in a `for` loop starting at line 50. Note that the continuation condition for the for loop is `SUCCEEDED( hr ) && hr !=` `S_ADS_NOMORE_ROWS`. Just using `SUCCEED(hr)` is insufficient because `SUCCEEDED( S_ADS_NOMORE_ROWS )` evaluates to `TRUE`.

At line 57, the program retrieves the `distinguishedName` attribute and prints it. Note that the program calls `IDirectorySearch::FreeColumn()` even though the `ADS_SEARCH_COLUMN` structure is declared on the stack. This is because `FreeColumn()` frees the values associated with the attribute, not the `ADS_SEARCH_COLUMN` structure itself.

The program likewise retrieves and prints the `cn` and `sn` attributes at lines 67 and 77.

At line 89, the program releases the search interface and then releases the `rootDSE` interface at line 93.

The program finally wraps up by calling `CoUninitialize()` at line 96.

Extended Searches Using Search Preferences

I've shown how you can construct Active Directory searches using the `IDirectorySearch` interface, and that will probably be sufficient for most of your searching needs. But what I've covered so far in this chapter doesn't begin to take advantage of the power and flexibility of the LDAP interface that ADSI exposes.

To provide a clean interface to some of the more powerful features of LDAP, the `IDirectorySearch` interface provides the ability to set search preferences on your directory searches. *Search preferences* are essentially options that alter the behavior of the underlying LDAP search. By using the search preferences mechanism, you can limit the scope of your search, or set limits on the amount of time the search will take or the number of entries the search will return. You can even take advantage of totally different LDAP search mechanisms by using asynchronous and/or paged searches.

To take advantage of these features, you call the `IDirectorySearch::SetSearchPreference()` function. The `SetSearchPreference()` function accepts an array of `ADS_SEARCHPREF_INFO` structures, and each `ADS_SEARCHPREF_INFO` structure lets you set a single search preference. The search preferences apply to all searches that you initiate using the same interface pointer.

The `IDirectorySearch::SetSearchPreference()` function looks like this:

```
HRESULT IDirectorySearch::SetSearchPreference(
                        PADS_SEARCHPREF_INFO psSearchPreference,
                        DWORD dwNumPrefs )
```

> `psSearchPreference` is a pointer to an array of `ADS_SEARCHPREF_INFO` structures.
>
> `dwNumPrefs` is a `DWORD` containing the number of entries in the array that `psSearchPreference` points to.

Returns: `IDirectorySearch::SetSearchPreference()` returns an ADSI or COM error code. Check the result with one of the COM error macros described in Chapter 11.

The `ADS_SEARCHPREF_INFO` structure contains an identifier for the particular search preference you are setting, an `ADSVALUE` structure that contains the value you are setting the preference to (generally an integer), and a status value that ADSI sets upon return indicating whether the particular preference was set properly. Table 13.3 shows the elements of the `ADS_SEARCHPREF_INFO` structure.

TABLE 13.3 ELEMENTS OF THE `ADS_SEARCHPREF_INFO` STRUCTURE

Field Name	Type	Description
dwSearchPref	ADS_SEARCHPREF	A value from the `ADS_SEARCHPREF` enumeration indicating which search preference you are setting.
vValue	ADSVALUE	An `ADSVALUE` containing the new value for the search preference.
dwStatus	ADS_STATUS	A value from the `ADS_STATUS` enumeration indicating the search preference was properly set. This element is set upon return from the `IDirectorySearch::SetSearchPreference()` function.

The possible values for the `dwSearchPref` element of the `ADS_SEARCHPREF_INFO` structure come from the `ADS_SEARCHPREF` enumeration and are described in Table 13.4. The Type column lists the `ADSTYPE` of the parameter that accompanies the particular search preference.

TABLE 13.4   VALUES OF THE ADS_SEARCHPREF ENUMERATION

Value Name	Type	Description
ADS_SEARCHPREF_ASYNCHRONOUS	ADSTYPE_BOOLEAN	Enables an asynchronous LDAP search. The default value is FALSE.
ADS_SEARCHPREF_DEREF_ALIASES	ADSTYPE_INTEGER	Indicates that the search should dereference aliases or not. The default is that aliases are not dereferenced. The values for this preference come from the ADS_DEREFENUM enumeration in iads.h.
ADS_SEARCHPREF_SIZE_LIMIT	ADSTYPE_INTEGER	Places a limit on the maximum number of entries the server will return for this search. The default is 0, indicating no limit.
ADS_SEARCHPREF_TIME_LIMIT	ADSTYPE_INTEGER	Places a limit on the amount of time the server will spend servicing the search. The value is an integer number of seconds. 0 is the default and indicates no time limit.
ADS_SEARCHPREF_ATTRIBTYPES_ONLY	ADSTYPE_BOOLEAN	Indicates that the server should return only the names of the attributes found in the search and not their values. The default is FALSE, indicating that attribute names and values will be returned.

Value Name	Type	Description
ADS_SEARCHPREF_SEARCH_SCOPE	ADSTYPE_INTEGER	Indicates the scope of the search. The value is an integer taken from the ADS_SCOPEENUM enumeration. The default is ADS_SCOPE_SUBTREE.
ADS_SEARCHPREF_TIMEOUT	ADSTYPE_INTEGER	Indicates the maximum amount of time the client will wait for a response from the server during a search before issuing a timeout error.
ADS_SEARCHPREF_PAGESIZE	ADSTYPE_INTEGER	If set to a nonzero value, indicates that the ADSI LDAP provider will used a paged search to retrieve the search results in small chunks. The page size is given as the number of entries to return on each call. The default is 0, indicating that paged searching is not enabled.
ADS_SEARCHPREF_PAGED_TIME_LIMIT	ADSTYPE_INTEGER	If paged searching is enabled (see ADS_SEARCHPREF_ PAGESIZE), determines the maximum amount of time, in seconds, the client will wait for the server to return a page of data. The default value is 0, indicating the client will wait forever for the next page of data.

13

SEARCHING ACTIVE DIRECTORY WITH ADSI

continues

TABLE 13.4 CONTINUED

Value Name	Type	Description
ADS_SEARCHPREF_CHASE_REFERRALS	ADSTYPE_BOOLEAN	If TRUE, the ADSI LDAP provider will chase referrals to other naming contexts. The default value is TRUE.
ADS_SEARCHPREF_SORT_ON	ADSTYPE_PROV_ SPECIFIC	Causes the server to sort the search results by a single search key. The default is no sorting.
ADS_SEARCHPREF_CACHE_RESULTS	ADSTYPE_BOOLEAN	Causes the ADSI LDAP provider to cache the search results on the client so that you can use the IDirectorySearch:: GetFirstRow() and IDirectorySearch:: GetPreviousRow() functions to renavigate the search results without having to reissue the search.

The following code snippet shows, in general, how to set a search preference:

```
IDirectorySearch* piSearch = NULL;
HRESULT hr = ADsGetObject( _bstr_t( "LDAP://" ) +
                           _bstr_t( varDefaultNamingContext ),
                           IID_IDirectorySearch,
                           ( void** )&piSearch
                         );
if( SUCCEEDED( hr ) )
{
    ADS_SEARCHPREF_INFO asPrefs[ 1 ];

    asPrefs[ 0 ].dwSearchPref = ADS_SEARCHPREF_TIME_LIMIT;
    asPrefs[ 0 ].vValue.dwType = ADSTYPE_INTEGER;
    asPrefs[ 0 ].vValue.Integer = 10;

    hr = piSearch->SetSearchPreference( asPrefs, 1 );
    if( SUCCEEDED( hr ) && asPrefs[ 0 ].dwStatus == ADS_STATUS_S_OK )
    {
```

```
        // call ExecuteSearch() here
    }
    piSearch->Release();
}
```

There are a few interesting things to note about this piece of code. First, note the declaration of asPrefs as an array of ADS_SEARCHPREF_INFO structures. SetSearchPreference() accepts an array of one or more preferences so that you can set several preferences at once. Although this sample only sets one preference, it must still handle it as an array.

The second thing to note is that you must explicitly set both the dwType element of the vValue structure, as well as the corresponding value element (in this case, the Integer element).

Finally, after calling SetSearchPreference(), the code checks not only the return code of the function, but it also checks the value of the dwStatus element of the ADS_SEARCHPREF_INFO structure. This value is set by the call to SetSearchPreference(), and indicates whether that particular preference was properly set. The values of the dwStatus element come from the ADS_STATUSENUM enumeration and are described in Table 13.5.

TABLE 13.5 VALUES OF THE ADS_STATUSENUM ENUMERATION

Value Name	Description
ADS_STATUS_S_OK	The search preference was properly set.
ADS_STATUS_INVALID_SEARCHPREF	The value of the dwSearchPref element was not valid.
ADS_STATUS_INVALID_SEARCHPREFVALUE	The value of the vValue element was invalid or of the wrong type.

The next several sections describe some of the search preferences you can use to enhance your directory searches.

Synchronous and Asynchronous Searching with IDirectorySearch

LDAP supports—and the IDirectorySearch interface provides access to—both synchronous and asynchronous searching facilities. Synchronous searches are the simplest searches, and IDirectorySearch uses synchronous searches by default. A synchronous search works as follows: The client sends a single request to the server, the server searches the directory and sends the results back to the client as it finds them. The client waits for all the results to come back from the server, and then gives all the results to the

application. From the application's viewpoint, it amounts to a single function call to get the results of the search—very neat and clean.

But synchronous searches have a couple of drawbacks. The first drawback is that the client must store all the results of the search in memory. It wouldn't be hard to exhaust the client's available memory with a large result set containing tens of thousands of entries. The second drawback is that the client application is idle while the server sends back the search results. That is a lot of wasted time and can cause unacceptable delays for the user.

Asynchronous searches work differently. Instead of waiting until all the search results come in from the server, the LDAP client periodically polls for any returned results. Although this makes the code for the application a little more complicated, it potentially solves the memory and excessive delay problems.

The `IDirectorySearch` interface effectively hides all this from you. You simply set the `ADS_SEARCHPREF_ASYNCHRONOUS` option to `TRUE` and call `ExecuteSearch()`, `GetFirstRow()`, and `GetNextRow()` as you normally would. The big difference is that you can start getting results before the search is complete.

> **NOTE**
>
> If you enable asynchronous searching, you must be sure to call `IDirectorySearch::AbanadonSearch()` if you terminate the search prematurely. This tells the server to free up the resources it allocated on behalf of your search.

Listing 13.5 shows how to enable asynchronous searching with `IDirectorySearch`.

LISTING 13.5 ASYNCHRONOUS SEARCHING

```
IDirectorySearch* piSearch = NULL;
HRESULT hr = ADsGetObject( _bstr_t( "LDAP://" ) +
                           _bstr_t( varDefaultNamingContext ),
                           IID_IDirectorySearch,
                           ( void** )&piSearch
                         );
if( SUCCEEDED( hr ) )
{
    ADS_SEARCHPREF_INFO asPrefs[ 1 ];

    asPrefs[ 0 ].dwSearchPref = ADS_SEARCHPREF_ASYNCHRONOUS;
    asPrefs[ 0 ].vValue.dwType = ADSTYPE_BOOLEAN;
```

```
    asPrefs[ 0 ].vValue.Boolean = TRUE;

    hr = piSearch->SetSearchPreference( asPrefs, 1 );
    if( SUCCEEDED( hr ) && asPrefs[ 0 ].dwStatus == ADS_STATUS_S_OK )
    {
        // call ExecuteSearch() here
    }
    piSearch->Release();
}
```

Paged Searches Using `IDirectorySearch`

The Active Directory LDAP implementation supports paged searches—that is, searches where the server returns the result set in chunks, or pages of several entries each. The client can process each page of results and then explicitly request the next page from the server.

Paged searches in Active Directory have several benefits, particularly when you are dealing with large result sets. The biggest advantage is that you can use a paged search to retrieve more result entries than are normally allowed by the administrative limit set on the server. If your directory administrator has lowered this limit to reduce the search load on the domain controller, using a paged search is the only way to ensure that you get all the search results you are expecting. Using a paged search also reduces the memory demand on both the client and server because they both treat the search as a sequence of smaller searches (see the section "Enabling and Disabling the Results Cache with `IDirectorySearch`"). Finally, a paged search spreads the network load out over time, so the network will not be swamped when the server returns a single huge result set.

Using paged searching with the `IDirectorySearch` interface is almost a complete no-brainer. All you have to do is set the `ADS_SEARCHPREF_PAGE_SIZE` search preference, and you're good to go. Listing 13.6 shows how to set the search preferences so that the server will return the search results in chunks of 100 entries.

LISTING 13.6 SETTING SEARCH PREFERENCES

```
IDirectorySearch* piSearch = NULL;
HRESULT hr = ADsGetObject( _bstr_t( "LDAP://" ) +
                           _bstr_t( varDefaultNamingContext ),
                           IID_IDirectorySearch,
                           ( void** )&piSearch
                         );
if( SUCCEEDED( hr ) )
{
    ADS_SEARCHPREF_INFO asPrefs[ 1 ];
```

continues

LISTING 13.6   CONTINUED

```
asPrefs[ 0 ].dwSearchPref = ADS_SEARCHPREF_PAGESIZE;
asPrefs[ 0 ].vValue.dwType = ADSTYPE_INTEGER;
asPrefs[ 0 ].vValue.Integer = 100;

hr = piSearch->SetSearchPreference( asPrefs, 1 );
if( SUCCEEDED( hr ) && asPrefs[ 0 ].dwStatus == ADS_STATUS_S_OK )
{
    // call ExecuteSearch() here
}
piSearch->Release();

}
```

Note that after you set the page size, you don't have to do anything special to handle the search results. You just use `GetNextRow()` and `GetColumn()` as you normally would.

Sorting Search Results with `IDirectorySearch`

The Active Directory LDAP implementation supports sorting of search results by the server. It allows you to sort the search result set by a single attribute in either ascending or descending order. See Chapter 22, "Extending LDAP Searches," for more about sorting.

The `IDirectorySearch` interface provides a search preference that lets you enable the Active Directory sorting feature. To sort your search results using `IDirectorySearch`, you must initialize an `ADS_SORTKEY` structure and initialize an `ADS_SEARCHPREF_INFO` structure using an `ADS_PROV_SPECIFIC` value that contains the `ADS_SORTKEY` structure.

Listing 13.7 is a sample program that retrieves all the user objects in the Users container, sorted by their common name (cn) attribute.

LISTING 13.7   RETRIEVING USER OBJECTS

```
 1: #include <windows.h>
 2: #include <activeds.h>
 3: #include <comutil.h>
 4: #include <stdio.h>
 5:
 6: int main(int argc, char* argv[])
 7: {
 8:     HRESULT hr = CoInitialize( NULL );
 9:
10:     if( SUCCEEDED( hr ) )
11:     {
12:         IADs* piIADs = NULL;
13:
14:         // Get rootDSE
```

```
15:              hr = ADsGetObject( L"LDAP://rootDSE", IID_IADs,
16:                                  ( void** )&piIADs );
17:          if( SUCCEEDED( hr ) )
18:          {
19:              _variant_t varDefaultNamingContext;
20:              _bstr_t strDefaultNamingContext;
21:
22:              // Get the domain naming context
23:              hr = piIADs->Get( L"defaultNamingContext",
24:                                &varDefaultNamingContext );
25:              if( SUCCEEDED( hr ) )
26:              {
27:                  IDirectorySearch* piSearch = NULL;
28:
29:                  // bind to the Users container and get an
30:                  // IDirectorySearch interface
31:                  hr = ADsGetObject( _bstr_t( "LDAP://CN=Users," ) +
32:                                      _bstr_t( varDefaultNamingContext),
33:                                      IID_IDirectorySearch,
34:                                      ( void** )&piSearch );
35:                  if( SUCCEEDED( hr ) )
36:                  {
37:                      // The sort key information
38:                      ADS_SORTKEY sKey = { L"cn", NULL, FALSE };
39:
40:                      // The search preference array
41:                      ADS_SEARCHPREF_INFO asPref[ 1 ];
42:
43:                      asPref[ 0 ].dwSearchPref= ADS_SEARCHPREF_SORT_ON;
44:                      asPref[ 0 ].vValue.dwType =ADSTYPE_PROV_SPECIFIC;
45:                      asPref[ 0 ].vValue.ProviderSpecific.dwLength =
46:                          sizeof( sKey );
47:                      asPref[ 0 ].vValue.ProviderSpecific.lpValue =
48:                          ( LPBYTE )&sKey;
49:
50:                      // Set the search preference
51:                      hr = piSearch->SetSearchPreference( asPref, 1 );
52:
53:                      // Retrieve these attributes for each user object
54:                      LPWSTR apszAttrNames[] =
55:                          { L"distinguishedName", L"cn", L"sn" };
56:                      ADS_SEARCH_HANDLE hSearch = NULL;
57:
58:                      // Initialize the search for user objects
59:                      piSearch->ExecuteSearch(
60:                          L"objectClass=user",
61:                          apszAttrNames,
62:                  sizeof( apszAttrNames ) / sizeof( apszAttrNames[ 0 ] ),
```

13

SEARCHING ACTIVE
DIRECTORY WITH
ADSI

continues

LISTING 13.7   CONTINUED

```
63:                          &hSearch
64:                      );
65:
66:                      // Get each row from the result table
67:                      for( hr = piSearch->GetFirstRow( hSearch );
68:                          SUCCEEDED( hr ) && hr != S_ADS_NOMORE_ROWS;
69:                          hr = piSearch->GetNextRow( hSearch ) )
70:                      {
71:                          ADS_SEARCH_COLUMN sColumn;
72:
73:                          // Get the DN column
74:                          hr = piSearch->GetColumn( hSearch,
75:                                  L"distinguishedName", &sColumn );
76:                          if( SUCCEEDED( hr ) )
77:                          {
78:                              printf( "dn: %S\n",
79:                                  sColumn.pADsValues[ 0
                                   ➡].CaseIgnoreString );
80:                              piSearch->FreeColumn( &sColumn );
81:                          }
82:
83:                          // Get the common name (cn) column
84:                          hr = piSearch->GetColumn( hSearch,
85:                                                  L"cn", &sColumn );
86:                          if( SUCCEEDED( hr ) )
87:                          {
88:                              printf( "cn: %S\n",
89:                                  sColumn.pADsValues[ 0
                                   ➡].CaseIgnoreString );
90:                              piSearch->FreeColumn( &sColumn );
91:                          }
92:
93:                          // Get the surname (sn) column
94:                          hr = piSearch->GetColumn( hSearch,
95:                                                  L"sn", &sColumn );
96:                          if( SUCCEEDED( hr ) )
97:                          {
98:                              printf( "sn: %S\n",
99:                                  sColumn.pADsValues[ 0
                                   ➡].CaseIgnoreString );
100:                             piSearch->FreeColumn( &sColumn );
101:                         }
102:
103:                         printf( "\n" );
104:                     }
105:
106:                     piSearch->Release();
107:                 }
108:             }
```

```
109:
110:                 piIADs->Release();
111:         }
112:
113:         ( void )CoUninitialize();
114:     }
115:
116:     return 0;
117: }
```

At line 15 the program gets an interface pointer to the rootDSE of a domain controller in the logged-in user's domain, and the program retrieves the domain naming context from the rootDSE at line 23.

The program gets an IDirectorySearch interface to the root of the domain naming context at line 31.

At line 38, the program starts setting up the parameters for setting the search preference. The program declares and initializes an ADS_SORTKEY structure to sort the cn attribute in ascending order.

At line 41, the program declares an array of one ADS_SEARCHPREF_INFO structure. At line 43, the program initializes the single entry in the array as an ADSTYPE_PROV_SPECIFIC value referring to the ADS_SORTKEY structure.

The program sets the search preference at line 51 and starts the search of the Users container at line 59 by calling ExecuteSearch().

The program then retrieves each row of the result table in the for loop starting at line 67 and retrieves the distinguished name, common name, and surname (sn) attributes at line 74, 84, and 94, respectively.

The program releases the search interface pointer at line 106, releases the rootDSE interface pointer at line 110, and finally shuts down the COM subsystem at line 113 by calling CoUninitialize().

Enabling and Disabling the Results Cache with IDirectorySearch

The IDirectorySearch interface provides a search results cache on the client side that lets you traverse the search results table more than once without resubmitting the search operation to the server. Using the cache can significantly increase the performance of your application if it has to reevaluate the search results over and over. By default, the search results cache is enabled, and to reenumerate the search results, you simply call IDirectorySearch::GetFirstRow() to start at the beginning of the results table again.

For searches with large result sets, caching the entire results set on the client might be prohibitive in terms of memory requirements. If you are using `IDirectorySearch` to perform searches that have large result sets (hundreds or thousands of entries), you might want to disable the cache before issuing the search. The following code segment shows how to disable the client-side results cache.

CAUTION

If you disable the client-side results cache, calling `IDirectorySearch::GetFirstRow()` more than once will not work properly, and calling `IDirectorySearch::GetPreviousRow()` will not work at all.

```
IDirectorySearch* piSearch = NULL;
HRESULT hr = ADsGetObject( _bstr_t( "LDAP://" ) +
                           _bstr_t( varDefaultNamingContext ),
                           IID_IDirectorySearch,
                           ( void** )&piSearch
                         );
if( SUCCEEDED( hr ) )
{
    ADS_SEARCHPREF_INFO asPrefs[ 1 ];

    asPrefs[ 0 ].dwSearchPref = ADS_SEARCHPREF_CACHE_RESULTS;
    asPrefs[ 0 ].vValue.dwType = ADSTYPE_BOOLEAN;
    asPrefs[ 0 ].vValue.Boolean = FALSE;

    hr = piSearch->SetSearchPreference( asPrefs, 1 );
    if( SUCCEEDED( hr ) && asPrefs[ 0 ].dwStatus == ADS_STATUS_S_OK )
    {
        // call ExecuteSearch() here
    }
    piSearch->Release();
}
```

Setting Limits on Searches with `IDirectorySearch`

Searching a large directory can be expensive in terms of disk performance on the server as well as processor and memory use on both the client and server. A directory search with a large result set can consume a prodigious amount of network bandwidth as well.

The most effective way to reduce the resources your directory searches consume is to limit them in some reasonable way. The `IDirectorySearch` interface provides several search preferences that limit your searches. The following sections show how you can make your searches quicker and less expensive in terms of the system resources they consume.

Limiting the Scope of a Search

One of the most effective things you can do to limit the amount of the directory namespace you have to search is to specify a *search scope.*

Active Directory is a hierarchical collection of objects, with each object in the directory potentially containing one or more additional objects. When you search Active Directory using the IDirectorySearch interface, you specify the starting location of the search in the directory (the search base). You can also specify a search scope that determines how much of the subtree beneath the search base to include in the search by using the ADS_SEARCHPREF_SEARCH_SCOPE search preference. LDAP (and therefore the IDirectorySearch interface) provide three possible search scopes, as shown in Table 13.6.

TABLE 13.6 VALUES OF THE ADS_SCOPEENUM ENUMERATION

Value Name	Description
ADS_SCOPE_BASE	Limits the search to the base object itself. A search with base scope will return, at most, the base object. You can accomplish the same thing more easily by using ADsGetObject().
ADS_SCOPE_ONELEVEL	Limits the search to the objects immediately contained by the base object. A one-level search does not include the base object.
ADS_SCOPE_SUBTREE	Does not limit the scope of the search. The search will include the entire directory subtree rooted at the base object, including the base object itself. This is the default setting for IDirectorySearch.

It is always a good idea to restrict the scope of your search as much as possible to reduce the search time and the load you put on the domain controller. For instance, if you are searching for user objects and you know they are all in the Users container, set the search scope to ADS_SCOPE_ONELEVEL.

The following code snippet shows how to set the search scope to ADS_SCOPE_ONELEVEL.

```
IDirectorySearch* piSearch = NULL;
HRESULT hr = ADsGetObject( _bstr_t( "LDAP://" ) +
                           _bstr_t( varDefaultNamingContext ),
                           IID_IDirectorySearch,
                           ( void** )&piSearch
                         );
```

```
if( SUCCEEDED( hr ) )
{
    ADS_SEARCHPREF_INFO asPrefs[ 1 ];

    asPrefs[ 0 ].dwSearchPref = ADS_SEARCHPREF_SEARCH_SCOPE;
    asPrefs[ 0 ].vValue.dwType = ADSTYPE_INTEGER;
    asPrefs[ 0 ].vValue.Integer = ADS_SCOPE_ONELEVEL;

    hr = piSearch->SetSearchPreference( asPrefs, 1 );
    if( SUCCEEDED( hr ) && asPrefs[ 0 ].dwStatus == ADS_STATUS_S_OK )
    {
        // call ExecuteSearch() here
    }
    piSearch->Release();
}
```

Limiting the Search to a Single Naming Context

When you start a directory search on a domain controller, the domain controller might send referrals back to the client indicating that the requested data lies in another naming context, possibly on another domain controller. To complete the search operation, the client must connect to these additional naming contexts or domain controllers and resubmit the search. Chapter 23, "Processing LDAP Referrals," gives a more complete description of LDAP referrals.

Connecting to other naming contexts and domain controllers to continue a search that has been referred is called *chasing the referral*. Chasing referrals can be extremely time-consuming, adding several seconds to the search time, depending on a variety of network and server configuration issues.

If limiting a search to a single naming context is acceptable, you can significantly improve your search time by disabling automatic referral chasing. You do this by setting the search preference ADS_SEARCHPREF_CHASE_REFERRALS to FALSE. The following code snippet shows how.

```
IDirectorySearch* piSearch = NULL;
HRESULT hr = ADsGetObject( _bstr_t( "LDAP://" ) +
                           _bstr_t( varDefaultNamingContext ),
                           IID_IDirectorySearch,
                           ( void** )&piSearch
                         );
if( SUCCEEDED( hr ) )
{
    ADS_SEARCHPREF_INFO asPrefs[ 1 ];

    asPrefs[ 0 ].dwSearchPref = ADS_SEARCHPREF_CHASE_REFERRALS;
    asPrefs[ 0 ].vValue.dwType = ADSTYPE_BOOLEAN;
    asPrefs[ 0 ].vValue.Boolean = FALSE;
```

```
    hr = piSearch->SetSearchPreference( asPrefs, 1 );
    if( SUCCEEDED( hr ) && asPrefs[ 0 ].dwStatus == ADS_STATUS_S_OK )
    {
        // call ExecuteSearch() here
    }
    piSearch->Release();
}
```

Limiting the Number of Entries Returned

In some applications, you might want to use only the first several directory entries that meet your search criteria. For instance, you might want to check that there is at least one user object for a user who lives in California. It would be a big waste of resources to have the search return potentially hundreds or thousands of entries when all you really want to know is that there is at least one. You can improve the performance of this kind of search by limiting the number of entries returned by the server setting the ADS_SEARCHPREF_SIZE_LIMIT search preference to the maximum number of entries you want the server to return. The following code snippet sets the search limit to 1.

```
IDirectorySearch* piSearch = NULL;
HRESULT hr = ADsGetObject( _bstr_t( "LDAP://" ) +
                           _bstr_t( varDefaultNamingContext ),
                           IID_IDirectorySearch,
                           ( void** )&piSearch
                         );
if( SUCCEEDED( hr ) )
{
    ADS_SEARCHPREF_INFO asPrefs[ 1 ];

    asPrefs[ 0 ].dwSearchPref = ADS_SEARCHPREF_SIZE_LIMIT;
    asPrefs[ 0 ].vValue.dwType = ADSTYPE_INTEGER;
    asPrefs[ 0 ].vValue.Integer = 1;

    hr = piSearch->SetSearchPreference( asPrefs, 1 );
    if( SUCCEEDED( hr ) && asPrefs[ 0 ].dwStatus == ADS_STATUS_S_OK )
    {
        // call ExecuteSearch() here
    }
    piSearch->Release();
}
```

13

SEARCHING ACTIVE
DIRECTORY WITH
ADSI

If you want to remove a previously set entry limit, set the ADS_SEARCHPREF_SIZE_LIMIT preference to zero.

Limiting the Time Spent Searching

If you have a directory search that you know from experience will take a long time and your application doesn't necessarily require the complete result set, you can explicitly limit the amount of time the domain controller will spend processing your search request.

The `ADS_SEARCHPREF_TIME_LIMIT` search preference lets you set the maximum number of seconds (of elapsed time) the server will spend on your search request. The following code snippet sets the search time limit to 5 seconds:

```
IDirectorySearch* piSearch = NULL;
HRESULT hr = ADsGetObject( _bstr_t( "LDAP://" ) +
                           _bstr_t( varDefaultNamingContext ),
                           IID_IDirectorySearch,
                           ( void** )&piSearch
                         );
if( SUCCEEDED( hr ) )
{
    ADS_SEARCHPREF_INFO asPrefs[ 1 ];

    asPrefs[ 0 ].dwSearchPref = ADS_SEARCHPREF_TIME_LIMIT;
    asPrefs[ 0 ].vValue.dwType = ADSTYPE_INTEGER;
    asPrefs[ 0 ].vValue.Integer = 10;

    hr = piSearch->SetSearchPreference( asPrefs, 1 );
    if( SUCCEEDED( hr ) && asPrefs[ 0 ].dwStatus == ADS_STATUS_S_OK )
    {
        // call ExecuteSearch() here
    }
    piSearch->Release();
}
```

If you want to remove a previously set time limit, set the `ADS_SEARCHPREF_TIME_LIMIT` preferences to zero.

Retrieving Attribute Names Only

If your application needs to know only the names of the attributes each entry has, as opposed to the values of the attributes, you can set the `ADS_SEARCHPREF_ATTRIBTYPES_ONLY` search preference to `TRUE`. This causes the domain controller to return only the names of the attributes for each directory entry meeting your search criteria. I must say that I'm hard-pressed to come up with a scenario where this would be useful, but there it is. The following code shows how to set the `ADS_SEARCHPREF_ATTRIBTYPES_ONLY` search preference.

```
IDirectorySearch* piSearch = NULL;
HRESULT hr = ADsGetObject( _bstr_t( "LDAP://" ) +
                           _bstr_t( varDefaultNamingContext ),
                           IID_IDirectorySearch,
                           ( void** )&piSearch
                         );
if( SUCCEEDED( hr ) )
{
    ADS_SEARCHPREF_INFO asPrefs[ 1 ];
```

```
asPrefs[ 0 ].dwSearchPref = ADS_SEARCHPREF_ATTRIBTYPES_ONLY;
asPrefs[ 0 ].vValue.dwType = ADSTYPE_BOOLEAN;
asPrefs[ 0 ].vValue.Boolean = TRUE;

hr = piSearch->SetSearchPreference( asPrefs, 1 );
if( SUCCEEDED( hr ) && asPrefs[ 0 ].dwStatus == ADS_STATUS_S_OK )
{
    // call ExecuteSearch() here
}
piSearch->Release();
}
```

CHAPTER 14

Accessing Users, Groups, and Organizations with ADSI

Probably the most popular thing to do with a directory is to manage user and group information. Almost every application that deals with the directory needs to access user and group information. ADSI provides three interfaces for simplifying access to Active Directory users and groups: `IADsUser`, `IADsGroup`, and `IADsMember`.

Active Directory organizes the user and group information within a domain in containers called localities, organizations, and organizational units, usually referred to as Ls, Os, and OUs. ADSI provides three interfaces for dealing with these containers: `IADsLocality`, `IsO`, and `IADsOU`.

The `IADsUser`, `IADsGroup`, `IADsO`, and `IADsOU` interfaces are all derived from the `IADs` interface I described in Chapter 12, "Basic Active Directory ADSI Interfaces." This means that if you get an `IADsUser` interface pointer to an object, you can use all the `IADsUser` functions with it, as well as all the `IADs` functions. You do not have to obtain a separate `IADs` pointer.

The fact that these four interfaces inherit from `IADs` also means they use the `IADs` property cache. The `IADs` property cache can improve network performance, but it's important that you understand how it works and how to use it effectively. You should check Chapter 12 for more information about the `IADs` property cache.

This chapter looks first at the IADsUser interface and then continues with the IADsGroup and IADsMember interfaces. This chapter finishes by discussing the IADsLocality, IADsOU and IADsO interfaces.

Accessing User Objects with ADSI

There are several ways to access user objects with ADSI. I've already described the IADs and IDirectoryObject interfaces in an earlier chapter. These interfaces provide generic access to the attributes and values of any directory object.

You can also use the IADsUser interface to access user objects. IADsUser provides easier-to-use functions for setting and retrieving the more common attributes of user objects. For instance, you can use the IADs::Get() and IADs::Put() functions to get and set the description attribute, which requires working with VARIANTs, or you can use the IADsUser::get_Description() and IADsUser::set_Description() functions that use BSTRs. The net effect is the same, but the IADsUser functions are sometimes a little more concise.

One big advantage of using IADsUser functions rather than their IADs counterparts is that IADsUser shields you somewhat from changes in the Active Directory schema. For instance, if you retrieve the last name of a user using the IADsUser::get_LastName() function, Microsoft could move the user's last name from the sn attribute to the lastName attribute, and you wouldn't have to modify your code.

Using the IADsUser interface also makes it much easier for you to write code that is portable between the different directory platforms supported by ADSI, such as the Windows NT Security Accounts Manager (SAM) database and Novell Directory Services (NDS).

IADsUser also provides a few functions that have no equivalents in the generic directory object interfaces. For instance, the IADsUser:SetPassword() function lets you set a user's password to a new value (provided you have the appropriate access rights). You can't do that using the generic directory object interfaces.

The IADsUser Interface

The IADsUser interface provides read and write access to the attributes of the Active Directory user object.

IADsUser inherits from the IADs interface, which means that all the functions of the IADs interface are also part of the IADsUser interface.

Because `IADsUser` inherits from `IADs`, `IADsUser` uses the property cache supported by the `IADs` interface, and consequently exhibits some of the same behaviors as the `IADs` interface. For instance, if you change an attribute using one of the `put_...()` functions that make up the `IADsUser` interface, you must call the `IADs::SetInfo()` function to write the changes to the directory. Refer to Chapter 12 for more information about the `IADs` property cache.

NOTE

Even though `SetInfo()` is part of the `IADs` interface, you do not need to obtain a separate `IADs` interface pointer to use. Because the `IADsUser` interface inherits from `IADs`, you can invoke the `SetInfo()` function by using the `IADsUser` interface pointer.

The `IADsUser` interface handles multivalued attributes in the same way that the `IADs` interface does. For instance, the function `IADsUser::get_LoginWorkstations()` returns a multivalue attribute containing the names of the workstations from which the user is allowed to log in. The `IADsUser` interface retrieves this attribute as a `VARIANT` array of `VARIANT`s. You can then use the `SafeArray...()` functions described in Chapter 12 to access the individual values of the attribute.

Sometimes one of the `IADsUser::get_...()` functions will return the ADSI error `E_ADS_PROPERTY_NOT_FOUND` (`0x8000500d`). This error indicates that the `get_...()` function is trying to obtain an attribute from the property cache that doesn't exist. This is not an infrequent occurrence with `IADsUser` because there are so many attributes defined in the schema for a user object, and administrators rarely give them all values.

Table 14.1 lists the functions that make up the `IADsUser` interface. For those functions that get and set a specific attribute of the user object, the table lists the attribute name in square brackets—for instance, `[description]`. You'll also notice that several of the functions defined as part of the `IADsUser` interface are not implemented by the ADSI LDAP provider for Active Directory. The table describes these functions as unsupported.

You'll notice that the `IADsUser` interface does not contain a function to create a new user object. You must use either the `IDirectoryObject::CreateDSObject()` or `IADsContainer::Create()` function, both of which are described in Chapter 12.

14

ACCESSING USERS,
GROUPS, AND
ORGANIZATIONS

TABLE 14.1   THE IADsUser INTERFACE

Function Name	Description
QueryInterface()	IUnknown interface.
AddRef()	IUnknown interface.
Release()	IUnknown interface.
GetTypeInfoCount()	IDispatch interface.
GetTypeInfo()	IDispatch interface.
GetIDsOfNames()	IDispatch interface.
Invoke()	IDispatch interface.
ChangePassword()	Sets the password for the user. You do not need the Administrator's security context for this call, but you do need the value of the current password.
get_AccountDisabled()/ put_AccountDisabled()	Retrieves/sets the account disabled flag in the userAccountControl attribute. ([userAccountControl])
get_AccountExpirationDate()/ put_AccountExpirationDate()	Retrieves/sets the account expiration date of the user account. If this attribute is missing or equal to zero, the account does not expire. ([accountExpirationDate])
get_BadLoginAddress()	Not supported by Active Directory.
get_BadLoginCount()	Retrieves the number of failed login attempts that occurred with the administrator-configured grace period *on this domain controller.*
get_Department()/put_Department()	Retrieves/sets the department name for the user. ([department])
get_Description()/ put_Description()	Retrieves/sets the user's department description. ([description])
get_Division()/put_Division()	Retrieves/sets the name of the division of which the user is a part. ([division])
get_EmailAddress()/ put_EmailAddress()	Retrieves/sets the user's email address. ([mail])
get_EmployeeID()/put_EmployeeID()	Retrieves/sets the user's employee ID. ([employeeID])
get_FaxNumber()/put_FaxNumber()	Retrieves/sets the user's fax number. ([facsimileTelephoneNumber])
get_FirstName()/put_FirstName()	Retrieves/sets the user's first name. ([givenName])

Function Name	Description
get_FullName()/put_FullName()	Retrieves/sets the user's full name. ([displayName])
get_GraceLoginsAllowed()/ put_GraceLoginsAllowed()	Not supported by Active Directory.
get_GraceLoginsRemaining()/ put_GraceLoginsRemaining()	Not supported by Active Directory.
get_HomeDirectory()/ put_HomeDirectory()	Retrieves/sets the user's home directory. The user's default directory will be set to this after he logs in. ([homeDirectory])
get_HomePage()/put_HomePage()	Retrieves/sets the user's WWW home page. ([wWWHomePage])
get_IsAccountLocked()/ put_IsAccountLocked()	Retrieves/sets the account locked flag for the user. It is one of the flags in the userAccountControl attribute. ([userAccountControl])
get_Languages()/put_Languages()	Not supported by Active Directory.
get_LastFailedLogin()	Retrieves the time and date of the last failed login attempt for this account *on this domain controller*. ([badPasswordTime])
get_LastLogin()	Retrieves the time and date of the last successful login for this user account *on this domain controller*. ([lastLogon])
get_LastLogoff()	Retrieves the time and date of the last logoff for this user account *on this domain controller*. ([lastLogoff])
get_LastName()/put_LastName()	Retrieves/sets the user's last name. ([sn])
get_LoginHours()/put_LoginHours()	Retrieves/sets the allowed login hours for this account as an array of BOOLEANs.
get_LoginScript()/ put_LoginScript()	Retrieves/sets the name of the file containing the user's login script. ([scriptPath])
get_LoginWorkstations()/ put_LoginWorkstations()	Retrieves/sets the names of the workstations from which the user is allowed to log in. ([userWorkstations])
get_Manager()/put_Manager()	Retrieves/sets the name of the user's manager. ([manager])
get_MaxLogins()/put_MaxLogins()	Not supported by Active Directory.

continues

14

ACCESSING USERS,
GROUPS, AND
ORGANIZATIONS

TABLE 14.1   CONTINUED

Function Name	*Description*
get_MaxStorage()/put_MaxStorage()	Retrieves/sets the maximum amount of disk storage the user is allowed to consume on the network. ([maxStorage])
get_NamePrefix()/put_NamePrefix()	Retrieves/sets the user's name prefix, such as Mr. or Dr. ([namePrefix])
get_NameSuffix()/put_NameSuffix()	Retrieves/sets the user's name suffix, such as PhD or III. ([generationQualifier])
get_OfficeLocations()/ put_OfficeLocations()	Retrieves the location of the office at which the user works. ([physicalDeliveryOfficeName])
get_OtherName()/put_OtherName()	Retrieves/sets the user's middle name. ([middleName])
get_PasswordExpirationDate()/ put_PasswordExpirationDate()	Retrieves/sets the password expiration date for the account.
get_PasswordLastChanged()	Retrieves the time and date the account password was last changed. ([pwdLastSet])
get_PasswordMinimumLength()/ put_PasswordMinimumLength()	Retrieves/sets the minimum length allowed for the user's password.
get_PasswordRequired()/ put_PasswordRequired()	Retrieves/sets the password required flag in the userAccountControl attribute. ([userAccountControl])
get_Picture()/put_Picture()	Retrieves/sets the user's picture in the directory. ([thumbnailPhoto])
get_PostalAddresses()/ put_PostalAddresses()	Retrieves/sets the user's mail address. ([postalAddress])
get_PostalCodes()/ put_PostalCodes()	Retrieves/sets the user's mail postal codes. ([postalCode])
get_Profile()/put_Profile()	Retrieves/sets the path of the profile file for the user. ([profilePath])
get_RequireUniquePassword()/ put_RequireUniquePassword()	Retrieves/sets the unique password required flag in the userAccountControl attribute. ([userAccountControl])
get_SeeAlso()/put_SeeAlso()	Retrieves/sets the user's see also name. ([seeAlso])
get_TelephoneHome()/ put_TelephoneHome()	Retrieves/sets the user's home phone number. ([homePhone])
get_TelephoneMobile()/ put_TelephoneMobile()	Retrieves/sets the user's mobile telephone number ([mobile])

Function Name	Description
get_TelephoneNumber()/ put_TelephoneNumber()	Retrieves/sets the user's primary phone number. ([telephoneNumber])
get_TelephonePager()/ put_TelephonePager()	Retrieves/sets the user's pager number. ([pager])
get_Title()/put_Title()	Retrieves/sets the user's title—for instance, Director. ([title])
Groups()	Retrieves the IADsMembers interface for the user, which will allow you to enumerate the groups of which the user is a member. ([memberOf])
SetPassword()	Sets the user's password to the specified value. This requires the Administrator's security context.

Getting a User's Name with IADsUser

Using the get_...() and put_...() functions from the IADsUser interface is extremely simple, and all the functions work pretty much the same way. The following sample shows how to use the get_FirstName() and get_LastName() functions for each of the user objects in the Users container.

HRESULT IADsUser::get_FirstName(BSTR* pstrFirstName)

    pstrFirstName is a pointer to a BSTR that will be set to the user's first name.

Returns: An ADSI or COM error code. Check the result with one of the COM error macros described in Chapter 11, "ADSI Fundamentals."

HRESULT IADsUser::get_LastName(BSTR* pstrLastName)

    pstrLastName is a pointer to a BSTR that will be set to the user's last name.

Returns: An ADSI or COM error code. Check the result with one of the COM error macros described in Chapter 11.

The sample program in Listing 14.1 demonstrates using the IADsUser interface to retrieve a user's first and last name.

LISTING 14.1 USING THE IADsUser INTERFACE TO RETRIEVE THE FIRST AND LAST NAME

```
1: #include <windows.h>
2: #include <activeds.h>
3: #include <comutil.h>
```

14

ACCESSING USERS,
GROUPS, AND
ORGANIZATIONS

continues

LISTING 14.1 CONTINUED

```
 4: #include <stdio.h>
 5:
 6: int main(int argc, char* argv[])
 7: {
 8:   HRESULT hr = CoInitialize( NULL );
 9:
10:   if( SUCCEEDED( hr ) )
11:   {
12:     IADs* piIADs = NULL;
13:
14:     // Get rootDSE
15:     hr = ADsGetObject( L"LDAP://rootDSE", IID_IADs, ( void** )
       ➥&piIADs );
16:     if( SUCCEEDED( hr ) )
17:     {
18:       // Get the domain NC
19:       _variant_t varDefaultNamingContext;
20:       hr = piIADs->Get( L"defaultNamingContext",
21:                         ➥&varDefaultNamingContext );
22:       if( SUCCEEDED( hr ) )
23:       {
24:         // Compose the DN of the User container in the domain
25:         _bstr_t strPath = _bstr_t( "LDAP://CN=Users," ) +
26:                           ➥_bstr_t( varDefaultNamingContext );
27:         IADsContainer* piContainer = NULL;
28:
29:         hr = ADsGetObject( strPath, IID_IADsContainer,
30:                           ➥( void** )&piContainer );
31:         if( SUCCEEDED( hr ) )
32:         {
33:           IEnumVARIANT* piEnum;
34:
35:           // Set filter
36:           LPWSTR apszClassNames[] = { L"user" };
37:           _variant_t varClassNames;
38:           ADsBuildVarArrayStr( apszClassNames,
39:             ➥sizeof( apszClassNames ) / sizeof(
40:             ➥apszClassNames[ 0 ] ), &varClassNames );
41:           hr = piContainer->put_Filter( varClassNames );
42:
43:           // Create an enumerator on the User container
44:           hr = ADsBuildEnumerator( piContainer, &piEnum );
45:           if( SUCCEEDED( hr ) )
46:           {
47:             ULONG ulCount;
48:             _variant_t varEntry;
49:
50:             // Enumerate the entries
51:             while( ( hr = ADsEnumerateNext( piEnum, 1, &varEntry,
```

```
52:            ➥&ulCount ) == S_OK ) && ulCount == 1 )
53:            {
54:              IADsUser* piUser = NULL;
55:
56:              // Get an IADUsers interface to the child object
57:              hr = ( ( IDispatch* )varEntry)->QueryInterface(
58:                      ➥IID_IADsUser, ( void** )&piUser );
59:              if( SUCCEEDED( hr ) )
60:              {
61:                BSTR strFirstName = L"";
62:                BSTR strLastName = L"";
63:
64:                ( void )piUser->get_FirstName( &strFirstName );
65:                ( void )piUser->get_LastName( &strLastName );
66:
67:                printf( "First: %S Last: %S\n",
68:                        ➥strFirstName, strLastName );
69:
70:                piUser->Release();
71:              }
72:
73:              ( ( IDispatch* )varEntry )->Release();
74:            }
75:
76:            piEnum->Release();
77:          }
78:
79:          piContainer->Release();
80:        }
81:      }
82:    }
83:
84:    ( void )CoUninitialize();
85:  }
86:
87:  return 0;
88: }
```

14

ACCESSING USERS,
GROUPS, AND
ORGANIZATIONS

From lines 1–30, the program in Listing 14.1 binds to the rootDSE, gets the default naming context, and also gets an IADsContainer interface to the Users container in the domain. This is the same code used in Chapter 12 to enumerate the Users container.

The program sets the search filter at line 41 so that the container enumerator will return only user objects.

At line 44, the program constructs a container enumerator by calling ADsBuildEnumerator. At line 51, the program starts enumerating the user objects in the Users container.

At line 57, the program gets an IADsUser interface pointer to each object returned by the enumerator.

The program then retrieves the first name and last name of each user object at lines 64 and 65 and then prints them at line 67.

The program then releases the various interface pointers, and shuts down the COM subsystem at line 84.

Locking a User Account with IADsUser

The next sample program shows how to lock a single user account using the IADsUser::set_IsAccountLocked() function. put_IsAccountLocked() sets the ADS_UF_LOCKOUT flag in the userAccountControl attribute of the user object. There are a couple interesting things to notice about this program.

First, the program uses serverless binding to bind directly to the user object. This is very convenient because you do not have to get the domain name for the user and then call DsGetDcName() to find an appropriate domain controller. ADsGetObject() does this for you automatically.

The other thing to notice is that the program calls IADs::SetInfo() after calling IADsUser::set_IsAccountLocked(). This causes ADSI to write change to the userAccountControl attribute to the directory. If you leave out this step, ADSI will not update the directory with your changes.

```
HRESULT IADsUser::put_IsAccountLocked( VARIANT_BOOL bLocked )
```

> bLocked is a VARIANT_BOOL that, if TRUE, indicates that the account is to be locked. If it's FALSE, bLocked indicates that the account is to be unlocked.

Returns: An ADSI or COM error code. Check the result with one of the COM error macros described in Chapter 11.

The sample application shown in Listing 14.2 demonstrates using the IADsUser interface to lock a user account.

LISTING 14.2   USING THE IADsUser INTERFACE TO LOCK A USER ACCOUNT

```
1: #include <windows.h>
2: #include <activeds.h>
3: #include <comutil.h>
4: #include <stdio.h>
5:
6: int main(int argc, char* argv[])
7: {
```

```
 8:    HRESULT hr = CoInitialize( NULL );
 9:
10:    if( SUCCEEDED( hr ) )
11:    {
12:      IADsUser* piUser = NULL;
13:      _bstr_t strPath =
14:      ➡L"LDAP://CN=Steve Calderon,CN=Users,DC=megacorp,DC=com";
15:
16:      hr = ADsGetObject( strPath, IID_IADsUser, ( void** )&piUser );
17:      if( SUCCEEDED( hr ) )
18:      {
19:        VARIANT_BOOL bLocked = TRUE;
20:
21:        ( void )piUser->put_IsAccountLocked( bLocked );
22:
23:        hr = piUser->SetInfo();
24:
25:        if( SUCCEEDED( hr ) )
26:        {
27:          printf( "Account locked\n" );
28:        }
29:        else
30:        {
31:          printf ( "Error %x locking out account\n", hr );
32:        }
33:
34:        piUser->Release();
35:      }
36:
37:      ( void )CoUninitialize();
38:    }
39:
40:    return 0;
41: }
```

14

The program in Listing 14.2 starts by initializing the COM subsystem at line 8. Then it gets an IADsUser interface pointer to the user
CN=SCalderon,CN=Users,DC=megacorp,DC=com.

At line 21, the program sets the account locked flag in the property cache by calling
IADsUser::put_IsAccountLocked() with a parameter of TRUE. The program then calls
IADs::SetInfo() to write the changed attribute from the cache to the directory.

The program releases the IADsUser interface at line 34 and wraps up the COM subsystem at line 37.

Setting a User Password with `IADsUser`

If you have administrative privileges, you can force the password of a user to a particular value. The sample program in Listing 14.3 uses the `IADsUser::SetPassword()` function to perform this operation.

The program uses the same binding technique as the preceding sample program, which doesn't require binding to a particular domain controller or domain.

Note that the program does not call the `IADs::SetInfo()` function after changing the password. The `IADs::SetPassword()` function does not modify the password in the property cache; it sends the change directly to the domain controller.

> **NOTE**
>
> The `IADsUser::SetPassword()` function requires administrative access to change a user's password. The `IADsUser::ChangePassword()` function also changes a user's password, but does not require administrative access rights. `IADsUser::ChangePassword()` does, however, require knowledge of the current password of the account being changed.

```
HRESULT IADsUser::SetPassword( BSTR strNewPassword )
```

> `strNewPassword` is the value of the new password. If there is to be no password, pass an empty BSTR.

Returns: An ADSI or COM error code. Check the result with one of the COM error macros described in Chapter 11.

The sample program shown in Listing 14.3 demonstrates using `IADsUser` to set a user's password.

LISTING 14.3 USING THE `IADsUser` INTERFACE TO SET A USER'S PASSWORD

```
 1: #include <windows.h>
 2: #include <activeds.h>
 3: #include <comutil.h>
 4: #include <stdio.h>
 5:
 6: int main(int argc, char* argv[])
 7: {
 8:   HRESULT hr = CoInitialize( NULL );
 9:
10:   if( SUCCEEDED( hr ) )
11:   {
```

```
12:     IADsUser* piUser = NULL;
13:     _bstr_t strPath =
14:   ➥L"LDAP://CN=JCarthey,CN=Users,DC=megacorp,dc=com";
15:
16:     hr = ADsGetObject( strPath, IID_IADsUser, ( void** )&piUser );
17:     if( SUCCEEDED( hr ) )
18:     {
19:       hr = piUser->SetPassword( L"foo" );
20:       if( SUCCEEDED( hr ) )
21:       {
22:         printf( "Password set\n" );
23:       }
24:       else
25:       {
26:         printf ( "Error %x setting password\n", hr );
27:       }
28:
29:       piUser->Release();
30:     }
31:
32:     ( void )CoUninitialize();
33:   }
34:
35:   return 0;
36: }
```

The program in Listing 14.3 gets an `IADsUser` interface pointer for the JCarthey user at line 16 and then calls the `IADsUser::SetPassword()` function at line 19, setting the new password for the account to "foo."

The program releases the `IADsUser` interface pointer at line 29 and shuts down the COM subsystem at line 32.

Accessing Groups with ADSI

In Windows 2000, a *group* is a collection of users who share some common characteristics. The Administrators group, for instance, contains the names of all the users who have administrative privileges in the domain. A group is a security principal, and a user inherits the access rights of the groups of which he is a member. A group can also contain other groups, so an administrator can create quite sophisticated groupings of users. Groups are the primary mechanism a network administrator uses to keep user privileges organized.

Active Directory creates a `group` object in the directory for every group the administrator defines. Each `group` object contains a multivalued attribute called `members` that contain the fully qualified names of each of the members of the group. Active Directory also implements an operational attribute of the user object named memberOf, which contains the fully qualified names of the groups of which the user is a member.

ADSI uses two separate interfaces to support groups in Active Directory. The first interface, IADsGroup, provides access to the nonmember information of the group, such as the group description. IADsGroup also provides functions for adding members to and removing members from the group.

ADSI provides a second class, named IADsMembers, that supports enumeration of the members of the group. The IADsMembers interface is similar to the IADsContainer interface in that it provides a way to create an enumerator for the group and a way to filter the results of the enumeration by class. The IADsGroup interface has a member function, IADsGroup::Members(), that retrieves the IADsMembers interface from a group.

The following sections describe how to use the IADsGroup and IADsMembers interfaces.

The IADsGroup Interface

The IADsGroup interface provides functions for getting and setting the description attribute of an Active Directory group object, as well as functions for adding group members, removing group members, and testing group membership. The IADsGroup::Members() function returns an IADsMembers interface pointer to the group (see Table 14.2).

TABLE 14.2   THE IADsGroup INTERFACE

Function Name	*Description*
QueryInterface()	IUnknown interface.
AddRef()	IUnknown interface.
Release()	IUnknown interface.
GetTypeInfoCount()	IDispatch interface.
GetTypeInfo()	IDispatch interface.
GetIDsOfNames()	IDispatch interface.
Invoke()	IDispatch interface.
get_Description()/put_Description()	Retrieves/sets the description for the group.
Members()	Returns an IADsMembers interface pointer for the group.
IsMember()	Determines whether a given name (expressed as an ADsPath) is a member of the group.
Add()	Adds a member to the group.
Remove()	Removes a member from the group.

There is no function in the `IADsGroup` interface to create a new group. You must use either the `IDirectoryObject::CreateDSObject()` or `IADsContainer::Create()` function, both of which are described in Chapter 12.

Adding a Member to a Group

The first function in the `IADsGroup` interface I'll cover is the `IADsGroup::Add()` function. The `IADsGroup::Add()` function adds a new name to an existing group. If the name already exists in the group, the add operation will fail. Also, both the group and the object you are adding to the group must exist in the directory; otherwise, the add operation will fail.

You can add objects from other domains to a group, subject to the limitations on the type of group. See Chapter 4, "Active Directory Security," for more information regarding local groups, global groups, and universal groups.

You can also add one group to another group, again subject to the limitations on the type of group.

```
HRESULT IADsGroup::Add( BSTR strPathToAdd )
```

> `strPathToAdd` is a `BSTR` containing the `ADsPath` of the object to add to the group. Note that this is a full `ADsPath` including the namespace qualifier—for instance, `"LDAP://CN=Randy Bradley,CN=Users,DC=megacorp,DC=com"`. Just using a fully qualified distinguished name is insufficient.

Returns: An ADSI or COM error code. Check the result with one of the COM error macros described in Chapter 11.

The sample program in Listing 14.4 shows you how to add a new member to an existing group.

LISTING 14.4   ADDING A MEMBER TO A GROUP

```
 1: #include <windows.h>
 2: #include <activeds.h>
 3: #include <comutil.h>
 4: #include <stdio.h>
 5:
 6: int main(int argc, char* argv[])
 7: {
 8:   HRESULT hr = CoInitialize( NULL );
 9:
10:   if( SUCCEEDED( hr ) )
11:   {
12:     IADs* piRootDSE = NULL;
13:
```

continues

14

ACCESSING USERS,
GROUPS, AND
ORGANIZATIONS

LISTING 14.4 CONTINUED

```
14:      hr = ADsGetObject( L"LDAP://rootDSE", IID_IADs,
15:                          ⟜( void** )&piRootDSE );
16:      if( SUCCEEDED( hr ) )
17:      {
18:        _variant_t varDefaultNamingContext;
19:
20:        hr = piRootDSE->Get( L"defaultNamingContext",
21:                              ⟜&varDefaultNamingContext );
22:        if( SUCCEEDED( hr ) )
23:        {
24:          IADsGroup* piGroup;
25:          _bstr_t strDomain = varDefaultNamingContext;
26:
27:          hr = ADsGetObject(
28:            ⟜bstr_t( L"LDAP://CN=Administrators,CN=Builtin," ) +
29:            ⟜strDomain, IID_IADsGroup, ( void** )&piGroup );
30:
31:          if( SUCCEEDED( hr ) )
32:          {
33:            _bstr_t strPath =
34:            ⟜_bstr_t( "LDAP://CN=Cindy McGee,CN=Users," ) + strDomain;
35:            hr = piGroup->Add( strPath );
36:            if( SUCCEEDED( hr ) )
37:            {
38:              printf( "Added user to group\n" );
39:            }
40:            else
41:            {
42:              printf( "Add failed with error %x\n", hr );
43:            }
44:
45:            piGroup->Release();
46:          }
47:        }
48:
49:        piRootDSE->Release();
50:      }
51:
52:      ( void )CoUninitialize();
53:    }
54:
55:    return 0;
56: }
```

The program in Listing 14.4 gets the domain naming context from the rootDSE at line 20 and gets an IADsGroup interface to the Administrators group for the domain at line 27.

At line 33, the program composes the name of a user in the domain (the user must already exist in the directory). At line 35, the program adds the user to the Administrators group.

The program releases the group interface and the `rootDSE` interface at lines 45 and 49, respectively, and shuts down the COM subsystem at line 52.

Testing a User's Membership in a Group

The `IADsGroup` interface provides the `IADsGroup::IsMember()` function for testing if a given name is a member of group.

`HRESULT IADsGroup::IsMember( BSTR strName, VARIANT_BOOL* pbIsMember )`

> `strName` is the `ADsPath` of the name to test membership of. Note that this is a full `ADsPath`, including the namespace qualifier—for instance, `"LDAP://CN=Doug Dickerson,CN=Users,DC=megacorp,DC=com"`. Just using a fully qualified distinguished name is insufficient.

> `pbIsMember` is the address of a `VARIANT_BOOL` that will be set to `TRUE` if the given name is a member of the group, and set to `FALSE` if the name is not a member of the group.

Returns: An ADSI or COM error code. Check the result with one of the COM error macros described in Chapter 11.

CAUTION

The `IADsGroup::IsMember()` function tests only for *direct* membership in a group. If a user is a member of another group and that other group is a member of the group you are testing membership in, `IADsGroup::IsMember()` will return `FALSE`.

The only way to accurately test group membership is to recursively check membership in all contained groups.

The sample program shown in Listing 14.5 demonstrates using `IADsGroup` to check membership in a group.

LISTING 14.5 TESTING MEMBERSHIP IN A GROUP

```
1: #include <windows.h>
2: #include <activeds.h>
3: #include <comutil.h>
```

14

ACCESSING USERS, GROUPS, AND ORGANIZATIONS

continues

LISTING 14.5 CONTINUED

```
 4: #include <stdio.h>
 5:
 6: int main(int argc, char* argv[])
 7: {
 8:    HRESULT hr = CoInitialize( NULL );
 9:
10:    if( SUCCEEDED( hr ) )
11:    {
12:      IADs* piRootDSE = NULL;
13:
14:      hr = ADsGetObject( L"LDAP://rootDSE", IID_IADs,
15:                           ➥( void** )&piRootDSE );
16:      if( SUCCEEDED( hr ) )
17:      {
18:        _variant_t varDefaultNamingContext;
19:
20:        hr = piRootDSE->Get( L"defaultNamingContext",
21:                               ➥&varDefaultNamingContext );
22:        if( SUCCEEDED( hr ) )
23:        {
24:          IADsGroup* piGroup;
25:          _bstr_t strDomain = varDefaultNamingContext;
26:
27:          hr = ADsGetObject(
28:             ➥_bstr_t( L"LDAP://CN=Administrators,CN=Builtin," ) +
29:             ➥strDomain, IID_IADsGroup, ( void** )&piGroup );
30:          if( SUCCEEDED( hr ) )
31:          {
32:            VARIANT_BOOL bIsMember;
33:            _bstr_t strName =
34:               ➥bstr_t( "LDAP://CN=Ralph Krausse,CN=Users," ) +
               ➥strDomain;
35:
36:            hr = piGroup->IsMember( strName, &bIsMember );
37:            if( SUCCEEDED( hr ) )
38:            {
39:              printf( "%s %s a member of the Administrators group\n",
40:                 ➥( const char* )strName, bIsMember ? "is" : "is not" );
41:            }
42:
43:            piGroup->Release();
44:          }
45:        }
46:
47:        piRootDSE->Release();
48:      }
49:
50:      ( void )CoUninitialize();
51:   }
```

```
52:
53:    return 0;
54: }
```

The program in Listing 14.5 starts by getting the domain naming context from the `rootDSE` at line 20. Then it retrieves an `IADsGroup` interface pointer to the Administrators group in that domain at line 27.

At line 33, the program composes the name of a user in the domain. Then it checks to see whether that user is a member of the Administrators group at line 36.

The program displays the results of the test at line 39, releases the group and `rootDSE` interface pointers at lines 43 and 47, and wraps up by calling `CoUninitialize()` at line 50.

The `IADsMembers` Interface

There are many cases in which you might want to list the members of a group in your application. The functions in the `IADsGroup` interface do not provide any way to enumerate the members of a group. These functions are provided instead by the `IADsMembers` interface. `IADsMembers` has functions to count the members in a group and to create an enumerator that you can use to list the members of the group. The `IADsGroup::Members()` function retrieves an `IADsMembers` interface that you can then use to get an enumerator for the group.

Table 14.3 describes the `IADsMembers` interface.

TABLE 14.3 THE `IADsMembers` INTERFACE

Function Name	Description
`QueryInterface()`	IUnknown interface.
`AddRef()`	IUnknown interface.
`Release()`	IUnknown interface.
`GetTypeInfoCount()`	IDispatch interface.
`GetTypeInfo()`	IDispatch interface.
`GetIDsOfNames()`	IDispatch interface.
`Invoke()`	IDispatch interface.
`get_Count()`	Returns the number of members in the group.

continues

TABLE 14.3 CONTINUED

Function Name	Description
get__NewEnum()	Creates a new enumerator for the group using the current filter settings. Note that the function name contains two underscore (_) characters.
get_Filter()	Retrieves the current class filter settings.
put_Filter()	Sets the current class filter settings to be used by subsequent enumerators created using this interface.

Table 14.4 describes the IEnumVARIANT interface.

TABLE 14.4 THE IEnumVARIANT INTERFACE

Function Name	Description
QueryInterface()	IUnknown interface.
AddRef()	IUnknown interface.
Release()	IUnknown interface.
GetTypeInfoCount()	IDispatch interface.
GetTypeInfo()	IDispatch interface.
GetIDsOfNames()	IDispatch interface.
Invoke()	IDispatch interface.
Next()	Retrieves the next object in the group.
Skip()	Skips the next object in the container.
Reset()	Resets the iterator back to the beginning of the group.
Clone()	Creates a new enumerator that has the same settings as this one.

The process of creating and using a group enumerator is identical to creating and using a container enumerator, as described in Chapter 12. Because the interface for creating an enumerator is identical in both cases, you can use the enumerator helper functions described in Chapter 12 to enumerate the members of a group.

```
HRESULT ADsBuildEnumerator( IADsContainer* piContainer, IEnumVARIANT**
➥ppiEnumerator )
```

> piContainer is a IADsContainer* interface pointer to the container object you want to enumerate.
>
> ppiEnumerator is the address of the IEnumVARIANT pointer to set to the new enumerator.

Returns: An ADSI or COM error code. Check the result with one of the COM error macros described in Chapter 11.

```
HRESULT ADsEnumerateNext( IEnumVARIANT* piEnumerator,
➥ULONG uCountRequested, VARIANT* pvarEntries, ULONG* puCountReturned )
```

piEnumerator is a IEnumVARIANT interface pointer to iterate.

uCountRequested is the number of entries you want to retrieve at one time.

pvarEntries is the address of a VARIANT that the function will set to contain the returned pointers to contained objects.

puCountReturned is the address of a ULONG variable to set to the actual number of entries returned in pvarEntries.

Returns: S_OK if it successfully retrieved one or more entries, or 1 if it did not.

CAUTION

Do not test the return value of ADsEnumerateNext() using the SUCCEEDED() macro. ADsEnumerateNext returns either S_OK or 1. The SUCCEEDED() macro evaluates to TRUE for both those values. Instead, you should explicitly compare the return value of ADsEnumerateNext() to S_OK.

```
HRESULT ADsFreeEnumerator( IEnumVARIANT* piEnumerator )
```

piEnumerator is a pointer to an IEnumVARIANT interface that was created with ADsBuildEnumerator.

Enumerating the Members of a Group

The sample program in Listing 14.6 shows how to use the enumerator helper functions to enumerate the members of a group. The program gets an interface pointer to the Administrators group and then lists all the direct members of the group.

LISTING 14.6 ENUMERATING THE MEMBERS OF A GROUP

```
1: #include <windows.h>
2: #include <activeds.h>
3: #include <comutil.h>
4: #include <stdio.h>
5:
6: int main(int argc, char* argv[])
7: {
8:   HRESULT hr = CoInitialize( NULL );
```

continues

LISTING 14.6 CONTINUED

```
 9:
10:   if( SUCCEEDED( hr ) )
11:   {
12:     IADs* piRootDSE = NULL;
13:
14:     hr = ADsGetObject( L"LDAP://rootDSE", IID_IADs,
15:                         ➥( void** )&piRootDSE );
16:     if( SUCCEEDED( hr ) )
17:     {
18:       _variant_t varDefaultNamingContext;
19:
20:       hr = piRootDSE->Get( L"defaultNamingContext",
21:                            ➥&varDefaultNamingContext );
22:       if( SUCCEEDED( hr ) )
23:       {
24:         IADsGroup* piGroup;
25:         IADsMembers* piMembers;
26:         _bstr_t strDomain = varDefaultNamingContext;
27:
28:         hr = ADsGetObject(
29:           ➥_bstr_t( L"LDAP://CN=Administrators,CN=Builtin," ) +
30:           ➥strDomain, IID_IADsGroup, ( void** )&piGroup );
31:         if( SUCCEEDED( hr ) )
32:         {
33:           hr = piGroup->Members( &piMembers );
34:           if( SUCCEEDED( hr ) )
35:           {
36:             IEnumVARIANT* piEnum = NULL;
37:
38:             hr = ADsBuildEnumerator( ( IADsContainer* )piMembers,
39:                                      ➥&piEnum );
40:             if( SUCCEEDED( hr ) )
41:             {
42:               ULONG ulCount;
43:               _variant_t varEntry;
44:
45:               // Enumerate the entries
46:               while( ADsEnumerateNext( piEnum, 1,
47:                     ➥&varEntry, &ulCount ) == S_OK && ulCount == 1 )
48:               {
49:                 IADs* piEntry = NULL;
50:
51:                 // Get an IADs interface to the child object
52:                 hr = ( ( IDispatch* )varEntry)->QueryInterface(
53:                       ➥IID_IADs,( void** )&piEntry );
54:                 if( SUCCEEDED( hr ) )
55:                 {
56:                   BSTR strName;
57:
```

```
58:                          piEntry->get_ADsPath( &strName );
59:                          printf( "%S\n", strName );
60:
61:                          piEntry->Release();
62:                     }
63:
64:                     ( ( IDispatch* )varEntry )->Release();
65:                 }
66:
67:                 piEnum->Release();
68:             }
69:
70:             piMembers->Release();
71:         }
72:     }
73:   }
74:
75:   piRootDSE->Release();
76:   }
77:
78:   ( void )CoUninitialize();
79: }
80:
81:   return 0;
82: }
```

The sample program in Listing 14.6 retrieves the domain naming context from the
rootDSE at line 20 and gets an IADsGroup interface to the Administrators group in the
domain at line 28.

At line 33, the sample program gets the IADsMembers interface pointer from the group
using the IADsGroup::Members() function.

At line 38, the program creates an enumerator using the IADsMembers interface and the
ADsBuildEnumerator() function. Note that the program explicitly casts the IADsMembers
interface pointer to an IADsContainer interface pointer. That is safe in this case because
the IADsMembers interface supports the same functions as the IADsContainer interface,
even though they do not inherit from each other.

14

ACCESSING USERS,
GROUPS, AND
ORGANIZATIONS

> **CAUTION**
>
> The casting of interface pointers as demonstrated in this program is quite
> dangerous; your program loses all concept of type-safety. Casting an interface
> pointer to an incompatible type can lead to GPFs and other program failures.
> In general, you should avoid doing this.

The while loop that starts at line 46 enumerates the members of the group, each time retrieving a VARIANT containing the IDispatch pointer to the next object in the group.

At line 52, the program calls QueryInterface on the IDispatch pointer to get an IADs interface pointer and then calls IADs::GetADsPath() to retrieve the ADsPath of the object.

The program releases the various interface pointers and then wraps up by calling CoUninitialize() at line 78.

Recursively Enumerating the Members of a Group

Because you can nest groups within other groups, it is often useful to list the members of a group recursively. That is, list all the members of a given group, and if any of those members are groups themselves, list out their members, and so on.

Listing 14.7 shows how you can list the members of a group recursively.

LISTING 14.7 RECURSIVELY ENUMERATING THE MEMBERS OF A GROUP

```
 1: #include <windows.h>
 2: #include <activeds.h>
 3: #include <comutil.h>
 4: #include <stdio.h>
 5:
 6: void EnumerateGroup( IADsGroup* piGroup );
 7:
 8: int main(int argc, char* argv[])
 9: {
10:   HRESULT hr = CoInitialize( NULL );
11:
12:   if( SUCCEEDED( hr ) )
13:   {
14:     IADs* piRootDSE = NULL;
15:
16:     hr = ADsGetObject( L"LDAP://rootDSE", IID_IADs,
17:                     ➥( void** )&piRootDSE );
18:     if( SUCCEEDED( hr ) )
19:     {
20:       _variant_t varDefaultNamingContext;
21:
22:       hr = piRootDSE->Get( L"defaultNamingContext",
23:                       ➥&varDefaultNamingContext );
24:       if( SUCCEEDED( hr ) )
25:       {
26:         IADsGroup* piGroup;
27:
28:         hr = ADsGetObject(
29:           ➥_bstr_t( L"LDAP://CN=Administrators,CN=Builtin," ) +
```

```
30:            ➥_bstr_t( varDefaultNamingContext ), IID_IADsGroup,
                 ➥( void** )&piGroup );
31:          if( SUCCEEDED( hr ) )
32:          {
33:            EnumerateGroup( piGroup );
34:
35:            piGroup->Release();
36:          }
37:        }
38:
39:        piRootDSE->Release();
40:      }
41:
42:      ( void )CoUninitialize();
43:    }
44:
45:    return 0;
46: }
47:
48: void EnumerateGroup( IADsGroup* piGroup )
49: {
50:    IADsMembers* piMembers = NULL;
51:
52:    HRESULT hr = piGroup->Members( &piMembers );
53:    if( SUCCEEDED( hr ) )
54:    {
55:      IEnumVARIANT* piEnum = NULL;
56:
57:      hr = ADsBuildEnumerator( ( IADsContainer* )piMembers, &piEnum );
58:      if( SUCCEEDED( hr ) )
59:      {
60:        ULONG ulCount;
61:        _variant_t varEntry;
62:
63:        // Enumerate the entries
64:        while( ADsEnumerateNext( piEnum, 1,
65:               ➥&varEntry, &ulCount ) == S_OK && ulCount == 1 )
66:        {
67:          IADs* piEntry = NULL;
68:
69:          // Get an IADs interface to the child object
70:          hr = ( ( IDispatch* )varEntry)->QueryInterface( IID_IADs,
71:                 ➥( void** )&piEntry );
72:          if( SUCCEEDED( hr ) )
73:          {
74:            BSTR strName;
75:
76:            piEntry->get_ADsPath( &strName );
77:            printf( "%S\n", strName );
78:
```

14

ACCESSING USERS,
GROUPS, AND
ORGANIZATIONS

continues

LISTING 14.7 CONTINUED

```
 79:              piEntry->Release();
 80:         }
 81:
 82:         IADsGroup* piMemberGroup = NULL;
 83:
 84:         hr = ( ( IDispatch* )varEntry)->QueryInterface(
            ➥IID_IADsGroup,( void** )&piMemberGroup );
 85:
 86:         if( SUCCEEDED( hr ) )
 87:         {
 88:            EnumerateGroup( piMemberGroup );
 89:
 90:            piMemberGroup->Release();
 91:         }
 92:
 93:         ( ( IDispatch* )varEntry )->Release();
 94:      }
 95:
 96:      piEnum->Release();
 97:    }
 98:
 99:    piMembers->Release();
100:   }
101: }
```

The program in Listing 14.7 is basically a rearrangement of the code in Listing 14.6. The main program gets an IADsGroup interface to the Administrators group and then calls the EnumerateGroup() function at line 33.

The EnumerateGroup() function starts at line 48. It accepts an IADsGroup interface pointer, and recursively lists the members of that group.

At line 52, the function gets the IADsMembers interface for the group, and at line 57, it builds the enumerator for the group. The EnumerateGroup() function starts enumerating the members of the group at line 64.

For each object in the group, EnumerateGroup() gets an IADs interface to the member object and displays the object's name. It then tries to get an IADsGroup interface to the object. If it can, EnumerateGroup() calls itself with the member group as a parameter.

EnumerateGroup() releases its interface pointers and returns to its caller. The main program releases its interface pointers at lines 35 and 39 and wraps up by calling CoUninitialize() at line 42.

Accessing Organizations, Localities, and Organizational Units with ADSI

A single Active Directory domain can contain tens of thousands—if not hundreds of thousands or millions—of objects. To provide a way to organize these objects within a domain, Active Directory, like other LDAP directories, uses *organizations, organizational units,* and *localities* to organize objects. These are commonly referred to as *Os, OUs,* and *Ls*. Organizations, organizational units, and localities are simply containers into which you can place other directory objects, including other organizational units.

Os are top-level entities; generally, an O will represent an entire company. OUs are subdivisions within an organization or organizational unit. A large directory might have an O that represents the company—for example, O=megacorp. Within that O might be OUs that represent the major business units of the company—for instance, OU=Aircraft and OU=Shipbuilding. There might also be localities representing geographic divisions of the company, such as L=New York and L=Northwest. Within those OUs and Ls might be other OUs representing functional areas in the organization, such as OU-=engineering and OU=accounting. Note that Os, OUs, and Ls always exist in the same domain as their parents.

Note that an O or L can contain OUs, but an OU can contain only other OUs. Os and Ls are generally contained directly by a domain.

Although ADSI provides separate interfaces for Os (IADsO), OUs (IADsOU), and Ls (IADsLocality), the interfaces are essentially identical. The only difference is that IADsOU provides an additional function for setting and getting the businessCategory attribute. Consult the Active Directory schema for the other differences between Os, Ls, and OUs.

14

ACCESSING USERS,
GROUPS, AND
ORGANIZATIONS

The IADsO, IADsOU, and IADsLocality Interfaces

Both the IADsO, IADsOU, and IADsLocality interfaces are all dual interfaces, supporting both IDispatch and IUnknown. They all inherit from IADs, so they use the property cache as well. See Chapter 12 for details about the IADs interface and handling the property cache.

Tables 14.5, 14.6, and 14.7 list the member functions of the IADsO, IADsOU, and IADsLocality interfaces, respectively. As you can see, the interfaces are essentially the same.

TABLE 14.5 THE IADsO INTERFACE

Function Name	Description
QueryInterface()	IUnknown interface.
AddRef()	IUnknown interface.
Release()	IUnknown interface.
GetTypeInfoCount()	IDispatch interface.
GetTypeInfo()	IDispatch interface.
GetIDsOfNames()	IDispatch interface.
Invoke()	IDispatch interface.
get_Description()/ put_Description()	Retrieves/sets the description of the organization. ([description])
get_LocalityName()/ put_LocalityName()	Retrieves/sets the name of the locality of the organization. ([localityName])
get_PostalAddress()/ put_PostalAddress()	Retrieves/sets the organization's postal address. ([postalAddress])
get_TelephoneNumber()/ put_TelephoneNumber()	Retrieves/sets the organization's telephone number. ([telephoneNumber])
get_FaxNumber()/put_FaxNumber()	Retrieves/sets the organization's fax number. ([facsimileTelephoneNumber])
get_SeeAlso()/put_SeeAlso()	Retrieves/sets the organization's see also attribute. ([seeAlso])

TABLE 14.6 THE IADsOU INTERFACE

Function Name	Description
QueryInterface()	IUnknown interface.
AddRef()	IUnknown interface.
Release()	IUnknown interface.
GetTypeInfoCount()	IDispatch interface.
GetTypeInfo()	IDispatch interface.
GetIDsOfNames()	IDispatch interface.
Invoke()	IDispatch interface.
get_Description()/ put_Description()	Retrieves/sets the description of the organizational unit. ([description])
get_LocalityName()/ put_LocalityName()	Retrieves/sets the name of the locality of the organizational unit. ([localityName])

Function Name	Description
get_PostalAddress()/ put_PostalAddress()	Retrieves/sets the postal address of the organizational unit. ([postalAddress])
get_TelephoneNumber()/ put_TelephoneNumber()	Retrieves/sets the telephone number of the organizational unit. ([telephoneNumber])
get_FaxNumber()/ put_FaxNumber()	Retrieves/sets the fax number of the organizational unit. ([facsimileTelephoneNumber])
get_SeeAlso()/put_SeeAlso()	Retrieves/sets the see also attribute of the organizational unit. ([seeAlso])
get_BusinessCategory()/ put_BusinessCategory()	Retrieves/sets the business category attribute of the organizational unit. ([businessCategory])

TABLE 14.7 THE IADsLocality INTERFACE

Function Name	Description
QueryInterface()	IUnknown interface.
AddRef()	IUnknown interface.
Release()	IUnknown interface.
GetTypeInfoCount()	IDispatch interface.
GetTypeInfo()	IDispatch interface.
GetIDsOfNames()	IDispatch interface.
Invoke()	IDispatch interface.
get_Description()/ put_Description()	Retrieves/sets the description of the organizational unit. ([description])
get_LocalityName()/ put_LocalityName()	Retrieves/sets the name of the locality of the organizational unit. ([localityName])
get_PostalAddress()/ put_PostalAddress()	Retrieves/sets the postal address of the organizational unit. ([postalAddress])
get_SeeAlso()/put_SeeAlso()	Retrieves/sets the see also attribute of the organizational unit. ([seeAlso])

Getting the Description of an Organization

After you get an interface to an O or OU, accessing the attributes of the object using the get_...() and put_...() functions is the same as with any of the other IADs interfaces.

The sample program in Listing 14.8 shows how to get the description of an OU using the
`IADsOU::get_Description()` function. You would access the attributes of an O in the
same way.

LISTING 14.8 GETTING THE DESCRIPTION OF AN OU

```
 1: #include <windows.h>
 2: #include <activeds.h>
 3: #include <comutil.h>
 4: #include <stdio.h>
 5:
 6: int main(int argc, char* argv[])
 7: {
 8:   HRESULT hr = CoInitialize( NULL );
 9:
10:   if( SUCCEEDED( hr ) )
11:   {
12:     IADs* piIADs = NULL;
13:
14:     // Get rootDSE
15:     hr = ADsGetObject( L"LDAP://rootDSE", IID_IADs,
16:                        ( void** )&piIADs );
17:     if( SUCCEEDED( hr ) )
18:     {
19:       // Get the domain NC
20:       _variant_t varDefaultNamingContext;
21:       hr = piIADs->Get( L"defaultNamingContext",
22:                         &varDefaultNamingContext );
23:       if( SUCCEEDED( hr ) )
24:       {
25:         // Compose the DN of the User container in the domain
26:         _bstr_t strPath = _bstr_t( "LDAP://OU=ShipBuilding," ) +
27:                           _bstr_t( varDefaultNamingContext );
28:         IADsO* piOU = NULL;
29:
30:         hr = ADsGetObject( strPath, IID_IADsOU, ( void** )&piOU );
31:         if( SUCCEEDED( hr ) )
32:         {
33:           BSTR strDesc;
34:
35:           hr = piOU->get_Description( &strDesc );
36:           if( SUCCEEDED( hr ) )
37:           {
38:             printf( "description: %S\n", strDesc );
39:           }
40:         }
41:
42:         piOU->Release();
43:       }
```

```
44:
45:
46:        piIADs->Release();
47:     }
48:
49:     ( void )CoUninitialize();
50:  }
51:
52:  return 0;
53: }
```

The program in Listing 14.8 gets the domain naming context from the rootDSE at line 21 and then composes the name of the ShipBuilding OU at line 26.

The program gets an interface to the OU at line 30 using the ADsGetObject() function and then gets the description attribute of the OU at line 35.

At line 38, the program prints the description of the OU. At line 42, the program releases the OU interface pointer.

The program wraps up by calling CoUninitialize() at line 49.

Enumerating the Contents of an O or OU

One of the most popular things to do with an O or OU is to list the objects it contains. The IADsO and IADsOU interfaces do not support any enumeration functions; you must use the IADsContainer interface or the IDirectorySearch interface to list the contents of an O or OU. Refer to Chapter 12 for more about the IADsContainer interface and to Chapter 13, "Searching Active Directory with ADSI," for information about the IDirectorySearch interface.

CHAPTER 15

Accessing the Active Directory Schema with ADSI

The schema is one of the most critical components of Active Directory. The Active Directory schema contains the rules that determine what sorts of objects can appear in the directory, and with what kind of hierarchical relationship. If the schema is screwed up in some way, there's a good chance Active Directory will stop working.

Fortunately, most application developers won't have much need for manipulating the schema. The schema that ships with Active Directory is quite rich, and generally you won't have to modify it.

If you do have to modify the schema for some reason—for instance, to add some configuration objects for your application—you can use either the Microsoft Management Console (MMC) Active Directory Schema snap-in or Microsoft's LDIFDE.EXE to update the schema from an LDAP Directory Interchange Format (LDIF) script.

However, there are some times when accessing or updating the schema programmatically is the only way to go—for instance, if you're building a schema maintenance utility. ADSI therefore provides a way for accessing and manipulating the Active Directory schema.

A Tale of Two Schemas

Active Directory actually stores its schema information in two places. The "true" schema is stored as a set of objects in the Schema naming context, which is replicated on every domain controller in the enterprise. You can access this version of the schema by using the ADSI generic object interfaces `IADs` and `IDirectoryObject`.

The second version of the schema is called the *subschema*. It is stored as a set of multi-valued attributes in the `CN=Aggregate` object in the Schema naming context—for instance, `CN=Aggregate,CN=Schema,CN=Configuration,DC=megacorp,DC=com`. The `Aggregate` object contains a summary of the true schema's information. ADSI provides access to this abstract schema through three special ADSI interfaces: `IADsClass`, `IADsProperty`, and `IADsSyntax`. These interfaces provide a slightly easier-to-use mechanism for getting to the schema, although they don't expose all the schema operations you might want to perform. You can also access the `Aggregate` object by using the generic object interfaces if you want. The big advantage to the subschema is that the lists of attributes that a class must have and may have include all the attributes inherited and included from other classes. If you try to access this information by using the generic object interfaces, you would have to follow the inheritance chains yourself—not an appealing prospect.

Which Version of the Schema Should You Use?

If you want to add new attributes or classes or if you want to modify existing classes or attributes, you should use generic object interfaces and simply add or modify the appropriate objects in the Schema naming context.

If all you want to do is inspect the schema—for instance, if you want to determine what the syntax of a specific attribute is—you should use the abstract schema and the `IADsProperty` interface. Likewise, if you want to see what attributes a class must have or may have, you should use the abstract schema and the `IADsClass` interface.

Using the Generic Object Interfaces to Access the Schema

Using the generic object interfaces `IADs` and `IDirectoryObject` to access the Active Directory schema objects is just like using them anywhere else. The only thing you need to know is what attributes each class or property object must have and how to properly initialize them. Refer to Chapter 9, "The Active Directory Schema": It describes the schema objects in some detail and also lays out the rules regarding what you can and can't change in the schema.

If you need to enumerate the schema objects—for instance, if you want to get a list of all the classes defined in the schema—you follow these steps:

1. Get the distinguished name of the Schema naming context from the `rootDSE` `schemaNamingContext` attribute.

2. Bind to the Schema naming context using `ADsGetObject()` or `ADsOpenObject()` and get an `IADsContainer` interface.

3. Use a container enumerator and a container filter to enumerate the class objects.

You could also issue a one-level search using the `IDirectorySearch` interface from the Schema container to get the same result.

You can access a specific schema object by composing its distinguished name and binding to the object directly, but there is a minor difficulty. The relative distinguished name of a schema object is not the `lDAPDisplayName` you normally use. For instance, to bind to the class schema object for the `acsPolicy` class, you would use the name `CN=ACS-Policy,CN=Schema,CN=Configuration,DC=megacorp,DC=com`, not `CN=acsPolicy,CN=Schema,CN=Configuration,DC=megacorp,DC=com`. If you don't know the relative distinguished name of a schema object, you can find the schema object using a one-level search from the Schema container and a search filter, as follows:

`lDAPDisplayName=acsPolicy`

Because the schema objects are indexed by `lDAPDisplayName`, this search is quite efficient. You don't have to explicitly search for `objectClass=classSchema` or `objectClass=attributeSchema` because the `lDAPDisplayName` attribute is unique across all class and attribute schema objects.

Enumerating Classes in the Schema Using the Generic Object Interfaces

The program in Listing 15.1 shows how to enumerate the class objects in the Schema naming context using the `IADsContainer` interface. The program gets the Schema naming context distinguished name, and uses the `IADsContainer` interface and the `ADsEnumerator...()` helper functions to enumerate the `classSchema` objects in the Schema naming context.

LISTING 15.1 ENUMERATING CLASS OBJECTS IN THE SCHEMA USING `IADsContainer`

```
1: #include <windows.h>
2: #include <activeds.h>
3: #include <comutil.h>
4: #include <stdio.h>
5:
6: int main(int argc, char* argv[])
7: {
```

continues

LISTING 15.1 CONTINUED

```
 8:    HRESULT hr = CoInitialize( NULL );
 9:
10:    if( SUCCEEDED( hr ) )
11:    {
12:      IADs* piRootDSE = NULL;
13:
14:      hr = ADsGetObject( L"LDAP://rootDSE", IID_IADs,
15:                         ( void** )&piRootDSE );
16:      if( SUCCEEDED( hr ) )
17:      {
18:        _variant_t varSchemaNC;
19:        _bstr_t strSchemaNC;
20:
21:        // get the schema naming context dn
22:        hr = piRootDSE->Get( L"schemaNamingContext", &varSchemaNC );
23:        if( SUCCEEDED( hr ) )
24:        {
25:          strSchemaNC = varSchemaNC;
26:
27:          // Get the schema container
28:          IADsContainer* piSchema = NULL;
29:
30:          hr = ADsGetObject( _bstr_t( "LDAP://" ) + strSchemaNC,
31:                   IID_IADsContainer, ( void** )&piSchema );
32:          if( SUCCEEDED( hr ) )
33:          {
34:            IEnumVARIANT* piEnum = NULL;
35:
36:            // Set filter to only get class objects
37:            LPWSTR apszClassNames[] = { L"classSchema" };
38:            _variant_t varClassNames;
39:
40:            ADsBuildVarArrayStr( apszClassNames,
41:              sizeof( apszClassNames ) / sizeof( apszClassNames[0] ),
42:              &varClassNames );
43:
44:            hr = piSchema->put_Filter( varClassNames );
45:
46:            // Build the enumerator
47:            hr = ADsBuildEnumerator( piSchema, &piEnum );
48:            if( SUCCEEDED( hr ) )
49:            {
50:              ULONG ulCount;
51:              _variant_t varEntry;
52:
53:              // Enumerate the entries
54:              while( ( hr = ADsEnumerateNext( piEnum, 1,
55:                &varEntry, &ulCount ) == S_OK ) && ulCount == 1 )
56:              {
```

```
57:                    IADs* piIADs = NULL;
58:
59:                    hr = ( ( IDispatch* )varEntry)->QueryInterface(
60:                            IID_IADs, ( void** )&piIADs );
61:                    if( SUCCEEDED( hr ) )
62:                    {
63:                      BSTR strName;
64:
65:                      hr = piIADs->get_Name( &strName );
66:                      if( SUCCEEDED( hr ) )
67:                      {
68:                        printf( "name: %S\n", strName );
69:                      }
70:
71:                      piIADs->Release();
72:                    }
73:
74:                    ( ( IDispatch* )varEntry )->Release();
75:                }
76:
77:                piEnum->Release();
78:            }
79:
80:            piSchema->Release();
81:          }
82:        }
83:
84:        piRootDSE->Release();
85:      }
86:
87:      ( void )CoUninitialize();
88:    }
89:
90:    return 0;
91: }
```

The program in Listing 15.1 first binds to the rootDSE of a domain controller in the currently logged-in user's domain. It then gets the distinguished name of the schema naming context by getting the schemaNamingContext attribute from the rootDSE at line 22.

At line 30, the program composes the ADsPath for the Schema naming context and binds to the Schema container using ADsGetObject(), obtaining an IADsContainer interface in the process.

The program sets up a filter from lines 36 to 44 so that the container enumeration will return only class objects (objects whose class is classSchema). If you want to get attribute objects, you set the filter to use attributeSchema instead of classSchema.

At line 47, the program creates an enumerator for the Schema container, using the filter created previously.

The loop that enumerates the class objects starts at line 54. For each object returned, the program gets an IADs interface pointer and retrieves the name of the class object at lines 59–65. The program prints the name of the class object at line 68.

The program releases all the interface pointers and cleans up the COM subsystem at line 87 by calling CoUninitialize().

Binding to the Schema Master

Because the schema is replicated on all domain controllers and is so critical to the proper operation of the directory, Active Directory allows updates to the schema on only a single domain controller (the administrator can change which one). Limiting updates to a single domain controller prevents potentially conflicting updates from occurring on multiple domain controllers. The domain controller that services the updates to the schema is called the *schema master* or the *schema FSMO role owner*.

You can determine the name of the schema master by reading the fSMORoleOwner attribute of the Schema naming context object. This attribute contains the distinguished name of the nTDSDSA object for the schema master. If you remove the first part of this object's distinguished name, you have the distinguished name of the site-local server object for the schema master. The site-local server object has an attribute named serverReference that contains the distinguished name of the real server object that represents the schema master. The dNSHostName attribute contains the DNS name of the schema master server that you use to compose the ADsPath. A sample program later in the chapter shows how to do this.

Before you attempt to modify the schema in any way, you must bind to the schema container on the domain controller that holds the schema FSMO. The process for doing this is somewhat convoluted, as shown in Listing 15.2.

LISTING 15.2 BINDING TO THE SCHEMA MASTER

```
 1: HRESULT BindToSchemaMaster( IUnknown** piUnknown )
 2: {
 3:   IADs* piRootDSE = NULL;
 4:
 5:   HRESULT hr = ADsGetObject( L"LDAP://rootDSE", IID_IADs,
 6:                              ( void** )&piRootDSE );
 7:   if( SUCCEEDED( hr ) )
 8:   {
 9:     _variant_t varSchemaNC;
10:     _bstr_t strSchemaNC;
11:
12:     hr = piRootDSE->Get( L"schemaNamingContext", &varSchemaNC );
13:     if( SUCCEEDED( hr ) )
14:     {
```

```
15:          strSchemaNC = varSchemaNC;
16:
17:          // Get the schema NC object
18:          IADs* piSchema = NULL;
19:
20:          hr = ADsGetObject( _bstr_t( "LDAP://" ) + strSchemaNC,
21:                             IID_IADs, ( void** )&piSchema );
22:          if( SUCCEEDED( hr ) )
23:          {
24:            _variant_t varFSMORoleOwner;
25:
26:            // get the dn of the schema master nTDSSettings object
27:            hr = piSchema->Get( L"fSMORoleOwner",
28:                                &varFSMORoleOwner );
29:            if( SUCCEEDED( hr ) )
30:            {
31:              IDirectoryObject* piDCSettings;
32:
33:              hr = ADsGetObject( _bstr_t( "LDAP://" ) +
34:                                 _bstr_t( varFSMORoleOwner ),
35:                                 IID_IDirectoryObject,
36:                                 ( void** )&piDCSettings );
37:              if( SUCCEEDED( hr ) )
38:              {
39:                ADS_OBJECT_INFO* psInfo = NULL;
40:
41:                // Get the DN of the parent of the nTDSSettings
42:                // object
43:                hr = piDCSettings->GetObjectInformation( &psInfo );
44:                if( SUCCEEDED( hr ) )
45:                {
46:                  IADs* piDC = NULL;
47:
48:                  hr = ADsGetObject( psInfo->pszParentDN,
49:                                     IID_IADs, ( void** )&piDC );
50:                  if( SUCCEEDED( hr ) )
51:                  {
52:                    _variant_t varServerDN;
53:
54:                    // Get the DN of the actual schema master DC
55:                    // (as opposed to the site local DC)
56:                    ( void )piDC->Get( L"serverReference",
57:                                       &varServerDN );
58:
59:                    IADs* piSchemaMaster = NULL;
60:
61:                    hr = ADsGetObject( _bstr_t( "LDAP://" ) +
62:                                       _bstr_t( varServerDN ),
63:                                       IID_IADs,
64:                                       ( void** )&piSchemaMaster );
```

continues

15

ACCESSING THE ACTIVE DIRECTORY SCHEMA

LISTING 15.2   CONTINUED

```
65:                    if( SUCCEEDED( hr ) )
66:                    {
67:                      _variant_t varHostName;
68:
69:                      // Get the DNS host name of the schema master
70:                      hr = piSchemaMaster->Get( L"dNSHostName",
71:                                                &varHostName );
72:                      if( SUCCEEDED( hr ) )
73:                      {
74:                        // Compose the ADsPath of the Schema NC on
75:                        // the schema master DC
76:                        _bstr_t strSchemaMasterPath =
77:                          _bstr_t( "LDAP://" ) +
78:                          _bstr_t( varHostName ) +
79:                          _bstr_t( "/" ) + strSchemaNC;
80:
81:                        hr = ADsGetObject( strSchemaMasterPath,
82:                              IID_IUnknown, ( void** )piUnknown );
83:                      }
84:
85:                      piSchemaMaster->Release();
86:                    }
87:
88:                    piDC->Release();
89:                  }
90:
91:                  FreeADsMem( psInfo );
92:                }
93:
94:              piDCSettings->Release();
95:            }
96:          }
97:
98:        piSchema->Release();
99:      }
100:
101:      piRootDSE->Release();
102:    }
103:  }
104:
105:  return hr;
106: }
```

The `BindToSchemaMaster()` function shown in Listing 15.2 accepts the address of an
`IUnknown` pointer, which the function will set to refer to the Schema NC on the domain
controller that holds the Schema FSMO. It is up to the caller to `Release()` this interface
pointer. `BindToSchemaMaster()` returns an HRESULT.

At line 5, the function gets the `rootDSE` interface from a domain controller in the currently logged-in user's domain. It then gets the distinguished name of the Schema naming context at line 12.

The function gets an `IADs` interface to the Schema naming context at line 20, and retrieves the `fSMORoleOwner` attribute from it at line 27. This contains the distinguished name of the `nTDSSettings` object of the domain controller that holds the Schema FSMO.

At line 33, the function gets an `IDirectoryObject` interface to the `nTDSSettings` object. The function uses this interface instead of `IADs` so that it can use the `GetObjectInformation()` function to get the distinguished name of the parent object.

`BindToSchemaMaster()` gets the distinguished name of the site-local server object and binds to this object at line 48. The function retrieves the `serverReference` attribute at line 56. This is the distinguished name of the actual server object for the schema master.

At line 61, the function binds to the actual server object. At line 70, it gets the `dNSHostName` attribute from the server object.

At line 76, `BindToSchemaMaster()` composes the `ADsPath` from the `dNSHostName` and the distinguished name of the Schema naming context. At line 81, the function binds to the Schema naming context on the domain controller that holds the Schema FSMO.

The function releases the various interface pointers and returns the result of the operation at line 105.

Adding a New Attribute Using the Generic Object Interfaces

Adding a new `attributeSyntax` object to the schema is quite straightforward. The only things you need to know are the initial values for a few attributes in the new object. Active Directory will default the rest of the attributes for you.

When you create a new attribute in the schema, you must specify the attributes listed in Table 15.1.

TABLE 15.1 REQUIRED ATTRIBUTES FOR A NEW ATTRIBUTE

Attribute Name	Description
`objectClass`	Indicates the class of the new object. Must be `"attributeSchema"`.
`lDAPDisplayName`	The LDAP display name of the new attribute. By convention, this name should begin with a lowercase letter and should not include any hyphens or spaces. The `lDAPDisplay` name must be unique across all objects in the schema.

continues

TABLE 15.1 CONTINUED

Attribute Name	Description
attributeID	The ITU OID string for the new attribute. This value must be unique across all objects in the schema. See Chapter 9 for information on obtaining OID strings.
attributeSyntax	The OID string of the syntax of the new attribute—for instance, "2.5.5.9" for an integer attribute. Chapter 9 lists the possible syntaxes and their OID strings.
oMSyntax	The OM syntax for the attribute. This value must correspond to the attributeSyntax, as described in Chapter 9.

The next sample program shows how to add a new attribute to the schema. Before attempting this, you should read Chapter 9, which describes some of the constraints Active Directory imposes on your program when modifying the schema.

Listing 15.3 first finds the Schema FSMO role owner (refer to Chapter 9 for more about the Schema FSMO) and binds to its Schema naming context. It then adds a single new property called foo to the schema.

LISTING 15.3 USING ADSI TO ADD AN ATTRIBUTE TO THE SCHEMA

```
 1: #include <windows.h>
 2: #include <activeds.h>
 3: #include <comutil.h>
 4: #include <stdio.h>
 5:
 6: HRESULT BindToSchemaMaster( IUnknown** piUnknown );
 7:
 8: int main(int argc, char* argv[])
 9: {
10:   HRESULT hr = CoInitialize( NULL );
11:
12:   if( SUCCEEDED( hr ) )
13:   {
14:     IUnknown* piunkSchema = NULL;
15:
16:     hr = BindToSchemaMaster( &piunkSchema );
17:     if( SUCCEEDED( hr ) )
18:     {
19:       IADsContainer* piSchema = NULL;
20:
21:       hr = piunkSchema->QueryInterface( IID_IADsContainer,
22:                                         ( void** )&piSchema );
```

```
23:        if( SUCCEEDED( hr ) )
24:        {
25:          IDispatch* pidispAttr = NULL;
26:
27:          hr = piSchema->Create( L"attributeSchema",
28:                                 L"CN=Foo", &pidispAttr );
29:          if( SUCCEEDED( hr ) )
30:          {
31:            IADs* piIADsAttr = NULL;
32:
33:            hr = pidispAttr->QueryInterface( IID_IADs,
34:                               ( void** )&piIADsAttr );
35:            if( SUCCEEDED( hr ) )
36:            {
37:              piIADsAttr->Put( L"objectClass",
38:                 _variant_t( L"attributeSchema" ) );
39:              piIADsAttr->Put( L"lDAPDisplayName",
40:                 _variant_t( L"foo" ) );
41:              piIADsAttr->Put( L"attributeID",
42:                 _variant_t( L"1.3.6.1.4.1.1593.4.2.1.1.2.29" ) );
43:              piIADsAttr->Put( L"attributeSyntax",
44:                 _variant_t( L"2.5.5.5" ) );
45:              piIADsAttr->Put( L"oMSyntax", _variant_t( "22" ) );
46:
47:              hr = piIADsAttr->SetInfo();
48:              if( ! SUCCEEDED( hr ) )
49:              {
50:                printf( "Error %x adding attribute to schema\n",
51:                        hr );
52:              }
53:
54:              piIADsAttr->Release();
55:            }
56:
57:            pidispAttr->Release();
58:          }
59:
60:          piSchema->Release();
61:        }
62:
63:        piunkSchema->Release();
64:      }
65:
66:      ( void )CoUninitialize();
67:   }
68:
69:   return 0;
70: }
```

15

The sample program in Listing 15.3 first uses the `BindToSchemaMaster()` function at line 16 to connect to the Schema naming context on the schema master domain controller.

At line 21, the program gets an `IADsContainer` interface pointer to the `Schema` naming context on the schema master in preparation for creating a new object in the Schema container.

The program creates the new `attributeSchema` object in the property cache at line 27. Note that the object has not yet been created on the server; it exists only in memory on the client.

At line 33, the program gets an `IADs` interface pointer to the new `attributeSchema` object, and at lines 37–45 the program adds the required attributes to the new object. Note that you must create a proper OID string for the `attributeID` attribute. Refer to Chapter 9 for more information on creating OID strings for schema objects.

At line 47, the program calls `SetInfo()` to store the new object on the schema master domain controller. It is at this point that the domain controller validates all the attributes of the new object.

> **NOTE**
>
> The `SetInfo()` function will fail if the schema master domain controller has not been configured to allow schema updates. Refer to Chapter 9 for information on allowing schema updates on a domain controller.

The program finally releases all the interface pointers and cleans up the COM subsystem by calling `CoUninitialize()`.

Adding a New Class Using the Generic Object Interfaces

Adding a new class to the schema works the same way as adding a new attribute. The only thing you really have to worry about is the initial values of the `classSchema` object you are creating.

Table 15.2 lists the attributes you must define when you create a new class. Even though there are other required attributes, Active Directory defaults them to reasonable values.

TABLE 15.2 REQUIRED ATTRIBUTES FOR A NEW CLASS

Attribute Name	Description
objectClass	Indicates the class of the new object. Must be "classSchema".
lDAPDisplayName	The LDAP display name of the new attribute. By convention, this name should begin with a lowercase letter and should not include any hyphens or spaces. The lDAPDisplay name must be unique across all objects in the schema.
governsID	The ITU OID string for the new class. This value must be unique across all objects in the schema. Refer to Chapter 9 for information on obtaining OID strings.
subClassOf	The lDAPDisplayName of the class the new class inherits from. This value should be single-valued; Active Directory will fill in the rest of the inheritance chain.
mayContain	A multivalue attribute containing the lDAPDisplayNames of the attributes that objects of this class may contain.

The sample program shown in Listing 15.4 adds a new class to the schema that must have the foo attribute we created with the preceding sample program. This program is a near clone of the preceding program that added an attribute. The only significant differences occur where the program creates the new object in the Schema container and then sets its attributes.

LISTING 15.4 USING ADSI TO ADD A CLASS TO THE SCHEMA

```
 1: #include <windows.h>
 2: #include <activeds.h>
 3: #include <comutil.h>
 4: #include <stdio.h>
 5:
 6:
 7: HRESULT BindToSchemaMaster( IUnknown** piUnknown );
 8:
 9: int main(int argc, char* argv[])
10: {
11:   HRESULT hr = CoInitialize( NULL );
12:
13:   if( SUCCEEDED( hr ) )
14:   {
15:     IUnknown* piunkSchema = NULL;
16:
17:     hr = BindToSchemaMaster( &piunkSchema );
```

continues

Listing 15.4   CONTINUED

```
18:      if( SUCCEEDED( hr ) )
19:      {
20:        IADsContainer* piSchema = NULL;
21:
22:        hr = piunkSchema->QueryInterface( IID_IADsContainer,
23:                                          ( void** )&piSchema );
24:        if( SUCCEEDED( hr ) )
25:        {
26:          IDispatch* piDisp = NULL;
27:
28:          hr = piSchema->Create( L"classSchema", L"CN=Bar",
29:                                 &piDisp );
30:          if( SUCCEEDED( hr ) )
31:          {
32:            IADs* piIADsClass = NULL;
33:
34:            hr = piDisp->QueryInterface( IID_IADs,
35:                                         ( void** )&piIADsClass );
36:            if( SUCCEEDED( hr ) )
37:            {
38:              piIADsClass->Put( L"objectClass",
39:                  _variant_t( L"classSchema" ) );
40:              piIADsClass->Put( L"lDAPDisplayName",
41:                  _variant_t( L"bar" ) );
42:              piIADsClass->Put( L"governsID",
43:                  _variant_t( L"1.3.6.1.4.1.1593.4.2.1.1.2.30" ) );
44:              piIADsClass->Put( L"subClassOf",
45:                  _variant_t( L"top" ) );
46:              piIADsClass->Put( L"possSuperiors",
47:                  _variant_t( "container" ) );
48:              piIADsClass->Put( L"mayContain",
49:                  _variant_t( L"foo" ) );
50:
51:              hr = piIADsClass->SetInfo();
52:              if( ! SUCCEEDED( hr ) )
53:              {
54:                printf( "Error %x adding class to Schema\n", hr );
55:              }
56:
57:              piIADsClass->Release();
58:
59:            }
60:
61:            piDisp->Release();
62:          }
63:
64:          piSchema->Release();
65:        }
66:
```

```
67:       piunkSchema->Release();
68:     }
69:
70:     ( void )CoUninitialize();
71:   }
72:
73:   return 0;
74: }
```

The sample program in Listing 15.4 binds to the Schema container on the schema master by calling the function `BindToSchemaMaster()` at line 17. The program then calls `QueryInterface` to get an `IADsContainer` interface pointer to the Schema naming context at line 22.

At line 28, the sample program creates a new `classSchema` object in the Schema container. This does not create the `classSchema` object on the server; it creates it only in memory on the client.

At line 34, the program gets an `IADs` interface pointer to the new `classSchema` object. At lines 38–49, the program adds the required attributes to the new object.

The program stores the new `classSchema` object on the domain controller at line 51 by calling `IADs::SetInfo()`. If there are any errors in the composition of the new `classSchema` object, the call to `IADs::SetInfo()` will return an error.

> **NOTE**
>
> The `SetInfo()` function will fail if the schema master domain controller has not been configured to allow schema updates. Refer to Chapter 9 for information on allowing schema updates on a domain controller.

The program then releases the various interface pointers and cleans up the COM subsystem at line 70 by calling `CoUninitialize()`.

Using the Abstract Schema Interface to Access the Schema

The abstract schema provides a somewhat simpler way to access the Active Directory schema than does the generic object interfaces. The abstract schema is based on the subschema object located at `CN=Aggregate,CN=Schema,CN=Configuration,DC=megacorp,DC=com`, for instance.

There are two ways to use the abstract schema interface in Active Directory. First, the LDAP ADSI provider implements an IADsContainer interface to the Aggregate object that lets you treat the multivalued attributes of the Aggregate object as if they were entries in a container. The IADsContainer interface lets you enumerate the classes and attributes defined in the abstract schema.

You can also use the abstract schema to get an IADsClass or IADsProperty interface to a particular schema object. Although both the IADsClass and IADsProperty interfaces provide functions to update the schema, I've had some peculiar results using them. As a general rule, I use the generic object interfaces to update objects in the schema, and the abstract schema interfaces to read the schema information.

Binding to the Abstract Schema

There are two ways to bind to the abstract schema. The first method binds to the entire schema and gives you a way to get an IADsContainer interface to enumerate the attributes and classes in the schema. The following piece of code shows how you bind to the abstract schema using the IADsContainer interface.

```
IADsContainer* piContainer = NULL;

HRESULT hr = ADsGetObject( L"LDAP://schema",
                           IID_IADsContainer,
                           ( void** )&piContainer );
if( SUCCEEDED( hr ) )
{
    // use the IADsContainer interface
    piContainer->Release();
}
```

This will bind to the abstract schema on some domain controller in the domain of the logged-in user. You can bind to a specific domain controller, as follows:

```
IADsContainer* piContainer = NULL;

HRESULT hr = ADsGetObject( L"LDAP://engserver.megacorp.com/schema",
                           IID_IADsContainer,
                           ( void** )&piContainer );
if( SUCCEEDED( hr ) )
{
    // use the IADsContainer interface
    piContainer->Release();
}
```

You can also bind to an individual schema object (either class or attribute) in the abstract schema by using the following binding syntax.

```
IADsClass* piClass = NULL;

HRESULT hr = ADsGetObject( L"LDAP://schema//user",
                           IID_IADsClass,
                           ( void** )&piClass );
if( SUCCEEDED( hr ) )
{
    // use the IADsClass interface
    piClass->Release();
}
```

This preceding bit of code gets an IADsClass interface to the User class in the abstract schema. Note that with this binding syntax, you specify the schema object name using its lDAPDisplayName—in this case class—not the distinguished name, such as CN=User, CN=Schema,CN=Configuration,DC=megacorp,DC=com. This by itself makes using the abstract schema a little easier than using the generic object interfaces.

Using the Abstract Schema Container Interface

The IADsContainer interface to the abstract schema provides access to a collection of entries that includes all the class in the schema, all the properties in the schema, and all the attribute syntaxes supported by the directory.

> **NOTE**
>
> The abstract schema exposes an incomplete implementation of the IADsContainer interface. For instance, the abstract schema's IADsContainer interface does not support filters or hints. If you want to enumerate only the classes or properties that make up the schema, you have to try to obtain the IADsClass interface on each entry returned by the enumerator. This isn't as inefficient as it might sound because there is no additional network traffic.

You can obtain an IADs interface to each entry in the abstract schema, but there is a surprise here. The "objects" you get from the abstract schema are not the true objects from the Schema naming context; they are virtual objects constructed from the attributes of the Aggregate object. Consequently, the objects in the abstract schema have only a few of the attributes the true schema objects have. Also, instead of retrieving the relative distinguished name, the IADs::get_Name() function returns the lDAPDisplayName. This all makes sense when you realize that the abstract schema is based entirely on the contents of the Aggregate object and not the Schema container, but it can be confusing nonetheless.

Because of this inconsistent behavior, you are better off sticking with the IADsClass and IADsProperty interfaces when inspecting objects in the abstract schema. The only problem with this strategy is that neither IADsClass nor IADsProperty provides a function to retrieve the name of the abstract schema object. So you have to use the IADs::get_Name() function. Sigh.

Hey, if this stuff were easy, you wouldn't be making the medium bucks now, would you?

The sample program in Listing 15.5 shows how to use the IADsContainer interface to the abstract schema to list the class objects. The program checks each entry returned from the enumerator using QueryInterface() to see whether the entry is a class entry; if it is, the program uses the IADs interface to display the object's name.

LISTING 15.5 ENUMERATING THE ABSTRACT SCHEMA WITH THE IADSCONTAINER INTERFACE

```
 1: #include <windows.h>
 2: #include <activeds.h>
 3: #include <comutil.h>
 4: #include <stdio.h>
 5:
 6: int main(int argc, char* argv[])
 7: {
 8:   HRESULT hr = CoInitialize( NULL );
 9:
10:   if( SUCCEEDED( hr ) )
11:   {
12:     IADsContainer* piSchema = NULL;
13:
14:     hr = ADsGetObject( L"LDAP://schema",
15:                        IID_IADsContainer,
16:                        ( void** )&piSchema );
17:     if( SUCCEEDED( hr ) )
18:     {
19:       IEnumVARIANT* piEnum = NULL;
20:
21:       // Build the enumerator
22:       hr = ADsBuildEnumerator( piSchema, &piEnum );
23:       if( SUCCEEDED( hr ) )
24:       {
25:         ULONG ulCount;
26:         _variant_t varEntry;
27:
28:         // Enumerate the entries
29:         while( ( hr = ADsEnumerateNext( piEnum, 1, &varEntry,
30:             &ulCount ) == S_OK ) && ulCount == 1 )
31:         {
32:           IADsClass* piClass = NULL;
33:
34:           // See if this is a class
```

```
35:                hr = ( ( IDispatch* )varEntry)->QueryInterface(
36:                     IID_IADsClass, ( void** )&piClass );
37:            if( SUCCEEDED( hr ) )
38:            {
39:              BSTR strName;
40:
41:              piClass->get_Name( &strName );
42:              printf( "class: %S\n", strName );
43:
44:              piClass->Release();
45:            }
46:
47:            ( ( IDispatch* )varEntry )->Release();
48:          }
49:
50:        piEnum->Release();
51:      }
52:
53:      piSchema->Release();
54:    }
55:
56:    ( void )CoUninitialize();
57:  }
58:
59:  return 0;
60: }
```

The sample program in Listing 15.5 starts by binding to the abstract schema container using the ADsPath LDAP://schema at line 14. This will bind to the Aggregate object in the Schema naming context on some domain controller in the domain of the logged-in user. The program obtains an IADsContainer interface pointer to the abstract schema

At line 22, the program builds an enumerator to the container interface. At line 29, it starts to enumerate the entries in the abstract schema container.

The program calls QueryInterface() at line 35 to determine whether the object is a class entry. If it is, the program calls IADs::get_Name() to retrieve the lDAPDisplayName of the class.

After printing the name of the class, the program releases the various interface pointers and cleans up by calling CoUninitialize() at line 56.

Accessing a Schema Class Object with IADsClass

Now that you can enumerate the abstract schema object, let's take a look at the special interfaces to the abstract schema objects that ADSI provides.

The first interface is the IADsClass interface. It is a dual-mode interface; that is, it supports the methods of both IUnknown and IDispatch. IADsClass provides access to the schema information that is available in the Aggregate object in the Schema container. Table 15.3 lists the functions that make up the IADsClass interface.

TABLE 15.3   THE IADsClass INTERFACE

Function Name	Description
QueryInterface()	IUnknown interface.
AddRef()	IUnknown interface.
Release()	IUnknown interface.
GetTypeInfoCount()	IDispatch interface.
GetTypeInfo()	IDispatch interface.
GetIDsOfNames()	IDispatch interface.
Invoke()	IDispatch interface.
get_PrimaryInterface()	Retrieves the COM interface GUID of the primary interface for this class.
get_CLSID()/put_CLSID()	Gets or sets the CLSID of the COM interface that implements this class.
get_OID()/put_OID()	Retrieves/sets the OID string for the class object. The OID uniquely identifies the class in the ITU identifier hierarchy.
get_Abstract()/put_Abstract()	Retrieves a Boolean indicating whether the class is abstract (used only for inheritance purposes) or not.
get_Auxiliary()/ put_Auxiliary()	Retrieves a Boolean indicating whether the class is an auxiliary class or not.
get_MandatoryProperties()/ put_MandatoryProperties()	Retrieves a VARIANT array of the attributes that are mandatory for this class. It includes mandatory attributes inherited or included from other classes.
get_OptionalProperties()/ put_OptionalProperties()	Retrieves a VARIANT array of the attributes that are optional for this class. It includes optional attributes inherited or included from other classes.
get_NamingProperties()/ put_NamingProperties()	Gets or sets a VARIANT array of the attributes that can be used as the relative distinguished name of objects of this class.
get_DerivedFrom()/ put_DerivedFrom()	Retrieves/sets the class(es) this class is derived from.

Function Name	*Description*
`get_AuxDerivedFrom()/` `put_AuxDerivedFrom()`	Retrieves/sets the auxiliary classes this class includes attributes from.
`get_PossibleSuperiors()/` `put_PossibleSuperiors()`	Retrieves/sets a `VARIANT` array of the class of objects that can contain this class of object.
`get_Containment()/` `put_Containment()`	Retrieves/sets the class(es) this container can contain.
`get_Container()/` `put_Container()`	Retrieves/sets the flag that specifies if this class is a container.
`get_HelpFileName()/` `put_HelpFileName()`	Retrieves/sets the name of an optional help file.
`get_HelpFileContext()/` `put_HelpFileContext()`	Retrieves/sets the context identifier for the optional help file.
`Qualifiers()`	Retrieves a collection of objects specifying provider-specific qualifiers for the schema.

The sample program in Listing 15.6 uses the code from the preceding program to enumerate the class objects in the abstract schema, and then uses the `IADsClass::get_MandatoryProperties()` function to retrieve the names of the mandatory properties for each class.

```
HRESULT IADsClass::get_MandatoryProperties( VARIANT* varPropertyNames )
```

> `varPropertyNames` is the address of a `VARIANT` that will be set to contain a `VARIANT` array of property names. These will be the names of the properties that each object of this class must have.

Returns: `IADsClass::get_MandatoryProperties()` returns an ADSI or COM error code. Check the result with one of the COM error macros described in Chapter 11, "ADSI Fundamentals."

LISTING 15.6 GETTING THE MANDATORY PROPERTIES FOR EACH CLASS USING THE `IADsClass` INTERFACE

```
1: #include <windows.h>
2: #include <activeds.h>
3: #include <comutil.h>
4: #include <stdio.h>
5:
6: int main(int argc, char* argv[])
7: {
8:   HRESULT hr = CoInitialize( NULL );
```

continues

15

ACCESSING THE ACTIVE DIRECTORY SCHEMA

LISTING 15.6   CONTINUED

```
 9:
10:    if( SUCCEEDED( hr ) )
11:    {
12:      IADsContainer* piSchema = NULL;
13:
14:      hr = ADsGetObject( L"LDAP://schema", IID_IADsContainer,
15:                          ( void** )&piSchema );
16:      if( SUCCEEDED( hr ) )
17:      {
18:        IEnumVARIANT* piEnum = NULL;
19:
20:        // Build the enumerator
21:        hr = ADsBuildEnumerator( piSchema, &piEnum );
22:        if( SUCCEEDED( hr ) )
23:        {
24:          ULONG ulCount;
25:          _variant_t varEntry;
26:
27:          // Enumerate the entries
28:          while( ( hr = ADsEnumerateNext( piEnum, 1,
29:              &varEntry, &ulCount ) == S_OK ) && ulCount == 1 )
30:          {
31:            IADsClass* piClass = NULL;
32:
33:            // See if this is a class
34:            hr = ( ( IDispatch* )varEntry)->QueryInterface(
35:                IID_IADsClass, ( void** )&piClass );
36:            if( SUCCEEDED( hr ) )
37:            {
38:              BSTR strName;
39:
40:              piClass->get_Name( &strName );
41:              printf( "class: %S\n", strName );
42:
43:              _variant_t varProps;
44:
45:              hr = piClass->get_MandatoryProperties( &varProps );
46:              if( SUCCEEDED( hr ) )
47:              {
48:                SAFEARRAY* aProps = V_ARRAY( &varProps );
49:                if( aProps != NULL )
50:                {
51:                  LONG lLBound;
52:                  LONG lUBound;
53:
54:                  ( void )SafeArrayGetLBound( aProps, 1, &lLBound );
55:                  ( void )SafeArrayGetUBound( aProps, 1, &lUBound );
56:
57:                  for( LONG lIndex = lLBound; lIndex <= lUBound;
```

```
58:                            lIndex++ )
59:                        {
60:                            _variant_t varProp;
61:
62:                            hr = SafeArrayGetElement( aProps, &lIndex,
63:                                &varProp );
64:                            if( SUCCEEDED( hr ) )
65:                            {
66:                                printf( "property: %s\n",
67:                                        ( const char* )_bstr_t( varProp ) );
68:                            }
69:                        }
70:                    }
71:                }
72:
73:                piClass->Release();
74:            }
75:
76:            ( ( IDispatch* )varEntry )->Release();
77:        }
78:
79:        piEnum->Release();
80:    }
81:
82:    piSchema->Release();
83:    }
84:
85:    ( void )CoUninitialize();
86:    }
87:
88:    return 0;
89: }
```

The sample program in Listing 15.6 starts by binding to the abstract schema container using the ADsPath LDAP://schema at line 14. This will bind to the Aggregate object in the Schema naming context on some domain controller in the domain of the logged-in user. The program obtains an IADsContainer interface pointer to the abstract schema.

At line 21, the program builds an enumerator to the container interface; at line 28, it starts to enumerate the entries in the abstract schema container.

The program calls QueryInterface() at line 34 to determine whether the object is a class entry. If it is, the program calls IADs::get_Name() to retrieve the lDAPDisplayName of the class. The program prints the name at line 41.

At line 45, the program retrieves the list of mandatory properties for the class by calling IADsClass::get_MandatoryProperties. get_MandatoryProperties() retrieves the list of property names as a VARIANT array of BSTRs.

The code from line 48 through 55 gets the VARIANT array pointer and array bounds. The for loop that starts at line 57 executes once for each property name in the array.

The program uses the SafeArrayGetElement() function at line 62 to retrieve each mandatory property name from the array. The program prints each property name at line 66.

Starting at line 73, the sample program releases its interface pointers, and it closes up shop at line 85 by calling CoUninitialize().

Accessing a Schema Property Object with IADsProperty

The IADsProperty interface can be used to retrieve and set the attribute definition(s) of a directory service property. Table 15.4 details the IADsProperty interface.

TABLE 15.4 THE IADsProperty INTERFACE

Function Name	*Description*
QueryInterface()	IUnknown interface.
AddRef()	IUnknown interface.
Release()	IUnknown interface.
GetTypeInfoCount()	IDispatch interface.
GetTypeInfo()	IDispatch interface.
GetIDsOfNames()	IDispatch interface.
Invoke()	IDispatch interface.
get_OID()/put_OID()	Retrieves/sets the ITU OID for the attribute.
get_Syntax()/put_Syntax()	Retrieves/sets the syntax identifier for the attribute.
get_MaxRange()/put_MaxRange()	Retrieves/sets the maximum value (for numeric attributes) or minimum size in characters (for string attributes).
get_MinRange()/put_MinRange()	Retrieves/sets the minimum value (for numeric attributes) or minimum size in characters (for string attributes).
get_MultiValued()/ put_MultiValued()	Retrieves/sets a flag indicating whether the property supports multiple values.
Qualifiers()	Optional provider-specific constraints on the property (none specified by Active Directory).

The sample program in Listing 15.7 enumerates the entries in the abstract schema. For each property entry, the program uses the IADsProperty interface to retrieve the property's syntax name.

LISTING 15.7 GETTING THE SYNTAX FOR EACH SCHEMA PROPERTY USING IADsProperty

```
 1: #include <windows.h>
 2: #include <activeds.h>
 3: #include <comutil.h>
 4: #include <stdio.h>
 5:
 6: int main(int argc, char* argv[])
 7: {
 8:   HRESULT hr = CoInitialize( NULL );
 9:
10:   if( SUCCEEDED( hr ) )
11:   {
12:     IADsContainer* piSchema = NULL;
13:
14:     hr = ADsGetObject( L"LDAP://schema", IID_IADsContainer,
15:                        ( void** )&piSchema );
16:     if( SUCCEEDED( hr ) )
17:     {
18:       IEnumVARIANT* piEnum = NULL;
19:
20:       // Build the enumerator
21:       hr = ADsBuildEnumerator( piSchema, &piEnum );
22:       if( SUCCEEDED( hr ) )
23:       {
24:         ULONG ulCount;
25:         _variant_t varEntry;
26:
27:         // Enumerate the entries
28:         while( ( hr = ADsEnumerateNext( piEnum, 1, &varEntry,
29:             &ulCount ) == S_OK ) && ulCount == 1 )
30:         {
31:           IADsProperty* piProperty = NULL;
32:
33:           hr = ( ( IDispatch* )varEntry )->QueryInterface(
34:               IID_IADsProperty, ( void** )&piProperty );
35:           if( SUCCEEDED( hr ) )
36:           {
37:             BSTR strName;
38:             BSTR strSyntax;
39:
40:             piProperty->get_Name( &strName );
41:             piProperty->get_Syntax( &strSyntax );
42:
43:             printf( "property: %S syntax: %S\n",
```

continues

LISTING 15.7   CONTINUED

```
44:               strName, strSyntax );
45:
46:          piProperty->Release();
47:        }
48:
49:        ( ( IDispatch* )varEntry )->Release();
50:      }
51:
52:      piEnum->Release();
53:    }
54:
55:    piSchema->Release();
56:  }
57:
58:  ( void )CoUninitialize();
59: }
60:
61:  return 0;
62: }
```

The program in Listing 15.7 starts by binding to the abstract schema container using the LDAP://schema ADsPath at line 14.

The program builds an enumerator for the abstract schema container starting at line 21 and starts enumerating the entries in the container at line 28.

At line 33, the program tries to obtain an IADsProperty interface on each entry in the abstract schema container. For those entries that represent properties in the schema, the program calls get_Name() and get_Syntax() to retrieve the lDAPDisplayName of the property and the property's syntax name, respectively. The program prints these two values at line 43.

At lines 46, 49, 52, and 55, the program releases the interface pointers it obtained, and then the program finally calls CoUninitialize() at line 58.

Accessing a Schema Syntax Object with IADsSchema

Unlike the "true" schema in the Schema naming context, the abstract also contains some information about the attribute syntaxes supported by Active Directory. You can list the supported syntaxes by enumerating the objects in the abstract schema container and then checking each with QueryInterface() using the interface ID IID_IADsSyntax.

The only thing you can do with an IADsSyntax interface is retrieve the OLE automation type that corresponds to the syntax. The type is returned as a long. The value returned corresponds to the OLE type defined in the VARENUM enumeration in wtypes.h.

This interface has one use I can think of. If you write a program that has no *a priori* knowledge of the syntaxes of the properties in the directory—for instance, a generic Active Directory browser—you can use IADsSyntax to determine how to handle each property you get from the directory. This would involve some big switch statement on the value returned by the IADsSyntax::get_OleAutoDataType() function. Table 15.5 details the IADsSyntax interface.

TABLE 15.5 THE IADsSyntax INTERFACE

Function Name	Description
QueryInterface()	IUnknown interface.
AddRef()	IUnknown interface.
Release()	IUnknown interface.
GetTypeInfoCount()	IDispatch interface.
GetTypeInfo()	IDispatch interface.
GetIDsOfNames()	IDispatch interface.
Invoke()	IDispatch interface.
get_OleAutoDataType()	Retrieves the Automation data type constant.
put_OleAutoDataType()	Sets the Automation data type constant.

Listing 15.8 builds on the preceding program. For each attribute the program gets from the abstract schema container, the program gets the OLE automation type and prints it.

LISTING 15.8 GETTING THE SYNTAX FOR EACH SCHEMA PROPERTY USING IADsProperty

```
 1: #include <windows.h>
 2: #include <activeds.h>
 3: #include <comutil.h>
 4: #include <stdio.h>
 5:
 6: int main(int argc, char* argv[])
 7: {
 8:   HRESULT hr = CoInitialize( NULL );
 9:
10:   if( SUCCEEDED( hr ) )
11:   {
12:     IADsContainer* piSchema = NULL;
13:
```

continues

LISTING 15.8 CONTINUED

```
14:     hr = ADsGetObject( L"LDAP://schema", IID_IADsContainer,
15:                         ( void** )&piSchema );
16:     if( SUCCEEDED( hr ) )
17:     {
18:       IEnumVARIANT* piEnum = NULL;
19:
20:       // Build the enumerator
21:       hr = ADsBuildEnumerator( piSchema, &piEnum );
22:       if( SUCCEEDED( hr ) )
23:       {
24:         ULONG ulCount;
25:         _variant_t varEntry;
26:
27:         // Enumerate the entries
28:         while( ( hr = ADsEnumerateNext( piEnum, 1, &varEntry,
29:             &ulCount ) == S_OK ) && ulCount == 1 )
30:         {
31:           IADsProperty* piProperty = NULL;
32:
33:           hr = ( ( IDispatch* )varEntry )->QueryInterface(
34:               IID_IADsProperty, ( void** )&piProperty );
35:           if( SUCCEEDED( hr ) )
36:           {
37:             BSTR strName;
38:             BSTR strSyntax;
39:
40:             piProperty->get_Name( &strName );
41:             piProperty->get_Syntax( &strSyntax );
42:
43:             _bstr_t strSyntaxPath = _bstr_t( "LDAP://schema/" ) +
44:                                     _bstr_t( strSyntax );
45:
46:             IADsSyntax* piSyntax = NULL;
47:
48:             hr = ADsGetObject( strSyntaxPath, IID_IADsSyntax,
49:                               ( void** )&piSyntax );
50:             if( SUCCEEDED( hr ) )
51:             {
52:               LONG lType;
53:
54:               piSyntax->get_OleAutoDataType( &lType );
55:
56:               printf( "property: %S syntax: %S OLE type: %d\n",
57:                   strName, strSyntax, lType );
58:
59:               piSyntax->Release();
60:             }
61:             piProperty->Release();
62:           }
```

```
63:
64:              ( ( IDispatch* )varEntry )->Release();
65:          }
66:
67:          piEnum->Release();
68:      }
69:
70:      piSchema->Release();
71:  }
72:
73:  ( void )CoUninitialize();
74:  }
75:
76:  return 0;
77: }
```

The sample program in Listing 15.8 binds to the abstract schema container at line 14, and builds an enumerator for the abstract container starting at line 21.

The program enumerates each entry in the abstract schema container in the `while` loop that starts at line 28. For each entry in the abstract schema container, the program tries to get an `IADsProperty` interface.

For each entry in the abstract schema container that actually is a property entry, the program gets the name and syntax string at lines 40 and 41.

At line 43, the program builds the `ADsPath` for the syntax entry. This `ADsPath` will look something like `"LDAP://schema/DN"`, which is the `ADsPath` for the abstract schema entry for the distinguished name syntax.

The program gets the `IADsSyntax` interface pointer for the syntax at line 48. At line 54, the program gets the OLE automation data type code. This number corresponds to one of the entries in the `VARENUM` enumeration in wtypes.h.

The program prints the property name, syntax name, and OLE automation data type number at line 56.

At lines 59, 61, 64, 67, and 70, the sample program releases the interface pointers it previously obtained. At line 73, the program wraps up by calling `CoUninitialize()`.

15

ACCESSING THE ACTIVE DIRECTORY SCHEMA

CHAPTER 16

Other Active Directory API Functions

Microsoft provides a host of non-ADSI API functions that simplify accessing Active Directory.

The first set of functions translates directory names from one form to another—for instance, from the LDAP name form (CN=Jenny Mulcahy,CN=Users,DC=megacorp,DC=com) to the canonical name form (megacorp.com/Users/Jenny Mulcahy).

The second set of functions accesses the information in the Active Directory Configuration naming context to list the sites in the enterprise, list the servers in a site, and get information about domain controllers.

The third set of functions manages the replication topology of Active Directory. You can use these functions to list the replication partners of a domain controller and to add and remove domain controllers from the replication partner list of a domain controller. There is also a function to force a replication event on a domain controller.

> **NOTE**
>
> To use the functions described in this chapter, you need to do two things. First, you must include the header file ntdsapi.h. Second, you must add the import library ntdsapi.lib to your project.

Connecting to an Active Directory Service

Most of the functions in this chapter use a directory service (DS) connection handle. A *DS connection handle* is simply a HANDLE that represents an authenticated connection with a particular domain controller. Before using any of the functions in this chapter, you must create a connection with a domain controller by calling DsBind() or DsBindWithCred(). When you are done with the connection, you must call DsUnBind() to free the connection. Table 16.1 lists the functions that deal with DS connection handles.

TABLE 16.1 DS CONNECTION MANAGEMENT FUNCTIONS

Function Name	*Description*
DsBind	Creates a connection with a specific domain controller using the current user's credentials.
DsBindWithCred	Creates a connection with a specific domain controller using the specified credentials.
DsUnBind	Frees a connection handle returned by DsBind() or DsBindWithCred().
DsMakePasswordCredentials	Creates a credentials structure from the specified username and password to be passed to DsBindWithCred().
DsFreePasswordCredentials	Frees a credentials structure created by DsMakePasswordCredentials().

The following code sample shows how you typically create a connection to a domain controller:

```
DWORD DsBind( TCHAR* pszDCAddress, TCHAR* pszDNSDomain, HANDLE* phDS )
```

pszDCAdress s a pointer to a NUL-terminated string containing the DNS host name or address of the domain controller you want to connect to. The format of the address string is, for instance, "\\208.192.112.23". If you specify NULL, DsBind() will connect to a domain controller in the domain specified by pszDNSDomain. You must specify a value for either the pszDCAddress or the pszDNSDomain parameter, but not for both parameters.

pszDNSDomain is a pointer to a NUL-terminated string containing the DNS name of the domain to which you want to connect. DsBind() will connect to a domain controller in that domain. You must specify a value for only one of the parameters pszDNSDomain and pszDCAddress. If you specify NULL, DsBind() will connect to the domain controller indicated by `pszDCAddress`. If `pszDCAddress` is `NULL`, `DsBind()` will connect to a domain controller in the currently logged-in user's domain.

`phDS` is the address of a `HANDLE` that will be set to the DS connection handle.

Returns: A Windows NT error code.

```
HANDLE hDS;

DWORD dwResult = DsBind( NULL, NULL, &hDS );
if( dwResult == ERROR_SUCCESS )
{
    // do stuff with the DS connection handle
    DsUnBind( &hDS );
}
```

Or, if you want to connect to the domain controller using a set of credentials different from those of the logged-in user, the code would look something like the following code sample.

```
DWORD DsMakePasswordCredentials( LPTSTR pszUserName, LPTSTR pszDomain,
➥LPTSTR pszPassword, RPC_AUTH_IDENTITY_HANDLE* phCredentials )
```

> `pszUserName` is a pointer to a NUL-terminated string containing the name of the user you want credentials for. If you specify `NULL`, the function will use the credentials of the logged-in user.
>
> `pszDomain` is a pointer to a NUL-terminated string containing the NetBIOS name of the domain containing the user given by `pszUserName`. If `pszUserName` is `NULL`, this parameter should be `NULL`.
>
> `pszPassword` is a pointer to a NUL-terminated string containing the password for the user. If `pszUserName` is `NULL`, this parameter should be `NULL` too.
>
> `phCredentials` is the address of a handle that will be set to contain the credentials for the user.

Returns: A Windows NT error code.

```
DWORD DsBindWithCred( TCHAR* pszDCAddress, TCHAR* pszDNSDomain,
➥RPC_AUTH_IDENTITY_HANDLE hCreds, HANDLE* phDS )
```

> `pszDCAddress` is a pointer to a NUL-terminated string containing the DNS host name or address of the domain controller to which you want to connect. The format of the address string is, for instance, `"\\208.192.112.23"`. If you specify `NULL`, `DsBind()` will connect to a domain controller in the domain specified by `pszDNSDomain`. You must specify a value for only one of the `pszDCAddress` and `pszDNSDomain` parameters.
>
> `pszDNSDomain` is a pointer to a NUL-terminated string containing the DNS name of a domain to which you want to connect. `DsBind()` will connect to a domain

controller in this domain. You must specify a value for only one of the parameters `pszDNSDomain` and `pszDCAddress`. If you specify NULL, `DsBind()` will connect to the domain controller indicated by `pszDCAddress`. If `pszDCAddress` is NULL, `DsBind()` will connect to a domain controller in the currently logged-in user's domain.

`hCreds` is a credentials handle returned by `DsMakePasswordCredentials`.

`phDS` is the address of a HANDLE that will be set to the DS connection handle.

Returns: A Windows NT error code.

```
DWORD DsFreePasswordCredentials( RPC_AUTH_IDENTITY_HANDLE hCreds )
```

`hCreds` is a credentials handle initialized by `DsMakePasswordCredentials()`.

Returns: A Windows NT error code.

```
RPC_AUTH_IDENTITY_HANDLE hCreds;

DWORD dwResult = DsMakePasswordCredentials( "Administrator", "MEGACORP",
➥"xyzzy", &hCreds );
if( dwResult == ERROR_SUCCESS )
{
HANDLE hDS;

DWORD dwResult = DsBindWithCred( "//208.192.221.32", NULL, hCreds, &hDS );
if( dwResult == ERROR_SUCCESS )
{
        // do stuff with the DS connection handle
    DsUnBind( &hDS );
}

DsFreePasswordCredentials( hCreds );
}
```

Translating Directory Service Names

Windows 2000 and Active Directory use several different naming systems to identify objects in the system. As I described in Chapter 3, "The Components of Active Directory," a user in Windows 2000 can be identified by several different names. For instance, a single user will have a distinguished name in the directory (`CN=Corbin Glowacki,CN=Users,DC=megacorp, DC=com`), a canonical name (`megacorp.com/users/Corbin Glowacki`), a user principal name (`CorbinG@megacorp.com`), a GUID, (`4fa050f0-f561-11cf-bdd9-0012a003a99b6`), and so forth.

Microsoft provides a function called `DsCrackNames()` to translate from one name form to another. `DsCrackNames()` accepts an array of names in one format and then, based on the parameters you pass, converts the names to a second format and returns the results in a `DS_NAME_RESULT` structure allocated by `DsCrackNames()`. After inspecting the names, you call `DsFreeNameResult()` to free the memory allocated for the result structure. Table 16.2 lists the various functions you can use to translate names.

TABLE 16.2 DS NAME TRANSLATION FUNCTIONS

Function Name	Description
DsCrackNames	Translates an array of directory service object names from one format to another.
DsFreeNameResult	Frees the translated names returned by DsCrackNames.

`DsCrackNames()` works in two modes. In the normal mode, `DsCrackNames()` accepts a handle to directory connection created with `DsBind()` or `DsBindWithCred()` and uses the directory to translate the names. In the "syntactical translation only" mode, `DsCrackNames()` attempts to translate the name without contacting the directory.

The syntactical translation only mode is limited in that it can perform translations only between a fully qualified distinguished name and a canonical name, and vice versa.

Table 16.3 lists the name formats supported by `DsCrackNames()`. These name format constants are defined in the `DS_NAME_FORMAT` enumeration in ntdsapi.h.

TABLE 16.3 POSSIBLE VALUES FOR DS_NAME_FORMAT

Name Format	Description
DS_UNKNOWN_NAME	Unknown name format. Not used.
DS_FQDN_1779_NAME	Fully qualified LDAP distinguished name, such as `CN=Jason Lockett,CN=Users,DC=megacorp,DC=com`.
DS_NT4_ACCOUNT_NAME	Windows NT 4 username, such as `GEORGEWILSON`.
DS_DISPLAY_NAME	The user-friendly display name for the user from the `displayName` attribute in the directory—for instance, Christofer Gendreau.
DS_DOMAIN_SIMPLE_NAME	Not used.
DS_ENTERPRISE_SIMPLE_NAME	Not used.
DS_UNIQUE_ID_NAME	The GUID of the object in string form, such as `{41d03010-e571-44cf-b3d9-0112b043a99b6}`.

continues

TABLE **16.3** CONTINUED

Name Format	Description
DS_CANONICAL_NAME	The canonical name of the object—for instance, megacorp.com/Users/Bill McClurg.
DS_USER_PRINCIPAL_NAME	The user principal name of the object—for instance, DPeterson@megacorp.com.
DS_CANONICAL_NAME_EX	The same as DS_CANONICAL_NAME except that the last forward slash is replaced by a newline character—for instance, megacorp.com/Users\nMatt Celupica.
DS_SID_OR_SID_HISTORY_NAME	The Windows NT Security Identifier (SID) for the user. You can't use it for the uFormatDesired parameter.
DS_SERVICE_PRINCIPAL_NAME	A service principal name—for instance, LDAP/engserver.megacorp.com/megacorp.

DsCrackNames() allocates a DS_NAME_RESULT structure containing the translated names. Table 16.4 describes the elements of the DS_NAME_RESULT structure. Table 16.5 describes the DS_NAME_RESULT_ITEM structure, which is contained within the DS_NAME_RESULT structure.

TABLE **16.4** THE DS_NAME_RESULT STRUCTURE

Element	Type	Description
cItems	DWORD	The number of entries in the rItems array.
rItems	PDS_NAME_RESULT_ITEM	A pointer to an array of DS_NAME_RESULT_ITEM structures containing the translated names.

The DS_NAME_RESULT structure contains an array of DS_NAME_RESULT_ITEM structures. Each DS_NAME_RESULT_ITEM contains the translated name string, a DWORD indicating the error encountered while translating the name or zero if there was no error, and a pointer to the DNS domain name that contains the name.

TABLE **16.5** THE DS_NAME_RESULT_ITEM STRUCTURE

Element	Type	Description
status	DWORD	A Windows NT error code if there was an error translating this name, or zero if there was no error.
pDomain	LPSTR	A pointer to a NUL-terminated string containing the DNS domain to which the translated name belongs.
pName	LPSTR	A pointer to a NUL-terminated string containing the translated name.

The function prototype for `DsCrackNames()` is as follows:

```
DWORD DsCrackNames( HANDLE hDS, DS_NAME_FLAGS uFlags,
➥DS_NAME_FORMAT uFormatOffered, DS_NAME_FORMAT uFormatDesired,
➥DWORD dwNames, LPTSTR* apszNames, PDS_NAME_RESULT* ppsResult )
```

> `hDS` is a connection handle to Active Directory created by `DsBind()` or `DsBindWithCred()`.
>
> `uFlags` is either `DS_NAME_NO_FLAGS`, indicating to use the directory to perform the name translation, or `DS_NAME_FLAG_SYNTACTICAL_ONLY`, indicating to perform a syntactical translation only.
>
> `uFormatOffered` is a `DS_NAME_FORMAT` value indicating the format of the names to be translated.
>
> `uFormatDesired` is a `DS_NAME_FORMAT` value indicating the desired format of the translated names.
>
> `dwNames` is the number of names in the `apszNames` array.
>
> `apszNames` is an array of NUL-terminated strings containing the names to be translated.
>
> `ppsResult` is the address of a `DS_NAME_RESULT` pointer that will be set by `DsCrackNames()`. You must free this pointer by passing it to `DsFreeNameResult()`.

Returns: A Windows NT error code.

After you have translated an array of names, you have to pass the result pointer `*ppsResult` to the `DsFreeNameResult()` function. The prototype for `DsFreeNameResult()` follows:

```
DWORD DsFreeNameResult( PDS_NAME_RESULT psResult )
```

> `psResult` is a pointer to a `DS_NAME_RESULT` structure created by `DsCrackNames()`.

Returns: A Windows NT error code.

The sample program in Listing 16.1 shows how to use the `DsCrackNames()` function. It connects to an Active Directory domain controller by using `DsBind()` and then calls `DsCrackNames()` to translate an LDAP-style distinguished name to a canonical name.

LISTING 16.1 TRANSLATING A DIRECTORY NAME WITH `DsCrackNames()`

```
1: #include <windows.h>
2: #include <ntdsapi.h>
3: #include <dsgetdc.h>
4: #include <stdio.h>
5:
6: int main(int argc, char* argv[])
7: {
```

continues

LISTING 16.1   CONTINUED

```
 8:      HANDLE hDS;
 9:
10:
11:      // Connect to a domain controller
12:      DWORD dwResult = DsBind( "engserver.megacorp.com", NULL, &hDS );
13:      if( dwResult == ERROR_SUCCESS )
14:      {
15:          // The array of names to translate
16:          char* apszNames[] = { "CN=Dana Wolf,CN=Users,DC=megacorp,
             ➥DC=com" };
17:          DS_NAME_RESULT* psNames;
18:
19:          // Translate the names
20:          dwResult = DsCrackNames( hDS, DS_NAME_NO_FLAGS,
             ➥DS_FQDN_1779_NAME, DS_CANONICAL_NAME, 1, apszNames,
             ➥&psNames );
21:          if( dwResult == ERROR_SUCCESS )
22:          {
23:              // Walk through the array of translated names
24:              for( unsigned int nName = 0; nName < psNames->cItems;
                 ➥nName++ )
25:              {
26:                  if( psNames->rItems[ nName ].status == ERROR_SUCCESS )
27:                  {
28:                      printf( "Name: %s Domain: %s\n", psNames->
                         ➥rItems[ nName ].pName, psNames->
                         ➥rItems[ nName ].pDomain );
29:                  }
30:              }
31:
32:              DsFreeNameResult( psNames );
33:          }
34:
35:          DsUnBind( &hDS );
36:      }
37:
38:      return 0;
39: }
```

The program in Listing 16.1 connects to a domain controller at line 11 by calling
DsBind(). The program then declares an array of directory names in LDAP distinguished
name format that contains a single name.

At line 20, the program calls DsCrackNames() passing DS_NAME_NO_FLAGS indicating the
program should consult the directory to translate the names.

The for loop at line 24 enumerates the translated name entries in the *psNames structure.
For each entry in the *psNames structure, the program checks the status code in the entry,

and if it is `ERROR_SUCCESS`, the program prints the translated name and the DNS domain that contains the name.

Discovering Sites, Servers, and Domains

Two things you will certainly do if you write any kind of directory administration tool are discovering and listing Active Directory sites and servers. You can find this information by searching the Active Directory Configuration naming context, but Microsoft makes the job a little easier by providing several functions that do all the hard work for you. Table 16.6 lists the functions that discover sites, servers, and domains in Active Directory.

TABLE 16.6   DS SITE, SERVER, AND DOMAIN DISCOVERY FUNCTIONS

Function Name	Description
DsGetDcName	Retrieves the name of a domain controller that meets specified search criteria.
DsListSites	Lists the sites in the Active Directory enterprise.
DsListServersInSite	Lists the servers in a specific Active Directory site.
DsListDomainsInSite	Lists the domains present on domain controllers in the specified Active Directory site.
DsListServersForDomainInSite	Lists the servers in a specific domain located in a specified Active Directory site.
DsListInfoForServer	Retrieves the DNS host name, DSA service name, and SAM account name for the specified server.
DsListRoles	Retrieves an array containing the names of the five FSMO role owners for the domain.
DsGetDomainControllerInfo	Retrieves name information for the specified domain controller, as well as whether or not the server is a down-level primary domain controller (PDC) or an Active Directory domain controller.
DsFreeDomainControllerInfo	Frees the results returned by `DsGetDomainControllerInfo()`.

Finding a Domain Controller

`DsGetDcName()` retrieves the name of an "appropriate" domain controller—that is, a domain controller that meets certain criteria you specify. For instance, you can request a domain controller in a particular site or domain, or you can request a domain controller that is both a global catalog server and exists in a particular site. Note that you do not need a domain controller connection before you call `DsGetDcName()`; in fact, you usually call `DsGetDcName()` to find the domain controller to which you want to connect and then pass the results from `DsGetDcName()` to `DsBind()` to create the connection.

Unlike the other functions this chapter describes, the function prototypes and other definitions for `DsGetDcName()` are in the dsgetdc.h header file. To build a program that uses `DsGetDcName()`, you must include dsgetdc.h as well as link in the library netapi32.lib.

```
DWORD DsGetDcName( LPCSTR pszComputerName, LPCSTR pszDomainName,
➥GUID* psDomainGuid, LPCSTR pszSiteName, ULONG uFlags,
➥PDOMAIN_CONTROLLER_INFO* ppsDCInfo )
```

`pszComputerName` is a pointer to a NUL-terminated string containing the NetBIOS name of the computer to execute this function. Pass NULL for this parameter to execute on the local machine.

`pszDomainName` is a pointer to a NUL-terminated string containing the name of the domain to find a domain controller in. You can use either the DNS name format, such as `engineering.megacorp.com`, or the NT 4 domain name format, such as ENGINEERING. If you specify NULL for this parameter, `DsGetDcName()` will look for a domain controller in the domain of the computer specified by `pszComputerName`. If you are looking for a global catalog and `pszDomainName` is NULL, `DsGetName()` will search for a global catalog in the same Active Directory tree as the computer specified `pszComputerName`.

`psDomainGuid` is a pointer to a GUID structure containing the GUID of the domain you want to find a domain controller. Normally, you specify a NULL for this parameter. You would specify a GUID if you previously saved the domain GUID and the domain had since been renamed.

`pszSiteName` is a pointer to a NUL-terminated string containing the name of the Active Directory site to find a domain controller in. If `pszSiteName` is NULL, `DsGetDcName()` will search for a domain controller in the same site as the computer specified by `pszComputerName`.

`uFlags` specifies the kind of domain controller to search for. The value of `uFlags` comes from ORing one or more values from the constants listed in Table 16.7.

`ppsDCInfo` is the address of a pointer to a `DOMAIN_CONTROLLER_INFO` structure. `DsGetDcName()` sets this pointer to refer to a newly allocated `DOMAIN_CONTROLLER_INFO` structure containing the result of your search. You must free this structure by passing the returned pointer to `NetApiBufferFree()`, which is defined in the lm.h header file.

Returns: A Windows NT error code.

Table 16.7 lists the possible value for the `uFlags` parameter of `DsGetDcName`. You can OR these flags together to indicate what kind of domain controller you want to find.

TABLE 16.7 VALUES FOR THE `uFlags` PARAMETER OF `DsGetDcName`

Flag Name	Description
DS_FORCE_REDISCOVERY	Forces the computer to flush its cache of domain controller names and requery DNS for domain controllers matching your criteria.
DS_DIRECTORY_SERVICE_REQUIRED	Requires that the returned domain controller be an Active Directory domain controller.
DS_DIRECTORY_SERVICE_PREFERRED	If a domain controller running Active Directory can be found, the function returns it. Otherwise, it returns a down-level Windows NT 4 domain controller.
DS_GC_SERVER_REQUIRED	Requires that the returned domain controller be a global catalog server.
DS_PDC_REQUIRED	Requires that the returned domain controller be a primary domain controller for the specified domain.
DS_IP_REQUIRED	Causes `DsGetDcName()` to return the IP address of the returned server.
DS_KDC_REQUIRED	Requires that the returned domain controller be a Kerberos key distribution center (KDC).
DS_TIMESERV_REQUIRED	Requires that the returned domain controller be running the Windows NT or 2000 time service.
DS_WRITABLE_REQUIRED	Requires that the returned domain controller have a writable copy of the directory or SAM database.
DS_GOOD_TIMESERV_PREFERRED	Requires that the returned domain controller be running the Windows NT or 2000 time service and that it have a connection to an external time source.
DS_AVOID_SELF	Makes sure the returned domain controller is not the computer from which the `DsGetDcName()` call was made.
DS_ONLY_LDAP_NEEDED	Returns any domain controller that is running an LDAP service.
DS_IS_FLAT_NAME	Indicates the domain name given by `pszDomainName` is a Windows NT 4–style flat domain name—for example, MEGACORP.

continues

TABLE 16.7 CONTINUED

Flag Name	Description
DS_IS_DNS_NAME	Indicates the domain name given by pszDomainName is a DNS style domain name—for example, megacorp.com.
DS_RETURN_DNS_NAME	Requests that DsGetDcName() return the domain controller name as a DNS host name—for instance, engserver.megacorp.com.
DS_RETURN_FLAT_NAME	Requests that the DsGetDcName() return the Windows NT 4–style flat name for the server—for instance, ENGSERVER.

DsGetDcName() returns its results in a DOMAIN_CONTROLLER_INFO structure whose address is placed at *ppsDCInfo. The definition of the DOMAIN_CONTROLLER_INFO structure is shown in Table 16.8.

TABLE 16.8 ELEMENTS OF THE DOMAIN_CONTROLLER_INFO STRUCTURE

Element	Description
DomainControllerName	A pointer to a NUL-terminated string containing the name of the returned domain controller, preceded by a double backslash—for instance, \\engserver.megacorp.com.
DomainControllerAddress	A pointer to a NUL-terminated string containing the network address of the returned server. The DomainControllerAddressType indicates whether the address is an IP address like \\208.192.123.45 or a NetBIOS address, such as \\ENGSERVER.
DomainControllerAddressType	Indicates the format of the DomainControllerAddress element. It is either DS_INET_ADDRESS or DS_NETBIOS_ADDRESS.
DomainGuid	The GUID of the domain containing the returned domain controller.
DomainName	A pointer to a NUL-terminated string containing the name of the domain containing the domain controller.
TreeName	A pointer to a NUL-terminated string containing the name of the Active Directory forest containing the domain controller.

Other Active Directory API Functions
CHAPTER 16

415

16

OTHER ACTIVE
DIRECTORY API
FUNCTIONS

Element	Description
Flags	A set of flags indicating the kind of domain controller returned. The possible values of the Flags field are given in Table 16.9. Note that the names of the flag values are similar to, but different from, the uFlags parameter of DsGetDcNames().
DcSiteName	A pointer to a NUL-terminated string containing the name of the Active Directory site in which the domain controller resides. The pointer will be NULL if the returned domain controller is not a Windows 2000 domain controller.
ClientSiteName	A pointer to a NUL-terminated string containing the name of the Active Directory site containing the computer given by the pszComputerName parameter in the call to DsGetDcName(). This value may be NULL if the computer is not assigned to an Active Directory site.

Table 16.9 lists the possible values of the Flags element of DOMAIN_CONTROLLER_INFO structure.

TABLE 16.9 VALUES FOR THE Flags ELEMENT OF THE DOMAIN_CONTROLLER_INFO STRUCTURE

Flag Name	Description
DS_PDC_FLAG	The returned domain controller is a down-level primary domain controller.
DS_GC_FLAG	The returned domain controller hosts an Active Directory global catalog.
DS_LDAP_FLAG	The returned domain controller is running an LDAP directory.
DS_DS_FLAG	The returned domain controller hosts a copy of the directory.
DS_KDC_FLAG	The returned domain controller is Kerberos Key Distribution Center (KDC).
DS_TIMESERV_FLAG	The returned domain controller is running Windows time service.
DS_CLOSEST_FLAG	The returned domain controller is the closest (in terms of response time) domain controller from which the request was made.

continues

TABLE 16.9 CONTINUED

Flag Name	Description
DS_WRITABLE_FLAG	The returned domain controller has a writable copy of the directory.
DS_GOOD_TIMESERV_FLAG	The returned domain controller is running the time service and it is connected to an external time source.
DS_DNS_CONTROLLER_FLAG	The name of the returned domain controller in DomainController is in DNS format.
DS_DNS_DOMAIN_FLAG	The name of the returned domain in DomainName is in DNS format.
DS_DNS_FOREST_FLAG	The name of the returned domain forest in TreeName is in DNS format.

This program in Listing 16.2 uses the DsGetDcName() function to get the name of a global catalog to connect to.

LISTING 16.2 FINDING A GLOBAL CATALOG SERVER WITH DsGetDcName()

```
 1: #include <windows.h>
 2: #include <ntdsapi.h>
 3: #include <dsgetdc.h>
 4: #include <lm.h>
 5: #include <stdio.h>
 6:
 7: int main(int argc, char* argv[])
 8: {
 9:     PDOMAIN_CONTROLLER_INFO psDCInfo;
10:     ULONG uFlags = DS_GC_SERVER_REQUIRED | DS_RETURN_DNS_NAME;
11:
12:     // Call DsGetDcName to find a global catalog
13:     DWORD dwResult = DsGetDcName(
14:         NULL,          // computer to execute search from
15:         NULL,          // domain
16:         NULL,          // domain GUID
17:         NULL,          // site name
18:         uFlags,         // search flags
19:         &psDCInfo      // pointer to DOMAIN_CONTROLLER_INFO struct
20:     );
21:
22:     if( dwResult == ERROR_SUCCESS )
23:     {
24:         printf( "DC: %s\n", psDCInfo->DomainControllerName );
25:         printf( "Address: %s\n", psDCInfo->DomainControllerAddress );
26:         printf( "Domain: %s\n", psDCInfo->DomainName );
```

```
27:          printf( "Forest: %s\n", psDCInfo->DnsForestName );
28:          printf( "Site: %s\n", psDCInfo->DcSiteName );
29:
30:
31:          NetApiBufferFree( psDCInfo );
32:      }
33:
34:      return 0;
35: }
```

The program in Listing 16.2 shows how to get the name of a nearby global catalog server. The program initializes the `DsGetDcName()` search flags by ORing the `DS_GC_SERVER_REQUIRED` and `DS_RETURN_DNS_NAME` flags. This causes `DsGetDcName()` to return the DNS host name of a global catalog server.

At line 13, the program actually calls `DsGetDcName()`, specifying the flags set on line 10, and NULL for all the other parameters. In this case, `DsGetDcName()` defaults the computer to search from to the current computer, the domain defaults to the domain of the computer executing the call, and the site defaults to the site the computer is in.

If the call succeeds, the program prints the domain controller name, the address, the domain of which the domain controller is a member, and the name of the forest containing the domain. The program also prints the name of the site containing the returned domain controller.

The sample program frees the `DOMAIN_CONTROLLER_INFO` structure at line 31 by calling `NetApiBufferFree()`.

Listing the Sites in Active Directory

The `DsListSites()` function does just that: It lists the Active Directory sites stored in the Configuration naming context in the Sites container. `DsListSites()` takes a domain controller connection handle and returns a `DS_NAME_RESULT` structure (refer to Table 16.4) that contains the full distinguished names of the sites in Active Directory.

`DWORD DsListSites( HANDLE hDS, PDS_NAME_RESULT* ppsResult )`

> hDS is a connection handle to Active Directory created by `DsBind()` or `DsBindWithCred()`.
>
> ppsResult is the address of a `DS_NAME_RESULT` pointer that will be set by `DsListSites`. You must free this pointer by passing it to `DsFreeNameResult()`.

Returns: A Windows NT error code.

The program in Listing 16.3 shows how to call `DsListSites()` to lists the Active Directory sites defined in the directory. It calls `DsListSites()` to get a list of the sites in Active Directory, and the program then prints all the site names.

LISTING 16.3   LIST ACTIVE DIRECTORY SITES WITH DsListSites()

```
 1: #include <windows.h>
 2: #include <ntdsapi.h>
 3: #include <dsgetdc.h>
 4: #include <stdio.h>
 5:
 6: int main(int argc, char* argv[])
 7: {
 8:     HANDLE hDS;
 9:
10:
11:     // Connect to a domain controller
12:     DWORD dwResult = DsBind( "engserver.megacorp.com", NULL, &hDS );
13:     if( dwResult == ERROR_SUCCESS )
14:     {
15:         DS_NAME_RESULT* psNames;
16:
17:         // Get the list of sites
18:         dwResult = DsListSites( hDS, &psNames );
19:         if( dwResult == ERROR_SUCCESS )
20:         {
21:             // Walk through the array of site names
22:             for( unsigned int nName = 0; nName < psNames->cItems;
             ➥nName++ )
23:             {
24:                 if( psNames->rItems[ nName ].status == ERROR_SUCCESS )
25:                 {
26:                     printf( "Site: %s\n", psNames->rItems[ nName]
                     ➥pName );
27:                 }
28:             }
29:
30:             DsFreeNameResult( psNames );
31:         }
32:
33:         DsUnBind( &hDS );
34:     }
35:
36:     return 0;
37: }
```

The sample program in Listing 16.3 starts by getting a DS connection to a domain controller at line 12.

The program then calls DsListSites() at line 18 to get a list of the Active Directory site names.

At line 21, the sample program iterates through the entries in the returned DS_NAME_RESULT structure and prints each one.

The program frees the DS_NAME_RESULT structure at line 29 with DsFreeNameResult(), and it disconnects from the domain controller at line 33 by calling DsUnBind().

Listing the Servers in a Site

DsListServersInSite() gives you an easy way to compose a list of Active Directory servers in a specific site. This is a useful thing to be able to do if you want to present your users with a list of servers that are physically near them.

The DsListServersInSite() function accepts a directory service connection handle and the full distinguished name of a site, and it returns a pointer to a DS_NAME_RESULT structure containing the distinguished names of the servers in that site. You must free the resulting structure with DsFreeNameResult().

```
DWORD DsListServersInSite( HANDLE hDS, LPCSTR pszSiteName,
➥PDS_NAME_RESULT* ppsResult )
```

> hDS is a connection handle to Active Directory created by DsBind() or DsBindWithCred().
>
> pszSiteName is a pointer to a NUL-terminated string containing the name of the site to list servers for.
>
> ppsResult is the address of a DS_NAME_RESULT pointer that will be set by DsListSites. You must free this pointer by passing it to DsFreeNameResult().

Returns: A Windows NT error code.

The program in Listing 16.4 is an extension of the preceding sample program. In this case, the program lists all the sites in Active Directory by calling DsListSites(), and for each site it finds, the program calls DsListServersInSite() to list the servers present in each site.

LISTING 16.4 LISTING SERVERS WITHIN ACTIVE DIRECTORY SITES WITH
DsListServersInSites()

```
 1: #include <windows.h>
 2: #include <lm.h>
 3: #include <ntdsapi.h>
 4: #include <stdio.h>
 5:
 6: int main( int argc, char** argv )
 7: {
 8:     HANDLE hDS;
 9:
10:
11:     // Connect to a domain controller
```

continues

LISTING 16.4   CONTINUED

```
12:    DWORD dwResult = DsBind( "engserver.megacorp.com", NULL, &hDS );
13:    if( dwResult == 0 )
14:    {
15:        DS_NAME_RESULT* psSiteNames;
16:
17:        dwResult = DsListSites( hDS, &psSiteNames );
18:        for( unsigned int nSiteName = 0; nSiteName <
           ➥psSiteNames->cItems; nSiteName++ )
19:        {
20:            if( psSiteNames->rItems[ nSiteName ].status ==
               ➥ERROR_SUCCESS )
21:            {
22:                printf( "Site: %s\n", psSiteNames->
                   ➥rItems[ nSiteName ].pName );
23:
24:                DS_NAME_RESULT* psServerNames;
25:
26:                dwResult = DsListServersInSite( hDS, psSiteNames->
                   ➥rItems[ nSiteName ].pName, &psServerNames );
27:                if( dwResult == ERROR_SUCCESS )
28:                {
29:                    for( unsigned int nServerName = 0; nServerName <
                       ➥psServerNames->cItems; nServerName++ )
30:                    {
31:                        if( psServerNames->rItems[ nServerName ]
                           ➥.status== ERROR_SUCCESS )
32:                        {
33:                            printf( "Server: %s\n", psServerNames->
                               ➥rItems[ nServerName ].pName );
34:                        }
35:                    }
36:
37:                    DsFreeNameResult( psServerNames );
38:                }
39:            }
40:        }
41:
42:        DsFreeNameResult( psSiteNames );
43:
44:        DsUnBind( &hDS );
45:    }
46:
47:    return 0;
48: }
```

The program in Listing 16.4 starts by getting a connection to an Active Directory domain controller at line 12.

The program then calls DsListSites(), as in Listing 16.3, to get a list of the distinguished names of all the sites in Active Directory.

At line 18, the program iterates through the names of the sites, and for each site, prints the site name. The program then calls DsListServersInSite() at line 26.

The for loop at line 29 iterates through the list of server names in the site, and at line 33 the program prints the distinguished name of each server in the site.

At line 37, the program frees the list of server names by calling DsFreeNameResult(). At line 42, it frees the list of site names as well.

The program wraps up by disconnecting from the domain controller when it calls DsUnBind() at line 44.

Lightweight Directory Access Protocol

PART
IV

CHAPTER 17

LDAP Fundamentals

LDAP is the core technology behind the explosion in the popularity of directories. As so often has been the case in the networking business, standardization has brought about increased development, commercialization, and deployment.

LDAP is unusual in that it is both an Internet-standard protocol for directory servers and a standard C language API.

> **NOTE**
>
> The LDAP API isn't, strictly speaking, a standard. RFC 1823, which documents the LDAP API, is an informational RFC.

Because this is a book about programming, I will discuss only LDAP the API and, more specifically, the Microsoft implementation of that API.

This chapter briefly describes the history of LDAP and then introduces the basic concepts underlying LDAP programming. If you have already done a bunch of LDAP programming, you can skip this chapter.

LDAP History

In the early 1990s, the creation of publicly accessible X.500 directory servers was a hot topic. The only problem was that X.500 required the complicated, resource-intensive, and wildly unpopular Open Systems Interconnection (OSI) protocols. There were several one-off projects that made X.500 work on non-OSI networks, but they were all either propri-etary or specific to a particular application. Wide implementation of X.500 directories was basically stuck because no one wanted to run the protocols X.500 required.

In 1990, researchers at the University of Michigan realized that the primary problem with X.500 was the complexity of the client software required for directory access. The low-powered PCs and workstations of the time just didn't have the horsepower to imple-ment the full-blown OSI/X.500 protocols.

The researchers' solution was to create a simplified protocol for the low-powered PCs to use and a high-powered proxy server that could service the PCs' requests and translate them to the relatively expensive X.500 protocol. This strategy resulted in two X.500 proxy servers: the Directory Assistant and DIXIE.

In 1992, some of the researchers realized that the old 90/10 rule applied to directory ser-vice implementation: You could get 90% of the benefit of a directory with only 10% of the implementation effort. This realization led to the first LDAP specification, defined in RFC 1487, which was submitted in 1993.

LDAP Version 1

LDAP version 1 exposed the most important aspects of an X.500 directory with some important simplifications. It was defined primarily as a protocol for an X.500 proxy server. Here were the main features of LDAPv1:

- The class/object/attribute/value data model from X.500
- The hierarchical namespace from X.500
- A subset of the sophisticated search capabilities in X.500
- A simplified representation of most data
- A simplified protocol defined over TCP

LDAPv1 left out several significant pieces:

- The ability to logically connect directory servers via chaining or referrals
- Support for secure connections

- Any support for schema access
- Any notion of access controls
- Any definition of a replication protocol

LDAP Version 2

LDAPv2 came out as RFC 1777 in March 1995 and changed almost nothing in the original protocol. The only significant change was to the semantics of the name-change operation. This version of the protocol went on to become the Internet standard. It is also the version that the not-quite-standardized LDAP API was developed around.

LDAP Version 3

RFC 2251 defines LDAPv3 and was originally published in December 1997. It attempts to address the shortcomings in LDAPv2—in particular, referrals, replication, and secure connections. LDAPv3 addresses nearly everything except replication and security. LDAPv3 is currently a proposed standard. LDAPv3 includes the following:

- The ability to logically connect multiple LDAP servers via referrals
- Authentication via the Simple Authentication and Security Layer (SASL)
- Access to the schema access using LDAP operations
- Functional extensibility via LDAP controls and extensions
- Access to server-specific operational parameters
- Unicode UTF-8 encodings for strings

Active Directory supports LDAPv3, with some omissions and extensions. The other LDAP chapters in this book all refer to the Microsoft implementation of LDAPv3.

Installing the LDAP Components

The files required for LDAP programming come on the Windows 2000 Platform SDK CD. Alternatively, you can install the Platform SDK directly from Microsoft's Web site at http://msdn.microsoft.com/downloads/sdks/platform/platform.asp. Installing the SDK is straightforward.

17

**LDAP
FUNDAMENTALS**

> **NOTE**
>
> Even though the SDK that comes with Microsoft's Visual Studio 6.0 includes some of the SDK files, including some of the LDAP files, you must install the current platform SDK. The files that come with Visual Studio 6.0 are incompatible with Windows 2000.

1. Run the SETUP.EXE program from the root of the Windows 2000 Platform SDK CD, or run the Platform SDK setup from the Microsoft Web site.

2. Click Next to get through the introductory screens.

3. Click I agree to indicate that you accept the license agreement, and then click Next.

4. Confirm your user name and organization name, and click Next.

5. Select the appropriate installation type. If you are tight on disk space and you want to install only those components needed for LDAP programming, select Custom. Otherwise, select Typical.

6. Check the Register Environment Variables box if you will be doing all your programming using the new SDK. Uncheck it if you will continue to use the older NT 4 SDKs, or if there is some other reason you don't want the installation process to modify your INCLUDE and LIB environment variables.

7. Check the Enable Microsoft Visual C++ Integration box if you want the installation process to automatically update your Visual C++ installation with new paths for libraries and include files. If you do not check this box, you will have to modify the include directories and library directories for your projects to refer to the Platform SDK include and lib directories.

8. On the next page, enter the drive and directory you want to install SDK in.

9. If you selected Custom in step 5, you now have to select the components of the Platform SDK you want to install. Expand the Build Environment entry and select the Win32 Build Environment option, the Minimum Build Tools option, the COM Headers and Libraries option, and the Active Directory Services Interface Headers and Libraries option. Click Next. This minimal installation will require about 20MB.

   If you can at all afford the disk space, install the SDK documentation as well. This will require an additional 117MB, but it's worth it.

10. Click Finish and wait for the installer to do its thing.

LDAP Programming Components

Even though the Platform SDK copied tens or maybe hundreds of megabytes of files to your hard disk, there are primarily three files you use to write and run LDAP programs: WINLDAP.H, WLDAP32.LIB, and WLDAP32.DLL. They are described in the following sections.

WINLDAP.H

WINLDAP.H is the header file for LDAP under Win32. It contains all of the #defines, typedefs, and function prototypes you need to communicate with an LDAP server. You must include WINLDAP.H in any source file that uses the LDAP library. This file is normally in the INCLUDE subdirectory under the directory where you installed the toolkit.

WLDAP32.LIB

WLDAP32.LIB is the import library for WLDAP32.DLL. It contains all the entry points for the LDAP library. You find this file in the LIB subdirectory under the directory you installed the toolkit in.

WLDAP32.DLL

WLDAP32.DLL is the Dynamic Link Library (DLL) that contains the executable code for the WIN32 LDAP library. You'll normally find it in the C:\WJNNT\SYSTEM32 directory.

Setting Up Visual Studio for LDAP Programming

You need to configure Visual Studio properly so that it can locate the three LDAP files. There are three methods for doing this. Use one method only; using multiple methods can be confusing, particularly if you try to build your projects on another machine.

Method One: Modify the Project Settings

Use this method if you need to share your project files with other developers, or if only some of your projects need access to the Windows 2000 SDK. You need to make sure that WLDAP32.DLL appears in a directory named in your PATH environment variable. This occurs by default during the SDK installation, so it shouldn't require any additional work on your part. Two areas in the IDE need to be modified to support LDAP—the compiler include path and the linker library path. The next two sections give the details for setting up the IDE to support LDAP.

Modify the Compiler Include Path

1. Select the Settings option from the Project menu.

2. Select All Configurations in the Settings For combo box.

3. Select the Preprocessor category on the C/C++ tab.

4. Add the Windows 2000 Platform SDK include directory to the Additional Include Directories edit control, as shown in Figure 17.1.

FIGURE 17.1

Setting the project include directory in Visual C++.

5. Click OK.

Modify the Linker Library Path

1. Select the Settings option from the Project menu.

2. Select All Configurations in the Settings For combo box.

3. Select the Input category on the Link tab.

4. Add WLDAP32.LIB to the Object/Library Modules edit control.

5. Add the Windows 2000 Platform SDK include directory to the Additional Library Path edit control, as shown in Figure 17.2.

FIGURE 17.2

Setting the project additional libraries and library directory options in Visual C++.

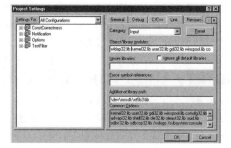

6. Click OK.

Method Two: Modify the Visual C++ Directories Options

Use this method if most of your projects will use the Windows 2000 SDK, and you can ensure that other developers who share these projects make these same changes. These option changes are not kept in the project or workspace files; they are kept in the workstation's registry. Like the preceding method, this one also has two areas in the IDE that need to be changed. These changes are described in the following two sections.

Modify the Include Files List

1. Select the Options option from the Tools menu.

2. Select the Directories tab.

3. Select Include files in the Show Directories For combo box.

4. Add the Windows 2000 Platform SDK include directory to the list of directories, as shown in Figure 17.3.

FIGURE 17.3

Setting the Visual C++ include directories list.

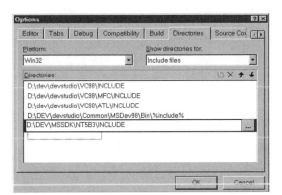

5. Click OK.

Modify the Library Files Directory List

1. Select the Options option from the Tools menu.

2. Select the Directories tab.

3. Select Library files in the Show Directories For combo box.

4. Add the Windows 2000 Platform SDK library directory to the list of directories, as shown in Figure 17.4.

FIGURE 17.4

Setting the Visual C++ library directories list.

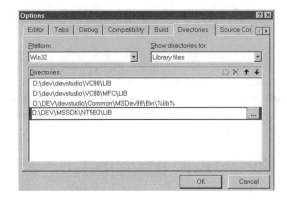

5. Click OK.

Method Three: Modify the System Environment Variables

Use this method if you have other tools that require the environment variables to be set to include the Windows 2000 SDK files, and you can guarantee that other developers sharing this project will set their environments the same way. This method requires a couple of changes to environment variables. The following sections describe these changes.

Modify the INCLUDE Environment Variable

1. Select the Settings option from the Start menu.

2. Select Control Panel.

3. Select the System icon from Control Panel.

4. Select the Advanced tab, and click the Environment Variables button. You see the Environment Variables dialog box, shown in Figure 17.5.

5. If the INCLUDE environment variable already exists, select it and click the Edit button. Otherwise, click the New button.

6. Add the Windows 2000 Platform SDK include directory to the path list.

7. Click OK.

FIGURE 17.5

Setting the system INCLUDE *environ-ment variable.*

Modify the LIB Environment Variable

1. Select the Settings option from the Start menu.

2. Select Control Panel.

3. Select the System icon from Control Panel.

4. Select the Advanced tab, and click the Environment Variables button.

5. If the LIB environment variable already exists, select it and click the Edit button. Otherwise, click the New button.

6. Add the Windows 2000 Platform SDK lib directory to the path list.

7. Click OK.

LDAP Programming Model

The LDAP API is the client-side API for a client/server system. It looks a lot like most other client/server APIs. LDAP breaks down into the following steps:

1. Initialize the client library.

2. Connect to an Active Directory server.

3. Issue LDAP requests.

4. Process the results.

5. Close the connection to the server.

Network programming just doesn't get any easier than that.

Figure 17.6 shows the programming model graphically.

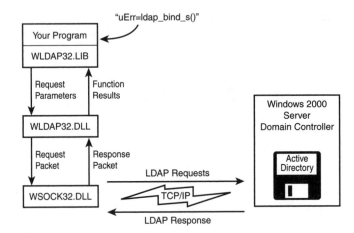

Figure 17.6
The LDAP programming model.

The next several sections go into more detail about these five steps.

Initializing the Client Library

You initialize the client library by calling ldap_init(). ldap_init() returns a pointer to an LDAP structure. The LDAP structure represents a single connection to an LDAP server. It contains all the information regarding the connection between your client and the server, including the results of the last function, the last error received, and the TCP socket information. Almost every LDAP API call accepts a pointer to an LDAP structure as its first argument. Each call to ldap_init() allocates a new LDAP structure.

Connecting to an Active Directory Server

After you have initialized the library and the LDAP structure, you need to connect and authenticate to the LDAP server. You can do this in one of two ways. The best way is to explicitly bind (authenticate) to a name in the directory using one of the ldap_bind() calls. This will connect to the domain controller and establish your credentials so that you can access the directory.

You can also skip the bind step entirely and just issue an LDAP request. This method works only if the domain controller allows anonymous access to the directory. By default, Active Directory domain controllers allow anonymous access only to the Root DSE attributes; access to the rest of the directory requires authentication.

Issuing LDAP Requests

The next step is to issue some LDAP requests. Generally you will issue search commands using ldap_search() and related calls, but this depends on your application. If you are writing a directory administration utility or a program to synchronize with some other directory, you will also use ldap_add() and ldap_modify().

Processing LDAP Results

Almost all LDAP functions return an integer error code of some sort. If this error code is not 0, the function call failed, and you'll probably have to give some indication to the user that all is not well.

If the call succeeded, the way you process the results depends on the specific call. For instance, if you made a call to one of the `ldap_search()` functions to read entries from the directory, you will use `ldap_first_entry()` and `ldap_next_entry()` to inspect the entries, and `ldap_first_attribute()` and `ldap_next_attribute()` to get the retrieved attributes. Finally, you will use `ldap_first_value()` and `ldap_next_value()` to get the values of the attributes.

After processing the results of a search operation, you will also have to free up the memory associated with the search by calling `ldap_memfree()` and `ldap_value_free()`.

Closing the Connection

After you are done with the connection to the server, you close the connection and free up the associated resources by calling `ldap_unbind()`.

Some General Notes About LDAP Programming for Active Directory

In general, the Microsoft implementation of the LDAP client library adheres to the API described in RFC 1823. But there are a few things you should know that either aren't completely spelled out in the RFC or are unique to the Microsoft LDAP implementation.

Creating an LDAP Connection

RFC 1823 defines the `ldap_open()` function as the way to create an LDAP connection. `ldap_open()` allocates an LDAP structure, resolves the DNS name of the LDAP server, opens a TCP connection to the server, and returns a pointer to the allocated LDAP structure. The latest IETF draft of the standard C API for LDAP deprecates the use of `ldap_open()` and recommends using `ldap_init()` instead. Even though Microsoft includes an implementation of `ldap_open()`, you should use `ldap_init()`.

The latest LDAP C API draft also deprecates the use of `ldap_bind()` and `ldap_bind_s()` and recommends that instead you use `ldap_simple_bind()` and `ldap_simple_bind_s()` or `ldap_sasl_bind()` and `ldap_sasl_bind_s()`, respectively.

```
LDAP* psLdap;
psLdap = ldap_init("server.megacorp.com", LDAP_PORT);
if(psLdap != NULL)
{
    // do something with pLdap
}
```

17

LDAP
FUNDAMENTALS

Error Handling

For the most part, LDAP functions return a 32-bit error code indicating the success or failure of the function call. But some do not. For instance, the `ldap_init()` function returns a pointer to an LDAP structure. If `ldap_init()` fails for some reason, it will return NULL. But how do you find out what went wrong? Microsoft has included the `LdapGetLastError()` function to help here. It retrieves the error returned by the last LDAP function call. You might be tempted to just retrieve the `ld_errno` value from the LDAP structure because that is the last error code returned for a particular LDAP connection, but this is problematic if you are using multiple threads on the same LDAP connection. Between the time you call a function and look at `ld_errno`, another thread could very well overwrite its value. It is much better to use `LdapGetLastError()`.

```
LDAP* pLdap;
psLdap = ldap_init("server.megacorp.com", LDAP_PORT);
if(psLdap == NULL)
{
    ULONG uErr = LdapGetLastError();
}
```

Microsoft has also included the `LdapMapErrorToWin32()` function in the LDAP library. This function converts an LDAP error to the Win32 error code that it is most similar to. This is useful if you already have error-handling routines in place for the stock Win32 error codes.

```
LDAP* psLdap;
psLdap = ldap_init("server.megacorp.com", LDAP_PORT);
if(psLdap == NULL)
{
    ULONG uErr = LdapGetLastError();
    ULONG uWin32Err = LdapMapErrorToWin32(uErr);
    // uWin32Err has the Win32 equivalent error code
}
```

ANSI and Unicode Character Sets

Most of the Microsoft LDAP functions (the ones that take character strings as arguments) come in two flavors: ANSI and Unicode. The ANSI functions support the single-byte ANSI character set, and the Unicode functions support the UTF-8 encoding of the Unicode character set. WLDAP32.DLL, the DLL that contains the LDAP client library, actually has three entry points for each of these functions. For example, the `ldap_init()` function appears as `ldap_init`, `ldap_initA` (A stands for ANSI character set), and `ldap_initW` (W stands for wide, or Unicode, character set). In order to be consistent with the standard, `ldap_init()` accepts ANSI character set parameters. `ldap_init()` then calls `ldap_initA()`. `ldap_initA` accepts ANSI parameters and converts them to UTF-8 and calls `ldap_initW()`. `ldap_initW()` is the "real" `ldap_init()` function, and it ultimately does the work.

If you define the UNICODE preprocessor macro when you build your LDAP program (using either #define UNICODE or /DUNICODE on the compiler command line), the WINLDAP.H header file will define all the LDAP API functions in terms of their UNICODE equivalents. For instance, if UNICODE is defined, the name "ldap_init" will be defined as ldap_initW. Your UNICODE parameters go directly to the "real" ldap_init function.

If you are building for the ANSI character set (the UNICODE preprocessor macro is not defined), WINLDAP.H doesn't play any preprocessor tricks. Your program calls ldap_init() in the DLL, which passes its arguments on to ldap_initA(). ldap_initA() converts its arguments to UTF-8 and calls ldap_initW(), which actually initializes the LDAP session.

This scheme has two nice characteristics. If you build an ANSI-flavored LDAP program, it will have external references to the standard LDAP functions, such as ldap_init(). You could theoretically link your ANSI program with another LDAP client library and everything would work just swell. If the external references were things like ldap_initA, you could never link your program with another library without recompiling it with a different LDAP header file. On the other hand, if you build a UNICODE-flavored LDAP program, the external references will be to the wide-character functions, such as ldap_initW. These will never link with a non-Microsoft library, which is appropriate because any other LDAP client library will define the LDAP API functions to use ANSI character strings.

If you have to write source code that works with both ANSI and Unicode character sets, you can use the macros defined in Microsoft's TCHAR.H header file. The Microsoft Developer Network (MSDN) CDs contain complete descriptions of UNICODE programming and TCHAR.H.

Object Identifiers (OIDs)

The ITU-T recommendation X.208 defines a mechanism for creating unique identifiers for software systems throughout the world. These object identifiers are simply strings of numbers separated by dots. The ISO delegates OIDs starting with 1.2.x to ISO member countries. ANSI (the United States representative to the ISO) delegates numbers starting with 1.2.840.x. Microsoft delegates numbers starting with 1.2.840.113556.x, and so forth.

Active Directory uses OIDs to identify client and server controls (extensions), as well as attribute syntaxes.

Synchronous and Asynchronous (Multithreaded) Functions

RFC 1823 defines a synchronous and an asynchronous variant of many of the LDAP API functions. The synchronous variant of these functions is named with a trailing _s. For instance, `ldap_simple_bind_s()` is the synchronous variant of the `ldap_simple_bind()` function.

The synchronous functions and their asynchronous counterparts are identical in all respects except for the way they return their results. The synchronous functions return their results directly to the caller through the return code and through the LDAP structure. Your program doesn't get control back until the operation is complete.

The asynchronous functions, on the other hand, return immediately with a message ID, which is essentially a handle you use to identify the actual results. You then call the `ldap_result()` function with the message ID to determine when the operation is complete.

The synchronous functions (those with the _s on the end) are generally easier to use because you don't have to worry about coordinating multiple threads or distinguishing between multiple replies. Most of the examples in this book are written using the synchronous functions.

The following two examples give you an idea of how this works.

```
//Synchronous search using ldap_search_s()
char* apszAttrs = {"name", "description", NULL};
LDAPMessage* pResults;

ULONG uErr = ldap_search_s(
    pLdap,                   // LDAP session
    "DC=megacorp,DC=com",    // base of search
    LDAP_SCOPE_SUBTREE,      // search the whole subtree
    "objectClass=user",      // all user objects
    apszAttrs,               // attributes to retrieve
    0                        // get attr names and values,
    &pResults                // address of pointer to set
);  // Search is complete; process results here

//Asynchronous search using ldap_search()
char* apszAttrs = {"name", "description", NULL};

ULONG hMsg = ldap_search(
    pLdap,                   // LDAP session
    "DC=megacorp,DC=com",    // base of search
    LDAP_SCOPE_SUBTREE,      // search the whole subtree
    "objectClass=user",      // all user objects
```

```
    apszAttrs,               // attributes to retrieve
    0                        // get attr names and values
);

// Search has started; check for results

bool bDone = false;
do
{
    struct timeval sTimeout = {1, 0};
    LDAPMessage* pResults;

    int nResult = ldap_result(pLdap, hMsg, 0, &sTimeout, &pResults);
    if(nResult > 0)
    {
        // Process partial results in pResults
        if(nResult == LDAP_RES_SEARCH_RESULT)
        {
            bDone = true;
        }
    }
    else if(nResult < 0)
    {
        // error
        bDone = true;
    }
    else
    {
        // timeout; try again
    }
} while( !bDone);
```

You can see from these two samples that using the asynchronous LDAP functions is somewhat more complicated than using their synchronous counterparts.

A Simple LDAP Program

Even though the LDAP API comprises more than fifty different functions, you can do useful things using only six or seven of them. For instance, Listing 17.1 lists the values of the attributes of the RootDSE. For simplicity, I've left out any error processing.

LISTING 17.1 A SIMPLE LDAP PROGRAM

```
1: #include <windows.h>
2: #include <winldap.h>
3: #include <iostream.h>
```

continues

LISTING 17.1 CONTINUED

```
4: int main( int argc, char** argv )
5: {
6:    // initialize an LDAP session
7:    LDAP* psLdap = ldap_init( NULL, LDAP_PORT );
8:    if( psLdap != NULL )
9:    {
10:        LDAPMessage* pmsgResult = NULL;
11:
12:        // read the Root DSE
13:        int nErr = ldap_search_s(
14:            psLdap,                // LDAP connection
15:            NULL,                  // NULL container name means root DSE
16:            LDAP_SCOPE_BASE,       // search scope
17:            "objectClass=*",       // search filter
18:            NULL,                  // return all attributes
19:            (ULONG)false,          // not attrs only
20:            &pmsgResult            // the result structure
21:        );
22:        if( nErr == LDAP_SUCCESS && pmsgResult != NULL )
23:        {
24:            // get the first (and only) entry
25:            LDAPMessage* pmsgObject = ldap_first_entry( psLdap,
              ➥pmsgResult );
26:            if( nErr == LDAP_SUCCESS && pmsgObject != NULL )
27:            {
28:                char* pszAttrName;
29:                BerElement* psberAttrValue;
30:
31:                // enumerate the attributes of root DSE
32:                for( pszAttrName = ldap_first_attribute( psLdap, pmsgObject,
                  ➥&psberAttrValue );
33:                     pszAttrName != NULL;
34:                     pszAttrName = ldap_next_attribute( psLdap, pmsgObject,
                      ➥psberAttrValue ) )
35:                {
36:                    // enumerate the values of the attribute
37:                    char** ppszValues = ldap_get_values( psLdap,
                      ➥pmsgResult, pszAttrName );
38:                    if( ppszValues != NULL )
39:                    {
40:                      for( int nVal = 0; ppszValues[ nVal ] != NULL;
                        ➥nVal++ )
41:                        {
42:                            cout << pszAttrName << ": " <<
                              ➥ppszValues[ nVal ] << endl;
43:                        }
44:
45:                        ldap_value_free( ppszValues );
46:                    }
```

```
47:                    }
48:            }
49:
50:            ldap_msgfree( pmsgResult );
51:        }
52:
53:            ldap_unbind( psLdap );
54:    }
55:
56: return 0;
57: }
```

Listing 17.1 is a complete LDAP program that reads the attributes of the Root DSE and displays them.

The program first initializes an LDAP session at line 7 by calling `ldap_init()`. At line 13, the program calls `ldap_search_s()` to search the Root DSE entry, and at line 33, the program actually retrieves each of the entry's attributes, one at a time. For each attribute it retrieves, the program gets each value of the attribute, starting at line 41. After freeing the memory allocated by the LDAP library at lines 49 and 53, the program closes the LDAP session at line 53 by calling `ldap_unbind()`.

Listing 17.1 is probably the simplest useful LDAP program you can write.

When you get right down to it, the LDAP protocol (the part that is actually standardized, not the unstandardized API) provides for only eight different directory operations: bind, unbind, search, add, modify, delete, rename, and compare. Although this is a fairly small number of operations, the LDAP API provides a rich set of functions for performing these operations in a convenient way.

17

LDAP FUNDAMENTALS

CHAPTER 18

Connecting to Active Directory with LDAP

This chapter discusses the LDAP API functions that are used to connect to an Active Directory domain controller. Every LDAP program performs the following five steps:

- Locating a domain controller
- Initializing the LDAP client library and connecting to the domain controller
- Authenticating with the domain controller (optional)
- Performing LDAP functions such as searching or updating
- Disconnecting from the domain controller

This chapter also describes the functions you use to find, connect to, and disconnect from domain controllers on the network. Table 18.1 lists the functions described in this chapter.

TABLE 18.1 LDAP FUNCTIONS FOR FINDING, CONNECTING TO, AND DISCONNECTING FROM DOMAIN CONTROLLERS

Function	Description
DsGetDcName	Returns the name of a domain controller that meets certain criteria. Note that this is a not strictly a LDAP function, and it is not part of the draft standard LDAP C API.

continues

TABLE 18.1 CONTINUED

Function	Description
ldap_init	Initializes the LDAP client library and allocates an LDAP session structure to use with subsequent LDAP API calls.
ldap_sslinit	Same as ldap_init(), except that communications with the LDAP server will be encrypted using Secure Sockets Layer (SSL). Note that this function is Microsoft-specific and is not part of the draft standard LDAPv3 C API.
ldap_connect	Forces the establishment of the TCP connection for a given LDAP session. Note that this function is Microsoft-specific and is not part of the draft standard LDAPv3 C API.
ldap_open	Initializes the LDAP client library and creates the TCP connection with the LDAP server. ldap_open() performs the same function as ldap_init() followed by ldap_connect(). Note that this function has been deprecated in the latest draft standard LDAPv3 C API. You should use ldap_init() instead.
cldap_open	Same as ldap_open(), except that the LDAP session is connection-less, using UDP instead of TCP. Note that this function is Microsoft-specific and is not part of the draft standard LDAPv3 C API.
ldap_unbind	Disconnects from a domain controller and frees any memory associated with the LDAP session.

This chapter describes the various ways you can accomplish these tasks by using the preceding functions.

A Note About Using the LDAP Library

In general, you can just link in the import library and let the NT loader take care of resolving the DLL entry points for you. But if you don't want to incur the delay of loading the LDAP DLL when your program loads, you can load it explicitly using the WIN32 LoadLibrary() function, and then resolve the function entry points with GetProcAddress. The following example shows how to do this. (Note that the LDAP DLL isn't any different than any other DLL in this regard. I just thought it would be nice to show how to do it.)

Listing 18.1 shows how to load the winldap32 DLL dynamically.

LISTING 18.1   USING `LoadLibrary()` AND `GetProcAddress()`

```
1:    #include <windows.h>
2:    #include <winldap.h>
3:    #include <iostream.h>
4:
5:    int main( int argc, char** argv )
6:    {
7:        typedef LDAP* ( *PF_INIT )( const PCHAR HostName,
          ➥ULONG PortNumber);
8:
9:        HINSTANCE hi = LoadLibrary( "wldap32.dll" );
10:       if( hi != NULL )
11:       {
12:           PF_INIT pfLdapInit = ( PF_INIT )GetProcAddress( hi,
              ➥"ldap_init" );
13:           if( pfLdapInit != NULL )
14:           {
15:             LDAP* psLdap = pfLdapInit( "engserver.megacorp.com",
              ➥LDAP_PORT );
16:               if( psLdap != NULL )
17:               {
18:                   cout << "We have a session" << endl;
19:               }
20:           }
21:
22:           FreeLibrary( hi );
23:       }
24:
25:       return 0;
26:   }
```

The program in Listing 18.1 starts at line 7 by declaring the type name `PF_INIT` for a pointer to a function with the same prototype as the `ldap_init()` function.

At line 9, the program loads the wldap32 DLL and gets an instance handle (which is the same as a module handle).

The program gets a pointer to the `ldap_init()` function in the DLL by calling `GetProcAddress()` at line 12.

The program finally calls the `ldap_init()` function through the `pfLdapInit` pointer at line 15.

At line 22, the program decrements the use count on the wldap32 DLL by calling the `FreeLibrary()` function.

18

CONNECTING TO ACTIVE DIRECTORY WITH LDAP

Locating a Domain Controller

Identifying the domain controller you want to connect to is highly application-dependent; just how you do it depends on what you are trying to accomplish. Just remember that the LDAP library requires either a fully qualified DNS name or the IP address of a domain controller. Whichever way you choose to obtain one of those is up to you.

There are three general strategies:

- Ask the user for a server name or IP address
- Get the server name or IP address from somewhere it was previously saved—for instance, a file or Registry entry
- Find an appropriate domain controller using DNS and Active Directory APIs

The first two strategies are the "traditional" solutions to locating a service on the network. The last one is more interesting.

Recall that Active Directory uses DNS as a domain controller locator service. When Active Directory needs to find the name and address of a particular domain controller, it finds it with DNS. (For more information about how Active Directory uses DNS, see Chapter 5, "Active Directory and DNS.")

You could write your own routines for getting the names and addresses of domain controllers from DNS, but there is no need. Microsoft has provided, in the Windows 2000 SDK, a set of functions for getting this information. The most useful of these functions is DsGetDcName().

```
DWORD DsGetDcName( LPCSTR ComputerName, LPCSTR DomainName, GUID *DomainGuid,
➥LPCSTR SiteName, ULONG Flags, DOMAIN_CONTROLLER_INFO*
➥DomainControllerInfo )
```

ComputerName is a pointer to a NUL-terminated string containing the name of the computer to process the request on. Set this to NULL, unless you want to get the domain controller information for some other computer.

DomainName is a pointer to a NUL-terminated string containing the name of the DNS domain to query. Set this to NULL to get the information from the primary domain of the workstation the function is being called from. Otherwise, set it to the DNS domain you want to query. The domain name can either be the DNS form, such as "megacorp.com" or the old NTLM form, such as "MEGACORP".

DomainGuid is a pointer to the GUID of the domain you want to query. The use of this is somewhat obscure. Each object in Active Directory, including each domain object, is assigned a GUID that acts as its unique identifier for the object's lifetime. If the domain is renamed, you would have difficulty finding it again unless you knew what it had been renamed to. However, you can find it by its GUID, which never changes. If you want to get domain controller information for a domain that has been renamed and you have the GUID of the domain, you can specify it here. As I said, it's a little obscure.

`SiteName` is a pointer to a NUL-terminated string containing the name of the site the returned domain controller should be a member of. Set this to `NULL` to indicate the site of the machine give by `ComputerName`. Otherwise, set it to the fully qualified distinguished name of the site object for the site.

`Flags` is a bit-mask of options indicating what kind of domain controller you are interested in, and what format the name parameters are in. The values you can `OR` together for this parameter are given in Table 18.2.

`DomainControllerInfo` is a pointer to a pointer to a structure to be set upon return. If the call succeeds (the return value is `0`), you must free the pointer with `NetApiBufferFree()`.

TABLE 18.2 POSSIBLE VALUES FOR `Flags`

Flag Name	*Description*
DS_FORCE_REDISCOVERY	Flushes the cache of known domain controllers and forces the PC to rediscover the domain controllers in its site. Don't specify this option unless you've already tried this function once and the returned domain controller was not available.
DS_DIRECTORY_SERVICE_REQUIRED	Specifies that you want a Windows 2000 domain controller, as opposed to an NT 4 domain controller.
DS_DIRECTORY_SERVICE_PREFERRED	Indicates that you want a Windows 2000 domain controller if one is available, but if one is not available to return an NT 4 domain controller.
DS_GC_SERVER_REQUIRED	Indicates that you want a domain controller with a global catalog running on it.
DS_PDC_REQUIRED	Indicates that the returned domain controller be a Primary Domain Controller (PDC) for the domain. Note that any Windows 2000 domain controller is considered a PDC for a domain, so this affects the results only if NT 4 domain controllers are available. You must not specify this flag if you specify DS_WRITABLE_REQUIRED, DS_FDC_REQUIRED, or DS_GC_SERVER_REQUIRED.

continues

18

CONNECTING TO
ACTIVE DIRECTORY
WITH LDAP

TABLE 18.2 CONTINUED

Flag Name	Description
DS_IP_REQUIRED	Indicates that you want the IP address for the returned domain controller, not just its name.
DS_KDC_REQUIRED	Indicates that you want a domain controller running the Kerberos Key Distribution Center service. This is appropriate if you need to perform some Kerberos functions, such as obtaining a ticket.
DS_TIMESERV_REQUIRED	Indicates that you want a domain controller that is running the Windows 2000 network time service. This is appropriate if you need ensure that you have the most up-to-date network time value.
DS_WRITABLE_REQUIRED	Indicates that you want a domain controller that can process directory updates. In general, any Windows 2000 domain controller can process updates, although global catalogs and NT 4 Backup Domain Controllers (BDCs) cannot.
DS_IS_FLAT_NAME	Indicates the domain name you specified in pszDomainName is the old NTLM or "flat" form, such as, "MEGACORP". You should specify this flag or DS_IS_DNS_NAME, but not both. If you specify neither, DsGetDcName will do two separate DNS queries to find the domain.
DS_IS_DNS_NAME	Indicates the domain name you specified in pszDomainName is in DNS format, such as, "megacorp.com". You should specify this flag or DS_IS_FLAT_NAME, but not both. If you specify neither, DsGetDcName will do two separate DNS queries to find the domain.
DS_RETURN_DNS_NAME	Indicates that you want the returned domain controller name to be in DNS format—for instance, "lithium.acctg.megacorp.com". You must specify either this flag or DS_RETURN_FLAT_NAME, but not both.

If the call to `DsGetDcName` is successful, the following structure (pointed to by `ppInfo`) will be filled with the information.

```
typedef struct _DOMAIN_CONTROLLER_INFOA {
    LPSTR DomainControllerName;
    LPSTR DomainControllerAddress;
    ULONG DomainControllerAddressType;
    GUID DomainGuid;
    LPSTR DomainName;
    LPSTR DnsForestName;
    ULONG Flags;
    LPSTR DcSiteName;
    LPSTR ClientSiteName;
} DOMAIN_CONTROLLER_INFO, *PDOMAIN_CONTROLLER_INFO;
```

Table 18.3 describes these fields in more detail.

TABLE 18.3   DOMAIN_CONTROLLER_INFO STRUCTURE

Field	Description
LPSTR DomainControllerName	The name of the returned domain controller.
LPSTR DomainControllerAddress	The IP address of the returned domain controller—for example, `\\208.111.234.123`. This will be returned only if you set the `DS_IP_REQUIRED` flag.
ULONG DomainControllerAddressType	Indicates the type of address in `DomainControllerAddress`. It will be either `DS_INET_ADDRESS`, indicating an IP address such as `\\208.111.234.123`, or `DS_NETBIOS_ADDRESS`, indicating a NetBIOS address such as `\\LITHIUM`.
GUID DomainGuid	The GUID of the primary domain of the returned domain controller.
LPSTR DomainName	The name of the primary domain of the returned domain controller. This will be the DNS format name if the domain is a Windows 2000 domain. If the domain is an NT 4 domain, it will be in NetBIOS format.

continues

18

CONNECTING TO
ACTIVE DIRECTORY
WITH LDAP

TABLE 18.3 CONTINUED

Field	Description
LPSTR DnsForestName	The name of the tree (top-level domain) of the returned domain. This will be the DNS format name if the domain is a Windows 2000 domain; otherwise, it will be an empty string.
ULONG Flags	A bit-mask indicating what kind of domain controller this is. See Table 18.4 for possible values.
LPSTR DcSiteName	The DN of the site the domain controller is in.
LPSTR ClientSiteName	The DN of the site of the machine the function was called from is in.

After the call to DsGetDcName is successful, the Flags variable in the preceding structure will be filled with a descriptive value about the domain controller. Table 18.4 shows the possible values for Flags.

TABLE 18.4 DomainControllerInfo Flags VALUES

Field	Description
DS_PDC_FLAG	The returned domain controller is the PDC of the domain.
DS_WRITABLE_FLAG	Domain controller hosts a writable DS (or SAM).
DS_FDC_FLAG	The returned domain controller is the FDC of the domain.
DS_GC_FLAG	The returned domain controller is a GC server for DnsForestName.
DS_DS_FLAG	The returned domain controller is a directory service server for the domain.
DS_KDC_FLAG	The returned domain controller is a Kerberos Key Distribution Center for the domain.
DS_TIMESERV_FLAG	The returned domain controller is running the Windows time service for the domain.
DS_DNS_CONTROLLER_FLAG	The returned DomainControllerName is in DNS format.
DS_DNS_DOMAIN_FLAG	DomainName is in DNS format.
DS_DNS_TREE_FLAG	DnsForestName is in DNS format.

It returns a Win32 error code or NO_ERROR if there was no error.

Listing 18.2 shows how to use DsGetDcName for the typical case of finding the nearest Global Catalog server for the local machine.

LISTING 18.2 USING THE DsGetDcName() FUNCTION

```
1:   #include <windows.h>
2:   #include <winldap.h>
3:   #include <dsgetdc.h>
4:   #include <lm.h>
5:   #include <iostream.h>
6:
7:   int main( int argc, char** argv )
8:   {
9:       PDOMAIN_CONTROLLER_INFO psInfo = NULL;
10:      DWORD dwErr = DsGetDcName(
11:          NULL,     // execute on this machine
12:          NULL,     // use this users domain
13:          NULL,     // no domain GUID
14:          NULL,     // no site name
15:          DS_GC_SERVER_REQUIRED, // we want a GC
16:          &psInfo );
17:      if( dwErr == NO_ERROR )
18:      {
19:          cout << "We found a GC at " << psInfo->DomainControllerName <<
             ➥endl;
20:
21:          // call ldap_init() using the name of the server
22:
23:          NetApiBufferFree( psInfo );
24:      }
25:
26:      return 0;
27:  }
```

This program declares a pointer to a DOMAIN_CONTROLLER_INFO structure at line 9, and then calls DsGetDcName() at line 10 with the arguments needed to find a global catalog server in the current site.

If the call to DsGetDcName() succeeds, the program prints the name of the domain controller at line 19, and then frees the DOMAIN_CONTROLLER_INFO structure at line 23.

Initializing the LDAP Client Library

The client-side LDAP library for Windows 2000 is contained in WLDAP32.DLL. You'll normally find WLDAP32.DLL in the \winnt\system32 directory.

> **CAUTION**
>
> Be sure that the WLDAP32.DLL file in your \WINNT\system32 directory is the latest version. Earlier Platform SDKs and Visual Studio 6 might have earlier, incompatible versions of WLDAP32.DLL. The earlier versions of WLDAP32.DLL will fail miserably on Windows 2000.

The import library for WLDAP32.DLL is, not surprisingly, WLDAP32.LIB, which you can find in the SDK \lib directory.

The `ldap_init()` Function

The `ldap_init()` function is the primary method for initializing the LDAP client library. Generally speaking, every LDAP program you write will call `ldap_init()` before making any other LDAP function calls. (There are some exceptions, as noted later in this chapter.) The description of `ldap_init()` follows.

```
LDAP* ldap_init( PCHAR HostName, ULONG PortNumber )
```

> `HostName` is a pointer to a NUL-terminated string that names one or more LDAP servers to connect to. The string contains a list of one or more host specifiers, separated by spaces. A host specifier is either the DNS host name of the LDAP server or the dotted-decimal string representation of its IP address. Each host specifier optionally includes a colon followed by an IP port number. So the following are all valid values for the `HostName` parameter:
>
> `"engserver.megacorp.com"`
>
> `"engserver.megacorp.com mktgserver.megacorp.com"`
>
> `"208.192.129.1 208.192.129.7"`
>
> `"engserver.megacorp.com:636 mktgserver.megacorp.com"`
>
> The LDAP library will try each host specifier in order until it successfully establishes a TCP connection with one of them.
>
> You can also pass a `NULL` for the `HostName` parameter. In this case, the LDAP library will use the default domain controller for the machine your program is running on. This is the simplest solution if you want to communicate with a domain controller in the current user's domain. However, using `NULL` to connect to a default domain controller is not part of the behavior defined in the draft standard LDAP C API, so if you are planning on making your code portable to other platforms, don't depend on this behavior.

> **NOTE**
>
> The `ldap_init()` function does not actually establish a connection with the LDAP server. The connection is established by the first call to LDAP function that attempts to communicate with the server—for instance, `ldap_simple_bind_s()`. That means `ldap_init()` will return successfully even if you specify an invalid host name or address. In this case, subsequent calls to LDAP functions will return the `LDAP_SERVER_DOWN` error.
>
> As odd as this behavior might seem, it has the advantage of letting you set global session options with `ldap_set_option()` before actually communicating with the server. See Chapter 28, "Extending LDAP with Options and Controls," for more information about `ldap_set_option()`.
>
> If you must determine that you can connect to the server you specified, you can use the `ldap_connect()` function, which I discuss later in this chapter.

`PortNumber` is an integer containing the IP port number to use when establishing the TCP connection to the server. Generally, you should use the constant `LDAP_PORT`, which is defined as 389 in winldap.h. 389 is the IETF standard LDAP port number, and is always used by Windows 2000 domain controllers. Some other LDAP server implementations might use an alternative port number.

Note that if you specify a port number as part of a host specifier in the `HostName` parameter, the LDAP library will ignore the value of `PortNumber` and use the port number given in the host specifier instead.

It returns a pointer to a newly allocated LDAP structure, or `NULL` if there is an error. `ldap_init()` allocates and initializes a new LDAP structure. You must pass this pointer (called an LDAP session handle or session pointer) to all LDAP functions that use this LDAP connection. When you are done with LDAP session, you must call `ldap_unbind()`, passing it this session handle. `ldap_unbind()` will close the session with the LDAP server and free any memory associated with the session.

If `ldap_init()` returns `NULL`, you should call `LdapGetLastError()` to find out the cause of the error.

The trivial program in Listing 18.3 shows how you would typically use the `ldap_init()` function.

LISTING 18.3   USING THE `ldap_init()` FUNCTION

```
1:   #include <windows.h>
2:   #include <winldap.h>
3:   #include <iostream.h>
```

continues

18

CONNECTING TO
ACTIVE DIRECTORY
WITH LDAP

LISTING 18.3 CONTINUED

```
4:
5:    int main( int argc, char** argv )
6:    {
7:        LDAP* psLdap = ldap_init( "engserver.megacorp.com", LDAP_PORT );
8:        if( psLdap != NULL )
9:        {
10:            cout << "We have a session" << endl;
11:
12:            ldap_unbind( psLdap );
13:        }
13:
14:        return 0;
15:    }
```

The program in Listing 18.3 calls `ldap_init()` at line 7 to initialize an LDAP session with the server `"engserver.megacorp.com"` on the default LDAP port 389.

If the call succeeds, the program prints a message and closes the session at line 12 by calling `ldap_unbind()`.

Note that because this program never actually called any LDAP functions that would communicate with the server, it doesn't generate any network traffic. In fact, the server `"engserver.megacorp.com"` may not even exist!

A Note on Port Numbers

By default all LDAP servers, including Active Directory domain controllers, listen for connections on port 389. You can use the constant `LDAP_PORT` in WINLDAP.H to specify this value. Active Directory domain controllers are not configurable with respect to the port number they use, so you can always use the `LDAP_PORT` constant when accessing Active Directory via LDAP.

Active Directory Global Catalogs listen on port 3268; the constant `LDAP_GC_PORT` in WINLDAP.H is defined as this value.

If the network administrator has configured Secure Sockets Layer for the domain controller, the domain controller will also listen on port 636 (`LDAP_SSL_PORT` in WINLDAP.H). If the domain controller is also a global catalog, the server will also listen on port 3269, which is given by the constant `LDAP_SSL_GC_PORT`.

The `ldap_sslinit()` Function

If you are particularly concerned about the security of your program's interactions with an LDAP server—for instance, if your application accesses sensitive personnel information in the directory—you might want to use LDAP over the Secure Sockets Layer (SSL) protocol. Using SSL encrypts the traffic between your client application and the LDAP server so that it is essentially impossible for unauthorized processes to identify the directory data passing over the wire.

Using LDAP over SSL is quite simple. Instead of using the `ldap_init()` function to initialize the LDAP session, you use the `ldap_sslinit()` function. All functions that use the LDAP session handle returned from `ldap_sslinit()` will then have their traffic encrypted over the network.

> **NOTE**
>
> SSL is a protocol developed by Netscape to provide secure Web transactions over the Internet. Although SSL is a de facto standard on the Internet, it is not a standard for LDAP in the IETF sense. Consequently, the `ldap_sslinit()` function is not part of the draft standard LDAP C API. The IETF is working on a session-level encryption standard called Transport Layer Security (TLS) that is based on SSL 3.0. Although this work isn't finished, ultimately, the standard way to encrypt LDAP traffic will be to use LDAP over TLS.
>
> That being said, the only way to encrypt LDAP traffic at this time with the Microsoft LDAP library is to use the `ldap_sslinit()` function.

```
LDAP* ldap_sslinit( PCHAR HostName, ULONG PortNumber, int secure )
```

`HostName` is a pointer to a NUL-terminated string that names one or more LDAP servers to connect to. It is identical to the `HostName` parameter for the `ldap_init()` function described earlier in this chapter.

`PortNumber` is an integer containing the IP port number to use when establishing the TCP connection to the server. Generally, you should use the constant `LDAP_SSL_PORT`, which is defined as 636 in winldap.h. 636 is always used by Windows 2000 domain controllers for SSL sessions. Some other LDAP server implementations might use an alternative port number.

> **CAUTION**
>
> You must specify the appropriate port number when you connect using Secure Sockets Layer. `ldap_sslinit()` will not succeed if you use the standard `LDAP_PORT` value.

18

CONNECTING TO ACTIVE DIRECTORY WITH LDAP

secure is an integer that enables or disables the encryption on the LDAP session. If you set secure to 1, the LDAP traffic for the session will be encrypted. If you set secure to 0, the traffic will not be encrypted.

Returns: A pointer to a newly allocated LDAP structure or NULL if there is an error. See the description of the return value of the ldap_init() function, described earlier in this chapter. Note that you must close the session and free its associated memory by calling ldap_unbind(), passing it the value returned by ldap_sslinit().

> **NOTE**
>
> You can't use an SSL LDAP session with a Windows 2000 domain controller unless the administrator for the domain controller has enabled Secure Sockets Layer for that domain controller.

Connecting to the Domain Controller

Normally the LDAP client library automatically creates a TCP connection to the domain controller the first time you call an LDAP function that communicates with the server. Therefore, you do not have to explicitly connect to the server; the LDAP functions do it for you.

However, the LDAP client library provides three ways of establishing an LDAP connection explicitly. These functions are ldap_connect(), ldap_open(), and cldap_open().

The ldap_connect() Function

The LDAP client library will normally establish a connection with the LDAP server automatically. However, you might find it desirable to establish the TCP connection directly, before executing any LDAP functions. In that case, you can use the ldap_connect() function to force the creation of the TCP (or SSL) connection with the server. The ldap_connect() function initializes a connection with the domain controller that you specified when you created the LDAP session with ldap_init() or ldap_sslinit(). The description of ldap_connect() follows.

`ULONG ldap_connect( LDAP* ld, struct l_timeval* timeout )`

> `ld` is a pointer to an LDAP structure that was returned from `ldap_init()` or `ldap_sslinit()`.

> The `l_timeval` structure is used in several different LDAP API functions. It has the fields described in Table 18.5.

> `timeout` is a pointer to an `l_timeval` structure containing the amount of time the client library should wait for a response from the server.

Returns: An LDAP error code or `LDAP_SUCCESS` if the call completed successfully.

TABLE 18.5   THE FIELDS OF THE `l_timeval` STRUCTURE

Field Name	Description
`LONG tv_sec`	The number of seconds the client library should wait for a response.
`LONG tv_usec`	The number of microseconds the client library should wait for a response. The Microsoft client library ignores this field.

The sample program in Listing 18.4 shows how you can use the `ldap_connect()` function.

LISTING 18.4   USING THE `ldap_connect()` FUNCTION

```
1:   #include <windows.h>
2:   #include <winldap.h>
3:   #include <iostream.h>
4:
5:   int main( int argc, char** argv )
6:   {
7:       LDAP* psLdap = ldap_init( NULL, LDAP_PORT );
8:       if( psLdap != NULL )
9:       {
10:          struct l_timeval sTimeout = { 5, 0 }; // 5 second timeout
11:
12:          ULONG uErr = ldap_connect( psLdap, &sTimeout );
```

continues

18

CONNECTING TO
ACTIVE DIRECTORY
WITH LDAP

LISTING 18.4   CONTINUED

```
13:            if( uErr == LDAP_SUCCESS )
14:            {
15:                cout << "We have established a connection" << endl;
16:            }
17:
18:            ldap_unbind( psLdap );
19:        }
20:
21:        return 0;
22:    }
```

The program in Listing 18.4 starts by initializing an LDAP session on the default domain controller by calling `ldap_init()` with a `NULL HostName` parameter.

At line 10, the program declares and initializes an `l_timeval` structure to represent a timeout value of five seconds (and zero microseconds).

The program creates a TCP connection with the default domain controller at line 12 by calling `ldap_connect()`, specifying a five-second timeout.

At line 18, the program closes the LDAP connection by calling `ldap_unbind()`.

The `ldap_open()` Function

The `ldap_open()` function initializes an LDAP session as `ldap_init()` does, but it also establishes a TCP connection with the LDAP server.

Earlier versions of the standard LDAP C API, as defined in RFC 1823, included a function called `ldap_open()`. Even though the current draft standard LDAP C API deprecates the use of `ldap_open()`, the Microsoft LDAP client library includes an implementation of `ldap_open()` for backward compatibility. `ldap_open()` both initializes the LDAP client library like `ldap_init()`, and establishes the connection with the LDAP server like `ldap_connect()`.

> **NOTE**
>
> Because `ldap_open()` is deprecated by the most current draft standard LDAP C API, you should avoid using it. Instead, you should use `ldap_init()` and, if necessary, `ldap_connect()`.

```
LDAP* ldap_open( const PCHAR HostName, ULONG PortNumber )
```

> HostName is a pointer to a NUL-terminated string that names one or more LDAP servers to connect to. It is identical to the HostName parameter for the ldap_init() function described earlier in this chapter.

> PortNumber is an integer containing the IP port number to use when establishing the TCP connection to the server. Generally, you should use the constant LDAP_PORT, which is defined as 389 in winldap.h. 389 is the IETF standard LDAP port number, and is always used by Windows 2000 domain controllers. Some other LDAP server implementations may use an alternative port number.

> Note that if you specify a port number as part of a host specifier in the HostName parameter, the LDAP library will ignore the value of PortNumber and use the port number given in the host specifier instead.

Returns: A pointer to a newly allocated LDAP structure or NULL if there is an error. See the description of the return value of the ldap_init() function, described earlier in this chapter. Note that you must close the session and free its associated memory by calling ldap_unbind(), passing it the value returned by ldap_open().

Connecting with UDP Using the `cldap_open()` Function

Creating a TCP connection can be expensive in terms of time and bandwidth, particularly over slow wide-area network (WAN) links. The problem is particularly annoying when you need to access only a small amount of data from the directory—for instance, if you simply want to validate a user's name and nothing else. In those situations where you want to keep the connection overhead to a minimum, you can connect to LDAP using the User Datagram Protocol, or UDP.

UDP is a very lightweight protocol that is used by many Internet services. It has the advantages of being fast and efficient, but it lacks TCP's reliability and ability to transmit arbitrarily large amounts of data. But if you can't afford the expense of a TCP connection and you don't need to get much data from the directory (less than about 500 bytes), you can create an LDAP connection using UDP.

The cldap_open() function (the "c" is for "connectionless") creates a LDAP session over UDP. It accepts the same parameters that ldap_open() does, and it generally works the same way. The only difference is that it is up to you to deal with the unreliability and size constraints of the resulting connection.

```
LDAP* cldap_open( PCHAR HostName, ULONG PortNumber )
```

> HostName is a pointer to a NUL-terminated string that names one or more LDAP servers to connect to. It is identical to the HostName parameter for the ldap_init() function described earlier in this chapter.

PortNumber is an integer containing the IP port number to use when establishing the TCP connection to the server. Generally, you should use the constant LDAP_PORT, which is defined as 389 in winldap.h. 389 is the IETF standard LDAP port number, and is always used by Windows 2000 domain controllers. Some other LDAP server implementations might use an alternative port number.

Note that if you specify a port number as part of a host specifier in the HostName parameter, the LDAP library will ignore the value of PortNumber and use the port number given in the host specifier instead.

Returns: A pointer to a newly allocated LDAP structure or NULL if there is an error. See the description of the return value of the ldap_init() function, described earlier in this chapter. Note that you must close the session and free its associated memory by calling ldap_unbind(), passing it the value returned by cldap_open().

Listing 18.5 shows how you can use cldap_open() to start a connectionless LDAP session and read the RootDSE of a domain controller.

LISTING 18.5   USING THE cldap_open() FUNCTION

```
 1:    #include <windows.h>
 2:    #include <winldap.h>
 3:    #include <iostream.h>
 4:
 5:    int main( int argc, char** argv )
 6:    {
 7:        // establish a connectionless LDAP session with the default DC
 8:        LDAP* psLdap = cldap_open( NULL, LDAP_PORT );
 9:        if( psLdap != NULL )
10:        {
11:            LDAPMessage* psResult = NULL;
12:
13:            // read the RootDSE
14:            ULONG uErr = ldap_search_s(
15:                psLdap,
16:                NULL,
17:                LDAP_SCOPE_BASE,
18:                "objectClass=*",
19:                NULL,
20:                false,
21:                &psResult
22:            );
23:
24:            if( uErr == LDAP_SUCCESS )
25:            {
26:                cout << "Read RootDSE over UDP" << endl;
27:                // free the rootDSE data
28:                ldap_msgfree( psResult );
29:            }
30:
```

```
31:            ldap_unbind( psLdap );
32:        }
33:
34:        return 0;
35:    }
```

The program in Listing 18.5 initializes a connectionless LDAP session by calling `cldap_open()` at line 8. The program specifies NULL for the HostName parameter, which causes the `cldap_open()` function to initialize a session with the default domain controller for the workstation.

At line 14, the program issues a search on the RootDSE. See Chapter 20, "Searching Active Directory with LDAP," for more information.

If the search was successful, the program prints a message at line 26 and frees the data returned from the search by calling `ldap_msgfree()` at line 28.

The program finally closes the connectionless LDAP session at line 31 by calling `ldap_unbind()`.

A Note on Active Directory Support for Connectionless LDAP

At the time this chapter was written (before the release of Windows 2000), Microsoft's support of connectionless LDAP was pretty limited. The only operation I could perform on a connectionless LDAP session was to read the RootDSE of the server I connected to. In particular, I couldn't authenticate, nor could I read any other object in the tree. This limitation might be removed by the time Windows 2000 ships.

This limits the utility of using connectionless LDAP with Active Directory. If your application can get the information it needs from the RootDSE, you certainly could use connectionless LDAP. Otherwise, connectionless LDAP doesn't really work with Active Directory.

Handling the Unreliability of UDP

The primary problem you will encounter with LDAP over UDP is that your request or the server's response might be lost. Either error results in your LDAP function call returning a timeout error.

The simplest solution to this is to retry the function call a number of times:

```
const int nRetries = 5;
LDAP* psLdap = NULL;
for( int nTry = 0; pLdap == NULL && nTry < Retries; nTry++ )
{
```

18

CONNECTING TO
ACTIVE DIRECTORY
WITH LDAP

```
    psLdap = cldap_open( "engserver.megacorp.com", LDAP_PORT );
}
if( psLdap != NULL )
{
    //do something with pLdap
    ldap_unbind( psLdap );
}
```

> **NOTE**
>
> Every API function you call using the UDP-based LDAP connection might time out even though the LDAP server is available. You should write your code to retry every operation that times out.

Handling the Size Limitation of UDP

You shouldn't use a UDP-based LDAP connection if you expect your client program or the server to transmit more than about 500 bytes during any single API call. But sometimes it's hard to know in advance. For instance, if you use a UDP-based connection to retrieve a list of email addresses for a user and that user had a large number of long email addresses, conceivably the server could not return the data in a single datagram. In that case, you will receive the LDAP_SIZELIMIT_EXCEEDED error from your search call.

If you absolutely have to retrieve the data, you can open a regular TCP-based LDAP connection and try the operation again.

Disconnecting from an Active Directory Domain Controller

When your program completes, or when it is finished using LDAP, you make sure that it closes the connection it created by calling ldap_unbind() or ldap_unbind_s(). Despite the name, you should use ldap_unbind() even on connections that were not authenticated. Calling ldap_unbind() or ldap_unbind_s() is simple; the only parameter is a pointer to the LDAP structure you want to disconnect.

```
ULONG ldap_unbind( LDAP* ld )
```

```
ULONG ldap_unbind_s( LDAP* ld )
```

> ld is a pointer to an LDAP structure returned from a call to ldap_init(), ldap_sslinit(), or ldap_open().

Returns: An LDAP error code or LDAP_SUCCESS if there is no error.

> **NOTE**
>
> ldap_unbind() and ldap_unbind_s() do exactly the same thing.
> ldap_unbind_s() (the _s indicates the call is synchronous) is included to mirror
> the other LDAP API functions that have synchronous and asynchronous versions.

CHAPTER 19

Authenticating with LDAP

Most network directories, and certainly Active Directory, contain information that is critical to the proper functioning of the network. For instance, Active Directory contains the names users log in to the network with. Consequently, making sure that only the appropriate people have access to the directory is very important. Establishing the identity of the processes accessing the directory is called *authentication* or *binding*, and LDAP provides three primary functions (along with their synchronous counterparts) for doing this.

Authentication Credentials

When your program authenticates with an LDAP server, your program asserts its identity by specifying a set of credentials. The credentials contain a distinguished name along with some sort of proof that the program is who it claims to be.

The distinguished name specified in the credentials must be the name of an object in Active Directory of class `securityPrincipal`. Typically, you would use the distinguished name of a User object. Active Directory grants access rights to the contents of the directory based on this distinguished name.

The credentials also include either a password or some other form of proof of identity, so that Active Directory can verify the identity of the process issuing the bind request.

Generally, you want to use the current user's credentials to authenticate with, thereby granting the access rights appropriate to the currently logged-in user. All the LDAP bind functions accept a NULL for the username and password to indicate that they should pass the credentials of the current user to the server for authentication.

Multiple Binds

You can authenticate multiple times on a given LDAP connection. When you issue a subsequent bind command, the server aborts any outstanding operations on the connection. Any operations performed after the bind command are in the context of the newly authenticated credentials.

Anonymous Connections

LDAPv2 required that you authenticate the connection before performing any other operation. This has changed in LDAPv3, which supports unauthenticated, or *anonymous,* connections. You can, in fact, perform LDAP functions without authenticating at all. By default, however, the only thing an anonymous process can do is read the RootDSE of the domain controller. The Active Directory access control mechanisms prohibit any other operations.

If you want, you can reauthenticate an LDAP connection as an anonymous connection by using an empty string for the username and password. This resets the credentials on the connection to those of an anonymous process.

LDAP Binding Functions

The Microsoft LDAP API provides three methods for authenticating with Active Directory. Each method is supported by a pair of binding functions, with each pair containing a synchronous and an asynchronous version of the binding function.

> **CAUTION**
>
> The draft standard LDAP C API provides both asynchronous and synchronous functions for authenticating to the directory server. The Microsoft LDAP client library provides both synchronous and asynchronous binding functions as well. However, as of Windows 2000 Release Candidate 3, the asynchronous binding functions are not implemented; they always return an error. You must therefore use the synchronous binding functions (those ending with _s) when using the Microsoft LDAP client library.

The first binding method, the *simple* binding method, is implemented by the ldap_simple_bind() and ldap_simple_bind_s() functions. The simple binding method is, as you might guess, the simplest way to authenticate with Active Directory, but it is also the least secure.

The second method uses the *Simple Authentication and Security Layer* (SASL) mechanism as defined by RFC 2222. SASL is a flexible and secure authentication mechanism in which the client and server can authenticate each other using a variety of strategies. The functions ldap_sasl_bind() and ldap_sasl_bind_s() support the SASL authentication mechanism.

The third method is the earlier LDAPv2 authentication scheme implemented by the functions ldap_bind() and ldap_bind_s(). In this method, you actually specify the authentication mechanism to use. Although most existing LDAP programs use ldap_bind() or ldap_bind_s() to authenticate to the directory, the most recent draft standard LDAP C API deprecates these two functions. You should instead use either the simple binding method or the SASL binding method.

Table 19.1 lists the binding functions described in this chapter.

TABLE 19.1 LDAP BINDING FUNCTIONS

Function	Description
ldap_simple_bind	Asynchronous function that implements the simple binding method. Not completely implemented in the Microsoft LDAP library.
ldap_simple_bind_s	Synchronous function that implements the simple binding method.
ldap_sasl_bind	Asynchronous function that implements the SASL binding method. Not completely implemented in the Microsoft LDAP library.
ldap_sasl_bind_s	Synchronous function that implements the SASL binding method.
ldap_bind	Asynchronous function that implements the LDAPv2 binding method. Not completely implemented in the Microsoft LDAP library.
ldap bind_s	Synchronous function that implements the LDAPv2 binding method.

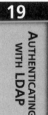

19

AUTHENTICATING
WITH LDAP

Simple LDAP Binding with ldap_simple_bind_s()

ldap_simple_bind_s() and its asynchronous counterpart, ldap_simple_bind(), provide the simplest, but least secure, mechanism for authenticating with the directory. With ldap_simple_bind_s(), you specify a username and a password. These are passed to the

LDAP server in clear text, and the LDAP server looks up your user object in the directory and compares the password provided with the one in the directory. The username you specify must be the distinguished name of a security principal in the directory.

ULONG ldap_simple_bind_s(LDAP *ld, PCHAR dn, PCHAR passwd)

> ld is the pointer to an LDAP structure returned from ldap_init(), ldap_ssl_init(), or ldap_open().

> dn is a pointer to a NUL-terminated string containing the distinguished name of the object in the directory to authenticate as. If you use an empty string, or if you specify a NULL pointer, ldap_simple_bind_s() makes the connection anonymous.

> passwd is a pointer to a NUL-terminated string containing the password for the object given by the dn parameter. If the dn parameter is an empty string or a NULL pointer, indicating an anonymous bind, passwd should also be an empty string or a NULL pointer.

> Returns: An LDAP error code or LDAP_SUCCESS if the bind was successful. Note that if the bind fails, the LDAP connection reverts to an anonymous connection.

Listing 19.1 contains a sample program that authenticates using a ldap_simple_bind_s() and a specific username and password.

LISTING 19.1   USING ldap_simple_bind_s() TO AUTHENTICATE TO ACTIVE DIRECTORY

```
1:    #include <windows.h>
2:    #include <winldap.h>
3:    #include <iostream.h>
4:
5:    int main( int argc, char** argv )
6:    {
7:        LDAP* psLdap = ldap_init( "engserver.megacorp.com", LDAP_PORT );
8:        if( psLdap != NULL )
9:        {
10:           ULONG uErr = ldap_simple_bind_s( psLdap,
11:           "CN=Administrator,CN=Users,DC=megacorp,DC=com", "secret" );
12:           if( uErr == LDAP_SUCCESS )
13:           {
14:               cout << "Bind succeeded" << endl;
15:               // do something with the LDAP session
16:           }
17:
18:           ldap_unbind( psLdap );
19:        }
20:
21:        return 0;
22:    }
```

The program in Listing 19.1 first creates an LDAP session by calling `ldap_init()` at line 7.

The program then authenticates the session using `ldap_simple_bind_s()` and the distinguished name and password of the Administrator account at line 10. If the bind succeeds, the program prints a message at line 14.

The program closes the LDAP session at line 18 by calling `ldap_unbind()`. Note that you must call `ldap_unbind()` even if the bind operation failed.

> **CAUTION**
>
> Don't forget that even though the Microsoft LDAP client implements the asynchronous `ldap_simple_bind()`, it always return an error. You must use the `ldap_simple_bind_s()` function instead.

You can also use the `ldap_simple_bind_s()` function to bind to Active Directory as an anonymous user. In that case, you simply specify NULL as the username and password. Listing 19.2 shows how to do this.

LISTING 19.2   USING `ldap_simple_bind_s()` TO AUTHENTICATE TO ACTIVE DIRECTORY AS AN ANONYMOUS USER

```
1:   #include <windows.h>
2:   #include <winldap.h>
3:   #include <iostream.h>
4:
5:   int main( int argc, char** argv )
6:   {
7:       LDAP* psLdap = ldap_init( NULL, LDAP_PORT );
8:       if( psLdap != NULL )
9:       {
10:          ULONG uErr = ldap_simple_bind_s( psLdap, NULL, NULL );
11:          if( uErr == LDAP_SUCCESS )
12:          {
13:              cout << "Bind succeeded" << endl;
14:              // do something with the LDAP session
15:          }
16:
17:          ldap_unbind( psLdap );
18:      }
19:
20:      return 0;
21:  }
```

19

AUTHENTICATING WITH LDAP

The program in Listing 19.2 initializes an LDAP session at line 7 by calling `ldap_init()`.

The program then authenticates as an anonymous user by calling `ldap_simple_bind_s()` and specifying `NULL` as the username and password. If the bind succeeds, the program prints a message at line 13.

The program closes the LDAP session by calling `ldap_unbind()` at line 17.

Using SASL to Authenticate with Active Directory

The SASL framework, as defined by RFC 2222, provides a secure and extensible mechanism for a client and server to authenticate each other, and optionally to negotiate a connection-oriented security protocol. Despite the similarity in acronyms, there is no relationship between Secure Sockets Layer (SSL) and Simple Authentication and Security Layer. In fact, you can initialize an SSL LDAP session for traffic encryption and use SASL for authentication to get the utmost in security.

Windows 2000 domain controllers support two SASL mechanisms, which are listed in the `supportedSASLMechanisms` attribute of each domain controller's `RootDSE`. The first mechanism is named `GSSAPI`, which indicates that both the LDAP client and the domain controller will use the Generic Security Service Application Programming Interface (GSSAPI). The GSSAPI is defined in RFCs 1508 and 2078. When Windows 2000 domain controllers use the `GSSAPI` mechanism, they will authenticate the client using Kerberos Version 5.

The second SASL mechanism supported by Windows 2000 domain controllers is called `GSS-SPNEGO`. This is a security negotiation mechanism that lets the client and server negotiate exactly which security scheme they will use. In this case, Windows 2000 domain controllers will use Kerberos Version 5 or the Windows NT LAN Manager Security Service Provider (NTLMSSP) to authenticate the client, depending on the kind of client making the connection.

The Windows 2000 LDAP client library provides two functions for SASL binding: `ldap_sasl_bind()` and `ldap_sasl_bind_s()`. Microsoft has included these functions primarily for compliance with the draft standard LDAP C API; the SASL bind functions aren't documented anywhere, and the Basic Encoding Rules support functions you need to encode the parameters aren't yet part of the platform SDK. So, even though the SASL bind functions exist in the LDAP client library, they aren't particularly useful.

```
INT ldap_sasl_bind_s( LDAP* ExternalHandle, const PCHAR DistName,
➥const PCHAR AuthMechanism, const BERVAL* cred, PLDAPControl* ServerCtrls,
➥PLDAPControl* ClientCtrls, PBERVAL ServerData )
```

ExternalHandle is a pointer to an LDAP structure previously returned by ldap_init(), ldap_sslinit(), or ldap_open().

DistName is a pointer to a NUL-terminated string containing the fully qualified distinguished name of the user as whom you want to authenticate. If you pass a NULL for DistName and NULL for the cred parameter, the function authenticates as an anonymous user.

AuthMechanism is a pointer to a NUL-terminated string containing the name of the SASL authentication mechanism to use. It must be either GSSAPI-SPNEGO or GSSAPI.

cred is a pointer to a BERVAL structure containing the credentials appropriate for the selected AuthMechanism. Set cred to NULL if you also set DistName to NULL to authenticate as an anonymous user.

ServerCtrls is a pointer to a NULL-terminated array of pointers to LDAPControl structures that specify any server controls for this call. For instance, you could disable referrals for the bind call. You can set this parameter to NULL if there are no server controls. See Chapter 28, "Extending LDAP with Options and Controls," for more information about LDAP controls.

ClientCtrls is a pointer to a NULL-terminated array of pointers to LDAPControl structures that specify any client controls for this call. You can set this parameter to NULL if there are no client controls. See Chapter 28 for more information about LDAP controls.

ServerData is a pointer to a BERVAL structure that will be filled out with the credentials returned by the server so that the client can authenticate the server. You should free the memory associated with the returned structure by passing the pointer to ber_bvfree(). If you set this pointer to NULL, ldap_sasl_bind_s() ignores the returned server credentials.

19

AUTHENTICATING WITH LDAP

Using `ldap_bind_s()` to Authenticate with Active Directory

The easiest way to take advantage of the sophisticated security mechanisms in Windows 2000—for example, Kerberos—is to use the `ldap_bind_s()` function. (Recall that the asynchronous `ldap_bind()` function is present but not supported.)

In addition to an LDAP session handle, a username, and a set of credentials, `ldap_bind_s()` accepts a parameter describing the authentication mechanism to use. Table 19.2 lists the constants for the different authentication mechanisms. One of these constants, `LDAP_AUTH_NEGOTIATE`, specifies that the LDAP client library should negotiate the best authentication mechanism using the GSSAPI-SPNEGO algorithm. As a result, your application will use Kerberos Version 5 if it is running under Windows 2000, or NTLM if it is running under Windows 98 or Windows NT 4. Binding with `ldap_bind_s()` and `LDAP_AUTH_NEGOTIATE` is the best way to go.

```
ULONG ldap_bind_s( LDAP *ld, PCHAR dn, PCHAR cred, ULONG method )
```

> `ld` is a pointer to an LDAP structure returned by `ldap_init()`, `ldap_sasl_init()`, or `ldap_open()`.

> `dn` is a pointer to a NUL-terminated string containing the DN of the user as whom you want to authenticate. If you specify NULL for `dn`, your program authenticates as the currently logged-in user, not an anonymous user. If you do so, you should also set the `cred` parameter to NULL.

> `cred` is a pointer to a structure containing the authentication credentials appropriate for the type of authentication specified in `method`. If you use the `LDAP_AUTH_NEGOTIATE` method (the most flexible mechanism), and you don't want to authenticate as the currently logged-in user, `cred` should point to an appropriately initialized SEC_WINNT_AUTH_IDENTITY structure. Set `cred` to NULL if you specified a NULL for the `dn` parameter.

> `method` is one of the authentication constants defined in WINLDAP.H. It can be one of the constant names shown in Table 19.2.

TABLE 19.2 AUTHENTICATION CONSTANTS FOR `ldap_bind_s()`

Constant Name	*Description*
LDAP_AUTH_SIMPLE	Use the simple LDAP authentication mechanism. Use `ldap_simple_bind_s()` instead.
LDAP_AUTH_SASL	Indicates the LDAP client should use the SASL layer to determine which authentication mechanism is used. You should use `LDAP_AUTH_NEGOTIATE` instead, unless you need to use this code with non-Microsoft LDAP servers.

Constant Name	Description
LDAP_AUTH_SICILY	Not used with Active Directory.
LDAP_AUTH_MSN	Authenticates using Microsoft Network login credentials. Not used in Active Directory.
LDAP_AUTH_NTLM	Authenticate using Windows NT 4 credentials. Use this if your client is running on an NT 4 system.
LDAP_AUTH_NEGOTIATE	Negotiate the appropriate authentication protocol using the Generic Security Service Application Program Interface Simple and Protected Negotiation (GSS-SPNEGO) mechanism.
LDAP_AUTH_DPA	Use the Microsoft Membership system's Distributed Password Authentication mechanism.

> **CAUTION**
>
> Don't forget that even though the Microsoft LDAP client implements the asynchronous `ldap_bind()`, it always returns an error. You must use the `ldap_bind_s()` function instead.

The simplest and most effective way of binding with an Active Directory domain controller is to use LDAP_AUTH_NEGOTIATE. This uses the GSSAPI to determine what kind of authentication to use.

Listing 19.3 shows how to authenticate to an Active Directory domain controller using the currently logged-in user's credentials.

LISTING 19.3 USING `ldap_bind_s()` TO AUTHENTICATE WITH THE CURRENT USER'S CREDENTIALS

```
1:   #include <windows.h>
2:   #include <winldap.h>
3:   #include <iostream.h>
4:
5:   int main( int argc, char** argv )
6:   {
7:       LDAP* psLdap = ldap_init( NULL, LDAP_PORT );
8:
9:       if( psLdap != NULL )
10:      {
```

19

AUTHENTICATING WITH LDAP

continues

LISTING 19.3 CONTINUED

```
11:          ULONG uErr = ldap_bind_s(
12:              psLdap,      // LDAP session
13:              NULL,        // user name (NULL = current)
14:              NULL,        // credentials (NULL = current)
15:              LDAP_AUTH_NEGOTIATE // auth mechanism
16:          );
17:
18:          if( uErr == LDAP_SUCCESS )
19:          {
20:              cout << "Bind succeeded" << endl;
21:          }
22:
23:          ldap_unbind( psLdap );
24:      }
25:
26:      return 0;
27: }
```

The program in Listing 19.3 initializes an LDAP session with the default domain controller by calling `ldap_init()` at line 7.

At line 11, the program authenticates using the currently logged-in user's credentials by calling `ldap_bind_s()` with NULL as the username and credentials. The program specifies `LDAP_AUTH_NEGOTIATE` as the authentication mechanism.

If the bind is successful, the program prints a message at line 20, and the program closes the LDAP session by calling `ldap_unbind()` at line 23.

Listing 19.4 shows how to bind to an Active Directory domain controller using credentials that are different from those of the currently logged-in user.

LISTING 19.4 USING `ldap_bind_s()` TO AUTHENTICATE WITH ANOTHER USER'S CREDENTIALS

```
1:  #include <windows.h>
2:  #include <winldap.h>
3:  #include <iostream.h>
4:  #include <rpcdce.h>
5:
6:  int main( int argc, char** argv )
7:  {
8:      LDAP* psLdap = ldap_init( "engserver.megacorp.com", LDAP_PORT );
9:
10:     if( psLdap != NULL )
11:     {
12:         ULONG uErr = LDAP_SUCCESS;
13:
```

```
14:            const PCHAR pszUserName = "CN=DaveS,CN=Users,DC=megacorp,
               ➥DC=com";
15:            const PCHAR pszDomainName = "MEGACORP";
16:            const PCHAR pszPassword = "secret-mcgw";
17:
18:            SEC_WINNT_AUTH_IDENTITY sIdentity;
19:
20:            sIdentity.User = ( unsigned char* )pszUserName;
21:            sIdentity.UserLength = strlen( pszUserName );
22:            sIdentity.Domain = ( unsigned char* )pszDomainName;
23:            sIdentity.DomainLength = strlen( pszDomainName );
24:            sIdentity.Password = ( unsigned char* )pszPassword;
25:            sIdentity.PasswordLength = strlen( pszPassword );
26:            sIdentity.Flags = SEC_WINNT_AUTH_IDENTITY_ANSI;
27:
28:            uErr = ldap_bind_s(
29:                psLdap,
30:                pszUserName,
31:                ( const PCHAR )&sIdentity,
32:                LDAP_AUTH_NEGOTIATE
33:            );
34:
35:            if( uErr == LDAP_SUCCESS )
36:            {
37:                cout << "Bind succeeded" << endl;
38:            }
39:
40:            ldap_unbind( psLdap );
41:        }
42:
43:    return 0;
44:    }
```

The program in Listing 19.4 starts by initializing an LDAP session at line 8 by calling

```
ldap_init().
```

At line 14–16, the program initializes some local variables to contain the username, domain, and password with which to authenticate.

At lines 18–26, the program declares and initializes the SEC_WINNT_AUTH_IDENTITY structure to contain the credentials of the user with which the program will authenticate.

The program calls ldap_bind_s() at lines 28–33, using the LDAP_AUTH_NEGOTIATE authentication method. If the bind succeeds, the program will print a message at line 37.

The program closes the LDAP session at line 40 by calling ldap_unbind().

19

AUTHENTICATING WITH LDAP

CHAPTER 20

Searching Active Directory with LDAP

Your most frequent interaction with Active Directory will almost certainly be searching the contents of the directory for specific objects. You'll either be listing usernames, finding configuration data, displaying the domain hierarchy, or some other such thing. The LDAP API makes searching the directory pretty straightforward.

This chapter describes the LDAP API functions you will need to perform basic directory searches. Table 20.1 lists these functions.

TABLE 20.1 LDAP FUNCTIONS FOR BASIC SEARCHES

Function	Description
ldap_search_s	Performs a synchronous search of the directory.
ldap_first_entry	Retrieves the first entry returned by a search operation.
ldap_next_entry	Retrieves subsequent entries returned by a search operation.
ldap_msgfree	Frees the memory associated with an entry returned by a search operation.
ldap_get_dn	Retrieves the distinguished name of an entry returned by a search operation.
ldap_first_attribute	Retrieves the first attribute of an entry returned by a search operation.

continues

TABLE 20.1 CONTINUED

Function	Description
ldap_next_attribute	Retrieves subsequent attributes of an entry returned by a search operation.
ldap_get_values	Retrieves the values of an attribute as NUL-terminated strings.
ldap_count_values	Returns a count of the number of values a specific attribute has.
ldap_free_values	Frees the memory associated with a set of attribute values.
ldap_get_values_len	Retrieves the values of an attribute in pointer/length format.
ldap_count_values_len	Counts the number of values in a set returned by ldap_get_values_len().
ldap_free_values_len	Frees the memory associated with values returned by ldap_get_values_len().

Specifying an LDAP Search

There are four fundamental components of every LDAP directory search. They are the starting point of the search, the depth of the search, the search criteria, and the requested attributes. You must specify all four of these when you use LDAP to search the directory.

The Starting Point of the Search

Unlike a conventional database search, an LDAP search does not implicitly search the entire directory. Instead, you specify a subtree of the directory to search. The subtree can start at any object in the directory, and the search will continue below that object in the hierarchy. You specify the starting point, or *search base*, by providing its distinguished name. For instance, a search starting at the container "CN=Users,DC=acctg, DC=megacorp,DC=com" would search all the objects in the Users container in the acctg domain of MegaCorp.com.

Search Depth

After you specify the starting point in the directory from which you want to start the search, you must specify how far down the hierarchy you want to search. LDAP searches let you specify one of three search depths, or *search scopes*. These are defined as constants in WINLDAP.H:

- LDAP_SCOPE_BASE indicates that the search starts and ends with the object you specified as the starting point of the search. A search with a scope of LDAP_SCOPE_BASE effectively reads one item from the directory.

- LDAP_SCOPE_ONELEVEL indicates that the search encompasses all objects in the directory that are immediately subordinate to the starting point of the search. This is analogous to searching for files in a single directory. A search that uses LDAP_SCOPE_ONELEVEL will not return the object given as the search base.

- LDAP_SCOPE_SUBTREE indicates that the search will encompass all objects in the tree below the starting point, all the way to the bottom of the directory tree. Searches that use LDAP_SCOPE_SUBTREE will include the object given as the base of the search.

Search Criteria

In addition to specifying a portion of the directory tree to search, LDAP provides a very flexible mechanism for specifying search criteria called *search filters*. LDAP filters let you search for objects that match very specific conditions. You can search for objects with or without specific attributes, whose attributes are equal to, less than, or greater than some constant, or whose attributes match a pattern or contain a substring. You can combine these conditions into complex queries using logical ANDs and ORs. The following are some examples of LDAP search filters:

"objectClass=server" indicates that you want retrieve all objects that are of class server.

"(&(objectClass=server)(cn=LITHIUM))" indicates that you want to retrieve the server object whose common name is LITHIUM.

"(&(objectClass=User)(lastLogon>=19990101))" would retrieve the user objects for all users who had logged in since the beginning of 1999.

These are just some simple examples to get started. Chapter 21, "Advanced Searching with LDAP," gives the complete syntax for LDAP search filters.

Requesting Attributes

The final component of a search specification is the list of attributes you want returned. You can specify a list of attributes to be returned for each object that meets the criteria, or you can specify that all of each object's attributes be returned.

You specify the attributes you want by providing a NULL-terminated array of pointers to NUL-terminated strings, where each string gives the display name of the attribute you want. For instance, the following array would request the logonCount and lastLogonTime attributes of a user object.

```
char* apszAttrNames[] =
{
    "description",
    "logonCount",
    "lastLogonTime",
    NULL
};
```

It's very important that you do not forget the terminating NULL at the end of the array. That is how the LDAP client library identifies the end of the list of attribute names. If you forget the terminating NULL, the LDAP library will wander off into random areas of memory looking for attribute names, and your program will fail miserably.

Note that you specify the LDAP display name of the attributes you want, not their relative distinguished name. Chapter 21 gives a complete description of specifying attributes in a search.

A Simple Search Using ldap_search_s()

The easiest search function to use is ldap_search_s(). It gives you all the search flexibility described previously, and you don't have to worry about processing the search results asynchronously.

```
ULONG ldap_search_s( LDAP* ld, const PCHAR base, ULONG scope,
➥const PCHAR filter, PCHAR attrs[], ULONG attrsonly, LDAPMessage** res )
```

> ld is a pointer to an LDAP structure that has been initialized with ldap_init(), ldap_sslinit(), or ldap_open().
>
> base is a pointer to a NUL-terminated string that specifies the distinguished name of the starting object for the search.
>
> scope is one of LDAP_SCOPE_BASE, LDAP_SCOPE_ONELEVEL, or LDAP_SCOPE_SUBTREE.
>
> filter is a pointer to a NUL-terminated string that contains the search filter. It cannot be NULL or a pointer to an empty string.

Tip

If you want to retrieve all objects in a search, you cannot specify a search filter of NULL or an empty string. The simplest way to indicate that you want all objects is to use the filter "objectClass=*", which indicates that you want all objects that have an attribute named "objectClass". All objects in Active Directory have an attribute named "objectClass".

attrs is a NULL-terminated array of pointers to NUL-terminated strings containing the names of the attributes to return. The search will return these attributes for each object, if they exist. You can specify NULL to indicate that you want to retrieve all attributes for each object satisfying the search filter.

attrsonly is a Boolean value that determines whether the search will return attribute values. If you set attrsonly to 1, the search will return only the names of the attributes satisfying the search filter. If you set attrsonly to 0, the search will return the attribute names and values.

res is the address of a pointer to a LDAPMessage structure. If the search function is successful, it sets this pointer to an allocated LDAPMessage structure containing the results of the search. You must free this structure when you are done with it by passing the pointer to ldap_msgfree().

Returns: An LDAP error code, or LDAP_SUCCESS if the search worked properly. Note that it is possible for a search to succeed (return LDAP_SUCCESS) but to return no entries. This can occur if no objects met the criteria specified by the search filter or if your program had insufficient access rights to see the objects.

The following code searches the entire directory for all the user objects. Assume that the LDAP connection represented by psLDAP has been initialized by calls to ldap_init() and ldap_bind_s().

```
char* apszAttrNames[] = { "cn", "description", NULL };
LDAPMessage* psResults = NULL;

ULONG uErr = ldap_search_s(
    psLdap,
    "CN=Users,DC=megacorp,DC=com",
    LDAP_SCOPE_SUBTREE,
    "objectClass=user",
    apszAttrNames,
    0,
    &psResults
);
```

Processing the Search Results

After you submit a search request with LDAP, you need to process the results. Conceptually, LDAP returns a list of objects, a list of attributes for each object, and a list of values for each attribute. Figure 20.1 shows the results of a search.

20

SEARCHING ACTIVE
DIRECTORY WITH
LDAP

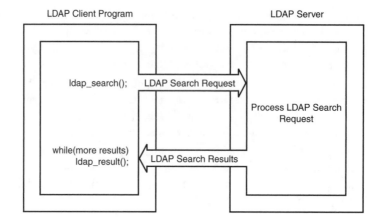

FIGURE 20.1

The structure of LDAP search results.

Given this kind of data structure, you can imagine what the code that processes it looks like:

```
FOREACH entry in result set
    FOREACH attribute in entry
        FOREACH value of attribute
            Do something
        NEXT value
    NEXT attribute
NEXT entry
```

Iterating the Returned Entries

LDAP provides two functions for retrieving each of the objects returned from a search: ldap_first_entry() and ldap_next_entry(). These functions form the outermost loop in the preceding pseudocode.

```
LDAPMessage* ldap_first_entry( LDAP* ld, LDAPMessage* res )
```

> ld is a pointer to the LDAP structure that was used to perform the search operation.

> res is a pointer to the LDAPMessage structure that was returned from ldap_search_s().

Returns: A pointer to an LDAPMessage structure that contains the first entry of the returned search results. It will be NULL if there are no entries that satisfy the search criteria or if an error is encountered in processing the search results. To determine the error code, you have to call LdapGetLastError().

You should *not* try to free the LDAPMessage structure returned by ldap_first_entry(). It is freed when you free the LDAPMessage structure containing the entire search result set.

```
LDAPMessage* ldap_next_entry( LDAP* ld, LDAPMessage* entry )
```

> `ld` is a pointer to the LDAP structure that was used to perform the search operation.
>
> `entry` is a pointer to the `LDAPMessage` structure returned from the preceding call to `ldap_first_entry()` or `ldap_next_entry()`.

Returns: A pointer to an `LDAPMessage` structure that contains the next entry of the returned search results. It will return `NULL` if there are no more entries in the result set, or if there was an error getting the next entry in the result set. You have to call `LdapGetLastError()` to determine which it is.

The following code enumerates the objects returned from a previous search:

```
// Assume that psLdap has been initialized by a call to ldap_init()
// Assume that psResults has been set by a call to ldap_search_s()
LDAPMessage* pEntry;

for( pEntry = ldap_first_entry( pLdap, pResults );
     pEntry != NULL;
     pEntry = ldap_next_entry( psLdap, pEntry ) )
{
    // pEntry refers to a returned LDAP object
}

ULONG uErr = LdapGetLastError( psLdap );
if( uErr != LDAP_SUCCESS )
{
    // some sort of error occurred
}
else
{
    // we processed all of the returned entries
}
```

Getting the Distinguished Name of a Returned Entry

Each object you retrieve with `ldap_first_entry()` and `ldap_next_entry()` has at least one attribute that you can check: its distinguished name. Even if you did not request any attributes, or even if the object has no attributes in the directory, you can always get an object's distinguished name. The function you use to obtain the distinguished name of a returned entry is `ldap_get_dn()`.

```
PCHAR ldap_get_dn( LDAP* ld, LDAPMessage* entry )
```

> `ld` is a pointer to the LDAP structure that was used for the search operation.
>
> `entry` is a pointer to an `LDAPMessage` struct that was returned by a call to `ldap_first_entry()` or `ldap_next_entry()`.

20

SEARCHING ACTIVE DIRECTORY WITH LDAP

Returns: A pointer to a NUL-terminated string containing the distinguished name of the returned entry. You must free this pointer when you are done with it by passing it to `ldap_memfree()`.

Retrieving the Returned Attributes

After you have retrieved an item from the directory, you will typically want to do something with its attributes. You use the functions `ldap_first_attribute()` and `ldap_next_attribute()` to iterate the list of returned attributes for each object. `ldap_first_attribute()` returns the name of the first attribute for a given search entry, and `ldap_next_attribute()` returns the name of subsequent attributes for a given search entry.

```
PCHAR ldap_first_attribute( LDAP* ld, LDAPMessage* entry, BerElement** ptr )
```

> `ld` is a pointer to the LDAP structure used in the search.
>
> `entry` is the `LDAPMessage` pointer returned by a call to `ldap_first_entry()` or `ldap_next_entry()`.
>
> `ptr` is the address of pointer to a `BerElement` structure to be set. The `BerElement` structure is an opaque type that represents a single attribute of an object that possibly contains multiple values. The `ldap_first_attribute()` and `ldap_next_attribute()` functions use the `BerElement` structure to maintain the state of the iteration through the attributes of an entry.

Returns: A pointer to a NUL-terminated string containing the name of the attribute.

Unless you specified TRUE for the `attrsonly` parameter to the search function, the search results will contain the names and the values of the attributes you specified in your search request. The search will return an object if it passes the search filter, even if it does not have one of the attributes you specified in `attrs` parameter of the `ldap_search_s()` function.

```
PCHAR ldap_next_attribute( LDAP* ld, LDAPMessage* entry, BerElement* ptr )
```

> `ld` is a pointer to the LDAP structure that was used in the search.
>
> `entry` is the `LDAPMessage` pointer returned by a call to `ldap_first_entry()` or `ldap_next_entry()`.
>
> `ptr` is the pointer to a `BerElement` structure returned from the call to `ldap_first_attribute()`. The `BerElement` structure is an opaque type that represents a single attribute of an object that possibly contains multiple values. The `ldap_first_attribute()` and `ldap_next_attribute()` functions use the `BerElement` structure to maintain the state of the iteration through the attributes of an entry.

> **CAUTION**
>
> The draft standard C API and the Microsoft documentation both say that you should free the string returned from `ldap_first_attribute()` and `ldap_next_attribute()` by passing it to `ldap_memfree()`. Don't do it! The pointer returned by these functions points to the middle of the returned result block, and attempting to free it will corrupt the heap. If you intend your code to be portable to other platforms, beware that you might cause a memory leak on these other platforms by not calling `ldap_memfree()`.
>
> Also be aware that `ldap_first_attribute()` and `ldap_next_attribute()` use the same buffer and return the same address. If you want to save the names of the attributes, you will have to copy the strings using a function such as `strdup()`.
>
> It appears that the memory associated with the attribute name is freed up when you free the result message with `ldap_msgfree()`.

> **CAUTION**
>
> The draft standard C API and the Microsoft documentation both say that you should free the allocated `BerElement` structure by calling `ldap_ber_free()`. As of Release Candidate 3, this function does not exist in the Microsoft LDAP client API. If you intend your code to be portable to other platforms, beware of this deficiency.
>
> It appears that the memory is freed up when you free the result message with `ldap_msgfree()`.

The following code snippet shows how to retrieve the attributes for an object. Assume pEntry has already been set by a call to `ldap_first_entry()` or `ldap_next_entry()`.

```
// psLdap has been set by a call to ldap_init()
// psEntry has been set by a call to ldap_first_entry() or
// ldap_next_entry()
char* pszAttrName = NULL;
BerElement* psValue = NULL;
for( pszAttrName = ldap_first_attribute( psLdap, psEntry, &psValue );
pszAttrName != NULL;
pszAttrName = ldap_next_attribute( psLdap, psEntry, psValue ) )
{
    // pszAttrName is the name of the attribute
}
```

20

SEARCHING ACTIVE
DIRECTORY WITH
LDAP

Processing the Attribute Values

After you've retrieved an attribute, you'll want to look at its values. Remember that in an LDAP directory, a single attribute can have one or more values, and they are all of the same type.

There are two ways to retrieve the attribute values. You can retrieve them as an array of NUL-terminated strings, or you can retrieve them as an array of `berval` structures, where each `berval` structure contains a pointer and a length.

The API function `ldap_get_values()` retrieves the attribute values as an array of pointers to NUL-terminated strings. The array itself is terminated with a NULL pointer. Use `ldap_get_values()` when you know that the attribute values are a NUL-terminated string—for instance, if the attribute has a syntax of Unicode or Numeric String.

The API function `ldap_get_values_len()` retrieves the attribute values as an array of pointers to `berval` structures, where each `berval` structure contains the length of the value and a pointer to the attribute data. Use `ldap_get_values_len()` when the attribute values may be binary—for instance, if the attribute syntax is Octet String or NT Security Descriptor.

```
PCHAR* ldap_get_values( LDAP* ld, LDAPMessage* entry, const PCHAR attr )
```

> `ld` is a pointer to the LDAP structure that was used in the search operation.
>
> `entry` is a pointer to an `LDAPMessage` that was returned by a previous call to `ldap_first_entry()` or `ldap_next_entry()`.
>
> `attr` is a pointer to a NUL-terminated string containing the name of the attribute whose values you want to get. This is typically the attribute name returned by `ldap_first_attribute()` or `ldap_next_attribute()`.

Returns: A pointer to a NUL-terminator array of pointers to NUL-terminated strings, where each entry in the array points to a value of the attribute. This value must be freed by calling `ldap_value_free()`. `ldap_get_values()` will return NULL if there was some sort of error. You should call `LdapGetLastError()` to determine the exact error code.

```
ULONG ldap_value_free( PCHAR* vals )
```

> `vals` is the pointer to an array of values that was returned by a call to `ldap_get_values()`.

Returns: An LDAP error code, or LDAP_SUCCESS if there was no error.

The following code sample retrieves each of the values of an attribute. Assume that the `pszAttrName` was returned by a call to `ldap_first_entry()`, and that `psLdap` and `psEntry` have been set by calls to `ldap_init()` and `ldap_first_entry()` or `ldap_next_entry()`, respectively.

```
// psLdap has been set by a call to ldap_init()
// psEntry has been set by a call to ldap_first_entry()
// pszAttrName has been set by a call to ldap_first_attribute()
PCHAR* apszValues = ldap_get_values( psLdap, psEntry, pszAttrName );

if( apszValues != NULL )
{
    for(int nEntry = 0; apszValues[ nEntry ] != NULL; nEntry++ )
    {

        // apszValues[ nEntry ] points to the attribute value
    }

    ldap_value_free( apszValues );
}
```

The function `ldap_count_values()` returns the number of non-NULL entries returned by `ldap_get_values()`. This is useful if you need to know the number of entries in the array without enumerating them one by one.

```
ULONG ldap_get_values( PCHAR* vals )
```

> vals is the pointer to an array of pointers to values returned by
> `ldap_get_values()`.

Returns: The number of non-NULL entries in `vals`.

The following sample does the same thing as the preceding sample.

```
// psLdap has been set by a call to ldap_init()
// psEntry has been set by a call to ldap_first_entry()
// pszAttrName has been set by a call to ldap_first_attribute()
PCHAR* apszValues = ldap_get_values( psLdap, psEntry, pszAttrName );

if( apszValues != NULL )
{
    nValues = ldap_count_values( apszValues );

    for(int nEntry = 0; nEntry < nValues; nEntry++ )
    {
        // apszValues[ nEntry ] points to the attribute value
    }

    ldap_value_free( apszValues );
}
```

We can put all this together to write a little program that will retrieve all the users in a domain and print out all their values. The program in Listing 20.1 does exactly that.

20

SEARCHING ACTIVE
DIRECTORY WITH
LDAP

LISTING 20.1 SEARCHING ACTIVE DIRECTORY WITH ldap_search_s()

```
1:  #include <windows.h>
2:  #include <winldap.h>
3:  #include <iostream.h>
4:
5:  int main( int argc, char** argv )
6:  {
7:      LDAP* psLdap = ldap_init( NULL, LDAP_PORT );
8:      if( psLdap != NULL )
9:      {
10:         ULONG uErr = ldap_bind_s( psLdap, NULL, NULL,
            ➥LDAP_AUTH_NEGOTIATE );
11:        if( uErr == LDAP_SUCCESS )
12:        {
13:            LDAPMessage* psResult = NULL;
14:
15:            // Issue the search
16:            uErr = ldap_search_s(
17:                psLdap,                       // LDAP session
18:                "CN=Users,DC=megacorp,DC=com", // base container
19:                LDAP_SCOPE_ONELEVEL,          // scope of search
20:                "objectClass=User",           // search filter
21:                NULL,                         // get all attributes
22:                false,                        // attribute names only?
23:                &psResult                     // result set
24:            );
25:
26:            if( uErr== LDAP_SUCCESS )
27:            {
28:                // Count the entries returned
29:                int nEntries = ldap_count_entries( psLdap, psResult );
30:                cout << nEntries << " entries found" << endl;
31:
32:                // Retrieve each of the returned entries
33:                for( LDAPMessage* psEntry = ldap_first_entry( psLdap,
                    ➥psResult );
34:                    psEntry != NULL;
35:                    psEntry = ldap_next_entry( psLdap, psEntry ) )
36:                {
37:                    cout << ldap_get_dn( psLdap, psEntry ) << endl;
38:
39:                    BerElement* psBerval;
40:
41:                    // Retrieve each of the attributes
42:                    for( char* pszAttrName = ldap_first_attribute
                        ➥(psLdap, psEntry, &psBerval );
43:                        pszAttrName != NULL;
44:                        pszAttrName = ldap_next_attribute( psLdap,
                        ➥psEntry, psBerval ) )
45:                    {
```

```
46:                          // Get all the attribute values
47:                          PCHAR* ppszAttrVals = ldap_get_values(
                           ➥psLdap, psEntry, pszAttrName );
48:                          if( ppszAttrVals != NULL )
49:                          {
50:                              // Print out each value
51:                              for( int nVal = 0;
                               ➥ppszAttrVals[ nVal ] != NULL; nVal++ )
52:                              {
53:                                  cout << "\t" << pszAttrName << "("
                                   ➥<< nVal <<"): " <<
                                   ➥ppszAttrVals[ nVal ] << endl;
54:                              }
55:
56:                              // Free the values of the attribute
57:                              ldap_value_free( ppszAttrVals );
58:                          }
59:                      }
60:                  }
61:
62:              ldap_msgfree( psResult );
63:          }
64:
65:      }
66:
67:      ldap_unbind( psLdap );
68:  }
69:
70:  return 0;
71: }
72:
```

The program in Listing 20.1 initializes an LDAP session by calling `ldap_init()` at line 7 and `ldap_bind_s()` at line 10. Note that it uses the credentials of the logged-in user.

At line 16, the program issues a synchronous LDAP search by calling `ldap_search_s()`. The base of the search is the Users container in the `CN=megacorp,CN=com`. To make this work on your network, you should change the base of the search to the equivalent container in your domain.

When the search returns (which might take several seconds), the program counts the number of entries returned by the search by calling `ldap_count_entries()` and specifying the results pointer `psResult`. The program prints the number of entries on the console.

At line 33, the program retrieves each entry from the result set by calling `ldap_first_entry()` and `ldap_next_entry()`. There are no more entries to retrieve when either of these functions returns `NULL`.

20

SEARCHING ACTIVE DIRECTORY WITH LDAP

The program retrieves the distinguished name of each entry and prints it out at line 37.

Starting at line 42, the program iterates through each of the attributes returned for each entry using `ldap_first_attribute()` and `ldap_next_attribute()`.

The program calls `ldap_get_values()` for each attribute at line 47, which sets the `ppszAttrVals` pointer to point to an NULL-terminated array of string pointers.

The `for` loop starting at line 51 prints out each attribute value.

The program frees the attribute values by calling `ldap_value_free()` at line 57 and then frees the entire chain of search results at line 62 by calling `ldap_msgfree()`.

The program finally wraps up by closing the LDAP connection at line 67 with `ldap_unbind()`.

Processing Binary Attribute Values

In general, attribute values in an LDAP directory are printable, NUL-terminated strings. The LDAP API even returns integers, Booleans, and times as printable strings. Most of the time, you can just get a pointer to the value of an attribute with `ldap_get_values()` and treat it as a string.

Some values in the directory are not translatable to NUL-terminated strings. For instance, it is fairly common to store images in an LDAP directory, which are, of course, not NUL-terminated strings. What to do?

The LDAP API provides another pair of value-retrieval functions for values that you can use with any type of attribute, not just NUL-terminated strings. `ldap_get_values_len()` returns a pointer to an array of pointers to `berval` structures. `ldap_free_values_len()` frees the memory associated with the array returned by `ldap_get_values_len()`.

The LDAP client library uses the `berval` structure to handle binary values. The `berval` structure contains a pointer to the data and a length indicating how many bytes of data there are. The `berval` structure is defined as follows:

```
typedef struct berval
{
    ULONG bv_len; // length of value
    PCHAR bv_val; // pointer to value
}
LDAP_BERVAL;
```

Table 20.2 describes the elements of the structure.

TABLE 20.2 berval STRUCTURE ELEMENTS

Element	Description
bv_len	Contains the length of the value, in bytes.
bv_val	Contains the address of the value data.

Even though ldap_get_values_len() and ldap_free_values_len() are oriented toward handling binary values, you can also use them to handle NUL-terminated string values, too. Just remember that the length of the value includes the NULL terminator.

```
struct berval ** ldap_get_values_len( LDAP* *ExternalHandle,
➥LDAPMessage* Message, const PCHAR attr )
```

ExternalHandle is a pointer to the LDAP structure that was used for the search.

Message is a pointer to an LDAPMessage struct that was returned by a previous call to ldap_first_entry() or ldap_next_entry().

attr is a pointer to a NUL-terminated string containing the name of the attribute whose values you want to retrieve. This is typically the value returned by ldap_first_attribute() or ldap_next_attribute().

Returns: A pointer to a NUL-terminated array of pointers to berval structures. The return value will be NULL if the entry does not have an attribute with the name you specified in pszAttrName, or if there was an internal error. You can call LdapGetLastError() to determine which. You must free the value returned from ldap_get_values_len() by passing it to ldap_value_free_len().

```
ULONG ldap_value_free_len( struct berval** vals )
```

vals is a pointer to an array of pointers to berval structures that was returned by a call to ldap_get_values_len().

Returns: An LDAP error code, or LDAP_SUCCESS if there was no error.

The following code will retrieve all the values of an attribute using ldap_get_values_len(). Assume that psLdap was initialized by a call to ldap_init(), psEntry was returned by a call to ldap_first_entry() or ldap_next_entry(), and pszAttrName was returned from a call to ldap_first_attribute() or ldap_next_attribute().

```
// psLdap has been set by a call to ldap_init()
// psEntry has been set by a call to ldap_first_entry()
// pszAttrName has been set by a call to ldap_first_attribute()
struct berval** ppberValues;

ppsberValues = ldap_get_values_len( psLdap, psEntry, pszAttrName );

if( ppsberValues != NULL )
{
```

```
    for( int nEntry = 0; ppsberValues[nEntry] != NULL; nEntry++ )
    {
        // ppsberValues[ nEntry ]->bv_val points to the value
        // ppsberValues[ nEntry ]->bv_len is the size of the value
    }

    ULONG uErr = ldap_value_free_len( ppsberValues );
}
```

Likewise, there is an API function for returning the count of non-NULL entries in the array returned by `ldap_get_values_len()`. It is called, not surprisingly, `ldap_count_values_len()`.

`ULONG ldap_count_values_len( struct berval** vals )`

> `vals` is a pointer to an array of pointers to `berval` structures returned by a call to `ldap_get_values_len()`.

Returns: The number of entries in the `vals` array.

This sample does essentially the same thing as the preceding example.

```
// psLdap has been set by a call to ldap_init()
// psEntry has been set by a call to ldap_first_entry()
// pszAttrName has been set by a call to ldap_first_attribute()
struct berval** ppsberValues;

ppsberValues = ldap_get_values_len( psLdap, psEntry, pszAttrName );

if( ppsberValues != NULL )
{
    ULONG uEntryCount = ldap_count_values_len( ppsberValues );

    for( int nEntry = 0; nEntry < uEntryCount; nEntry++ )
    {
        // ppsberValues[ nEntry ]->bv_val points to the value
        // ppberValues[ nEntry ]->bv_len is the size of the value
    }

    ULONG uErr = ldap_value_free_len(ppberValues);
}
```

The program in Listing 20.2 is essentially the same as that in Listing 20.1, except that it uses the `ldap_get_values_len()` to retrieve the attribute values.

LISTING 20.2 SEARCHING ACTIVE DIRECTORY WITH `ldap_search_s()` AND `ldap_get_values_len()`

```
1:    #include <windows.h>
2:    #include <winldap.h>
3:    #include <iostream.h>
```

```
4:
5:    int main( int argc, char** argv )
6:    {
7:        LDAP* psLdap = ldap_init( NULL, LDAP_PORT );
8:        if( psLdap != NULL )
9:        {
10:           ULONG uErr = ldap_bind_s( psLdap, NULL, NULL,
          ➥LDAP_AUTH_NEGOTIATE );
11:           if( uErr == LDAP_SUCCESS )
12:           {
13:               LDAPMessage* psResult = NULL;
14:
15:               // Issue the search
16:               uErr = ldap_search_s(
17:                   psLdap,                     // LDAP session
18:                   "CN=Users,DC=megacorp,DC=com", // base container
19:                   LDAP_SCOPE_ONELEVEL,        // scope of search
20:                   "objectClass=User",         // search filter
21:                   NULL,                       // get all attributes
22:                   false,                      // attribute names only?
23:                   &psResult                   // result set
24:               );
25:
26:               if( uErr== LDAP_SUCCESS )
27:               {
28:                   // Count the entries returned
29:                   int nEntries = ldap_count_entries( psLdap, psResult );
          ➥cout << nEntries << " entries found" << endl;
30:
31:                   // Retrieve each of the returned entries
32:                   for( LDAPMessage* psEntry = ldap_first_entry( psLdap,
          ➥psResult );
33:                       psEntry != NULL;
34:                       psEntry = ldap_next_entry( psLdap, psEntry ) )
35:                   {
36:                       cout << ldap_get_dn( psLdap, psEntry ) << endl;
37:
38:                       BerElement* psBerval;
39:
40:                       // Retrieve each of the attributes
41:                       for( char* pszAttrName = ldap_first_attribute(
          ➥psLdap, psEntry, &psBerval );
42:                           pszAttrName != NULL;
43:                           pszAttrName = ldap_next_attribute( psLdap,
          ➥psEntry, psBerval ) )
44:                       {
45:                           // Get all the attribute values
46:                           LDAP_BERVAL** ppsAttrVals =
          ➥ldap_get_values_len( psLdap,
          ➥psEntry, pszAttrName );
47:                           if( ppsAttrVals != NULL )
```

20

SEARCHING ACTIVE
DIRECTORY WITH
LDAP

continues

LISTING 20.2   CONTINUED

```
48:                          {
49:                              // Print out each value
50:                              for( int nVal = 0;
                                 ➥ppsAttrVals[ nVal ] != NULL; nVal++ )
51:                              {
52:                                  cout << "\t" << pszAttrName << "("
                                     ➥<< nVal << " " << ppsAttrVals
                                     ➥[ nVal ]->bv_len << " bytes):"
                                     ➥<< ppsAttrVals[ nVal ]->bv_val <<
                                     ➥endl;
53:                              }
54:
55:                              // Free the values of the attribute
56:                              ldap_value_free_len( ppsAttrVals );
57:                          }
58:                      }
59:                  }
60:
61:              ldap_msgfree( psResult );
62:          }
63:
64:      }
65:
66:      ldap_unbind( psLdap );
67:  }
68:
69:  return 0;
70: }
```

Searching with a Timeout Value

ldap_search_s() is very simple to use, but it has one annoying drawback: It can take an arbitrarily long time to complete. The delay might be due to network problems, or server load, or it could be that there are lots of objects that satisfy your search criteria. Whatever the reason, ldap_search_s() can sometimes take a long time to complete. ldap_search_st() offers a simple solution.

ldap_search_st() is essentially equivalent to ldap_search_s(), except that it lets you specify a client-side timeout value. So, if you are unwilling to have your program wait more than, say, five seconds for the search to complete, you can use ldap_search_st() and specify a five-second timeout.

```
ULONG ldap_search_st( LDAP* ld, const PCHAR base, ULONG scope,
➥const PCHAR filter, PCHAR attrs[], ULONG attrsonly,
➥struct l_timeval* timeout, LDAPMessage** res )
```

ld is a pointer to an LDAP structure that has been initialized with ldap_init(), ldap_sslinit(), or ldap_open().

base is a pointer to a NUL-terminated string that specifies the distinguished name of the starting object for the search.

scope indicates the scope of the search and is one of LDAP_SCOPE_BASE, LDAP_SCOPE_ONELEVEL, or LDAP_SCOPE_SUBTREE.

filter is a pointer to a NUL-terminated string that contains the search filter. It cannot be NULL or a pointer to an empty string.

attrs is a NUL-terminated array of pointers to NUL-terminated strings containing the attribute names to return. The search will return these attributes for each object, if they exist. You can specify NULL to indicate that you want to retrieve all attributes for each object satisfying the search filter.

attrsonly is a Boolean value that determines whether the search will return attribute values. If attrs is set to 1, the search will return only the names of the attributes satisfying the search filter. If attrs is set to 0, the search will return the attribute names and values.

timeout is a pointer to an initialized l_timeval structure that specifies the maximum amount of time the client should wait for the search to complete. If the search does not complete in the specified amount of time, the search is cancelled and ldap_search_st() returns the error LDAP_TIMEOUT. No partial results are returned. Table 20.3 describes the members of the l_timeval structure.

res is the address of a pointer to an LDAPMessage structure. If the search function is successful, it will set this pointer to an allocated LDAPMessage structure containing the results of the search. You must free this structure when you are done with it by passing the pointer to ldap_msgfree().

TABLE 20.3 THE l_timeval STRUCTURE

Member	Description
LONG tv_sec	The number of seconds.
LONG tv_usec	The number of microseconds. This value is generally ignored by the LDAP API functions.

Returns: An LDAP error code, or LDAP_SUCCESS if the search worked properly. Note that it is possible for a search to succeed (return LDAP_SUCCESS), but to return no entries. This can occur if no objects met the criteria specified by the search filter, or if your program had insufficient access rights to see the objects.

ldap_search_st() works just like ldap_search_s(), except that you have to specify the additional timeout parameter. The following code sample would initiate a search for all

20

SEARCHING ACTIVE
DIRECTORY WITH
LDAP

of the user objects in the domain DC=megacorp,DC=com, and return after, at most, 10 seconds. Assume that psLdap has been initialized by a call to ldap_init() and that the connection has been authenticated with ldap_bind_s().

The program in Listing 20.3 performs a subtree search on the entire megacorp.com domain using ldap_search_st() and a timeout value of 1 second. This search should fail on all but the fastest servers, and the program will print an error message.

LISTING 20.3 USING ldap_search_st() TO PERFORM A SEARCH WITH A TIMEOUT VALUE

```
 1:   #include <windows.h>
 2:   #include <winldap.h>
 3:   #include <iostream.h>
 4:
 5:   int main( int argc, char** argv )
 6:   {
 7:       LDAP* psLdap = ldap_init( NULL, LDAP_PORT );
 8:       if( psLdap != NULL )
 9:       {
10:           ULONG uErr = ldap_bind_s( psLdap, NULL, NULL,
              ➥LDAP_AUTH_NEGOTIATE );
11:           if( uErr == LDAP_SUCCESS )
12:           {
13:               LDAPMessage* psResult = NULL;
14:
15:               // Issue the search with a one second timeout
16:               struct l_timeval sTimeout = { 1, 0 };
17:
18:               uErr = ldap_search_st(
19:                   psLdap,                   // LDAP session
20:                   "DC=megacorp,DC=com", // base container
21:                   LDAP_SCOPE_SUBTREE,    // scope of search
22:                   "objectClass=*",     // search filter
23:                   NULL,                  // get all attributes
24:                   false,                 // attribute names only?
25:                   &sTimeout,             // timeout value
26:                   &psResult              // result set
27:               );
28:
29:               if( uErr == LDAP_TIMEOUT )
30:               {
31:                   cout << "Timeout error" << endl;
32:               }
33:               else if( uErr == LDAP_SUCCESS )
34:               {
35:                   // Count the entries returned
36:                   int nEntries = ldap_count_entries( psLdap, psResult );
37:                   cout << nEntries << " entries found" << endl;
38:
```

```
39:                    // Retrieve each of the returned entries
40:            for( LDAPMessage* psEntry = ldap_first_entry( psLdap,
        ➥psResult );
41:                    psEntry != NULL;
42:                    psEntry = ldap_next_entry( psLdap, psEntry ) )
43:                {
44:                    cout << ldap_get_dn( psLdap, psEntry ) << endl;
45:                }
46:
47:                ldap_msgfree( psResult );
48:            }
49:
50:        }
51:
52:        ldap_unbind( psLdap );
53:    }
54:
55:    return 0;
56: }
```

The program in Listing 20.3 starts in the usual way by calling `ldap_init()` at line 7 to initialize an LDAP session, and by calling `ldap_bind_s()` at line 10.

At line 16, the program initializes an `l_timeval` structure to represent a timeout value of one second.

The program calls `ldap_search_st()` at line 18, performing a subtree search starting at the root of the `megacorp.com` domain. The search will retrieve all objects in the domain, and uses the `l_timeval` structure declared on line 16.

At line 29, the program checks to see whether the search timed out. (It should in most cases.) If the search did time out, the program prints a message to that effect at line 31.

If the search succeeds, the program enumerates the returned items and displays the distinguished name of each at line 44. At line 47, the program frees the memory associated with the result set.

Finally, the program closes the LDAP session at line 52 by calling `ldap_unbind()`.

20

Advanced Searching with LDAP

The preceding chapter showed you how to perform basic directory searches using the LDAP function `ldap_search_s()` and simple search filters using the EQUAL (=), AND (&), and OR (|) filter operators. In this chapter, we'll go through the full breadth of LDAP search filter syntax, as well as specify different sets of attributes for the search to return. We'll also go over how to set limits on searches, how to use LDAP controls to perform extended searches, and finally how to perform asynchronous searches using `ldap_search()` and `ldap_result()`.

Complex Search Criteria

I only scratched the surface of the LDAP search filter syntax in the preceding chapter. The full search filter syntax as defined in RFC 2251 is fairly extensive. This section will review all the components of the LDAPv3 search filter syntax used by Active Directory.

> **NOTE**
>
> Because ADSI for Active Directory uses the LDAP protocol, ADSI searches using the `IDirectorySearch` interface have the same semantics and use the same search filters as described in this chapter.

How LDAP Processes Search Filters

LDAP uses the mechanisms defined by the X.511 when evaluating a search filter against an object in the directory. Specifically, each search filter (and component of a search filter) must yield a result of TRUE, FALSE, or UNDEFINED. LDAP searches will return the attributes of an object only if the result of evaluating the search filter against that object is TRUE.

For instance, when LDAP evaluates the filter expression "givenName=Bob" against Bob Kelly's User object, the result is TRUE. When LDAP evaluates the filter "givenName=Waldo" against Bob Kelly's User object, the result is FALSE. And when LDAP evaluates the filter "givenGnome=Bob" against Bob Kelly's User object, the result is UNDEFINED. If Bob Kelly's User object has no givenName attribute, the result is also UNDEFINED. If you do not have sufficient access rights to read the givenName attribute of Bob Kelly's User object, the result is also UNDEFINED.

> **NOTE**
>
> If you specify a bogus attribute name in an LDAP search filter, the search operation will succeed, but the LDAP search might not return any objects.

The Full LDAP Search Filter Syntax

The full syntax of an LDAP search filter is given in section 4.5.1 of RFC 2251. The following extended Backus-Naur Form description comes from that document.

```
Filter ::= CHOICE {
            and                 [0] SET OF Filter,
            or                  [1] SET OF Filter,
            not                 [2] Filter,
            equalityMatch       [3] AttributeValueAssertion,
            substrings          [4] SubstringFilter,
            greaterOrEqual      [5] AttributeValueAssertion,
            lessOrEqual         [6] AttributeValueAssertion,
            present             [7] AttributeDescription,
            approxMatch         [8] AttributeValueAssertion,
            extensibleMatch     [9] MatchingRuleAssertion
    }

    SubstringFilter ::= SEQUENCE {
        type    AttributeDescription,
        SEQUENCE OF CHOICE {
            initial         [0] LDAPString,
            any             [1] LDAPString,
            final           [2] LDAPString
        }
    }
```

```
AttributeValueAssertion ::= SEQUENCE {
        attributeDesc   AttributeDescription,
        attributeValue  AttributeValue
}

MatchingRuleAssertion ::= SEQUENCE {
        matchingRule    [1] MatchingRuleID OPTIONAL,
        type            [2] AttributeDescription OPTIONAL,
        matchValue      [3] AssertionValue,
        dnAttributes    [4] BOOLEAN DEFAULT FALSE
}

AttributeDescription ::= LDAPString

AttributeValue ::= OCTET STRING

MatchingRuleID ::= LDAPString

AssertionValue ::= OCTET STRING

LDAPString ::= OCTET STRING
```

From this syntax description, you can see that a search filter is one of the following, possibly ANDed or ORed with other search filters:

- An equality match
- A substring match
- A greater-than comparison
- A less-than comparison
- An attribute-present test
- An approximate-match test
- An extensible-match test

To construct any of these filters, you specify an attribute name to test, an operator symbol such as = or <=, and a match value to compare the attribute with. The following sections describe exactly how you do this for different kinds of attributes.

LDAP Matching Rules

LDAP uses *matching rules* to determine how to compare an attribute value to a search filter. Each attribute syntax used by Active Directory has at least one matching rule defined for it. That means you can search for objects in Active Directory using any attribute as selection criteria. Each matching rule has a name and an OID that uniquely identifies it. A matching rule can define an equality match or an ordering match (less than or greater than), or both.

LDAPv3 allows the directory implementer to support additional matching rules beyond those defined by RFC 2252. Microsoft has implemented two additional matching rules, which I discuss in the section "Extensible Matching."

Search Filters and Multivalued Attributes

When an LDAP search tests a multivalued attribute, it applies the filter to each value in the attribute. The filter value is considered TRUE if the filter evaluates to TRUE on any value in the attribute.

For instance, a User object in Active Directory has a multivalued attribute called memberOf that contains the distinguished names of all the groups of which the user is a member. You can retrieve all the users that are members of the Administrators group of the megacorp.com domain with the following search filter:

```
"(&(objectClass=User)(memberOf=CN=Administrators,CN=Builtin,DC=megacorp,
➥DC=com))"
```

Even if a user is a member of multiple groups (which means the memberOf attribute has multiple values), this filter still evaluates to TRUE if one of the values is the distributed name of the Administrators group.

Specifying Attribute Names in Search Filters

To identify the attribute you want to test in a match filter, simply specify the lDAPDisplayName (not the relative distinguished name) of the attribute. For example:

```
char* pszGoodFilter = "sn=Kelly"; // Right! Uses attr ldapDisplayName

char* pszBadFilter = "Surname=Kelly"; // Wrong! Uses attr RDN
```

The first line of code specifies a filter that tests the Surname attribute (denoted by "sn") for equality with the string value "Kelly". "sn" is the ldapDisplayName for the Surname attribute.

You can also specify the attribute by giving its Object ID (OID) as given in the attributeSchema object attributeID attribute. For instance:

```
char* pszGoodFilter = "2.5.5.4=Kelly"; // Uses OID of surname attribute
```

Why would you do this? There are two reasons. First, it is possible in some LDAP implementations (though not in Active Directory) to have attributes defined in the schema that do not have an lDAPDisplayName. Second, it is possible to change the lDAPDisplayName value of attributes—for instance, to reflect local language conventions. Using the OID of the attribute insulates your code from attribute name changes.

Advanced Searching with LDAP

CHAPTER 21

503

21

ADVANCED
SEARCHING WITH
LDAP

> **TIP**
>
> In general, use the lDAPDisplay name for attributes in your search filters. It is highly unlikely that users will change the lDAPDisplayNames in their schemas, and using the lDAPDisplayName makes your code much easier to read.

The Equality Filter Operator

After you specify the attribute name in a filter, you then specify the operator you want to use. Each filter operator has a symbol that you use in the filter string. The symbol for the equality operator is, not surprisingly, the equal sign (=).

> **CAUTION**
>
> You'll notice that there are no spaces between the attribute name and the equal sign or between the equal sign and the attribute value. This is not just a convention. The *spaces are significant* in a search filter. If you put in a space, LDAP will either look for an attribute name with a space at the end of its name, or look for an object value with a space at its beginning. Likely neither exists, and your search will fail silently.
>
> For instance:
>
> ```
> char* pszGoodFilter = "sn=Kelly"; // Good! no spaces
> char* pszBadFilter = "sn = Kelly"; // Bad! Spaces are significant
> ```

The Substring Filter Operator

One very useful feature of LDAP search filters, particularly when it comes to looking up usernames, is the substring filter operator. The substring operator looks like the equality operator combined with the UNIX shell pattern-matching character, *. For instance:

```
char* pszGoodFilter1 = "sn=K*"; // Find all last names starting with K
```

This search filter would return all objects with the Surname attribute beginning with the letter K.

Note that the case of the match value might or might not be significant, depending on the matching rule in effect. This depends on the syntax of the attribute you are testing. If the attribute has the Print Case String syntax, the match value will be case sensitive. Otherwise, the case of the match string does not matter.

You can use more than one asterisk in a substring search filter. For instance:

```
char* pszGoodFilter2 = "sn=*smith*"; // Find all surnames with smith in
                                     // them
```

This filter would return objects with surnames of Smith, Smithson, Blacksmith, and Porsmithelm.

You can use the substring filter operator with all string-valued attributes, but not with integers, distinguished names, or OIDs. The following sections on filters for different attribute syntaxes will indicate whether or not you can use substring matching.

The Existence Filter Operator

Many times you merely want to determine whether an object has an attribute, without regard to its specific value. The existence filter operator lets you select objects that have any value at all for an attribute.

The syntax of the existence filter operator is similar to the equality filter operator, except that the match value is a single asterisk (*). The following filter would select objects that had any value at all for the Surname attribute:

```
char* pszGoodFilter1 = "(sn=*)"; // GOOD! Selects all objects with sn
                                 // attribute
```

All objects in Active Directory must have a value for the objectClass attribute, so if you want to select all objects in a search, regardless of their objectClass, you can use the following:

```
char* pszGoodFilter2 = "objectClass=*"; // GOOD! Selects all objects
```

The Greater-Than-Or-Equal Filter Operator

The greater-than-or-equal filter operator lets you select objects from the directory if an attribute value is greater than or equal to the filter value. The symbol for the greater-than-or-equal filter operator is >=.

```
char* pszGoodFilter = "(&(objectClass=User)(badPwdCount>=1));
```

The filter in this example would select User objects where someone specified at least one invalid password during the login process.

Advanced Searching with LDAP

CHAPTER 21

505

21

ADVANCED
SEARCHING WITH
LDAP

> **NOTE**
>
> LDAP does not define a greater-than operator. If you need to select objects with attributes that are strictly greater than some value, you have to use the AND (&), EQUAL (=), and NOT (!) operators in a compound filter. For instance:
>
>   (&(whenChanged>=19981231000000.0Z)(!(whenChanged=19981231000000.0Z)))
>
> would select objects (presumably users) with a lastLogon time after midnight on December 31, 1998. Of course, you could also write this as
>
>   (whenChanged>19990101000000.0Z)

The Less-Than-Or-Equal Filter Operator

The less-than-or-equal filter operator selects objects with attributes that are less than or equal to the filter value you specify. The symbol for the less-than-or-equal filter operator is <=.

The following filter selects all User objects that have not been changed since August 1.

```
char* pszGoodFilter =
"(&(objectClass=User)(whenChanged<=19990801000000.0Z))
```

The Approximate Match Operator

The LDAPv3 RFCs specify an "approximate match" operator that will evaluate to TRUE if the attribute value approximately matches the match value. The symbol for the approximate match filter operator is ~=.

Active Directory does not support the approximate match operator. Well, that's not exactly true. Active Directory treats the approximate match operator the same as a regular equality filter operator. The filters

```
char* pszMediocreFilter = "sn~=Kelly";
```

and

```
char* pszGoodFilter = "sn=Kelly";
```

are equivalent.

The AND Filter Operator

You can combine LDAP search filters to produce fairly sophisticated filters by using the AND, OR, and NOT filter operators. Because of the three-valued logic LDAP search filters follow, the meanings of these filters are somewhat different from what you are used to in C or C++.

The AND filter operator evaluates to TRUE if all of its filter arguments evaluate to TRUE. The AND filter operator evaluates to FALSE if any of its filter arguments evaluate to FALSE or UNDEFINED.

The syntax of the AND filter operator is as follows:

```
(&(<filter 1>)(<filter 2>)...(<filter n>))
```

You can see from this syntax that the AND filter operator doesn't just accept two arguments the way typical programming language AND operators do; the LDAP AND operator accepts an entire list of arguments.

For example, the following filter would select User objects that have a last name of Kelly and a first name of Bob.

```
char* pszGoodFilter = "(&(objectClass=User)(sn=Kelly)(givenName=Bob));
// AND filter with three arguments
```

The OR Filter Operator

The OR LDAP filter operator works in much the same way as the AND filter operator. The OR filter operator evaluates to TRUE if any one of its arguments evaluates to TRUE. It will evaluate to FALSE only if *all* of its arguments evaluate to UNDEFINED or FALSE.

The syntax of the OR filter operator is as follows:

```
(|(<filter 1>)(<filter 2>)...(<filter n>))
```

Like the AND operator, the OR filter operator accepts an arbitrary number of arguments.

The following search filter will find all User objects that have a first name of Bob, Rob, or Robert.

```
char* pszGoodFilter ="(|(givenName=Bob)(givenName=Rob)(givenName=Robert))";
// OR filter with three arguments
```

The NOT Filter Operator

The NOT filter operator reverses the sense of its single argument. If the argument of the NOT filter operator is TRUE, the result is FALSE. If the argument of the NOT filter operator is FALSE, the result is TRUE. And if the argument of the NOT filter operator is UNDEFINED, the result of the NOT filter is also UNDEFINED.

The syntax of the NOT filter operator is

```
(!(<filter>))
```

For example, the following would select User objects that have a last name not equal to Kelly.

```
char* pszGoodFilter = "(!(sn=Kelly))"; // NOT operator will select all but
                                       // Kelly
```

CAUTION

As of Windows 2000 Release Candidate 1, applying the NOT filter operator to an UNDEFINED argument results in TRUE, not UNDEFINED as indicated by the RFC. This bug might or might not be fixed in the released version of Windows 2000.

This bug can result in some truly unexpected behavior. Let's say you mistype an attribute name in a search filter that uses the NOT filter operator. For instance:

```
char* pszBadFilter = "(!(sirname=Kelly))";
// BAD! sirname is not a valid attribute name
```

The LDAP search engine in Release Candidate 1 will evaluate the subfilter (sirname=Kelly) as UNDEFINED because it does not recognize the attribute sirname (the attribute name should be sn). Because its argument is UNDEFINED, the NOT operator will incorrectly evaluate to TRUE, with the result that this filter will select all objects, including those with the Surname attribute equal to Kelly! Certainly not what one would expect.

Combining Search Filters with AND, OR, and NOT

You might have gathered from the preceding sections that you can combine filters using AND, OR, and NOT to an arbitrary level of complexity. And you would be right. There is no arbitrary limit to how deep or complicated you can make LDAP search filters.

For instance, the following filter would find all User objects in the Administrators group that had been created since July 1, 1999.

```
char* pszGoodFilter1 = "(&(objectClass=User)(memberOf=CN=Administrators,
➥CN=Builtin,DC=MegaCorp,DC=com)(whenCreated>=19990701000000.0Z));
```

The next filter would select all User objects whose first name is Bob, Rob, or Robert and who are members of the Administrators group.

```
char* pszGoodFilter2 = "(&(|(givenName=Bob)(givenName=Robert)
➥(givenName=Rob)|(memberOf=CN=Administrators,CN=Builtin,DC=MegaCorp,
➥DC=com))";
```

You can mix and match filters to your heart's content.

Specifying Match Values for String Attributes

When you construct a filter that tests a string-valued attribute such as `Surname`, specifying the match string is easy. You just specify the string normally.

```
char* pszGoodFilter="sn=Kelly"; // Kelly is string value to match
```

If you are testing a Unicode attribute, you can specify an ANSI string as the match value and the LDAP libraries will do the right thing.

Whether or not the case is significant depends on the matching rule in effect, which in turn depends on the syntax of the attribute you are testing. If the attribute has the `Printable Case String` syntax (`attributeSyntax 2.5.5.5`), the case of the match string will be significant; otherwise, the case doesn't matter.

Specifying Match Values for Distinguished Name Attributes

There are many times where you want to see whether an attribute contains a particular distinguished name. The most popular case is to see whether a Group object contains a particular username, or a `User` object's `memberOf` attribute contains a particular group name.

When you specify the match value for a distinguished name attribute, you must specify the entire distinguished name. You can't use the substring matching operators or use the relative distinguished name. For instance:

```
char* pszGoodFilter = "(member=CN=Bob Kelly,CN=Users,DC=Megacorp,DC=com)";
// GOOD! Filter value has entire DN

char* pszBadFilter1 = "(member=CN=Bob Kelly)"; // BAD! uses RDN

char* pszBadFilter2 = "(member=CN=Bob*)"; // BAD! uses substring match
```

The case of the match string is not important. For instance, both of these filters will match Bob Kelly if his DN is in the `member` attribute.

```
char* pszGoodFilter1 = "(member=CN=bob
➥kelly,cn=users,dc=megacorp,dc=com)";   // GOOD! Lowercase is ok
char* pszGoodFilter1 = "(member=CN=BOB
➥KELLY,CN=USERS,DC=MEGACORP,DC=COM)";   // GOOD! Uppercase is ok too
```

Specifying Object ID (OID) Match Values

There are several attributes in Active Directory that have the OID syntax. All are associated with the Schema in some way. For instance, the `attributeSyntax` attribute of the `attributeSchema` object specifies the syntax of an attribute, and the `mustContain` and `mayContain` attributes of the `classSchema` object contain OIDs of the attributes the class must and may contain, respectively.

When you specify an OID string, you simply give it as a string of digits separated by dots. For instance:

```
char* = pszGoodFilter1 = "(mayContain=1.2.840.113556.1.2.459)";
// GOOD! Filter value specifies OID string
```

The preceding filter string, when applied to the Schema container, would match on all of the `classSchema` objects that can have the `networkAddress` attribute (`1.2.840.113556.1.2.459` being the `attributeID` of the `networkAddress` schema object).

In the cases where the object identified by the OID also has an `lDAPDisplayName` attribute, you can use `lDAPDisplayName` instead of the OID. The following filter is effectively the same as the previous one:

```
char* = pszGoodFilter2 = "(mayContain=networkAddress)";
// GOOD! Filter value specifies lDAPDisplayName string
```

This works out nicely because by default, LDAP will return attributes that have the OID syntax in `lDAPDisplayName` format. So, as far as LDAP programs are concerned, attributes that have OID syntax really act as string attributes containing names instead of OIDs.

Dealing with OID-syntax attributes as strings works pretty well, except for one thing. You can't use substring matching on OID attributes.

```
char* = pszBadFilter = "(mayContain=network*)";
// BAD! Filter value specifies substring match
```

In the cases where the object the OID refers to is not part of the directory (for instance, the `attributeSyntax` attribute refers to the syntax of an attribute, which is not represented by an object in the directory), you have to use the OID string in the filter match value.

Specifying Integer Match Values

When you want to test an integer-valued attribute, you just specify the integer match value as a decimal string in your search filter. For instance, to search for `User` objects that have had five or more invalid logon attempts, you could use the following filter:

```
char* pszGoodFilter = "(&(objectClass=user)(padPwdCount>=5))";
// GOOD! Integer specified as string
```

Not surprisingly, you can't use the substring operators with integer match values. For instance, the following search filter is not valid.

```
char* pszBadFilter1 = "(&(objectClass=user)(padPwdCount=1*))";
// BAD! Can't use substring match with integer
```

Active Directory stores integer-syntax attributes as 32-bit unsigned integers, but you can write your search filters using either signed or unsigned values. For instance, if the badPwdCount attribute of a user was 2147483650 (which is 0x80000002 in hex, a negative signed value), you could retrieve the User object with both of the following filters.

```
char* pszGoodFilter1 = "(&(objectClass=user)(badPwdCount=2147483650))";
// GOOD! Unsigned value matches
```

```
char* pszGoodFilter2 = "(&(objectClass=user)(badPwdCount=-2147483646))";
// GOOD! Signed value matches too
```

> **NOTE**
>
> Active Directory stores all Integer syntax values as 32-bit unsigned integers, but when you retrieve an Integer value, Active Directory will return it as a string formatted as a signed 32-bit integer. So, you can store the value 2147483650 (which is 0x80000002 in hex), but what you will get back is -2147483646.

Specifying Large Integer Match Values

Specifying a match value for a large integer attribute is exactly the same as specifying a match value for a regular integer. The only difference is that you can specify larger numbers.

Just as with regular integers, you cannot use substring matching or negative match values with large integers.

Here is a bit of code to find the User objects that are about to expire. Note that in this case, the attribute we are testing contains a DSTIME, the number of seconds since January 1, 1601. Active Directory stores DSTIMEs as 64-bit integers using the Large Integer syntax.

```
FILETIME sNow;

GetSystemTimeAsFileTime( &sNow ); // get current time into FILETIME
__int64 nNow = *( __int64* )&sNow; // copy to large integer
nNowPlusAWeek = nNow + ( 7 * 86400 ); // add a weeks worth of seconds

char szFilter[ 256 ];
sprintf( szFilter, "(&(objectClass=user)(accountExpires>=%I64d))",
➥nNowPlusAWeek );
```

Advanced Searching with LDAP

CHAPTER 21

511

21

ADVANCED
SEARCHING WITH
LDAP

Specifying Boolean Match Values

Boolean values are easy to search for. There are only two values for which you can test, TRUE and FALSE, so the syntax for specifying Boolean match values is pretty simple. For instance, the following would select all the critical system objects.

```
char* pszGoodFilter1 = "(criticalSystemObject=TRUE)";
// GOOD! Specifies attribute match on TRUE
```

Testing a Boolean attribute for a FALSE value works the same way:

```
char* pszGoodFilter2 = "(criticalSystemObject=FALSE)";
// GOOD! Specifies attribute match on FALSE
```

You can't use substring matching on Boolean attributes, so the following is not valid:

```
char* pszBadFilter1 = "(criticalSystemObject=F*)";
// BAD! Can't use substring match on Boolean attr
```

More importantly, you have to specify TRUE or FALSE using all uppercase letters. Lowercase true or mixed-case True will not work. The following is an invalid search filter.

```
char* pszBadFilter2 = "(criticalSystemObject=False)";
// BAD! Have to use FALSE, not False
```

Specifying DN-With-String Match Values

The DN-With-String syntax stores a distinguished name reference to another directory object, along with a string value that you specify. Active Directory keeps the distinguished name up-to-date, even though the object it refers to is moved or renamed.

You can use the equality filter operator to search for objects with a specific distinguished name and string value. The following search filter searches for objects with a specific value of the (fictitious) userLink attribute.

```
char* pszGoodFilter = "userLink=cn=Bob Kelly,cn=users,dc=megacorp,dc=com:
➥S:xyzzy"; // GOOD! Specifies full DN and string
```

You cannot search for DN-With-String attributes using either of the inequality operators or the substring matching operator.

```
char* pszBadFilter1 = "userLink=Bob*:S:xyzzy";
// BAD! Can't use substring match operator

char* pszBadFilter2 = "userLink>=cn=Bob Kelly,cn=users,dc=megacorp,
➥dc=com:S:xyzzy"; // BAD! Can't use greater than or equal operator
```

Specifying Binary Match Values

One of the really nice things about LDAP is that you can handle almost all attribute values as strings. The LDAP specification stops just short of requiring a string representation for all syntaxes. Treating everything as a string makes creating search filters much easier. But what about those attributes that don't have a string representation? How do you look up a User object given its Security ID (SID), a binary structure?

RFC 2254 describes how to encode LDAP search filters as NUL-terminated strings. Part of the encoding rules for filters is a scheme for escaping metacharacters—characters that are part of the search filter syntax, such as * and (—and nonprinting characters. To escape a character, you simply use a backslash followed by the two hex characters that represent the value of the byte. For instance, to specify a search filter that looks for a left parenthesis in a User object's Surname attribute, you would use the following:

```
char* pszGoodFilter1 = "(&(objectClass=user)(sn=*\28*))";
//28 is the hex value for a left paren
```

To search for a surname enclosed in parentheses, you would use the following:

```
char* pszGoodFilter2 = "(&(objectClass=user)(sn=\28*\29))";
//28 is the hex value for a left paren, 29 for right paren
```

If you wanted to search for the four-byte string 0x00 0x01 0x2e 0x00, the encoding would be

```
char* pszGoodFilter3 = "(someAttr=\00\01\2e\00)";
```

To find a streetAddress with an asterisk in it, you would use the following search filter:

```
char* pszGoodFilter4 = "(streetAddress=*\2a*)"; // 2a is hex value for
                                                 // asterisk
```

The Microsoft LDAP library also provides a way for encoding binary match values into strings so that you can use them in an LDAP search filter. The function ldap_escape_filter_element() does the trick.

```
ULONG ldap_escape_filter_element( PCHAR sourceFilterElement,
➥ULONG sourceLength, PCHAR destFilterElement, ULONG destLength )
```

sourceFilterElement is a pointer to the binary data you want to use as a filter match value.

sourceLength is the size, in bytes, of the binary data.

destFilterElement is a pointer to a buffer into which the function will store the encoded binary data as a NUL-terminated string. If this pointer is NULL, the function will not encode any data but will return the size of the filter buffer required.

destLength is the size in bytes of the buffer destFilterElement points to. The function will not write more than this number of bytes to the buffer.

Returns: The LDAP error code, if any, or LDAP_SUCCESS if the function succeeded. If you specified NULL for destFilterElement, the return value will be the number of bytes required for the destination filter buffer.

The following piece of code looks up a User object in the directory given its GUID.

```
GUID guidUser; // assume this has been assigned a value somehow

char szGuidString[ ( 3 * sizeof GUID ) + 1 ]; // 3 chars per byte + NUL
➡ULONG uBytesUsed = ldap_escape_filter_element( &guidUser, sizeof
➡( guidUser ),pszGuidString, uBytesNeeded + 1 ); // encode the guid

char szFilter[ 4096 ]; // should be big enough
sprintf( szFilter, "(&(objectClass=user)(objectGuid=%s))",
➡pszGuidString );

LDAPMessage* pMsg;
ULONG uErr = ldap_search_s( pLdap, LDAP_SEARCH_BASE, szFilter, NULL,
➡false, &pMsg );
```

You can also search for users by Security ID (SID). The basic strategy is the same as for searching for a user by GUID. The only difference is that the SID is of variable length. In this sample, we'll call `ldap_escape_filter_element()` twice—first to find out how big the buffer needs to be, and then to actually encode the SID.

```
PSID pSID; // assume this has been assigned a value somehow
ULONG uBytesNeeded = ldap_escape_filter_element( ( char* )pSID,
➡GetLengthSid( pSID ), NULL, 0 );
char* pszSidString = new char[ uBytesNeeded + 1 ]; // +1 for NUL
ULONG uBytesUsed = = ldap_escape_filter_element( ( char* )pSID,
➡GetLengthSid( pSID ), pszSidString, uBytesNeeded + 1 ); // encode the SID
char szFilter[ 4096 ]; // should be big enough
sprintf( szFilter, "(&(objectClass=user)(objectSid=%s))", pszSidString );
LDAPMessage* pMsg;
ULONG uErr = ldap_search_s( pLdap, LDAP_SEARCH_BASE, szFilter, NULL,
➡false, &pMsg );
```

Extensible Matching

LDAPv3 defines an extensible-match mechanism that lets you choose the matching rule you want to apply in a search filter. This lets you, for instance, perform case-insensitive matches on case-sensitive string attributes.

The extensible-match mechanism even allows the directory implementer (in this case, Microsoft) to define new matching rules that go beyond the scope of the basic matching rules defined in the LDAP RFCs.

Each matching rule is identified by a unique Object ID (OID). The built-in matching rules (integer, case-sensitive string, and so forth) have their OIDs defined by the X.500 specification or the LDAP RFCs. Directory vendors assign their own OIDs to new matching rules.

The syntax to use an extensible match filter in a search looks like this:

`<attribute name>[":dn"][":"<match rule OID>]":="<match value>`

or

`[":dn"]":"<match rule OID>":="<match value>`

> `<attribute name>` is the name of the attribute to match.
>
> `":dn"` indicates that LDAP should apply the matching rule to the attributes of the distinguished name of the object as well as the attribute specified by `<attribute type>`.
>
> `<match rule OID>` is the OID of the matching rule to apply.
>
> `<match value>` is the match value to compare with the attribute value.

The second form does not contain an attribute name; it causes LDAP to apply the specified matching rule to all the attributes of the object that support the matching rule.

CAUTION

As of Windows 2000 Release Candidate 1, Active Directory does not fully support extensible matching rules. In particular, you cannot use the `":dn"` syntax to include the attributes of the object's distinguished name in the match. You also cannot specify any of the standard matching rules; you can use only the two nonstandard matching rules for bitwise AND and bitwise OR matching.

This behavior might or might not be fixed by the time Windows 2000 actually ships.

Here are some examples of search filters using the extensible match facility:

```
char* pszGoodFilter1 = "(&(objectClass=User)(sn:2.5.13.2:=Kelly))";
//GOOD! Case-insensitive tests for sn="Kelly";
```

This filter would select all the User objects whose Surname attribute contained Kelly, kelly, KELLY, and so forth.

```
char* pszGoodFilter2 = (&(objectClass=User)(cn:dn: 2.5.13.4:=*bob*))
```

This filter would select all the User objects whose common name (cn) or distinguished name contained the word bob.

Searching for Bit-Field Attributes

There are many attributes in Active Directory that are stored as integers but are actually bit masks. For instance, the `userAccountControl` attribute of a `User` object contains various flags that describe the user account. The `systemFlags` attribute of any directory object contains bits that describe the state of that object.

The problem is that because these attributes are stored as integers, there is no reasonable way to search for objects with a particular bit set. To test for a `userAccountControl` attribute with the account disabled bit (`0x02`) flag set, you would have to write something like this:

```
(&(objectClass=User)(|(userAccountControl=2)(userAccountControl=3)
➥(userAccountControl=6)(userAccountControl=7)...
```

You get the idea. It's basically not workable.

To solve this problem, Microsoft has created two extensible matching rules for matching bit-mask attributes: the bitwise `AND` and bitwise `OR` matching rules.

Using the Bitwise OR Matching Rule

The OID for the bitwise `OR` matching rule is `1.2.840.113556.1.4.804`. When you use the bitwise `OR` matching rule, you specify the attribute you want to match, the matching rule OID, and a bit mask value to match. The bitwise `OR` matching rule will evaluate to `TRUE` for an object if the object has the attribute you specified, and *any one of* the bits in your bit mask match value is set in the object's attribute.

Let's look at the previous example of testing the `userAccountControl` attribute for the account disabled bit. Using the bitwise `OR` matching rule, the search filter would look like this:

```
(&(objectClass=User)(userAccountControl:1.2.840.113556.1.4.804:=2))
```

This filter will evaluate to `TRUE` for each object that is of class `User` and has the account disabled bit set in its `userAccountControl` attribute. Note that the match value is expressed in decimal. You can't use hexadecimal notation in LDAP search filters, so you always have to convert your match values to decimal.

If you want to search for all `User` objects that have either the account disabled bit set, the lockout bit set (`0x10`), or the can't change password bit set (`0x40`), first `OR` the masks together to get `0x52`, and then convert the hexadecimal value to decimal, which gives us 82. The search filter would then look like this:

```
(&(objectClass=User)(userAccountControl:1.2.840.113556.1.4.804:=82))
```

This search filter would evaluate to TRUE if the User object had set the account disabled bit, the lockout bit, or the can't change password bit in the userAccountControl attribute.

Using the Bitwise AND Matching Rule

The OID for the bitwise AND matching rule is 1.2.840.113556.1.4.803. When you use the bitwise AND matching rule, you specify the attribute you want to match, the matching rule OID, and a bit mask value to match. The bitwise AND matching rule will evaluate to TRUE for an object if the object has the attribute you specified, and *all* the bits in your bit mask match value are set in the object's attribute. Note that the bitwise AND and bitwise OR matching rules behave identically if you are only testing for a single bit.

Let's try a different example this time. Let's say you want to find all the Windows 2000 universal groups in the CN=Users container. Each group object has a groupType attribute that contains bits identifying the type of the group (global, domain local, local, and universal). There is an additional bit that indicates the group is a security group.

The bit value for the universal group type is 0x08, so the match value in decimal is 8. The search filter to locate all universal groups would then be

(&(objectClass=group)(groupType:1.2.840.113556.1.4.803:=8))

This filter will evaluate to TRUE for each object that is of class group and has the universal group type bit set in its groupType attribute. Note again that the match value must be expressed in decimal.

Let's try searching for all group objects that have both the global group type bit set (0x02) and the security group bit set (0x80000000). First, OR the two masks together to get 0x80000002. Then convert the mask to decimal, giving 2147483650. This gives us a search filter that looks like this:

(&(objectClass=group)(groupType:1.2.840.113556.1.4.803:=2147483650))

This search filter will evaluate to TRUE if the group object has both the global group bit and the security group bit set in the groupType attribute.

Checking the Validity of an LDAP Search Filter

One difficulty with LDAP search filters is that they are easy to screw up. The unconventional syntax, combined with the lack of white space, makes it very easy to use a filter that looks right but is really invalid.

The function ldap_check_filter() can check your filter strings and help ensure that they are at least syntactically valid.

Advanced Searching with LDAP

CHAPTER 21

517

21

ADVANCED
SEARCHING WITH
LDAP

```
ULONG ldap_check_filter( LDAP* ld, char* SearchFilter )
```

ld is a pointer to an LDAP session that has been initialized with ldap_open(),
ldap_init(), or ldap_sslinit(). The LDAP session does not have to be authenticated.

> SearchFilter is a pointer to a NUL-terminated string containing a candidate
> search filter.

Returns: An LDAP error code or LDAP_SUCCESS if the filter string is syntactically valid.

ldap_check_filter() does not check for things such as valid attribute names, valid
match values, or valid extensible matching rule OIDs. It just makes sure that your search
filter is syntactically valid. This is unfortunate, particularly because you pass a pointer to
an LDAP session to ldap_check_filter(); it could query the schema and the rootDSE
to check these things. Ah well, it's merely another cross we Active Directory LDAP programmers have to bear.

The following snippet of code calls ldap_check_filter() twice, once with a valid filter
and once with an invalid one.

```
ULONG uErr;

uErr = ldap_check_filter( pLdap, "(&(objectClass=user)
➥(userAccountControl=10))" );
// GOOD! Filter should be valid

uErr= ldap_check_filter( pLdap, "&(objectClass=User)" );
// BAD! Missing AND clause
```

Asynchronous LDAP Searches

The first important variation on the LDAP searches we discussed in Chapter 20,
"Searching Active Directory with LDAP," are asynchronous searches using
ldap_search(). ldap_search() does not return any search results to your program.
Instead, ldap_search() starts the search process on the LDAP server and returns a handle (called a message ID) to your program. As the LDAP server finds objects in the
directory that meet the criteria you specified, the LDAP server returns them to your program, one at a time.

If you can't get the results back through the parameter list of ldap_search(), how do
you get them back? You get them back by repeatedly calling ldap_result(), specifying
the message ID returned by ldap_search(). Figure 21.1 shows how this happens.

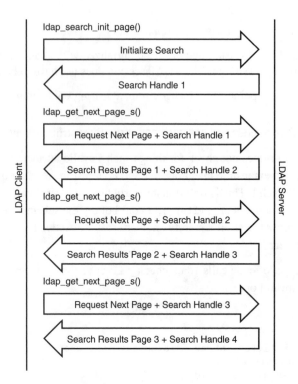

Figure 21.1

Control flow with asynchronous LDAP searches.

If you've done any multithreaded programming with the Win32 API, you might be wondering why LDAP provides special functions to do asynchronous searching. Because Win32 threads are pre-emptive, you could easily start up a separate background thread and have it call ldap_search_s(). The program's main thread could continue to do something useful while the search progressed in the background. This is true, but it misses an important distinction between synchronous and asynchronous LDAP searches. A synchronous search doesn't return until the entire search is complete, and it returns all the results at one time. Even though your program processes the search results one at a time, the LDAP client assembles the entire result set of a synchronous search in the client's memory before returning control to your program. Often this isn't a problem, but if your program is doing a search that results in thousands or millions of result objects, the amount of memory the results would require (and the time required to assemble them in memory) could be prohibitive.

Starting an Asynchronous Search

Starting an asynchronous LDAP search is essentially the same as performing a synchronous LDAP search. The parameters for `ldap_search()` and `ldap_search_s()` are quite similar.

```
ULONG ldap_search( LDAP* ld, PCHAR base, ULONG scope, PCHAR filter,
➥PCHAR attrs[], ULONG attrsonly, LDAPMessage** res )
```

> `ld` is a pointer to an LDAP structure that has been initialized with `ldap_init()`, `ldap_sslinit()`, or `ldap_open()`.
>
> `base` is a pointer to a NUL-terminated string that specifies the distinguished name of the starting object for the search.
>
> `scope` indicates the depth of the search and is one of the following: `LDAP_SCOPE_BASE`, `LDAP_SCOPE_ONELEVEL`, or `LDAP_SCOPE_SUBTREE`.
>
> `filter` is a pointer to a NUL-terminated string that contains the search filter. It cannot be `NULL` or a pointer to an empty string.

> **NOTE**
>
> If you want to retrieve all objects in a search, don't specify a NULL search filter or an empty string. The simplest way to indicate that you want all objects is to use the filter `objectClass=*`, which indicates that you want all objects that have an attribute named `objectClass`. All objects in Active Directory have an attribute named `objectClass`, so the search will return all objects in the scope you specified.

> `attrs` is an array of pointers to a NUL-terminated string containing attribute names, terminated with a NULL pointer. The search will return these attributes for each object, if they exist. You can specify `NULL` to indicate that you want to retrieve all attributes for each object satisfying the search filter.

> **NOTE**
>
> Specifying NULL for the list of attributes in a search will return all the normal attributes for an object; it will not return operational attributes. To obtain operational attributes, you have to specify them explicitly.

`attrsonly` is a Boolean value that determines whether the search will return attribute values or not. If `attrsonly` is set to 1, the search will return only the names of the attributes satisfying the search filter. If `attrsonly` is set to 0, the search will return the attribute names and values.

Returns: An integer search handle that you use with `ldap_result()` to retrieve the search results. A return value of -1 indicates an error.

> ### NOTE
>
> The Microsoft version of the LDAP APIs defines `ldap_search()` as returning an unsigned long value (as do almost all the Microsoft LDAP functions). The draft LDAP API standard defines the return value as an integer. Because -1 is defined as the error return for `ldap_search()`, you will have to cast the result before checking it.

The following sample code starts an asynchronous LDAP search to retrieve every item in the `megacorp.com` domain.

```
ULONG uMsgID = ldap_search(
    pLdap,                  // LDAP session
    "DC=megacorp,DC=com",   // search base
    LDAP_SCOPE_SUBTREE,     // search scope
    "objectClass=*",        // all objects
    NULL,                   // which attributes
    false                   // attrs only?
);
if( uMsgID != -1 )
{
    // check for search results
}
```

Processing Asynchronous Search Results

After you start an asynchronous search, you need to check for incoming results. To do this, you call `ldap_result()` from within a loop, processing whatever results have come in since the previous call to `ldap_result()`.

When the directory service sends back results for your search, it can send back several kinds of result messages:

- A search entry that contains one or more objects.
- A search result indicating there are no more objects to be returned.

- A referral indicating that you must perform the search on another naming context. If referral chasing by the client is enabled (it is by default), you will not receive a referral message; the LDAP client software will chase the referral for you.

You obtain the returned results by repeatedly calling `ldap_result()`. Even though you write your code as if you were polling for results on the server, `ldap_result()` doesn't generate any network traffic; it simply checks the local result buffer to see whether results have come in.

```
ULONG ldap_result( LDAP* ld, ULONG msgid, ULONG all,
➥struct l_timeval* timeout, LDAPMessage** res )
```

> `ld` is a pointer to an LDAP structure that has been initialized with `ldap_init()`, `ldap_sslinit()`, or `ldap_open()`. It must be the same LDAP structure that you used to start the search.

> `msgid` is the handle to the search that was returned by `ldap_search()`. If you specify `LDAP_RES_ANY`, `ldap_result()` will return results for any outstanding asynchronous operation that were started on the LDAP session given by `ld`.

> `all` specifies how many of the result objects you want returned. It must be one of three constants defined in WINLDAP.H:

Constant	Description
LDAP_MSG_ONE	Indicates that `ldap_result()` should return a single search result object.
LDAP_MSG_ALL	Indicates that `ldap_results()` should wait until all the search results have been received from the server. (This is essentially the same as performing a synchronous search with `ldap_search_s()`.)
LDAP_MSG_RECEIVED	Indicates that `ldap_results()` should return all the result objects that have been received so far.

> If you specify `LDAP_MSG_ALL` or `LDAP_MSG_RECEIVED`, `ldap_result()` will actually return the first message in a list of messages. You then need to use `ldap_first_entry()` and `ldap_next_entry()` to iterate the list.

> `timeout` is a pointer to an `l_timeval` structure that contains the timeout value for the `ldap_result()` call. If there are no messages to retrieve within the time specified by the `l_timeval` structure, `ldap_result()` will return a 0.

> `res` is the address of an `LdapMessage` pointer to be set by `ldap_result()`. This pointer must be freed by passing it to `ldap_msgfree()` after you are done with it.

Returns: The type of the message retrieved. There are eleven possible returned messages. Only the first three, `LDAP_RES_SEARCH_ENTRY`, `LDAP_RES_SEARCH_RESULT`, and `LDAP_RES_REFERRAL` will be returned as the result of a search operation.

`LDAP_RES_SEARCH_ENTRY` indicates the message is an object returned in response to an LDAP search request. If you did not specify `LDAP_MSG_ONE`, you should parse the message using `ldap_first_entry()` and `ldap_next_entry()`.

`LDAP_RES_SEARCH_RESULT` indicates the search is complete. If you did not specify `LDAP_MSG_ONE`, you should parse the message using `ldap_first_entry()` and `ldap_next_entry()`.

`LDAP_RES_REFERRAL` indicates the message contains one or more referrals to other naming contexts.

`0` indicates the call to `ldap_result()` timed out. This means there were no results sent from the server within the timeout period. You should retry the call to `ldap_result()`.

`-1` indicates an error of some sort. Call `LdapGetLastError()` to get the corresponding error code. You should not call `ldap_result()` after receiving an error.

The following code snippet shows how you would typically use `ldap_result()` to get and process the results of an asynchronous LDAP search. Note that, in this example, the code uses the `LDAP_MSG_ONE` parameter to make sure that we process one search result at a time. This will simplify your code substantially. Listing 21.1 uses `LDAP_MSG_RECEIVED`, and you can see how the code for processing the asynchronous results becomes more complicated.

LISTING 21.1   USING `ldap_search()`, `ldap_result()`, AND `LDAP_MSG_ONE`

```
1:   #include <windows.h>
2:   #include <winldap.h>
3:   #include <iostream.h>
4:
5:   int main( int argc, char** argv )
6:   {
7:       LDAP* psLdap = ldap_init( NULL, LDAP_PORT );
8:       if( psLdap != NULL )
9:       {
10:          ULONG uErr = ldap_bind_s( psLdap, NULL, NULL,
            ➥LDAP_AUTH_NEGOTIATE );
11:          if( uErr == LDAP_SUCCESS )
12:          {
13:              ULONG uMsgID = ldap_search(
14:                  psLdap,                    // LDAP session
15:                  "CN=Users,DC=megacorp,DC=com",  // search base
16:                  LDAP_SCOPE_ONELEVEL,   // search scope
17:                  "objectClass=*",       // all objects
18:                  NULL,                  // which attributes
19:                  false                  // attrs only?
20:              );
```

21

```
21:
22:                     if( uMsgID != -1 )
23:                     {
24:                         // check for search results
25:                         LDAP_TIMEVAL sTimeout = { 1, 0 };
                            // one-second timeout for ldap_result()
26:
27:                         bool bDone = false;
28:                         while( ! bDone )
29:                         {
30:                             LDAPMessage* psMsg;
31:
32:                             // Poll for result
33:                             ULONG uResult = ldap_result( psLdap, uMsgID,
                            ➥LDAP_MSG_ONE, &sTimeout, &psMsg );
34:
35:                             switch( uResult )
36:                             {
37:                                 char* pszDN;
38:
39:                                 case 0: // timeout, just continue
40:                                     break;
41:
42:                                 case 0xffffffff: // error, just ignore for now
43:                                     cout << "Error " << LdapGetLastError() <<
                                    ➥endl;
44:                                     bDone = true;
45:                                     break;
46:
47:                                 case LDAP_RES_SEARCH_ENTRY:
48:                                     pszDN = ldap_get_dn( psLdap, psMsg );
                                    // get the object's DN
49:                                     cout << "Search returned: " << pszDN <<
                                    ➥endl;
50:                                     ldap_msgfree( psMsg ); // free the message
51:                                     break;
52:
53:                                 case LDAP_RES_SEARCH_RESULT:
54:                                     cout << "End of search" << endl;
55:                                     ldap_msgfree( psMsg );
                                    // no more items, free the message
56:                                     bDone = true;
57:                                     break;
58:
59:                                 case LDAP_RES_REFERRAL:
60:                                     cout << "Got a referral" << endl;
61:                                     ldap_msgfree( psMsg );
                                    // shouldn't happen by default
62:                                     break;
63:
```

continues

LISTING 21.1   CONTINUED

```
64:                             default:
65:                                 cout << "Unexpected search result "
                                   ➥<< uResult << endl;
66:                                 bDone = true;
67:                                 break;
68:                         }
69:                     }
70:                 }
71:             }
72:
73:         ldap_unbind( psLdap );
74:     }
75:
76:     return 0;
77: }
```

The program in Listing 21.1 starts by calling ldap_init() at line 7 to initialize the LDAP session, and then calls ldap_bind_s() at line 10 to authenticate as the currently logged-in user.

At line 13, the program starts an asynchronous search of the Users container by calling ldap_search(). uMsgID contains the message ID that the program uses later with ldap_result().

If the search was started successfully (uMsgID is not equal to -1), the program enters a while loop at line 28 and will exit the loop when the bDone flag is set to TRUE. Each time through the loop, the program calls ldap_result() to retrieve another entry from the search results.

At line 33, the program calls ldap_result(), specifying LDAP_RES_ONE so that it will retrieve one result entry at a time. uResult contains the type of entry returned.

The switch statement at line 35 switches on the type of message retrieved.

If the uResult is 0, ldap_result() timed out and the loop continues around to try again.

If uResult is 0xffffffff (-1), there was some sort of error and the program sets the bDone flag to exit the loop.

If uResult is LDAP_RES_SEARCH_ENTRY, the program gets the distinguished name for the entry and prints it. It then frees the message structure by calling ldap_msgfree().

If uResult is LDAP_RES_SEARCH_RESULT, the search is complete, and the program sets the bDone flag to exit the loop.

Advanced Searching with LDAP

CHAPTER 21

525

21

ADVANCED
SEARCHING WITH
LDAP

If uResult is LDAP_RES_REFERRAL, the program prints an error and sets the bDone flag to exit the loop. This program should never get LDAP_RES_REFERRAL because the LDAP client will chase them by default.

The program wraps up at line 73 by calling ldap_unbind() to close the LDAP session.

Listing 21.2 shows how you would typically process asynchronous search results use the LDAP_MSG_RECEIVED parameter. Note that when you get a return value of LDAP_RES_SEARCH_ENTRY, you may have received several entries at once, and you have to enumerate them with ldap_first_entry()/ldap_next_entry(). Likewise, if you get a return value of LDAP_RES_SEARCH_RESULT, indicating the end of the search, the final result message may contain more search entries that you have to enumerate with ldap_first_entry() and ldap_next_entry().

LISTING 21.2 USING ldap_search(), ldap_result(), AND LDAP_MSG_RECEIVED

```
1:    #include <windows.h>
2:    #include <winldap.h>
3:    #include <iostream.h>
4:
5:    int main( int argc, char** argv )
6:    {
7:        LDAP* psLdap = ldap_init( NULL, LDAP_PORT );
8:        if( psLdap != NULL )
9:        {
10:           ULONG uErr = ldap_bind_s( psLdap, NULL, NULL,
             ➥LDAP_AUTH_NEGOTIATE );
11:           if( uErr == LDAP_SUCCESS )
12:           {
13:               ULONG uMsgID = ldap_search(
14:                   psLdap,                      // LDAP session
15:                   "CN=Users,DC=megacorp,DC=com", // search base
16:                   LDAP_SCOPE_ONELEVEL,    // search scope
17:                   "objectClass=*",        // all objects
18:                   NULL,                   // which attributes
19:                   false                   // attrs only?
20:               );
21:
22:               if( uMsgID != -1 )
23:               {
24:                   // check for search results
25:                   LDAP_TIMEVAL sTimeout = { 1, 0 };
                      // one second timeout for ldap_result()
26:
27:                   bool bDone = false;
28:                   while( ! bDone )
29:                   {
30:                       LDAPMessage* psMsg;
31:
```

continues

LISTING 21.2   CONTINUED

```
32:                     // Poll for result
33:                     ULONG uResult = ldap_result( psLdap, uMsgID,
                    ➥LDAP_MSG_RECEIVED, &sTimeout, &psMsg );
34:
35:                     switch( uResult )
36:                     {
37:                         char* pszDN;
38:
39:                         case 0: // timeout, just continue
40:                             break;
41:
42:                         case 0xffffffff: // error, just ignore for now
43:                             cout << "Error " << LdapGetLastError() <<
                            ➥endl;
44:                             bDone = true;
45:                             break;
46:
47:                         case LDAP_RES_SEARCH_ENTRY:
48:                             {
49:                                 cout << "Got an entry" << endl;
50:                                 for( LDAPMessage* psEntry =
                                ➥ldap_first_entry( psLdap, psMsg );
51:                                     psEntry != NULL;
52:                                     psEntry = ldap_next_entry
                                    ➥( psLdap, psEntry ) )
53:                                 {
54:                                     pszDN = ldap_get_dn( psLdap,
                                    ➥psEntry );
                                     // get the object's DN
55:                                     cout << "Search returned: "
                                    ➥<< pszDN << endl;
56:                                 }
57:
58:                                 ldap_msgfree( psMsg ); // free the
                                                        // message
59:                             }
60:                             break;
61:
62:                         case LDAP_RES_SEARCH_RESULT:
63:                             {
64:                                 cout << "End of search" << endl;
65:                                 for( LDAPMessage* psEntry =
                                ➥ldap_first_entry( psLdap, psMsg );
66:                                     psEntry != NULL;
67:                                     psEntry = ldap_next_entry
                                    ➥( psLdap, psEntry ) )
68:                                 {
69:                                     pszDN = ldap_get_dn( psLdap,
                                    ➥psEntry );
```

Advanced Searching with LDAP

CHAPTER 21

527

21

**ADVANCED
SEARCHING WITH
LDAP**

```
                                           // get the object's DN
70:                                        cout << "Search returned: "
                                         ➡<< pszDN << endl;
71:                                    }
72:
73:                                    ldap_msgfree( psMsg );
                                       // free the message
74:                                }
75:
76:                                bDone = true;
77:                                break;
78:
79:                            case LDAP_RES_REFERRAL:
80:                                cout << "Got a referral" << endl;
81:                                ldap_msgfree( psMsg );
                                   // shouldn't happen by default
82:                                break;
83:
84:                            default:
85:                                cout << "Unexpected search result "
                                 ➡<< uResult << endl;
86:                                bDone = true;
87:                                break;
88:                        }
89:                    }
90:                }
91:            }
92:
93:        ldap_unbind( psLdap );
94:    }
95:
96:    return 0;
97: }
```

The program in Listing 21.2 calls ldap_init() at line 7 to initialize the LDAP session, and calls ldap_bind_s() at line 10 to authenticate as the currently logged-in user.

At line 13, the program starts an asynchronous search of the Users container by calling ldap_search(). uMsgID contains the message ID that the program uses later with ldap_result().

If the search was started successfully (uMsgID is not equal to -1), the program enters a while loop at line 28 and will exit the loop when the bDone flag is set to TRUE. Each time through the loop, the program calls ldap_result() to retrieve another entry from the search results.

At line 33, the program calls ldap_result(), specifying LDAP_RES_ONE so that it will retrieve one result entry at a time. uResult contains the type of entry returned.

The switch statement at line 35 switches on the type of message retrieved.

If the uResult is 0, ldap_result() timed out and the loop continues around to try again.

If uResult is 0xffffffff (-1), there was some sort of error and the program sets the bDone flag to exit the loop.

If uResult is LDAP_RES_SEARCH_ENTRY, the program received one or more result entries that the program enumerates using ldap_first_entry() and ldap_next_entry(). For each entry, the program gets the distinguished name for the entry and prints it. It then frees the message structure by calling ldap_msgfree().

If uResult is LDAP_RES_SEARCH_RESULT, the program received one or more result entries, including the last result entry for the search. The program enumerates the entries using ldap_first_entry() and ldap_next_entry(). For each entry, the program gets the distinguished name for the entry and prints it. It then frees the message structure by calling ldap_msgfree(). The program sets the bDone flag to exit the loop.

If uResult is LDAP_RES_REFERRAL, the program prints an error and sets the bDone flag to exit the loop. This program should never get LDAP_RES_REFERRAL because the LDAP client will chase them by default.

The program wraps up at line 93 by calling ldap_unbind() to close the LDAP session.

Abandoning an Asynchronous Search

Sometimes you need to cancel an asynchronous search when you are in the middle of processing search results. One way to do this is to kill the LDAP session by calling ldap_unbind(). But then you have to re-create the LDAP session with the server, which is expensive and error-prone.

You can also call the ldap_abandon() function. This function accepts an LDAP session pointer and a message ID as returned from a call to ldap_search(). After a successful call to ldap_abandon, you are guaranteed that your asynchronous search will not receive any more search results.

```
ULONG ldap_abandon( LDAP* ld, ULONG msgid )
```

> ld is a pointer to the LDAP session you started the asynchronous search on.
>
> msgid is the message ID returned by the call to ldap_search().

Returns: An LDAP error code or LDAP_SUCCESS if the function completed successfully.

Listing 21.3 shows how you can abandon a search after retrieving a specific number of objects. This program keeps a count of the number of entries it has retrieved from the search. When the number exceeds a certain maximum, the program uses ldap_abandon() to terminate the search.

LISTING 21.3   USING `ldap_abandon()` TO TERMINATE AN ASYNCHRONOUS SEARCH

```
1    #include <windows.h>
2    #include <winldap.h>
3    #include <iostream.h>
4
5    int main( int argc, char** argv )
6    {
7        LDAP* psLdap = ldap_init( NULL, LDAP_PORT );
8        if( psLdap != NULL )
9        {
10           ULONG uErr = ldap_bind_s( psLdap, NULL, NULL,
            ➥LDAP_AUTH_NEGOTIATE );
11           if( uErr == LDAP_SUCCESS )
12           {
13               ULONG uMsgID = ldap_search(
14                   psLdap,                     // LDAP session
15                   "CN=Users,DC=redrock,DC=home,DC=netpro,DC=com",
                                                 // search base
16                   LDAP_SCOPE_SUBTREE,    // search scope
17                   "objectClass=*",       // all objects
18                   NULL,                  // which attributes
19                   false                  // attrs only?
20               );
21
22               if( uMsgID != -1 )
23               {
24                   // check for search results
25                   LDAP_TIMEVAL sTimeout = { 1, 0 };
                     // one second timeout for ldap_result()
26
27                   const int MAX_ENTRIES = 10;
28                   int nEntries = 0;
29
30                   bool bDone = false;
31                   while( ! bDone )
32                   {
33                       LDAPMessage* psMsg;
34
35                       // Poll for result
36                       ULONG uResult = ldap_result( psLdap, uMsgID,
                         ➥LDAP_MSG_ONE, &sTimeout, &psMsg );
37
38                       switch( uResult )
39                       {
40                           char* pszDN;
41
42                           case 0: // timeout, just continue
43                               break;
44
```

continues

LISTING 21.3   CONTINUED

```
45                              case 0xffffffff: // error, just ignore for now
46                                  cout << "Error " << LdapGetLastError() <<
                                    ➥endl;
47                                  bDone = true;
48                                  break;
49
50                              case LDAP_RES_SEARCH_ENTRY:
51
52                                  nEntries++;
53                                  pszDN = ldap_get_dn( psLdap, psMsg );
                                    // get the object's DN
54                                  cout << "Search returned: " << pszDN <<
                                    ➥endl;
55
56                                  // check if we seen enough entries
57                                  if( nEntries >= MAX_ENTRIES )
58                                  {
59                                      ldap_abandon( psLdap, uMsgID );
60                                      bDone = true;
61                                  }
62
63                                  ldap_msgfree( psMsg ); // free the message
64                                  break;
65
66                              case LDAP_RES_SEARCH_RESULT:
67                                  cout << "End of search" << endl;
68                                  ldap_msgfree( psMsg );
                                    // no more items; free the message
69                                  bDone = true;
70                                  break;
71
72                              case LDAP_RES_REFERRAL:
73                                  cout << "Got a referral" << endl;
74                                  ldap_msgfree( psMsg );
                                    // shouldn't happen by default
75                                  break;
76
77                              default:
78                                  cout << "Unexpected search result "
                                    ➥<< uResult << endl;
79                                  bDone = true;
80                                  break;
81                          }
82                      }
83                  }
84              }
85
86          ldap_unbind( psLdap );
87      }
```

```
88
89      return 0;
90  }
```

The program in Listing 21.3 starts by calling `ldap_init()` at line 7 to initialize the LDAP session and then calls `ldap_bind_s()` at line 10 to authenticate as the currently logged-in user.

At line 13, the program starts an asynchronous search of the Users container by calling `ldap_search()`. `uMsgID` contains the message ID that the program uses later with `ldap_result()`.

At line 27, the program declares the constant `MAX_ENTRIES` that is the maximum number of entries the program will retrieve. The integer `nEntries` declared at line 28 is the count of the entries retrieved so far.

If the search was started successfully (`uMsgID` is not equal to `-1`), the program enters a `while` loop at line 31 and exits the loop when the `bDone` flag is set to `TRUE`. Each time through the loop, the program calls `ldap_result()` to retrieve another entry from the search results.

At line 36, the program calls `ldap_result()`, specifying `LDAP_RES_ONE` so that it retrieves one result entry at a time. `uResult` contains the type of entry returned.

The `switch` statement at line 38 switches on the type of message retrieved.

If `uResult` is `0`, `ldap_result()` timed out and the loop continues around to try again.

If `uResult` is `0xffffffff` (`-1`), there was some sort of error and the program sets the `bDone` flag to exit the loop.

If `uResult` is `LDAP_RES_SEARCH_ENTRY`, the program gets the distinguished name for the entry, prints it, and increments the count of entries retrieved. If the count is greater than or equal to the maximum, the program calls `ldap_abandon()` at line 59 to terminate the search and sets the `bDone` flag to exit the loop. It then frees the message structure by calling `ldap_msgfree()`.

If `uResult` is `LDAP_RES_SEARCH_RESULT`, the search is complete, and the program sets the `bDone` flag to exit the loop.

If `uResult` is `LDAP_RES_REFERRAL`, the program prints an error and sets the `bDone` flag to exit the loop. This program should never get `LDAP_RES_REFERRAL` because the LDAP client will chase them by default.

The program wraps up at line 86 by calling `ldap_unbind()` to close the LDAP session.

Attribute Requests

When you search the directory for objects that meet your search criteria, you generally want to retrieve one or more of the attributes of the selected objects. As I showed in the preceding chapter, you can specify the list of attributes you want to retrieve in the ldap_search...() commands. But LDAP provides some additional capabilities with respect to retrieving attributes that I will discuss in the following sections.

Requesting All Attributes

The simplest case is when you want to retrieve all the attributes for each object that meets your selection criteria. In this case, you simply pass NULL for the attribute list to the LDAP search function. For instance:

```
ULONG uErr = ldap_search_s(
    pLdap,                  // ptr to LDAP session
    pszContainerDN,         // DN of container to search
    LDAP_SCOPE_ONELEVEL,    // scope of search
    "objectClass=*",        // select all objects
    NULL,                   // return all attributes
    false,                  // attrs only?
    &pMsg                   // result message
); // GOOD! Gets ALL attributes for selected objects
```

The NULL in the fifth parameter indicates that you want to retrieve all the attributes for each object in the container given by pszContainerDN.

> **TIP**
>
> Don't specify NULL for the list of attributes to return unless you really need all the attributes for each object. The extra network bandwidth this consumes can be substantial. Try to specify just the attributes you need.

Requesting Specific Attributes

Retrieving a specific list of attributes during a search is easy too, and we touched on it in the preceding chapter. You simply name the attributes you want in a NULL-terminated array of string pointers. For instance, this search will return the Surname and givenName attributes of a User object.

```
char* apszAttrNames[] = { "sn", "givenName", NULL };
ULONG uErr = ldap_search_s(
    pLdap,                      // LDAP session
    pszContainerDN,             // container DN
    LDAP_SCOPE_ONELEVEL,        // search scope
    "(objectClass=*)",          // search filter
    apszAttrNames,              // list of attributes
    false,                      // attrs only?
    &pMsg                       // result message
);
```

You can also name the attributes you want to retrieve by specifying the Object IDs (OIDs) for the attributes. For instance, the following search function will produce the same results as the preceding one.

```
char* apszAttrNames[] = { "2.5.4.4", "2.5.5.42", NULL };
ULONG uErr = ldap_search_s(
    pLdap,                      // LDAP session
    pszContainerDN,             // container DN
    LDAP_SCOPE_ONELEVEL,        // search scope
    "(objectClass=*)",          // search filter
    apszAttrNames,              // list of attributes
    false,                      // attrs only?
    &pMsg                       // result message
);
```

The primary reason for using OIDs instead of the lDAPDisplayNames of the attributes is to protect your programs from Active Directory administrators who change the lDAPDisplayNames of some of their attributes.

> **NOTE**
>
> Note that even when you specify the attributes to retrieve by using OIDs, LDAP returns the attributes with their lDAPDisplayNames (assuming the attributes have them). When you get the attribute values from the LDAP search results, you still have to use the lDAPDisplayNames of the attributes when you call ldap_get_values() or ldap_get_values_len().

Requesting Operational Attributes

Operational attributes are attributes defined in the schema and supported by LDAP that are not attributes in the real sense. Users don't store operational attributes (in fact, they are not writable); Active Directory instead synthesizes these attributes when needed.

Aside from not being writable, operational attributes behave just like regular attributes, except for one thing: LDAP does not return operational attributes to you in a search unless you explicitly ask for them. This behavior makes sense because operational attributes generally exist for the use of Active Directory itself, and are not generally intended for public consumption.

For instance, the following will *not* return any operational attributes:

```
ULONG uErr = ldap_search_s(
    pLdap,                    // ptr to LDAP session
    pszContainerDN,           // DN of container to search
    LDAP_SCOPE_ONELEVEL,      // scope of search
    "objectClass=*",          // select all objects
    NULL,                     // return all attributes
    false,                    // attrs only?
    &pMsg                     // result message
);    // BAD! Does not get operational attributes
```

The following code, on the other hand, will retrieve the update sequence number (USN) information for each object:

```
char* apszAttrNames[] = { "uSNChanged", "uSNCreated", NULL };

ULONG uErr = ldap_search_s(
    pLdap,                    // LDAP session
    pszContainerDN,           // container DN
    LDAP_SCOPE_ONELEVEL,      // search scope
    "(objectClass=*)",        // search filter
    apszAttrNames,            // list of attributes
    false,                    // attrs only?
    &pMsg                     // result message
);    // GOOD! Retrieve operational attributes in apszAttrNames
```

Requesting All Attributes and Operational Attributes

What if you want all the attributes for an object—in other words, all the normal attributes *and* all the operational attributes? The obvious way is to specify a list of attribute names that includes all the attributes the object might have, but that would be pretty boneheaded. A User object has potentially hundreds of attributes; naming them all just to get the few attributes that the User object actually has would be a waste.

LDAP provides a way to get all the normal attributes and whatever operational attributes you want in the same search. You simply specify an attribute name list that includes an asterisk (*) as the first entry. For instance:

```
char* apszAttrNames[] = { "*", uSNChanged, uSNCreated, NULL };
ULONG uErr = ldap_search_s(
```

Advanced Searching with LDAP

CHAPTER 21

535

21

ADVANCED
SEARCHING WITH
LDAP

```
    pLdap,               // LDAP session
    pszContainerDN,      // container DN
    LDAP_SCOPE_ONELEVEL, // search scope
    "(objectClass=*)",   // search filter
    apszAttrNames,       // list of attributes
    false,               // attrs only?
    &pMsg                // result message
);   // GOOD! Retrieve all normal attributes and specified operational
➥attributes
```

This search will return all the normal attributes for each object in the containers given by pszContainerDN, and it will return the two operational attributes uSNChanged and uSNCreated as well.

Requesting No Attributes

Sometimes you don't want LDAP to return any attributes at all from a search. Perhaps you are just counting entries that meet your search criteria, or you only want to display the distinguished name. How can you tell the LDAP search to return no attributes? Passing NULL for the attribute list won't work because passing NULL returns all attributes.

The answer is a surprising kludge. You specify an attribute name list whose only entry is the OID string "1.1". No, really. I'm not making this up. For instance:

```
char* apszAttrNames[] = { "1.1", NULL };
ULONG uErr = ldap_search_s(
    pLdap,               // LDAP session
    pszContainerDN,      // container DN
    LDAP_SCOPE_ONELEVEL, // search scope
    "(objectClass=*)",   // search filter
    apszAttrNames,       // list of attributes
    false,               // attrs only?
    &pMsg                // result message
);   // GOOD! Retrieve no attributes whatsoever
```

The OID 1.1 is guaranteed to not correspond to any real attribute, so although it is awkward, this scheme works just fine.

Time-Limited LDAP Searches

Sometimes you may not know how long a search is going to take. You don't know how large the directory is, or how loaded the LDAP server is, or whether the user is entering search criteria, or how complex your program's search requests will be. In these cases, you might want to place a limit on how long you are willing to wait for search results.

There are two ways to limit the amount of time a search takes. You can limit the amount of time the server will spend on the search, or you can limit the amount of time the LDAP client will wait for a result from the server. The distinction is subtle, but important. In particular, you can specify any time limit you want for the client, but you cannot set the server search time limit greater than the administrative limit set in the queryPolicyObject for the server. See Chapter 8, "The Configuration Naming Context," for more about the queryPolicyObject.

Setting a Server Time Limit for a Search

The LDAP protocol requires that the LDAP client send a maximum search time in each search request. But normally you don't specify a maximum search time when you perform a search. Where does this number come from?

The LDAP client library associates a maximum search time with each LDAP session. By default, the LDAP client library sends this value along with each search. You can get or set this default search time by calling ldap_get_option() or ldap_set_option using the LDAP_OPT_TIMELIMIT option identifier.

For instance, to set the default session time limit to one minute, you would execute the following code:

```
int nLimit = 60; // default search time limit in seconds
ULONG uErr = ldap_set_option( pLdap, LDAP_OPT_TIMELIMIT, &nLimit );
```

> **NOTE**
>
> Note that setting the maximum server search time does not take into account any network delays or client delays. It limits only the clock time the server will spend executing the search.
>
> Because the LDAP client chases referrals, your search might complete on one server within the timeout value, but your total search time might exceed the limit you set because the client starts other searches on other servers.

The search functions `ldap_search_ext()` and `ldap_search_ext_s()` let you specify a server search time limit. These functions pass the timeout value you specify to the server along with the search request, effectively overriding the default search time limit for the session. The synchronous function `ldap_search_ext_s()` also uses this timeout value to determine how long the client will wait for a search result.

```
ULONG ldap_search_ext( LDAP* ld, const PCHAR base, ULONG scope,
➥const PCHAR filter, PCHAR attrs[], ULONG attrsonly, PLDAPControl*
➥ServerControls, PLDAPControl* ClientControls, ULONG TimeLimit,
➥ULONG SizeLimit, ULONG* MessageNumber )
```

`ld` is a pointer to an LDAP session that has been initialized with `ldap_open()`, `ldap_init()`, or `ldap_sslinit()`.

`base` is a NUL-terminated string containing the distinguished name of the object in the tree at which to start the search.

`scope` is one of the following: `LDAP_SCOPE_BASE`, indicating that the search will return only the object given by `base`; `LDAP_SCOPE_ONELEVEL`, indicating that the search will return only entries immediately subordinate to `base`; or `LDAP_SCOPE_SUBTREE`, indicating that the search will retrieve all entries below `base`.

`filter` is a NUL-terminated string containing the search filter string for the search. Use `objectClass=*` to retrieve all items within the search scope.

`attrs` is a NULL-terminated array of pointers to NUL-terminated strings, each string naming an attribute to retrieve.

`attrsonly` is a Boolean that, if `TRUE`, will cause the search to return only the names of the attributes for each entry, and not attribute values themselves.

`ServerControls` is a NULL-terminated array of pointers to `LDAPControl` structures that specify LDAP extensions that will apply to this search. Specify `NULL` if there are no server controls.

`ClientControls` is a NULL-terminated array of pointers to `LDAPControl` structures that specify LDAP extensions that will apply to this search. Specify `NULL` if there are no client controls.

`TimeLimit` gives the maximum number of seconds the search will be allowed to take before returning a page of results. If you specify `0` for `TimeLimit`, the LDAP library will use the default client timeout for the session.

`SizeLimit` is the maximum number of entries the search will return. If you set `SizeLimit` to `0`, LDAP will not limit the number of entries returned by the search operation.

`MessageNumber` is the address of a `ULONG` to set to the returned message ID. Use this value when you call `ldap_result()` to get the results of the search.

Returns: An LDAP error or `LDAP_SUCCESS` if the search operation was started successfully.

> **CAUTION**
>
> The current draft API for LDAPv3 indicates that the time limit parameter (uTimeLimit) for ldap_search_ext() is a pointer to a timeval structure, not an integer number of seconds. Be aware of this incompatibility if you expect your code to be portable.

The sample program in Listing 21.4 shows how to limit the amount of time a search will take by specifying a search time limit with ldap_search_ext().

LISTING 21.4 USING ldap_search_ext() TO LIMIT SEARCH TIME

```
1:    #include <windows.h>
2:    #include <winldap.h>
3:    #include <time.h>
4:    #include <iostream.h>
5:
6:    int main( int argc, char** argv )
7:    {
8:        LDAP* psLdap = ldap_init( NULL, LDAP_PORT );
9:        if( psLdap != NULL )
10:       {
11:           //set the protocol version
12:           int nVersion = LDAP_VERSION3;
13:           ldap_set_option( psLdap, LDAP_OPT_VERSION, &nVersion );
14:
15:           // turn off referrals chasing
16:           int nChaseReferrals = 0;
17:           ldap_set_option( psLdap, LDAP_OPT_REFERRALS,
                 ➥&nChaseReferrals);
18:
19:           ULONG uErr = ldap_bind_s( psLdap, NULL, NULL,
              ➥LDAP_AUTH_NEGOTIATE );
20:           if( uErr == LDAP_SUCCESS )
21:           {
22:               // Don't retrieve any attributes
23:               char* apszAttrs[] = { "1.1", NULL };
24:               ULONG uMsgID;
25:
26:               // Use ldap_search_ext and set a 1 second time limit to
                  // show how the search is limited
27:               uErr = ldap_search_ext( psLdap, "megacorp.com",
                  ➥LDAP_SCOPE_SUBTREE, "objectClass=*", apszAttrs, false,
                  ➥NULL, NULL, 1, 0, &uMsgID );
28:               if( uErr == LDAP_SUCCESS )
29:               {
30:                   bool bDone = false;
```

Advanced Searching with LDAP

CHAPTER 21

539

21

ADVANCED
SEARCHING WITH
LDAP

```
31:                    int nEntries = 0;
32:
33:                    time_t tStart = time( NULL );
34:                    while( ! bDone )
35:                    {
36:                        LDAPMessage* pEntry;
37:
38:                        int nResult = ldap_result( psLdap, uMsgID,
                       ➥LDAP_MSG_ONE, NULL, &pEntry );
39:                        switch( nResult )
40:                        {
41:                            default: // ??
42:                            case 0: // timeout
43:                                break;
44:
45:                            case -1: // error
46:                                cout << "Error " << LdapGetLastError()
                               ➥<< " from ldap_result()" << endl;
47:                                bDone = true;
48:                                break;
49:
50:                            case LDAP_RES_SEARCH_ENTRY:
51:                                ldap_msgfree( pEntry );
52:                                nEntries++;
53:                                break;
54:
55:                            case LDAP_RES_SEARCH_RESULT:
56:                                ldap_msgfree( pEntry );
57:                                bDone = true;
58:                                break;
59:                        }
60:                    }
61:
62:                    ULONG uDuration = time( NULL ) - tStart;
63:
64:                    cout << "NENTRIES: " << nEntries << endl;
65:                    cout << "DURATION: " << uDuration << endl;
66:                }
67:            }
68:
69:        ldap_unbind( psLdap );
70:    }
71:
72:    return 0;
73: }
```

At lines 8–20, the program initializes and authenticates the LDAP session and sets the
LDAP options to use the LDAPv3 protocol and to not chase referrals.

The program starts the asynchronous search at line 27 by calling `ldap_search_ext()`. In this case, the program specifies a maximum time value of one second. It also specifies `1.1` for the attribute list, meaning the search should return no attribute data whatsoever.

The program starts processing the results in the loop starting at line 34.

Lines 39–59 retrieve and process the results from the search. For each entry `ldap_result()` returns, the program increments a counter.

When the loop terminates, the program displays the number of entries and the elapsed time. The elapsed time will generally be one second. (Occasionally it is two seconds due to not starting on a one-second boundary.)

The program closes the LDAP session at line 69 by calling `ldap_unbind()`.

Setting a Client Time Limit for a Search

In the preceding section, I showed how you could limit the amount of time the domain controller spent on your search operation. In this section, I'll show how you can use `ldap_search_ext_s()` to limit how long the client waits for the search to complete.

> **NOTE**
>
> You can also used the function `ldap_search_st()`, which was covered in Chapter 20, to limit the amount of time the client waits for the search to complete.

You can set the client time limit for a search by using the `ldap_search_st()` function, discussed in Chapter 20, or you can use the extended synchronous search function `ldap_search_ext_s()`. There is a subtle distinction between the two functions, however. `ldap_search_st()` sets a limit on the amount of time the client waits for a response, but it uses the session default value for the server search time limit. `ldap_search_ext_s()`, on the other hand, sets both the client time limit and the server time limit to the value you specify. From a practical standpoint, this doesn't make much difference.

```
ULONG ldap_search_ext_s( LDAP* ld, const PCHAR base, ULONG scope,
➥const PCHAR filter, PCHAR attrs[], ULONG attrsonly, PLDAPControl*
➥ServerControls, PLDAPControl* ClientControls, struct l_timeval* timeout,
➥ULONG SizeLimit, LDAPMessage** res )
```

ld is a pointer to an LDAP session that has been initialized with `ldap_open()`, `ldap_init()`, or `ldap_sslinit()`.

base is a NUL-terminated string containing the distinguished name of the object in the tree at which to start the search.

scope is one of the following: LDAP_SCOPE_BASE, indicating that the search will return only the object given by base; LDAP_SCOPE_ONELEVEL, indicating that the search will return only entries immediately subordinate to base; or LDAP_SCOPE_SUBTREE, indicating that the search will retrieve all entries below base.

filter is a NUL-terminated string containing the search filter string for the search. Use objectClass=* to retrieve all items within the search scope.

attrs is a NULL-terminated array of pointers to NUL-terminated strings, each string naming an attribute to retrieve.

attrsonly is a Boolean that, if TRUE, will cause the search to return only the names of the attributes for each entry, and not attribute values themselves.

ServerControls is a NULL-terminated array of pointers to LDAPControl structures that specify LDAP extensions that will apply to this search. Specify NULL if there are no server controls.

ClientControls is a NULL-terminated array of pointers to LDAPControl structures that specify LDAP extensions that will apply to this search. Specify NULL if there are no client controls.

timeout is a pointer to an l_timeval structure that contains the client timeout value for the search operation. This value will be used as the server search timeout value. If you set timelimit to NULL, the LDAP client library will wait indefinitely and will use the default timeout for the session as the server search timeout.

SizeLimit is the maximum number of entries the search will return. If you set this to 0, LDAP will not limit the number of entries returned by the search.

res is the address of a pointer to an LDAPMessage structure. ldap_search_ext_s will set *ppResult to point to the returned search results. You must free this pointer with ldap_msgfree() when you are done processing the returns result entries.

Returns: An LDAP error or LDAP_SUCCESS if the search operation was successful.

Listing 21.5 shows how to use ldap_search_ext_s() to perform a search that is time-limited on both the client and the server.

LISTING 21.5 LIMIT CLIENT AND SERVER SEARCH TIMES WITH ldap_search_ext_s()

```
1:   #include <windows.h>
2:   #include <winldap.h>
3:   #include <time.h>
4:   #include <iostream.h>
5:
6:   int main( int argc, char** argv )
7:   {
8:       LDAP* psLdap = ldap_init( NULL, LDAP_PORT );
```

continues

LISTING 21.5 CONTINUED

```
 9:      if( psLdap != NULL )
10:        {
11:          ULONG uErr = ldap_bind_s( psLdap, NULL, NULL,
              ➡LDAP_AUTH_NEGOTIATE );
12:          if( uErr == LDAP_SUCCESS )
13:            {
14:                // set LDAP API version
15:                int nVersion = LDAP_VERSION3;
16:                ldap_set_option( psLdap, LDAP_OPT_VERSION, &nVersion );
17:
18:                // turn off referrals chasing
19:                int nChaseReferrals = 0;
20:                ldap_set_option( psLdap, LDAP_OPT_REFERRALS,
                  ➡&nChaseReferrals );
21:
22:                LDAPMessage* psMsg = NULL;
23:
24:                // don't retrieve any attributes
25:                char* apszAttrs[] = { "1.1", NULL };
26:
27:                // Now use ldap_search_ext_s and try to limit the search
                  // time that way
28:                struct l_timeval sTimeout = { 1, 0 }; // 1 second
29:
30:                time_t tStart = time( NULL );
31:                uErr = ldap_search_ext_s( psLdap, "DC=megacorp,DC=com",
                  ➡LDAP_SCOPE_SUBTREE, "objectClass=*", apszAttrs,
                  ➡false, NULL, NULL, &sTimeout, 0, &psMsg );
32:                if( uErr == LDAP_SUCCESS )
33:                  {
34:                      ULONG uDuration = time( NULL ) - tStart;
35:                      cout << "DURATION: " << uDuration << endl;
36:
37:                      ldap_msgfree( psMsg );
38:                  }
39:            }
40:
41:          ldap_unbind( psLdap );
42:        }
43:
44:      return 0;
45: }
```

The program in Listing 21.5 starts in the usual way by initializing an LDAP session with `ldap_init()` and authenticating it with `ldap_bind_s()`.

At line 16, the program sets the LDAP protocol version to 3, indicating it will use the LDAPv3 protocol. At line 20, the program turns off referral chasing in the LDAP client library.

The program sets the l_timeval structure at line 28 to one second. This will be the timeout value for both the client and server.

The program calls ldap_search_ext_s() at line 31, specifying the timeout value set at line 28. When the search returns, the program prints the elapsed time at line 36 and frees the returned results at line 37 by calling ldap_msgfree().

The program closes the LDAP session at line 41 by calling ldap_unbind().

Changing the Server Search Time Limits

You can set two server search time limits through LDAP. The LDAP client library manages the first timeout value. When you create an LDAP session, the library sets a default timeout value for the session. By default, the LDAP client library sends this value to the server every time you issue a search. You can change this session timeout value by calling ldap_set_option() with the LDAP_OPT_TIMELIMIT constant. See Chapter 28, "Extending LDAP with Options and Controls," for more information about LDAP options.

The network administrator can set another time limit for the domain controller itself. This *administrative limit* is a maximum value for all searches processed on the domain controller for all LDAP sessions.

Each domain controller in Windows 2000 refers to a queryPolicy object that contains its LDAP administrative limits. After initial installation, all domain controllers refer to the same queryPolicy object, CN=Default Query Policy,CN=Query Policies, CN=DirectoryService,CN=Windows NT,CN=Services, in the Configuration naming context.

The LDAP administrative limits are in the multivalued lDAPAdminLimits attribute; each value of the attribute contains a limit of the form *<parameter name>=<value>*. One of the parameter names is MaxQueryDuration. This value gives the maximum number of seconds each LDAP search is allowed to take.

You can change this value by writing an LDAP or ADSI program, or by using the NTDSUTIL.EXE program that comes with Windows 2000 Server.

Entry-Limited LDAP Searches

Another useful (or annoying, depending on your point of view) limitation you can place on LDAP searches is the *entry limit*. The LDAP protocol includes with each search request a maximum number of entries that the server should return as a result of the search. The LDAP server will stop processing the search if the search finds more entries than are specified in the search request.

Why Entry Limits Aren't

There is a subtle point here that I would like to reiterate. The LDAP server terminates the search after it *exceeds* the entry limit, not when it has *met* the entry limit. So, let's say only one object in the directory has a common name (cn attribute) equal to "Bob". Your program issues a search request with the filter "(cn=Bob)" and an entry limit of 1. The LDAP server will start the search, find the one entry with a common name of "Bob", and search the rest of the directory until it has searched the entire directory, or until it finds another matching entry that would cause the search to exceed the entry limit.

Here's some more unexpected behavior: Let's say you are searching the megacorp domain, and this domain has three subordinate domains named Eng, Sales, and Mktg. Furthermore, you want to get a maximum of 10 user objects from the directory using a subtree-scope search. If you issue the search with a filter of something like "objectClass=user", you won't just get *10* entries; you will get *40* entries! Why? Because the entry limit is implemented by the LDAP server, not the client. When your LDAP client chases referrals to the subordinate domains, it reissues the search for each domain, each time with an entry limit of 10. The result is that your program will get 10 entries from each domain controller.

Setting Search Entry Limits

As with search time limits, there are several ways you can limit the number of entries you get in a search. You can set the default search entry limit for all searches using a particular LDAP session by using ldap_set_option(). You can set the limit by setting the SizeLimit parameter in ldap_search_ext() or ldap_search_ext_s(). And you set an administrative limit on the server itself by modifying the queryPolicy object for the server.

Note that, in any case, you cannot exceed the administrative limit for the server as set in the server's queryPolicy object.

Setting the LDAP_OPT_SIZELIMIT Option

If you want to limit the number of entries returned by any search using a particular LDAP session, you can set the default entry limit for the session by using ldap_set_option with the LDAP_OPT_SIZELIMIT identifier. For instance, the following code will set the default entry limit to 10.

```
int nLimit = 10;
ULONG uErr = ldap_set_option( pLdap, LDAP_OPT_SIZELIMIT, &nLimit );
```

Any search that your program executes using pLdap will return a maximum of 10 entries (per server; refer to the earlier section "Why Entry Limits Aren't"). Chapter 28 has more information about setting LDAP options.

Changing the Default Server Search Entry Limit

As with search time limits, you (or your administrator) can set the maximum search size limit by modifying the queryPolicy object for the server. This is the same object that contains the time limit setting, by default CN=Default Query Policy, CN=Query-Policies,CN=Directory Service,CN=Windows NT,CN=Services in the Configuration naming context.

You can change this value by assigning a new queryPolicy object to the server, or by modifying the value of the lDAPAdminLimits attribute containing the MaxResultSetSize entry. You can also use NTDSUTIL.EXE, which comes with Windows 2000 Server.

CHAPTER 22

Extending LDAP Searches

LDAP provides a very flexible scheme for extending the behavior of LDAP functions. This extension scheme lets directory vendors add advanced features to their directory servers without sacrificing compatibility with existing standards-compliant LDAP clients and applications.

This chapter describes the various enhancements Microsoft has provided to the LDAP searching mechanism in Active Directory, and shows how you can take advantage of these powerful extensions.

Extending LDAP Searches with LDAP Controls

LDAPv3 adds an extension mechanism that allows LDAP providers to add capabilities to LDAP beyond the scope of what the LDAP RFCs specify. Any LDAP operation can be extended by using this mechanism.

To invoke an LDAP extension, you must specify an *LDAP control*. An LDAP control is a data structure that includes a unique OID that identifies the particular extension you want to use, a flag that indicates whether your application considers the extension critical, and a Basic Encoding Rules (BER)–encoded value that contains additional parameters required by the extension.

Client and Server Controls

LDAP extensions can be either client or server extensions. Client extensions invoke some special behavior by the LDAP client libraries. Chasing (or not chasing) referrals is an example of a function that can be modified with a client control.

Server controls change the behavior of the directory server. Making the server return deleted objects as part of the search results is an example of functionality that can be invoked with a server control.

The `LDAPControl` Structure

LDAP uses the following structure to pass LDAP control information to an extended LDAP API. Table 22.1 describes the elements of the `LDAPControl` structure.

```
Typedef struct ldapcontrolA {
    PCHAR         ldctl_oid;
    struct berval ldctl_value;
    BOOLEAN       ldctl_iscritical;
} LDAPControlA, *PLDAPControlA;
```

TABLE 22.1 ELEMENTS OF THE LDAPControl STRUCTURE

Element	Description
ldctl_oid	A pointer to the NULL-terminated OID string that identifies the control. For instance, the OID string `"1.2.840.113556.1.4.616"` represents the referrals control.
ldctl_value	An LDAP_BERVAL structure that contains data to pass along with the control. The form of the data is defined by the extension and is encoded using Abstract Syntax Notation 1 (ASN.1) Basic Encoding Rules. If the extension does not require additional data, set the bv_len element of ldctl_value to 0 and the bv_val element to NULL.
ldctl_iscritical	A Boolean value that indicates whether the control is critical. If you set this element to TRUE, the extended operation will fail if the extension is not available or some problem is associated with the control. If you specify FALSE and the control is not supported or there is a problem with the control, the operation will default to the nonextended behavior.

> **NOTE**
>
> Microsoft has not exposed its BER-encoding functions such as `ber_printf()` in the Platform SDK, so if the LDAP control you need requires additional data, you will have to encode it by hand. Consult the X.680 specification for ASN.1 for more information about BER encoding.

The Extended LDAP Functions

To use a client control or server control, you have to employ one of the special extended API functions. Each primary LDAP function has a related function that accepts an array of client controls and an array of server controls as arguments. Table 22.2 lists those functions.

TABLE 22.2 LDAP FUNCTIONS AND THEIR EXTENDED COUNTERPARTS

Basic Function	*Extended Function*
`ldap_search()`	`ldap_search_ext()`
`ldap_search_s()`	`ldap_search_ext_s()`
`ldap_modify()`	`ldap_modify_ext()`
`ldap_modify_s()`	`ldap_modify_ext_s()`
`ldap_rename()`	`ldap_rename_ext()`
`ldap_rename_s()`	`ldap_rename_ext_s()`
`ldap_add()`	`ldap_add_ext()`
`ldap_add_s()`	`ldap_add_ext_s()`
`ldap_compare()`	`ldap_compare_ext()`
`ldap_compare_s()`	`ldap_compare_ext_s()`
`ldap_delete()`	`ldap_delete_ext()`
`ldap_delete_s()`	`ldap_delete_ext_s()`

This chapter covers only the extended search functions; later chapters describe the other extended functions.

Introduction to Active Directory Search Controls

This chapter describes six LDAP search controls supported by Active Directory. There might be others, but these are the only ones I could find any information about.

The notification search control lets you register for notifications so that Active Directory notifies your program when objects in the directory are changed.

The deleted items search control retrieves items that have been deleted but for which *tombstones* (or placeholders) still exist.

The security descriptor search control retrieves the Windows NT security descriptor associated with an object in the directory.

The extended name control retrieves the GUID and SID of an object along with the object's distinguished name.

The paged search control gives you a way to retrieve search results a few at a time. This is the only way to get around administrative limits that restrict the number of entries the domain controller will return in a single search operation.

Finally, the sorted search control returns your search results in sorted order.

Some of these controls—for instance, the sorted search and paged search controls—are described by IETF Internet Drafts. Others, such as the security descriptor search control, are specific to Active Directory.

Getting Notifications of Directory Changes

The notification control is probably the most useful extension to LDAP that Microsoft has created. The notifications control lets you issue a search operation. Then, instead of returning objects that pass the search filter, the search function returns objects that have been changed in the directory. This feature lets you write applications that register with the directory server for change notifications, and then do something useful when a specific object or container changes.

> **NOTE**
>
> The Active Directory notification search control provides a subset of the functionality of the persistent search control described in the Internet Draft draft-ietf-ldapext-psearch-00.txt.

> **NOTE**
>
> The notification search control works only with asynchronous searches using `ldap_search_ext()`.

Here's what happens when you make an extended search call with the notification control (see Figure 22.1 for a visual explanation):

1. The LDAP program sends the search request to the server. The search includes a base DN to search from.

2. The Active Directory service adds your search request to a registration list associated with the DN specified in the search. Each LDAP session can, by default, have up to eight outstanding notification searches.

3. The LDAP program periodically calls `ldap_result()` using `LDAP_MSG_ONE` to see whether there is a result. Generally this call will time out.

4. When Active Directory makes a change to the object your search specified, it checks the registration list for the LDAP session and sends a search result to each registration entry in the list that is registered for the changed object.

5. The LDAP client library receives the search result.

6. The LDAP program calls `ldap_result()`, gets the search result, and processes it as if it were a normal response to a search request.

22

EXTENDING LDAP
SEARCHES

FIGURE 22.1

Notification search flow of control.

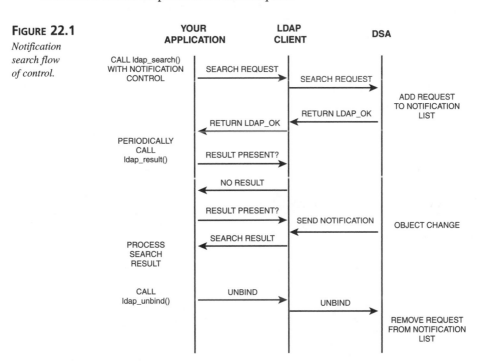

The notification registration remains in effect until you unbind the LDAP session. Every time the object you registered for changes, the directory server sends another search result to the client, and your program is notified.

As one of the Microsoft lead directory engineers puts it, "It's the search that keeps on giving."

Even though the client application has to "poll" for the notification by periodically calling `ldap_result()`, it is a very low-overhead operation and does not generate any network traffic.

Listing 22.1 shows how to register for changes to a user object in the directory.

> **NOTE**
>
> You can use `LDAP_SCOPE_BASE` or `LDAP_SCOPE_ONELEVEL` only when you issue a notification search. Using `LDAP_SCOPE_BASE` generates a notification when the specific object you specified is changed. `LDAP_SCOPE_ONELEVEL` generates a notification when any object contained by the object you specified is changed. The directory server will return the DN of the modified object so that you can tell which specific object in the container changed.

The program in Listing 22.1 will issue a notification search on the Users container of the currently logged-in user's domain and print a message any time a user object is changed.

Note that even if you change a user object on another domain controller, this program will indicate the change when Active Directory replicates the change to the domain controller to which the program is connected.

LISTING 22.1   USING THE NOTIFICATION SEARCH CONTROL

```
1:   #include <windows.h>
2:   #include <iostream.h>
3:   #include <winldap.h>
4:   #include <conio.h>
5:
6:   int main(int argc, char* argv[])
7:   {
8:       LDAP* pLdap = ldap_init( NULL, LDAP_PORT );
9:       if( pLdap != NULL )
10:        {
11:            ULONG uErr = ldap_bind_s( pLdap, NULL, NULL,
             ➥LDAP_AUTH_NEGOTIATE );
12:            if( uErr == LDAP_SUCCESS )
13:            {
```

```
14:              // DN of object we will register for changes to
15:              char szUserDN[ 1024 ] = "CN=Users,";
16:
17:              LDAPMessage* pMsg = NULL;
18:
19:              // Get rootDSE attr defaultNamingContext
20:              uErr = ldap_search_s( pLdap, NULL, LDAP_SCOPE_BASE,
            ➥"objectClass=*", NULL, false, &pMsg );
21:              if( uErr == LDAP_SUCCESS )
22:              {
23:                  char** ppszDomain = ldap_get_values( pLdap, pMsg,
                ➥"defaultNamingContext" );
24:                  if( ppszDomain != NULL )
25:                  {
26:                      strcat( szUserDN, ppszDomain[ 0 ] );
27:                  }
28:                  ldap_msgfree( pMsg );
29:              }
30:
31:              // LDAPControl for notification search
32:              LDAPControl sControl =
33:              {
34:                  "1.2.840.113556.1.4.528",   // OID for notification
                                              // search
35:                  { 0, NULL },                // BERval structure; no
                                              // data
36:                  true                        // control is critical
37:              };
38:
39:              // array of pointers to server controls
40:              LDAPControl* apsServerControls[] = { &sControl, NULL };
41:
42:              ULONG uMsgID;
43:
44:              // Issue notification search
45:              uErr = ldap_search_ext( pLdap, szUserDN,
            ➥LDAP_SCOPE_ONELEVEL, "objectClass=*", NULL, false,
            ➥apsServerControls, NULL, 0, 0, &uMsgID );
46:              if( uErr == LDAP_SUCCESS )
47:              {
48:                  // wait for notifications
49:                  cout << "Waiting for changes to " << szUserDN
                ➥<< ", press a key to quit..." << endl;
50:
51:                  while( _kbhit() == 0 )
52:                  {
53:                      LDAP_TIMEVAL sTimeout = { 1, 0 }; // one-second
                                                      // timeout for
                                                      // ldap_result()
```

continues

LISTING 22.1   CONTINUED

```
54:
55:                          // Poll for result
56:                          ULONG uResult = ldap_result( pLdap, uMsgID,
                            ➥LDAP_MSG_ONE, &sTimeout, &pMsg );
57:                          switch( uResult )
58:                          {
59:                          case 0: // timeout, just continue
60:                              break;
61:
62:                          case 0xffff: // error, just ignore for now
63:                              cout << "Error " << LdapGetLastError() <<
                                ➥endl;
64:                              break;
65:
66:                          case LDAP_RES_SEARCH_ENTRY:
67:                              char* pszDN = ldap_get_dn( pLdap, pMsg );
68:                              cout << "Object changed: " << pszDN << endl;
69:                              ldap_msgfree( pMsg );
70:                              break;
71:                          }
72:                      }
73:                  }
74:              }
75:
76:          ( void )ldap_unbind( pLdap );
77:      }
78:
79:      return 0;
80: }
```

This program connects to the DSA by first initializing an LDAP session by calling
ldap_init() using NULL for the server name. This will select a domain controller in the
same domain as the logged-in user. The program then authenticates to the directory by
calling ldap_bind_s() with NULL for the username and password, indicating that
ldap_bind_s() should use the logged-in user's credentials.

Next, at line 20, the program reads the rootDSE entry and gets the
defaultNamingContext attribute, which is the name of the domain hosted on the domain
controller.

At line 29, the program constructs the distinguished name of the Users container in that
domain.

At line 37, the program initializes the LDAPControl structure that represents the notification search control, and puts this structure's address in the apsServerControls array at
line 45.

At line 50, the program issues the asynchronous extended search by calling `ldap_search_ext()`.

The polling loop starts at line 56. The program repeatedly calls `ldap_result()` with a one second timeout to see whether any results have been returned for the notification search.

The `switch` statement at line 62 starts the processing of any returned results. The `case LDAP_RES_SEARCH_ENTRY` at line 71 prints the DN of the modified object.

Searching for Deleted Objects

When you delete an object from Active Directory, Active Directory does not actually remove the object from the directory. Instead, Active Directory moves the object to a container named Deleted Objects in the root of the naming context containing the object. Active Directory then marks the item deleted by setting the object's `isDeleted` attribute to `TRUE`. Active Directory actually removes the object from the directory 60 days after it is deleted. This 60-day period helps ensure that replication has occurred properly and that all replicas are consistent with respect to the deleted object.

The Deleted Objects container is itself marked as "deleted," so it will not appear in a normal search.

You can list the contents of the Deleted Objects container and even recover deleted objects and restore them to the directory (with some limitations) by using the Show Deleted Objects control. The distinguished names of the objects in the Deleted Objects are not the original distinguished names of the objects; Active Directory changes the distinguished names to the following:

`<old RDN>\<newline>"DEL:"<object GUID>",CN=Deleted Objects,<NC Name>`
> `<old RDN>` is the old relative distinguished name of the object.
>
> `<object GUID>` is the GUID that identifies the object—in other words, the value of the `objectGUID` attribute.
>
> `<NC Name>` is the name of the NC that contained the object.

For example, if you deleted the object `CN=Bob Kelly,CN=Users,DC=megacorp,DC=com`, the distinguished name of the object in the Deleted Objects container would be

```
CN=Bob Kelly\<newline>DEL:dd0cbd70-3720-11d3-a0c6-006097311f72,
➥CN=Deleted Objects,DC=megacorp,DC=com
```

Note that the original distinguished name does not appear in the deleted object; there is no way to recover the object's original distinguished name.

The Show Deleted Objects control lets the search operators (and, presumably, the other extended LDAP operations, although I haven't tried them) operate on deleted objects that are still in the Deleted Objects container.

The OID for the Show Deleted Objects control is 1.2.840.113556.1.4.417, and it does not require you to provide any additional data in the BER structure in the LDAP control.

Listing 22.2 lists the items in the Deleted Objects container of the domain naming context.

LISTING 22.2   USING THE DELETED ITEMS SEARCH CONTROL

```
1:   #include <windows.h>
2:   #include <iostream.h>
3:   #include <winldap.h>
4:
5:   int main(int argc, char* argv[])
6:   {
7:       LDAP* psLdap = ldap_init( NULL, LDAP_PORT );
8:       if( psLdap != NULL )
9:       {
10:          ULONG uErr = ldap_bind_s( psLdap, NULL, NULL,
             ➥LDAP_AUTH_NEGOTIATE );
11:          if( uErr == LDAP_SUCCESS )
12:          {
13:              // DN of object we will get deleted items of
14:              char szContainerDN[ 1024 ] = "CN=Deleted Objects,";
15:
16:              LDAPMessage* psMsg = NULL;
17:
18:              // Get rootDSE attr defaultNamingContext
19:              uErr = ldap_search_s( psLdap, NULL, LDAP_SCOPE_BASE,
                 ➥"objectClass=*", NULL, false, &psMsg );
20:              if( uErr == LDAP_SUCCESS )
21:              {
22:                  LDAPMessage* pEntry = ldap_first_entry( psLdap,
                     ➥psMsg );
23:                  if( pEntry != NULL )
24:                  {
25:                    char** ppszDomain = ldap_get_values( psLdap, psEntry
                       ➥"defaultNamingContext" );
26:                    if( ppszDomain != NULL )
27:                    {
28:                        strcat( szContainerDN, ppszDomain[ 0 ] );
29:                        ldap_value_free( ppszDomain );
30:                    }
31:                  }
32:                  ldap_msgfree( psMsg );
33:              }
34:
35:              // LDAPControl for deleted items search
36:              LDAPControl sControl =
37:              {
```

```
38:                "1.2.840.113556.1.4.417",   // OID for deleted items
                                               // search
39:                { 0, NULL },                // BERval structure; no
                                               // data
40:                true                        // control is critical
41:            };
42:
43:            // array of pointers to server controls
44:            LDAPControl* apsServerControls[] = { &sControl, NULL };
45:
46:            // Issue deleted items search
47:            uErr = ldap_search_ext_s(
48:                psLdap,                     // session
49:                szContainerDN,              // base of search
50:                LDAP_SCOPE_ONELEVEL,        // scope
51:                "objectClass=*",            // filter
52:                NULL,                       // attrs to get
53:                false,                      // attrs only?
54:                apsServerControls,          // server controls
55:                NULL,                       // client controls
56:                0,                          // time limit
57:                0,                          // size limit
58:                &psMsg                      // results
59:            );
60:
61:            if( uErr == LDAP_SUCCESS )
62:            {
63:                for( LDAPMessage* pEntry = ldap_first_entry( psLdap,
          ➡psMsg );
64:                     pEntry != NULL;
65:                     pEntry = ldap_next_entry( psLdap, pEntry ) )
66:                {
67:                    char* pszDN = ldap_get_dn( psLdap, pEntry );
68:                    cout << "DN: " << pszDN << endl;
69:                }
70:
71:                ldap_msgfree( psMsg );
72:            }
73:        }
74:
75:        ( void )ldap_unbind( psLdap );
76:    }
77:
78:    return 0;
79: }
```

Lines 9–12 initialize the LDAP session and authenticate to a domain controller in the domain of the logged-in user.

Line 14 initializes the distinguished name of the Deleted Objects container, and lines 19–33 construct the full DN using the defaultNamingContext attribute from rootDSE.

Lines 21–30 get the name of the domain for the domain controller from the rootDSE.

Lines 36–41 initialize the LDAPControl structure for the Show Deleted Items control, and line 44 creates the array of pointers to the LDAP control structures.

The program issues a synchronous one-level search on the Deleted Objects container at line 47 using ldap_search_ext_s().

Lines 63–73 enumerate the deleted objects in the Deleted Objects container and display the distinguished name of each object.

The program closes the LDAP session at line 75 by calling ldap_unbind().

Retrieving Security Descriptors for Directory Objects

Every object in the directory has an attribute containing its security descriptor, but, by default, Active Directory does not return this attribute with any search. If you want to inspect or manipulate an object's security descriptor, you must use the Security Descriptor control with an LDAP search operation.

The OID for Security Descriptor control is 1.2.840.113556.1.4.801, and it requires a BER-encoded bit mask that indicates which parts of the security descriptor to retrieve (Owner Security ID, Group Security ID, Discretionary Access Control List, or System Access Control List). Refer to Chapter 4, "Active Directory Security," for more information about Windows NT security descriptors and how to manipulate them.

The additional data value that you specify with the control is a 32-bit integer bit mask that contains any or all of the following four settings (these are defined in the winnt.h header file). Table 22.3 describes the different bit values you can use.

TABLE 22.3 CONSTANTS FOR ACCESSING COMPONENTS OF AN ACTIVE DIRECTORY SECURITY DESCRIPTOR

Name	*Value*	*Description*
OWNER_SECURITY_INFORMATION	0X00000001	Retrieves the owner SID from the security descriptor.
GROUP_SECURITY_INFORMATION	0X00000002	Retrieves the group SID from the security descriptor.
DACL_SECURITY_INFORMATION	0X00000004	Retrieves the DACL from the security descriptor.
SACL_SECURITY_INFORMATION	0X00000008	Retrieves the SACL from

the security descriptor.

After you set the bit mask indicating the portions of the security descriptor you want to retrieve, you must encode the bit mask using the basic encoding rules of ASN.1. The Microsoft LDAP implementation does not yet export functions to perform this encoding (as of Windows 2000 Release Candidate 1), although they might be available by the time Windows 2000 actually ships. The following function will encode a single 32-bit bit mask according to the basic encoding rules.

```
#define N_SD_BER_BYTES 5
int BEREncodeSecurityBits( ULONG uBits, char* pBuffer )
{
    *pBuffer++ = 0x30;    // Universal, constructed sequence
    *pBuffer++ = 0x03;    // Universal, primitive, bitstring
    *pBuffer++ = 0x02;    // Two content octets
    *pBuffer++ = 0x00;    // Zero unused bits
    *pBuffer = uBits & 0x0f; // The value

    return N_SD_BER_BYTES; // length of the BER encoding
}
```

Listing 22.3 reads the security descriptor from the root object of the domain naming context, converts the security descriptor to string format, and prints it.

LISTING 22.3 USING THE SECURITY DESCRIPTOR SEARCH CONTROL

```
1:   #include <windows.h>
2:   #include <iostream.h>
3:   #include <winldap.h>
4:
5:   // sddl is mostly Win2000 only
6:   #define _WIN32_WINNT 0x0500
7:   #include <sddl.h>
8:
9:   #define N_SD_BER_BYTES 5
10:
11:  // function to BER-encode a bitstring
12:  int BEREncodeSecurityBits( ULONG uBits, char* pBuffer )
13:  {
14:      *pBuffer++ = 0x30;    // Universal, constructed sequence
15:      *pBuffer++ = 0x03;    // Universal, primitive, bitstring
16:      *pBuffer++ = 0x02;    // Two content octets
17:      *pBuffer++ = 0x00;    // Zero unused bits
18:      *pBuffer = uBits & 0x0f; // The value
19:
20:      return N_SD_BER_BYTES; // length of the BER encoding
21:  }
22:
```

continues

22

EXTENDING LDAP
SEARCHES

LISTING 22.3 CONTINUED

```
23:  int main( int argc, char** argv )
24:  {
25:      LDAP* psLdap = ldap_init( NULL, LDAP_PORT );
26:      if( psLdap != NULL )
27:      {
28:          ULONG uErr = ldap_bind_s( psLdap, NULL, NULL,
             ➥LDAP_AUTH_NEGOTIATE );
29:          if( uErr == LDAP_SUCCESS )
30:          {
31:              // DN of object we will register for changes to
32:              char szDomainDN[ 1024 ] = { 0 };
33:
34:              LDAPMessage* psMsg = NULL;
35:
36:              // Get rootDSE attr defaultNamingContext
37:              uErr = ldap_search_s(
38:                  psLdap,                 // session
39:                  NULL,                   // base
40:                  LDAP_SCOPE_BASE,        // scope
41:                  "objectClass=*",        // filter
42:                  NULL,                   // attrs
43:                  false,                  // attrsonly?
44:                  &psMsg                  // results
45:              );
46:              if( uErr == LDAP_SUCCESS )
47:              {
48:                  LDAPMessage* pEntry = ldap_first_entry( psLdap,
                     ➥psMsg );
49:                  if( pEntry != NULL )
50:                  {
51:                      char** ppszDomain = ldap_get_values( psLdap,
                         ➥pEntry,
                         ➥"defaultNamingContext" );
52:                      if( ppszDomain != NULL )
53:                      {
54:                          strcat( szDomainDN, ppszDomain[ 0 ] );
55:                          ldap_value_free( ppszDomain );
56:                      }
57:                  }
58:                  ldap_msgfree( psMsg );
59:              }
60:
61:              char acBERBuf[ N_SD_BER_BYTES ];
62:              ULONG dwInfo = OWNER_SECURITY_INFORMATION
63:                  | GROUP_SECURITY_INFORMATION
64:                  | DACL_SECURITY_INFORMATION
65:                  | SACL_SECURITY_INFORMATION;
66:
67:              BEREncodeSecurityBits( dwInfo, acBERBuf );
```

```
68:
69:              // LDAPControl for security descriptor
70:              LDAPControl sControl =
71:              {
72:                  "1.2.840.113556.1.4.801", // OID for SD items search
73:                  {
74:                      N_SD_BER_BYTES,    // number of bytes in ber val
75:                      acBERBuf           // ber encoded data
76:                  },
77:                  true                   // control is critical
78:              };
79:
80:              // array of pointers to server controls
81:              LDAPControl* apsServerControls[] = { &sControl, NULL };
82:
83:              // Issue search
84:              uErr = ldap_search_ext_s(
85:                  psLdap,          // session
86:                  szDomainDN,      // base
87:                  LDAP_SCOPE_BASE,// scope
88:                  "objectClass=*",// filter
89:                  NULL,            // attrs
90:                  false,           // attrsonly?
91:                  apsServerControls, // server controls
92:                  NULL,            // client controls
93:                  NULL,            // time limit
94:                  0,               // size limit
95:                  &psMsg
96:              );
97:              if( uErr == LDAP_SUCCESS )
98:              {
99:                  for( LDAPMessage* pEntry = ldap_first_entry( psLdap,
                ➥psMsg );
100:                     pEntry != NULL;
101:                     pEntry = ldap_next_entry( psLdap, pEntry ) )
102:                  {
103:                      char* pszDN = ldap_get_dn( psLdap, pEntry );
104:                      cout << "DN: " << pszDN << endl;
105:
106:                      struct berval** ppsValues = ldap_get_values_len(
                  ➥psLdap, pEntry, "nTSecurityDescriptor" );
107:
108:                      if( ppsValues != NULL )
109:                      {
110:                          for( int nVal = 0; ppsValues[ nVal ] != NULL;
                      ➥ nVal++ )
111:                          {
112:                              SECURITY_DESCRIPTOR* pSD = (
                          ➥SECURITY_DESCRIPTOR* )
                          ➥ppsValues[ nVal ]->bv_val;
```

22

EXTENDING LDAP
SEARCHES

continues

LISTING 22.3   CONTINUED

```
113:                         char* pszSDString;
114:                         ULONG uSDStringLen;
115:
116:                     ConvertSecurityDescriptorToStringSecurity
               ➥Descriptor(
117:                         pSD,             // security descriptor
118:                         SDDL_REVISION,   // version
119:                         dwInfo,          // bits we want
120:                         &pszSDString,    // ptr to result
121:                         &uSDStringLen    // length of result
122:                         );
123:
124:                     cout << pszSDString << endl;
125:
126:                     LocalFree( pszSDString ); // free the
                                                   // string
127:                 }
128:
129:                 ldap_value_free_len( ppsValues );
130:             }
131:         }
132:
134:         ldap_msgfree( psMsg );
135:     }
136:   }
137:
138:   ( void )ldap_unbind( psLdap );
139:   }
140:
141:   return 0;
142: }
```

Lines 5–7 include the sddl.h header file. This file contains the security descriptor string conversion routines. Note that the #define of _WIN32_WINNT to 0x0500 is necessary to pull in the function declarations because most of the functions defined in sddl.h are for Windows 2000 only.

Lines 9–21 contain the function that will BER-encode a string of bits.

The program initializes the LDAP session and authenticates it with ldap_bind_s() at lines 25–28.

At line 37, the program retrieves the domain name from the rootDSE of the domain controller. This is the object for which we retrieve the security descriptor.

At lines 61-67, the program encodes the requested portions of the security descriptor using the BER.

The program sets up the LDAPControl structure and the array of pointers to controls at lines 70-81.

Lines 84–112 actually perform the synchronous search, retrieve the object from the directory, and get the `ntSecurityDescriptor` attribute from the object. Note that you have to use `ldap_get_values_len()` because the `nTSecurityDescriptor` attribute is binary and is not expressed as a string.

The program gets a pointer to the security descriptor at line 107 and converts the security descriptor to a string and prints it at lines 111–119. The program frees the memory associated with the string at line 121 by calling `LocalFree()`.

Retrieving Extended Name Information

Active Directory identifies objects in the directory in several ways. Objects can be identified by distinguished name, by GUID, and by SID (if the object is a security principal like a user or group). Chapter 3, "The Components of Active Directory," discusses all the ways Active Directory identifies objects.

The Extended Name control provides a way to get all this identifying information at once, without actually retrieving any of the object's attributes.

When you use the Extended Name control, instead of returning the normal distinguished name, Active Directory returns a string that has the following format:

```
"<GUID=" <object GUID> ">;<SID=" <object SID> ">;" <object DN>.
```

For example:

```
<GUID=8c4cdbc0002dd311a0c6006097311f72>;<SID=0105000000000000515000000
➥f536454245e6975b9755449060000>;CN=Administrator,CN=Users,DC=megacorp,DC=com.
```

If the object is not a security principal and therefore does not have a SID, the extended name will include only the GUID and distinguished name. For instance:

```
<GUID=2bb226fd5f0ad311995200609779521e>;CN=System,DC=megacorp,DC=com
```

The OID for the Extended Name control is `1.2.840.113556.1.4.529` and it does not require you to specify any data in the `BER` structure in the control.

Listing 22.4 lists the extended names of all the objects in the Users container of the domain of the currently logged-in user.

LISTING 22.4 USING THE EXTENDED NAMES SEARCH CONTROL

```
1:   #include <windows.h>
2:   #include <winldap.h>
3:   #include <iostream.h>
4:
```

continues

LISTING 22.4   CONTINUED

```
 5:    int main( int argc, char** argv )
 6:    {
 7:        LDAP* psLdap = ldap_init( NULL, LDAP_PORT );
 8:        if( psLdap != NULL )
 9:        {
10:            ULONG uErr = ldap_bind_s( psLdap, NULL, NULL,
          ➥LDAP_AUTH_NEGOTIATE );
11:            if( uErr == LDAP_SUCCESS )
12:            {
13:                // DN of search base
14:                char szDomainDN[ 1024 ] = { 0 };
15:
16:                LDAPMessage* psMsg = NULL;
17:
18:                // Get rootDSE attr defaultNamingContext
19:                uErr = ldap_search_s(
20:                    psLdap,            // session
21:                    NULL,              // base
22:                    LDAP_SCOPE_BASE,// scope
23:                    "objectClass=*",// filter
24:                    NULL,              // attrs
25:                    false,             // attrsonly?
26:                    &psMsg             // result
27:                );
28:
29:                // Get default domain name
30:                if( uErr == LDAP_SUCCESS )
31:                {
32:                    LDAPMessage* pEntry = ldap_first_entry( psLdap, psMsg );
33:                    if( pEntry != NULL )
34:                    {
35:                        char** ppszDomain = ldap_get_values( psLdap,
                      ➥pEntry, "defaultNamingContext" );
36:                        if( ppszDomain != NULL )
37:                        {
38:                            strcat( szDomainDN, ppszDomain[ 0 ] );
39:                            ldap_value_free(ppszDomain );
40:                        }
41:                        ldap_msgfree( psMsg );
42:                    }
43:                }
44:                // LDAPControl for deleted items search
45:                LDAPControl sControl =
46:                {
47:                    "1.2.840.113556.1.4.529", // Extended DN OID
48:                    { 0, NULL },              // BERval structure, no data
49:                    true                      // control is critical
50:                };
51:
52:                // array of pointers to server controls
53:                LDAPControl* apsServerControls[] = { &sControl, NULL };
```

```
54:
55:            // Issue search
56:            uErr = ldap_search_ext_s(
57:                psLdap,                // session
58:                szDomainDN,            // base
59:                LDAP_SCOPE_ONELEVEL,// scope
60:                "objectClass=*",      // filter
61:                NULL,                  // attrs
62:                false,                 // attrsonly?
63:                apsServerControls,    // server controls
64:                NULL,                  // client controls
65:                NULL,                  // time limit
66:                0,                     // size limit
67:                &psMsg                 // results
68:            );
69:            if( uErr == LDAP_SUCCESS )
70:            {
71:              for( LDAPMessage* psEntry = ldap_first_entry( psLdap,
        ➥psMsg );
72:                    psEntry != NULL;
73:                    psEntry = ldap_next_entry( psLdap, psEntry ) )
74:                {
75:                    char* pszDN = ldap_get_dn( psLdap, psEntry );
76:                    cout << pszDN << endl;
77:                }
78:
79:                ldap_msgfree( psMsg );
80:            }
81:        }
82:
83:        ldap_unbind( psLdap );
84:    }
85:
86:    return 0;
87: }
```

The program in Listing 22.4 starts in the usual way by calling ldap_init() to initialize an LDAP session, and then calls ldap_bind_s() to authenticate the session using the credentials of the currently logged-in user.

At lines 19–43, the program retrieves the domain name of the domain controller from the rootDSE.

The program initializes the LDAPControl structure for the Extended Name control at lines 45–50, and initializes the array of LDAPControl pointers at line 53.

At line 56, the program calls ldap_search_ext_s() with the LDAPControl array. At lines 71-77, it prints the extended distinguished name of each entry returned by the search.

The program frees the search results by calling ldap_msgfree() at line 79, and closes the LDAP session with ldap_unbind() at line 83.

Getting Search Results—A Page at a Time

When you are searching (and retrieving) a large number of entries, you might run into a couple problems. The first, and most annoying, problem is that you might attempt to retrieve more entries from the directory than the domain controller's administrative limits allow. By default, the maximum number of entries a domain controller will return for a search is 262,144—but it is quite possible that the administrator will set this down to a smaller value, such as 1,000. The consequence of this reduction is that your search will return the first 1,000 objects that pass the filter, and no more.

The second problem is a performance issue. If you issue a synchronous search that will return a large number of entries, your LDAP program might wait several minutes before it receives any results. It is quite possible that retrieving thousands of entries, combined with retrieving all the attributes for each entry, will cause your application to run out of memory.

The Microsoft LDAP client provides a *paged search* facility to avoid these problems. A paged search works like a regular search, except that the server returns the search items in relatively small blocks, or pages. Performing a paged search avoids the problem of running into the administrative limits of the server, and it also limits the amount of client memory required by the search.

Why is this? Why don't administrative limits apply to paged searches? They actually do apply. However, a paged search is really a sequence of small searches, each one starting where the other left off. Therefore, each search fits comfortably within the administrative limits for the server.

> **NOTE**
>
> The Microsoft implementation of the protocol for a paged search is described by the Internet Draft draft-ietf-asid-ldapv3-simplepaged-03.txt.

Two Ways to Perform a Paged Search

Microsoft implemented paged searches as an extension to the regular LDAP search. The OID for the control is 1.2.840.113556.1.4.319, and the additional data provided with the control is a BER-encoded sequence containing an integer indicating the number of entries to return per page and an empty octet string. However, building the extended search yourself isn't really an option because Microsoft has not exposed the BER encoding functions you would need to initialize the LDAPControl structure.

Fortunately, Microsoft has supplied several helper functions that handle all the gory details for you. There are five functions you need for performing paged searches.

You can perform paged searches in one of two ways. The easy way is to use the `ldap_search_init_page()`, `ldap_get_next_page()`, and `ldap_get_paged_count()` functions to do the paged search. You do not have to worry about setting up the `LDAPControl` structures for the search.

The second way is more difficult. In this case, you set up an `LDAPControl` structure for the paged search using the `ldap_create_page_control()` function. You then issue the search using `ldap_search_ext()` and process the results when they come back, including a returned `LDAPControl` structure from the server. The `BER` value in the `LDAPControl` structure contains a cookie that represents the state of the search on the server. You have to pass this cookie back to the server for the next page of the search. This whole process is quite a bit more difficult and error-prone, and it doesn't provide any advantage over the helper functions. I'll leave the `ldap_create_page_control()`/`ldap_search_ext()` method as an exercise for the reader.

Setting Up the Paged Search

```
PLDAPSearch ldap_search_init_page( PLDAP ExternalHandle,const PCHAR
➡DistinguishedName, ULONG ScopeOfSearch, const PCHAR SearchFilter,
➡PCHAR AttributeList[], ULONG AttributesOnly, PLDAPControl*
➡ServerControls,PLDAPControl* ClientControls, ULONG PageTimeLimit,
➡ULONGTotalSizeLimit,PLDAPSortKey* SortKeys )
```

> `ExternalHandle` is a pointer to an LDAP session that has been initialized and authenticated.

> `DistinguishedName` is a NUL-terminated string containing the distinguished name of the object in the tree at which to start the search.

> `ScopeOfSearch` is one of these three choices: `LDAP_SCOPE_BASE`, indicating that the search will return only the object given by `DistinguishedName`; `LDAP_SCOPE_ONELEVEL`, indicating that the search will return only entries immediately subordinate to `DistinguishedName`; or `LDAP_SCOPE_SUBTREE`, indicating that the search will retrieve all entries below `DistinguishedName`.

> `SearchFilter` is a NUL-terminated string containing the search filter string for the search. Use `"objectClass=*"` to retrieve all items within the search scope.

> `AttributeList` is a NULL-terminated array of pointers to NUL-terminated strings, each string naming an attribute to retrieve.

> `AttributesOnly` is a `BOOLEAN` that if `TRUE` will cause the search to return only the names of the attributes for each entry, and not attributes values themselves.

> `ServerControls` is a NULL-terminated array of pointers to `LDAPControl` structures that specify LDAP extensions that will apply to this search. Set this to `NULL` if you do not want to specify any additional server controls.

> **NOTE**
>
> You do not need to specify the Paged Search control if you use the
> `ldap_search_init_page()` function. The `ldap_search_init_page()` function
> includes the Paged Search control for you automatically.

`ClientControls` is a NULL-terminated array of pointers to `LDAPControl` structures
that specify LDAP extensions that will apply to this search. Set this to NULL if you
do not want to specify any additional server controls.

`PageTimeLimit` gives the maximum number of seconds the search is allowed to
take before returning a page of results. Set this to zero if you want to use the
default time limit for the session.

`TotalSizeLimit` is the maximum number of total entries the search will return. Set
this to zero to use the default size limit for the session.

`SortKeys` is a NULL-terminated array of pointers to `LDAPSortKey` structures. See
the section on sorted search for more information about LDAP sort keys. Pass NULL
for this parameter if you do not want to sort the search results.

Returns: A pointer to an `LDAPSearch` structure. The `LDAPSearch` structure is opaque. You
pass the returned pointer as a handle to the other paged search functions.

Here is an example of starting a paged search:

```
char* apszAttrs[] = { "1.1", NULL }; // return no attributes
char* pszDomainDN = "DC=engineering,DC=megacorp,DC=com";

LDAPSearch* pSearch = ldap_search_init_page(
    psLdap,              // LDAP session
    pszDomainDN,         // search base
    LDAP_SCOPE_SUBTREE,  // search scope
    "objectClass=*",     // search filter
    apszAttrs,           // attrs to get
    false,               // attrs only?
    NULL,                // server controls
    NULL,                // client controls
    60,                  // page time limit
    0,                   // total size limit
    NULL                 // sort keys
);
if( pSearch != NULL )
{
    // get pages search results here
}
```

Retrieving Pages of Entries

Processing the results of a paged search is essentially the same as processing the results of a normal search. However, you first must retrieve a page of results using the `ldap_get_next_page()` function, and then you can use `ldap_first_entry()` and `ldap_next_entry()` in the usual way.

After you have started a paged search, you can retrieve a page of results either synchronously by using `ldap_get_next_page_s()` or asynchronously by using `ldap_get_next_page()`. `ldap_get_next_page_s()` is somewhat easier to use, but your choice really depends on how you've structured your program.

```
ULONG ldap_get_next_page_s( PLDAP ExternalHandle, PLDAPSearch
➥SearchHandle,struct l_timeval* timeout, ULONG PageSize,
➥ULONG* TotalCount, LDAPMessage** Results)
```

> `ExternalHandle` is a pointer to the LDAP session that was used by the call to `ldap_search_init_page()`.
>
> `SearchHandle` is the pointer returned by `ldap_search_init_page()`.
>
> `timeout` is a pointer to an appropriately initialized `l_timeval` structure. It determines how long `ldap_get_next_page_s()` will wait for the entries from the server.
>
> `PageSize` is the number of entries to return in this page. It should be smaller than the search entry limit for the session.
>
> `TotalCount` is the address of a `ULONG` that will be set to the server's estimate of the total number of entries to be returned by the search. Active Directory sets this to 0.
>
> `Results` is the address of a pointer to an `LDAPMessage` structure that will be set to the address of the returned results. You must free this pointer with `ldap_msgfree()`.

Returns: An LDAP error code or `LDAP_SUCCESS` if the function completes properly.

```
ULONG ldap_get_paged_count( PLDAP ExternalHandle, PLDAPSearch SearchBlock,
➥ULONG* TotalCount, PLDAPMessage Results )
```

> `ExternalHandle` is a pointer to the LDAP session that was used by the call to `ldap_search_init_page()`.
>
> `SearchBlock` is the pointer returned by `ldap_search_init_page()`.
>
> `TotalCount` is the address of a `ULONG` that will be set to the total number of entries to be returned by the search.
>
> `Results` is the pointer to the last set of results returned by `ldap_get_next_page_s()`.

Returns: An LDAP error code or `LDAP_SUCCESS` if the function completes properly.

Listing 22.5 is a code snippet that shows how to process the results of a paged search using the synchronous function `ldap_get_next_page_s()`.

LISTING 22.5   RETRIEVING A PAGE OF RESULTS WITH `ldap_get_next_page_s()`

```
 1:    struct l_timeval sTimeout = { 60, 0 };
 2:    ULONG uTotal;
 3:    LDAPMessage* psMsg = NULL;
 4:    bool bDone = false;
 5:
 6:    while( ! bDone )
 7:    {
 8:        uErr = ldap_get_next_page_s(
 9:            pLdap,       // LDAP session
10:            pSearch,     // search handle from ldap_search_init_page
11:            &sTimeout,   // how long to wait for the next page
12:            10,          // max number of entries for the next page
13:            &uTotal,     // total number of entries
14:            &psMsg       // address of LDAPMessage pointer
15:        );
16:
17:        if( uErr != LDAP_SUCCESS )          // error returned at end of
                                               // search
18:        {
19:            bDone = true;
20:        }
21:        else
22:        {
23:            uErr = ldap_get_paged_count( psLdap, pSearch, &uTotal, psMsg
          ➡ );
24:            for( LDAPMessage* psEntry = ldap_first_entry( psLdap, psMsg );
25:                 psEntry != NULL;
26:                 psEntry = ldap_next_entry( psLdap, psEntry ) )
27:            {
28:                char* pszDN = ldap_get_dn( psLdap, psEntry );
29:                cout << pszDN << endl;
30:            }
31:
32:            ldap_msgfree( pMsg );
33:        }
34:    }
```

At line 8, the code calls `ldap_get_next_page_s()` to get the next page in the search results. It is a synchronous call, so `ldap_get_next_page_s()` will wait until an entire page comes from the server or until the timeout value is reached, whichever comes first.

`ldap_get_next_page_s()` returns `LDAP_NO_RESULTS_RETURNED` when there are no more search results. The test at line 17 checks this.

Line 23 has a call to `ldap_get_paged_count()`. This function is a bit of a hack. I mentioned earlier that the server returns a cookie containing the state of the search with each page of results. The client must pass this cookie into the next paged search so that the server can start at the right place. According to the Microsoft documentation, `ldap_get_paged_count()` performs this task by taking the cookie from its last argument and squirreling it away in the LDAP library so that the next call to `ldap_get_next_page()` or `ldap_get_next_page_s()` can use it. That being said, I removed this call from my test programs, and it did not seem to make a bit of difference. Go figure.

Lines 24–28 process the returned search results just as with any other search.

Line 30 has the call to `ldap_msgfree()` to free the `LDAPMessage` structure allocated by `ldap_get_next_page_s()`. Don't forget this call!

If you've organized your code to use asynchronous functions and you find yourself needing to use the Paged Search facility, you can use the `ldap_get_next_page()` function. It is essentially the same as `ldap_get_next_page_s()`, except that instead of returning a page of results, it returns a message ID. You handle the message ID just as you would an asynchronous search using `ldap_search()`—by repeatedly calling `ldap_result()` to get the search results.

```
ULONG ldap_get_next_page( PLDAP ExternalHandle, PLDAPSearch SearchHandle,
➥ULONG PageSize, ULONG* MessageNumber )
```

> `ExternalHandle` is a pointer to the LDAP session that was used by the call to `ldap_search_init_page()`.
>
> `SearchHandle` is the pointer returned by `ldap_search_init_page()`.
>
> `PageSize` is the number of entries to return in this page.
>
> `MessageNumber` is the address of a `ULONG` that will be set to the asynchronous search message ID. You use this message ID when you call `ldap_result()` to get the results of the asynchronous search operation.

Returns: An LDAP error code or `LDAP_SUCCESS` if the function completes properly.

Listing 22.6 does essentially the same thing as Listing 22.5, except that it uses `ldap_get_next_page()` instead of `ldap_get_next_page_s()`.

LISTING 22.6 RETRIEVING A PAGE OF RESULTS WITH ldap_get_next_page()

```
 1:    struct l_timeval sTimeout = { 60, 0 };
 2:    ULONG uTotal;
 3:    LDAPMessage* psMsg = NULL;
 4:
 5:    ULONG uMsgID;
 6:    bool bMorePages = true;
 7:
 8:    while( bMorePages )
 9:    {
10:        uErr = ldap_get_next_page( psLdap, pSearch, 10, &uMsgID );
11:        if( uErr != LDAP_SUCCESS )
12:        {
13:            bMorePages = false;
14:        }
15:        else
16:        {
17:            bool bDone = false;
18:            while( ! bDone )
19:            {
20:                // get result entries one at a time
21:                int nResult = ldap_result( psLdap, uMsgID, LDAP_MSG_ONE,
          ➥&sTimeout, &psMsg );
22:
23:                // get the page count to save the cookie
24:                ldap_get_paged_count( psLdap, pSearch, &uTotal, psMsg );
25:
26:                switch( nResult )
27:                {
28:                    case LDAP_RES_SEARCH_ENTRY:
29:                    {
30:                        char* pszDN = ldap_get_dn( psLdap, psMsg );
31:                        cout << pszDN << endl;
32:                        ldap_msgfree( psMsg );
33:                    }
34:                    break;
35:
36:                    case LDAP_RES_SEARCH_RESULT:
37:                    {
38:                        ldap_msgfree( psMsg );
39:                        bDone = true;
40:                    }
41:                    break;
42:
43:                    case 0: // timeout
44:                    break;
45:
46:                    case -1: // error
47:                    {
48:                        cout << "Error " << LdapGetLastError() << endl;
```

```
49:                          bDone = true;
50:                      }
51:                      break;
52:                  }
53:              }
54:          }
55:      }
```

At line 10, the code calls `ldap_get_next_page()`. This performs an asynchronous search operation for the next page of results. `ldap_get_next_page()` will return `LDAP_NO_RESULTS_RETURNED` when it is done with the search.

The loop at line 18 executes once for each result entry by calling `ldap_result()`.

Line 21 contains the call to `ldap_result()`. In this case, I used the `LDAP_MSG_ONE` parameter to retrieve the results one at a time. You can also use `LDAP_MSG_RECEIVED` or `LDAP_MSG_ALL`. See the section on asynchronous searches for more information on `ldap_result()`.

Line 24 has the call to `ldap_get_paged_count()` to copy the cookie from the returned result to someplace in the LDAP library. In this case, this call seems to be important; I removed this call from the test program and it failed to get the second page of search results.

The `switch` statement at line 25 starts the processing of the results message from `ldap_result()`. The handling of the paged search results here is identical to handling search results from a call to `ldap_search()`. Note the calls to `ldap_msgfree()`. Don't leave them out; otherwise, your program will leak memory.

Abandoning a Paged Search

After your paged search is complete, or any time you want to terminate the search, you must call `ldap_search_abandon_page()` to terminate the search activity on the server and to clean up the search state information stored in the LDAP client library.

```
ULONG ldap_search_abandon_page( LDAP* ExternalHandle,
➥LDAPSearch*SearchBlock )
```

> `ExternalHandle` is a pointer to the LDAP session that was used by the call to `ldap_search_init_page()`.
>
> `SearchBlock` is the pointer returned by `ldap_search_init_page()`.

Returns: An LDAP error code or `LDAP_SUCCESS` if the function completes properly.

You can call the `ldap_search_abandon_page()` function at any time during the search process.

Getting Search Results in Sorted Order

The last extended search topic I'll cover is the *sorted search*. Active Directory supports a sorted search control that lets you retrieve the results of a normal search sorted by the attributes you specify. If you need your search results sorted, and you don't have enough processing power or memory on the client to handle it (or you just don't want to write yet another sorting function), you can get the LDAP server to sort the search results for you.

> **NOTE**
>
> The sorted search function as implemented in Active Directory provides a subset of the features of the Internet Draft sorted search as described in draft-ietf-ldapext-sorting-02.txt.

Sorting Oddities and Limitations

The LDAP sorting extension as implemented in Active Directory is fairly basic, and it has some quirks you need to be aware of before using it.

Only One Sort Key

The most important limitation is that the current implementation allows you to sort by only a single attribute. The sorted search control and the function that builds it (`ldap_create_sort_control()`) both support multiple sort keys, but the server implementation currently supports only one.

Sorting in the Presence of Referrals

If you perform a sorted search that chases referrals—for instance, if you perform a sub-tree search on a domain that has two subordinate domains—the search results will not come back completely sorted.

The reason for this is similar to the reason why specifying an entry limit on a search that chases referrals doesn't really work either. Because each server is sorting its own entries separately from the others, you will get the batch of entries for the top-level domain properly sorted, followed by the entries from the first subordinate domain, also sorted, followed by the entries of the second subordinate domain, also sorted. But the entire result set is not sorted as a single set.

You can remedy this by using a merge sort to sort the results from the separate referred-to servers, but if you're going to go through the effort, and you have the memory to do it, you might as well sort the whole mess yourself to begin with.

Entries Without the Sort Key Attribute

If you use the sort control to sort a bunch of entries, and some of the entries do not have the attribute you specified as a sort key, the LDAP server will sort them all to the end of your result set. This isn't necessarily bad, but you need to be aware of it.

Sorting with Multivalued Keys

This is easy. You can't. The search will return an error if you try to sort by a multivalued attribute. This isn't really a problem, because the semantics of sorting by a multivalued attribute aren't obvious. Sort by the highest value? The first value?

The difficulty comes when you sort by an attribute that is defined in the schema as multivalued but none of the entries has multiple values. In this case, you're stuck. You'll have to do the sorting yourself on the client.

Ordering Rules

According to the Internet Draft for sorted LDAP searches (and according to Microsoft's own documentation), you can specify the ordering rule for each sort key by putting the OID of the matching rule you want to use in the `sk_matchruleoid` field of the `LDAPSortKey` structure. You could then perform, for instance, a case-insensitive sort on a directory string attribute.

As of Windows 2000 Release Candidate 1, this capability was not functioning. In particular, you can only specify a NULL for the matching rule OID in the `LDAPSortKey` structure. Active Directory will use the matching rule appropriate to the syntax of the sort key attribute.

This isn't much of a limitation because most of the time you want to use the default matching rule anyway. But it is a problem if you want to perform a case-insensitive sort on an attribute that is normally case-sensitive.

This problem might or might not be fixed by the time Windows 2000 actually ships.

Sort Control Returned from Server

The LDAPv3 definition doesn't just provide for LDAP controls to be sent from the client to the server; it also provides for controls to be sent from the server back to the client. When you make a sorted search request, not only does the LDAP client (your program) send an LDAP control to the server specifying the sort criteria, but the server also returns an LDAP control structure containing the results of the sorting activity. Microsoft provides functions to get and parse the returned control, which I'll discuss in a later section.

The Sorted Search Functions

Performing a sorted search is pretty straightforward. It breaks down into the following steps:

1. Create an `LDAPControl` structure containing the sort key information using the `ldap_create_sort_control()` function.

2. Issue the sorted search using `ldap_search_ext()` or `ldap_search_ext_s()`.

3. Process the results in the usual way by using `ldap_result()` if you issued an asynchronous search, and `ldap_first_entry()` and `ldap_next_entry()` if you used a synchronous search.

4. Call `ldap_parse_result()` and `ldap_parse_sort_control()` to inspect the returned `LDAPControl` structure containing the results of the search.

Initializing the Sort Controls

The first step in executing a sorted search is to set up the `LDAPControl` structures for the sort operation. You could do the BER encoding yourself, but Microsoft has made the process much easier by supplying the `ldap_create_sort_control()` function.

> **NOTE**
>
> The `ldap_create_sort_control()` function supercedes `ldap_encode_sort_control()`, which did basically the same thing. `ldap_create_sort_control()` tracks the Internet Draft for LDAP sorting.

When you create the `LDAPControl` structures for the extended search operation, you first define an array of pointers to `LDAPSortKey` structures. Each `LDAPSortKey` structure defines the attribute to sort by, the ordering rule to use for that attribute, and whether you want to sort in inverse order. Details for the structures are given in Table 22.4.

```
typedef struct ldapsortkey
{
    PCHAR   sk_attrtype;        // name or OID of attribute
    PCHAR   sk_matchruleoid;    // OID of matching rule, or NULL for
                                // default
    BOOLEAN sk_reverseorder;    // FALSE for normal order, TRUE for
                                // reverse
}
LDAPSortKeyW, *PLDAPSortKeyW;
```

TABLE 22.4 ELEMENTS OF THE `ldapsortkey` STRUCTURE

Element	Description
sk_attrtype	A NUL-terminated string containing the name of the attribute to use as a sort key. It can also be the attribute's OID string.
sk_matchruleoid	A NUL-terminated string containing the OID of the matching rule to use in the sorting process. This must always be set to NULL in the current implementation.
sk_reverseorder	A Boolean value that, if TRUE, will cause Active Directory to reverse the sort order of this attribute.

For example, the following LDAPSortKey definition would set up sorting entries by the common name (cn) attribute.

```
LDAPSortKey sKey = { "cn", NULL, FALSE };
```

After you define the sort keys you want by initializing LDAPSortKey structures, you use the ldap_create_sort_control() function to encode the sort key information into LDAPControl structures that you then pass to ldap_search_ext() or ldap_search_ext_s().

```
ULONG ldap_create_sort_control( PLDAP ExternalHandle, PLDAPSortKey*
➡SortKeys, UCHAR IsCritical, PLDAPControl* Control )
```

> ExternalHandle is a pointer to the LDAP session on which you are going to issue the search.

> SortKeys is a NULL-terminated array of pointers to LDAPSortKey structures. In this version of Active Directory, you can have only one entry, plus the NULL pointer, in this array.

> IsCritical is a Boolean value that if set to TRUE will set the IsCritical flag in the returned LDAPControl structure. This will cause the search to fail if the server does not support the requested sort operation.

> Control is the address of a pointer that the function will set to point to an LDAPControl structure. You add this pointer to the array of pointers to server controls that you pass to ldap_search_ext() or ldap_search_ext_s(). You should free this pointer after the search by passing it to ldap_control_free().

Returns: An LDAP error code, or LDAP_SUCCESS if the function executed properly.

After you create the LDAPControl structure by calling ldap_create_sort_control(), you must add its address to the array of LDAPControl pointers you pass to the extended search function. The following code snippet shows how to set it all up.

22

EXTENDING LDAP
SEARCHES

```
LDAPSortKey sKey = { "cn", NULL, FALSE };          // sort key structure
LDAPSortKey* apsSortKeys[] = { &sKey, NULL }; // array of pointers to sort
                                              // keys

LDAPControl* pSortControl;          // pointer to newly create sort control

ULONG uErr = ldap_create_sort_control( pLdap, apsSortKeys, TRUE,
➥&pSortControl );
if( uErr == LDAP_SUCCESS )
{
    LDAPControl* apsServerControls[] = { pSortControl, NULL };

    // call search routine and process results

    ldap_control_free( pSortControl );
}
```

Issuing the Sorted Search and Retrieving the Entries

You perform a sorted search just as you would perform any other extended search: by calling `ldap_search_ext()` for an asynchronous search or `ldap_search_ext_s()` for a synchronous search. You retrieve the search results the same way, too—by calling `ldap_result()` for an asynchronous search or `ldap_first_entry()` and `ldap_next_entry()` for a synchronous search. After you have the `LDAPControl` structure set up properly, performing a sorted search is just like performing any other search. Listing 22.7 shows how to start a synchronous sorted search by using `ldap_search_ext_s()`.

LISTING 22.7 USING `ldap_search_ext_s()` TO PERFORM A SORTED SEARCH

```
 1: LDAPSortKey sKey = { "cn", NULL, FALSE };          // sort key structure
 2:
 3: LDAPSortKey* apsSortKeys[] = { &sKey, NULL };       // array of pointers
                                                        // to sort keys
 4:
 5: LDAPControl* psSortControl;          // pointer to newly create sort
                                         // control
 6:
 7: ULONG uErr = ldap_create_sort_control( psLdap, apsSortKeys, TRUE,
    ➥&psSortControl );
 8: if( uErr == LDAP_SUCCESS )
 9: {
10:     LDAPControl* apsServerControls[] = { psSortControl, NULL };
11:     LDAPMessage* psMsg;
12:
13:     uErr = ldap_search_ext_s(
14:         psLdap,                  // session
```

```
15:            szDomainDN,            // search base
16:            LDAP_SCOPE_SUBTREE,    // scope
17:            "objectClass=*",       // filter
18:            apszAttrs,             // attributes to get
19:            false,                 // attrs only?
20:            apsServerControls,     // server controls
21:            NULL,                  // client controls
22:            NULL,                  // timelimit
23:            0,                     // size limit
24:            &psMsg                 // result
25:        );
26:
27:     if( uErr == LDAP_SUCCESS )
28:     {
29:         for( LDAPMessage* psEntry = ldap_first_entry( psLdap, psMsg );
30:              psEntry != NULL;
31:              psEntry = ldap_next_entry( psLdap, psEntry ) )
32:         {
33:             // process the search entry
34:         }
35:
36:         ldap_msgfree( psMsg );
37:     }
38:
39:     ldap_control_free( pSortControl );
40: }
```

Retrieving the Sort Results

One significant difference between a sorted search and a regular search is that a sorted search can return an LDAPControl structure to the client along with the search results. This LDAPControl structure indicates whether the sort was successful. If the sort was not successful, the LDAPControl structure contains the error code and the name of the sort key that caused the problem. Given that you can have only one sort key, this isn't a huge win, but in preparation for the day when Active Directory supports multiple sort keys, inspecting the returned LDAPControl structure is a good idea.

Getting the results of the sort is surprisingly involved. You must first get the final result message from the server. This is returned by the synchronous search ldap_search_ext_s(). In the case of an asynchronous search using ldap_search_ext(), you get the final result message when ldap_result() returns a message type of LDAP_RES_SEARCH_RESULT.

After you get the final result message, you use the ldap_parse_result() function to extract the LDAPControl structures returned by the server. Finally, you use the ldap_parse_sort_control() function to get the error information from the BER-encoded data in the LDAPControl structure.

```
ULONG ldap_parse_result( LDAP* Connection, LDAPMessage* ResultMessage,
➥ULONG* ReturnCode, PCHAR* MatchedDNs, PCHAR* ErrorMessage, PCHAR**
➥Referrals,PLDAPControl** ServerControls, BOOLEAN Freeit )
```

Connection is a pointer to the LDAP session the search was issued on.

ResultMessage is a pointer to the final result LDAPMessage returned by either ldap_search_ext_s() or ldap_result().

ReturnCode is the address of a ULONG to set to the returned result of the search. This is the same value returned by ldap_search_ext_s(). You can pass a NULL to ignore the returned error code.

MatchedDNs: If the search returned the error LDAP_NO_SUCH_OBEJCT, ldap_parse_result() will set the pointer at this address to point to a string containing the portion of the DN that actually was matched. You could reissue the same search starting at this location in the tree with different search criteria to find the object in question. If *MatchedDNs is non-NULL after calling ldap_parse_result(), you must free it by passing it to ldap_memfree(). If you want to ignore the matched DNs returned by the server, you can pass a NULL for MatchedDNs.

ErrorMessage is the address of a pointer set to point to an error message string that corresponds to the error returned in *ReturnCode. If *ErrorMessage is non-NULL after calling ldap_parse_result(), you must free it by passing it to ldap_memfree(). You can pass a NULL for ErrorMessage if you want to ignore the returned error message string.

Referrals is the address of a pointer that will be set to point to a NULL-terminated array of pointers to NUL-terminated strings. ldap_parse_result() will set this to point to an array of referral URLs, if any were returned by the server. If *Referrals is non-NULL after calling ldap_parse_result(), you must free it by passing *Referrals to ldap_value_free(). You can pass a NULL for Referrals to ignore any returned referral strings.

ServerControls is the address of a pointer that will be set to point to a NULL-terminated array of pointers to LDAPControl structures. ldap_parse_result() will set this to point to the LDAPControl structures returned from the server. If ldap_parse_result() returns more than one LDAPControl structure, you must inspect the OID string of each to determine which control is which. (This doesn't happen with a simple sorted search.) Pass Controls[0] to ldap_parse_sort_control() to retrieve the sort results. If *Controls is non-NULL after calling ldap_parse_result(), you must pass *Controls to ldap_controls_free() to free the memory associated with the control structures. You can pass a NULL for Controls if you want to ignore the LDAPControl structures returned by the server.

Freeit is a Boolean value that, if set to TRUE, will cause ldap_parse_result() to free the memory associated with the ResultMsg parameter. If you set Freeit to TRUE, be sure that you don't later free ResultMsg with ldap_msgfree().

Returns: An LDAP error code or LDAP_SUCCESS if the function succeeded.

> **NOTE**
>
> It's a good idea to set all the pointers whose addresses you pass to ldap_parse_result() to NULL before you pass them in. After calling ldap_parse_result(), you can check each pointer to see whether it is NULL, and if it is not, free it with the appropriate function.

After you have the final result message, you use the function ldap_parse_result() to get the LDAPControl structures returned by the server. The LDAPControl structure returned by ldap_parse_result() contains the result of the sorting operation. To get useful information from the LDAPControl structure (it is BER-encoded), you have to pass a pointer to the LDAPControl structure to ldap_parse_sort_control().

```
ULONG ldap_parse_sort_control( PLDAP ExternalHandle, PLDAPControl*
➡Control,ULONG* Result, PCHAR* Attribute
```

ExternalHandle is a pointer to the LDAP session that you used to perform the sorted search operation.

Control is the address of a pointer to an LDAPControl structure that ldap_parse_sort_control will set to point to the returned sort control. If ldap_parse_sort_control() is successful and *Control is not NULL, you must free the returned control structure by passing *Control to ldap_control_free().

Result is the address of a ULONG that ldap_parse_sort_control() will set to the sort error. This error is distinct from the error returned with the search. *Result is strictly the error (if any) associated with the sorting operation.

Attribute is the address of a pointer that ldap_parse_sort_control() will set to point to the name of the sort key attribute that caused the problem, if any. If ldap_parse_sort_control() returns successfully, and *Attribute is non-NULL, you must free the returned string by passing *Attribute to ldap_memfree().

Returns: An LDAP error code or LDAP_SUCCESS if the function is successful.

The code to do this is shown in Listing 22.8.

LISTING 22.8 USING THE `ldap_parse_result()` FUNCTION

```
1:   //psLdap is an LDAP session pointer
2:   //psMsg is an LDAPMessage* that contains the final result message
3:
4:   LDAP* psLdap = NULL;
5:   ULONG uReturnErr = 0;          // the sort error, if any
6:   char* pszMatchedDNs = NULL;    // not used for sort
7:   char* pszErrorMsg = NULL;          // text error message
8:   char** ppszReferrals = NULL;    // referrals not chased
9:   LDAPControl** ppsServerControls;     // returned controls from server
10:
11:  ULONG uErr = ldap_parse_result( psLdap, psMsg, &uReturnErr,
     ➥&pszMatchedDNs,
12:      &pszErrorMsg, &ppszReferrals, &ppsServerControls, false );
13:  if( uErr == LDAP_SUCCESS )
14:  {
15:      cout << "RETURNERR: " << uReturnErr << endl;
16:      if( pszMatchedDNs != NULL )
17:      {
18:          cout << "MATCHEDDNS: " << pszMatchedDNs << endl;
19:          ldap_memfree( pszMatchedDNs );
20:      }
21:      if( pszErrorMsg != NULL )
22:      {
23:          cout << "ERRORMSG: " << pszErrorMsg << endl;
24:          ldap_memfree( pszErrorMsg );
25:      }
26:      if( ppszReferrals != NULL )
27:      {
28:          for( int nRefs = 0; ppszReferrals[ nRefs ] != NULL; nRefs++ )
29:          {
30:              cout << "REFERRAL: " << ppszReferrals[ nRefs ] << endl;
31:          }
32:          ldap_value_free( ppszReferrals );
33:      }
34:      if( ppsServerControls != NULL )
35:      {
36:          ULONG uSortResult = 0;
37:          char* pszAttrResult = NULL;
38:          ldap_parse_sort_control( psLdap, ppsServerControls,
             ➥&uSortResult,
39:              &pszAttrResult );
40:          cout << "SORTRESULT: " << uSortResult << " "
             ➥<< pszAttrResult << endl;
41:          ldap_controls_free( ppsServerControls );
42:      }
43:  }
```

If you're going to use an asynchronous search, processing the results and getting the sort control from the server is essentially the same. The following piece of code is equivalent to the preceding listing, except that it uses ldap_result() to get the search results for a search started with ldap_search_ext(). Listing 22.9 is the code you would use following the call to ldap_search_ext().

LISTING 22.9 USING THE ldap_parse_result() FUNCTION WITH AN ASYNCHRONOUS SEARCH

```
1:    // psLdap initialized by ldap_init()
2:    // uMsgID initialized by ldap_search()
3:    // uErr initialized by ldap_search()
4:
5:    if( uErr == LDAP_SUCCESS )
6:    {
7:        bool bDone = false;
8:        struct l_timeval sTimeout = { 1, 0 };
9:
10:        while( ! bDone )
11:        {
12:            LDAPMessage* psEntry;
13:            int nResult = ldap_result( psLdap, uMsgID, LDAP_MSG_ONE,
              ➥&sTimeout, &psEntry );
14:
15:            switch( nResult )
16:            {
17:                case -1:
18:                    // error
19:                    cout << "Error is " << LdapGetLastError() << endl;
20:                    bDone = true;
21:                    break;
22:                case 0:
23:                // timeout
24:                    break;
25:
26:                case LDAP_RES_SEARCH_ENTRY:
27:                {
28:                    char* pszDN = ldap_get_dn( psLdap, psEntry );
29:
30:                    char** ppszValues = ldap_get_values( psLdap, psEntry,
                      ➥"cn" );
31:                    if( ppszValues != NULL )
32:                    {
33:                        for( int nVal = 0; ppszValues[ nVal ] != NULL;
                          ➥nVal++ )
34:                        {
35:                            cout << ppszValues[ nVal ] << " " << pszDN <<
                              ➥endl;
```

continues

LISTING 22.9   CONTINUED

```
36:                            }
37:                        }
38:                    else
39:                    {
40:                        // entry did not have a "cn" attribute
41:                        ➥cout << "*" << pszDN << endl;
42:                    }
43:
44:                    ldap_msgfree( psEntry );
45:                }
46:            break;
47:
48:            case LDAP_RES_SEARCH_RESULT:
49:            {
50:                ULONG uReturnErr = 0;
51:                char* pszMatchedDNs = NULL;
52:                char* pszErrorMsg = NULL;
53:                char** ppszReferrals = NULL;
54:                LDAPControl** ppsServerControls;
55:
56:                uErr = ldap_parse_result( psLdap, psEntry,
                    ➥&uReturnErr,
                    ➥&pszMatchedDNs, &pszErrorMsg, &ppszReferrals,
                    ➥&ppsServerControls, false );
57:                if( uErr == LDAP_SUCCESS )
58:                {
59:                    cout << "RETURNERR: " << uReturnErr << endl;
60:                    if( pszMatchedDNs != NULL )
61:                    {
62:                        cout << "MATCHEDDNS: " << pszMatchedDNs <<
                        ➥endl;
63:                        ldap_memfree( pszMatchedDNs );
64:                    }
65:                    if( pszErrorMsg != NULL )
66:                    {
67:                        cout << "ERRORMSG: " << pszErrorMsg << endl;
68:                        ldap_memfree( pszErrorMsg );
69:                    }
70:                    if( ppszReferrals != NULL )
71:                    {
72:                        for( int nRefs = 0; ppszReferrals[ nRefs ]
                        ➥!= NULL; nRefs++ )
73:                        {
74:                            cout << "REFERRAL: " <<
                            ➥ppszReferrals[ nRefs ] << endl;
75:                        }
76:                        ldap_value_free( ppszReferrals );
77:                    }
```

```
78:                    if( ppsServerControls != NULL )
79:                    {
80:                        ULONG uSortResult = 0;
81:                        char* pszAttrResult = NULL;
82:
83:                        ldap_parse_sort_control( psLdap,
                           ➥ppsServerControls,
                           ➥ &uSortResult, &pszAttrResult );
84:
85:                        // pszAttrResult has the name of the sort
                           // attribute
86:                        // uSortResult has the sort error
87:
88:                        ldap_memfree( pszAttrResult );
89:                        ldap_controls_free( ppsServerControls );
90:                    }
91:                }
92:
93:                ldap_msgfree( psEntry );
94:                bDone = true;
95:            }
96:            break;
97:
98:            default:
99:            {
100:            }
101:            break;
102:        }
103:    }
104: }
```

In this case, the code to process the returned search entries starting at line 22 is essentially the same as in any other asynchronous search. The major difference shows up in the handling of the final result message, starting at line 41. In the case of an asynchronous search using `ldap_search_ext()`, the program doesn't call `ldap_parse_result()` until the final message comes in. Otherwise, the code is the same as in the preceding example.

A Sample Program

Listing 22.10 is a complete program that performs a subtree search on the domain naming context for the domain of the logged-in user. It sorts the results by common name (cn).

LISTING 22.10 A COMPLETE PROGRAM USING THE SORTED SEARCH CONTROL

```
1:    #include <iostream.h>
2:    #include <windows.h>
3:    #include <winldap.h>
4:
5:    int main( int argc, char* argv[] )
6:    {
7:        LDAP* psLdap = ldap_init( NULL, LDAP_PORT );
8:        if( psLdap != NULL )
9:        {
10:           int nVersion = LDAP_VERSION3;
11:           ldap_set_option( psLdap, LDAP_OPT_VERSION, &nVersion );
12:
13:           int nReferrals = 0;
14:           ldap_set_option( psLdap, LDAP_OPT_REFERRALS, &nReferrals );
15:
16:           ULONG uErr = ldap_bind_s( psLdap, NULL, NULL,
          ➥LDAP_AUTH_NEGOTIATE );
17:           if( uErr == LDAP_SUCCESS )
18:           {
19:               // DN of object we will search
20:               char szDomainDN[ 1024 ] = "CN=Users,";
21:
22:               LDAPMessage* psMsg = NULL;
23:
24:               // Get rootDSE attr defaultNamingContext
25:               uErr = ldap_search_s( psLdap, NULL, LDAP_SCOPE_BASE,
          ➥"objectClass=*", NULL, false, &psMsg );
26:               if( uErr == LDAP_SUCCESS )
27:               {
28:                   LDAPMessage* pEntry = ldap_first_entry( psLdap,
          ➥psMsg);
29:                   if( pEntry != NULL )
30:                   {
31:                       char** ppszDomain = ldap_get_values( psLdap,
                          pEntry,
          ➥"defaultNamingContext" );
32:                       if( ppszDomain != NULL )
33:                       {
34:                           strcat( szDomainDN, ppszDomain[ 0 ] );
35:                           ldap_value_free( ppszDomain );
36:                       }
37:                       ldap_msgfree( psMsg );
38:                   }
39:               }
40:
41:               char* pszSortKey = "cn";
42:
43:               LDAPSortKey sKey;
44:               sKey.sk_attrtype = pszSortKey;
45:               sKey.sk_matchruleoid = NULL;
```

```
46:                    sKey.sk_reverseorder = false;
47:
48:                    LDAPSortKey* apsSortKeys[2];
49:                    apsSortKeys[0] = &sKey;
50:                    apsSortKeys[1] = NULL;
51:
52:                    LDAPControl* psSortControl;
53:
54:                    uErr =  ldap_create_sort_control(
55:                        psLdap,
56:                        apsSortKeys,
57:                        true,
58:                        &psSortControl
59:                    );
60:
61:                    LDAPControl* apsControls[2];
62:                    apsControls[0] = psSortControl;
63:                    apsControls[1] = NULL;
64:
65:                    char* apszAttrs[] = { pszSortKey, NULL };
66:
67:                    if(uErr == 0)
68:                    {
69:                        uErr = ldap_search_ext_s(
70:                            psLdap,                  // session
71:                            szDomainDN,              // search base
72:                            LDAP_SCOPE_ONELEVEL,     // scope
73:                            "objectClass=User",      // filter
74:                            apszAttrs,               // attributes to get
75:                            false,                   // attrs only?
76:                            apsControls,             // server controls
77:                            NULL,                    // client controls
78:                            NULL,                    // timelimit
79:                            0,                       // size limit
80:                            &psMsg                   // result
81:                        );
82:
83:                        if( uErr == LDAP_SUCCESS )
84:                        {
85:                        for( LDAPMessage* psEntry = ldap_first_entry( psLdap,
                    ➥psMsg );
86:                                  psEntry != NULL;
87:                                  psEntry = ldap_next_entry( psLdap, psEntry ) )
88:                            {
89:                                char** ppszValues = ldap_get_values( psLdap,
                        ➥psEntry, pszSortKey );
90:                                if( ppszValues != NULL )
91:                                {
92:                                for( int nVal = 0; ppszValues[ nVal ] != NULL;
                    ➥nVal++ )
```

continues

LISTING 22.10   CONTINUED

```
93:                              {
94:                                  cout << ppszValues[ nVal ] << endl;
95:                              }
96:                          }
97:                          else
98:                          {
99:                              char* pszDN = ldap_get_dn( psLdap, psEntry );
100:
101:                              cout << "*" << pszDN << endl;
102:                          }
103:                      }
104:
105:                  ULONG uReturnErr = 0;
106:                  char* pszMatchedDNs = NULL;
107:                  char* pszErrorMsg = NULL;
108:                  char** ppszReferrals = NULL;
109:                  LDAPControl** ppsServerControls;
110:
111:                  // Parse the final result message
112:                  uErr = ldap_parse_result(
113:                      psLdap,
114:                      psMsg,
115:                      &uReturnErr,
116:                      &pszMatchedDNs,
117:                      &pszErrorMsg,
118:                      &ppszReferrals,
119:                      &ppsServerControls,
120:                      false
121:                  );
122:
123:                  if( uErr == LDAP_SUCCESS )
124:                  {
125:                      cout << "RETURNERR: " << uReturnErr << endl;
126:                      if( pszMatchedDNs != NULL )
127:                      {
128:                          cout << "MATCHEDDNS: " << pszMatchedDNs
                                  << ➥endl;
129:                          ldap_memfree( pszMatchedDNs );
130:                      }
131:                      if( pszErrorMsg != NULL )
132:                      {
133:                          cout << "ERRORMSG: " << pszErrorMsg <<
                                  ➥endl;
134:                          ldap_memfree( pszErrorMsg );
135:                      }
136:                      if( ppszReferrals != NULL )
137:                      {
138:                          for( int nRefs = 0; ppszReferrals[ nRefs ]
                                  ➥!= NULL; nRefs++ )
```

```
139:                                  {
140:                                   cout << "REFERRAL: " << ppszReferrals[
                                  ➥nRefs ] << endl;
141:                                  }
142:                                  ldap_value_free( ppszReferrals );
143:                              }
144:                          if( ppsServerControls != NULL )
145:                          {
146:                              ULONG uSortResult = 0;
147:                              char* pszAttrResult = NULL;
148:
149:                              ldap_parse_sort_control(
150:                                  psLdap,                 // session
151:                                  ppsServerControls,  // returned
                                                          // controls
152:                                  &uSortResult,           // sort error
                                                          // code
153:                                  &pszAttrResult       // name of sort
                                                          // attr
154:                              );
155:
156:                              if( pszAttrResult != NULL )
157:                              {
158:                                  cout << "ATTR: " << pszAttrResult <<
                                      ➥" SORT RESULT: " << uSortResult <<
                                      ➥endl;
159:
160:                                  ldap_memfree( pszAttrResult );
161:                              }
162:
163:                              ldap_controls_free( ppsServerControls );
164:                          }
165:                      }
166:
167:                      ldap_msgfree( psMsg );
168:                  }
169:              }
170:          }
171:
172:          ( void )ldap_unbind( psLdap );
173:      }
174:
175:      return 0;
176: }
```

At lines 7–16, the program initializes and authenticates the LDAP session. Note that it also disables referrals. This avoids the awkward behavior of having two separate sets of results that are not sorted together.

From line 19 to 39, the program gets the domain naming context from the rootDSE. It builds the distinguished name of the Users container of the default domain in the variable szDomainDN.

Lines 41-59 contain the code to initialize the LDAPSortKey structure and to convert it into an LDAPControl structure.

The program sets up the array of server controls at lines 61-63.

Finally, at line 69, the program calls ldap_search_ext_s() with the sort control created by ldap_create_sort_control().

From lines 85-103, the program gets the sorted results from the search operation and prints the distinguished name and the cn attribute value for each object.

Starting at line 112, the program parses the result data returned from the server by calling ldap_parse_result(). If any returned server controls potentially contain error information regarding the sort operation, the program extracts them at line 149 by calling ldap_parse_sort_control().

Finally, the program cleans up by freeing the result message at line 167 with ldap_msgfree() and closing the LDAP session with ldap_unbind() at line 172.

Using Paged and Sorted Searches Together

If you need your search results sorted for you, and you also need to get them a page at a time, you can use the LDAPControl structure created by ldap_create_sort_control() with the paged search functions I discussed earlier in the chapter.

I won't go into great detail describing this because the code is just the same as before. Listing 22.11 shows how you can use a sorted search and results paging together in the same search operation. In this program, I used the asynchronous search function ldap_get_next_page() instead of ldap_get_next_page_s(), just to show how to get the sort results from an asynchronous search.

LISTING 22.11   A COMPLETE PROGRAM FOR AN ASYNCHRONOUS PAGED AND SORTED SEARCH

```
1:   #include <iostream.h>
2:   #include <windows.h>
3:   #include <winldap.h>
4:
5:   int main(int argc, char* argv[])
6:   {
```

```
 7:          LDAP* psLdap = ldap_init( NULL, LDAP_PORT );
 8:          if( psLdap != NULL )
 9:          {
10:              int nReferrals = 0;
11:              ldap_set_option( psLdap, LDAP_OPT_REFERRALS, &nReferrals );
12:
13:              int nVersion = LDAP_VERSION3;
14:              ldap_set_option( psLdap, LDAP_OPT_VERSION, &nVersion );
15:
16:          ULONG uErr = ldap_bind_s( psLdap, NULL, NULL,
            ➥LDAP_AUTH_NEGOTIATE );
17:          if( uErr == LDAP_SUCCESS )
18:          {
19:              // DN of object we search
20:              char szDomainDN[ 1024 ] = "CN=Users,";
21:
22:              LDAPMessage* psMsg = NULL;
23:
24:              // Get rootDSE attr defaultNamingContext
25:              uErr = ldap_search_s(
26:                  psLdap,          // session
27:                  NULL,            // base
28:                  LDAP_SCOPE_BASE,// scope
29:                  "objectClass=*",// filter
30:                  NULL,            // attrs
31:                  false,           // attrs only?
32:                  &psMsg           // result msg
33:              );
34:              if( uErr == LDAP_SUCCESS )
35:              {
36:                  LDAPMessage* pEntry = ldap_first_entry(psLdap, psMsg);
37:                  if( pEntry != NULL )
38:                  {
39:                      char** ppszDomain = ldap_get_values( psLdap,
                        ➥pEntry, "rootDomainNamingContext" );
40:                      if( ppszDomain != NULL )
41:                      {
42:                          // make the CN=Users,DC=... DN
43:                          strcat( szDomainDN, ppszDomain[ 0 ] );
44:                          ldap_value_free( ppszDomain );
45:                      }
46:                  }
47:                  ldap_msgfree( psMsg );
48:              }
49:
50:              if( uErr == LDAP_SUCCESS )
51:              {
52:                  char* pszSortKey = "cn";
53:
54:                  // set up LDAPSortKey structure
```

continues

LISTING 22.11 CONTINUED

```
55:                LDAPSortKey sKey;
56:                sKey.sk_attrtype = pszSortKey;
57:                sKey.sk_matchruleoid = NULL;
58:                sKey.sk_reverseorder = false;
59:
60:                // set up array of LDAPSortKey structures
61:                LDAPSortKey* apsSortKeys[2];
62:                apsSortKeys[0] = &sKey;
63:                apsSortKeys[1] = NULL;
64:
65:                LDAPControl* psSortControl;
66:
67:                // create an LDAPControl
68:                uErr = ldap_create_sort_control(
69:                    psLdap,
70:                    apsSortKeys,
71:                    true,
72:                    &psSortControl
73:                );
74:
75:                // set up array of LDAPControl structures
76:                LDAPControl* apsControls[2];
77:                apsControls[0] = psSortControl;
78:                apsControls[1] = NULL;
79:
80:                char* apszAttrs[] = { pszSortKey, NULL };
81:
82:                // start paged, sorted search
83:                LDAPSearch* pSearch = ldap_search_init_page(
84:                    psLdap,               // LDAP session
85:                    szDomainDN,           // search base
86:                    LDAP_SCOPE_SUBTREE,// search scope
87:                    "objectClass=User",// search filter
88:                    apszAttrs,            // attrs to get
89:                    false,                // attrs only?
90:                    apsControls,          // server controls
91:                    NULL,                 // client controls
92:                    60,                   // page time limit
93:                    0,                    // total size limit
94:                    NULL                  // sort keys
95:                );
96:
97:                if( uErr == LDAP_SUCCESS && pSearch != NULL )
98:                {
99:                    bool bMorePages = true;
100:
101:                    while( bMorePages )
102:                    {
103:                        ULONG uMsgID;
104:
```

```
105:                    // get the next page of 10 entries
106:                    uErr = ldap_get_next_page( psLdap, pSearch,
                        ➡10, &uMsgID );
107:                    if( uErr != LDAP_SUCCESS )
108:                    {
109:                        bMorePages = false;
110:                    }
111:                    else
112:                    {
113:                        bool bDone = false;
114:                        while( ! bDone )
115:                        {
116:                            // timeout for next
117:                            struct l_timeval sTimeout = { 60, 0 };
118:                            LDAPMessage* psEntry;
119:
120:                            // get next entry from page
121:                            int nResult = ldap_result( psLdap,
                            ➡uMsgID,
                            ➡LDAP_MSG_ONE, &sTimeout, &psEntry );
122:
123:                            switch( nResult )
124:                            {
125:                            case LDAP_RES_SEARCH_ENTRY:
126:                                {
127:                                    // get the value of the sort
128:                                    // key and print it
129:                                    char** ppszValues =
                                    ➡ldap_get_values(
130:                                        psLdap,
131:                                        psEntry,
132:                                        pszSortKey
133:                                    );
134:                                    if( ppszValues != NULL )
135:                                    {
136:                                        for( int nVal = 0;
137:                                            ppszValues[ nVal ] !=
                                            ➡NULL;
138:                                            nVal++ )
139:                                        {
140:                                        cout << ppszValues[ nVal ] <<
                                        ➡endl;
141:                                        }
142:                                    }
143:                                    else
144:                                    {
145:                                        // object didn't have the
                                        // sort key attr, so print dn
```

continues

LISTING 22.11   CONTINUED

```
146:                                    char* pszDN = ldap_get_dn(
                                        ➥psLdap, psEntry );
147:
148:                                    cout << "*" << pszDN <<
                                        ➥endl;
149:                                }
150:
151:                                ldap_msgfree( psEntry );
152:                            }
153:                        break;
154:                    case LDAP_RES_SEARCH_RESULT:
155:                        {
156:                    // we will execute this once for  each
                        // page
157:                            ULONG uReturnErr = 0;
158:                            char* pszMatchedDNs = NULL;
159:                            char* pszErrorMsg = NULL;
160:                            char** ppszReferrals = NULL;
161:                            ULONG uTotal;
162:                        LDAPControl** ppsServerControls =
                            ➥NULL;
163:
164:                            // Save the paged search
                                ➥cookie
165:                            ldap_get_paged_count(
166:                                psLdap,
167:                                pSearch,
168:                                &uTotal,
169:                                psEntry
170:                            );
171:
172:                            uErr = ldap_parse_result(
173:                                psLdap, // session
174:                                psEntry, // entry
175:                                &uReturnErr, // error for
                                    ➥page
176:                                &pszMatchedDNs, // best
                                    ➥match DN
177:                                &pszErrorMsg, // errmsg
178:                                &ppszReferrals, //
                                    ➥referrals
179:                                &ppsServerControls, //
                                    ➥control
180:                                false // free psEntry?
181:                            );
182:                            if( uErr == LDAP_SUCCESS )
183:                            {
184:                                cout << "RETURNERR: "
185:                                    << uReturnErr
```

```
186:                                   << endl;
187:                              if( pszMatchedDNs != NULL )
188:                              {
189:                                  cout << "MATCHEDDNS: "
190:                                       << pszMatchedDNs
191:                                       << endl;
192:                               ldap_memfree(
                                  ➥pszMatchedDNs );
193:                              }
194:                              if( pszErrorMsg != NULL )
195:                              {
196:                                  cout << "ERRORMSG: "
197:                                       << pszErrorMsg
198:                                       << endl;
199:                                  ldap_memfree(
                                  ➥pszErrorMsg );
200:                              }
201:                              if( ppszReferrals != NULL )
202:                              {
203:                                  for( int nRefs = 0;
204:                              ppszReferrals[ nRefs ] !=
                              ➥NULL;
205:                                      nRefs++ )
206:                                  {
207:                                    cout << "REFERRAL: "
208:                                   << ppszReferrals[
                                  ➥nRefs ]
209:                                          << endl;
210:                                  }
211:                          ldap_value_free(
                          ➥ppszReferrals );
212:                              }
213:                              if( ppsServerControls !=
                              ➥NULL )
214:                              {
215:                                  ULONG uSortResult = 0;
216:                                  char* pszAttrResult =
                                  ➥NULL;
217:
218:                                  ldap_parse_sort_control(
219:                                      psLdap,
220:                                      ppsServerControls,
221:                                      &uSortResult,
222:                                      &pszAttrResult
223:                                  );
224:
225:                                  if( pszAttrResult !=
                                  ➥NULL )
226:                                  {
```

continues

LISTING 22.11   CONTINUED

```
227:                                             cout << "ATTR: "
228:                                                << pszAttrResult
229:                                                << " SORT RESULT: "
230:                                                   << uSortResult
231:                                                      << endl;
232:
233:                                      ldap_memfree(
                                         ➥pszAttrResult );
234:                                             }
235:
236:                                ldap_controls_free(
                                   ➥ppsServerControls );
237:                                         }
238:                             }
239:
240:                             ldap_msgfree( psEntry );
241:                             bDone = true;
242:                         }
243:                      break;
244:
245:                      case 0: // timeout
246:                         break;
247:
248:                      default:
249:                      case -1: // error
250:                         {
251:                             cout << "Error " <<
                                 ➥LdapGetLastError() << endl;
252:                             bDone = true;
253:                         }
254:                      break;
255:                   }
256:                }
257:             }
258:          }
259:       }
260:
261:          ldap_control_free( psSortControl );
262:       }
263:    }
264:
265:    ( void )ldap_unbind( psLdap );
266: }
267:
268: return 0;
269: }
```

The program in Listing 22.11 starts in the usual way by initializing an LDAP session with ldap_init() and authenticating it with ldap_bind_s(). Note also that this program turns off referral-chasing because that can make for unexpected sorting results.

At line 25, the program reads the rootDSE to obtain the name of the domain naming context. It creates the distinguished name of the Users container for the domain at line 40.

At lines 55-73, the program sets up an LDAPSortKey structure so that the search will sort by the "cn" attribute. It converts the LDAPSortKey structure to an LDAPControl structure by calling ldap_create_sort_control() at line 68.

The program initializes the LDAPControl array at lines 76-80.

Finally, at line 83, the program issues the asynchronous paged search request, including the array of LDAPControl pointers that will make the server sort the results of the search by the "cn" attribute.

If the search request was successful, the program calls ldap_get_next_page() at line 106 to retrieve the next page of results. The program then uses the ldap_result() function to retrieve the entries from the page one at a time. For each entry the program retrieves, it prints the value of the "cn" attribute at line 140. If the entry does not have a "cn" attribute, the program prints the distinguished name at line 148.

When the program retrieves the last entry from the page (nResult is equal to LDAP_RES_SEARCH_RESULT), the program calls ldap_get_paged_count() at line 165 to save the paged search cookie. Note that you only make this call when you get the final search result for each page, not for each entry on the page.

The program also retrieves the search result information from the page by calling ldap_parse_result() at line 172. The program prints any information ldap_parse_result() extracted from the result message at lines 184-212.

If ldap_parse_result() retrieved an LDAPControl structure from the search results, the program parses the sort control with ldap_parse_sort_control(). The program then prints any of the information it obtained from the sort control returned by the server.

The program frees the psSortControl structure created at line 49 by calling ldap_control_free() at line 261. It then closes the LDAP session at line 265 by calling ldap_unbind().

This program demonstrates most of the mechanisms shown in this chapter: asynchronous searching, server controls, sorting, paged searches, and processing control structures returned by the server. This code is about as complicated as LDAP searches can get.

22

EXTENDING LDAP SEARCHES

CHAPTER 23

Processing LDAP Referrals

One thing that inhibited the adoption of LDAPv2 as an enterprise directory standard was its inherent single-server nature. There was no notion of multiple LDAP servers working together to provide a distributed enterprise directory service. Because partitioning and replication are the two primary schemes for building large, robust directories, LDAP single-server orientation was a substantial limitation.

LDAPv3 addressed the problem with a mechanism called a referral. A *referral* is a response to an LDAP function that essentially says, "The object you want is not on this server; look for it on these other servers instead." The referral mechanism provides a way for LDAP operations to span servers.

This chapter covers the different ways you can handle referrals in your program. It also describes how to use the APIs listed in Table 23.1.

TABLE 23.1 LDAP FUNCTIONS FOR PROCESSING REFERRALS

Function	Description
ldap_first_reference	Retrieves the first referral entry in the results returned from the server.
ldap_next_reference	Retrieves the next referral entry in the results returned from the server.
ldap_count_references	Returns the number of referral entries in the results returned from the server.

continues

TABLE 23.1   CONTINUED

Function	Description
ldap_parse_reference	Parses a referral entry into its component parts.
QUERYFORCONNECTION	Typedef for a user-defined callback function that will be called whenever the LDAP client library chases a referral to another naming context.
NOTIFYOFNEWCONNECTION	Typedef for a user-defined callback function that will be called whenever the LDAP client library creates a new LDAP connection when chasing a referral.
DEREFERENCECONNECTION	Typedef for a user-defined callback function that will be called whenever the LDAP client is done with a connection that it used while chasing a referral.

Two Kinds of Referrals

Active Directory domain controllers generate two kinds of referrals. The first kind of referral is called a subordinate referral. You will get a subordinate referral if you try to access an object that exists in a naming context that is subordinate to the one you are currently searching. Figure 23.1 shows how a subordinate referral can occur.

FIGURE 23.1

A subordinate reference.

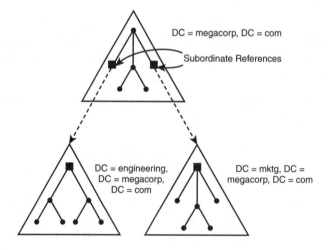

DC = megacorp, DC = com

Subordinate References

DC = engineering,
DC = megacorp,
DC = com

DC = mktg, DC =
megacorp, DC = com

Active Directory can generate another kind of referral, called an external referral. This occurs if the directory administrator has created external connections or cross-references from Active Directory to other LDAP directories or other Active Directory trees. Figure 23.2 shows an example of an external referral.

FIGURE 23.2

An external reference.

Active Directory Forest

Other LDAP Tree or Active Directory Forest

External Reference

When Are Referrals Generated?

Active Directory generates a referral whenever an operation is targeted to a naming context different than the current one—that is, the domain naming context on the domain controller with which you started your LDAP session. For instance, if there are two naming contexts called `megacorp.com` and `acctg.megacorp.com`, and you issue a search on `megacorp.com` with the scope parameter set to `LDAP_SCOPE_SUBTREE`, Active Directory will search all the objects in `DC=megacorp,DC=com` and return a subordinate referral to `DC=acctg,DC=megacorp,DC=com`. If `megacorp.com` was the first domain in the first tree in the enterprise (the root domain), Active Directory will return referrals to `DC=acctg,DC=megacorp,DC=com` and `CN=Configuration,DC=acctg,DC=megacorp,DC=com` because the Configuration naming context is always subordinate to the first domain in the enterprise.

You might think this last referral is a little odd. Isn't there a copy of the Configuration naming context on every domain controller? Why would Active Directory generate a referral to a naming context that is available on the current server? Why doesn't it just do the search?

The answer is consistency. Active Directory currently supports exactly three naming contexts on each domain controller: the Domain naming context, the Configuration naming context, and the Schema naming context. But Microsoft intends to support an arbitrary set of naming contexts per domain controller in future versions of Active Directory. That

23

PROCESSING LDAP REFERRALS

is, a domain controller could have replicas of three, or five, or ten different naming contexts. Let's say domain controller A has replicas of the naming contexts `DC=megacorp,DC=com` and `DC=acctg,DC=megacorp,DC=com`, and domain controller B has a replica of `DC=megacorp,DC=com`. If a client performed a search on domain controller A with a scope of `LDAP_SCOPE_SUBTREE`, you might expect that Active Directory would just perform the search all the way down through the `DC=acctg` naming context. But, if you issued the same search against domain controller B, Active Directory would have to generate a referral. That means you would get different results depending on what domain controller you happened to be connected to, which is certainly unexpected behavior. The solution is that Active Directory generates a referral whenever a search goes out of the scope of the current naming context, even if the naming context is on the same server.

Two Strategies for Handling Referrals

There are two strategies for dealing with references. You can tell the LDAP client to chase them for you, or you can tell the LDAP client to return the referrals to your application and you can write the code to chase them yourself.

Configuring the LDAP Client to Chase Referrals

The simplest way to handle referrals is to let LDAP chase them for you. The LDAP client library does this by default, so if you want the LDAP client to chase referrals, you really don't have to do anything special.

> **CAUTION**
>
> Having the LDAP client automatically chase referrals seems to be a hit-or-miss operation as of Windows 2000 Release Candidate 1. The behavior I've seen is that the client will chase at least one subordinate referral, but if there is more than one subordinate domain, the LDAP client will not chase the second referral. The LDAP client instead will return the referral to your application.
>
> This might or might not be fixed by the time Windows 2000 ships.

The `LDAP_OPT_REFERRALS` session option controls the chasing of referrals by the LDAP client. You can turn the chase referrals option off and on by using the `ldap_set_option()` functions as shown in the following code:

```
// Turn off referral chasing
ULONG uOptReferrals = false;
ULONG uErr = ldap_set_option( pLdap, LDAP_OPT_REFERRALS, &uOptReferrals );
if( uErr == LDAP_SUCCESS )
{
    // Do LDAP function without chasing referrals

    // Turn referral chasing back on
    uOptReferrals = true;
    ldap_set_option( pLdap, LDAP_OPT_REFERRALS, &uOptReferrals );
}
```

You can also specify the kinds of referrals the LDAP client will chase. For instance, if you only want the client to chase subordinate referrals, you can do the following:

```
ULONG uOptReferrals = LDAP_CHASE_SUBORDINATE_REFERRALS;
ULONG uErr = ldap_set_option( pLdap, LDAP_OPT_REFERRALS, &uOpts );
```

The following code will set the client to chase only external referrals:

```
ULONG uOptReferrals = LDAP_CHASE_EXTERNAL_REFERRALS;
ULONG uErr = ldap_set_option( pLdap, LDAP_OPT_REFERRALS, &uOptReferrals );
```

You can OR together the LDAP_CHASE_EXTERNAL_REFERRALS and LDAP_CHASE_SUBORDINATE_REFERRALS flags, in which case the effect is exactly the same as setting the options to TRUE.

```
ULONG uOptReferrals = LDAP_CHASE_EXTERNAL_REFERRALS
➥| LDAP_CHASE_SUBORDINATE_REFERRALS;
ULONG uErr = ldap_set_option( pLdap, LDAP_OPT_REFERRALS, &uOptReferrals );
```

Using ldap_set_option to tell LDAP to chase referrals will cause the LDAP client to chase referrals for all subsequent operations on that LDAP connection. If you want to chase referrals on just one operation, you can specify a special LDAP client control in an extended LDAP API function, such as ldap_search_ext_s(). For instance, the search in Listing 23.1 will chase referrals down through any subordinate naming contexts.

LISTING 23.1 USING A CLIENT CONTROL WITH ldap_search_ext_s() TO CHASE REFERRALS

```
1: ULONG uFlags = LDAP_CHASE_SUBORDINATE_REFERRALS;
2: LDAPControl sReferralControl =
3: {
4:     "1.2.840.113556.1.4.1339",          // control OID
5:     {
6:         sizeof( uFlags ),
7:         ( char* )&uFlags
8:     }, // control data
9:     true // critical?
```

continues

23

PROCESSING
LDAP REFERRALS

LISTING 23.1   CONTINUED

```
10: };
11:
12: PLDAPControl apsClientControls[] =
13: {
14:     &sReferralControl,
15:     NULL
16: };
17:
18: LDAPMessage* psResult;
19:
20: ULONG uErr = ldap_search_ext_s(
21:     psLdap,                  // ldap session
22:     "DC=megacorp,DC=com",    // search base
23:     LDAP_SCOPE_SUBTREE,      // scope
24:     "objectClass=*",         // filter
25:     NULL,                    // attrs (all)
26:     false,                   // attrs only?
27:     NULL,                    // server controls
28:     apsClientControls,       // client controls
29:     NULL,                    // timeout = none
30:     0,                       // size limit = none
31:     &psResult                // result pointer
32: );
```

Chasing Referrals from Search Results

The second option for handling referrals is to configure the LDAP client to not chase them, and for your application to get the referrals and handle them itself. The code to do this can be a little involved, but it gives you complete control over what referrals you chase and how you chase them.

There are four functions in the Microsoft LDAP client library that you can use to handle referrals. ldap_first_reference() and ldap_next_reference() return the referral entries from the search results returned by ldap_search_s(). ldap_count_references() counts the number of referrals contained in a search result. ldap_parse_reference() parses a referral entry into a list of LDAP URLs that you can then use to continue the search.

LDAPMessage* ldap_first_reference(LDAP* psLdap, LDAPMessage* psResult)
    psLdap is a pointer to the LDAP session that generated the referral.

    psResult is a pointer to the LDAPMessage structure that was returned by
    ldap_result(), ldap_search_s(), or whatever other function you called that generated the referral.

Returns: A pointer to the referral message. You can pass this pointer to `ldap_parse_referral()` to obtain the servers and naming contexts the program was referred to. You do not need to explicitly free this pointer; it is freed when you free the original `LDAPMessage*` returned from the function that generated the referral. A return value of `NULL` indicates there are no more referrals or an error of some sort. You must call `LdapGetLastError()` to determine which is indicated by the `NULL` value.

`LDAPMessage* ldap_next_reference( LDAP* psLdap, LDAPMessage psReferral )`

> `psLdap` is a pointer to the LDAP session that generated the referral.

> `psReferral` is a pointer to the `LDAPMessage` structure that was returned by a previous call to `ldap_first_reference()` or `ldap_next_reference()`.

Returns: A pointer to the referral message. You can pass this pointer to `ldap_parse_referral()` to obtain the servers and naming contexts to which the program was referred. You do not need to explicitly free this pointer; it is freed when you free the original `LDAPMessage*` returned from the function that generated the referral. A return value of `NULL` indicates there are no more referrals or an error of some sort. You must call `LdapGetLastError()` to determine which is indicated by the `NULL` value.

`ULONG ldap_count_references( LDAP* psLdap, LDAPMessage* psResult )`

> `psLdap` is a pointer to the LDAP session that generated the list of referrals.

> `psResult` is a pointer to the LDAP result structure returned by `ldap_result()`, `ldap_search_s()`, or by whatever other LDAP function you used that generated the referral.

Returns: The number of referral structures in the referral result list.

Each referral result contains one or more strings that contain the server name and naming context of each referral. You can get this information by calling `ldap_parse_reference()`.

`ULONG ldap_parse_reference( LDAP* psLdap, LDAPMessage* psReferenceMessage,`
`➥PCHAR** pppReferrals )`

> `psLdap` is a pointer to the LDAP session that generated the referrals.

> `psReferenceMessage` is a pointer to a reference message returned by `ldap_first_referral()`, `ldap_next_referral()`, or `ldap_result()`.

> `pppReferrals` is the address of a pointer to an array of pointers to NUL-terminated strings. `ldap_parse_reference()` will set `*pppReferrals` to point to the array of referral strings, each string containing a server name and naming context. You must free this array by passing `*pppReferrals` to `ldap_value_free()`.

Returns: The LDAP error, if any, or `LDAP_SUCCESS` if the call succeeded.

23

PROCESSING LDAP REFERRALS

> **CAUTION**
>
> The Microsoft implementation of `ldap_parse_reference()` is not consistent with the definition given in the current Internet draft for the C language LDAP API. Take appropriate precautions if you expect your source code to be portable.

There are four steps in handling referrals:

- Turn off automatic referral-chasing
- Issue a search or other function that will generate referrals
- Retrieve the referral information
- Chase the referrals

Configuring the LDAP client not to chase referrals is straightforward, as you have seen in the previous sections. You simply call `ldap_set_option()` using the `LDAP_OPT_REFERRALS` option identifier and pass the address of an integer that is set to `0`.

```
// Turn off referral chasing
ULONG uOptReferrals = false;
ULONG uErr = ldap_set_option( psLdap, LDAP_OPT_REFERRALS, &uOptReferrals
➥);
```

When you issue a search that generates referrals, the LDAP client no longer chases them for you. It's up to you to retrieve the referral information from the LDAP client.

The referral information comes back from the server along with the search results. The LDAP client builds a list of the returned referrals, and you can enumerate the referral entries in the list using the functions `ldap_first_reference()` and `ldap_next_reference()`. You then must parse each referral entry using the `ldap_parse_reference()` function, which gives you an array of pointers to LDAP URLs that contain the names of the referred-to naming contexts. Typically, the code to do this looks something like Listing 23.2.

LISTING 23.2 PROCESSING REFERRALS WITH `ldap_first_reference()` AND `ldap_next_reference()`

```
1:   #include <windows.h>
2:   #include <winldap.h>
3:   #include <time.h>
4:   #include <iostream.h>
5:
6:   int main( int argc, char** argv )
7:   {
```

```
8:        LDAP* psLdap = ldap_init( NULL, LDAP_PORT );
9:        if( psLdap != NULL )
10:       {
11:          ULONG uErr = ldap_bind_s( psLdap, NULL, NULL,
          ➥LDAP_AUTH_NEGOTIATE );
12:          if( uErr == LDAP_SUCCESS )
13:          {
14:              // set LDAP API version
15:              int nVersion = LDAP_VERSION3;
16:              ldap_set_option( psLdap, LDAP_OPT_VERSION, &nVersion );
17:
18:              // turn off referrals chasing
19:              int nChaseReferrals = 0;
20:              ldap_set_option( psLdap, LDAP_OPT_REFERRALS,
              ➥&nChaseReferrals );
21:
22:              // DN of search base
23:              char szDomainDN[ 1024 ] = { 0 };
24:
25:              LDAPMessage* psMsg = NULL;
26:
27:              // Get rootDSE attr rootDomainNamingContext
28:              uErr = ldap_search_s(
29:                  psLdap,
30:                  NULL,
31:                  LDAP_SCOPE_BASE,
32:                  "objectClass=*",
33:                  NULL,
34:                  false,
35:                  &psMsg
36:              );
37:              if( uErr == LDAP_SUCCESS )
38:              {
39:                  char** ppszDomain = ldap_get_values( psLdap, psMsg,
                  ➥"rootDomainNamingContext" );
40:                  if( ppszDomain != NULL )
41:                  {
42:                      strcat( szDomainDN, ppszDomain[ 0 ] );
43:                  }
44:                  ldap_msgfree( psMsg );
45:              }
46:
47:              ULONG uErr = ldap_search_s(
48:                  psLdap,
49:                  szDomainDN,
50:                  LDAP_SCOPE_SUBTREE,
51:                  "objectClass=*",
52:                  NULL,
53:                  false,
54:                  &psMsg
```

23

PROCESSING
LDAP REFERRALS

continues

Listing 23.2   CONTINUED

```
55:              );
56:              if( uErr == LDAP_SUCCESS )
57:              {
58:                  // print the search results
59:                  for( LDAPMessage* psEntry = ldap_first_entry( psLdap,
                 ➥psMsg );
60:                      psEntry != NULL;
61:                      psEntry = ldap_next_entry( psLdap, psEntry ) )
62:                  {
63:                      char* pszDN = ldap_get_dn( psLdap, psEntry );
64:                      cout << "DN: " << pszDN << endl;
65:                  }
66:
67:                  // count the referrals
68:                  int nRefs = ldap_count_references( psLdap, psMsg );
69:                  cout << "nRefs: " << nRefs << endl;
70:
71:                  // enumerate the referrals
72:                  for( LDAPMessage* psReferralEntry =
                 ➥ldap_first_reference(psLdap, psMsg );
73:                      psReferralEntry != NULL;
74:                      psReferralEntry = ldap_next_reference( psLdap,
                 ➥psReferralEntry ) )
75:                  {
76:                      char** ppszReferrals;
77:
78:                      uErr = ldap_parse_reference( psLdap,
                 ➥psReferralEntry,&ppszReferrals );
79:                      if( uErr == LDAP_SUCCESS )
80:                      {
81:                          for( int nRef = 0; ppszReferrals[ nRef ] !=
                 ➥NULL; nRef++ )
82:                          {
83:                              // print the referral LDAP URL
84:                              cout << "REF: " << ppszReferrals[ nRef ]
                 <<endl;
85:                          }
86:
87:                          ldap_value_free( ppszReferrals );
88:                      }
89:                  }
90:              }
91:          }
92:
93:          ldap_unbind( psLdap );
```

```
94:    }
95:
96:    return 0;
97: }
```

The program in Listing 23.2 starts by initializing an LDAP session with `ldap_init()` and authenticating the session with `ldap_bind_s()`.

At lines 28 through 45, the program gets the `rootDomainNamingContext` attribute from the `rootDSE` of the domain controller. This is the distinguished name of the topmost domain in the forest.

At line 47, the program starts a subtree search of the top domain, which will generate referrals to any subordinate domains.

The program prints the distinguished name of all the entries it found in the search at lines 59–65.

At line 72, the program starts a loop to process the referral entries returned by the server. For each referral, the program calls `ldap_parse_reference()` to get the referral information. At line 84, the program prints the referral string.

The program frees the referral strings by calling `ldap_value_free()` at line 87 and closes the LDAP session by calling `ldap_unbind()` at line 93.

After you have parsed the referral URLs from the search results, you have to parse the URL itself into a useful form. The LDAP URL returned for referrals has the following format:

```
"LDAP:\\" <DNS domain name> "\" <domain DN>
```

You must parse this string and then use the `DsGetDcName()` function to get the name of a domain controller that can handle that domain. Listing 23.3 is a function that parses the URL into its DNS domain name and naming context distinguished name parts.

LISTING 23.3   FUNCTION TO GET THE DOMAIN AND DISTINGUISHED NAME FROM A REFERRAL URL

```
1: ULONG GetDomainAndNCNameForURL( char* pszURL, char* pszDNSDomain,
   ➥char* pszNCDN )
2: {
3:     ULONG uErr = LDAP_SUCCESS;
4:     const int nIDBytes = 7;
5:     char szID[ nIDBytes + 1 ];
6:
7:     int nChars = 0;
```

continues

LISTING 23.3   CONTINUED

```
 8:
 9:     while( *pszURL && nChars < nIDBytes )
10:         szID[ nChars++ ] = *pszURL++;
11:     szID[ nChars ] = '\0';
12:
13:     if( stricmp( szID, "LDAP://" ) != 0 )
14:     {
15:         uErr = LDAP_INVALID_DN_SYNTAX; // as good an error as any, I
                                           // guess
16:     }
17:     else
18:     {
19:         // Get the DNS domain
20:         nChars = 0;
21:         while( *pszURL && *pszURL != '/' )
22:             *pszDNSDomain++ = *pszURL++;
23:         *pszDNSDomain = '\0';
24:
25:         // Get the NC DN
26:         nChars = 0;
27:         pszURL++;
28:         while( *pszURL && *pszURL != '/' )
29:             *pszNCDN++ = *pszURL++;
30:         *pszNCDN = '\0';
31:     }
32:
33:     return uErr;
34: }
```

The function in Listing 23.4 accepts an LDAP URL as returned from the
ldap_parse_reference() function and returns an LDAP session pointer to a domain
controller that contains the referred-to domain. Given a domain name, it uses
DsGetDcName to find an appropriate domain controller.

LISTING 23.4   FUNCTION TO CREATE AN LDAP SESSION FROM A REFERRAL URL

```
1: ULONG GetHostAndNCForURL( char* pszURL, char* pszHostName, char*
   ➡pszNCDN )
2: {
3:     char szDNSDomain[ 256 ];
4:
5:     ULONG uErr = GetDomainAndNCNameForURL( pszURL, szDNSDomain,
       ➡pszNCDN );
6:     if( uErr == 0 )
7:     {
8:         DOMAIN_CONTROLLER_INFO* psDCInfo;
9:
```

```
10:            uErr = DsGetDcName(
11:                NULL,                 // computer name
12:                szDNSDomain,     // domain name
13:                NULL,                 // domain GUID
14:                NULL,                 // site name
15:                DS_DIRECTORY_SERVICE_REQUIRED | DS_IS_DNS_NAME
                   ➥| DS_RETURN_DNS_NAME, // flags
16:                &psDCInfo           // addr of pointer to set
17:            );
18:
19:            if( uErr == 0 )
20:            {
21:                strcpy( pszHostName, psDCInfo->DomainControllerName + 2 );
22:                NetApiBufferFree( psDCInfo );
23:            }
24:        }
25:
26:        return uErr;
27: }
```

The sample program in Listing 23.5 ties all these ideas together. The program gets the root domain naming context, turns off referrals, and starts a subtree search on the root domain naming context. It prints the distinguished names of all the returned search items, and then gets the referrals and processes them recursively.

LISTING 23.5 EXPLICITLY CHASING LDAP REFERRALS

```
1:     #include <iostream.h>
2:     #include <windows.h>
3:     #include <winldap.h>
4:     #include <DSGetDC.h>
5:     #include <LM.h>
6:
7:     // prototypes
8:     LDAP* InitializeSession( char* pszHost );
9:     ULONG GetDomainAndNCNameForURL( char* pszURL, char* pszDNSDomain,
       ➥char*pszNCDN );
10:    ULONG GetHostAndNCForURL( char* pszURL, char* pszHostName,
       ➥char*pszNCDN );
11:    void SearchNC( LDAP* psLdap, char* pszDomainDN );
12:
13:    int main(int argc, char* argv[])
14:    {
15:        // Get an LDAP session and set all the options
16:        LDAP* psLdap = InitializeSession( NULL );
17:
18:        if( psLdap != NULL )
19:        {
```

23
PROCESSING
LDAP
REFERRALS

continues

LISTING 23.5   CONTINUED

```
20:          // DN of root domain NC to search
21:          char szDomainDN[ 1024 ] = { 0 };
22:
23:          LDAPMessage* psMsg = NULL;
24:
25:          // Get rootDSE attr defaultNamingContext
26:          ULONG uErr = ldap_search_s( psLdap, NULL, LDAP_SCOPE_BASE,
        ➥"objectClass=*", NULL, false, &psMsg );
27:          if( uErr == LDAP_SUCCESS )
28:          {
29:              char** ppszDomain = ldap_get_values( psLdap, psMsg,
            ➥"rootDomainNamingContext" );
30:              if( ppszDomain != NULL )
31:              {
32:                  strcat( szDomainDN, ppszDomain[ 0 ] );
33:              }
34:              ldap_msgfree( psMsg );
35:          }
36:
37:          // start the search
38:          SearchNC( psLdap, szDomainDN );
39:
40:          // clean up the session
41:          ( void )ldap_unbind( psLdap );
42:      }
43:
44:      return 0;
45: }
46:
47: //
48: // Search the given NC using the give LDAP session. Chase any
    //referrals
49: //
50: void SearchNC( LDAP* psLdap, char* pszDomainDN )
51: {
52:      // Don't retrieve any attributes
53:      char* apszAttrs[] = { "1.1", NULL };
54:      LDAPMessage* psMsg;
55:
56:      cout << "Searching " << pszDomainDN << endl;
57:
58:      // Do a subtree search
59:      ULONG uErr = ldap_search_s( psLdap, pszDomainDN,
        ➥LDAP_SCOPE_SUBTREE,"objectClass=*", apszAttrs, false, &psMsg );
60:      if( uErr == LDAP_SUCCESS )
61:      {
62:          // enumerate the search results, but do anything with them
```

```
63:             for( LDAPMessage* psEntry = ldap_first_entry( psLdap, psMsg );
64:                  psEntry != NULL;
65:                  psEntry = ldap_next_entry( psLdap, psEntry ) )
66:             {
67:                 char* pszDN = ldap_get_dn( psLdap, psEntry );
68:             }
69:
70:             // Get the number of referrals
71:             int nRefs = ldap_count_references( psLdap, psMsg );
72:             cout << "NREFS: " << nRefs << endl;
73:
74:             // Enumerate the referrals
75:             for( LDAPMessage* pReferral = ldap_first_reference( psLdap,
         ➥psMsg );
76:                  pReferral != NULL;
77:                  pReferral = ldap_next_reference( psLdap, pReferral ) )
78:             {
79:                 char** ppszReferrals;
80:
81:                 uErr = ldap_parse_reference( psLdap, pReferral,
         ➥&ppszReferrals );
82:                 if( uErr == LDAP_SUCCESS )
83:                 {
84:                     for( int nRef = 0; ppszReferrals[ nRef ] != NULL;
         ➥nRef++ )
85:                     {
86:                         char szHostName[ 256 ];
87:                         char szNCDN[ 256 ];
88:
89:                         // Parse the URL into a host name and an NC name
90:                         uErr = GetHostAndNCForURL( ppszReferrals[ nRef ],
         ➥szHostName, szNCDN );
91:                         if( uErr == 0 )
92:                         {
93:                             // Get a session on the host
94:                             LDAP* psLdapRef = InitializeSession(
         ➥szHostName );
95:                             if( psLdapRef )
96:                             {
97:                                 // Search the NC
98:                                 SearchNC( psLdapRef, szNCDN );
99:
100:                                ldap_unbind( psLdapRef );
101:                            }
102:                        }
103:                    }
104:
105:                    ldap_value_free( ppszReferrals );
106:                }
107:            }
```

continues

LISTING 23.5   CONTINUED

```
108:        }
109: }
110:
111: //
112: // Initialize an LDAP session for the specified host
113: //
114: LDAP* InitializeSession( char* pszHost )
115: {
116:     LDAP* psLdap = ldap_init( pszHost, LDAP_PORT );
117:
118:     if( psLdap != NULL )
119:     {
120:         // set LDAPv3
121:         int nVer = LDAP_VERSION3;
122:         ldap_set_option( psLdap, LDAP_OPT_VERSION, &nVer );
123:
124:         // disable referral chasing
125:         int nOpts = 0;
126:         ldap_set_option( psLdap, LDAP_OPT_REFERRALS, &nOpts );
127:
128:         // authenticate
129:         ULONG uErr = ldap_bind_s( psLdap, NULL, NULL,
             ➥LDAP_AUTH_NEGOTIATE );
130:         if( uErr != LDAP_SUCCESS )
131:         {
132:             ldap_unbind( psLdap );
133:             psLdap = NULL;
134:         }
135:     }
136:
137:     return psLdap;
138: }
139:
140: //
141: // Given a LDAP URL, return the host name and the NC DN
142: //
143: ULONG GetHostAndNCForURL( char* pszURL, char* pszHostName, char*
     ➥pszNCDN )
144: {
145:     char szDNSDomain[ 256 ];
146:
147:     // Parse the URL
148:     ULONG uErr = GetDomainAndNCNameForURL( pszURL, szDNSDomain,
         ➥pszNCDN );
149:     if( uErr == 0 )
150:     {
151:         DOMAIN_CONTROLLER_INFO* psDCInfo;
152:
153:         // Get a DC for the domain parsed from the URL
```

```
154:        uErr = DsGetDcName(
155:            NULL,                // computer name
156:            szDNSDomain,         // domain name
157:            NULL,                // domain GUID
158:            NULL,                // site name
159:            DS_DIRECTORY_SERVICE_REQUIRED | DS_IS_DNS_NAME |
                ➥DS_RETURN_DNS_NAME, // flags
160:            &psDCInfo            // addr of pointer to set
161:        );
162:
163:        if( uErr == 0 )
164:        {
165:            strcpy( pszHostName, psDCInfo->DomainControllerName + 2 );
166:            NetApiBufferFree( psDCInfo );
167:        }
168:    }
169:
170:    return uErr;
171: }
172:
173: //
174: // Parse a URL string into a DNS domain name and an NC DN
175: //
176: ULONG GetDomainAndNCNameForURL( char* pszURL, char* pszDNSDomain,
     ➥char* pszNCDN )
177: {
178:    ULONG uErr = LDAP_SUCCESS;
179:    const int nIDBytes = 7;
180:    char szID[ nIDBytes + 1 ];
181:
182:    int nChars = 0;
183:
184:    // Get the LDAP:// part and make sure this is a valid URL
185:    while( *pszURL && nChars < nIDBytes )
186:        szID[ nChars++ ] = *pszURL++;
187:    szID[ nChars ] = '\0';
188:
189:    if( stricmp( szID, "LDAP://" ) != 0 )
190:    {
191:        uErr = LDAP_INVALID_DN_SYNTAX; // as good an error as any, I
                                           //   guess
192:    }
193:    else
194:    {
195:        // Get the DNS domain
196:        nChars = 0;
197:        while( *pszURL && *pszURL != '/' )
198:            *pszDNSDomain++ = *pszURL++;
199:        *pszDNSDomain = '\0';
200:
```

continues

23

PROCESSING
LDAP REFERRALS

LISTING 23.5 CONTINUED

```
201:          // Get the NC DN
202:          nChars = 0;
203:          pszURL++;
204:          while( *pszURL && *pszURL != '/' )
205:              *pszNCDN++ = *pszURL++;
206:          *pszNCDN = '\0';
207:      }
208:
209:      return uErr;
210: }
```

Line 16 initializes an LDAP session on the default domain controller for the domain of which the currently logged-in user is a member. The InitializeSession() function calls ldap_init and ldap_bind, and sets the options on the session to use LDAPv3 facilities and to disable referrals.

Lines 26–35 get the root domain naming context for the domain of the currently logged-in user. This is the naming context in which the program will start the search.

At line 38, the program calls SearchNC(). This function calls ldap_search_s() on the specified naming context, enumerates the results, and also picks up any referrals that were returned by the server.

SearchNC() executes the subtree search at line 59 and enumerates the results at lines 63–68. At lines 71–72, SearchNC() counts the referrals in the results message and prints out the number of referrals returned.

SearchNC enumerates the referrals in a for loop starting at line 75. This loop calls ldap_first_reference() and ldap_next_reference() to get the referral entries from the search results.

At line 81, SearchNC() parses each referral entry into an array of LDAP URL strings.

At line 90, SearchNC() calls GetHostAndNCForURL() to parse the URL into a host name and an NC name to search.

At line 94, SearchNC() calls InitializeSession() to initialize a new LDAP session for the referred-to host, and starts another subtree search by calling SearchNC() recursively at line 98.

GetHostAndNCForURL() starts at line 143. It calls GetDomainAndNCNameForURL() to parse the URL string, and then calls DsGetDcName() to find a domain controller for the domain it found in the URL string.

GetDomainAndNCNameForURL() at line 176 simply parses the incoming URL into its two components.

Caching Connections for Referrals

One disadvantage of having the LDAP client chase referrals automatically is that the LDAP client might create and destroy LDAP sessions with the same servers over and over again. This can be a fairly expensive operation, particularly if the connections are to domain controllers located in different sites than the client. Ideally, you would like to cache LDAP connections so that the LDAP client could reuse them as needed.

The Microsoft LDAP client library provides a set of callback functions for exactly this purpose. There are three callback functions you can set up.

The first callback function is the Query For Connection callback. The LDAP client will call this function when it is about to chase a referral. Your callback function can return a connection (a pointer to a valid LDAP structure) for the client to use, or your callback can tell the LDAP client to open its own connection.

The second callback function is the Notify New Connection callback function. The LDAP client will call this function when it has successfully created a connection when chasing a referral. This is your opportunity to squirrel away the LDAP connection for later use.

The third callback function is the Connection Done callback (or the Dereference callback if you read the header file). The LDAP client will call the Connection Done callback when it is done with the referral. This is an indication that you can get rid of the connection from the connection cache if you want.

Figures 23.3 and 23.4 show the control flow for the callback functions.

FIGURE 23.3

The control flow for referral callback functions with no cached connection.

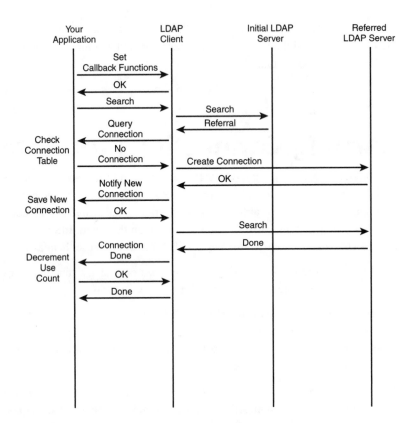

FIGURE 23.4

The control flow for referral callback functions with a cached connection.

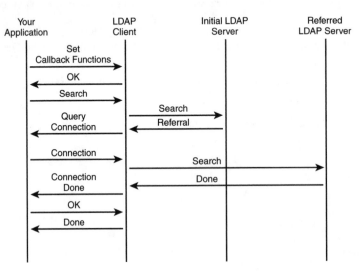

The following are the function prototypes and structure definitions you need to set up referral callbacks. Note that these are functions that *you* have to implement; the LDAP client library will call them at the appropriate times.

```
ULONG _cdecl QueryForConnection( LDAP* pPrimaryConnection,
➥LDAP* pReferralFromConnection, wchar_t* pszNewDN, char* pszHostName,
➥ULONG uPort, void* pvSecAuthIdentity, void* pvCurrentUserToken,
➥LDAP** ppConnectionToUse )
```

pPrimaryConnection is a pointer to the LDAP session on which the original operation (for instance, a search) was started.

pReferralFromConnection is a pointer to the LDAP session that generated the referral. This will be the same as pPrimaryConnection in cases in which this is a referral from the naming context where the original operation occurred.

pszNewDN is a pointer to a NUL-terminated Unicode string containing the fully qualified distinguished name of the referred-to naming context.

pszHostName is a pointer to a NUL-terminated ANSI string containing the DNS name of the domain (not the DNS name of the domain controller!) containing the naming context given by pszNewDN. You have to call a function such as DsGetDcNames to get a domain controller for this domain.

uPort is the TCP port on which the operation was started. If you cached LDAP sessions for both the global catalog and the regular DSA, you could use the port value to differentiate them.

pvSecAuthIdentity is a pointer to the SEC_WINNT_AUTH_IDENTITY or SEC_WINNT_AUTH_IDENTITY_EX structure containing the credentials for the user who initiated the operation. You can pass this pointer to ldap_bind_s() to authenticate an LDAP connection. If this parameter is NULL, indicating that the operation was started by the currently logged-in user, the pvCurrentUserToken contains the current logged-in user's access token. Refer to Chapter 4, "Active Directory Security," for more on credentials and access tokens.

pvCurrentUserToken is a pointer to the current user's access token.

ppConnectionToUse is the address of an LDAP session pointer for you to set. If your code has an LDAP connection the LDAP client can use to chase the referral, set *ppConnectionToUse to this session pointer.

Returns: LDAP_SUCCESS if the LDAP client should continue to chase the referral, and any other error if it should not.

```
BOOLEAN _cdecl NotifyNewConnection( LDAP* pPrimaryConnection,
➥LDAP* pReferralFromConnection, wchar_t* pszNewDN, char* pszHostName,
➥LDAP* pNewConnection, ULONG uPort, void* pvSecAuthIdentity,
➥void* pvUserLUID, ULONG uBindError )
```

pPrimaryConnection is a pointer to the LDAP session on which the original operation (for instance, a search) was started.

pReferralFromConnection is a pointer to the LDAP session that generated the referral. This will be the same as pPrimaryConnection in the case that this is a referral from the naming context where the original operation occurred.

pszNewDN is a pointer to a NUL-terminated Unicode string containing the fully qualified distinguished name of the referred-to naming context.

pszHostName is a pointer to a NUL-terminated ANSI string containing the DNS name of the domain (not the DNS name of the domain controller!) containing the naming context given by pszNewDN. You have to call a function such as DsGetDcNames to get a domain controller for this domain.

pNewConnection is a pointer to the LDAP session that the LDAP client is using to chase the referral.

uPort is the TCP port on which the operation was started.

pvSecAuthIdentity is a pointer to the SEC_WINNT_AUTH_IDENTITY or SEC_WINNT_AUTH_IDENTITY_EX structure containing the credentials for the user who initiated the operation. You can pass this pointer to ldap_bind_s() to authenticate an LDAP connection. This parameter may be NULL, indicating that the operation was started by the currently logged-in user.

pvUserLUID is a pointer to the current user's locally unique ID (LUID).

uBindError is the error code returned from the bind attempt on the referred-to server. If it is equal to LDAP_SUCCESS, the bind completed successfully.

Returns: Your function should return TRUE if you want to cache the connection. In that case, the LDAP library will not destroy the connection when it is done with the connection. If you return FALSE, the LDAP library will destroy the connection when it has completed the referred operation on this server.

```
ULONG _cdecl UnreferenceConnection( LDAP* pPrimaryConnection,
➥LDAP* pConnectionToUnreference )
```

pPrimaryConnection is a pointer to the LDAP session on which the original operation (for instance, a search) was started.

pConnectionToUnreference is a pointer to the LDAP session that the LDAP library is finished with.

Returns: Your function should return LDAP_SUCCESS, or an appropriate error code if an error occurs.

To install your callback routines, you must initialize the LDAP_REFERRAL_CALLBACK structure with the addresses of your routines, and then call ldap_set_option() using the LDAP_OPT_REFERRAL_CALLBACK option identifier, passing the address of the LDAP_REFERRAL_CALLBACK structure as the argument.

You can uninstall the callback functions by calling `ldap_set_option()` using the `LDAP_OPT_REFERRAL_CALLBACK` identifier, passing `NULL` for the third argument.

The `LDAP_REFERRAL_CALLBACK` structure looks like this:

```
typedef struct LdapReferralCallback
{
    ULONG SizeOfCallbacks;
    QUERYFORCONNECTION *QueryForConnection;
    NOTIFYOFNEWCONNECTION *NotifyRoutine;
    DEREFERENCECONNECTION *DereferenceRoutine;
} LDAP_REFERRAL_CALLBACK, *PLDAP_REFERRAL_CALLBACK;
```

Its elements are described in Table 23.2.

TABLE 23.2 ELEMENTS OF THE `LdapReferralCallback` STRUCTURE

Element	Description
`SizeOfCallback`	The size of the `LDAP_REFERRAL_CALLBACK` structure. You should set this to `sizeof( LDAP_REFERRAL_CALLBACK )`.
`QueryForConnection`	A pointer to your `QueryForConnection` callback function.
`NotifyRoutine`	A pointer to your `NotifyNewConnection` callback routine.
`DereferenceRoutine`	A pointer to your `UnreferenceConnection` routine.

Listing 23.6 installs a set of callback functions and then issues a subtree search on the root domain naming context. If there are any subordinate domains, the LDAP library calls the callback functions.

LISTING 23.6 HANDLING REFERRAL CONNECTIONS WITH REFERRAL CALLBACK FUNCTIONS

```
1:  #include <iostream.h>
2:  #include <windows.h>
3:  #include <winldap.h>
4:
5:  // This function will be called when the LDAP client is about to chase
    // a referral
6:  ULONG _cdecl QueryForConnection(
7:      PLDAP          PrimaryConnection,
8:      PLDAP          ReferralFromConnection,
9:      PWCHAR         NewDN,
10:     PCHAR          HostName,
11:     ULONG          PortNumber,
12:     PVOID          SecAuthIdentity,
13:     PVOID          CurrentUserToken,
14:     PLDAP          *ConnectionToUse
```

continues

23

PROCESSING
LDAP REFERRALS

LISTING 23.6 CONTINUED

```
15:  )
16:  {
17:      cout << "QueryForConnection " << HostName << endl;
18:      *ConnectionToUse = NULL; // we don't have a connection for the
                                  // client to use
19:      return LDAP_SUCCESS;
20:  }
21:
22:  BOOLEAN _cdecl NotifyNewConnection(
23:      PLDAP       PrimaryConnection,
24:      PLDAP       ReferralFromConnection,
25:      PWCHAR      NewDN,
26:      PCHAR       HostName,
27:      PLDAP       NewConnection,
28:      ULONG       PortNumber,
29:      PVOID       SecAuthIdentity,
30:      PVOID       CurrentUser,
31:      ULONG       ErrorCodeFromBind
32:  )
33:  {
34:      cout << "New connection " << HostName << endl;
35:      return FALSE; // LDAP client will destroy the session when done
36:  }
37:
38:  ULONG _cdecl UnreferenceConnection(
39:      PLDAP       PrimaryConnection,
40:      PLDAP       ConnectionToDereference
41:  )
42:  {
43:      cout << "Unreference" << endl;
44:      return LDAP_SUCCESS;
45:  }
46:
47:  int main( int argc, char** argv )
48:  {
49:      LDAP* psLdap = ldap_init( NULL, LDAP_PORT );
50:      if( psLdap != NULL )
51:      {
52:          ULONG uErr = ldap_bind_s( psLdap, NULL, NULL,
            ➥LDAP_AUTH_NEGOTIATE );
53:          if( uErr == LDAP_SUCCESS )
54:          {
55:              // set LDAP API version
56:              int nVersion = LDAP_VERSION3;
57:              ldap_set_option( psLdap, LDAP_OPT_VERSION, &nVersion );
58:
59:              // DN of search base
60:              char szDomainDN[ 1024 ] = { 0 };
61:
```

```
62:                 LDAPMessage* psMsg = NULL;
63:
64:                 // Get rootDSE attr rootDomainNamingContext
65:                 uErr = ldap_search_s(
66:                     psLdap,
67:                     NULL,
68:                     LDAP_SCOPE_BASE,
69:                     "objectClass=*",
70:                     NULL,
71:                     false,
72:                     &psMsg
73:                 );
74:                 if( uErr == LDAP_SUCCESS )
75:                 {
76:                     char** ppszDomain = ldap_get_values( psLdap, psMsg,
                    ➥"rootDomainNamingContext" );
77:                     if( ppszDomain != NULL )
78:                     {
79:                         strcat( szDomainDN, ppszDomain[ 0 ] );
80:                     }
81:                     ldap_msgfree( psMsg );
82:                 }
83:
84:                 LDAP_REFERRAL_CALLBACK sCallbacks =
85:                 {
86:                     sizeof( LDAP_REFERRAL_CALLBACK ),
87:                     QueryForConnection,
88:                     NotifyNewConnection,
89:                     UnreferenceConnection
90:                 };
91:
92:                 // set up the callback functions
93:                 ldap_set_option( psLdap, LDAP_OPT_REFERRAL_CALLBACK,
                ➥&sCallbacks );
94:
95:                 char* apszAttrs[] = { "cn", NULL };
96:
97:                 uErr = ldap_search_s(
98:                     psLdap,
99:                     szDomainDN,
100:                    LDAP_SCOPE_SUBTREE,
101:                    "objectClass=*",
102:                    apszAttrs,
103:                    false,
104:                    &psMsg
105:                );
106:                if( uErr == LDAP_SUCCESS )
107:                {
```

23

continues

LISTING 23.6 CONTINUED

```
108:                         // don't have to do anything; the referrals will be
                             // chased anyway
109:                 }
110:         }
111:
112:         ldap_unbind( psLdap );
113:     }
114:
115:     return 0;
116: }
```

At line 49 in Listing 23.6, the program starts by calling ldap_init() and
ldap_bind_s() to initialize an LDAP session.

At line 65, the program calls ldap_search_s() on the rootDSE to get the name of the
topmost domain in the forest into szDomainDN.

The program sets up the LDAP_REFERRAL_CALLBACK structure with pointers to the callback functions at lines 84–90. It then establishes the callback functions by calling
ldap_set_option() with the LDAP_OPT_REFERRAL_CALLBACK parameter at line 93.

At line 97, the program starts a subtree search on the topmost domain in the forest,
which should generate subordinate referrals for any subdomains that exist. The LDAP
library will invoke the callback functions defined at the top of the program for each of
the subordinate domains found.

CHAPTER 24

Modifying Active Directory Objects with LDAP

After searching for objects in the directory, modifying objects in the directory will probably be your most common directory programming task.

There are two primary kinds of modifications you can make to an object with LDAP. The first kind (and the one you will use most often) modifies the object's attributes. This includes adding new attributes, adding new values to existing attributes, and removing values of existing attributes. There are four APIs for modifying the attributes of an object: `ldap_modify()`, `ldap_modify_s()`, `ldap_modify_ext()`, and `ldap_modify_ext_s()`. The second kind of modification involves renaming an object. There are four APIs for renaming an object. (Well, there are actually eight, but four of them are obsolete.) They are `ldap_rename()`, `ldap_rename_s()`, `ldap_rename_ext()`, and `ldap_rename_ext_s()`.

This chapter covers the LDAP functions listed in Table 24.1.

TABLE 24.1 LDAP FUNCTIONS AND DATA STRUCTURES FOR MODIFYING OBJECTS

Function	Description
`ldap_modify()`	Asynchronous function to modify an existing directory object.
`ldap_modify_s()`	Synchronous function to modify an existing directory object.

continues

TABLE 24.1   CONTINUED

Function	Description
ldap_modify_ext()	Asynchronous function to modify an existing directory object. This function includes parameters for specifying client controls and server controls.
ldap_modify_ext_s()	Synchronous function to modify an existing directory object. This function includes parameters for timeout values, client controls, and server controls.
ldap_rename_ext()	Asynchronous function for renaming or moving an existing directory object.
ldap_rename_ext_s()	Synchronous function for renaming or moving an existing directory object.
ldap_result2error()	Extracts the error code from an asynchronous response message retrieved by ldap_result().
ldap_parse_message()	Parses an asynchronous response message retrieved by ldap_result().
ldap_msgfree()	Frees the memory associated with an LDAP response message.
ldap_rename_ext()	Asynchronous function that renames or moves an object in the directory.
ldap_rename_ext_s()	Synchronous function that renames or moves an object in the directory.
struct ldapmod (LDAPMod)	Structure that defines an attribute modification operation.
struct berval (LDAP_BERVAL)	Structure that contains a binary attribute value.

Things to Know Before You Go

There are several underlying concepts that you should understand before modifying objects in the directory. They are generally straightforward, but understanding them will make your programming task a lot easier, and will save you a lot of head-scratching.

First, I'll describe the general mechanisms you use to modify directory objects, including handling multivalued attributes. Then I'll cover the different constraints the directory places on modifications, including schema and access rights enforcement. Finally, I'll look at the different LDAP data structures and API functions you can use to modify objects in the directory.

Multiple Modification Operations

When you modify a directory object with LDAP, you actually specify a list of modification operations, all of which are performed on the same object at the same time. This is good from a network traffic standpoint because LDAP will send several modification operations at once as opposed to one operation at a time. LDAP will ensure that it either makes all the modifications you specified, or it will make none of them. This helps prevent you from creating inconsistent or incomplete directory objects.

Multivalued Attributes

Recall from Chapter 3, "The Components of Active Directory," that LDAP allows you to store multiple values for each attribute. The attributes must all be of the same type, or syntax. Furthermore, and this is a little surprising, each value in the multivalued attribute *must be unique.* For instance, the otherLoginWorkstations attribute of a User object contains a list of workstations that the user may login from. You could store the values LUCY and ARMITAGE, but if you tried to add the value ARMITAGE again, the LDAP modification function would fail with the error LDAP_ATTRIBUTE_OR_VALUE_EXISTS. You have to keep in mind that the values in a multivalued attribute must be unique.

Modification Operations

LDAP provides three ways to modify an attribute. You can

- Add values to an attribute (creating the attribute if necessary and assuming there are no duplicate values)
- Replace all the existing values with a new set of values (creating the attribute if it doesn't exist)
- Delete some or all of any existing values

These three modification operations cover all the ways you would like to modify an attribute.

No Empty Attributes

LDAP does not allow attributes with no values, so if you remove the last value of an attribute, the directory service will remove the entire attribute. There is no such thing as an "empty" or "NULL" attribute or value in LDAP.

Schema Rules

The schema controls what sorts of objects and attributes can appear in the directory and how they can be organized. Any changes you make to directory objects have to observe these rules. The following sections describe the ways that the schema constrains the kinds of modifications you can make.

Attribute Syntaxes

The schema defines what type of data each attribute in the directory may contain. The directory service will deny any attempt on your part to store attribute values that are of a different syntax than the one specified in the schema. For the most part, you can express LDAP values as strings, so this isn't a big deal; just be sure you know what the syntax of an attribute is *before* you try to modify it. You can usually find the syntax of an attribute by checking Microsoft's MSDN Web site, although it is occasionally out-of-date or incorrect.

You can also find the syntax of an attribute by using the DSBrowser utility from the enclosed CD-ROM to look directly in the Active Directory schema. For instance, if you want to know the syntax of the `accountExpires` attribute, run the `DSBrowser` utility and select the `Account-Expires` object in the Schema container. The `attributeSyntax` attribute of the `accountExpires` object will contain the string `"2.5.5.16"`, which represents the large integer syntax. (Chapter 9, "The Active Directory Schema," describes all the possible syntaxes.) Each `accountExpires` attribute in the directory contains a 64-bit integer that represents the time and date a user's account will expire.

Multivalued or Single-Valued?

The schema defines whether or not an attribute may be single-valued or multivalued. If you try to violate this constraint by adding multiple values to a single-valued attribute, LDAP will return an `LDAP_CONSTRAINT_VIOLATION` error. Once again, you must know whether an attribute is single-valued or multivalued *before* you try to add additional values to it.

To determine whether an attribute is single-valued or multivalued, you can again look at Microsoft's Web site, or you can use the DSBrowser utility and check the `isSingleValued` attribute of the schema object.

Must Contain and May Contain

The schema also defines what attributes each class of object *must* contain and what attributes each class of object *may* contain. The directory service will not allow you to delete an attribute that the schema says the object *must* contain. Similarly, you won't be able to add an attribute that the schema does not name in them *must* or *may* contain lists for that class of object.

Don't forget that an object inherits the must and may contain lists from all its superclasses. You have to satisfy the schema constraints for all the classes in the inheritance hierarchy, not just those for the class of the object you are modifying.

System Attributes

The directory service reserves some attributes for its own use. These attributes are generally marked as SYSTEM-ONLY or NO-USER-MODIFICATION, meaning that only Active Directory can modify the attribute.

Access Rights

You can't modify anything in the directory unless you have sufficient access rights. Each attribute in Active Directory has its own access control list (ACL), and each object has its own ACL as well. ACLs for an object are also propagated down from its containing objects. All these ACLs are merged to determine what access you actually have to an object. Be sure your program authenticates to the directory with a username that has sufficient access rights to make the modifications you need to make.

Data Structures for Modifying Objects with LDAP

LDAP implements a fairly sophisticated data model; consequently, setting up the data structures to define an update operation is a little complicated.

You have to set up four fundamental data structures for any modification operation:

- An array of pointers to ldapmod structures—This array must be terminated with a NULL pointer. Each pointer refers to an ldapmod structure which specifies a single modification operation on a single attribute.

- One or more ldapmod structures that specify the modifications to be made— Each ldapmod structure contains a modification operation code (LDAP_MOD_ADD, LDAP_MOD_REPLACE, or LDAP_MOD_DELETE), an attribute name, and a pointer to an array of pointers to values. The modification operation code includes a bit that indicates that the values are specified as strings or binary (berval structure) values.

- An array of pointers to values—The array must be terminated with a NULL pointer. The array entries all point to either string values or berval structures.

- Zero or more values—Each value is either a NUL-terminated string or a berval structure containing a length and a pointer to an arbitrary block of data.

Figure 24.1 gives you an idea of what these data structures look like.

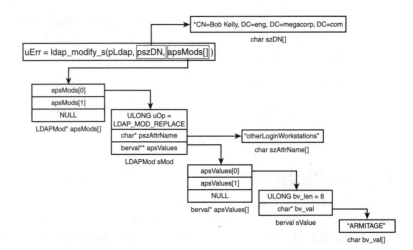

FIGURE 24.1

Data structures for modifying directory entries with LDAP.

Selecting the Appropriate API Function

There are four APIs you can choose from when you need to update LDAP objects. Which one should you use? Well, the four modification APIs mirror the `ldap_search()` and `ldap_add()` APIs in that there are both basic and extended flavors of `ldap_modify`, and there are synchronous and asynchronous versions of each as well. Here are some guidelines you can use.

In general, use the synchronous calls `ldap_modify_s()` or `ldap_modify_ext_s()`. They have the simpler calling sequence, and they block until the modification operation completes or encounters an error. You will have to write many fewer lines of code if you use one of these two functions.

If you have a bunch of modification operations you want to fire off at one time and you don't want to wait for each one to complete, use `ldap_modify()` or `ldap_modify_ext()`. You can look for the results of the operations using `ldap_result()` while your program is doing something else.

If you need to specify a special LDAP control when performing the modification, you have to use `ldap_modify_ext()` or `ldap_modify_ext_s()`. (You could also set the control as the default for the entire session using `ldap_set_option()`, but using one of the `ext()` functions might be simpler.) One control you might want to use is the lazy commit control (defined as `LDAP_SERVER_LAZY_COMMIT_OID` in ntldap.h). Using this control with `ldap_modify_ext()` or `ldap_modify_ext_s()` turns off the immediate flush to disk that normally follows any LDAP operation. This is just the ticket when you have to do a mass update of the entire directory; the performance increase can be substantial.

API Data Structures for Modifying Objects with LDAP

There are structures you need to know about to modify objects with LDAP. They are both defined in WINLDAP.H.

The `berval` Structure

You use the `berval` structure (BER is the acronym for Basic Encoding Rules) when you need to specify attribute values that do not have a string representation. For instance, if you wanted to store a JPEG image of each user in an attribute of each user object, you would have to use the `berval` structure to pass the JPEG value to LDAP.

The `berval` structure is very simple: It is just a length field and a pointer that points to a block of arbitrary data. The `berval` structure is defined as follows:

```
typedef struct berval {
    ULONG   bv_len;
    PCHAR   bv_val;
} LDAP_BERVAL, * PLDAP_BERVAL, BERVAL, * PBERVAL;
```

Table 24.2 describes the elements of the structure.

TABLE 24.2 THE ELEMENTS OF THE `berval` STRUCTURE

Element	Description
bv_len	An unsigned long indicating the length of the represented data. It can be 0, indicating that the value is empty.
bv_val	A pointer to the represented data. It cannot be NULL.

The `ldapmod` Structure

The `ldapmod` structure defines a single attribute modification operation. Each `ldapmod` structure includes the type of modification operation to be performed, the name of the attribute to be modified, and a pointer to an array of value pointers. If the attribute to be modified is defined with a syntax that provides a string representation, the pointer refers to an array of string pointers. If the syntax does not have a string representation, the pointer refers to an array of pointers to `berval` structures. The following is the definition of the `ldapmod` structure:

```
typedef struct ldapmod {
    ULONG       mod_op;
    PCHAR       mod_type;
```

```
    union {
       PCHAR* modv_strvals;
       struct berval** modv_bvals;
    } mod_vals;
} LDAPMod, *PLDAPMod;
```

Table 24.3 describes the elements of the structure.

TABLE 24.3 THE ELEMENTS OF THE ldapmod STRUCTURE

Element	Description
mod_op	The type of modification operation to perform. It must be one of the values listed in Table 24.4.
mod_type	A pointer to a NUL-terminated string containing the name of the attribute to be modified. This name may be the lDAPDisplayName or the OID string of the attribute.
modv_strvals	A pointer to a NULL-terminated array of pointers to NUL-terminated strings. Each string contains one of the attribute values. This is part of a union with modv_bvals.
modv_bvals	A pointer to a NULL-terminated array of pointers to berval structures. Each berval structure contains one of the attribute values. This is part of a union with modv_strvals.

TABLE 24.4 POSSIBLE VALUES FOR THE mod_op ELEMENT OF THE ldapmod STRUCTURE

Value	Meaning
LDAP_MOD_REPLACE	The specified attributes values will replace any and all existing attribute values. If the attribute does not exist, it will be added. If the modv_strvals pointer (or the modv_bvals pointer if you are using berval structures) is NULL, the entire attribute will be removed. This is similar to the behavior of LDAP_MOD_DELETE, except that LDAP_MOD_DELETE will fail if the attribute does not exist.
LDAP_MOD_ADD	The specified attribute values will be added to the attribute values that already exist in the directory. If the attribute does not already exist, it will be created automatically. Remember that the values of a multivalued attribute must be unique; you will receive an error from LDAP if you try to add a value that already exists.

Value	Meaning
LDAP_MOD_DELETE	The specified values will be deleted from the attribute. If the value does not exist, you will receive an error. If the modv_strvals (or modv_bvals) pointer is NULL, LDAP will delete the entire attribute. This is similar to the behavior of LDAP_MOD_REPLACE, except that LDAP_MOD_REPLACE will not return an error if the attribute does not exist.
LDAP_MOD_BVALUES	This is a bit flag that you OR with one of the preceding values to indicate that you are specifying the attribute values with an array of pointers to berval structures.

Modifying an Existing Attribute

Let's look at a simple case of updating an existing attribute of an object in the directory. The following sample will update the description attribute of a user object in the directory. This attribute is created by default when you create the user object with the Windows 2000 Active Directory Users and Computers snap-in.

For this program, we'll use the ldap_modify_s() API call.

```
ULONG ldap_modify_s( LDAP* ld, PCHAR dn, LDAPMod* mods )
```

> ld is a pointer to the LDAP session created with ldap_init(). The session must be appropriately authenticated with one of the bind functions before calling ldap_modify_s().

> dn is a NUL-terminated string containing the distinguished name of the object to be modified. The object with this name must already exist in the directory.

> mods is a NULL-terminated array of pointers to appropriately initialized ldapmod structures. Each of the ldapmod structures represents a separate attribute modification operation.

Returns: LDAP_SUCCESS if the call succeeded, or an LDAP error number if the call failed. If the call returns an error, the server will have executed none of the operations.

The sample program in Listing 24.1 uses ldap_modify_s() to modify the description attribute of a User object. I've left out the error handling to make the code a little clearer.

24

MODIFYING ACTIVE DIRECTORY OBJECTS WITH LDAP

LISTING 24.1 USING THE `ldap_modify_s()` FUNCTION TO MODIFY AN EXISTING ATTRIBUTE

```
1:    #include <windows.h>
2:    #include <winldap.h>
3:    #include <iostream.h>
4:
5:    int main( int argc, char** argv )
6:    {
7:        LDAP* psLdap = ldap_init( NULL, LDAP_PORT );
8:        if( psLdap != NULL )
9:        {
10:           ULONG uErr = ldap_bind_s( psLdap, NULL, NULL,
          ➥LDAP_AUTH_NEGOTIATE );
11:          if( uErr == LDAP_SUCCESS )
12:          {
13:              // set LDAP API version
14:              int nVersion = LDAP_VERSION3;
15:              ldap_set_option( psLdap, LDAP_OPT_VERSION, &nVersion );
16:
17:              // DN of user to modify
18:              char szDN[ 1024 ] = "CN=BobK,CN=Users,";
19:
20:              LDAPMessage* psMsg = NULL;
21:
22:              // Get rootDSE attr defaultNamingContext
23:              uErr = ldap_search_s(
24:                  psLdap,
25:                  NULL,
26:                  LDAP_SCOPE_BASE,
27:                  "objectClass=*",
28:                  NULL,
29:                  false,
30:                  &psMsg
31:              );
32:              if( uErr == LDAP_SUCCESS )
33:              {
34:                  char** ppszDomain = ldap_get_values( psLdap,
                  ➥ldap first entry( psLdap, psMsg ),
                  ➥"defaultNamingContext" );
35:                  if( ppszDomain != NULL )
36:                  {
37:                      strcat( szDN, ppszDomain[ 0 ] );
38:                      ldap value free( ppszDomain );
39:                  }
40:                  ldap_msgfree( psMsg );
41:              }
42:
43:              // A single value for the description attribute
44:              char* apszAttrVals[] =
45:              {
46:                  "Bob's new description",    // the new value
47:                  NULL                        // the NULL terminator
```

```
48:                    };
49:
50:                    // The single LDAPMod structure representing
51:                    // a single update
52:                    LDAPMod sMod =
53:                    {
54:                        LDAP_MOD_REPLACE, // The modification operation
55:                        "description",    // The attribute to replace
56:                        apszAttrVals      // The list of values to replace
57:                                          // it with
58:                    };
59:
60:                    // The list of pointers to operations
61:                    LDAPMod* asMods[] =
62:                    {
63:                        &sMod,    // one operation
64:                        NULL    // the NULL terminator
65:                    };
66:
67:                    // Do the modification synchronously
68:                    uErr = ldap_modify_s( psLdap, szDN, asMods );
69:                    if( uErr == LDAP_SUCCESS )
70:                    {
71:                        cout << "Success!" << endl;
72:                    }
73:                    else
74:                    {
75:                        cout << "Error " << uErr << endl;
76:                    }
77:            }
78:
79:            ldap_unbind( psLdap );
80:        }
81:
82:        return 0;
83:    }
```

The program in Listing 24.1 starts by initializing an LDAP session with `ldap_init()`
and authenticating with `ldap_bind_s()`. It then sets the LDAP protocol version to 3.

Lines 18–41 compose the name of the User object to modify. In this case, it is the user
`CN=BobK,CN=Users,<domain>`. If you want to run this program, be sure to change the
`BobK` to a username that exists in your domain.

From lines 44–65, the program defines the structures needed for the `ldap_modify_s()`
function. The `apszAttrVals` array at line 43 contains the new values (just one in this
case) for the description attribute. The `LDAPMod` structure at line 50 defines the modification operation and the name of the attribute to be modified. This example uses the
`LDAP_MOD_REPLACE` operation, which overwrites any existing description attribute or

creates a new description attribute if one does not already exist. The `LDAPMod*` array at line 61 contains all the attribute modification operations (there is only one) that we will make.

The program actually calls `ldap_modify_s()` at line 68 and prints the resulting error.

The program closes the LDAP session at line 79 by calling `ldap_unbind()`.

Adding a New Attribute to an Existing Object

Adding a new attribute to an existing object is essentially a repeat of the preceding procedure. The only difference is that you use the `LDAP_MOD_ADD` constant in the `ldapmod` structure. The sample program in Listing 24.2 adds two values to the `otherLoginWorkstations` attribute of a User object.

> **NOTE**
>
> Remember that all the values you add must be unique within the attribute; LDAP does not allow duplicate values in a multivalued attribute.

LISTING 24.2   USING `ldap_modify_s()` TO ADD A NEW ATTRIBUTE

```
1:   #include <windows.h>
2:   #include <winldap.h>
3:   #include <iostream.h>
4:
5:   int main( int argc, char** argv )
6:   {
7:       LDAP* psLdap = ldap_init( NULL, LDAP_PORT );
8:       if( psLdap != NULL )
9:       {
10:          ULONG uErr = ldap_bind_s( psLdap, NULL, NULL,
             ➥LDAP_AUTH_NEGOTIATE );
11:          if( uErr == LDAP_SUCCESS )
12:          {
13:              // set LDAP API version
14:              int nVersion = LDAP_VERSION3;
15:              ldap_set_option( psLdap, LDAP_OPT_VERSION, &nVersion );
16:
17:              // DN of user to modify
18:              char szDN[ 1024 ] = "CN=KristelD,CN=Users,";
19:
```

```
20:                 LDAPMessage* psMsg = NULL;
21:
22:                 // Get rootDSE attr defaultNamingContext
23:                 uErr = ldap_search_s(
24:                     psLdap,
25:                     NULL,
26:                     LDAP_SCOPE_BASE,
27:                     "objectClass=*",
28:                     NULL,
29:                     false,
30:                     &psMsg
31:                 );
32:                 if( uErr == LDAP_SUCCESS )
33:                 {
34:                     char** ppszDomain = ldap_get_values( psLdap,
                            ↪ldap first entry( psLdap, psMsg ),
                            ↪"defaultNamingContext" );
35:                     if( ppszDomain != NULL )
36:                     {
37:                         strcat( szDN, ppszDomain[ 0 ] );
38:                         ldap value free(ppszDomain );
39:                     }
40:                     ldap_msgfree( psMsg );
41:                 }
42:
43:                 // Three values for the otherLoginWorkstations attribute
44:                 char* apszAttrVals[] =
45:                 {
46:                     "WORKSTATION1", // the new values
47:                     "WORKSTATION2",
48:                     "WORKSTATION3",
49:                     NULL            // the NULL terminator
50:                 };
51:
52:         // The single LDAPMod structure representing a single update
53:         // operation
54:                 LDAPMod sMod =
55:                 {
56:                     LDAP_MOD_ADD,                 // The modification operation
57:                     "otherLoginWorkstations", // The attribute to replace
58:                     apszAttrVals                 // The list of values to
59:                                                  // replace
60:                 };
61:
62:                 // The list of pointers to operations
63:                 LDAPMod* asMods[] =
64:                 {
65:                     &sMod, // one operation
66:                     NULL   // the NULL terminator
67:                 };
68:
69:                 // Do the modification synchronously
70:                 uErr = ldap_modify_s( psLdap, szDN, asMods );
```

continues

LISTING 24.2 CONTINUED

```
71:                    if( uErr == LDAP_SUCCESS )
72:                    {
73:                        cout << "Success!" << endl;
74:                    }
75:                    else
76:                    {
77:                        cout << "Error " << uErr << endl;
78:                    }
79:            }
80:
81:            ldap_unbind( psLdap );
82:        }
83:
84:        return 0;
85:    }
```

The program in Listing 24.2 is exactly the same as the one in Listing 24.1 all the way up to line 44, where it defines the data structures for the update operation.

At line 44, the program defines three values for the otherLoginWorkstations attribute.

The program uses the LDAP_MOD_ADD constant in the ldapmod structure at line 54. This causes the program to add the specified attribute.

> **NOTE**
>
> You can also use the LDAP_MOD_REPLACE constant to add a new attribute. The only difference is in the behavior if the attribute already exists. LDAP_MOD_ADD will append its values to any existing attribute; LDAP_MOD_REPLACE will replace the entire attribute with the values you specify.

At line 63, the program creates a list of operations (there is only one). At line 70, the program calls ldap_modify_s() to add the new attribute.

> **NOTE**
>
> If you add a new attribute to an existing object, you must make sure that the attribute is specified in the schema for the class of object you are modifying. The name of the attribute you are adding must appear in one of the systemMustContain, systemMayContain, mustContain, or mayContain attributes of the class object in the schema. The attribute can also appear in one of the *...Contain attributes of class objects that your class inherits from.

The program closes the LDAP session at line 78 by calling ldap_unbind().

Adding a New Attribute Using the berval Structure

There are some attribute syntaxes that don't lend themselves to being expressed as NUL-terminated strings. For instance, some directories might include attributes that contain pictures of the users (syntax `"JPEG"`, `OID 1.3.6.1.4.1.1466.115.121.1.28`). When you are manipulating these types of attributes, you have to use the `berval` structure to pass the attribute value to the LDAP API.

> **NOTE**
>
> There is no restriction as to what types of attributes you can use `berval` structures with. For instance, you can use the `berval` structure to specify NUL-terminated string values.

The sample program in Listing 24.3 shows how to add new values to an attribute using a `berval` structure to specify the values. Normally you would use this to store binary values, but in this sample, I use string values for clarity and to show how you can use `berval` structures with NUL-terminated strings.

LISTING 24.3   USING berval STRUCTURES WITH ldap_modify_s()

```
1:    #include <windows.h>
2:    #include <winldap.h>
3:    #include <iostream.h>
4:
5:    int main( int argc, char** argv )
6:    {
7:        LDAP* psLdap = ldap_init( NULL, LDAP_PORT );
8:        if( psLdap != NULL )
9:        {
10:           ULONG uErr = ldap_bind_s( psLdap, NULL, NULL,
          ➥LDAP_AUTH_NEGOTIATE );
11:            if( uErr == LDAP_SUCCESS )
12:            {
13:                // set LDAP API version
14:                int nVersion = LDAP_VERSION3;
15:                ldap_set_option( psLdap, LDAP_OPT_VERSION, &nVersion );
16:
```

continues

24

MODIFYING ACTIVE
DIRECTORY OBJECTS
WITH LDAP

LISTING 24.3 CONTINUED

```
17:              // DN of user to modify
18:              char szDN[ 1024 ] = "CN=TonyM,CN=Users,";
19:
20:              LDAPMessage* psMsg = NULL;
21:
22:              // Get rootDSE attr defaultNamingContext
23:              uErr = ldap_search_s(
24:                  psLdap,
25:                  NULL,
26:                  LDAP_SCOPE_BASE,
27:                  "objectClass=*",
28:                  NULL,
29:                  false,
30:                  &psMsg
31:              );
32:              if( uErr == LDAP_SUCCESS )
33:              {
34:                  char** ppszDomain = ldap_get_values( psLdap,
                     ➥ldap first entry( psLdap, psMsg ),
                     ➥"defaultNamingContext" );
35:                  if( ppszDomain != NULL )
36:                  {
37:                      strcat( szDN, ppszDomain[ 0 ] );
38:                      ldap value free( ppszDomain );
39:                  }
40:                  ldap_msgfree( psMsg );
41:              }
42:
43:              LDAP_BERVAL sValue1;
44:              sValue1.bv_val = "WORKSTATION4";
45:              sValue1.bv_len = ::strlen( sValue1.bv_val );
46:
47:              LDAP_BERVAL sValue2;
48:              sValue2.bv_val = "WORKSTATION5";
49:              sValue2.bv_len = ::strlen( sValue2.bv_val );
50:
51:              LDAP_BERVAL sValue3;
52:              sValue3.bv_val = "WORKSTATION6";
53:              sValue3.bv_len = ::strlen( sValue3.bv_val );
54:
55:              // Three values for the otherLoginWorkstations attribute
56:              LDAP_BERVAL* asAttrVals[] =
57:              {
58:                  &sValue1, // the new values
59:                  &sValue2,
60:                  &sValue3,
61:                  NULL      // the NULL terminator
62:              };
63:
64:              // The single LDAPMod structure representing a single
65:              // update operation
```

```
66:                LDAPMod sMod =
67:                {
68:                    LDAP_MOD_ADD
69:                        | LDAP_MOD_BVALUES,    // The modification
70:                                               // operation
71:                    "otherLoginWorkstations",  // The attribute to replace
72:                    NULL,
73:                };
74:                sMod.mod_vals.modv_bvals = asAttrVals; // The list of
75:                                                       // values
76:
77:                // The list of pointers to operations
78:                LDAPMod* asMods[] =
79:                {
80:                    &sMod, // one operation
81:                    NULL    // the NULL terminator
82:                };
83:
84:                // Do the modification synchronously
85:                uErr = ldap_modify_s( psLdap, szDN, asMods );
86:                if( uErr == LDAP_SUCCESS )
87:                {
88:                    cout << "Success!" << endl;
89:                }
90:                else
91:                {
92:                    cout << "Error " << uErr << endl;
93:                }
94:            }
95:
96:            ldap_unbind( psLdap );
97:        }
98:
99:        return 0;
100:    }
```

The program in Listing 24.3 starts out the same as the previous two sample programs, and is essentially the same up to line 43.

At line 43, the program in Listing 24.3 initializes three berval (LDAP_BERVAL) structures with new values for the otherLoginWorkstations attribute. Note that each berval structure contains a pointer to the value data as well as the length of the value data. Even though the sample program is using NUL-terminated strings, the length does *not* include the terminating NUL. If it did, the NUL character would actually be stored as part of the data.

The asAttrVals structure defined at line 56 contains pointers to the three berval structures and a terminating NULL pointer.

24

MODIFYING ACTIVE
DIRECTORY OBJECTS
WITH LDAP

The LDAPMod structure at line 66 defines the modify operation using LDAP_MOD_ADD (to add the values) ORed with LDAP_MOD_BVALUES, which indicates that the values are expressed as berval structures instead of as NUL-terminated strings. The LDAPMod structure also includes otherLoginWorkstations as the name of the attribute to modify.

The rest of the program functions just as the previous sample programs do.

Deleting an Existing Attribute

Deleting an attribute isn't a common activity, but the need comes up occasionally. The code to delete an attribute is essentially the same as other modification operations; in fact, it is a little simpler because you don't have to specify a list of values.

There are actually two ways to delete an attribute. The first way is to use the LDAP_MOD_DELETE operator and specify NULL for the array of value pointers. This will delete the entire attribute if it exists, but it will generate an error if the attribute does not exist.

The second method is to use the LDAP_MOD_REPLACE operator and specify NULL for the array of value pointers. This method will delete the entire attribute if it exists, but it will not generate an error if the attribute doesn't exist.

CAUTION

The draft LDAP API specification says that you must specify NULL for the modv_strvals or modv_bvals pointer in the LDAPMod structure to delete an attribute. In some of the earlier version of the Windows 2000 LDAP implementation, you actually have to specify a pointer to an array of values that contains a single NULL pointer. This nonstandard behavior might not be fixed before the release of Windows 2000.

Listing 24.4 shows how to delete an attribute with the LDAP_MOD_REPLACE operator.

LISTING 24.4 USING THE ldap_modify_s() FUNCTION WITH LDAP_MOD_REPLACE TO DELETE AN ATTRIBUTE

```
1:   #include <windows.h>
2:   #include <winldap.h>
3:   #include <iostream.h>
4:
5:   int main( int argc, char** argv )
6:   {
7:       LDAP* psLdap = ldap_init( NULL, LDAP_PORT );
8:       if( psLdap != NULL )
```

```
 9:        {
10:            ULONG uErr = ldap_bind_s( psLdap, NULL, NULL,
         ➥LDAP_AUTH_NEGOTIATE );
11:            if( uErr == LDAP_SUCCESS )
12:            {
13:                // set LDAP API version
14:                int nVersion = LDAP_VERSION3;
15:                ldap_set_option( psLdap, LDAP_OPT_VERSION, &nVersion );
16:
17:                // DN of user to modify
18:                char szDN[ 1024 ] = "CN=Scott Sobotka,CN=Users,";
19:
20:                LDAPMessage* psMsg = NULL;
21:
22:                // Get rootDSE attr defaultNamingContext
23:                uErr = ldap_search_s(
24:                    psLdap,
25:                    NULL,
26:                    LDAP_SCOPE_BASE,
27:                    "objectClass=*",
28:                    NULL,
29:                    false,
30:                    &psMsg
31:                );
32:                if( uErr == LDAP_SUCCESS )
33:                {
34:                    char** ppszDomain = ldap_get_values( psLdap,
                    ldap first entry( psLdap, psMg ),
                    ➥"defaultNamingContext" );
35:                    if( ppszDomain != NULL )
36:                    {
37:                        strcat( szDN, ppszDomain[ 0 ] );
38:                        ldap value free( ppszDomain );
39:                    }
40:                    ldap_msgfree( psMsg );
41:                }
42:
43:                // No values for the otherLoginWorkstations attribute
44:                char* apszAttrVals[] =
45:                {
46:                    NULL // the NULL terminator
47:                };
48:
49:                // The single LDAPMod structure representing a single
50:                // update
51:                LDAPMod sMod =
52:                {
53:                    LDAP_MOD_REPLACE,            // The modification operation
54:                    "otherLoginWorkstations", // The attribute to replace
55:                    apszAttrVals              // The list of values to
```

continues

24

MODIFYING ACTIVE
DIRECTORY OBJECTS
WITH LDAP

LISTING 24.4 CONTINUED

```
56:                                            // replace
57:                   };
58:
59:                   // The list of pointers to operations
60:                   LDAPMod* asMods[] =
61:                   {
62:                       &sMod,  // one operation
63:                       NULL    // the NULL terminator
64:                   };
65:
66:                   // Do the modification synchronously
67:                   uErr = ldap_modify_s( psLdap, szDN, asMods );
68:                   if( uErr == LDAP_SUCCESS )
69:                   {
70:                       cout << "Success!" << endl;
71:                   }
72:                   else
73:                   {
74:                       cout << "Error " << uErr << endl;
75:                   }
76:             }
77:
78:             ldap_unbind( psLdap );
79:         }
80:
81:       return 0;
82: }
```

The program in Listing 24.4 starts out by initializing an LDAP session with `ldap_init()` and authenticating it with `ldap_bind_s()`. The program then constructs the distinguished name of the User object to modify—in this case, `"CN=Scott Sobotka,CN=Users, <domain name>"`.

At line 44, the program creates an empty list of values with which to replace the `otherLoginWorkstations` attribute. Note that the draft standard does not require this; it is required to work around a bug in some of the earlier versions of the Windows 2000 LDAP client library implementation.

At line 51, the program initializes the `ldapmod` structure with `LDAP_MOD_REPLACE`, the attribute name `"otherLoginWorkstations"`, and a pointer to the empty list of values. The draft standard indicates this pointer should be `NULL`; however, earlier versions of the LDAP client implementation in Windows 2000 require a non-NULL value.

The program creates an array of modification operations at line 60—in this case, this array contains a single operation.

Finally, at line 67 the program calls `ldap_modify_s()` to delete the `otherLoginWork` stations attribute.

The program closes the LDAP session at line 78 by calling `ldap_unbind()`.

You can delete an attribute using the `LDAP_MOD_DELETE` operation as well. In this case, the code to set up the data structures would look like the following:

```
// No values for the otherLoginWorkstations attribute
// Needed to work around bug in Beta 3 client
char* apszAttrVals[] =
{
    NULL // the NULL terminator
};

// The single LDAPMod structure representing a single update
LDAPMod sMod =
{
    LDAP_MOD_DELETE,            // Use the delete operation
    "otherLoginWorkstations",  // The attribute to delete
    apszAttrVals               // Ignored, should be NULL
};

// The list of pointers to operations
LDAPMod* asMods[] =
{
    &sMod,  // one operation
    NULL    // the NULL terminator
};

// Do the modification synchronously
uErr = ldap_modify_s( psLdap, szDN, asMods );
```

This code would also delete the `otherLoginWorkstations` attribute. It differs from using `LDAP_MOD_REPLACE` in that it will generate an error if the `otherLoginWorkstations` attribute does not exist.

Note that again because of a bug in earlier versions of the Microsoft LDAP client in Windows 2000, the code does not specify `NULL` for the attribute values pointer in the `ldapmod` structure, as specified in the draft standard. The code instead specifies a pointer to an empty list of values.

Adding Additional Values to an Existing Attribute

Adding additional values to an attribute that already exists is exactly the same as adding a new attribute. The only difference is that you must make sure that the values you specify do not already exist for the attribute. The values in a multivalued LDAP attribute must all be unique. See the sample code in the earlier section "Adding a New Attribute to an

Existing Object." The following code snippet shows how to set up the data structures to add an additional value to an existing attribute:

```
// One new values for the otherLoginWorkstations attribute
// Needed to work around bug in Beta 3 client
char* apszAttrVals[] =
{
    "NEWWORKSTATION",
    NULL // the NULL terminator
};

// The single LDAPMod structure representing a single update
LDAPMod sMod =
{
    LDAP_MOD_ADD,             // Add the values
    "otherLoginWorkstations", // The attribute to modify
    apszAttrVals              // The new values to add
};

// The list of pointers to operations
LDAPMod* asMods[] =
{
    &sMod, // one operation
    NULL   // the NULL terminator
};

// Do the modification synchronously
uErr = ldap_modify_s( psLdap, szDN, asMods );
```

Deleting a Value from a Multivalued Attribute

Deleting a single value from a multivalued attribute is probably a rare operation. Nevertheless, LDAP supports this functionality. Again, this type of operation is essentially the same as all the other modification operations. The only difference is that you specify LDAP_MOD_DELETE for the operation constant in the LDAPMod structure, and you must specify the values you want to delete (not the values you want to keep) in the modv_strvals or modv_bvals array.

> **NOTE**
>
> The values you specify to be deleted must all exist in the attribute you are modifying. If one of the attributes is missing, the entire operation will fail with an LDAP_NO_SUCH_ATTRIBUTE error, and the LDAP server will throw out all your modifications.

The program in Listing 24.5 shows the code to delete some of the existing values from an attribute. You'll see that this code looks essentially the same as the other sample programs presented in this chapter.

LISTING 24.5   USING `ldap_modify_s()` TO DELETE EXISTING VALUES

```
1:    #include <windows.h>
2:    #include <winldap.h>
3:    #include <iostream.h>
4:
5:    int main( int argc, char** argv )
6:    {
7:        LDAP* psLdap = ldap_init( NULL, LDAP_PORT );
8:        if( psLdap != NULL )
9:        {
10:           ULONG uErr = ldap_bind_s( psLdap, NULL, NULL,
           ➡LDAP_AUTH_NEGOTIATE );
11:          if( uErr == LDAP_SUCCESS )
12:          {
13:              // set LDAP API version
14:              int nVersion = LDAP_VERSION3;
15:              ldap_set_option( psLdap, LDAP_OPT_VERSION, &nVersion );
16:
17:              // DN of user to modify
18:              char szDN[ 1024 ] = "CN=Mitzi Parkins,CN=Users,";
19:
20:              LDAPMessage* psMsg = NULL;
21:
22:              // Get rootDSE attr defaultNamingContext
23:              uErr = ldap_search_s(
24:                  psLdap,
25:                  NULL,
26:                  LDAP_SCOPE_BASE,
27:                  "objectClass=*",
28:                  NULL,
29:                  false,
30:                  &psMsg
31:              );
32:              if( uErr == LDAP_SUCCESS )
33:              {
34:                  char** ppszDomain = ldap_get_values( psLdap,
                  ➡ldap first entry( psLdap, psMsg ),
                  ➡"defaultNamingContext" );
35:                  if( ppszDomain != NULL )
36:                  {
37:                      strcat( szDN, ppszDomain[ 0 ] );
38:                      ldap value free( ppszDomain );
39:                  }
40:                  ldap_msgfree( psMsg );
41:              }
42:
```

continues

LISTING 24.5   CONTINUED

```
43:                 // The values to delete from the otherLoginWorkstations
                    // attribute
44:                 char* apszAttrVals[] =
45:                 {
46:                     "WORKSTATION1",
47:                     "WORKSTATION2",
48:                     NULL // the NULL terminator
49:                 };
50:
51:                 // The single LDAPMod structure representing a single
52:                 // update operation
53:                 LDAPMod sMod =
54:                 {
55:                     LDAP_MOD_DELETE,            // The modification
56:                                                 // operation
57:                     "otherLoginWorkstations",  // The attribute to modify
58:                     apszAttrVals               // The list of values to
59:                                                 // delete
60:                 };
61:
62:                 // The list of pointers to operations
63:                 LDAPMod* asMods[] =
64:                 {
65:                     &sMod,     // one operation
66:                     NULL       // the NULL terminator
67:                 };
68:
69:                 // Do the modification synchronously
70:                 uErr = ldap_modify_s( psLdap, szDN, asMods );
71:                 if( uErr == LDAP_SUCCESS )
72:                 {
73:                     cout << "Success!" << endl;
74:                 }
75:                 else
76:                 {
77:                     cout << "Error " << uErr << endl;
78:                 }
79:             }
80:
81:         ldap_unbind( psLdap );
82:         }
83:
84:     return 0;
85: }
```

The program in Listing 24.5 starts out the same way as the previous sample programs in this chapter; in fact, the code is identical up to line 44.

At line 44, the program in Listing 24.5 initializes the value array to contain the values *to be deleted* from the otherLoginWorkstations attribute. Note that the call to ldap_modify_s() will fail if any one of the specified values does not exist in the directory.

The ldapmod structure at line 53 uses the LDAP_MOD_DELETE operation, indicating that the values are to be deleted, not added. The array of modification operations at line 59 contains a pointer to the single structure representing the delete operation.

The program executes the ldap_modify_s() function at line 70, prints a message, and then closes the LDAP session with a call to ldap_unbind() at line 81.

Performing Bulk Directory Updates with the Lazy Commit Control

A fairly common administration task is to update a large number of directory objects at one time. For instance, if your company changed the name of the company's email server, you might have to write a program to change the mail attribute for every user object in the directory. In a large environment with thousands of users, that could take quite a bit of time. The most significant component of the time the directory server spends updating the objects is writing the changes to disk. That is because Active Directory by default forces the modified attributes to disk after every successful modification operation.

One way to reduce the amount of time the server spends writing the modifications to disk is to enable the lazy commit control for the modification operation. This control causes the directory server to leave the modifications in cache and not write the modifications to disk until they're paged out. This can improve update performance substantially.

To enable the lazy commit control for a modification operation, you have to use either the ldap_modify_ext_s() function or its asynchronous counterpart, ldap_modify_ext().

```
ULONG ldap_modify_ext_s( LDAP* ld, char* PCHAR dn, LDAPMod* mods[],
➥PLDAPControl* ServerControls, PLDAPControl* ClientControls )
```

> ld is a pointer to the LDAP session to use. It must have been initialized by ldap_init() and authenticated with ldap_bind_s().

> dn is a NUL-terminated string containing the distinguished name of the object to modify. An object with this name must exist in the directory.

mods is a NULL-terminated array of pointers to appropriately initialized LDAPMod structures. Each of the LDAPMod structures represents a separate attribute modification operation.

ServerControls is a NULL-terminated array of pointers to appropriately initialized LDAPControl structures. Each LDAPControl structure represents a single LDAP server control.

ClientControls is a NULL-terminated array of pointers to appropriately initialized LDAPControl structures. Each LDAPControl structure represents a single LDAP client control.

Returns: LDAP_SUCCESS if the call succeeded or an LDAP error code if an error occurred.

The program in Listing 24.6 uses ldap_search_s() to find all the user objects in the directory and sets their description attributes to the string "A new description". It uses the lazy commit control and ldap_modify_ext_s() to update the attribute. Once again, I've left out error handling to make the code a little clearer.

LISTING 24.6 MODIFYING OBJECTS WITH ldap_modify_ext_s() AND THE LAZY COMMIT CONTROL

```
1:    #include <windows.h>
2:    #include <winldap.h>
3:    #include <time.h>
4:    #include <iostream.h>
5:
6:    int main( int argc, char** argv )
7:    {
8:        LDAP* psLdap = ldap_init( NULL, LDAP_PORT );
9:        if( psLdap != NULL )
10:       {
11:           ULONG uErr = ldap_bind_s( psLdap, NULL, NULL,
              ➥LDAP_AUTH_NEGOTIATE );
12:           if( uErr == LDAP_SUCCESS )
13:           {
14:               // set LDAP API version
15:               int nVersion = LDAP_VERSION3;
16:               ldap_set_option( psLdap, LDAP_OPT_VERSION, &nVersion );
17:
18:               // turn off referrals chasing
19:               int nChaseReferrals = 0;
20:               ldap_set_option( psLdap, LDAP_OPT_REFERRALS,
                  ➥&nChaseReferrals );
21:
22:               // DN of search base
23:               char szDomainDN[ 1024 ] = "CN=Users,";
24:
25:               LDAPMessage* psMsg = NULL;
```

```
26:
27:                 // Get rootDSE attr defaultNamingContext
28:                 uErr = ldap_search_s(
29:                     psLdap,
30:                     NULL,
31:                     LDAP_SCOPE_BASE,
32:                     "objectClass=*",
33:                     NULL,
34:                     false,
35:                     &psMsg
36:                 );
37:                 if( uErr == LDAP_SUCCESS )
38:                 {
39:                     char** ppszDomain = ldap_get_values( psLdap,
                         ➥ldap first entry( psLdap, psMsg ),
                         ➥"defaultNamingContext" );
40:                     if( ppszDomain != NULL )
41:                     {
42:                         strcat( szDomainDN, ppszDomain[ 0 ] );
43:                         ldap value free( ppszDomain );
44:                     }
45:                     ldap_msgfree( psMsg );
46:                 }
47:
48:                 // Set up an asynchronous search for all the users
49:                 // in CN=Users
50:                 char* apszAttrs[] =
51:                 {
52:                     "1.1",  // Get NO attributes
53:                     NULL    // NULL terminator for array
54:                 };
55:
56:                 ULONG uSearchHandle = ldap_search(
57:                     psLdap,                 // LDAP session
58:                     szDomainDN,             // Search base
59:                     LDAP_SCOPE_ONELEVEL,// Search entire tree
60:                     "objectClass=user", // Only retrieve users
61:                     apszAttrs,              // attributes to get
62:                     false                   // not attrs only
63:                 );
64:
65:                 // Now retrieve each entry from the asynchronously
66:                 bool bDone = false;
67:                 while( !bDone )
68:                 {
69:                     // timeout value for ldap_result() function
70:                     l_timeval sTimeout = { 10, 0 }; // 10 seconds
71:
72:                     LDAPMessage* psResult = NULL;
73:
74:                     int nResult = ldap_result(
75:                         psLdap,
```

continues

24

MODIFYING ACTIVE
DIRECTORY OBJECTS
WITH LDAP

LISTING 24.6   CONTINUED

```
76:                     uSearchHandle,
77:                     LDAP_MSG_ONE,
78:                     &sTimeout,
79:                     &psResult
80:                 );
81:                 switch( nResult )
82:                 {
83:                     case -1:    // an error
84:                         bDone = true;
85:                         break;
86:
87:                     case 0:        // timed out
88:                         break;
89:
90:                     case LDAP_RES_SEARCH_RESULT: // search is complete
91:                         bDone = true;
92:                         break;
93:
94:                     case LDAP_RES_SEARCH_ENTRY: // got a search entry
95:                         {
96:                             // first get the user's DN
97:                             char* pszDN = ldap_get_dn( psLdap,
                        ➥psResult );
98:
99:                             // A single value for the description
100:                            // attribute
101:                             char* apszAttrVals[] =
102:                             {
103:                                 "A new description", // the new value
104:                                 NULL             // the NULL terminator
105:                             };
106:
107:                             // The single LDAPMod structure
108:                             LDAPMod sMod =
109:                             {
110:                                 LDAP_MOD_REPLACE, // The modification
111:                                                   // operation
112:                                 "description",    // The attribute to
113:                                                   // replace
114:                                 apszAttrVals      // The list of values
115:                                                   // to replace it with
116:                             };
117:
118:                             // The array of pointers to operations
119:                             LDAPMod* asMods[] =
120:                             {
121:                                 &sMod, // one operation
122:                                 NULL   // the NULL terminator
123:                             };
```

```
124:
125:                          // The server control for lazy commit
126:                          LDAPControl sLazyCommitControl =
127:                          {
128:                              "1.2.840.113556.1.4.619",  // the lazy
129:                                                  // commit control OID
130:                              NULL, // no data for this control
131:                              false // control is not critical
132:                          };
133:
134:                          // The array of pointers to controls
135:                          LDAPControl* apzServerControls[] =
136:                          {
137:                              &sLazyCommitControl,
138:                              NULL
139:                          };
140:
141:                          // Do the modification synchronously
142:                          uErr = ldap_modify_ext_s(
143:                              psLdap, // the LDAP session
144:                              pszDN, // the DN of the object
145:                                      // to modify
146:                              asMods, // the list of mod operations
147:                              apzServerControls, // server controls
148:                              NULL // no client controls
149:                          );
150:
151:                          if( uErr == 0 )
152:                          {
153:                              cout << "Updated description for %s"
                              ➥<< pszDN <<endl;
154:                          }
155:
156:                          ldap_msgfree( psResult );
157:                     // free the message returned by ldap_result()
158:                          }
159:                  }
160:              }
161:          }
162:
163:          ldap_unbind( psLdap );
164:      }
165:
166:      return 0;
167: }
```

This sample program is notably different than the previous examples. Instead of modifying the attributes of a single object, this program uses an asynchronous search to find all the user objects in the Users container and then modifies the description attribute of each.

The program in Listing 24.6 starts out in the usual way by calling `ldap_init()` to initialize an LDAP session and `ldap_bind_s()` to authenticate it. The program then composes the distinguished name of the Users container in the domain.

At line 56, the program issues an asynchronous search of the Users container using `ldap_search_s()`. It is a one-level search that retrieves no attributes, just the distinguished name.

The program then enters a loop at line 67 and calls `ldap_result()` repeatedly to retrieve the results of the search. For each entry the search returns, the program performs a modification operation.

At line 101, the program defines the single new value for the description attribute. At line 108, it defines the `ldapmod` structure that represents the modification operation. It uses the `LDAP_MOD_REPLACE` operation so that the single new value will replace all existing values of the description attribute. The array of `ldapmod` pointers defined at line 119 contains the address of the single `ldapmod` structure.

The program defines the Lazy Commit control at line 126. The `LDAPControl` structure contains the Lazy Commit OID string, no additional data (as represented by the NULL data pointer), and a Boolean value indicating that the control is not critical.

At line 142, the program calls `ldap_modify_ext_s()` to replace the description attribute of the current user object. The program specifies the Lazy Commit control so that Active Directory will not flush each modification to disk immediately.

At line 156, the program frees the `LDAPMessage` pointer associated with the entry returned from the search operation. At line 163, the program closes the LDAP session by calling `ldap_unbind()`.

Asynchronous Directory Modifications

Another way to increase performance (well, the *apparent* performance, anyway) of LDAP modifications is to use the asynchronous `ldap_modify()` or `ldap_modify_ext()` function. These functions work in the same way that `ldap_search()` does, in that instead of returning a error value, they return a handle. It is then up to you to check that handle periodically by calling `ldap_result()` to see whether the operation has completed.

Asynchronous modifications don't necessarily execute any faster than synchronous searches. However, an asynchronous modification operation decouples the client from the server; the client doesn't have to wait for the server to complete the modification before the client can continue with its processing. The client can handle the responses to the modification operations in the background. That way, the modifications appear to complete more quickly.

```
ULONG ldap_modify( LDAP* ld, PCHAR dn, LDAPMod* mods[] )
```

> `ld` is a pointer to the LDAP session created with `ldap_init()`. The session must be appropriately authenticated with one of the bind functions before calling `ldap_modify()`.
>
> `dn` is a NUL-terminated string containing the distinguished name of the object to be modified. The object with this name must already exist in the directory.
>
> `mods` is a NULL-terminated array of pointers to appropriately initialized `ldapmod` structures. Each of the `ldapmod` structures represents a separate attribute modification operation.

Returns: A handle to the modify operation. If there was an error initiating the modify operation, the handle will be `-1`. Otherwise, you must use `ldap_result()` to check the status of the modify operation. `ldap_result()` will return a value of `LDAP_RES_MODIFY` to indicate the completion of the modification operation.

```
ULONG ldap_modify_ext( LDAP* ld, PCHAR dn, LDAPMod* mods[], PLDAPControl*
➥ServerControls, PLDAPControl* ClientControls )
```

> `ld` is a pointer to the LDAP session created with `ldap_init()`. The session must be appropriately authenticated with one of the bind functions before calling `ldap_modify_ext()`.
>
> `dn` is a NUL-terminated string containing the distinguished name of the object to be modified. The object with this name must already exist in the directory.
>
> `mods` is a pointer to a NULL-terminated array of pointers to appropriately initialized `ldapmod` structures. Each of the `ldapmod` structures represents a separate attribute modification operation.
>
> `ServerControls` is a pointer to a NULL-terminated array of pointers to initialized LDAP server control structures. Each entry refers to a single server control. `NULL` indicates there are no server controls for this operation. See Chapter 28, "Extending LDAP with Options and Controls," for details on the LDAP controls.
>
> `ClientControls` is a pointer to a NULL-terminated array of pointers to initialized LDAP client control structures. Each entry refers to a single client control. `NULL` indicates there are no client controls for this operation. See Chapter 28 for details on the LDAP controls.

Returns: A handle to the modify operation. If there was an error initiating the modify operation, the handle will be `-1`. Otherwise, you must use `ldap_result()` to check the status of the modify operation. `ldap_result()` will return a value of `LDAP_RES_MODIFY` to indicate the completion of the modification operation.

24

MODIFYING ACTIVE DIRECTORY OBJECTS WITH LDAP

The `LDAPControl` structure represents a single LDAP control. It has three members, as shown in this structure declaration:

```
typedef struct ldapcontrol {

    PCHAR         ldctl_oid;
    struct berval ldctl_value;
    BOOLEAN       ldctl_iscritical;

} LDAPControl, *PLDAPControl;
```

Table 24.5 describes these members in detail.

TABLE 24.5 THE `ldapcontrol` STRUCTURE

Member	Use
`ldctl_oid`	A pointer to a NUL-terminated string containing the object ID (OID) of the control. See Chapter 28 for a list of controls appropriate to a modification operation.
`ldctl_value`	A `berval` structure that contains data specific to the specified control. See Chapter 28 for the data requirements for LDAP controls.
`ldctl_iscritical`	`TRUE` indicates the support of the specified control is critical to the application. The call will fail if the client or server doesn't support the specified control. `FALSE` indicates the support of the specified control is not supported, and the operation will continue as if no control had been specified.

```
ULONG ldap_result( LDAP* ld, ULONG msgid, ULONG all,
➥struct l_timeval* timeout, LDAPMessage** res )
```

`ld` is a pointer to an LDAP structure that has been initialized with `ldap_init()`, `ldap_sslinit()`, or `ldap_open()`. It must be the same LDAP structure that you used to do the modification.

`msgid` is the handle to the search that was returned by `ldap_modify()` or `ldap_modify_ext()`. If you specify `LDAP_RES_ANY`, `ldap_result()` will return results for any outstanding asynchronous operation that were started on the LDAP session given by `ld`.

`all` specifies how many of the result objects you want returned. It must be one of three constants defined in WINLDAP.H. These constants are described in Table 24.6.

TABLE 24.6 POSSIBLE VALUES OF THE all PARAMETER OF ldap_result()

Constant	Meaning
LDAP_MSG_ONE	Indicates that ldap_result() should return a single operation result.
LDAP_MSG_ALL	Indicates that ldap_result() should wait until all the results have been received from the server. Because the modify operation only returns a single result, this value isn't very useful for modifications.
LDAP_MSG_RECEIVED	Indicates that ldap_result() should return all the result objects that have been received so far. Because the modify operation only returns a single result, this value isn't very useful for modifications.

> **NOTE**
>
> Modify operations will generate only one response message, so unless you spec-ify LDAP RES ANY for the msgid parameter you might as well use LDAP_MSG_ONE for the all parameter of ldap_result().

timeout is a pointer to an l_timeval structure that contains the timeout value for the ldap_result() call. If there are no messages to retrieve within the time speci-fied by the l_timeval structure, ldap_result() will return a 0.

res is the address of an LDAPMessage pointer to be set by ldap_result(). This pointer must be freed by passing it to ldap_msgfree() after you are done with it.

Returns: The type of the message retrieved. There are 11 possible returned messages; however, only LDAP_RES_MODIFY or LDAP_RES_REFERRAL will be returned as the result of a search operation.

LDAP_RES_MODIFY indicates the message contains the results of a modify operation.

LDAP_RES_REFERRAL indicates the message contains one or more referrals to other naming contexts. See the section on processing referrals for information on how to handle this message.

0 indicates the call to ldap_result() timed out. This means there were no results sent from the server within the timeout period. You should retry the call to ldap_result().

-1 indicates an error of some sort. Call LdapGetLastError() to get the corre-sponding error code. You should not call ldap_result() after receiving an error.

After you call ldap_result() successfully and it returns a pointer to an LDAPMessage structure in *res, you must free the LDAPMessage structure by calling ldap_msgfree(), passing it the pointer that was returned. You can also free the message by calling ldap_result2error() and setting the freeit parameter to true.

24

MODIFYING ACTIVE DIRECTORY OBJECTS WITH LDAP

```
ULONG ldap_msgfree( LDAPMessage* msg )
```

> msg is a pointer to an LDAPMessage structure that was returned by ldap_result().

Returns: 0 if it successfully freed the LDAPMessage structure or an LDAP error code if there was an error.

> **CAUTION**
>
> ldap_result() returns a valid pointer in *res only if its return value was greater than 0. Therefore, you should call ldap_msgfree() only if ldap_result() returned a value greater than 0. Calling ldap_msgfree() with an invalid LDAPMessage pointer will cause memory corruption.

Retrieving the Results of an Asynchronous Modification

When you issue an asynchronous search operation, the results you retrieve are the entries that matched your search criteria. When you issue an asynchronous modification operation using ldap_modify() or ldap_modify_ext(), the LDAPMessage pointer returned by ldap_result() contains the result of the asynchronous modification operation.

There are two functions you can use to get the results of an asynchronous modification operation, ldap_result2error() and ldap_parse_result(). Both functions accept the LDAPMessage pointer returned by ldap_result() as an argument.

Getting the Error Code with `ldap_result2error()`

The ldap_result2error() function accepts the LDAPMessage pointer returned from ldap_result() in *res, extracts the error code from the result message, and returns the LDAP error code associated with that particular modification operation.

```
ULONG ldap_result2error( LDAP* ld, LDAPMessage* res, ULONG freeit )
```

> ld is a pointer to the LDAP session you used when you called ldap_result().
>
> res is the LDAPMessage pointer that ldap_result() returned in *res.
>
> freeit is a Boolean that, if set to true, will cause ldap_result2error() to free the LDAPMessage structure. If freeit is false, ldap_result2error() will not free the message structure.

Returns: The error code extracted from the LDAPMessage structure.

> **CAUTION**
>
> If you free an LDAPMessage structure by setting the `freeit` parameter in `ldap_result2error()` to true, be sure that you do not subsequently try to free the message again by calling `ldap_msgfree()`. Doing so will likely cause memory corruption.

Just getting the error code for an asynchronous operation is fine, but what happens if the error is nonzero, indicating an actual failure? What object was being modified? `ldap_result2error()` can't give you that information. There are two solutions.

The first strategy is more complicated. In this case, you store in an array each operation handle returned by `ldap_modify()` or `ldap_modify_ext()`. Then you poll for the results for each handle by iterating through the array and calling `ldap_result()`, passing the operation handle for the `msgid` parameter. This is somewhat complicated, and it incurs the storage and lookup overhead of the array of operation handles.

The second strategy is simpler. In this case, you use `ldap_parse_result()` to retrieve the operation information from the LDAPMessage pointer returned by `ldap_result()`. `ldap_parse_result()` is described in the following section.

Getting Information About an Asynchronous Operation with `ldap_parse_result()`

If you want to know which modification operation generated an error code, `ldap_result2error()` is insufficient; it tells you what the error was, but not which object modification caused the error. `ldap_parse_result()` can retrieve this information for you.

```
ULONG ldap_parse_result( LDAP* Connection, LDAPMessage* ResultMessage,
➥ULONG* ReturnCode, PCHAR* MatchedDNs, PCHAR* ErrorMessage,
➥PCHAR** Referrals, PLDAPControl** ServerControls, BOOLEAN Freeit )
```

Connection is a pointer to the LDAP session the modification was issued on.

ResultMessage is a pointer to the result LDAPMessage returned by `ldap_result()`.

ReturnCode is the address of a ULONG to set to the returned result of the modification operation. You can pass a NULL to ignore the returned error code.

MatchedDNs is the address of a pointer that `ldap_parse_result()` will set to point to a string containing the distinguished name of the object that was being modified. If *MatchedDNs is non-NULL after calling `ldap_parse_result()`, you must free it by passing it to `ldap_memfree()`. If you want to ignore the matched distinguished names returned by the server, you can pass a NULL for MatchedDNs.

ErrorMessage is the address of a pointer set to point to an error message string that corresponds to the error returned in *ReturnCode. If *ErrorMessage is non-NULL after calling ldap_parse_result(), you must free it by passing it to ldap_memfree(). You can pass a NULL for ErrorMessage if you want to ignore the returned error message string.

Note that the distinguished name contained in the error message string is the "closest match" found in the directory. If the object you attempted to modify did not exist in the directory, this name will not be the name you specified, but the closest name in the directory tree to it.

Referrals is the address of a pointer that will be set to point to a NULL-terminated array of pointers to NUL-terminated strings. ldap_parse_result() will set this to point to an array of referral URLs, if any were returned by the server. If *Referrals is non-NULL after calling ldap_parse_result(), you must free it by passing *Referrals to ldap_value_free(). You can pass a NULL for Referrals to ignore any returned referral strings.

ServerControls is the address of a pointer that will be set to point to a NULL-terminated array of pointers to LDAPControl structures. ldap_parse_result() will set this to point to the LDAPControl structures returned from the server. If ldap_parse_result() returns more than one LDAPControl structure, you must inspect the OID string of each to determine which control is which. (This doesn't happen with a simple sorted search.) If *Controls is non-NULL after calling ldap_parse_result(), you must pass *Controls to ldap_controls_free() to free the memory associated with the control structures. You can pass a NULL for Controls if you want to ignore the LDAPControl structures returned by the server. None of the server controls you might use with ldap_modify_ext() return any control information, so you might as well set this parameter to NULL.

Freeit is a Boolean value that, if set to TRUE, will cause ldap_parse_result() to free the memory associated with the ResultMsg parameter. If you set Freeit to TRUE, be sure that you don't later free ResultMsg with ldap_msgfree().

Returns: An LDAP error code or LDAP_SUCCESS if the function succeeded.

> **NOTE**
>
> It's a good idea to set all the pointers whose addresses you pass to ldap_parse_result() to NULL before you pass them in. After calling ldap_parse_result(), you can check each pointer to see whether it is NULL, and if it is not, free it with the appropriate function.

When you use `ldap_parse_result()` to inspect the results returned by `ldap_result()` for an asynchronous modification operation, `*ReturnCode` will contain the result code for the operation, `*MatchedDNs` will contain the distinguished name of the modified object, and `*ErrorMessage` will contain a text string error message. You can use this information to format a meaningful error message without the overhead of keeping track of every modification operation.

Using Asynchronous Search and Modifications Together

Listing 24.7 shows how you can use asynchronous modifications to update objects in Active Directory. This sample uses `ldap_modify()`; using `ldap_modify_ext()` is essentially the same except that you must specify client and server controls.

This program uses an interesting scheme for retrieving search results and modification results. It is essentially the same as the preceding program, except that it issues the modification operations asynchronously using `ldap_modify()`.

After it issues the asynchronous search operation, it initializes a counter called `nOutstandingMods` to `0`. This variable contains the number of modification operations the program has submitted, but for which it has not received a response. It then goes into a loop, calling `ldap_result()` each time through. Instead of specifying a search or modification handle, the program calls `ldap_result()` with the constant `LDAP_RES_ANY`. This lets `ldap_result()` return results for both the `ldap_search()` and `ldap_modify()` functions.

Each time the program calls `ldap_modify()`, it increments the `nOutstandingMods` counter. Each time it receives an `LDAP_RES_MODIFY` message, it decrements `nOutstandingMods`.

The loop terminates when `ldap_result()` returns the `LDAP_RES_SEARCH_RESULT` message, indicating the search has completed, and when `nOutstandingMods` goes to `0`, indicating that the program has received all the responses to the `ldap_modify()` calls.

In practice, you would probably want to keep track of the outstanding modification handles, so if there were an error you could tell which modification operation caused it. But this is a good example of how you can combine asynchronous searching and modification in a single loop. Listing 24.7 shows how to use an asynchronous search and an asynchronous modification together.

LISTING 24.7   USING ASYNCHRONOUS SEARCHES AND MODIFICATIONS TOGETHER

```
1:    #include <windows.h>
2:    #include <winldap.h>
3:    #include <iostream.h>
4:
5:    int main( int argc, char** argv )
6:    {
7:        LDAP* psLdap = ldap_init( NULL, LDAP_PORT );
8:        if( psLdap != NULL )
9:        {
10:           ULONG uErr = ldap_bind_s( psLdap, NULL, NULL,
          ➥LDAP_AUTH_NEGOTIATE );
11:          if( uErr == LDAP_SUCCESS )
12:          {
13:              // set LDAP API version
14:              int nVersion = LDAP_VERSION3;
15:              ldap_set_option( psLdap, LDAP_OPT_VERSION, &nVersion );
16:
17:              // turn off referrals chasing
18:              int nChaseReferrals = 0;
19:             ldap_set_option( psLdap, LDAP_OPT_REFERRALS,
             ➥&nChaseReferrals );
20:
21:              // DN of search base
22:              char szDomainDN[ 1024 ] = "CN=Users,";
23:
24:              LDAPMessage* psMsg = NULL;
25:
26:              // Get rootDSE attr defaultNamingContext
27:              uErr = ldap_search_s(
28:                  psLdap,
29:                  NULL,
30:                  LDAP_SCOPE_BASE,
31:                  "objectClass=*",
32:                  NULL,
33:                  false,
34:                  &psMsg
35:              );
36:              if( uErr == LDAP_SUCCESS )
37:              {
38:                  char** ppszDomain = ldap_get_values( psLdap,
                  ➥ldap first entry( psLdap, psMsg ),
                  ➥"defaultNamingContext" );
39:                  if( ppszDomain != NULL )
40:                  {
41:                      strcat( szDomainDN, ppszDomain[ 0 ] );
42:                      ldap value free( ppszDomain );
43:                  }
44:                  ldap_msgfree( psMsg );
45:              }
46:
47:              // Set up an asynchronous search for all the users in
48:              // the domain
```

```
49:            char* apszAttrs[] =
50:            {
51:                "1.1",    // get no attributes
52:                NULL     // NULL terminator for array
53:            };
54:
55:            // Asynchronous search for users
56:            ULONG uSearchHandle = ldap_search(
57:                psLdap,              // LDAP session
58:                szDomainDN,          // Search base
59:                LDAP_SCOPE_SUBTREE,  // Search entire tree
60:                "objectClass=user",  // Only retrieve users
61:                apszAttrs,           // attributes to get
62:                false                // not attrs only
63:            );
64:
65:            // Now retrieve each entry from the asynchronous search
66:            // or mod
67:            int nOutstandingMods = 0;
68:            bool bDone = false;
69:
70:            while( !bDone || nOutstandingMods > 0 )
71:            {
72:                l_timeval sTimeout = { 10, 0 }; // 10 seconds
73:
74:                LDAPMessage* psResult;
75:
76:                int nResult = ldap_result( psLdap, LDAP_RES_ANY,
           ➥LDAP_MSG_ONE, &sTimeout, &psResult );
77:                switch( nResult )
78:                {
79:                    case -1: // an error
80:                        bDone = true;
81:                        break;
82:
83:                    case 0: // timed out
84:                        break;
85:
86:                    case LDAP_RES_MODIFY:
87:                        nOutstandingMods--;
88:
89:                        // check if there was an error
90:                        uErr = ldap_result2error( psLdap, psResult,
           ➥false );
91:                        if( uErr != LDAP_SUCCESS )
92:                        {
93:                            ULONG uModifyErr;
94:                            char* pszDNs = NULL;
95:                            char* pszErrmsg = NULL;
96:
```

continues

LISTING 24.7 CONTINUED

```
97:                          ldap_parse_result( psLdap, psResult,
                         ➥&uModifyErr, &pszDNs, &pszErrmsg, NULL,
                         ➥NULL, FALSE );
98:
99:                          cout << "Got error " << pszErrmsg <<
                         ➥" for "<< pszDNs << endl;

100:                           ldap_memfree( pszDNs );
101:                           ldap_memfree( pszErrmsg );
102:                      }
103:
104:              ldap_msgfree( psResult ); // free the message
105:              break;
106:
107:          case LDAP_RES_SEARCH_RESULT: // search is complete
108:              bDone = true;
109:              ldap_msgfree( psResult ); // free msg
110:              break;
111:
112:          case LDAP_RES_SEARCH_ENTRY: // got a search entry
113:                  {
114:                      // first get the user's DN
115:                      char* pszDN = ldap_get_dn( psLdap,
                      ➥psResult );
116:
117:                      // A single value for the
118:                      // description attribute
119:                      char* apszAttrVals[] =
120:                      {
121:                          "A new description", // the new value
122:                          NULL                 // the NULL
123:                                               // terminator
124:                      };
125:
126:                      // A single update operation
127:                      LDAPMod sMod =
128:                      {
129:                          LDAP_MOD_REPLACE, // Modification
130:                                            // operation
131:                          "description",    // Attribute to
132:                                            // replace
133:                          apszAttrVals      // Values to replace
134:                      };
135:
136:                      // The array of pointers to operations
137:                      LDAPMod* asMods[] =
138:                      {
139:                          &sMod, // one operation
140:                          NULL   // the NULL terminator
141:                      };
```

```
142:
143:                              // The server control for lazy commit
144:                              LDAPControl sLazyCommitControl =
145:                              {
146:                              "1.2.840.113556.1.4.619",
147:                              // Lazy commit OID
148:                              NULL,                        // no data
149:                              false                        // not critical
150:                              };
151:
152:                              // The array of pointers to controls
153:                              LDAPControl* apzServerControls[] =
154:                              {
155:                                  &sLazyCommitControl,
156:                                  NULL
157:                              };
158:
159:                              // Do the modification asynchronously
160:                              ULONG uModHandle = ldap_modify(
161:                                  psLdap, // the LDAP session
162:                                  pszDN,  // the DN of the object
163:                                          // to modify
164:                              asMods  // the list of mod operations
165:                                      // to perform
166:                              );
167:
168:                              if( uModHandle != -1 )
169:                              {
170:                         cout << "Updated description for " << pszDN <<
                         ➥endl;
171:                                  nOutstandingMods++;
172:                              }
173:
174:                              ldap_msgfree( psResult );
175:                              // free the message
176:                          }
177:                      }
178:                  }
179:              }
180:
181:          ldap_unbind( psLdap );
182:      }
183:
184:      return 0;
185: }
```

The program in Listing 24.7 sets up the LDAP session in the usual way at lines 7–45. The distinguished name of the Users container in the domain is in szDomainDN.

At line 56, the program issues an asynchronous search for user objects, and it starts a loop at line 70 to retrieve the search results with ldap_result().

The call to `ldap_result()` at line 76 specifies `LDAP_RES_ANY` so that it will retrieve the results of the search operation and the results of the modification operation issued later in the program.

The program handles search results starting at line 112. For each entry returned by the search, the program sets up an asynchronous modification of the description attribute starting at line 119. For each entry for which it issues a modification, the program increments the `nOutstandingMods` counter. The program frees the search entry at line 174 by calling `ldap_msgfree()`.

At line 86, the program handles results from modification operations. It decrements the `nOutstandingMods` counter, and then checks the result of the operation by calling `ldap_result2error()`. If the result of the modification was not `LDAP_SUCCESS`, indicating an error during the modification operation, the program calls `ldap_parse result()` to get the information about the modification. The information includes the distinguished name of the object being modified, the error code, and a text description of the error itself. The program prints the distinguished name and the error message text.

The program frees the distinguished name and error message string at lines 100 and 101 and frees the result pointer at line 104 by calling `ldap_msgfree()`.

The loop terminates when there are no more search entries (`bDone` is `true`) and the count of outstanding modifications has gone to `0`.

The program closes the LDAP session at line 181 by calling `ldap_unbind()`.

Moving and Renaming Active Directory Objects

Moving objects in the directory from one container to another is something that comes up quite often in directory administration. Whenever there is any kind of departmental reorganization, the directory administrator has to move all the user objects from one place to another in the tree.

Recall that—conceptually, at least—any object in the directory can be a container. Consequently, if you move or rename an object that is a container, you effectively move or rename the entire subtree it contains.

LDAP supports moving and renaming objects with the same set of functions. The two moving and renaming functions are `ldap_rename_ext()` and `ldap_rename_ext_s()`.

> **NOTE**
>
> The current draft LDAP API standard specifies that the renaming functions are called `ldap_rename()` and `ldap_rename_s()`. The current Microsoft implementation deviates from the draft standard by naming the functions `ldap_rename_ext()` and `ldap_rename_ext_s()`. Be aware of this if you are hoping to write code that is portable to different LDAP platforms.

Renaming an object within its current container is a straightforward operation. Moving an object to another container has a few restrictions you need to be aware of.

- You can move an object only to an existing container. This only makes sense because the directory service would have no idea how to create the missing containers.

- The schema determines what kind of container you can move the object to. Remember that essentially any object in the directory can be a container. For each class of object, the schema indicates what classes of objects can contain it in the class's `possibleSuperiors` attribute. The directory service will not let you move objects to containers that are not allowed to contain that class of object.

- You can only move an object within the current domain. You can get around this restriction by using the Active Directory–specific cross-domain move control.

> **NOTE**
>
> The LDAPv2 C API defined four other functions for renaming objects: `ldap_modrdn()`, `ldap_modrdn_s()`, `ldap_modrdn2()`, and `ldap_modrdn2_s()`. These functions could rename an object only within its container; they could not move the object to another container. These four functions exist in the current Microsoft LDAP implementation for backward compatibility, but their use has been deprecated. Use the `ldap_rename_ext_s()` and `ldap_rename_ext()` functions instead.

Renaming an Active Directory Object with LDAP

When you rename an object in the directory within its current container, you use the ldap_rename_ext_s() function or its asynchronous variant, ldap_rename_ext().

```
ULONG ldap_rename_ext_s( LDAP* ld, char* dn, char* NewRDN,
➥char* NewParent, INT DeleteOldRDN, LDAPControl* ServerControls[],
➥LDAPControl* ClientControls[] )
```

> ld is a pointer to an LDAP session. It must have been initialized with ldap_init() and appropriately authenticated with one of the bind functions.
>
> dn is a NUL-terminated string containing the distinguished name of the object to be moved or renamed.
>
> NewRDN is a NUL-terminated string containing the new relative distinguished name of the object. It includes the attribute type—for instance, "CN=Bob Kelly" instead of just "Bob Kelly". Note that you cannot leave this parameter NULL in an attempt to move an object from one container to another while retaining the object's original relative distinguished name. You must always specify the new relative distinguished name, even if it is the same as the original.
>
> NewParent is a NUL-terminated string containing the distinguished name of the new container for the object. The container must already exist, and it must be in the same domain as the object being moved, unless you specify the cross-domain move server control. If you leave this parameter NULL, the function will simply rename the object with the new name given by NewRDN within the object's current container.
>
> DeleteOldRDN is a Boolean value that, if true, indicates that the old RDN value should be removed from the object. If DeleteOldRDN is false, the old relative distinguished name will be retained as a separate value in the naming attribute of the object, in addition to the value of the new relative distinguished name. The schema must define the naming attribute of the object to be multivalued for this to occur. Note that the cn (common name) and dc (domain component) attributes are defined as single-valued in the schema; so, in general, you must always set DeleteOldRDN to true.
>
> ServerControls is a pointer to a NULL-terminated array of pointers to appropriately initialized server LDAPControl structures. Set this parameter to NULL if you are not using any server controls.
>
> ClientControls is a pointer to a NULL-terminated array of pointers to appropriately initialized client LDAPControl structures. Set this parameter to NULL if you are not using any client controls.

Returns: LDAP_SUCCESS if the move or rename operation succeeded; otherwise, it returns an LDAP error code.

The sample program in Listing 24.8 demonstrates using ldap_rename_ext_s() to rename a single object within the Users container.

LISTING 24.8 USING ldap_rename_ext_s() TO RENAME AN OBJECT

```
1:   #include <windows.h>
2:   #include <winldap.h>
3:   #include <iostream.h>
4:
5:   int main( int argc, char** argv )
6:   {
7:       LDAP* psLdap = ldap_init( NULL, LDAP_PORT );
8:       if( psLdap != NULL )
9:       {
10:          ULONG uErr = ldap_bind_s( psLdap, NULL, NULL,
             ➥LDAP_AUTH_NEGOTIATE );
11:          if( uErr == LDAP_SUCCESS )
12:          {
13:              // set LDAP API version
14:              int nVersion = LDAP_VERSION3;
15:              ldap_set_option( psLdap, LDAP_OPT_VERSION, &nVersion );
16:
17:              // turn off referrals chasing
18:              int nChaseReferrals = 0;
19:              ldap_set_option( psLdap, LDAP_OPT_REFERRALS,
                 ➥&nChaseReferrals );
20:
21:              char* pszOldDN = "CN=GlobalGroup2,CN=Users,DC=redrock,
                 ➥DC=home,DC=netpro,DC=com";
22:              char* pszNewRDN = "CN=GlobalGroup1";
23:
24:              uErr = ldap_rename_ext_s(
25:                  psLdap,      // LDAP session
26:                  pszOldDN,    // DN of object to rename
27:                  pszNewRDN,   // new RDN
28:                  NULL,        // new container
29:                  true,        // delete old RDN value
30:                  NULL,        // client controls
31:                  NULL         // server controls
32:              );
33:
34:              cout << "Error for rename was " << uErr << endl;
35:          }
36:
37:          ldap_unbind( psLdap );
38:      }
39:
40:      return 0;
41:  }
```

24

MODIFYING ACTIVE
DIRECTORY OBJECTS
WITH LDAP

The program in Listing 24.8 initializes and authenticates the LDAP session using `ldap_init()` and `ldap_bind_s()` at lines 7–10.

At lines 21 and 22, the program defines the distinguished name of the object to be renamed, as well as the new relative distinguished name of the object.

The program renames the object within its existing container at line 24 by calling `ldap_rename_ext_s()` with the distinguished name, the new relative distinguished name, and a `NULL` for the `NewParent` parameter.

The program prints the result at line 34 and closes the LDAP session with `ldap_unbind()` at line 37.

Renaming Active Directory Objects Asynchronously

You can rename objects in the directory asynchronously using the `ldap_rename_ext()` function. It behaves like all the other asynchronous functions in that it returns an operation handle. It is then up to you to check the status of the operation by repeatedly calling `ldap_result()` with the operation handle. When `ldap_result()` returns the response message for the server for the operation, you can check the error by using `ldap_result2error()` and `ldap_parse_result()` as described earlier in this chapter.

Note that the rename operation returns only a single server response with the type equal to `LDAP_RES_MODRDN`. You should therefore pass `LDAP_MSG_ONE` as the value for the uAll parameter when you call `ldap_result()`.

```
ULONG ldap_rename_ext( LDAP* ld, const PCHAR dn, const PCHAR NewRDN,
➥const PCHAR NewParent, INT DeleteOldRDN, PLDAPControl* ServerControls,
➥PLDAPControl* ClientControls, ULONG* MessageNumber )
```

> `ld` is a pointer to an LDAP session. It must have been initialized with `ldap_init()` and appropriately authenticated with one of the bind functions.
>
> `dn` is a NUL-terminated string containing the distinguished name of the object to be moved or renamed.
>
> `NewRDN` is a NUL-terminated string containing the new relative distinguished name of the object. It includes the attribute type—for instance, `"CN=Bob Kelly"` instead of just `"Bob Kelly"`. Note that you cannot leave this parameter `NULL` in an attempt to move an object from one container to another while retaining the object's original relative distinguished name. You must always specify the new relative distinguished name, even if it is the same as the original.
>
> `NewParent` is a NUL-terminated string containing the distinguished name of the new container for the object. The container must already exist, and it must be in the same domain as the object being moved, unless you specify the cross-domain

move server control. If you leave this parameter NULL, the function will simply rename the object with the new name given by NewRDN within the object's current container.

DeleteOldRDN is a Boolean value that, if true, indicates that the old RDN value should be removed from the object. If DeleteOldRDN is false, the old relative distinguished name will be retained as a separate value in the naming attribute of the object, in addition to the value of the new relative distinguished name. The schema must define the naming attribute of the object to be multivalued for this to occur. Note that the cn (common name) and dc (domain component) attributes are defined as single-valued in the schema; so, in general, you must always set DeleteOldRDN to true.

ServerControls is a pointer to a NULL-terminated array of pointers to appropriately initialized server LDAPControl structures. Set this parameter to NULL if you are not using any server controls.

ClientControls is a pointer to a NULL-terminated array of pointers to appropriately initialized client LDAPControl structures. Set this parameter to NULL if you are not using any client controls.

MessageNumber is a pointer to an operation handle that ldap_rename_ext() will set after successfully initiating the rename operation. You must check the results of the rename operation by repeatedly calling ldap_result() and passing this operation handle.

Returns: LDAP_SUCCESS if the rename operation was initiated properly or an LDAP error code if there was some sort of problem.

The sample program in Listing 24.9 asynchronously renames an object in the Users container from "CN=Keely Dryer" to "CN=Christy Cleveland", and moves the object to the "CN=On Leave" container in the same operation.

LISTING 24.9 USING ldap_rename_ext() TO RENAME A USER

```
1:    #include <windows.h>
2:    #include <winldap.h>
3:    #include <iostream.h>
4:
5:    int main( int argc, char** argv )
6:    {
7:        LDAP* psLdap = ldap_init( NULL, LDAP_PORT );
8:        if( psLdap != NULL )
9:        {
10:           ULONG uErr = ldap_bind_s( psLdap, NULL, NULL,
          ➥LDAP_AUTH_NEGOTIATE );
11:           if( uErr == LDAP_SUCCESS )
12:           {
```

24

MODIFYING ACTIVE
DIRECTORY OBJECTS
WITH LDAP

continues

Listing 24.9 CONTINUED

```
13:                // set LDAP API version
14:                int nVersion = LDAP_VERSION3;
15:                ldap_set_option( psLdap, LDAP_OPT_VERSION, &nVersion );
16:
17:                // turn off referrals chasing
18:                int nChaseReferrals = 0;
19:                ldap_set_option( psLdap, LDAP_OPT_REFERRALS,
        ➥&nChaseReferrals );
20:
21:                char* pszOldDN =
        ➥"CN=Keely Dryer,CN=Users,DC=megacorp",DC=com";
22:                char* pszNewRDN = "CN=Christy Cleveland";
23:                char* pszNewContainer =
        ➥"CN=On Leave,DC=megacorp,DC=com";
24:
25:                ULONG uHandle = 0;
26:
27:                uErr = ldap_rename_ext(
28:                    psLdap,            // LDAP session
29:                    pszOldDN,          // DN of object to rename
30:                    pszNewRDN,         // new RDN
31:                    pszNewContainer,   // new container
32:                    true,              // delete old RDN value
33:                    NULL,              // client controls
34:                    NULL,              // server controls
35:                    &uHandle
36:                );
37:
38:                if( uErr == LDAP_SUCCESS )
39:                {
40:                    bool bDone = false;
41:
42:                    while( ! bDone )
43:                    {
44:                        struct l_timeval sTimeout = { 10, 0 };
45:                        LDAPMessage* psResult = NULL;
46:
47:                        int nResult = ldap_result(
48:                            psLdap,            // LDAP session
49:                            uHandle,           // operation handle
50:                            LDAP_MSG_ONE,      // get one message
51:                            &sTimeout,         // timeout value
52:                            &psResult          // result
53:                        );
54:
55:                        switch( nResult )
56:                        {
57:                            case -1: // error
58:                                bDone = true;
```

```
59:                              break;
60:
61:                      default:
62:                      case 0: // timeout
63:                          break;
64:
65:                      case LDAP_RES_MODRDN:
66:                          uErr = ldap_result2error( psLdap,
                            ➥psResult, false );
67:                          if( uErr == LDAP_SUCCESS )
68:                          {
69:                              cout << "Rename succeeded" << endl;
70:                          }
71:                          else
72:                          {
73:                              ULONG uRenameErr;
74:                              char* pszDNs = NULL;
75:                              char* pszErrmsg = NULL;
76:
77:                              ldap_parse_result(
78:                                  psLdap,      // LDAP session
79:                                  psResult,    // result to parse
80:                                  &uRenameErr, // result
81:                                  &pszDNs,     // name of object
82:                                  &pszErrmsg,  // error msg
83:                                  NULL,        // referrals
84:                                  NULL,        // server controls
85:                                  FALSE        // free it?
86:                              );
87:
88:                              cout << "Got error " << pszErrmsg <<
                                ➥" for " << pszDNs << endl;
89:
90:                              ldap_memfree( pszDNs );
91:                              ldap_memfree( pszErrmsg );
92:                          }
93:                          break;
94:                  }
95:              }
96:          }
97:      }
98:
99:      ldap_unbind( psLdap );
100:    }
101:
102:    return 0;
103: }
```

After initializing an LDAP session at line 7 and authenticating it at line 10, the program in Listing 24.9 declares the old distinguished name, the new relative distinguished name, and the new container at lines 21–23.

The program issues the asynchronous rename operation at line 27 by calling `ldap_rename_ext_s()`, specifying the distinguished name, the new relative distinguished name, and the new container.

At line 42, the program starts a loop, calling `ldap_result()` each time around to see whether the rename operation has completed. If the returned result is `LDAP_RES_MODRDN`, the program uses `ldap_result2error()` to check the error code for the rename operation.

If there was an error during the rename operation, the program calls `ldap_parse_result()` to get the distinguished name and error message string for the error. It prints them at line 88.

The program closes the LDAP session at line 99 by calling `ldap_unbind()`.

CHAPTER 25

Adding Active Directory Objects with LDAP

Directories provide a powerful solution to the complexities of managing a large enterprise network. Because it is a centralized repository of network configuration information, a directory can simplify network administration by creating a consistent configuration and security framework that supports all network services. Windows 2000 simplifies enterprise network administration by integrating all its basic network services with the directory.

But administering basic network services is only part of the difficulty of managing a large network. In order to realize the full potential benefit that a directory can provide, all applications, not just the basic services, need to use the directory for configuration and management. To extend the use of the directory beyond what it came with out of the box, you have to add objects to the directory.

This chapter covers adding objects to and deleting objects from the directory, and it will also describe how to programmatically update the schema using LDAP.

The API functions covered in this chapter are listed in Table 25.1.

TABLE 25.1 LDAP FUNCTIONS AND DATA STRUCTURES FOR ADDING OBJECTS

Function	Description
ldap_add()	Asynchronous function to add an object to the directory.
ldap_add_s()	Synchronous function to add a function to the directory.
ldap_add_ext()	Asynchronous function to add an object to the directory. This function includes parameters for specifying client controls and server controls.
ldap_add_ext_s()	Synchronous function to add an object to the directory. This function includes parameters for timeout values, client controls, and server controls.
ldap_result2error()	Extracts the error code from an asynchronous response message retrieved by ldap_result().
ldap_parse_message()	Parses an asynchronous response message retrieved by ldap_result().
ldap_msgfree()	Frees the memory associated with an LDAP response message.
struct ldapmod (LDAPMod)	Structure that defines an attribute modification operation.
struct berval (LDAP_BERVAL)	Structure that contains a binary attribute value.

Things to Know Before You Go

This next section describes some basic concepts that are important for you to understand before you attempt to add objects to the directory with LDAP. Read through this section before you start writing any code; it will save you time later.

Adding Objects Is a Lot Like Modifying Them

The way you add objects to the directory is substantially similar to the way you modify them. The ldap_add...() APIs parallel the ldap_modify...() APIs, the add APIs use the same data structures to define attributes and values, and the security and schema rules that control the modification of directory objects are the same that control the addition of them. If you've successfully updated directory objects with LDAP, you're 90% of the way to understanding how to add new ones.

> **NOTE**
>
> Much of the material in this chapter is similar to that in Chapter 24, "Modifying Active Directory Objects with LDAP." It's repeated here for completeness.

Adding Multiple Attributes at Once

When you add an object to the directory with LDAP, you don't so much add an object as you add a set of attributes. You specify a list of attributes and values, and the directory server will create a new object and add all the attributes to it. Or, if there is some sort of an error, the directory server will reject the entire transaction. The server will never create an object and add just some of the attributes you specified.

Multivalued Attributes

The attributes of an LDAP object are potentially multivalued, depending, of course, on the schema. When you add an object to the directory, you can specify multiple values for these attributes. Remember, though, that the values in a multivalued attribute have to be unique. A single multivalued attribute cannot have two equal values.

Existence of the Parent Container

Before you add a new object to the directory, you must make sure that its container already exists in the directory. If the new object's container doesn't already exist, LDAP will return an error when you attempt to add the new object. It's up to you to create the container hierarchy for your new objects; the directory service will not create it for you.

Schema Rules

Just as in a relational database, the schema defines what sorts of objects and attributes you store in the directory, and in what ways they can be organized in the directory hierarchy. This section describes the schema rules you have to follow when you add objects to the directory.

Attribute Syntaxes

The schema defines what type of data each attribute in the directory may contain. When you add an object to the directory, you need to make sure that the values you specify for the attributes obey the appropriate syntax rules. If you don't, the add operation will fail. You can specify values as strings for almost all LDAP syntaxes, but you have to make sure the strings are in the right format. Be sure you know what the syntax of an attribute is *before* you try to add it.

Multivalued or Single-Valued?

The schema defines whether or not an attribute may be single-valued or multivalued. If you try to violate this constraint by adding multiple values to a single-valued attribute, LDAP will reject the entire add operation. Be sure you know whether an attribute is single-valued or multivalued *before* you try to add additional values to it.

Must Contain and May Contain

The schema also defines what attributes each class of object *must* contain and what attributes each class of object *may* contain. When you add an object to the directory, you have to provide values for *all* the must contain attributes; if you don't, the add operation will fail. Likewise, you can't specify values for attributes of an object you are adding unless the class definition names that attribute in the must have or may have list.

Remember that the must have and may have lists are inherited from the parent classes (those classes named in the subClassOf attribute of the class object) *and* the auxiliary classes. When you add a new object to the directory, make sure you specify values for all the must have attributes for all the parent classes and auxiliary classes of the class of object you are adding.

The directory service itself will create some of the must contain properties for you. In particular, the directory service will automatically assign values to the properties listed in Table 25.2. For a simple class, such as container, you need to specify a value only for the objectClass attribute of the new object. This attribute determines the class of the object you created. Other classes of objects might default other values for you as well, but the objects listed here seem to be used in objects of all classes.

TABLE 25.2   ATTRIBUTES THAT ARE AUTOMATICALLY ASSIGNED VALUES BY ACTIVE DIRECTORY

Attribute Name	Description
cn	The common name of the object. If not specified, Active Directory will use the relative distinguished name of the object.
instanceType	Used internally by Active Directory. Indicates how the object is to be replicated, among other things.
name	An alternative name for the object. Active Directory defaults this to the object's relative distinguished name.
nTSecurityDescriptor	The security descriptor containing the access control list for the object. If you do not specify this attribute, Active Directory defaults it to the value specified for this class of object in the schema.

Attribute Name	Description
objectCategory	An indication of the category of class of object of which this is a member. Unless you specify otherwise, Active Directory defaults this to the class of the object.
objectClass	The lDAPDisplayName of the class of object that the new object is. Although you must specify a single value for objectClass, Active Directory will figure out the inheritance chain and store the other parent classes in this attribute.
objectGUID	The globally unique identifier for the object. Active Directory generates a GUID for this attribute when it creates the object.
showInAdvancedViewOnly	Indicates whether the Microsoft Management Console (MMC) should show this attribute if the Advanced View is not enabled. Active Directory defaults this value to TRUE.
uSNChanged	The Update Sequence Number (USN) at which the object was last changed. This value is used to determine whether the object must be replicated to other domain controllers.
uSNCreated	The Update Sequence Number (USN) at which the object was created. This value is also used in the replication process.
whenChanged	The time and date the object was last changed. Active Directory sets this to the current time and date on the domain controller where the object was first created.
whenCreated	The time and date the object was created. Active Directory sets this to the current time and date on the domain controller where the object was first created.

Defining the New Object's Class

One major difference between adding a new object to the directory and simply modifying an existing one is that you have to define the object's class. You do this by specifying a value for the objectClass property. The value is a string, and it must be the lDAPDisplayName of a class defined in the schema; that is, there must be a classSchema object with that name in the Schema naming context.

In fact, the objectClass attribute is multivalued. The objectClass attribute contains the entire inheritance hierarchy for the class, not just the immediate parent class. However, you just specify the actual class for the object; the directory service will fill in the remainder of the inheritance hierarchy for you automatically.

25

ADDING ACTIVE DIRECTORY OBJECTS WITH LDAP

Possible Superiors

The Active Directory schema also defines what class of objects can contain the object you are adding. When you add an object, the container you are adding the object to has to be of a class that is named in the possible superiors list for the class of object you are adding. Classes inherit their possible superiors lists from their parent classes, but not from the auxiliary class list.

Access Rights

You can't add an object to the directory unless you have sufficient access rights to the container in which you are adding it. Each container in Active Directory has its own ACL. ACLs for a container are also propagated down from its containing objects. All these ACLs are merged together to determine what access you actually have to the container. Be sure your program authenticates to the directory with a username that has sufficient access rights to make the additions you need to make.

API Data Structures for Adding Objects with LDAP

This section describes the API data structures you need to set up to use any of the ldap_add...() API functions. All of the add functions use the same data structures. They are the same as the ones used by the ldap_modify...() functions, with one small difference. For completeness, this section repeats the description of these data structures.

You have to set up four fundamental data structures to add an object to the directory. These structures define the attributes and values for the object you are adding:

- An array of pointers to LDAPMod structures—This array must be terminated with a NULL pointer. Each LDAPMod structure specifies an attribute to add with your new object.

- One or more LDAPMod structures that specify the attributes to create—Each LDAPMod structure contains an operation code, an attribute name, and a pointer to an array of pointers to values. The ldap_add...() functions ignore the operation code except for the LDAP_MOD_BVALUES bit that indicates whether the values are specified as strings or binary values. For clarity, you should set this member to either LDAP_MOD_ADD or (LDAP_MOD_ADD | LDAP_MOD_BVALUES).

- An array of pointers to values—The array must be terminated with a NULL pointer. The array entries all point to either string values or berval structures.

- One or more values—Each value is either a NUL-terminated string or a `berval` structure containing a length and a pointer to an arbitrary block of data. Remember that the LDAP data model does not allow empty attributes, so you must always specify at least one value.

Figure 25.1 gives you an idea of what these data structures look like.

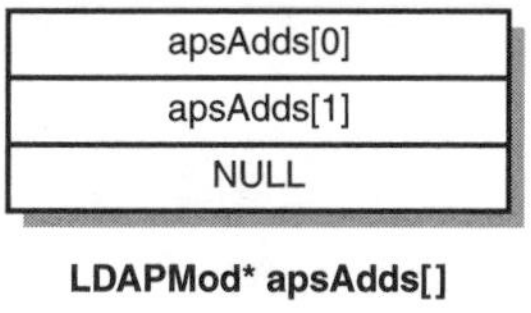

FIGURE 25.1

Data structures for adding directory entries with LDAP.

| apsAdds[0] |
| apsAdds[1] |
| NULL |

LDAPMod* apsAdds[]

The `berval` Structure

You use the `berval` structure (BER is the acronym for Basic Encoding Rules) when you need to specify attribute values that do not have a string representation. For instance, if you wanted to store a JPEG image of each user in an attribute of each user object, you would have to use the `berval` structure to pass the JPEG value to LDAP.

The `berval` structure is very simple: It is just a length field and a pointer that points to an arbitrary block of data. The `berval` structure is defined as follows:

```
typedef struct berval {
    ULONG  bv_len;
    PCHAR  bv_val;
} LDAP_BERVAL, * PLDAP_BERVAL, BERVAL, * PBERVAL;
```

Table 25.3 describes the elements of the structure.

TABLE 25.3 THE ELEMENTS OF THE `berval` STRUCTURE

Element	Description
bv_len	An unsigned long indicating the length of the represented data. It can be 0, indicating the value is empty.
bv_val	A pointer to the represented data. It cannot be NULL.

The `ldapmod` Structure

The `ldapmod` structure defines a single attribute addition operation. Each `ldapmod` structure includes the type of addition operation to be performed, the name of the attribute to be added, and a pointer to an array of value pointers. If the attribute to be added is defined with a syntax that provides a string representation, the pointer refers to an array of string pointers. If the syntax does not have a string representation, the pointer refers to an array of pointers to `berval` structures. The following is the definition of the `ldapmod` structure:

```
typedef struct ldapmod {
    ULONG     mod_op;
    PCHAR     mod_type;
    union {
        PCHAR* modv_strvals;
        struct berval** modv_bvals;
    } mod_vals;
} LDAPMod, *PLDAPMod;
```

Table 25.4 describes the elements of the `ldapmod` structure.

TABLE 25.4   THE ELEMENTS OF THE `ldapmod` STRUCTURE

Element	Description
mod_op	The type of addition operation to perform. It must be one of the values listed in Table 25.5.
mod_type	A pointer to a NUL-terminated string containing the name of the attribute to be modified. This name may be the `lDAPDisplayName` or the OID string of the attribute.
modv_strvals	A pointer to a NULL-terminated array of pointers to NUL-terminated strings. Each string contains one of the attribute values. This is part of a union with `modv_bvals`.
modv_bvals	A pointer to a NULL-terminated array of pointers to `berval` structures. Each `berval` structure contains one of the attribute values. This is part of a union with `modv_strvals`.

TABLE 25.5   POSSIBLE VALUES FOR THE `mod_op` ELEMENT OF THE `ldapmod` STRUCTURE

Value	Description
LDAP_MOD_ADD	The specified attribute values will be added with the object.
LDAP_MOD_BVALUES	This is a bit flag that you OR with one of the preceding values to indicate that you are specifying the attribute values with an array of pointers to `berval` structures.

Selecting the Appropriate API Function

Selecting the appropriate LDAP function to use to add an object is straightforward. There are four add API functions to choose from. `ldap_add_s()` and `ldap_add()` are the basic synchronous and asynchronous add functions, respectively. `ldap_add_ext_s()` and `ldap_add_ext()` are the corresponding extended functions that allow you to specify a set of client and server controls.

If you don't have to add a lot of objects, and you have no need to specify LDAP controls for the add operation, use `ldap_add_s()`. It has the simplest interface, and because it is synchronous, you'll have to write a lot less code.

If you must add many objects to the directory all at once, use `ldap_add()` or `ldap_add_ext()`. Managing the asynchronous interface is more cumbersome than with `ldap_add()`, but your program can issue a bunch of add operations and then handle the results in the background by calling `ldap_result()` periodically. This can improve the perceived performance of your application.

If you have to specify some extended functionality with an LDAP control, you'll have to use one of the extended functions, either `ldap_add_ext()` or `ldap_add_ext_s()`. There are two controls in particular that you might find useful when you are adding objects to the directory: the lazy commit control and the verify name control. The lazy commit control turns off the directory service's automatic cache flushing, which will improve the performance of the add operations. The verify name control is useful if the objects you are adding contain attributes that are the distinguished names of other objects in the directory. Normally, the directory service will verify each distinguished name attribute through the closest global catalog when the attribute is added or modified. You can use the verify name control to specify a particular server to use for such validation, or for even more performance, you can turn off the validation entirely. Refer to Chapter 28, "Extending LDAP with Options and Controls," for the details of the Microsoft Active Directory LDAP controls.

Adding Objects Synchronously by Using `ldap_add_s()`

The sample program in Listing 25.1 adds a single container object to the directory. It uses the `ldap_add_s()` function to add the object synchronously. Although the program isn't wonderfully useful by itself, it shows how to set up the data structures appropriately for `ldap_add_s()`.

The container class inherits only from top. The top class specifies four must-contain attributes: instanceType, nTSecurityDescriptor, objectCategory, and objectClass. The container class specifies one additional must-contain attribute: cn.

The code, however, defines only two of the properties. How can this be? The directory service automatically defines instanceType, nTSecurityDescriptor, and objectCategory (and the other attributes given in Table 25.2). To keep the sample program short, I've left these attributes undefined so that the directory service will define them automatically.

ULONG ldap_add_s(LDAP* ld, char* dn, LDAPMod* attrs[])

> ld is a pointer to an LDAP session that was created with ldap_init() and authenticated with ldap_bind_s(). Note that the bind must be done with a username that has sufficient access rights to add an object to the directory.

> dn is a pointer to a NUL-terminated string containing the full distinguished name of the new object. The container for the object (everything in the DN past the first comma) must already exist in the directory.

> attrs is a NULL-terminated array of pointers to appropriately initialized LDAPMod structures. Each LDAPMod structure represents an attribute of the new object. There must be one LDAPMod structure for each must-contain attribute defined for the class of object, except for those listed in Table 25.2. You must always specify a value for the objectClass attribute.

Returns: LDAP_SUCCESS if the object was added to the directory, and an LDAP error code if it failed. ldap_add_s() will not add the new object if any of the attribute definitions is in error.

LISTING 25.1   ADDING A CONTAINER WITH ldap_add_s()

```
1:   #include <windows.h>
2:   #include <winldap.h>
3:   #include <iostream.h>
4:
5:   int main( int argc, char** argv )
6:   {
7:       LDAP* psLdap = ldap_init( NULL, LDAP_PORT );
8:       if( psLdap != NULL )
9:       {
10:          ULONG uErr = ldap_bind_s( psLdap, NULL, NULL,
             ➥LDAP_AUTH_NEGOTIATE );
11:          if( uErr == LDAP_SUCCESS )
12:          {
13:              // set LDAP API version
14:              int nVersion = LDAP_VERSION3;
15:              ldap_set_option( psLdap, LDAP_OPT_VERSION, &nVersion );
16:
```

```
17:            // turn off referrals chasing
18:            int nChaseReferrals = 0;
19:           ldap_set_option( psLdap, LDAP_OPT_REFERRALS,
             ➥&nChaseReferrals );
20:
21:            // DN of new container
22:            char szNewDN[ 1024 ] = "CN=NewContainer,CN=Users,";
23:
24:            LDAPMessage* psMsg = NULL;
25:
26:            // Get rootDSE attr defaultNamingContext
27:            uErr = ldap_search_s(
28:                psLdap,
29:                NULL,
30:                LDAP_SCOPE_BASE,
31:                "objectClass=*",
32:                NULL,
33:                false,
34:                &psMsg
35:            );
36:            if( uErr == LDAP_SUCCESS )
37:            {
38:                char** ppszDomain = ldap_get_values( psLdap,
                   ➥ldap_first_entry( psLdap,psMsg),
                   ➥"defaultNamingContext" );
39:                if( ppszDomain != NULL )
40:                {
41:                    strcat( szNewDN, ppszDomain[ 0 ] );
42:                    ldap_value_free( ppszDomain );
43:                }
44:                ldap_msgfree( psMsg );
45:            }
46:
47:            // values for the objectClass attribute
48:            char* apszObjectClassVals[] =
49:            {
50:                "container", // a single value for the objectClass
51:                             // attribute
52:                NULL
53:            };
54:
55:            // operation for the objectClass attribute
56:            LDAPMod sAddObjectClass =
57:            {
58:                LDAP_MOD_ADD, // the operation
59:                "objectClass", // the name of the attribute
60:                apszObjectClassVals // pointer to array of values
61:            };
62:
63:            // values for the cn attribute
64:            char* apszCNVals[] =
65:            {
```

continues

25

ADDING ACTIVE DIRECTORY OBJECTS WITH LDAP

LISTING 25.1   CONTINUED

```
66:                   "NewContainer", // a single value for the cn attribute
67:                   NULL
68:              };
69:
70:              // operation for the cn attribute
71:              LDAPMod sAddCN =
72:              {
73:                   LDAP_MOD_ADD, // the operation
74:                   "cn", // the name of the attribute
75:                   apszCNVals
76:              };
77:
78:              // list of attributes to add
79:              LDAPMod* asAttrsToAdd[] =
80:              {
81:                   &sAddObjectClass,
82:                   &sAddCN,
83:                   NULL
84:              };
85:
86:              // add the new container
87:              uErr = ldap_add_s( psLdap, szNewDN, asAttrsToAdd );
88:
89:              cout << "Error is " << uErr << endl;
90:         }
91:
92:         ldap_unbind( psLdap );
93:    }
94:
95:    return 0;
96: }
```

Lines 7–10 of the program create an LDAP session with ldap_init() and then authenticate the session using ldap_bind_s(). The program then uses ldap_set_option() to disable referrals and to set the protocol to LDAPv3.

Lines 22–45 initialize the distinguished name for the new object by getting the default domain name from the rootDSE and prepending "CN=NewContainer,CN=Users" to it. This will create a new container called NewContainer in the Users container of the domain.

Lines 48–53 define a single value for the objectClass attribute. In this case, the value is "container" because that is the class of object we are creating.

Lines 56–61 define the LDAPMod structure for the objectClass attribute. It specifies the name of the attribute, the operation (which is ignored), and a pointer to the list of values.

Lines 64–76 repeat the setup for the cn attribute. Because the cn attribute is the naming attribute for container objects, the value for the cn attribute has to be the same as the value specified in the distinguished name.

The program specifies the list of attributes for the new object at lines 79–84, and then finally adds the object at line 87.

The program closes the LDAP session at line 92 by calling ldap_unbind().

Adding Objects Asynchronously by Using `ldap_add()`

The sample program in Listing 25.2 shows how to use the ldap_add() API function to add objects to the directory asynchronously. This sample program only adds one object, which isn't very useful, but it shows how to set everything up and how to poll for the results returned by the server.

```
ULONG ldap_add( LDAP* ld, char* dn, LDAPMod* attrs[] )
```

ld is a pointer to an LDAP session that was created with ldap_init() and authenticated with ldap_bind_s(). Note that the bind must be done with a username that has sufficient access rights to add an object to the directory.

dn is a pointer to a NUL-terminated string containing the full distinguished name of the new object. The container for the object (everything in the DN past the first comma) must already exist in the directory.

attrs is a NULL-terminated array of pointers to appropriately initialized LDAPMod structures. Each LDAPMod structure represents an attribute of the new object. There must be one LDAPMod structure for each must-contain attribute defined for the class of object. This always includes the objectClass attribute.

Returns: An operation handle if it initiated the add operation. You pass this handle to ldap_result() to determine whether the add operation actually succeeded. If there was some error in initiating the add operation, ldap_add() returns 0xffffffff. You must call LdapGetLastError() to determine the exact error code.

```
ULONG ldap_result( LDAP* ld, ULONG msgid, ULONG all,
➥struct l_timeval* timeout, LDAPMessage** res )
```

ld is a pointer to an LDAP structure that has been initialized with ldap_init(), ldap_sslinit(), or ldap_open(). It must be the same LDAP structure that you used to perform the addition.

msgid is the handle to the search that was returned by ldap_search(). If you specify LDAP_RES_ANY, ldap_result() will return results for any outstanding asynchronous operation that were started on the LDAP session given by ld.

25

ADDING ACTIVE DIRECTORY OBJECTS WITH LDAP

all specifies how many of the result objects you want returned. It must be one of three constants defined in Table 25.6.

TABLE 25.6   POSSIBLE VALUES OF THE all PARAMETER OF ldap_result()

Constant	Description
LDAP_MSG_ONE	Indicates that ldap_result() should return a single operation result.
LDAP_MSG_ALL	Indicates that ldap_result() should wait until all the results have been received from the server. Because an add operation returns only a single result, this value isn't very useful for additions.
LDAP_MSG_RECEIVED	Indicates that ldap_result() should return all the result objects that have been received so far. Because an add operation returns only a single result, this value isn't very useful for additions.

> **NOTE**
>
> Add operations will generate only one response message, so you might as well use LDAP_MSG_ONE for the all parameter of ldap_result().

timeout is a pointer to an l_timeval structure that contains the timeout value for the ldap_result() call. If there are no messages to retrieve within the time specified by the l_timeval structure, ldap_result() will return a 0.

res is the address of an LDAPMessage pointer to be set by ldap_result(). This pointer must be freed by passing it to ldap_msgfree() after you are done with it.

> **CAUTION**
>
> Failure to call ldap_msgfree() for each LDAPMessage pointer returned by ldap_result() will cause your program to leak memory and eventually fail.

Returns: The type of the message retrieved. There are 11 possible returned messages. Only LDAP_RES_ADD or LDAP_RES_REFERRAL will be returned as the result of a search operation. You can use ldap_result2error() or ldap_parse_result() to get the results of the add operation.

LDAP_RES_ADD indicates the message contains the results of an addition operation.

LDAP_RES_REFERRAL indicates the message contains one or more referrals to other naming contexts. See the section on processing referrals for information on how to handle this message.

0 indicates the call to ldap_result() timed out. This means there were no results sent from the server within the timeout period. You should retry the call to ldap_result().

-1 indicates an error of some sort. Call LdapGetLastError() to get the corresponding error code.

After you call ldap_result() successfully and it returns a pointer to an LDAPMessage structure in *res, you must free the LDAPMessage structure by calling ldap_msgfree(), passing it the pointer that was returned. You can also free the message by calling ldap_result2error() or ldap_parse_result() and setting the freeit parameter to TRUE.

ULONG ldap_msgfree(LDAPMessage* res)

res is a pointer to an LDAPMessage structure that was returned by ldap_result().

Returns: 0 if it successfully freed the LDAPMessage structure or an LDAP error code if there was some error.

> ### CAUTION
>
> ldap_result() returns a valid pointer in *res only if its return value was greater than 0. Therefore, you should call ldap_msgfree() only if ldap_result() returned a value greater than 0. Calling ldap_msgfree() with an invalid LDAPMessage pointer will cause memory corruption.

Retrieving the Results of an Asynchronous Addition

When you issue an asynchronous search operation, the results you retrieve are the entries that matched your search criteria. When you issue an asynchronous addition using ldap_add() or ldap_add_ext(), you generally want to know whether the server completed the addition successfully, or if there was some sort of error. The LDAPMessage pointer returned by ldap_result() contains the result of the asynchronous addition operation.

There are two functions you can use to get the results of an asynchronous addition operation, ldap_result2error() and ldap_parse_result(). Both functions accept the LDAPMessage pointer returned by ldap_result() as an argument.

Getting the Error Code with `ldap_result2error()`

The `ldap_result2error()` function accepts the `LDAPMessage` pointer returned from `ldap_result()` in `*res`, extracts the error code from the result message, and returns the LDAP error code associated with that particular addition operation.

```
ULONG ldap_result2error( LDAP* ld, LDAPMessage* res, ULONG freeit )
```

> `ld` is a pointer to the LDAP session you used when you called `ldap_result()`.
>
> `res` is the `LDAPMessage` pointer that `ldap_result()` returned in `*res`.
>
> `freeit` is a Boolean that, if set to `true`, will cause `ldap_result2error()` to free the `LDAPMessage` structure. If `freeit` is `false`, `ldap_result2error()` will not free the message structure.

Returns: The error code extracted from the `LDAPMessage` structure.

> **CAUTION**
>
> If you free an `LDAPMessage` structure by setting the `freeit` parameter in `ldap_result2error()` to `true`, be sure that you do not subsequently try to free the message again by calling `ldap_msgfree()`. Doing so will likely cause memory corruption.

Just getting the error code for an asynchronous operation is fine, but what happens if the error is nonzero, indicating an actual failure? What object was being added? `ldap_result2error()` can't give you that information. There are two solutions.

The first strategy is more complicated. In this case, you store in an array each operation handle returned by `ldap_add()` or `ldap_add_ext()`. Then you poll for the results for each handle by iterating through the array and calling `ldap_result()`, passing the operation handle for the `msgid` parameter. This is somewhat complicated, and it incurs the storage and lookup overhead of the array of operation handles.

The second strategy is simpler. In this case, you use `ldap_parse_result()` to retrieve the operation information from the `LDAPMessage` pointer returned by `ldap_result()`. `ldap_parse_result()` is described in the following section.

Getting Information About an Asynchronous Operation with `ldap_parse_result()`

If you want to know which add operation generated an error code, `ldap_result2error()` is insufficient; it tells you what the error was, but not which object addition caused the error. `ldap_parse_result()` can retrieve this information for you.

```
ULONG ldap_parse_result( LDAP* Connection, LDAPMessage* ResultMessage,
➥ULONG* ReturnCode, PCHAR* MatchedDNs, PCHAR* ErrorMessage,
➥PCHAR** Referrals, PLDAPControl** ServerControls, BOOLEAN Freeit )
```

Connection is a pointer to the LDAP session on which the add was issued.

ResultMessage is a pointer to the final result LDAPMessage returned by either ldap_result().

ReturnCode is the address of a ULONG to set to the returned result of the addition operation. You can pass a NULL to ignore the returned error code.

MatchedDNs is the address of a pointer that ldap_parse_result() will set to point to a string containing the distinguished name of the object that was being added. If *MatchedDNs is non-NULL after calling ldap_parse_result(), you must free it by passing it to ldap_memfree(). If you want to ignore the matched distinguished names returned by the server, you can pass a NULL for MatchedDNs.

ErrorMessage is the address of a pointer to set to point to an error message string that corresponds to the error returned in *ReturnCode. If *ErrorMessage is non-NULL after calling ldap_parse_result(), you must free it by passing it to ldap_memfree(). You can pass a NULL for ErrorMessage if you want to ignore the returned error message string.

Referrals is the address of a pointer that will be set to point to a NULL-terminated array of pointers to NUL-terminated strings. ldap_parse_result() will set this to point to an array of referral URLs, if any were returned by the server. If *Referrals is non-NULL after calling ldap_parse_result(), you must free it by passing *Referrals to ldap_value_free(). You can pass a NULL for Referrals to ignore any returned referral strings.

ServerControls is the address of a pointer that will be set to point to a NULL-terminated array of pointers to LDAPControl structures. ldap_parse_result() will set this to point to the LDAPControl structures returned from the server. If ldap_parse_result() returns more than one LDAPControl structure, you must inspect the OID string of each to determine which control is which. (This doesn't happen with a simple sorted search.) If *Controls is non-NULL after calling ldap_parse_result(), you must pass *Controls to ldap_controls_free() to free the memory associated with the control structures. You can pass a NULL for Controls if you want to ignore the LDAPControl structures returned by the server. None of the server controls you might use with ldap_add_ext() return any control information, so you may as well just set this parameter to NULL.

Freeit is a Boolean value that, if set to TRUE, will cause ldap_parse_result() to free the memory associated with the ResultMsg parameter. If you set Freeit to TRUE, be sure that you don't later free ResultMsg with ldap_msgfree().

Returns: An LDAP error code or LDAP_SUCCESS if the function succeeded.

> **NOTE**
>
> It's a good idea to set all the pointers whose addresses you pass to
> ldap_parse_result() to NULL before you pass them in. After calling
> ldap_parse_result(), you can check each pointer to see whether it is NULL,
> and if it is not, free it with the appropriate function.

When you use ldap_parse_result() to inspect the results returned by ldap_result() for an asynchronous addition operation, *ReturnCode will contain the result code for the operation, *MatchedDNs will contain the distinguished name of the new object, and *ErrorMessage will contain a text string error message. You can use this information to format a meaningful error message without the overhead of keeping track of every addition operation.

The next sample program shown in Listing 25.2 is equivalent to the previous sample program, except that it uses ldap_add() to add the container asynchronously.

LISTING 25.2   ADDING A CONTAINER BY USING ldap_add()

```
1:    #include <windows.h>
2:    #include <winldap.h>
3:    #include <iostream.h>
4:
5:    int main( int argc, char** argv )
6:    {
7:        LDAP* psLdap = ldap_init( NULL, LDAP_PORT );
8:        if( psLdap != NULL )
9:        {
10:           ULONG uErr = ldap_bind_s( psLdap, NULL, NULL,
          ➡LDAP_AUTH_NEGOTIATE );
11:          if( uErr == LDAP_SUCCESS )
12:          {
13:              // set LDAP API version
14:              int nVersion = LDAP_VERSION3;
15:              ldap_set_option( psLdap, LDAP_OPT_VERSION, &nVersion );
16:
17:              // turn off referrals chasing
18:              int nChaseReferrals = 0;
19:              ldap_set_option( psLdap, LDAP_OPT_REFERRALS,
              ➡&nChaseReferrals );
20:
21:              // DN of new container
22:              char szNewDN[ 1024 ] = "CN=NewerContainer,CN=Users,";
23:
24:              LDAPMessage* psMsg = NULL;
25:
```

```
26:          // Get rootDSE attr defaultNamingContext
27:          uErr = ldap_search_s(
28:              psLdap,
29:              NULL,
30:              LDAP_SCOPE_BASE,
31:              "objectClass=*",
32:              NULL,
33:              false,
34:              &psMsg
35:          );
36:          if( uErr == LDAP_SUCCESS )
37:          {
38:              char** ppszDomain = ldap_get_values( psLdap,
                 ➥ldap first entry( psLdap,psMsg)
                 ➥"defaultNamingContext" );
39:              if( ppszDomain != NULL )
40:              {
41:                  strcat( szNewDN, ppszDomain[ 0 ] );
42:                ldap value free( ppszDomain);
43:              }
44:              ldap_msgfree( psMsg );
45:          }
46:
47:          // values for the objectClass attribute
48:          char* apszObjectClassVals[] =
49:          {
50:              "container", // a single value for the objectClass
51:                           // attribute
52:              NULL
53:          };
54:
55:          // operation for the objectClass attribute
56:          LDAPMod sAddObjectClass =
57:          {
58:              LDAP_MOD_ADD, // the operation
59:              "objectClass", // the name of the attribute
60:              apszObjectClassVals // pointer to array of values
61:          };
62:
63:          // values for the cn attribute
64:          char* apszCNVals[] =
65:          {
66:              "NewerContainer", // a single value for the
67:                                // cn attribute
68:              NULL
69:          };
70:
71:          // operation for the cn attribute
62:          LDAPMod sAddCN =
73:          {
74:              LDAP_MOD_ADD, // the operation
75:              "cn", // the name of the attribute
```

continues

LISTING 25.2   CONTINUED

```
76:              apszCNVals
77:          };
78:
79:          // list of attributes to add
80:          LDAPMod* asAttrsToAdd[] =
81:          {
82:              &sAddObjectClass,
83:              &sAddCN,
84:              NULL
85:          };
86:
87:          // add the new container
88:          ULONG uAddHandle = ldap_add( psLdap, szNewDN,
           ➥asAttrsToAdd );
89:
90:          bool bDone = false;
91:
92:          while( !bDone )
93:          {
94:              l_timeval sTimeout = { 10, 0 }; // 10 seconds
95:
96:              LDAPMessage* psResult;
97:
98:              int nResult = ldap_result( psLdap, LDAP_RES_ANY,
               ➥LDAP_MSG_ONE, &sTimeout, &psResult );
99:              switch( nResult )
100:               {
101:                  case -1: // an error
102:                      bDone = true;
103:                      break;
104:
105:                  default:
106:                  case 0: // timed out
107:                      break;
108:
109:                  case LDAP_RES_ADD:
110:                      // check if there was an error
111:                      uErr = ldap_result2error( psLdap, psResult,
                       ➥false );
112:                      if( uErr != LDAP_SUCCESS )
113:                      {
114:                          ULONG uModifyErr;
115:                          char* pszDNs = NULL;
116:                          char* pszErrmsg = NULL;
117:
118:                          ldap_parse_result( psLdap, psResult,
                           ➥&uModifyErr, &pszDNs, &pszErrmsg,
                           ➥NULL, NULL, FALSE );
```

```
119:
120:                                    cout << "Got error " << pszErrmsg <<
                                        ➡" for " << pszDNs << endl;
121:
122:                                    ldap_memfree( pszDNs );
123:                                    ldap_memfree( pszErrmsg );
124:                           }
125:
126:                           ldap_msgfree( psResult ); // free the message
127:
128:                           bDone = true;
129:                           break;
130:                    }
131:             }
132:         }
133:
134:         ldap_unbind( psLdap );
135:     }
136:
137:     return 0;
138: }
```

The program in Listing 25.2 is essentially the same as the sample program for ldap_add_s(), up to the point where it calls ldap_add() at line 88. Instead of returning an error code as does ldap_add_s(), ldap_add() returns an operation handle that the program saves in uAddHandle.

The program then enters a polling loop at line 92, calling ldap_result() each time through. It calls ldap_result() with a pointer to the LDAP session and the operation handle returned from ldap_add(). The program passes LDAP_MSG_ONE as the all parameter to ldap_result(), indicating that ldap_result() should return one result code at a time. This makes sense because there should be only one result. The sTimeout structure is set to 10 seconds, which means that ldap_result() will wait up to 10 seconds for a result response from the server each time it is called. ldap_result() returns a pointer to an LDAPMessage structure in psResult.

The sample program retrieves the error code for the add operation by calling ldap_result2error() at line 111 with the LDAP session and the pointer to the LDAPResult structure returned by ldap_result().

If there is an error, the program then calls ldap_parse_result() to get the rest of the information regarding the add operation, including the distinguished name of the object being added and a text string containing the error message. The program frees the items retrieved by ldap_parse_result() at lines 122 and 123, and it frees the LDAPMessage structure returned by ldap_result() at line 126.

The program closes the LDAP session at line 134 by calling ldap_unbind().

Adding Objects in Bulk by Using the Lazy Commit Control

The sample program in Listing 25.3 shows how to use the `ldap_add_ext()` function in combination with the lazy commit control. This is the ideal way to write a directory migration program that must add a bunch of objects to the directory at one time. This example is pretty contrived, because it doesn't actually create multiple objects in the directory, but it shows how to set up the parameters to the APIs.

```
ULONG ldap_add_ext( LDAP* ld, PCHAR dn, LDAPMod* mods[],
➥PLDAPControl* ServerControls, PLDAPControl* ClientControls )
```

> `ld` is a pointer to the LDAP session created with `ldap_init()`. The session must be appropriately authenticated with one of the bind functions before calling `ldap_add_ext()`.

> `dn` is a NUL-terminated string containing the distinguished name of the object to be added. The object with this name must not already exist in the directory.

> `mods` is a pointer to a NULL-terminated array of pointers to appropriately initialized `ldapmod` structures. Each of the `ldapmod` structures represents a separate attribute to be added with the new object.

> `ServerControls` is a pointer to a NULL-terminated array of pointers to initialized LDAP server control structures. Each entry refers to a single server control. NULL indicates there are no server controls for this operation. See Chapter 28 for details on the LDAP controls.

> `ClientControls` is a pointer to a NULL-terminated array of pointers to initialized LDAP client control structures. Each entry refers to a single client control. NULL indicates there are no client controls for this operation. See Chapter 28 for details on the LDAP controls.

Returns: A handle to the add operation. If there was an error initiating the add operation, the handle will be -1. Otherwise, you must use `ldap_result()` to check the status of the add operation. `ldap_result()` will return a value of LDAP_RES_ADD to indicate the completion of the add operation.

LISTING 25.3   ADDING OBJECTS WITH `ldap_add_ext()` AND THE LAZY COMMIT CONTROL

```
1:  #include <windows.h>
2:  #include <winldap.h>
3:  #include <iostream.h>
4:
5:  int main( int argc, char** argv )
6:  {
```

```
 7:        LDAP* psLdap = ldap_init( NULL, LDAP_PORT );
 8:        if( psLdap != NULL )
 9:        {
10:          ULONG uErr = ldap_bind_s( psLdap, NULL, NULL,
          ➥LDAP_AUTH_NEGOTIATE );
11:          if( uErr == LDAP_SUCCESS )
12:          {
13:              // set LDAP API version
14:              int nVersion = LDAP_VERSION3;
15:              ldap_set_option( psLdap, LDAP_OPT_VERSION, &nVersion );
16:
17:              // turn off referrals chasing
18:              int nChaseReferrals = 0;
19:             ldap_set_option( psLdap, LDAP_OPT_REFERRALS,
              ➥&nChaseReferrals );
20:
21:              // DN of new container
22:              char szNewDN[ 1024 ] = "CN=NewestContainer,CN=Users,";
23:
24:              LDAPMessage* psMsg = NULL;
25:
26:              // Get rootDSE attr defaultNamingContext
27:              uErr = ldap_search_s(
28:                  psLdap,
29:                  NULL,
30:                  LDAP_SCOPE_BASE,
31:                  "objectClass=*",
32:                  NULL,
33:                  false,
34:                  &psMsg
35:              );
36:              if( uErr == LDAP_SUCCESS )
37:              {
38:                  char** ppszDomain = ldap_get_values( psLdap,
                  ➥ldap_first_entry( psLdap, psMsg ),
                  ➥"defaultNamingContext" );
39:                  if( ppszDomain != NULL )
40:                  {
41:                      strcat( szNewDN, ppszDomain[ 0 ] );
42:                      ldap_value_free( ppszDomain );
43:                  }
44:                  ldap_msgfree( psMsg );
45:              }
46:
47:              // values for the objectClass attribute
48:              char* apszObjectClassVals[] =
49:              {
50:                  "container", // a single value for the objectClass
51:                                  // attribute
52:                  NULL
53:              };
54:
```

continues

LISTING 25.3 CONTINUED

```
55:                    // operation for the objectClass attribute
56:                    LDAPMod sAddObjectClass =
57:                    {
58:                        LDAP_MOD_ADD, // the operation
59:                        "objectClass", // the name of the attribute
60:                        apszObjectClassVals // pointer to array of values
61:                    };
62:
63:                    // values for the cn attribute
64:                    char* apszCNVals[] =
65:                    {
66:                        "NewestContainer", // a single value for the
67:                                           // cn attribute
68:                        NULL
69:                    };
70:
71:                    // operation for the cn attribute
72:                    LDAPMod sAddCN =
73:                    {
74:                        LDAP_MOD_ADD, // the operation
75:                        "cn",  // the name of the attribute
76:                        apszCNVals
77:                    };
78:
79:                    // list of attributes to add
80:                    LDAPMod* asAttrsToAdd[] =
81:                    {
82:                        &sAddObjectClass,
83:                        &sAddCN,
84:                        NULL
85:                    };
86:
87:                    LDAPControl sLazyCommitControl =
88:                    {
89:                        "1.2.840.113556.1.4.619", // OID string
90:                        { 0, NULL }, // no additional data
91:                        false // not critical
92:                    };
93:
94:                    LDAPControl* apsServerControls[] =
95:                    {
96:                        &sLazyCommitControl,
97:                        NULL
98:                    };
99:
100:                    ULONG uAddHandle;

101:                    // add the new container
102:                    uErr = ldap_add_ext(
```

```
103:            psLdap, // LDAP session
104:            szNewDN, // DN of new object
105:            asAttrsToAdd, // attributes of new object
106:            apsServerControls, // array of server controls
107:            NULL, // array of client controls
108:            &uAddHandle // operation handle to set
109:        );
110:
111:        if( uErr == LDAP_SUCCESS )
112:        {
113:            bool bDone = false;
114:
115:            while( !bDone )
116:            {
117:                l_timeval sTimeout = { 10, 0 }; // 10 seconds
118:
119:                LDAPMessage* psResult;
120:
121:                int nResult = ldap_result( psLdap, LDAP_RES_ANY,
     ➥LDAP_MSG_ONE, &sTimeout, &psResult );
122:                switch( nResult )
123:                {
124:                    case -1: // an error
125:                        bDone = true;
126:                        break;
127:
128:                    default:
129:                    case 0: // timed out
130:                        break;
131:
132:                    case LDAP_RES_ADD:
133:                        // check if there was an error
134:                        uErr = ldap_result2error( psLdap,
     ➥psResult,false );
135:                        if( uErr != LDAP_SUCCESS )
136:                        {
137:                            ULONG uModifyErr;
138:                            char* pszDNs = NULL;
139:                            char* pszErrmsg = NULL;
140:
141:                            ldap_parse_result( psLdap, psResult,
     ➥&uModifyErr, &pszDNs, &pszErrmsg,
     ➥NULL, NULL, FALSE );
142:
143:                            cout << "Got error " << pszErrmsg <<
     ➥" for " << pszDNs << endl;
144:
145:                            ldap_memfree( pszDNs );
```

continues

25

**ADDING ACTIVE
DIRECTORY OBJECTS
WITH LDAP**

LISTING 25.3   CONTINUED

```
146:                                     ldap_memfree( pszErrmsg );
147:                            }
148:
149:                            ldap_msgfree( psResult ); // free the
                                                          // message
150:
151:                            bDone = true;
152:                            break;
153:                        }
154:                    }
155:                }
156:            }
157:
158:        ldap_unbind( psLdap );
159:    }
160:
161:    return 0;
162: }
```

The program in Listing 25.3 starts by calling `ldap_init()` to create an LDAP session and `ldap_bind_s()` to authenticate it. The program then calls `ldap_set_open()` to set the protocol version to LDAPv3 and to disable referrals.

The code from lines 27–45 reads the `rootDSE defaultNamingContext` attribute to get the name of the domain. It assembles the name of the new container in `szNewDN`. The new container will be called `"CN=NewestContainer,CN=Users,<domain DN>"`.

The code from lines 46–85 is identical to the code in Listing 25.2. This code initializes the data structures needed for the add operation, including the values for the `objectClass` and `cn` attributes.

The program defines the lazy commit server control at line 87, using the OID string `"1.2.840.113556.1.4.619"`. The control has no additional data, as indicated by the `NULL` berval structure, and for the purposes of this program we set the `is_critical` flag to `false`.

The program calls `ldap_add_ext()` at line 102, specifying the LDAP session, the new distinguished name in `szNewDn`, the list of attributes to add with the object, and the list of server controls containing the lazy commit control.

At line 115, the program enters a polling loop, calling `ldap_result()` each time. If `ldap_result()` returns `LDAP_RES_ADD`, indicating the add operation completed, the program then calls `ldap_result2error()` at line 134 to get the error from the add operation. If there was an error, the program then calls `ldap_parse_result()` at line 141 to get the distinguished name of the object that failed and an error message string.

At lines 145 and 146, the program calls `ldap_memfree()` to free the strings returned by `ldap_parse_message()`. At line 149, the program calls `ldap_msgfree()` to free the `LDAPResult` message returned by `ldap_result()`.

The program wraps up by calling `ldap_unbind()` at line 158.

Adding Objects to the Directory with `ldap_add_ext_s()`

The last LDAP add function to discuss is `ldap_add_ext_s()`. As you would expect, it is a synchronous version of `ldap_add_ext()`. It returns control to your program after the add operation has been performed on the server (or not, if there was an error). `ldap_add_ext_s()` lets you specify client and server controls so you can take advantage of special Active Directory extensions.

```
ULONG ldap_add_ext_s( LDAP* ld, char* PCHAR dn, LDAPMod* mods[],
➥PLDAPControl* ServerControls, PLDAPControl* ClientControls )
```

> `ld` is a pointer to the LDAP session to use. It must have been initialized by `ldap_init()` and authenticated with `ldap_bind_s()`.

> `dn` is a NUL-terminated string containing the distinguished name of the object to add. An object with this name must not already exist in the directory.

> `mods` is a NULL-terminated array of pointers to appropriately initialized `LDAPMod` structures. Each of the `LDAPMod` structures represents a separate attribute to add with the object.

> `ServerControls` is a NULL-terminated array of pointers to appropriately initialized `LDAPControl` structures. Each `LDAPControl` structure represents a single LDAP server control.

> `ClientControls` is a NULL-terminated array of pointers to appropriately initialized `LDAPControl` structures. Each `LDAPControl` structure represents a single LDAP client control.

Returns: `LDAP_SUCCESS` if the call succeeded or an LDAP error code if an error occurred.

The sample program in Listing 25.4 is somewhat nonsensical in that it uses the lazy commit control to add a single object to the directory, but it shows how to set up the parameters for `ldap_add_ext_s()`.

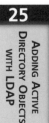

25

ADDING ACTIVE DIRECTORY OBJECTS WITH LDAP

LISTING 25.4   ADDING OBJECTS WITH `ldap_add_ext_s()` AND THE LAZY COMMIT
CONTROL

```
1:    #include <windows.h>
2:    #include <winldap.h>
3:    #include <iostream.h>
4:
5:    int main( int argc, char** argv )
6:    {
7:        LDAP* psLdap = ldap_init( NULL, LDAP_PORT );
8:        if( psLdap != NULL )
9:        {
10:           ULONG uErr = ldap_bind_s( psLdap, NULL, NULL,
            ➥LDAP_AUTH_NEGOTIATE );
11:          if( uErr == LDAP_SUCCESS )
12:          {
13:              // set LDAP API version
14:              int nVersion = LDAP_VERSION3;
15:              ldap_set_option( psLdap, LDAP_OPT_VERSION, &nVersion );
16:
17:              // turn off referrals chasing
18:              int nChaseReferrals = 0;
19:              ldap_set_option( psLdap, LDAP_OPT_REFERRALS,
              ➥&nChaseReferrals );
20:
21:              // DN of new container
22:              char szNewDN[ 1024 ] = "CN=MoreNewestContainer,CN=Users,";
23:
24:              LDAPMessage* psMsg = NULL;
25:
26:              // Get rootDSE attr defaultNamingContext
27:              uErr = ldap_search_s(
28:                  psLdap,
29:                  NULL,
30:                  LDAP_SCOPE_BASE,
31:                  "objectClass=*",
32:                  NULL,
33:                  false,
34:                  &psMsg
35:              );
36:              if( uErr == LDAP_SUCCESS )
37:              {
38:                  char** ppszDomain = ldap_get_values( psLdap,
                  ➥ldap first entry( psLdap, psMsg ),
                  ➥"defaultNamingContext" );
39:                  if( ppszDomain != NULL )
40:                  {
41:                      strcat( szNewDN, ppszDomain[ 0 ] );
42:                    ldap value free( ppszDomain );
43:                  }
44:                  ldap_msgfree( psMsg );
45:              }
46:
```

```
47:                // values for the objectClass attribute
48:                char* apszObjectClassVals[] =
49:                {
50:                    "container", // a single value for the objectClass
51:                                 // attribute
52:                    NULL
53:                };
54:
55:                // operation for the objectClass attribute
56:                LDAPMod sAddObjectClass =
57:                {
58:                    LDAP_MOD_ADD, // the operation
59:                    "objectClass", // the name of the attribute
60:                    apszObjectClassVals // pointer to array of values
61:                };
62:
63:                // values for the cn attribute
64:                char* apszCNVals[] =
65:                {
66:                    "MoreNewestContainer", // a single value cn attribute
67:                    NULL
68:                };
69:
70:                // operation for the cn attribute
71:                LDAPMod sAddCN =
72:                {
73:                    LDAP_MOD_ADD, // the operation
74:                    "cn",  // the name of the attribute
75:                    apszCNVals
76:                };
77:
78:                // list of attributes to add
79:                LDAPMod* asAttrsToAdd[] =
80:                {
81:                    &sAddObjectClass,
82:                    &sAddCN,
83:                    NULL
84:                };
85:
86:                LDAPControl sLazyCommitControl =
87:                {
88:                    "1.2.840.113556.1.4.619", // OID string
89:                    { 0, NULL }, // no additional data
90:                    false // not critical
91:                };
92:
93:                LDAPControl* apsServerControls[] =
94:                {
95:                    &sLazyCommitControl,
96:                    NULL
```

continues

Listing 25.4   CONTINUED

```
97:                 };
98:
99:                 // add the new container
100:                uErr = ldap_add_ext_s(
101:                    psLdap, // LDAP session
102:                    szNewDN, // DN of new obejct
103:                    asAttrsToAdd, // list of attrs to add
104:                    apsServerControls, // server controls
105:                    NULL // client controls
106:                );
107:
108:                cout << "Error is " << uErr << endl;
109:
110:            }
111:
112:        ldap_unbind( psLdap );
113:    }
114:
115:    return 0;
116: }
```

This sample program starts the same way as all the others, by calling ldap_init() to initialize an LDAP session and ldap_bind_s() to authenticate it. The program then calls
ldap_set_option() to set the protocol to LDAPv3 and to turn off referral chasing by the
client.

The program then gets the distinguished name of the domain from the rootDSE at lines
27–45, building the distinguished name of the new container object in szNewDN at line 41.

Lines 48–84 set up the attributes for the new container the same way the preceding sample programs did. It specifies a single value for the objectClass attribute and the cn
attribute for the new container.

The program defines the lazy commit control at line 86, using the OID string
1.2.840.113556.1.4.619. The lazy commit control does not require any additional
BER-encoded data, and we are making it noncritical for this program.

The program adds the new container to the directory at line 100 by calling
ldap_add_ext_s(), specifying the LDAP session, the distinguished name of the new
container, the list of attribute operations, the list of server controls, and a NULL indicating
no client controls.

At line 112, the program closes the LDAP session by calling ldap_unbind().

Deleting Active Directory Objects with LDAP

Like any good database system, LDAP provides a set of functions for deleting objects from the directory. Granted, it's not something you're likely to do very often, but if you write enough directory applications, eventually you'll need to delete some objects. At the very least, you'll want to delete the objects you've created using the test programs in this book!

The LDAP functions that delete objects from the directory are listed in Table 26.1.

TABLE 26.1 LDAP FUNCTIONS FOR DELETING OBJECTS

Function	Description
ldap_delete()	Asynchronous function that deletes a single object.
ldap_delete_s()	Synchronous function that deletes a single object.
ldap_delete_ext()	Asynchronous function that deletes a single object. This function includes parameters for specifying client controls and server controls.
ldap_delete_ext_s()	Synchronous function that deletes a single object. This function includes parameters for timeout values, client controls, and server controls.

Things to Know Before You Go

The next section describes some basic concepts that are important for you to understand before you attempt to delete objects from the directory with LDAP. Read through this section before you start writing any code; it will save you time later.

Access Rights

Just as with all other LDAP operations, you have to be sure you have the appropriate access rights to an object and its container before you can delete the object.

Containers Must Be Empty Before You Can Delete Them

Before you can delete an object from the directory, the Active Directory requires that you delete all the objects that it contains. LDAP does not (normally) support a "tree-delete" function.

However, Microsoft has created a special LDAP server control that will, in fact, let you delete an entire subtree from the directory. This chapter will show how to use that control.

Selecting the Appropriate API Function

There are four LDAP functions that delete objects from the directory. Which one should you use?

The four `ldap_delete_...()` functions parallel the `ldap_modify_...()` and `ldap_add_...()` functions, and the same general rules for selecting an appropriate API function apply. But you should note that deleting objects is generally a pretty quick process, and in any case the speed at which you can delete objects usually isn't very important.

Because deleting an object is relatively quick, you might as well stick with `ldap_ delete_s()` or `ldap_delete_ext_s()`. These are generally simpler to use, and they make your client code somewhat less complicated. Only use the asynchronous `ldap_delete()` and `ldap_delete_ext()` if they fit in well with your program architecture. There is no legitimate performance reason to use them.

The choice between `ldap_delete_s()` and `ldap_delete_ext_s()` is simple: If you need to use an LDAP control when you perform the delete operation (for instance, you want to delete an object and all its subordinates), you have to use `ldap_delete_ext_s()`. Otherwise, use `ldap_delete_s()`; it has a simpler interface.

Deleting Objects Synchronously by Using `ldap_delete_s()`

The sample program in Listing 26.1 deletes a single object from the directory using `ldap_delete_s()`. It's quite simple, as you can see from the code.

```
ULONG ldap_delete_s( LDAP* ld, char* dn )
```

> `ld` is a pointer to an LDAP session that was created with `ldap_init()` and authenticated with `ldap_bind_s()`. Note that the bind must be done with a username that has sufficient access rights to delete the object from the directory.

> `dn` is a pointer to a NUL-terminated string containing the full distinguished name of the object to be deleted. The object must exist, and it must have no subordinate objects; that is, the object to be deleted cannot contain any other objects.

Returns: `LDAP_SUCCESS` if it deleted the object from the directory and an LDAP error code if it failed.

LISTING 26.1 DELETING A DIRECTORY OBJECT WITH `ldap_delete_s()`

```
1:    #include <windows.h>
2:    #include <winldap.h>
3:    #include <iostream.h>
4:
5:    int main( int argc, char** argv )
6:    {
7:        LDAP* psLdap = ldap_init( NULL, LDAP_PORT );
8:        if( psLdap != NULL )
9:        {
10:           ULONG uErr = ldap_bind_s( psLdap, NULL, NULL,
          ➥LDAP_AUTH_NEGOTIATE );
11:           if( uErr == LDAP_SUCCESS )
12:           {
13:               // set LDAP API version
14:               int nVersion = LDAP_VERSION3;
15:               ldap_set_option( psLdap, LDAP_OPT_VERSION, &nVersion );
16:
17:               // turn off referrals chasing
18:               int nChaseReferrals = 0;
```

continues

LISTING 26.1   CONTINUED

```
19:             ldap_set_option( psLdap, LDAP_OPT_REFERRALS,
                ➥&nChaseReferrals );
20:
21:             // DN of search base
22:             char szDNToDelete[ 1024 ] = "CN=NewContainer,CN=Users,";
23:
24:             LDAPMessage* psMsg = NULL;
25:
26:             // Get rootDSE attr defaultNamingContext
27:             uErr = ldap_search_s(
28:                 psLdap,
29:                 NULL,
30:                 LDAP_SCOPE_BASE,
31:                 "objectClass=*",
32:                 NULL,
33:                 false,
34:                 &psMsg
35:             );
36:             if( uErr == LDAP_SUCCESS )
37:             {
38:                 char** ppszDomain = ldap_get_values( psLdap,
                    ➥ldap first entry( psLdap, psMsg ),
                    ➥"defaultNamingContext" );
39:                 if( ppszDomain != NULL )
40:                 {
41:                     strcat( szDNToDelete, ppszDomain[ 0 ] );
42:                     ldap value free( ppszDomain );
43:                 }
44:                 ldap_msgfree( psMsg );
45:             }
46:
47:             uErr = ldap_delete_s( psLdap, szDNToDelete );
48:
49:             cout << "Error is " << uErr << endl;
50:         }
51:
52:         ldap_unbind( psLdap );
53:     }
54:
55:     return 0;
56: }
```

The program in Listing 26.1 starts by initializing an LDAP session with `ldap_init()` and then authenticating it with `ldap_bind_s()`. At lines 14–19, the program sets the protocol to LDAPv3 and turns off referral chasing by the client.

The code from lines 22–45 constructs the distinguished name of the object to delete by getting the domain name from the rootDSE of the domain controller. The name of the object to delete will be "CN=NewContainer,CN=Users,*<domain name>*", which is, not coincidentally, the name of the object we added in the previous chapter.

At line 47, the program deletes the object by calling ldap_delete_s(), specifying the LDAP session pointer and the distinguished name of the object to delete.

The program closes the LDAP session with ldap_unbind_s() at line 52.

Deleting a Container and Its Subordinate Objects Using ldap_delete_ext_s()

Many times when you decide to delete an object, you just want to get rid of it, even if it has subordinate objects. Unfortunately (or fortunately, depending on how risk-averse you are), the LDAP delete functions won't let you delete an object that has subordinates.

One solution is to search through all the subordinate objects and delete each one individually, and then delete the original object. This is certainly possible, but it becomes more complicated (that is, recursive) if the subtree beneath the object to delete has more than one level.

A much simpler solution is to use the Tree Delete LDAP server control supported by Active Directory. If you perform a delete operation using this control, Active Directory deletes the object you specify, along with all its subordinates.

The sample program in Listing 26.2 shows how to use the Tree Delete server control with ldap_delete_ext_s().

```
ULONG ldap_delete_ext_s( LDAP* ld, char* dn, LDAPControl*ServerControls[],
➥LDAPControl* ClientControls[])
```

> ld is a pointer to an LDAP session that was created with ldap_init() and authenticated with ldap_bind_s(). Note that the bind must be done with a username that has sufficient access rights to delete the object from the directory.
>
> dn is a pointer to a NUL-terminated string containing the full distinguished name of the object to delete.
>
> ServerControls is a pointer to a NUL-terminated array of pointers to appropriately initialized LDAPControl structures representing LDAP server controls to use for the delete operation. If you don't want to use any server controls, pass a NULL.
>
> ClientControls is a pointer to a NUL-terminated array of pointers to appropriately initialized LDAPControl structures representing LDAP client controls to use for the delete operation. If you don't want to use any server controls, pass a NULL.

Returns: LDAP_SUCCESS if the object was deleted from the directory or an LDAP error code if the deletion failed.

LISTING 26.2 DELETING A SUBTREE WITH THE TREE DELETE CONTROL

```
1:   #include <windows.h>
2:   #include <winldap.h>
3:   #include <iostream.h>
4:
5:   int main( int argc, char** argv )
6:   {
7:       LDAP* psLdap = ldap_init( NULL, LDAP_PORT );
8:       if( psLdap != NULL )
9:       {
10:          ULONG uErr = ldap_bind_s( psLdap, NULL, NULL,
        ➥LDAP_AUTH_NEGOTIATE );
11:          if( uErr == LDAP_SUCCESS )
12:          {
13:              // set LDAP API version
14:              int nVersion = LDAP_VERSION3;
15:              ldap_set_option( psLdap, LDAP_OPT_VERSION, &nVersion );
16:
17:              // turn off referrals chasing
18:              int nChaseReferrals = 0;
19:              ldap_set_option( psLdap, LDAP_OPT_REFERRALS,
        ➥&nChaseReferrals );
20:
21:              // DN of search base
22:              char szDNToDelete[ 1024 ] = "CN=NewerContainer,CN=Users,";
23:
24:              LDAPMessage* psMsg = NULL;
25:
26:              // Get rootDSE attr defaultNamingContext
27:              uErr = ldap_search_s(
28:                  psLdap,
29:                  NULL,
30:                  LDAP_SCOPE_BASE,
31:                  "objectClass=*",
32:                  NULL,
33:                  false,
34:                  &psMsg
35:              );
36:              if( uErr == LDAP_SUCCESS )
37:              {
38:                  char** ppszDomain = ldap_get_values( psLdap,
        ➥ldap_first_entry( psLdap, psMsg),
        ➥"defaultNamingContext" );
39:                  if( ppszDomain != NULL )
40:                  {
41:                      strcat( szDNToDelete, ppszDomain[ 0 ] );
42:                      ldap_value_free( ppszDomain );
43:                  }
```

Deleting Active Directory Objects with LDAP

711

CHAPTER 26

26

DELETING ACTIVE
DIRECTORY OBJECTS
WITH LDAP

```
44:                     ldap_msgfree( psMsg );
45:                 }
46:
47:             LDAPControl sTreeDelete =
48:             {
49:                 "1.2.840.113556.1.4.805", // OID of tree delete
                                               // control
50:                 { 0, NULL }, // no BER data
51:                 true // is critical
52:             };
53:
54:             LDAPControl* apsServerControls[] =
55:             {
56:                 &sTreeDelete,
57:                 NULL
58:             };
59:
60:             uErr = ldap_delete_ext_s(
61:                 psLdap, // LDAP session
62:                 szDNToDelete, // DN to delete
63:                 apsServerControls, // array of server controls
64:                 NULL // array of client controls
65:             );
66:
67:             cout << "Error is " << uErr << endl;
68:         }
69:
70:         ldap_unbind( psLdap );
71:     }
72:
73:     return 0;
74: }
```

This sample program initializes the LDAP session in the usual way and then authenticates the LDAP session with `ldap_bind_s()` at line 10.

The code in lines 14–19 sets the LDAPv3 protocol option and disables referral chasing by the client.

Lines 22–45 compose the distinguished name of the container to delete by concatenating the distinguished name of the domain onto `"CN=NewerContainer,CN=Users,"`. This is one of the containers created in the preceding chapter.

The program initializes the Tree Delete server control at lines 47–52, using the OID string `"1.2.840.113556.1.4.805"`, which is the identifier for the Tree Delete control. The control does not require any additional BER-encoded data, and for the purpose of this program we make the control critical, meaning that the delete operation will fail if the Tree Delete control is not supported for some reason.

The program creates a NULL-terminated array of `LDAPControl` pointers at lines 54–58.

At line 60, the program calls `ldap_delete_ext_s()`, specifying the LDAP session pointer, the distinguished name of the object to delete, the array of server controls, and a NULL for the client controls.

After printing the result of the operation, the program calls `ldap_unbind()` at line 70 to close the LDAP session.

Deleting Objects Asynchronously Using `ldap_delete()`

If your program really lends itself to using the asynchronous LDAP APIs, there is an asynchronous version of the delete functions you can use. Unlike `ldap_delete_s()`, `ldap_delete()` returns immediately with an operation handle. You have to use `ldap_result()` to repeatedly check the handle to determine when the delete operation actually completes and retrieve the error code returned by the server. In general, `ldap_delete()` behaves just like the other asynchronous LDAP APIs.

```
ULONG ldap_delete( LDAP* ld, char* dn )
```

> `ld` is a pointer to an LDAP session that was created with `ldap_init()` and authenticated with `ldap_bind_s()`. Note that the bind must be done with a username that has sufficient access rights to delete the object from the directory.
>
> `dn` is a pointer to a NUL-terminated string containing the full distinguished name of the object to delete.

Returns: An operation handle that you use to check the status of the delete operation. You pass this handle to `ldap_result()`.

After you call `ldap_delete()`, you have to call `ldap_result()` repeatedly until it returns the result of the asynchronous delete operation.

```
ULONG ldap_result( LDAP* ld, ULONG msgid, ULONG all,
➥struct l_timeval* timeout, LDAPMessage** res )
```

> `ld` is a pointer to an LDAP structure that has been initialized with `ldap_init()`, `ldap_sslinit()`, or `ldap_open()`. It must be the same LDAP structure that you used to perform the deletion.
>
> `msgid` is the handle to the delete operation that was returned by `ldap_delete()` or `ldap_delete_ext()`. If you specify `LDAP_RES_ANY`, `ldap_result()` will return results for any outstanding asynchronous operation that were started on the LDAP session given by `ld`.

all specifies how many result objects you want returned. It must be one of three constants defined in WINLDAP.H and described in Table 26.2.

TABLE 26.2 POSSIBLE VALUES OF THE all PARAMETER OF ldap_result()

Constant	Description
LDAP_MSG_ONE	Indicates that ldap_result() should return a single operation result.
LDAP_MSG_ALL	Indicates that ldap_result() should wait until all the results have been received from the server. Because a delete operation returns only a single result, this value isn't very useful for deletions.
LDAP_MSG_RECEIVED	Indicates that ldap_result() should return all the result objects that have been received so far. Because a delete operation returns only a single result, this value isn't very useful for deletions.

timeout is a pointer to an l_timeval structure that contains the timeout value for the ldap_result() call. If there are no messages to retrieve within the time specified by the l_timeval structure, ldap_result() will return a 0.

res is the address of an LDAPMessage pointer to be set by ldap_result(). This pointer must be freed by passing it to ldap_msgfree() after you are done with it.

Returns: The type of the message retrieved. There are eleven possible returned messages, but only LDAP_RES_DELETE or LDAP_RES_REFERRAL will be returned as the result of a search operation.

LDAP_RES_DELETE indicates the message contains the results of a delete operation.

LDAP_RES_REFERRAL indicates the message contains one or more referrals to other naming contexts. See the section on processing referrals for information on how to handle this message.

0 indicates the call to ldap_result() timed out. This means there were no results sent from the server within the timeout period. You should retry the call to ldap_result().

-1 indicates an error of some sort. Call LdapGetLastError() to get the corresponding error code. You should not call ldap_result() after receiving an error.

After you call ldap_result() successfully and it returns a pointer to an LDAPMessage structure in *res, you must free the LDAPMessage structure by calling ldap_msgfree(), passing it the pointer that was returned. You can also free the message by calling ldap_result2error() and setting the freeit parameter to true.

```
ULONG ldap_msgfree( LDAPMessage* msg )
```

msg is a pointer to an LDAPMessage structure that was returned by ldap_result().

Returns: LDAP_SUCCESS if it successfully freed the LDAPMessage structure or an LDAP error code if there was an error.

> **CAUTION**
>
> ldap_result() returns a valid pointer in *res only if its return value was greater than 0. Therefore, you should call ldap_msgfree() only if ldap_result() returned a value greater than 0. Calling ldap_msgfree() with an invalid LDAPMessage pointer will cause memory corruption.

Retrieving the Results of an Asynchronous Deletion

When you issue an asynchronous search operation, the results you retrieve are the entries that matched your search criteria. When you issue an asynchronous delete operation using ldap_delete() or ldap_delete_ext(), you generally want to know whether the server completed the deletion successfully, or if there was some sort of an error. The LDAPMessage pointer returned by ldap_result() contains the result of the asynchronous deletion operation.

There are two functions you can use to get the results of an asynchronous delete operation, ldap_result2error() and ldap_parse_result(). Both functions accept the LDAPMessage pointer returned by ldap_result() as an argument.

Getting the Error Code with ldap_result2error()

The ldap_result2error() function accepts the LDAPMessage pointer returned from ldap_result() in *res, extracts the error code from the result message, and returns the LDAP error code associated with that particular delete operation.

```
ULONG ldap_result2error( LDAP* ld, LDAPMessage* res, ULONG freeit )
```

> ld is a pointer to the LDAP session you used when you called ldap_result().
>
> res is the LDAPMessage pointer that ldap_result() returned in *res.
>
> freeit is a Boolean that, if set to true, will cause ldap_result2error() to free the LDAPMessage structure. If freeit is false, ldap_result2error() will not free the message structure.

Returns: The error code extracted from the LDAPMessage structure.

Deleting Active Directory Objects with LDAP

CHAPTER 26

715

26

DELETING ACTIVE
DIRECTORY OBJECTS
WITH LDAP

> **CAUTION**
>
> If you free an `LDAPMessage` structure by setting the `freeit` parameter in `ldap_result2error()` to true, be sure that you do not subsequently try to free the message again by calling `ldap_msgfree()`. Doing so will likely cause memory corruption.

Just getting the error code for an asynchronous operation is fine, but what happens if the error is nonzero, indicating an actual failure? What object was being deleted? `ldap_result2error()` can't give you that information. There are two solutions.

The first strategy is more complicated. In this case, you store each operation handle returned by `ldap_delete()` or `ldap_delete_ext()` in an array, and then poll for the results for each handle by iterating through the array and calling `ldap_result()`, passing the operation handle for the `msgid` parameter. This is somewhat complicated, and incurs the storage and lookup overhead of the array of operation handles.

The second strategy is simpler. In this case, you use `ldap_parse_result()` to retrieve the operation information from the `LDAPMessage` pointer returned by `ldap_result()`. `ldap_parse_result()` is described in the following section.

Getting Information About an Asynchronous Operation with `ldap_parse_result()`

If you want to know which delete operation generated an error code, `ldap_result2error()` is insufficient; it tells you what the error was, but not which object deletion caused the error. `ldap_parse_result()` can retrieve this information for you.

```
ULONG ldap_parse_result( LDAP* Connection, LDAPMessage* ResultMessage,
➡ULONG* ReturnCode, PCHAR* MatchedDNs, PCHAR* ErrorMessage, PCHAR**
➡ Referrals, PLDAPControl** ServerControls, BOOLEAN Freeit )
```

`Connection` is a pointer to the LDAP session the deletion was issued on.

`ResultMessage` is a pointer to the result `LDAPMessage` returned by `ldap_result()`.

`ReturnCode` is the address of a `ULONG` to set to the returned result of the delete operation. You can pass a `NULL` to ignore the returned error code.

`MatchedDNs` is the address of a pointer that `ldap_parse_result()` will set to point to a string containing the distinguished name of the object that was being deleted. If `*MatchedDNs` is non-NULL after calling `ldap_parse_result()`, you must free it by passing it to `ldap_memfree()`. If you want to ignore the matched distinguished names returned by the server, you can pass a `NULL` for `MatchedDNs`.

Note that the distinguished name contained in the error message string is the "closest match" found in the directory. If the object you attempted to delete did not exist in the directory, this name will not be the name you specified, but the closest name in the directory tree to it.

ErrorMessage is the address of a pointer to set to point to an error message string that corresponds to the error returned in *ReturnCode. If *ErrorMessage is non-NULL after calling `ldap_parse_result()`, you must free it by passing it to `ldap_memfree()`. You can pass a NULL for ErrorMessage if you want to ignore the returned error message string.

Referrals is the address of a pointer that will be set to point to a NULL-terminated array of pointers to NUL-terminated strings. `ldap_parse_result()` will set this to point to an array of referral URLs, if any were returned by the server. If *Referrals is non-NULL after calling `ldap_parse_result()`, you must free it by passing *Referrals to `ldap_value_free()`. You can pass a NULL for Referrals to ignore any returned referral strings.

ServerControls is the address of a pointer that will be set to point to a NULL-terminated array of pointers to LDAPControl structures. `ldap_parse_result()` will set this to point to the LDAPControl structures returned from the server. If `ldap_parse_result()` returns more than one LDAPControl structure, you must inspect the OID string of each to determine which control is which. If *Controls is non-NULL after calling `ldap_parse_result()`, you must pass *Controls to `ldap_controls_free()` to free the memory associated with the control structures. You can pass a NULL for Controls if you want to ignore the LDAPControl structures returned by the server. None of the server controls you might use with `ldap_delete_ext()` return any control information, so you might as well set this parameter to NULL.

Freeit is a Boolean value that, if set to TRUE, will cause `ldap_parse_result()` to free the memory associated with the ResultMsg parameter. If you set Freeit to TRUE, be sure that you don't later free ResultMsg with `ldap_msgfree()`.

Returns: An LDAP error code or LDAP_SUCCESS if the function succeeded.

NOTE

It's a good idea to set all the pointers whose addresses you pass to `ldap_parse_result()` to NULL before you pass them in. After calling `ldap_parse_result()`, you can check each pointer to see whether it is NULL, and if it is not, free it with the appropriate function.

When you use `ldap_parse_result()` to inspect the results returned by `ldap_result()` for an asynchronous operation, `*ReturnCode` will contain the result code for the operation, `*MatchedDNs` will contain the distinguished name of the modified object, and `*ErrorMessage` will contain a text string error message. You can use this information to format a meaningful error message, without the overhead of keeping track of every delete operation.

The program shown in Listing 26.3 demonstrates how to use `ldap_delete()` and `ldap_result()` to perform an asynchronous delete operation.

LISTING 26.3   USING `ldap_` TO DELETE AN OBJECT

```
1:     #include <windows.h>
2:     #include <winldap.h>
3:     #include <iostream.h>
4:
5:     int main( int argc, char** argv )
6:     {
7:         LDAP* psLdap = ldap_init( NULL, LDAP_PORT );
8:         if( psLdap != NULL )
9:         {
10:            ULONG uErr = ldap_bind_s( psLdap, NULL, NULL,
              ➥LDAP_AUTH_NEGOTIATE );
11:            if( uErr == LDAP_SUCCESS )
12:            {
13:                // set LDAP API version
14:                int nVersion = LDAP_VERSION3;
15:                ldap_set_option( psLdap, LDAP_OPT_VERSION, &nVersion );
16:
17:                // turn off referrals chasing
18:                int nChaseReferrals = 0;
19:                ldap_set_option( psLdap, LDAP_OPT_REFERRALS,
                  ➥&nChaseReferrals );
20:
21:                // DN of search base
22:                char szDNToDelete[ 1024 ] = "CN=NewestContainer,CN=Users,";
23:
24:                LDAPMessage* psMsg = NULL;
25:
26:                // Get rootDSE attr defaultNamingContext
27:                uErr = ldap_search_s(
28:                    psLdap,
29:                    NULL,
30:                    LDAP_SCOPE_BASE,
31:                    "objectClass=*",
32:                    NULL,
```

continues

LISTING 26.3   CONTINUED

```
33:                false,
34:                &psMsg
35:            );
36:            if( uErr == LDAP_SUCCESS )
37:            {
38:                char** ppszDomain = ldap_get_values( psLdap,
                   ➡ldap first entry( psLdap, psMsg ),
                   ➡"defaultNamingContext" );
39:                if( ppszDomain != NULL )
40:                {
41:                    strcat( szDNToDelete, ppszDomain[ 0 ] );
42:                }
43:                ldap_msgfree( psMsg );
44:            }
45:
46:            ULONG uDeleteHandle = ldap_delete( psLdap, szDNToDelete );
47:            if( uDeleteHandle != -1 )
48:            {
49:                bool bDone = false;
50:
51:                while( ! bDone )
52:                {
53:                    l_timeval sTimeout = { 10, 0 };
54:
55:                    LDAPMessage* psResult = NULL;
56:
57:                    int nResult = ldap_result( psLdap, uDeleteHandle,
                       ➡LDAP_MSG_ONE, &sTimeout, &psResult );
58:
59:                    switch( nResult )
60:                    {
61:                        case -1: // error
62:                            bDone = true;
63:                            break;
64:
65:                        default:
66:                        case 0: // timeout
67:                            break;
68:
69:                        case LDAP_RES_DELETE:
70:                            {
71:                                uErr = ldap_result2error( psLdap,
                                   ➡psResult, false );
72:                                if( uErr != LDAP_SUCCESS )
73:                                {
74:                                    ULONG uDeleteErr;
75:                                    char* pszDNs = NULL;
76:                                    char* pszErrmsg = NULL;
77:
```

Deleting Active Directory Objects with LDAP

CHAPTER 26

719

26

DELETING ACTIVE
DIRECTORY OBJECTS
WITH LDAP

```
78:                                  ldap_parse_result( psLdap,
                                   ↪psResult, &uDeleteErr, &pszDNs,
                                   ↪&pszErrmsg, NULL, NULL,
                                   ↪FALSE );
79:
80:                                  cout << "Got error " << pszErrmsg
                                   ↪<< "for " << pszDNs << endl;
81:
82:                                  ldap_memfree( pszDNs );
83:                                  ldap_memfree( pszErrmsg );
84:                              }
85:
86:                          ldap_msgfree( psResult );
87:
88:                          bDone = true;
89:                      }
90:                  break;
91:              }
92:          }
93:      }
94:  }
95:
96:      ldap_unbind( psLdap );
97:  }
98:
99:      return 0;
100: }
```

These sample programs all look pretty similar, don't they? The one in Listing 26.3 starts like all the others by calling `ldap_init()` and `ldap_bind_s()` to initialize the session. It then calls `ldap_set_option()` to set the protocol to LDAPv3 and to disable referrals.

At line 27, the program searches the `rootDSE` to get the distinguished name of the domain so that it can compose the name of the container to delete. In this case, it will be `"CN=MoreNewestContainer,CN=Users,<domain name>"`, which was created with one of the sample programs in Chapter 25, "Adding Active Directory Objects with LDAP."

At line 47, the program initiates the delete operation by calling `ldap_delete()` with the LDAP session pointer and the distinguished name of the object to delete. The returned values are the operation handle, which it stores in `uDeleteHandle`.

The program enters a polling loop at line 51, calling `ldap_result()` with `uDeleteHandle` each time around.

If `ldap_result()` returns `LDAP_RES_DELETE`, indicating it received the results of the delete operation, the program checks the error for the delete operation by calling `ldap_result2error()`.

If the error value is not LDAP_SUCCESS, the program calls ldap_parse_result()
to get the details of the error condition. It then prints the error message and the
distinguished name involved, and frees the strings by using ldap_memfree().

The program frees the result message returned by ldap_result() at line 86 by calling
ldap_msgfree() and then closes the LDAP session with ldap_unbind() at line 97.

Deleting Objects Asynchronously Using LDAP Controls with ldap_delete_ext()

Our final sample program for deleting objects uses the asynchronous extended API variant ldap_delete_ext(). This program, shown in Listing 26.4, shows how to delete an
object asynchronously while specifying an LDAP server control. In this case, we use the
Tree Delete server control so that we can delete the object and any subordinate objects in
one operation.

LISTING 26.4   USING ldap_delete_ext() TO DELETE AN OBJECT

```
1:    #include <windows.h>
2:    #include <winldap.h>
3:    #include <iostream.h>
4:
5:    int main( int argc, char** argv )
6:    {
7:        LDAP* psLdap = ldap_init( NULL, LDAP_PORT );
8:        if( psLdap != NULL )
9:        {
10:           ULONG uErr = ldap_bind_s( psLdap, NULL, NULL,
          ➥LDAP_AUTH_NEGOTIATE );
11:          if( uErr == LDAP_SUCCESS )
12:          {
13:              // set LDAP API version
14:              int nVersion = LDAP_VERSION3;
15:              ldap_set_option( psLdap, LDAP_OPT_VERSION, &nVersion );
16:
17:              // turn off referrals chasing
18:              int nChaseReferrals = 0;
19:              ldap_set_option( psLdap, LDAP_OPT_REFERRALS,
          ➥&nChaseReferrals );
20:
21:              // DN of search base
22:              char szDNToDelete[ 1024 ] = "CN=MoreNewestContainer,
          ➥CN=Users,";
```

```
23:
24:                LDAPMessage* psMsg = NULL;
25:
26:                // Get rootDSE attr defaultNamingContext
27:                uErr = ldap_search_s(
28:                    psLdap,
29:                    NULL,
30:                    LDAP_SCOPE_BASE,
31:                    "objectClass=*",
32:                    NULL,
33:                    false,
34:                    &psMsg
35:                );
36:                if( uErr == LDAP_SUCCESS )
37:                {
38:                    char** ppszDomain = ldap_get_values( psLdap,
                   ➥ldap first entry( psLdap, psMsg ),
                   ➥"defaultNamingContext" );
39:                    if( ppszDomain != NULL )
40:                    {
41:                        strcat( szDNToDelete, ppszDomain[ 0 ] );
42:                        ldap value free( ppszDomain );
43:                    }
44:                    ldap_msgfree( psMsg );
45:                }
46:
47:                LDAPControl sTreeDelete =
48:                {
49:                    "1.2.840.113556.1.4.805", // OID of tree delete
50:                                              // control
51:                    { 0, NULL }, // no BER data
52:                    true // is critical
53:                };
54:
55:                LDAPControl* apsServerControls[] =
56:                {
57:                    &sTreeDelete,
58:                    NULL
59:                };
60:
61:                ULONG uDeleteHandle;
62:
63:            uErr = ldap_delete_ext( psLdap, szDNToDelete,
               ➥apsServerControls, NULL, &uDeleteHandle );
64:                if( uErr == LDAP_SUCCESS )
65:                {
66:                    bool bDone = false;
67:
68:                    while( ! bDone )
69:                    {
70:                        l_timeval sTimeout = { 10, 0 };
71:
```

continues

LISTING 26.4   CONTINUED

```
72:                      LDAPMessage* psResult = NULL;
73:
74:                      int nResult = ldap_result( psLdap, uDeleteHandle,
          ➥LDAP_MSG_ONE, &sTimeout, &psResult );
75:
76:                  switch( nResult )
77:                  {
78:                      case -1: // error
79:                          bDone = true;
80:                          break;
81:
82:                      default:
83:                      case 0: // timeout
84:                          break;
85:
86:                      case LDAP_RES_DELETE:
87:                          {
88:                              uErr = ldap_result2error( psLdap,
              ➥psResult, false );
89:                              if( uErr != LDAP_SUCCESS )
90:                              {
91:                                  ULONG uDeleteErr;
92:                                  char* pszDNs = NULL;
93:                                  char* pszErrmsg = NULL;
94:
95:                                  ldap_parse_result( psLdap,
                  ➥psResult, &uDeleteErr, &pszDNs,
                  ➥&pszErrmsg, NULL, NULL, FALSE );
96:
97:                                  cout << "Got error " << pszErrmsg
                  ➥<< " for " << pszDNs << endl;
98:
99:                                  ldap_memfree( pszDNs );
100:                                  ldap_memfree( pszErrmsg );
101:                              }
102:
103:                              ldap_msgfree( psResult );
104:
105:                              bDone = true;
106:                          }
107:                          break;
108:                  }
109:              }
110:          }
111:      }
112:
113:      ldap_unbind( psLdap );
114:  }
115:
116:  return 0;
117: }
```

Again, the sample program starts out using `ldap_init()` and `ldap_bind_s()` to start the LDAP session. It then sets the protocol option to LDAPv3 and turns off referral chasing by the client by calling `ldap_set_option()`.

The code from lines 22–45 compose the distinguished name of the container to delete— in this case, `"CN=MoreNewestContainer,CN=Users,<domain name>"`. This is the name of a container created by a sample program in Chapter 25.

The program initializes the `LDAPControl` structure for the Tree Delete control at lines 47–53, using the OID string `"1.2.840.113556.1.4.805"`, no `BER` data, and setting the `is_critical` flag to `TRUE`. The program builds the array of `LDAPControl` pointers at lines 55–59.

At line 63, the program calls `ldap_delete_ext()` to initiate the delete operation. If this call is successful, the program enters a loop, calling `ldap_result()` each time around.

If the value returned from `ldap_result()` is `LDAP_RES_DELETE`, indicating it received a result for the delete operation, the program then calls `ldap_result2error()` at line 88 to retrieve the result code from the operation.

If the result code is not `LDAP_SUCCESS`, the program calls `ldap_parse_result()` at line 93 to get more information about the failure. It prints the error message and the closest matching distinguished name at line 95, and then frees the strings retrieved by `ldap_parse_result()` by calling `ldap_memfree()` at lines 99 and 100.

At line 103, the program frees the `LDAPMessage` returned by `ldap_result()`, and the program closes the LDAP session at line 113 by calling `ldap_unbind()`.

CHAPTER 27

Comparing Active Directory Objects with LDAP

The LDAP compare operations are oddballs in an otherwise wonderfully useful set of API functions. The LDAP compare operation simply lets you determine whether an object has an attribute that is equal to a specific value. In other words, you can get a true or false response to the question "Does attribute X of object Y equal Z?" That seems straightforward enough, but don't the LDAP search operations let you do exactly that? Well, yes, the LDAP search functions let you do that and a whole lot more (as you have seen). In fact, the LDAP search functions can do pretty much anything the compare functions can do. So what's the point? Why do the compare functions even exist?

Good question. I don't know. My guess is that it is a holdover from X.500, or that in some early incarnations of LDAP, having a separate comparison function seemed like a good idea. In any case, the LDAP compare functions don't really provide any capabilities beyond those provided by the search functions. This chapter is included for completeness.

This chapter describes the four LDAP compare functions listed in Table 27.1.

TABLE 27.1 THE LDAP COMPARE FUNCTIONS

Function	Description
ldap_compare_s()	Synchronous function that checks an attribute assertion on a specific object.
ldap_compare()	Asynchronous function that checks an attribute assertion on a specific object.
ldap_compare_ext_s()	Synchronous function that checks an attribute assertion on a specific object. This function accepts both client controls and server controls.
ldap_compare_ext()	Asynchronous function that checks an attribute assertion on a specific object. This function accepts both client controls and server controls.

Things to Know Before You Go

There are a handful of useful things to know about the LDAP compare functions before you try to use them:

- The differences between compare and search
- Network traffic
- Missing attribute semantics
- Matching rules
- Access rights
- Comparing binary values
- Testing multivalued attributes

The Differences Between Compare and Search

There are a handful of small differences between the LDAP compare functions and the equivalent search functions. The differences aren't sufficiently important to make using the compare functions much "better" than using the search functions, but here they are.

Network Traffic

Both the request and the response packets of the LDAP compare operation are smaller than the request and response packets of the LDAP search operation. This means that using the compare functions generates a little less network traffic than the equivalent search functions.

Missing Attribute Semantics

When you perform an LDAP search operation, if you specify a search filter that tests the value of an attribute that the object does not have, the search operation will skip that entry because it does not match the search filter. The LDAP compare operation, on the other hand, will return the error `LDAP_NO_SUCH_ATTRIBUTE`.

Matching Rules

The LDAP compare operation uses the same equality matching rules that the LDAP search functions use.

Access Rights

The Active Directory access rights rules apply the compare operation just as they do to all the other operations. You must have at least read access rights to an object before you can issue a comparison operation against it.

Comparing Binary Values

For the most part, you can compare LDAP attributes to an ASCII string, and this is what the `ldap_compare()` and `ldap_compare_s()` functions let you do. (Remember that LDAP handles numeric values as strings, too.) However, in the case where you must test a binary-valued attribute, you must use one of the extended versions of the compare functions, either `ldap_compare_ext()` or `ldap_compare_ext_s()`. These two functions provide for specifying a `berval` structure to which to compare an attribute.

Testing Multivalued Attributes

The compare function works the same way with multivalued attributes that the search functions do. That is, if any one of the multiple values is equal to the value you specified, the object compares successfully.

Using `ldap_compare_s()` to Test Attribute Assertions

The LDAP compare APIs follow the same pattern as add, search, modify, and delete. You can choose from four flavors of compare: synchronous, synchronous with extensions, asynchronous, and asynchronous with extensions. This section describes how to use the simplest compare API, `ldap_compare_s()`.

> **NOTE**
>
> ldap_compare_s() can only test attributes whose values are represented by strings. If you must use one of the compare operations to test a binary value, use ldap_compare_ext_s() or ldap_compare_ext() instead.

```
ULONG ldap_compare_s( LDAP* ld, const PCHAR dn, const PCHAR attr,
➡const PCHAR value )
```

ld is a pointer to an LDAP session that was initialized by a call to ldap_init() and authenticated with ldap_bind_s().

dn is a pointer to a NUL-terminated string containing the full distinguished name of the object to test.

attr is a pointer to a NUL-terminated string containing the name of the attribute to test.

value is a pointer to a NUL-terminated string containing the value to compare.

Returns: An LDAP error code. ldap_compare_s() does *not* return LDAP_SUCCESS. If the call is successful (if all the parameters are valid), ldap_compare_s() returns either LDAP_COMPARE_FALSE or LDAP_COMPARE_TRUE. These constants are defined as 5 and 6, respectively, in WINLDAP.H.

> **CAUTION**
>
> The values returned by the ldap_compare_s() and ldap_compare_ext_s() functions are at odds with the draft LDAP C API standard. The draft standard states that the compare functions will return LDAP_SUCCESS if the attribute assertion is true. The Microsoft implementation returns either LDAP_COMPARE_TRUE or LDAP_COMPARE_FALSE. It never returns LDAP_SUCCESS.

Listing 27.1 demonstrates how to set up and use ldap_compare_s().

LISTING 27.1 TESTING AN ATTRIBUTE ASSERTION WITH ldap_compare_s()

```
1:   #include <windows.h>
2:   #include <winldap.h>
3:   #include <iostream.h>
4:
5:   int main( int argc, char** argv )
6:   {
7:       LDAP* psLdap = ldap_init( NULL, LDAP_PORT );
```

```
8:       if( psLdap != NULL )
9:       {
10:        ULONG uErr = ldap_bind_s( psLdap, NULL, NULL,
          ↪LDAP_AUTH_NEGOTIATE );
11:        if( uErr == LDAP_SUCCESS )
12:        {
13:            // set LDAP API version
14:            int nVersion = LDAP_VERSION3;
15:            ldap_set_option( psLdap, LDAP_OPT_VERSION, &nVersion );
16:
17:            // turn off referrals chasing
18:            int nChaseReferrals = 0;
19:           ldap_set_option( psLdap, LDAP_OPT_REFERRALS,
              ↪&nChaseReferrals );
20:
21:            // DN of search base
22:            char szDN[ 1024 ] = "";
23:
24:            LDAPMessage* psMsg = NULL;
25:
26:            // Get rootDSE attr defaultNamingContext
27:            uErr = ldap_search_s(
28:                psLdap,
29:                NULL,
30:                LDAP_SCOPE_BASE,
31:                "objectClass=*",
32:                NULL,
33:                false,
34:                &psMsg
35:            );
36:            if( uErr == LDAP_SUCCESS )
37:            {
38:                char** ppszDomain = ldap_get_values( psLdap,
                  ↪ldap_first_entry( psLdap, psMsg ),
                  ↪"defaultNamingContext" );
39:                if( ppszDomain != NULL )
40:                {
41:                    strcat( szDN, ppszDomain[ 0 ] );
42:                    ldap_value_free( ppszDomain );
43:                }
44:                ldap_msgfree( psMsg );
45:            }
46:
47:            uErr = ldap_compare_s( psLdap, szDN, "nTMixedDomain",
              ↪"1" );
48:            if( uErr == LDAP_COMPARE_TRUE )
49:            {
50:                cout << "The domain " << szDN << " is in mixed mode"
                  ↪<< endl;
51:            }
52:            else if( uErr == LDAP_COMPARE_FALSE )
53:            {
```

continues

LISTING 27.1 CONTINUED

```
54:                     cout << "The domain " << szDN <<
                     ➥" is not in mixed mode" << endl;
55:                 }
56:                 else
57:                 {
58:                     cout << "Error " << uErr << " occurred" << endl;
59:                 }
60:             }
61:
62:             ldap_unbind( psLdap );
63:
64:         }
65:
66:         return 0;
67:     }
```

The program shown in Listing 27.1 starts by initializing an LDAP session with
`ldap_init()` and authenticating it with `ldap_bind_s()`.

At lines 14–19, the program sets the options on the LDAP session to use the LDAPv3
protocol and to disable referral chasing.

From there through line 45, the program gets the distinguished name of the domain in
the variable szDN. This will be the object the program tests with `ldap_compare_s()`.

The program calls `ldap_compare_s()` at line 47 to check whether the nTMixedDomain
attribute is equal to 1 and then prints the result. Note that the program checks explicitly
for LDAP_COMPARE_TRUE or LDAP_COMPARE_FALSE because `ldap_compare_s()` will not
return LDAP_SUCCESS.

The program calls `ldap_unbind()` at line 62 to close the LDAP session.

Using `ldap_compare_ext_s()` to Test Attribute Assertions

`ldap_compare_ext_s()` provides the synchronous-with-extensions flavor of the compare
operation. You use it in essentially the same way as `ldap_compare_s()`, except that the
calling sequence is a bit different. `ldap_compare_ext_s()` has two separate parameters
that specify the value to compare against. The first parameter is a string pointer that is
equivalent to the value parameter to `ldap_compare_s()`. The second parameter is a pointer to a BER structure. You use the string pointer to compare a string value, and you use
the BER structure pointer to compare to a binary value. You can specify only one or the
other of these parameters; the other must be NULL.

```
ULONG ldap_compare_ext_s( LDAP* ld, PCHAR dn, PCHAR Attr, PCHAR Value,
➥struct berval* Data, LDAPControl* ServerControls[], LDAPControl*
➥ClientControls[] )
```

ld is a pointer to a properly initialized and authenticated LDAP session.

dn is a pointer to a NUL-terminated string containing the distinguished name of the object to test.

Attr is a pointer to a NUL-terminated string containing the name of the attribute to test.

Value is a pointer to a NUL-terminated string value to compare the specified attribute to. Value must be NULL, and Data must be non-NULL, if you want to test a binary-valued attribute.

Data is a pointer to a properly initialized berval structure containing the value to compare against. Data must be NULL, and Value must be non-NULL, if you want to compare a string-valued attribute.

ServerControls is a pointer to a NUL-terminated array of pointers to LDAPControl structures. Each control specifies a particular LDAP server extension to use for the compare operation.

ClientControls is a pointer to a NULL-terminated array of pointers to LDAPControl structures. Each control specifies a particular LDAP client extension to use for the compare operation.

Returns: An LDAP error code. ldap_compare_s() does *not* return LDAP_SUCCESS. If the call is successful (if all the parameters are valid) ldap_compare_ext_s() returns either LDAP_COMPARE_FALSE or LDAP_COMPARE_TRUE. These constants are defined as 5 and 6, respectively, in WINLDAP.H.

> **CAUTION**
>
> The values returned by the ldap_compare_s() and ldap_compare_ext_s() functions are at odds with the draft LDAP C API standard. The draft standard states that the compare functions will return LDAP_SUCCESS if the attribute assertion is true. The Microsoft implementation returns either LDAP_COMPARE_TRUE or LDAP_COMPARE_FALSE. It never returns LDAP_SUCCESS.

The program in Listing 27.2 shows how to use the ldap_compare_ext_s() function to test the value of the objectGUID attribute. Because objectGUID is a binary attribute (its syntax is Octet String), you cannot use the ldap_compare_s() function to test the objectGUID attribute; you have to use ldap_compare_ext_s() or ldap_compare_ext().

Listing 27.2 compares the `objectGUID` attribute of the domain object to a specific value. (This GUID is the one from the domain object in my directory; your domain's GUID will be different.)

This sample program initializes the LDAP session and then sets up the parameters for the call to `ldap_compare_ext_s()`. Because this program is comparing a binary attribute and a value (GUIDs are basically 128-bit structures), it leaves the string parameter of `ldap_compare_ext_s()` NULL and specifies a value for the `berval` structure pointer instead. If this program were comparing a string value, it would specify a value for the string parameter and leave the `berval` structure pointer NULL.

LISTING 27.2   COMPARING AN OBJECT'S GUID TO A SPECIFIC VALUE

```
1:   #include <windows.h>
2:   #include <winldap.h>
3:   #include <iostream.h>
4:
5:   int main( int argc, char** argv )
6:   {
7:       LDAP* psLdap = ldap_init( NULL, LDAP_PORT );
8:       if( psLdap != NULL )
9:       {
10:          ULONG uErr = ldap_bind_s( psLdap, NULL, NULL,
            ➥LDAP_AUTH_NEGOTIATE );
11:          if( uErr == LDAP_SUCCESS )
12:          {
13:              // set LDAP API version
14:              int nVersion = LDAP_VERSION3;
15:              ldap_set_option( psLdap, LDAP_OPT_VERSION, &nVersion );
16:
17:              // turn off referrals chasing
18:              int nChaseReferrals = 0;
19:              ldap_set_option( psLdap, LDAP_OPT_REFERRALS,
                ➥&nChaseReferrals );
20:
21:              // DN of search base
22:              char szDN[ 1024 ] = "";
23:
24:              LDAPMessage* psMsg = NULL;
25:
26:              // Get rootDSE attr defaultNamingContext
27:              uErr = ldap_search_s(
28:                  psLdap,
29:                  NULL,
30:                  LDAP_SCOPE_BASE,
31:                  "objectClass=*",
32:                  NULL,
33:                  false,
```

```
34:                    &psMsg
35:                );
36:                if( uErr == LDAP_SUCCESS )
37:                {
38:                    char** ppszDomain = ldap_get_values( psLdap,
                       ➥ldap first entry( psLdap, psMsg ),
                       ➥"defaultNamingContext" );
39:                    if( ppszDomain != NULL )
40:                    {
41:                        strcat( szDN, ppszDomain[ 0 ] );
42:                        ldap value free( ppszDomain );
43:                    }
44:                    ldap_msgfree( psMsg );
45:                }
46:
47:                // The GUID value to test
48:                unsigned char acGuid[] =
49:                {
50:                    0x67, 0x6E, 0x2E, 0xF7,
51:                    0x5F, 0x0A,
52:                    0xD3, 0x11,
53:                    0x99,
54:                    0x52,
55:                    0x00,
56:                    0x60,
57:                    0x97,
58:                    0x79,
59:                    0x52,
60:                    0x1E
61:                };
62:
63:                LDAP_BERVAL sGuidToCheck =
64:                {
65:                    sizeof( acGuid ),
66:                    ( char* )acGuid
67:                };
68:
69:                // do the comparison
60:                uErr = ldap_compare_ext_s(
71:                    psLdap,
72:                    szDN,
73:                    "objectGUID",
74:                    NULL,
75:                    &sGuidToCheck,
76:                    NULL,
77:                    NULL
78:                );
79:
80:                if( uErr == LDAP_COMPARE_TRUE )
81:                {
82:                    cout << "The GUID for " << szDN << " matches" << endl;
83:                }
```

continues

LISTING 27.2   CONTINUED

```
84:              else if( uErr == LDAP_COMPARE_FALSE )
85:              {
86:                  cout << "The GUID for " << szDN << " does not match"
                     ➥<< endl;
87:              }
88:              else
89:              {
90:                  cout << "Error " << uErr << " occurred" << endl;
91:              }
92:          }
93:
94:          ldap_unbind( psLdap );
95:      }
96:
97:      return 0;
98: }
```

The program in Listing 27.2 starts in the usual way by calling `ldap_init()`, `ldap_bind_s()`, and `ldap_set_option()` to initialize the LDAP session.

Lines 27–45 read the distinguished name of the domain from the `rootDSE` of the domain controller, and save the distinguished name in `szDN`.

The program initializes an array of bytes containing the value of the GUID to compare against starting at line 48. Lines 63–67 initialize the `berval` structure defining the value to compare against.

The program actually calls `ldap_compare_ext_s()` at line 70, passing the current LDAP session, the DN of the domain object, and the name of the attribute to compare. It also passes a `NULL` for the string value to compare against, and sets the `Data` parameter to the address of the initialized `berval` structure. We don't use any LDAP client or server controls in this example, so we pass `NULL` for these two parameters.

Lines 80–90 check the return code from the call to `ldap_compare_ext_s()`. The return value will be either `LDAP_COMPARE_TRUE` if the value of the `objectGUID` attribute matches the value specified, `LDAP_COMPARE_FALSE` if it didn't match, and some other value if there was an error.

The program closes the LDAP session at line 94 by calling `ldap_unbind()`.

Using `ldap_compare()` to Test Attribute Assertions

The next two LDAP compare functions are the asynchronous versions of the two we've discussed already. They work the same way that other asynchronous LDAP functions work. You must first call the API function (ldap_compare(), in this case), which returns an operation handle. You then must call ldap_result() repeatedly using this operation handle to obtain the results of the comparison.

ULONG ldap_compare(LDAP* ld, PCHAR dn, PCHAR Attr, PCHAR Value)

> ld is a pointer to a properly initialized and authenticated LDAP session.
>
> dn is a pointer to a NUL-terminated string containing the distinguished name of the object to test.
>
> Attr is a pointer to a NUL-terminated string containing the name of the attribute to test.
>
> Value is a pointer to a NUL-terminated string value to compare the specified attribute to.

Returns: An LDAP operation handle. You must call ldap_result with this handle to obtain the result of the comparison operation.

After you call ldap_compare(), you have to call ldap_result() repeatedly until it returns the result of the asynchronous compare operation.

ULONG ldap_result(LDAP* ld, ULONG msgid, ULONG all,
➥struct l_timeval* timeout, LDAPMessage** res)

> ld is a pointer to an LDAP structure that has been initialized with ldap_init(), ldap_sslinit(), or ldap_open(). It must be the same LDAP structure that you used to do to compare.
>
> msgid is the handle to the compare operation that was returned by ldap_compare() or ldap_compare_ext(). If you specify LDAP_RES_ANY, ldap_result() will return results for any outstanding asynchronous operation that was started on the LDAP session given by ld.
>
> all specifies how many of the result objects you want returned. It must be one of three constants defined in WINLDAP.H and described in Table 27.2.

TABLE 27.2 POSSIBLE VALUES OF THE all PARAMETER OF ldap_result()

Constant	Description
LDAP_MSG_ONE	Indicates that ldap_result() should return a single operation result.
LDAP_MSG_ALL	Indicates that ldap_result() should wait until all the results have been received from the server. Because a compare operation returns only a single result, this value isn't very useful for compare operations.
LDAP_MSG_RECEIVED	Indicates that ldap_result() should return all the result objects that have been received so far. Because a compare operation only returns a single result, this value isn't very useful for compare operations.

timeout is a pointer to an l_timeval structure that contains the timeout value for the ldap_result() call. If there are no messages to retrieve within the time specified by the l_timeval structure, ldap_result() will return a 0.

res is the address of an LDAPMessage pointer to be set by ldap_result(). This pointer must be freed by passing it to ldap_msgfree() after you are done with it.

Returns: The type of the message retrieved. There are 11 possible returned messages, but only LDAP_RES_COMPARE or LDAP_RES_REFERRAL will be returned as the result of a search operation.

LDAP_RES_COMPARE indicates that the message contains the results of a compare operation.

LDAP_RES_REFERRAL indicates that the message contains one or more referrals to other naming contexts. See the section on processing referrals for information on how to handle this message.

0 indicates that the call to ldap_result() timed out. This means there were no results sent from the server within the timeout period. You should retry the call to ldap_result().

-1 indicates an error of some sort. Call LdapGetLastError() to get the corresponding error code. You should not call ldap_result() after receiving an error.

After you call ldap_result() successfully and it returns a pointer to an LDAPMessage structure in *res, you must free the LDAPMessage structure by calling ldap_msgfree(), passing it the pointer that was returned. You can also free the message by calling ldap_result2error() and setting the freeit parameter to true.

ULONG ldap_msgfree(LDAPMessage* msg)

msg is a pointer to an LDAPMessage structure that was returned by ldap_result().

Returns: LDAP_SUCCESS if it successfully freed the LDAPMessage structure or an LDAP error code if there was an error.

CAUTION

ldap_result() returns a valid pointer in *res only if its return value was greater than 0. Therefore, you should call ldap_msgfree() only if ldap_result() returned a value greater than 0. Calling ldap_msgfree() with an invalid LDAPMessage pointer will cause memory corruption.

Retrieving the Results of an Asynchronous Comparison

When you issue an asynchronous search operation, the results you retrieve are the entries that matched your search criteria. When you issue an asynchronous compare operation using ldap_compare() or ldap_compare_ext(), you generally want to know the results of the comparison, or if there was some sort of an error. The LDAPMessage pointer returned by ldap_result() contains the result of the asynchronous comparison operation.

There are two functions you can use to get the results of an asynchronous comparison operation, ldap_result2error() and ldap_parse_result(). Both functions accept the LDAPMessage pointer returned by ldap_result() as an argument.

Getting the Error Code with `ldap_result2error()`

The ldap_result2error() function accepts the LDAPMessage pointer returned from ldap_result() in *res, extracts the error code from the result message, and returns the LDAP error code associated with that particular compare operation.

```
ULONG ldap_result2error( LDAP* ld, LDAPMessage* res, ULONG freeit )
```

> ld is a pointer to the LDAP session you used when you called ldap_result().
>
> res is the LDAPMessage pointer that ldap_result() returned in *res.
>
> freeit is a Boolean that, if set to true, will cause ldap_result2error() to free the LDAPMessage structure. If freeit is false, ldap_result2error() will not free the message structure.

Returns: The error code extracted from the LDAPMessage structure.

> **CAUTION**
>
> If you free an LDAPMessage structure by setting the freeit parameter in ldap_result2error() to true, be sure that you do not subsequently try to free the message again by calling ldap_msgfree(). Doing so will likely cause memory corruption.

Just getting the error code for an asynchronous operation is fine, but what happens if the error is nonzero, indicating an actual failure? What object was being compared? ldap_result2error() can't give you that information. There are two solutions.

The first strategy is more complicated. In this case, you store each operation handle returned by ldap_compare() or ldap_compare_ext() in an array, and then poll for the results for each handle by iterating through the array and calling ldap_result(), passing the operation handle for the msgid parameter. This is somewhat complicated, and incurs the storage and lookup overhead of the array of operation handles.

The second strategy is simpler. In this case, you use ldap_parse_result() to retrieve the operation information from the LDAPMessage pointer returned by ldap_result(). ldap_parse_result() is described in the following section.

Getting Information About an Asynchronous Operation with ldap_parse_result()

If you want to know which delete operation generated an error code, ldap_result2error() is insufficient; it tells you what the error was, but not which object comparison caused the error. ldap_parse_result() can retrieve this information for you.

```
ULONG ldap_parse_result( LDAP* Connection, LDAPMessage* ResultMessage,
➥ULONG* ReturnCode, PCHAR* MatchedDNs, PCHAR* ErrorMessage, PCHAR**
➥Referrals, PLDAPControl** ServerControls, BOOLEAN Freeit )
```

Connection is a pointer to the LDAP session on which the compare operation was issued.

ResultMessage is a pointer to the result LDAPMessage returned by ldap_result().

ReturnCode is the address of a ULONG to set to the returned result of the compare operation. You can pass a NULL to ignore the returned error code.

MatchedDNs is the address of a pointer that ldap_parse_result() will set to point to a string containing the distinguished name of the object that was being deleted. If *MatchedDNs is non-NULL after calling ldap_parse_result(), you must free it by passing it to ldap_memfree(). If you want to ignore the matched distinguished names returned by the server, you can pass a NULL for MatchedDNs.

Note that the distinguished name contained in the error message string is the "closest match" found in the directory. If the object you attempted to compare did not exist in the directory, this name will not be the name you specified, but the closest name in the directory tree to it.

ErrorMessage is the address of a pointer to set to point to an error message string that corresponds to the error returned in *ReturnCode. If *ErrorMessage is non-NULL after calling ldap_parse_result(), you must free it by passing it to ldap_memfree(). You can pass a NULL for ErrorMessage if you want to ignore the returned error message string.

Referrals is the address of a pointer that will be set to point to a NULL-terminated array of pointers to NUL-terminated strings. ldap_parse_result() will set this to point to an array of referral URLs, if any were returned by the server. If *Referrals is non-NULL after calling ldap_parse_result(), you must free it by passing

*Referrals to ldap_value_free(). You can pass a NULL for Referrals to ignore any returned referral strings.

ServerControls is the address of a pointer that will be set to point to a NULL-terminated array of pointers to LDAPControl structures. ldap_parse_result() will set this to point to the LDAPControl structures returned from the server. If ldap_parse_result() returns more than one LDAPControl structure, you must inspect the OID string of each to determine which control is which. (This doesn't happen with a simple sorted search.) If *Controls is non-NULL after calling ldap_parse_result(), you must pass *Controls to ldap_controls_free() to free the memory associated with the control structures. You can pass a NULL for Controls if you want to ignore the LDAPControl structures returned by the server. None of the server controls you might use with ldap_compare_ext() return any control information, so you might as well set this parameter to NULL.

Freeit is a Boolean value that, if set to TRUE, will cause ldap_parse_result() to free the memory associated with the ResultMsg parameter. If you set Freeit to TRUE, be sure that you don't later free ResultMsg with ldap_msgfree().

Returns: An LDAP error code or LDAP_SUCCESS if the function succeeded.

> **NOTE**
>
> It's a good idea to set all the pointers whose addresses you pass to ldap_parse_result() to NULL before you pass them in. After calling ldap_parse_result(), you can check each pointer to see whether it is NULL, and if it is not, free it with the appropriate function.

When you use ldap_parse_result() to inspect the results returned by ldap_result() for an asynchronous modification operation, *ReturnCode will contain the result code for the operation, *MatchedDNs will contain the distinguished name of the modified object, and *ErrorMessage will contain a text string error message. You can use this information to format a meaningful error message, without the overhead of keeping track of every compare operation.

Listing 27.3 does exactly the same thing as the program in Listing 27.1, except that it uses ldap_compare() instead of ldap_compare_s().

LISTING 27.3 USING ldap_compare_s() TO TEST AN ATTRIBUTE ASSERTION

```
1:    #include <windows.h>
2:    #include <winldap.h>
```

continues

LISTING 27.3   CONTINUED

```
3:    #include <iostream.h>
4:
5:    int main( int argc, char** argv )
6:    {
7:        LDAP* psLdap = ldap_init( NULL, LDAP_PORT );
8:        if( psLdap != NULL )
9:        {
10:           ULONG uErr = ldap_bind_s( psLdap, NULL, NULL,
              ➥LDAP_AUTH_NEGOTIATE );
11:          if( uErr == LDAP_SUCCESS )
12:          {
13:              // set LDAP API version
14:              int nVersion = LDAP_VERSION3;
15:              ldap_set_option( psLdap, LDAP_OPT_VERSION, &nVersion );
16:
17:              // turn off referrals chasing
18:              int nChaseReferrals = 0;
19:              ldap_set_option( psLdap, LDAP_OPT_REFERRALS,
                 ➥&nChaseReferrals );
20:
21:              // DN of search base
22:              char szDN[ 1024 ] = "";
23:
24:              LDAPMessage* psMsg = NULL;
25:
26:              // Get rootDSE attr defaultNamingContext
27:              uErr = ldap_search_s(
28:                  psLdap,
29:                  NULL,
30:                  LDAP_SCOPE_BASE,
31:                  "objectClass=*",
32:                  NULL,
33:                  false,
34:                  &psMsg
35:              );
36:              if( uErr == LDAP_SUCCESS )
37:              {
38:                  char** ppszDomain = ldap_get_values( psLdap,
                     ➥ldap first entry( psLdap, psMsg ),
                     ➥"defaultNamingContext" );
39:                  if( ppszDomain != NULL )
40:                  {
41:                      strcat( szDN, ppszDomain[ 0 ] );
42:                      ldap value free( ppszDomain );
43:                  }
44:                  ldap_msgfree( psMsg );
45:              }
46:
47:              // Issue the compare operation
48:              ULONG uCompareHandle = ldap_compare(
49:                  psLdap, // LDAP session
```

```
50:                      szDN, // DN to test
51:                      "nTMixedDomain", // attribute to test
52:                      "0" // value to compare
53:                  );
54:
55:              if( uCompareHandle != -1 )
56:              {
57:                  bool bDone = false;
58:
59:                  while( ! bDone )
60:                  {
61:                      l_timeval sTimeout = { 10, 0 }; // 10-second
62:                                                      // timeout
63:
64:                      LDAPMessage* psResult = NULL;
65:
66:                      int nResult = ldap_result( psLdap, uCompareHandle,
                         ➥LDAP_MSG_ONE, &sTimeout, &psResult );
67:
68:                      switch( nResult )
69:                      {
70:                      case -1: // error
71:                          bDone = true;
72:                          break;
73:
74:                      case 0: // timeout
75:                          break;
76:
77:                      case LDAP_RES_COMPARE: // operation result
78:                          {
79:                          uErr = ldap_result2error( psLdap, psResult,
                             ➥false );
80:                              if( uErr == LDAP_COMPARE_TRUE )
81:                              {
82:                               cout << "The domain " << szDN <<
                                 ➥" is in mixed mode" << endl;
83:                              }
84:                              else if( uErr == LDAP_COMPARE_FALSE )
85:                              {
86:                                cout << "The domain " << szDN <<
                                 ➥" is not in mixed mode" << endl;
87:                              }
88:                              else
89:                              {
90:                                  cout << "Error " << uErr <<
                                     ➥"occurred" << endl;
91:
92:                                  ULONG uCompareErr;
93:                                  char* pszDNs = NULL;
```

continues

LISTING 27.3   CONTINUED

```
 94:                                    char* pszErrmsg = NULL;
 95:
 96:                                    ldap_parse_result( psLdap,
 97:                                        psResult,
 98:                                        &uCompareErr,
 99:                                        &pszDNs,
100:                                         &pszErrmsg,
101:                                         NULL,
102:                                        NULL,
103:                                        FALSE
104:                                    );
105:
106:                                cout << "Got error " << pszErrmsg <<
                                    ➥" for " << pszDNs << endl;
107:
108:                                    ldap_memfree( pszDNs );
109:                                    ldap_memfree( pszErrmsg );
110:                                }
111:
112:                                ldap_msgfree( psResult );
113:
114:                                bDone = true;
115:                            }
116:
117:                        break;
118:                    }
119:                }
120:            }
121:        }
122:
123:        ldap_unbind( psLdap );
124:    }
125:
126:    return 0;
127: }
```

Listing 27.3 looks suspiciously like the other sample programs that use asynchronous LDAP functions. It initializes, authenticates, and configures the LDAP session at lines 7–19.

Lines 27–45 read the name of the domain from the rootDSE of the domain controller and save the distinguished name in szDN. This is the object against which the program will issue the compare operation.

The program calls ldap_compare() at line 48, in this case to test the nTMixedDomain attribute being equal to 1.

At line 59, the program goes into a loop, calling `ldap_result()` each time through. If the value returned by `ldap_result()` is `LDAP_RES_COMPARE`, indicating the client has received the results of the compare operation, the program extracts the result of the compare at line 79 by calling `ldap_result2error()`.

If the result was either `LDAP_COMPARE_TRUE` or `LDAP_COMPARE_FALSE`, the program prints the result of the comparison. If the result is any other value, the program calls `ldap_parse_result()` to get the details of the error condition. Note that the program frees the strings allocated by `ldap_parse_result()` at lines 108 and 109 by calling `ldap_memfree()`.

The program finally closes the LDAP session at line 123 by calling `ldap_unbind()`.

Using `ldap_compare_ext()` to Test Attribute Assertions

The last of the four compare functions is `ldap_compare_ext()`. Like `ldap_compare()`, it is an asynchronous function; it returns immediately with an operation handle, and the program has to check the status of the operation by calling `ldap_result()` repeatedly until the operation completes. Like `ldap_compare_ext_s()`, `ldap_compare_ext()` lets you test either string or binary valued attributes by providing two value parameters: one a pointer to a string and the other a pointer to a `berval` structure. Because it is an extended function, `ldap_compare_ext()` also provides client and server controls parameters so that you can take advantage of any appropriate LDAP extensions during the compare operation.

```
ULONG ldap_compare_ext( LDAP* ld, PCHAR dn, PCHAR Attr, PCHAR Value,
➡struct berval* Data, LDAPControl* ServerControls[],
➡LDAPControl* ClientControls[], ULONG* MessageNumber )
```

> `ld` is a pointer to a properly initialized and authenticated LDAP session.
>
> `dn` is a pointer to a NUL-terminated string containing the distinguished name of the object to test.
>
> `Attr` is a pointer to a NUL-terminated string containing the name of the attribute to test.
>
> `Value` is a pointer to the NUL-terminated string value to which to compare the specified attribute. If you want to compare a binary-valued attribute, set this parameter to `NULL` and pass the address of a properly initialized `berval` structure in `Data`. One of these two parameters must be non-`NULL`; the other must be `NULL`.
>
> `Data` is a pointer to a properly initialized `berval` structure. If you are comparing a string-valued attribute, you can specify the value in `Value` and set this parameter to `NULL`. If you are comparing a binary-valued attribute, set `Value` to `NULL` and use `Data` instead.

`ServerControls` is a pointer to a NULL-terminated array of properly initialized pointers to `LDAPControl` structures. Each `LDAPControl` structure specifies an LDAP server extension to use during the compare operation.

`ClientControls` is a pointer to a NULL-terminated array of properly initialized pointers to `LDAPControl` structures. Each `LDAPControl` structure specifies an LDAP client extension to use during the compare operation.

`MessageNumber` is a pointer to an unsigned long integer that will be set to the operation ID you must use when calling `ldap_result()` to determine the results of the compare operation.

Returns: `LDAP_SUCCESS` if the compare operation was properly initiated, or some other LDAP error if there was a problem with the parameters passed to the function. If `ldap_compare_ext()` returns `LDAP_SUCCESS`, `*MessageNumber` will be set to an LDAP operation handle. You should pass this handle to `ldap_result()` to determine the results of the compare operation.

Listing 27.4 is similar to the preceding program that used `ldap_compare()`, except that it tests against a binary-valued attribute (a GUID in this case).

LISTING 27.4   USING `ldap_compare_ext()` TO TEST A BINARY ATTRIBUTE ASSERTION
ASYNCHRONOUSLY

```
1:   #include <windows.h>
2:   #include <winldap.h>
3:   #include <iostream.h>
4:
5:   int main( int argc, char** argv )
6:   {
7:       LDAP* psLdap = ldap_init( NULL, LDAP_PORT );
8:       if( psLdap != NULL )
9:       {
10:          ULONG uErr = ldap_bind_s( psLdap, NULL, NULL,
          ➡LDAP_AUTH_NEGOTIATE );
11:          if( uErr == LDAP_SUCCESS )
12:          {
13:              // set LDAP API version
14:              int nVersion = LDAP_VERSION3;
15:              ldap_set_option( psLdap, LDAP_OPT_VERSION, &nVersion );
16:
17:              // turn off referrals chasing
18:              int nChaseReferrals = 0;
19:              ldap_set_option( psLdap, LDAP_OPT_REFERRALS,
              ➡&nChaseReferrals );
20:
21:              // DN of search base
22:              char szDN[ 1024 ] = "";
```

```
23:
24:                LDAPMessage* psMsg = NULL;
25:
26:                // Get rootDSE attr defaultNamingContext
27:                uErr = ldap_search_s(
28:                    psLdap,
29:                    NULL,
30:                    LDAP_SCOPE_BASE,
31:                    "objectClass=*",
32:                    NULL,
33:                    false,
34:                    &psMsg
35:                );
36:                if( uErr == LDAP_SUCCESS )
37:                {
38:                    char** ppszDomain = ldap_get_values( psLdap,
                       ➥ldap first entry( psLdap, psMsg ),
                       ➥"defaultNamingContext" );
39:                    if( ppszDomain != NULL )
40:                    {
41:                        strcat( szDN, ppszDomain[ 0 ] );
42:                        ldap value free( ppszDomain );
43:                    }
44:                    ldap_msgfree( psMsg );
45:                }
46:
47:                // The GUID value to test
48:                unsigned char acGuid[] =
49:                {
50:                    0x67, 0x6E, 0x2E, 0xF7,
51:                    0x5F, 0x0A,
52:                    0xD3, 0x11,
53:                    0x99,
54:                    0x52,
55:                    0x00,
56:                    0x60,
57:                    0x97,
58:                    0x79,
59:                    0x52,
60:                    0x1E
61:                };
62:
63:                // The berval for the GUID
64:                LDAP_BERVAL sGuidToCheck =
65:                {
66:                    sizeof( acGuid ),
67:                    ( char* )acGuid
68:                };
69:
70:                ULONG uCompareHandle;
71:
72:                // Issue the compare operation
```

continues

LISTING 27.4 CONTINUED

```
73:                  uErr = ldap_compare_ext(
74:                      psLdap,
75:                      szDN,
76:                      "objectGUID",
77:                      NULL,
78:                      &sGuidToCheck,
79:                      NULL,
80:                      NULL,
81:                      &uCompareHandle
82:                  );
83:
84:              if( uErr == LDAP_SUCCESS )
85:              {
86:                  bool bDone = false;
87:
88:                  while( ! bDone )
89:                  {
90:                      l_timeval sTimeout = { 10, 0 }; // 10-second
91:                                                      // timeout
92:
93:                      LDAPMessage* psResult = NULL;
94:
95:                      int nResult = ldap_result( psLdap, uCompareHandle,
       ➥LDAP_MSG_ONE, &sTimeout, &psResult );
96:
97:                      switch( nResult )
98:                      {
99:                      case -1: // error
100:                          bDone = true;
101:                          break;
102:
103:                      case 0: // timeout
104:                          break;
105:
106:                      case LDAP_RES_COMPARE: // operation result
107:                          {
108:                              uErr = ldap_result2error( psLdap,
       ➥psResult, false );
109:                              if( uErr == LDAP_COMPARE_TRUE )
110:                              {
111:                                  cout << "The GUIDs are the same" <<
       ➥endl;
112:                              }
113:                              else if( uErr == LDAP_COMPARE_FALSE )
114:                              {
115:                                  cout << "The GUIDs are different"
       ➥<< endl;
116:                              }
```

```
117:                              else
118:                              {
119:                                  cout << "Error " << uErr <<
                                     ➡" occurred" << endl;
120:
121:                                  ULONG uCompareErr;
122:                                  char* pszDNs = NULL;
123:                                  char* pszErrmsg = NULL;
124:
125:                                  ldap_parse_result( psLdap,
126:                                      psResult,
127:                                      &uCompareErr,
128:                                      &pszDNs,
129:                                      &pszErrmsg,
130:                                      NULL,
131:                                      NULL,
132:                                      FALSE
133:                                  );
134:
135:                                  cout << "Got error " << pszErrmsg <<
                                     ➡" for " << pszDNs << endl;
136:
137:                                  ldap_memfree( pszDNs );
138:                                  ldap_memfree( pszErrmsg );
139:                              }
140:
141:                              ldap_msgfree( psResult );
142:
143:                              bDone = true;
144:                          }
145:
146:                      break;
147:                  }
148:              }
149:          }
150:      }
151:
152:      ldap_unbind( psLdap );
153:  }
154:
155:  return 0;
156: }
```

The program in Listing 27.4 starts like the others, by calling `ldap_init()` and
`ldap_bind_s()`. It sets the protocol version to LDAPv3 and disables referral chasing by
calling `ldap_set_option()` at lines 15 and 19.

At line 27, the program calls `ldap_search_s()` to get the distinguished name of the domain. It stores the name in the `szDN` variable. This will be the object against which it will test the value of the `objectGUID` attribute.

Lines 48–68 declare and initialize the structures that defined the GUID value the program will use for the compare operation. The `acGUID` array contains the bytes of the GUID, and the `sGuidToCheck` structure is a `LDAP_BERVAL` structure the program will pass to `ldap_compare_ext()`.

The call to `ldap_compare_ext()` at line 73 issues the comparison operation, and the program enters into a loop at line 87 that calls `ldap_result()` repeatedly until it receives the results of the comparison.

At line 108, the program retrieves the result of the comparison operation from the message returned by `ldap_result()` by calling `ldap_result2error()`. It prints a message if the comparison was true or false.

If some other error was returned, the program calls `ldap_parse_result()` to retrieve the rest of the information regarding the error.

At lines 137 and 138 the program calls `ldap_memfree()` to free the strings returned by `ldap_parse_result()`. At line 152, it closes the LDAP session by calling `ldap_unbind()`.

CHAPTER 28

Extending LDAP with Options and Controls

The network software business is very dynamic, with the technology changing seemingly daily. Standards are a way of slowing down the rapid changes so that the marketplace can enjoy some synergy between competing technologies. The problem with software standards is that by the time a software standard becomes widely adopted, it becomes obsolete. When it becomes obsolete, some clever vendor will extend the standard to provide additional value and gain market share.

The LDAP designers were very smart in that they provided three mechanisms within the standard LDAP API where vendors could provide extensions to LDAP in an organized way, and software developers could take advantage of them in a way that would not lock their products to a single LDAP implementation. These three mechanisms are LDAP options, LDAP controls, and LDAP extensions.

Only some of the LDAP options have been specified in the current LDAP API draft standard. Most options are vendor-specific. Options are defined by constants in the vendor's LDAP header file (WINLDAP.H in Microsoft's case), and they often vary from implementation to implementation. If you write code that takes advantage of Microsoft's LDAP options, your code might not even compile, much less run, in another vendor's environment.

LDAP options apply to an entire LDAP session. For instance, if you establish an LDAP session with two different servers, and set the LDAP_OPT_REFERRALS option on one of them, the other LDAP session will remain unchanged.

LDAP controls, on the other hand, apply to single LDAP operations. For instance, one LDAP control disables referrals. If you pass this control to the `ldap_search_ext_s()` function, LDAP will not chase referrals on that one search operation. All the basic LDAP functions, such as `ldap_add()`, `ldap_delete()`, `ldap_rename()`, `ldap_modify()`, and `ldap_compare()` have variants that accept LDAP controls. These variant functions generally have _ext as part of their names, such as `ldap_add_ext()`.

LDAP controls are uniquely identified using OIDs, and different directory vendors implement their own sets of controls. Some of these controls are being semi-standardized through Internet Drafts in the IETF.

LDAP extensions provide a way of implementing completely new functions within the LDAP framework. Directory vendors can define new extended operations, again identified by OIDs, that you can perform on their directory servers.

Unfortunately, the Microsoft LDAP client library does not implement the `ldap_extended_operation()` or `ldap_extended_operation_s()` functions defined in the latest C API draft, so outside of constructing and parsing your own packets, there isn't a good way to invoke using the Microsoft LDAP client API. In any case, Microsoft has not documented any extended functions supported by Active Directory.

This chapter shows how to use the LDAP APIs listed in Table 28.1.

TABLE 28.1   LDAP FUNCTIONS FOR SETTING SESSION OPTIONS

Function	Description
ldap_get_option	Retrieves the value of an LDAP session option.
ldap_set_option	Sets the value of an LDAP session option.

LDAP Options

LDAP options apply to a single LDAP session. They are usually stored in the LDAP structure itself.) You can get and set LDAP options with two LDAP API functions: `ldap_get_option()` and `ldap_set_option()`.

Reading the Options

The `ldap_get_option` function is called whenever you want to read the current LDAP settings. It is shown in the following code line:

```
ULONG ldap_get_option( LDAP *ld, int option, void *invalue )
```

ld is a pointer to a valid LDAP connection structure previously returned by
ldap_init().

option is a number indicating which option should be returned. Valid values for
option are defined in WINLDAP.H and are described later in the section
"'Standard' LDAP Options."

invalue is a pointer to a variable or structure appropriate to the specific option
being returned.

Returns: LDAP_SUCCESS if the call succeeded and an LDAP error code if an error
occurred.

The following example shows how to use ldap_get_option() to return the current TCP
socket associated with an LDAP session.

```
char* pszHost = "lithium.megacorp.com;
LDAP* psLdap = ldap_init( pszHost, LDAP_PORT );
if( psLdap != NULL )
{
    int nSocket = 0;
    ULONG errLdap;

    errLdap = ldap_get_option(psLdap, LDAP_OPT_DESC, (void*)&nSocket);
    if(errLdap == LDAP_SUCCESS)
    {
        // nSocket now has the TCP socket number
    }
}
```

Setting the Options

To change a LDAP option, the ldap_set_option function is used. The function looks
like this:

```
ULONG ldap_set_option( LDAP *ld, int option, void *outvalue )
```

ld is a pointer to a valid LDAP connection structure previously returned by
ldap_init().

option is a number indicating which option should be returned. Valid values for
option are defined in WINLDAP.H and described later in the section "'Standard'
LDAP Options."

outvalue is a pointer to a variable or structure appropriate to the specific option
being set.

Returns: LDAP_SUCCESS if the call succeeded and an LDAP error code if an error
occurred.

The following example shows how to set the maximum number of entries returned by search operations using the current LDAP session.

```
char* pszHost = "lithium.megacorp.com;
LDAP* psLdap = ldap_init( pszHost, LDAP_PORT );

if( psLdap != NULL )
{
    int nMaxEntries = 100; // max entries for search operations
     ULONG errLdap;

    errLdap = ldap_set_option( psLdap, LDAP_OPT_SIZELIMIT,
             ➥( void* )&nMaxEntries );

    if( errLdap == LDAP_SUCCESS )
    {
        // search operations will return a max of 100 entries
    }
}
```

Turning Options On and Off

Some LDAP options are Boolean in nature; they can either be on or off. WINLDAP.H includes two defined constants for setting these parameters: LDAP_OPT_ON and LDAP_OPT_OFF. They are (void*) casts of the integers 1 and 0, respectively. The following code snippet makes this a little clearer:

```
// the wrong way to set a boolean option

int nSetting = 1; // set to TRUE
errLdap = ldap_set_option( psLdap, LDAP_OPT_RESTART, ( void* )&nSetting );
// the right way to set a boolean option
errLdap = ldap_set_option( psLdap, LDAP_OPT_RESTART, LDAP_OPT_ON );
```

"Standard" LDAP Options

The following LDAP options are part of the current draft LDAP "C" API Standard and are supported by the Microsoft LDAP implementation. These options are used in the ldap_set_option function and are returned in the ldap_get_option function, as described earlier.

LDAP_OPT_DESC

The LDAP_OPT_DESC option provides access to the LDAP session's TCP (or UDP if you used cldap_open()) socket descriptor. You can use appropriate Winsock functions, such as getpeername() or getsockopt(), to get more information about the LDAP session's TCP connection with the server.

You can also set the TCP socket number by calling ldap_set_option(). There probably isn't a great reason for doing this, but you can do it if you need to. The following code fragment shows how to use the LDAP_OPT_DESC option to retrieve the socket number:

```
int nSocket = 0;
ULONG errLdap;
errLdap = ldap_get_option( psLdap, LDAP_OPT_DESC, (void*)&nSocket );
if( errLdap == LDAP_SUCCESS )
{
    // nSocket now has the TCP socket number
}
```

LDAP_OPT_DEREF

Alias objects in Active Directory are pointers that refer to other objects. You can set how the LDAP routines will treat searches that encounter alias objects by calling ldap_set_option() with the LDAP_OPT_DEREF option value.

Table 28.2 shows the allowed values for the LDAP_OPT_DEREF option.

TABLE 28.2   ALLOWED VALUES FOR THE LDAP_OPT_DEREF OPTION

Value	*Description*
LDAP_DEREF_NEVER	Never dereferences alias entries to their targets. Always treats aliases as independent objects.
LDAP_DEREF_SEARCHING	Dereferences alias objects only during search operations, but not when locating the base object of the search.
LDAP_DEREF_FINDING	Dereferences alias objects when locating the base object of a search, but not during the search itself.
LDAP_DEREF_ALWAYS	Dereferences alias objects at all times during a search.

The following code sample shows how to set the LDAP session options so that LDAP will always dereference alias objects.

```
ULONG errLdap;
int nOption = LDAP_DEREF_ALWAYS;
errLdap = ldap_set_option( psLdap, LDAP_OPT_DEREF, ( void* )&nOption );
if( errLdap == LDAP_SUCCESS )
{
    // Searches will now always dereference alias entries
}
```

28

EXTENDING LDAP
WITH OPTIONS
AND CONTROLS

You can inspect the current value of the `LDAP_OPT_DEREF` option by call `ldap_get_option()`.

LDAP_OPT_SIZELIMIT

It's quite possible that an LDAP search operation will return thousands or even millions of entries. If your application requires only the first few entries that meet your search criteria, you can limit the amount of time the domain controller spends searching by using `ldap_set_option()` with the `LDAP_OPT_SIZELIMIT` option. The following code fragment shows how to limit the search entry to 1,000:

```
ULONG errLdap;
int nMaxEntries = 1000;
errLdap = ldap_set_option( psLdap, LDAP_OPT_SIZELIMIT,
        ➥( void* )&nMaxEntries );
if( errLdap == LDAP_SUCCESS )
{
    // Searches will now return a maximum of 1000 entries
}
```

You can inspect the current value of the `LDAP_OPT_SIZELIMIT` option by calling `ldap_get_option()`.

> **NOTE**
>
> Using `ldap_set_option` to place a limit on the number of entries returned by `ldap_search()` affects all search operations that use that LDAP connection. If you want to limit the number of entries returned by a single search, you can use the `ldap_search_ext()` function instead.
>
> Also note that the number of entries returned by a search operation might be limited by an administrative limit on the server itself.

LDAP_OPT_TIMELIMIT

When you search a large directory, or if the domain controller you are using is heavily loaded, a large search operation might take quite a long time (more than several minutes). You can limit the amount of time a server will spend on search operations by using `ldap_set_option()` with the `LDAP_OPT_TIMELIMIT` option. Note that this is different than the amount of time the client will wait for a response, as you can specify with `ldap_search_st()` or `ldap_result()`.

The following code snippet shows how to set the timeout limit to 10 seconds:

```
ULONG errLdap;
int nMaxSeconds = 10;
errLdap = ldap_set_option( psLdap, LDAP_OPT_TIMELIMIT,
          ➥( void* )&nMaxSeconds );
if(errLdap == LDAP_SUCCESS)
{
    // Searches will now return after a maximum of 10 seconds
}
```

You can inspect the current value of the LDAP_OPT_TIMELIMIT option by calling
ldap_get_option().

> **NOTE**
>
> Using ldap_set_option to place a limit on the amount of time used by
> ldap_search() affects all search operations that use that LDAP connection. If
> you want to limit the amount of time used by a single search, you can use the
> ldap_search_ext() function instead.

LDAP_OPT_REFERRALS

When you are doing a search on an Active Directory domain controller, it is quite possible
that the server will refer your search to another server to handle the request. For instance,
imagine you have a domain named PARENT with a subordinate domain called CHILD. If you
initiate a search on a domain controller that contains PARENT, and you specify a scope of
LDAP_SCOPE_SUBTREE (refer to Chapter 21, "Advanced Searching with LDAP"), eventually
the PARENT domain controller will issue a referral to the domain controller called CHILD. By
default, LDAP will only search through the PARENT naming context and then return an
error. If you want the LDAP client to "chase" (connect and bind to the referred-to domain
controller) the referrals to the other's domain controller, you should set the
LDAP_OPT_REFERRALS option to on, as shown in the following code snippet:

```
ULONG errLdap;
errLdap = ldap_set_option( psLdap, LDAP_OPT_REFERRALS, LDAP_OPT_ON );
if( errLdap == LDAP_SUCCESS )
{
    // Searches will now automatically chase referrals
}
```

There are two types of referrals that Active Directory domain controllers can return:
subordinate referrals and external referrals. Table 28.3 describes the differences between
these two referral methods.

28

EXTENDING LDAP WITH OPTIONS AND CONTROLS

TABLE 28.3 SUBORDINATE AND EXTERNAL REFERRALS

Referral Method	Description
Subordinate referrals	These referrals occur when the domain controller you are searching has the data you are searching for, but because you specified LDAP_SCOPE_SUBTREE, the search operation has to be referred to other domain controllers that handle the subordinate naming contexts.
External referrals	These referrals occur when the data you are searching for doesn't exist in the current naming context, and the search must be started on some other domain controller, or possibly a non–Active Directory server.

Chapter 23, "Processing LDAP Referrals," discusses referrals in more detail.

You can direct the Microsoft LDAP client to chase either subordinate referrals, external referrals, or both. WINLDAP.H contains the constants LDAP_CHASE_SUBORDINATE_REFERRALS and LDAP_CHASE_EXTERNAL_REFERRALS that can be passed to ldap_set_option to control the chasing of referrals. You can OR these two constants together to chase all referrals. This is equivalent to using LDAP_OPT_ON, as in the previous example.

The following code fragment directs LDAP to chase only subordinate referrals:

```
ULONG errLdap;
ULONG ulOptions = LDAP_CHASE_SUBORDINATE_REFERRALS;
errLdap = ldap_set_option( psLdap, LDAP_OPT_REFERRALS, &ulOptions );
if( errLdap == LDAP_SUCCESS )
{
    // Searches will now automatically chase subordinate referrals only
}
```

LDAP_OPT_RESTART

It is possible that some network or operating system event such as a signal will interrupt the transmission of an LDAP request or the receipt of an LDAP response from the domain controller. If you set the LDAP_OPT_RESTART option on, the LDAP client will automatically restart any operation that was interrupted by the signal. This is a Boolean option, so you can use LDAP_OPT_ON or LDAP_OPT_OFF as the value to ldap_set_option(). The following code fragment sets this option on:

```
ULONG errLdap;
errLdap = ldap_set_option( psLdap, LDAP_OPT_RESTART, LDAP_OPT_ON );
if( errLdap == LDAP_SUCCESS )
{
    // Interrupted options will be retried
}
```

LDAP_OPT_PROTOCOL_VERSION and LDAP_OPT_VERSION

Even though Active Directory domain controllers are LDAPv3 compliant, the Microsoft LDAP API uses the LDAPv2 protocol by default. (This behavior is defined by RFC 2251.) If you need to use LDAPv3 features, such as server-side sorting or referrals, you must direct the client to use the LDAPv3 protocol by calling `ldap_set_option` and setting the `LDAP_OPT_PROTOCOL_VERSION` to `LDAP_VERSION3`. Most of the sample programs in this book set this option. The following code fragment shows how to set LDAP to `LDAP_VERSION3`:

> **NOTE**
>
> You must use the `ldap_set_option` function to set the protocol version to `LDAP_VERSION3` before you issue any LDAPv3-specific operations on an LDAP connection.

```
int nVersion = LDAP_VERSION3;
ULONG errLdap;
errLdap = ldap_set_option( psLdap, LDAP_OPT_PROTOCOL_VERSION,
        ➡( void* )&nVersion );
if( errLdap == LDAP_SUCCESS )
{
    // Client is now using LDAPv3 protocol
}
```

LDAP_OPT_HOST_NAME

Sometimes it's useful to know the DNS host name of the LDAP server you are currently connected to. For instance, if you specify a NULL server name in `ldap_init()`, the LDAP client will find the "best" domain controller to connect to, but it won't tell you which domain controller it is. The easiest way to find this information is to use the `ldap_get_option()` function with the option value set to `LDAP_OPT_HOST_NAME`. The data parameter is the address of a pointer to be set. The following code fragment shows how to get the DNS host name:

```
char* pszHostName = NULL;
ULONG errLdap;
errLdap = ldap_get_option( psLdap, LDAP_OPT_HOST_NAME,
        ➡( void* )&pszHostName );

if( errLdap == LDAP_SUCCESS )
{
    // pszHostName points to the LDAP server's DNS name
}
```

> **CAUTION**
>
> The pointer you get from calling `ldap_get_option()` with the
> `LDAP_OPT_HOST_NAME` option value points to a string inside the LDAP structure.
> You must *not* free this pointer with `ldap_memfree()` or any other function.
> Doing so would likely cause a GPF.

LDAP_OPT_ERROR_NUMBER

You can retrieve the last error code returned on a particular LDAP connection by calling `ldap_get_option` with the `LDAP_OPT_ERROR_NUMBER` option value. The following code shows how:

```
ULONG uLastError = 0;
ULONG errLdap;
errLdap = ldap_get_option( psLdap, LDAP_OPT_ERROR_NUMBER,
        ➡(void*)&uLastError );
if( errLdap == LDAP_SUCCESS )
{
    // uLastError has the last error encountered on this LDAP connection
}
```

> **CAUTION**
>
> If you want to get the error code for the last completed LDAP operation, use
> `LdapGetLastError()` instead of `ldap_get_option()`. Getting the error code
> from the LDAP structure is not thread-safe, and you could potentially get the
> error code from the action of some other thread.

LDAP_OPT_ERROR_STRING

You can get an error message string for the most recently encountered error on
an LDAP connection by calling `ldap_get_option()` with the option parameter set to
`LDAP_OPT_ERROR_STRING`. The following code fragment shows how to make this call:

```
char* pszErrorMsg = NULL;
ULONG errLdap;
errLdap = ldap_get_option( psLdap, LDAP_OPT_ERROR_STRING, ( void* )
        ➡&pszErrorMsg );
if( errLdap == LDAP_SUCCESS )
{
    // pszErrorMsg points to the message for the last error
}
```

> **CAUTION**
>
> The pointer you get from calling `ldap_get_option()` with the `LDAP_OPT_ERROR_STRING` option value points to a static string inside the LDAP client. You must *not* free this pointer with `ldap_memfree()` or any other function. Doing so would likely cause a GPF.

The preceding LDAP options are all defined by the current draft standard C API for LDAP. The next section describes some of the options that Microsoft supplies as part of the LDAP client software. Use these options with caution if you expect to port your LDAP program to use other LDAP client libraries or servers.

Microsoft-Specific LDAP Options

The following LDAP option constants are defined in WINLDAP.H, but do not appear in the current draft "C" API standard. They are Microsoft specific, and might not exist in other vendors' LDAP implementations.

LDAP_OPT_SSL

You can specify that the LDAP client establishes a secure connection with the domain controller via Secure Sockets Layer (SSL) by calling `ldap_set_option` with the `LDAP_OPT_SSL` option value. This is equivalent to creating a session with `ldap_sslinit()`.

`LDAP_OPT_SSL` is a Boolean option, so you can use `LDAP_OPT_ON` or `LDAP_OPT_OFF` as a value passed to the `ldap_set_option` as shown in the following code fragment:

```
ULONG errLdap;
errLdap = ldap_set_option( psLdap, LDAP_OPT_SSL, LDAP_OPT_ON );
if( errLdap == LDAP_SUCCESS )
{
    // Make first LDAP call like ldap_bind_s() to create connection
    // over SSL
}
```

> **NOTE**
>
> You must set the SSL option on the session before you make any LDAP functions calls using that session. After the TCP connection is established, changing the SSL option will have no effect.

28

EXTENDING LDAP
WITH OPTIONS
AND CONTROLS

LDAP_OPT_REFERRAL_HOP_LIMIT

If you have enabled any of the "chase referral" options, you can specify a limit to the number of referrals in a single operation that the client will process. You do this by calling ldap_set_option() with the LDAP_OPT_REFERRAL_HOP_LIMIT option value. The following code fragment shows how to set the hop limit to 2:

```
int nHopLimit = 2;
ULONG errLdap;
errLdap = ldap_set_option( psLdap, LDAP_OPT_REFERRAL_HOP_LIMIT, ( void* )
        ➥&nHopLimit );
if( errLdap == LDAP_SUCCESS )
{
    // Client will chase only two referrals in an operation
}
```

LDAP_OPT_PING_KEEP_ALIVE, LDAP_OPT_PING_WAIT_TIME, and LDAP_OPT_PING_LIMIT

For the entire time that you keep an LDAP connection open (you don't call ldap_unbind()), the LDAP client library keeps the connection alive by periodically sending ICMP ping messages to the domain controller. The client library will close the TCP connection if the domain controller fails to respond to the ping messages in an appropriate amount of time.

The LDAP_OPT_PING_KEEP_ALIVE option lets you specify the number of seconds the LDAP connection must be idle before the client will send a ping message. By default, this value is 120 seconds. The minimum value is 5 seconds.

The LDAP_OPT_PING_WAIT_TIME option specifies how long the client will wait for a response to a ping. It is an integer number of milliseconds, and by default is set to 2000 (which is equal to two seconds). You can set the value to anything between 10 and 60000 (one minute).

The LDAP_OPT_PING_LIMIT is the number of unanswered pings the client will accept before it closes the connection. The default value is 4. You can set the value to any integer.

The following code fragment shows how to set the LDAP_OPT_PING_KEEP_ALIVE option; you can set LDAP_OPT_PING_WAIT_TIME and LDAP_OPT_PING_LIMIT in a similar fashion.

```
int nPingSeconds = 30;
ULONG errLdap;
errLdap = ldap_set_option( psLdap, LDAP_OPT_PING_KEEP_ALIVE,
        ➥( void* )&nPingSeconds );
if(errLdap == LDAP_SUCCESS)
{
    // ping messages will start after 30 seconds of idle time
}
```

LDAP_OPT_DNSDOMAIN_NAME

If you want to know the DNS domain name for the domain controller you are currently connected to, you can call `ldap_get_option` with the `LDAP_OPT_DNSDOMAIN_NAME` option value. The following code fragment shows how to retrieve the DNS domain name:

```
char* pszDomainName = NULL;
ULONG errLdap;
errLdap = ldap_get_option( psLdap, LDAP_OPT_GETDSNAME_FLAGS, ( void* )
        ➥&pszDomainName );

if( errLdap == LDAP_SUCCESS )
{
    // pszDomainName points to the domain name of the current
    // domain controller
}
```

> **CAUTION**
>
> The pointer you get from calling `ldap_get_option()` with the `LDAP_OPT_DNSDOMAIN_NAME` option value points to a string inside the LDAP structure. You must *not* free this pointer with `ldap_memfree()` or any other function. Doing so would likely cause your program to GPF.

LDAP_OPT_GETDSNAME_FLAGS

You can easily find out some of the characteristics of the domain controller you are connected to by calling `ldap_get_option` with the `LDAP_OPT_GETDSNAME_FLAGS` option value. The returned value is a bit mask identical to that returned by `DsGetDCName()` (see Chapter 18, "Connecting to Active Directory with LDAP," for more details on `DsGetDCName()`). Here is a code fragment that shows how to get the characteristics of the domain:

```
ULONG uFlags = 0;
ULONG errLdap;
errLdap = ldap_get_option( psLdap, LDAP_OPT_GETDSNAME_FLAGS,
        ➥( void* )&uFlags);
if( errLdap == LDAP_SUCCESS )
{
    // uFlags contains the option flags from DsGetDCName()
    if( uFlags & DS_GC_FLAG )
    {
        // The current DC is a global catalog
    }
}
```

LDAP_OPT_PROMPT_CREDENTIALS

If you are using ldap_bind() with the DPA or NTLM authentication mechanism, you can direct the LDAP client to display a dialog box to prompt for a username, domain, and password if they have not already been established.

This is a Boolean option, so you can use the LDAP_OPT_ON and the LDAP_OPT_OFF constant value as the parameter to ldap_set_option, as shown in the following code:

```
ULONG errLdap;
errLdap = ldap_set_option( psLdap, LDAP_OPT_PROMPT_CREDENTIALS,
          ➥LDAP_OPT_ON );
if( errLdap == LDAP_SUCCESS )
{
    // Client will prompt for credentials upon initial connection
}
```

LDAP_OPT_AUTO_RECONNECT

The Microsoft LDAP client will automatically attempt to reconnect to a domain controller if the TCP link is dropped. The LDAP_OPT_AUTO_RECONNECT option lets you turn this facility on and off.

Refer to the descriptions of the LDAP_OPT_PING_KEEP_ALIVE, LDAP_OPT_PING_WAIT_TIME, and LDAP_OPT_PING_LIMIT options for information on how LDAP determines that a connection has been dropped.

This is a Boolean option, so you can use LDAP_OPT_ON and LDAP_OPT_OFF constants, as the following code fragment shows:

```
ULONG errLdap;
errLdap = ldap_set_option( psLdap, LDAP_OPT_AUTO_RECONNECT, LDAP_OPT_ON );
if( errLdap == LDAP_SUCCESS )
{
    // Client will automatically reconnect dropped TCP connections
}
```

LDAP_OPT_SSPI_FLAGS

When you authenticate with a domain controller using any mechanism other than LDAP_AUTH_SIMPLE, the LDAP client calls the Windows 2000 function InitializeSecurity Context(). You can specify the flags you want LDAP to pass to InitializeSecurityContext() by calling ldap_set_option() with the LDAP_OPT_SSPI_FLAGS option value. The following code fragment shows how to set flags:

```
ULONG uOptions = REPLAY_DETECT | SEQUENCE_DETECT | MUTUAL_AUTH;
ULONG errLdap;
errLdap = ldap_set_option( psLdap, LDAP_OPT_SSPI_FLAGS,
➥(void*)&uOptions );
if( errLdap == LDAP_SUCCESS )
{
    // ldap_bind() will call InitializeSecurityContext()
    // with the above flags
}
```

This section covered all the options you can adjust on an LDAP session. The next section describes a way you can alter the behavior of individual LDAP function calls by using LDAP controls.

LDAP Controls

LDAP controls are another mechanism that allows you to take advantage of the extended features of an LDAP server. As opposed to LDAP options, which tend to be vendor-specific and must be known at compile time, LDAP controls can easily be checked at run time. LDAP options also affect the entire LDAP session; LDAP controls can be used to alter the behavior of a single API call.

LDAP controls fall into two categories: *server controls,* which can be sent to the server with any request and that alter the behavior of the LDAP server, and *client controls,* which modify the behavior of the LDAP client.

Every LDAP control is uniquely identified by an object ID. Each directory vendor assigns a unique OID to each control it develops, so there is little danger of specifying one control that works with one directory server and having it do something completely different on a different vendor's server. All LDAPv3-compliant directories list the OIDs of controls they support in the `supportedControls` attribute of the `rootDSE`. You specify this object ID when you enable the control.

When you specify a control, you also pass information to LDAP along with the control. For instance, if you specify the server-side sorting control with a search operation, the information you pass along includes the sort keys you want the server to use. Unfortunately, Microsoft hasn't supplied these BER-encoding functions defined in the draft standard LDAP C API, so you have to encode these structures by hand according to the BER encoding rules defined in ITU Recommendation X.690, "Abstract Syntax Notation One (ASN.1): Encoding Rules: Specification of Basic Encoding Rules (BER), Canonical Encoding Rules (CER), and Distinguished Encoding Rules (DER)."

Microsoft has implemented 13 server-side controls.

The paged search and sorted search controls are described in Chapter 21.

This section lists the controls and what data they require. Refer to the earlier chapters on the specific LDAP functions such as `ldap_search_ext()` to see how to pass these controls to the server.

Paged Search

The Paged Search control provides a way to obtain search results from the server a few entries at a time, instead of all at once. It is the only way to get complete search results from a domain controller with administrative limits set to limit the number of entries returned in a single search. The Paged Search control is defined by an Internet Draft `draft-ietf-asid-ldapv3-simplepaged-03.txt`; however, the Microsoft implementation does not completely implement the extension defined in the draft.

Microsoft has supplied special API functions for performing paged searches. See Chapter 21 for more information.

The OID for the Paged Search control is `1.2.840.113556.1.4.319`. The BER-encoded data you need to supply with the control is given by the following BNF notation. Note that you do not have to build the control yourself. The paged search API functions take care of this for you.

```
realSearchControlValue ::= SEQUENCE {
      size              INTEGER (0..maxInt),
                                -- requested page size from client
                                -- result set size estimate from server
      cookie            OCTET STRING
}
```

Sorted Search

The Sorted Search control is also defined by an Internet Draft, which can be found on the IETF Web site under the name `draft-ietf-ldapext-sorting-02.txt`. The Microsoft implementation is, again, an incomplete implementation of this draft.

Microsoft has supplied special API functions for performing sorted searches. See Chapter 21 for more information on how to use these functions.

The OID for the sorted search request is `1.2.840.113556.1.4.474`. Consult the draft standard for the structure of the control data.

Get Security Descriptor

The Get Security Descriptor control allows you to retrieve the nTSecurityDescriptor attribute during a search. Active Directory normally does not return this attribute, even if you explicitly request it. See Chapter 22, "Extending LDAP Searches," for an example of how to use this control.

The OID for the Get Security Descriptor control is 1.2.840.113556.1.4.801. The data is a set of flags passed as an integer indicating which portions of the security descriptor to return.

```
getSDFlagsValue = SEQUENCE {
        Flags          INTEGER
}
```

The value of Flags is the result of ORing one or more of the following flags listed in Table 28.4. These values are defined in the winnt.h header file.

TABLE 28.4 FLAGS TO USE WITH THE GET SECURITY DESCRIPTOR CONTROL

Name	Value	Description
OWNER_SECURITY_INFORMATION	0x01	Retrieves the owner security information from the security descriptor.
GROUP_SECURITY_INFORMATION	0x02	Retrieves the group security information from the security descriptor.
DACL_SECURITY_INFORMATION	0x04	Retrieves the discretionary access control list from the security descriptor.
SACL_SECURITY_INFORMATION	0x08	Retrieves the system access control list from the security descriptor.

Change Notification (Persistent Search)

The Change Notification control provides a way for your program to receive notifications from the server whenever a specific directory object is changed. You use this control in conjunction with an asynchronous extended search operation. Chapter 22 describes how to use this control.

The OID for this control is 1.2.840.113556.1.4.528. It requires no additional encoded data.

Show Deleted Objects

The Show Deleted Objects control lets you retrieve objects that have been deleted but not yet physically removed from the directory. These objects, called *tombstones,* are purged automatically by Active Directory after about 60 days. This control is used with an extended LDAP search. See Chapter 22 for an example of how to use this control.

The OID for the Show Deleted Objects control is 1.2.840.113556.1.4.417. It requires no additional data.

Lazy Commit

Normally, Active Directory will flush its database cache to disk after every update operation. This helps to ensure the integrity of the database in the case of a server failure. However, it also slows down directory updates. Normally, this isn't a problem, but if you are importing a lot of data into the directory or modifying a large number of objects, it can really hurt performance. If you specify the Lazy Commit control with your update operation, Active Directory defers flushing the cache. See Chapter 24, "Modifying Active Directory Objects with LDAP," or Chapter 25, "Adding Active Directory Objects with LDAP," for more examples of how to use this control.

The OID for the Lazy Commit is 1.2.840.113556.1.4.619. It requires no additional data.

DirSync Control

The DirSync Control provides a way for a program to search Active Directory for those objects (including deleted and renamed objects) that have been changed since a specific point in time. This is the control to use if you want to synchronize another directory or database with an Active Directory replica.

Generally, you use the DirSync Control with a subtree search, starting at the root of a naming context.

The OID for the DirSync control is 1.2.840.113556.1.4.841. The DirSync control requires additional BER-encoded data of the following form:

```
DirSyncData = SEQUENCE {
        Flags INTEGER,
        Size INTEGER,
        Cookie OCTET STRING
}
```

I've been unable to find out how the Flags value is used. The Size value indicates how many entries to return for each search operation, and the Cookie value is used to maintain the search state between DirSync searches. You initially set the `Cookie` to an empty octet string, and then retrieve the value returned by the server by using `ldap_parse_result()`. You must pass the returned `Cookie` value back to the server on the next DirSync search.

Return Extended DN

The Return Extended DN control causes the server to return the `objectGUID` and `objectSID` attributes along with each distinguished name when retrieving the results of a search. These values are concatenated together, as in the following example:

```
<GUID=676e2ef75f0ad311995200609779521e>;<SID=0104045e6975b97554>;DC
=megacorp,DC=com
```

You do not have to specify the `objectGUID` and `objectSID` attributes in your search attribute list; Active Directory will return them as part of the distinguished name of each entry.

The OID for the Return Extended DN is `1.2.840.113556.1.4.529`, and it requires no additional data.

Tree Delete

The Tree Delete control lets you delete an object from the directory even if it has subordinate objects (assuming you have appropriate access rights). You specify this control with an extended delete operation by using `ldap_delete_ext()` or `ldap_delete_ext_s()`. Refer to Chapter 26, "Deleting Active Directory Objects with LDAP," for an example of using this control.

The OID for the control is `1.2.840.113556.1.4.805`, and it requires no additional data.

Cross Domain Move

The Cross Domain Move control lets you extend the `ldap_rename_ext()` and `ldap_rename_ext_s()` functions so that they will move an object from one domain to another. See Chapter 25 for an example of using this control.

The OID for the Cross Domain Move control is `1.2.840.113556.1.4.521`. It requires the following additional BER-encoded data:

```
CrossDomainMoveData = SEQUENCE {
        Name OCTET STRING
}
```

`Name` is an octet string containing the distinguished name of the domain to which to move the object.

28

EXTENDING LDAP WITH OPTIONS AND CONTROLS

Verify Server Name

The Verify Server Name control lets you change the global catalog server Active Directory uses to validate distinguished names that are stored as references in objects. Normally, Active Directory verifies each distinguished name through a global catalog. This control lets you specify which global catalog.

The OID for the Verify Server Name control is 1.2.840.113556.1.4.1338. It requires additional BER-encoded data of the following form:

```
VerifyServerData = SEQUENCE {
        Flags    INTEGER,
        ServerName OCTET STRING
}
```

The Flags value indicates which kinds of validations should be enabled. I haven't found out what the appropriate values for this value are. The ServerName value contains the distinguished name (in Unicode) of the server to which to refer the validations.

Search with Local Scope

The Search with Local Scope control lets you disable referral generation by the server during a search, as distinct from disabling referral chasing by the client. This can substantially speed up some searches. Specifying this control will limit the scope of a search to the naming context containing the base of the search operation.

The OID for the Search with Local Scope control is 1.2.840.113556.1.4.1339. It requires no additional data.

Permissive Modify

The Permissive Modify control disables Active Directory's normal process of validating all distinguished name–valued attributes against a global catalog. This can speed up mass updates substantially. You specify this control when you are doing an add or a modify operation.

The OID for the Permissive Modify control is 1.2.840.113556.1.4.1413. It does not require any additional data.

CHAPTER 29

LDAP Error-Handling Functions

Error processing is one of the aspects of an API that tends to be left out of the design process, with the result that there are several different ways to detect and handle error conditions through the API. LDAP is no exception in this regard.

This chapter describes how to retrieve error codes resulting from LDAP API function calls and also how to translate those error codes into meaningful error messages.

Handling LDAP Errors

Unlike ADSI, the LDAP APIs don't return error or status information to your application in a consistent way. This is probably due to LDAP's UNIX and C heritage, where explicit error handling is at best an afterthought and at worst nonexistent.

There are three primary ways of retrieving error information from an LDAP function call. Many LDAP functions return an error value. For instance, ldap_bind_s() returns an unsigned long that contains the error code or zero if the call was successful. But many other functions, such as ldap_search(), return a handle or –1 if there is an error, and the problem becomes how to determine what the real error code is.

The traditional method is to inspect the ld_errno member of the LDAP structure for the session on which you made the API call. Although this seems simple and harmless, *don't do it*. The IETF is in the process of deprecating this scheme for retrieving error information.

In any case, it is not thread-safe because a thread can change the value of ld_errno between the time your program calls the LDAP API call and the time you check its value.

The best way to retrieve an error is to call the Microsoft-specific function LdapGetLastError(). This function retrieves the error code from the last LDAP API call from thread-local storage, which makes the call thread-safe. The following code snippet shows how this is done.

```
LDAP* pLdap  = ldap_init( "engserver.megacorp.com", LDAP_PORT );
if( pLdap == NULL )
{
    ULONG uErr = LdapGetLastError();
    // handle error here
}
else
{
    // handle success here
}
```

LDAP Error Codes

LDAP errors are represented by a single integer. The enumeration LDAP_RETCODE, defined in winldap.h, contains the symbolic definitions of all LDAP errors. Table 29.1 contains these definitions and their descriptions.

TABLE 29.1   LDAP ERROR CODES

LDAP Error Constant	*Value (Hex)*	*Description*
LDAP_SUCCESS	0x00	The operation succeeded.
LDAP_OPERATIONS_ERROR	0x01	An unspecified error occurred on the server processing an LDAP request.
LDAP_PROTOCOL_ERROR	0x02	The server received a request packet that was incorrectly formatted or out of sequence.
LDAP_TIMELIMIT_EXCEEDED	0x03	The time limit on the operation was exceeded. This is distinct from a time-out error detected by the client when the server does not respond in time.
LDAP_SIZELIMIT_EXCEEDED	0x04	The number of entries to return from a search exceeded either the administrative limit or the request limit.

LDAP Error Constant	Value (Hex)	Description
LDAP_COMPARE_FALSE	0x05	An LDAP comparison function (such as ldap_compare()) evaluated to FALSE.
LDAP_COMPARE_TRUE	0x06	An LDAP comparison function (such as ldap_compare()) evaluated to TRUE.
LDAP_AUTH_METHOD_NOT_SUPPORTED	0x07	The authentication method requested in a bind operation (such as ldap_bind()) is not supported by the server. This could occur if you use a non-Microsoft LDAP client to communicate with Active Directory.
LDAP_STRONG_AUTH_REQUIRED	0x08	The server requires a string authentication method other than a simple password.
LDAP_REFERRAL_V2	0x09	The search results contain LDAP v2 referrals or a partial result set.
LDAP_REFERRAL	0x0a	The requested operation must be handled by another server that has a copy of the appropriate naming context.
LDAP_ADMIN_LIMIT_EXCEEDED	0x0b	An administrative limit was exceeded. For instance, a search operation took longer than the maximum time allowed for the server.
LDAP_UNAVAILABLE_CRIT_EXTENSION	0x0c	The client requested an LDAP extension and indicated it was critical, but the server does not support the extension.
LDAP_CONFIDENTIALITY_REQUIRED	0x0d	The operation requires some level of encryption to perform.
LDAP_SASL_BIND_IN_PROGRESS	0x0e	A bind operation was requested while a SASL bind was already in progress with the client.
LDAP_NO_SUCH_ATTRIBUTE	0x10	The client attempted to modify or delete an attribute of an entry that does not exist.
LDAP_UNDEFINED_TYPE	0x11	Undefined type.

continues

29

LDAP ERROR-HANDLING FUNCTIONS

TABLE 29.1   CONTINUED

LDAP Error Constant	Value (Hex)	Description
LDAP_INAPPROPRIATE_MATCHING	0x12	The matching rule supplied is inappropriate for the search or is inappropriate for the attribute.
LDAP_CONSTRAINT_VIOLATION	0x13	The client requested an operation that would violate a semantic constraint on the directory. A common cause of this is an inappropriate change to the schema—for instance, supplying a duplicate OID when adding a new class.
LDAP_ATTRIBUTE_OR_VALUE_EXISTS	0x14	The client attempted to add an attribute or value that already exists.
LDAP_INVALID_SYNTAX	0x15	The syntax of the search filter is invalid.
LDAP_NO_SUCH_OBJECT	0x20	The client attempted to delete or modify an entry in the directory that does not exist.
LDAP_ALIAS_PROBLEM	0x21	The server encountered an error processing an alias.
LDAP_INVALID_DN_SYNTAX	0x22	The format of the distinguished name specified in the request is invalid.
LDAP_IS_LEAF	0x23	The entry specified in the function is a leaf entry in the directory tree.
LDAP_ALIAS_DEREF_PROBLEM	0x24	The server encountered an error dereferencing an alias. For instance, the target entry does not exist.
LDAP_INAPPROPRIATE_AUTH	0x30	The level of authentication is insufficient for the operation.
LDAP_INVALID_CREDENTIALS	0x31	The credentials supplied in the bind request are invalid—for instance, an invalid password.
LDAP_INSUFFICIENT_RIGHTS	0x32	You have insufficient access rights to perform the operation.
LDAP_BUSY	0x33	The server is too busy to service your request. Try again later.

LDAP Error Constant	Value (Hex)	Description
LDAP_UNAVAILABLE	0x34	The directory service is temporarily unavailable. Try again later.
LDAP_UNWILLING_TO_PERFORM	0x35	The server will not perform the operation due to an administrative or policy constraint—for instance, if you attempt to modify the schema when schema modifications have not been enabled or you are not connected to the schema master.
LDAP_LOOP_DETECT	0x36	In the process of chasing referrals, the client was referred back to a server it had been referred from.
LDAP_NAMING_VIOLATION	0x40	The client specified an incorrect distinguished name for an object.
LDAP_OBJECT_CLASS_VIOLATION	0x41	The operation violates the semantic rules defined by the class definition.
LDAP_NOT_ALLOWED_ON_NONLEAF	0x42	The requested operation may be performed only on a leaf (noncontainer) object.
LDAP_NOT_ALLOWED_ON_RDN	0x43	The operation is not allowed on the relative distinguished name attribute.
LDAP_ALREADY_EXISTS	0x44	The client tried to add an object that already existed.
LDAP_NO_OBJECT_CLASS_MODS	0x45	The client attempted to modify the class of an object by changing its objectClass attribute.
LDAP_RESULTS_TOO_LARGE	0x46	The result set of a search operation is too large for the server to process.
LDAP_AFFECTS_MULTIPLE_DSAS	0x47	The requested operation would affect multiple DSAs—for instance, performing a subtree delete where the subtree contains a subordinate reference to another naming context.
LDAP_OTHER	0x50	Some other LDAP error occurred.
LDAP_SERVER_DOWN	0x51	The LDAP server is down.

29

LDAP ERROR-
HANDLING
FUNCTIONS

continues

TABLE 29.1   CONTINUED

LDAP Error Constant	Value (Hex)	Description
LDAP_LOCAL_ERROR	0x52	Some other unspecified error occurred on the client.
LDAP_ENCODING_ERROR	0x53	An error occurred while encoding an LDAP request into ASN.1.
LDAP_DECODING_ERROR	0x54	The ASN.1-encoded data received from the server was invalid.
LDAP_TIMEOUT	0x55	The server failed to respond to the client within the time specified.
LDAP_AUTH_UNKNOWN	0x56	An unknown authentication mechanism was specified in a bind request.
LDAP_FILTER_ERROR	0x57	The search filter was erroneous in some way.
LDAP_USER_CANCELLED	0x58	The user cancelled the operation.
LDAP_PARAM_ERROR	0x59	One of the parameters specified to the function was incorrect. For instance, passing a NULL pointer to a LDAP API function that does not expect it can generate this error.
LDAP_NO_MEMORY	0x5a	The client tried to allocate memory and failed.
LDAP_CONNECT_ERROR	0x5b	The client attempted to establish a TCP connection to the server and failed.
LDAP_NOT_SUPPORTED	0x5c	The requested operation is not supported by this version of the LDAP protocol.
LDAP_CONTROL_NOT_FOUND	0x5d	The data received from the server indicated there was an LDAP control present, but none was found in the data.
LDAP_NO_RESULTS_RETURNED	0x5e	A response was received from the server, but it contained no results.
LDAP_MORE_RESULTS_TO_RETURN	0x5f	There are more results for the client to retrieve.
LDAP_CLIENT_LOOP	0x60	The client detected a loop while processing referrals.
LDAP_REFERRAL_LIMIT_EXCEEDED	0x61	The number of referrals chased by the client exceeded the limit.

Getting String Descriptions of LDAP Errors

Generally, you want to present a descriptive error message to your users when an error occurs, instead of a number such as 5. LDAP provides a way to translate LDAP error messages to strings with the `ldap_err2string()` function. `ldap_err2string()` accepts an LDAP error code as its only parameter, and returns a `const` pointer to a static string.

Note that many LDAP client libraries provide the `ldap_perror()` function to return the textual representation of the current error in the LDAP session structure. Microsoft includes this function for compatibility, but it doesn't do anything. The IETF is deprecating `ldap_perror()` in LDAPv3 anyway, so there's no good reason to use it in your code.

```
PCHAR ldap_err2string( ULONG uLdapError )
```

    `uLdapError` is an LDAP error return code.

Returns: A pointer to a static, NUL-terminated string containing the error message corresponding to the specified LDAP error code.

```
LDAP* pLdap = ldap_init( "engserver.megacorp.com", LDAP_PORT )
if( pLdap == NULL )
{
    ULONG uLdapErr = LdapGetLastError();
    const char* pszErrorMsg = ldap_err2string( uLdapErr );
    printf( "Error %x occurred: %s\n", uLdapErr, pszErrorMsg );
}
```

There is another way you can get a string message corresponding to an LDAP error code. You can translate the LDAP error return to an equivalent Win32 error code, and use the Win32 `FormatMessage()` function to get a message for the Win32 error code. The following section describes how to translate an LDAP error return to a Win32 error code.

Converting LDAP Errors to Win32 Errors

If your program already has some built-in error handling infrastructure that uses Win32 error codes, you can use the `LdapMapErrorToWin32()` function to translate LDAP error return codes to almost-equivalent Win32 error codes.

`LdapMapErrorToWin32()` accepts the LDAP error number as a parameter and returns the appropriate Win32 error code. The following code snippet shows how to use `LdapMapErrorToWin32()`.

```
DWORD LdapMapErrorToWin32( ULONG uLdapError )
```

    `uLdapError` is an LDAP error return code.

Returns: The Win32 error code that is closest to the same meaning as the specified LDAP error return code.

```
LDAPMessage* pMsg;

LONG uErr = ldap_search( pLdap, pszDomainNamingContext,
            ➡LDAP_SCOPE_ONELEVEL, "objectClass=*", NULL, false, &pMsg );
if( uErr == -1 )
{
    DWORD dwWin32Err = LdapMapErrorToWin32( uErr );
    if( dwWin32Error != 0 )
    {
        // call Win32 error handler here
    }
}
```

Appendixes

PART

V

IN THIS PART

APPENDIX A

ADSI Interfaces for Active Directory

IADs Interface

The IADs interface provides basic object and attribute services for any directory object. Chapter 12, "Basic Active Directory ADSI Interfaces," describes the IADs interface.

```
HRESULT get_Name(BSTR* retval)

HRESULT get_Class(BSTR* retval)

HRESULT get_GUID(BSTR* retval)

HRESULT get_ADsPath(BSTR* retval)

HRESULT get_Parent(BSTR* retval)

HRESULT get_Schema(BSTR* retval)

HRESULT GetInfo(void)

HRESULT SetInfo(void)

HRESULT Get(BSTR bstrName, VARIANT* pvProp)

HRESULT Put(BSTR bstrName, VARIANT vProp)

HRESULT GetEx(BSTR bstrName, VARIANT* pvProp)

HRESULT PutEx(long lnControlCode, BSTR bstrName, VARIANT vProp)

HRESULT GetInfoEx(VARIANT vProperties, long lnReserved)
```

IADsAccessControlEntry Interface

The IADsAccessControlEntry interface provides functions to manipulate an entry in an access control list. You retrieve an IADsAccessControlEntry interface pointer through the get_NewEnum() function of an IADsAccessControlList interface.

HRESULT get_AccessMask(long* retval)

HRESULT put_AccessMask(long lnAccessMask)

HRESULT get_AceType(long* retval)

HRESULT put_AceType(long lnAceType)

HRESULT get_AceFlags(long* retval)

HRESULT put_AceFlags(long lnAceFlags)

HRESULT get_Flags(long* retval)

HRESULT put_Flags(long lnFlags)

HRESULT get_ObjectType(BSTR* retval)

HRESULT put_ObjectType(BSTR bstrObjectType)

HRESULT get_InheritedObjectType(BSTR* retval)

HRESULT put_InheritedObjectType(BSTR bstrInheritedObjectType)

HRESULT get_Trustee(BSTR* retval)

HRESULT put_Trustee(BSTR bstrTrustee)

IADsAccessControlList Interface

The IADsAccessControlList interface provides functions for manipulating the discretionary access control list (DACL) or security access control list (SACL) of a security descriptor. You retrieve an IADsAccessControlList interface by calling get_DiscretionaryAcl() or get_SystemAcl() on an IADsSecurityDescriptor interface.

HRESULT get_AclRevision(long* retval)

HRESULT put_AclRevision(long lnAclRevision)

HRESULT get_AceCount(long* retval)

HRESULT put_AceCount(long lnAceCount)

HRESULT AddAce(IDispatch* pAccessControlEntry)

```
HRESULT RemoveAce(IDispatch* pAccessControlEntry)

HRESULT CopyAccessList(IDispatch * ppAccessControlList)

HRESULT get__NewEnum(IUnknown * retval)
```

IADsADSystemInfo Interface

The IADsADSystemInfo interface provides a way to get system information about a particular server or computer that the interface is created on. You must create an instance of the object using the following code:

```
IADsADSystemInfo* piInfo = NULL;
hr = CoCreateInstance(
    CLSID_ADSystemInfo,
    NULL,
    CLSCTX_INPROC_SERVER,
    IID_IADsADSystemInfo,
    (void**)&piInfo
);
HRESULT get_UserName(BSTR* retval)

HRESULT get_ComputerName(BSTR* retval)

HRESULT get_SiteName(BSTR* retval)

HRESULT get_DomainShortName(BSTR* retval)

HRESULT get_DomainDNSName(BSTR* retval)

HRESULT get_ForestDNSName(BSTR* retval)

HRESULT get_PDCRoleOwner(BSTR* retval)

HRESULT get_SchemaRoleOwner(BSTR* retval)

HRESULT get_IsNativeMode(VARIANT_BOOL* retval)

HRESULT GetAnyDCName(BSTR* pszDCName)

HRESULT GetDCSiteName(BSTR szServer, BSTR* pszSiteName)

HRESULT RefreshSchemaCache(void)

HRESULT GetTrees(VARIANT* pvTrees)
```

IADsCaseIgnoreList Interface

The IADsCaseIgnoreList interface is not supported by the Active Directory LDAP provider.

```
HRESULT get_CaseIgnoreList(VARIANT* retval)

HRESULT put_CaseIgnoreList(VARIANT vCaseIgnoreList)
```

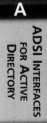

IADsClass Interface

The IADsClass interface provides access to class objects in the abstract schema of Active Directory. Chapter 15, "Accessing the Active Directory Schema with ADSI," describes the IADsClass interface.

```
HRESULT get_PrimaryInterface(BSTR* retval)

HRESULT get_CLSID(BSTR* retval)

HRESULT put_CLSID(BSTR bstrCLSID)

HRESULT get_OID(BSTR* retval)

HRESULT put_OID(BSTR bstrOID)

HRESULT get_Abstract(VARIANT_BOOL* retval)

HRESULT put_Abstract(VARIANT_BOOL fAbstract)

HRESULT get_Auxiliary(VARIANT_BOOL* retval)

HRESULT put_Auxiliary(VARIANT_BOOL fAuxiliary)

HRESULT get_MandatoryProperties(VARIANT* retval)

HRESULT put_MandatoryProperties(VARIANT vMandatoryProperties)

HRESULT get_OptionalProperties(VARIANT* retval)

HRESULT put_OptionalProperties(VARIANT vOptionalProperties)

HRESULT get_NamingProperties(VARIANT* retval)

HRESULT put_NamingProperties(VARIANT vNamingProperties)

HRESULT get_DerivedFrom(VARIANT* retval)

HRESULT put_DerivedFrom(VARIANT vDerivedFrom)

HRESULT get_AuxDerivedFrom(VARIANT* retval)

HRESULT put_AuxDerivedFrom(VARIANT vAuxDerivedFrom)

HRESULT get_PossibleSuperiors(VARIANT* retval)

HRESULT put_PossibleSuperiors(VARIANT vPossibleSuperiors)

HRESULT get_Containment(VARIANT* retval)

HRESULT put_Containment(VARIANT vContainment)

HRESULT get_Container(VARIANT_BOOL* retval)

HRESULT put_Container(VARIANT_BOOL fContainer)

HRESULT get_HelpFileName(BSTR* retval)

HRESULT put_HelpFileName(BSTR bstrHelpFileName)

HRESULT get_HelpFileContext(long* retval)
```

```
HRESULT put_HelpFileContext(long lnHelpFileContext)
```

```
HRESULT Qualifiers(IADsCollection * ppQualifiers)
```

IADsContainer Interface

The IADsContainer interface provides a way to enumerate the objects contained by an Active Directory object. Other ADSI interfaces return an IADsContainer interface pointer to iterate through elements of the objects they manage. Chapter 12 describes the IADsContainer interface.

```
HRESULT get_Count(long* retval)
```

```
HRESULT get__NewEnum(IUnknown* retval)
```

```
HRESULT get_Filter(VARIANT* pVar)
```

```
HRESULT put_Filter(VARIANT Var)
```

```
HRESULT get_Hints(VARIANT* pvFilter)
```

```
HRESULT put_Hints(VARIANT vHints)
```

```
HRESULT GetObject(BSTR ClassName, BSTR RelativeName, IDispatch* ppObject)
```

```
HRESULT Create(BSTR ClassName, BSTR RelativeName, IDispatch* ppObject)
```

```
HRESULT Delete(BSTR bstrClassName, BSTR bstrRelativeName)
```

```
HRESULT CopyHere(BSTR SourceName, BSTR NewName, IDispatch* ppObject)
```

```
HRESULT MoveHere(BSTR SourceName, BSTR NewName, IDispatch* ppObject)
```

IADsDeleteOps Interface

The IADsDeleteOps interface is supported by all Active Directory objects. It exports a single function that provides a simple way to delete an object or a subtree. Chapter 12 describes the IADsDeleteOps interface.

```
HRESULT DeleteObject(long lnFlags)
```

IADsDNWithBinary Interface

The IADsDNWithBinary interface provides a way to access the components of a value that has DN-with-binary syntax. IADsDNWithBinary is not supported by the current version of ADSI.

```
HRESULT get_BinaryValue(VARIANT* retval)
```

```
HRESULT put_BinaryValue(VARIANT vBinaryValue)
```

A

ADSI INTERFACES FOR ACTIVE DIRECTORY

```
HRESULT get_DNString(BSTR* retval)

HRESULT put_DNString(BSTR bstrDNString)
```

IADsDNWithString Interface

The IADsDNWithString interface provides a way to access the components of a value that has DN-with-string syntax. IADsDNWithString is not supported by the current version of ADSI.

```
HRESULT get_StringValue(BSTR* retval)

HRESULT put_StringValue(BSTR bstrStringValue)

HRESULT get_DNString(BSTR* retval)

HRESULT put_DNString(BSTR bstrDNString)
```

IADsGroup Interface

The IADsGroup interface provides access to the attributes of an Active Directory group object, including a simple way to get an interface pointer to the list of members of the group. Chapter 14, "Accessing Users, Groups, and Organizations with ADSI," describes the IADsGroup interface.

```
HRESULT get_Description(BSTR* retval)

HRESULT put_Description(BSTR bstrDescription)

HRESULT Members(IADsMembers * ppMembers)

HRESULT IsMember(BSTR bstrMember, VARIANT_BOOL* bMember)

HRESULT Add(BSTR bstrNewItem)

HRESULT Remove(BSTR bstrItemToBeRemoved)
```

IADsLargeInteger Interface

The IADsLargeInteger provides access to the high and low words of a large (64-bit) integer. The IADsLargeInteger interface is not supported by the current version of ADSI.

```
HRESULT get_HighPart(long* retval)

HRESULT put_HighPart(long lnHighPart)

HRESULT get_LowPart(long* retval)

HRESULT put_LowPart(long lnLowPart)
```

IADsLocality Interface

The IADsLocality interface provides access to the properties of a Locality container in Active Directory. Chapter 14 describes the IADsLocality interface.

HRESULT get_Description(BSTR* retval)

HRESULT put_Description(BSTR bstrDescription)

HRESULT get_LocalityName(BSTR* retval)

HRESULT put_LocalityName(BSTR bstrLocalityName)

HRESULT get_PostalAddress(BSTR* retval)

HRESULT put_PostalAddress(BSTR bstrPostalAddress)

HRESULT get_SeeAlso(VARIANT* retval)

HRESULT put_SeeAlso(VARIANT vSeeAlso)

IADsMembers Interface

The IADsMembers interface provides a way to enumerate the members of a group. You get an IADsMembers interface from an IADsGroup interface by using the IADsGroup::Members() function. Chapter 14 describes the IADsMembers interface.

HRESULT get_Count(long* plCount)

HRESULT get__NewEnum(IUnknown * ppEnumerator)

HRESULT get_Filter(VARIANT* pvFilter)

HRESULT put_Filter(VARIANT pvFilter)

IADsNameSpaces Interface

The IADsNameSpaces interface retrieves information about a specific ADSI namespace provider.

HRESULT get_DefaultContainer(BSTR* retval)

HRESULT put_DefaultContainer(BSTR bstrDefaultContainer)

IADsNameTranslate Interface

The IADsNameTranslate interface provides access to a name-translation mechanism that lets you translate names to and from LDAP distinguished names and Windows NT 4–style domain and object names.

A

ADSI INTERFACES
FOR ACTIVE
DIRECTORY

```
HRESULT put_ChaseReferral(long lnChaseReferral)

HRESULT Init(long lnSetType,BSTR bstrADsPath)

HRESULT InitEx(long lnSetType, BSTR bstrADsPath, BSTR bstrUserID,
➥BSTR bstrDomain, BSTR bstrPassword)

HRESULT Set(long lnSetType, BSTR bstrADsPath)

HRESULT Get(long lnFormatType, BSTR* pbstrADsPath)

HRESULT SetEx(long lnFormatType, VARIANT pvar)

HRESULT GetEx(long lnFormatType, VARIANT* pvar)
```

IADsO Interface

The IADsO interface provides access to the properties of a Organization container in Active Directory. Chapter 14 describes the IADsO interface.

```
HRESULT get_Description(BSTR* retval)

HRESULT put_Description(BSTR bstrDescription)

HRESULT get_LocalityName(BSTR* retval)

HRESULT put_LocalityName(BSTR bstrLocalityName)

HRESULT get_PostalAddress(BSTR* retval)

HRESULT put_PostalAddress(BSTR bstrPostalAddress)

HRESULT get_TelephoneNumber(BSTR* retval)

HRESULT put_TelephoneNumber(BSTR bstrTelephoneNumber)

HRESULT get_FaxNumber(BSTR* retval)

HRESULT put_FaxNumber(BSTR bstrFaxNumber)

HRESULT get_SeeAlso(VARIANT* retval)

HRESULT put_SeeAlso(VARIANT vSeeAlso)
```

IADsObjectOptions Interface

The IADsObjectOptions interface provides a way to get and set certain Active Directory LDAP provider options.

```
HRESULT GetOption(long lnOption, VARIANT* pvValue)

HRESULT SetOption(long lnOption, VARIANT vValue)
```

IADsOpenDSObject Interface

The IADsOpenDSObject interface provides a way to get a new interface pointer to an Active Directory object. Chapter 11, "ADSI Fundamentals," describes the IADsOpenDSObject interface.

```
HRESULT OpenDSObject(BSTR lpszDNName, BSTR lpszUserName,
➥BSTR lpszPassword, long lnReserved, IDispatch * ppOleDsObj)
```

IADsOU Interface

The IADsOU interface provides access to the properties of an Organizational Unit container in Active Directory.

```
HRESULT get_Description(BSTR* retval)
```

```
HRESULT put_Description(BSTR bstrDescription)
```

```
HRESULT get_LocalityName(BSTR* retval)
```

```
HRESULT put_LocalityName(BSTR bstrLocalityName)
```

```
HRESULT get_PostalAddress(BSTR* retval)
```

```
HRESULT put_PostalAddress(BSTR bstrPostalAddress)
```

```
HRESULT get_TelephoneNumber(BSTR* retval)
```

```
HRESULT put_TelephoneNumber(BSTR bstrTelephoneNumber)
```

```
HRESULT get_FaxNumber(BSTR* retval)
```

```
HRESULT put_FaxNumber(BSTR bstrFaxNumber)
```

```
HRESULT get_SeeAlso(VARIANT* retval)
```

```
HRESULT put_SeeAlso(VARIANT vSeeAlso)
```

```
HRESULT get_BusinessCategory(BSTR* retval)
```

```
HRESULT put_BusinessCategory(BSTR bstrBusinessCategory)
```

IADsPathname Interface

The IADsPathname interface provides a way to access the elements of an Active Directory ADsPath.

```
HRESULT Set(BSTR bstrADsPath, long lnSetType)
```

```
HRESULT SetDisplayType(long lnDisplayType)
```

```
HRESULT Retrieve(long lnFormatType, BSTR* pbstrADsPath)
```

```
HRESULT GetNumElements(long* plnNumPathElements)
```

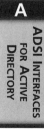

A

ADSI INTERFACES FOR ACTIVE DIRECTORY

```
HRESULT GetElement(long lnElementIndex, BSTR* pbstrElement)

HRESULT AddLeafElement(BSTR bstrLeafElement)

HRESULT RemoveLeafElement(void)

HRESULT CopyPath(IDispatch * ppAdsPath)

HRESULT GetEscapedElement(long lnReserved, BSTR bstrInStr,
➡BSTR* pbstrOutStr)

HRESULT get_EscapedMode(long* retval)

HRESULT put_EscapedMode(long lnEscapedMode)
```

IADsPrintQueue Interface

The IADsPrintQueue interface provides access to information about a specific printer on the network, such as the type of printer, its description, and its location.

```
HRESULT get_PrinterPath(BSTR* retval)

HRESULT put_PrinterPath(BSTR bstrPrinterPath)

HRESULT get_Model(BSTR* retval)

HRESULT put_Model(BSTR bstrModel)

HRESULT get_Datatype(BSTR* retval)

HRESULT put_Datatype(BSTR bstrDatatype)

HRESULT get_PrintProcessor(BSTR* retval)

HRESULT put_PrintProcessor(BSTR bstrPrintProcessor)

HRESULT get_Description(BSTR* retval)

HRESULT put_Description(BSTR bstrDescription)

HRESULT get_Location(BSTR* retval)

HRESULT put_Location(BSTR bstrLocation)

HRESULT get_StartTime(DATE* retval)

HRESULT put_StartTime(DATE daStartTime)

HRESULT get_UntilTime(DATE* retval)

HRESULT put_UntilTime(DATE daUntilTime)

HRESULT get_DefaultJobPriority(long* retval)

HRESULT put_DefaultJobPriority(long lnDefaultJobPriority)

HRESULT get_Priority(long* retval)

HRESULT put_Priority(long lnPriority)
```

```
HRESULT get_BannerPage(BSTR* retval)

HRESULT put_BannerPage(BSTR bstrBannerPage)

HRESULT get_PrintDevices(VARIANT* retval)

HRESULT put_PrintDevices(VARIANT vPrintDevices)

HRESULT get_NetAddresses(VARIANT* retval)

HRESULT put_NetAddresses(VARIANT vNetAddresses)
```

IADsPrintQueueOperations Interface

The IADsPrintQueueOperations interface provides functions for stopping, starting, and inspecting the contents of the print queue.

```
HRESULT get_Status(long* retval)

HRESULT PrintJobs(IADsCollection * pObject)

HRESULT Pause(void)

HRESULT Resume(void)

HRESULT Purge(void)
```

IADsProperty Interface

The IADsProperty interface provides a way to access attribute definition information in the abstract schema. Chapter 15 describes the IADsProperty interface.

```
HRESULT get_OID(BSTR* retval)

HRESULT put_OID(BSTR bstrOID)

HRESULT get_Syntax(BSTR* retval)

HRESULT put_Syntax(BSTR bstrSyntax)

HRESULT get_MaxRange(long* retval)

HRESULT put_MaxRange(long lnMaxRange)

HRESULT get_MinRange(long* retval)

HRESULT put_MinRange(long lnMinRange)

HRESULT get_MultiValued(VARIANT_BOOL* retval)

HRESULT put_MultiValued(VARIANT_BOOL fMultiValued)

HRESULT Qualifiers(IADsCollection * ppQualifiers)
```

A

ADSI INTERFACES FOR ACTIVE DIRECTORY

IADsPropertyEntry Interface

The IADsPropertyEntry interface lets you access individual properties of an object in the property cache. Chapter 12 describes the IADsPropertyEntry interface.

```
HRESULT Clear(void)

HRESULT get_Name(BSTR* retval)

HRESULT put_Name(BSTR bstrName)

HRESULT get_ADsType(long* retval)

HRESULT put_ADsType(long lnADsType)

HRESULT get_ControlCode(long* retval)

HRESULT put_ControlCode(long lnControlCode)

HRESULT get_Values(VARIANT* retval)

HRESULT put_Values(VARIANT vValues)
```

IADsPropertyList Interface

The IADsPropertyList interface provides a way to access the attributes of an object in the property cache as a collection of attributes. IADsPropertyList is described in Chapter 12.

```
HRESULT get_PropertyCount(long* plCount)

HRESULT Next(VARIANT* pVariant)

HRESULT Skip(long cElements)

HRESULT Reset(void)

HRESULT Item(VARIANT varIndex, VARIANT* pVariant)

HRESULT GetPropertyItem(BSTR bstrName, LONG lnADsType, VARIANT* pVariant)

HRESULT PutPropertyItem(VARIANT varData)

HRESULT ResetPropertyItem(VARIANT varEntry)

HRESULT PurgePropertyList(void)
```

IADsPropertyValue Interface

The IADsPropertyValue interface provides access to the individual attribute values in the property cache. You obtain an IADsPropertyValue interface from the IADsPropertyList interface. Chapter 12 describes the IADsPropertyValue interface.

```
HRESULT Clear(void)

HRESULT get_ADsType(long* retval)

HRESULT put_ADsType(long lnADsType)

HRESULT get_DNString(BSTR* retval)

HRESULT put_DNString(BSTR bstrDNString)

HRESULT get_CaseExactString(BSTR* retval)

HRESULT put_CaseExactString(BSTR bstrCaseExactString)

HRESULT get_CaseIgnoreString(BSTR* retval)

HRESULT put_CaseIgnoreString(BSTR bstrCaseIgnoreString)

HRESULT get_PrintableString(BSTR* retval)

HRESULT put_PrintableString(BSTR bstrPrintableString)

HRESULT get_NumericString(BSTR* retval)

HRESULT put_NumericString(BSTR bstrNumericString)

HRESULT get_Boolean(long* retval)

HRESULT put_Boolean(long lnBoolean)

HRESULT get_Integer(long* retval)

HRESULT put_Integer(long lnInteger)

HRESULT get_OctetString(VARIANT* retval)

HRESULT put_OctetString(VARIANT vOctetString)

HRESULT get_SecurityDescriptor(IDispatch * retval)

HRESULT put_SecurityDescriptor(IDispatch* pSecurityDescriptor)

HRESULT get_LargeInteger(IDispatch * retval)

HRESULT put_LargeInteger(IDispatch* pLargeInteger)

HRESULT get_UTCTime(DATE* retval)

HRESULT put_UTCTime(DATE daUTCTime)
```

IADsPropertyValue2 Interface

The IADsPropertyValue2 interface provides an alternative mechanism to access
values in the property cache. You obtain an IADsPropertyValue interface from the
IADsPropertyList interface. Chapter 12 describes the IADsPropertyValue2 interface.

```
HRESULT GetObjectProperty(long* lnADsType, VARIANT* pvProp)

HRESULT PutObjectProperty(long lnADsType, VARIANT vProp)
```

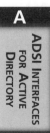

A

ADSI INTERFACES FOR ACTIVE DIRECTORY

IADsSecurityDescriptor Interface

The IADsSecurityDescriptor interface provides access to the elements of Active Directory security descriptor.

```
HRESULT get_Revision(long* retval)

HRESULT put_Revision(long lnRevision)

HRESULT get_Control(long* retval)

HRESULT put_Control(long lnControl)

HRESULT get_Owner(BSTR* retval)

HRESULT put_Owner(BSTR bstrOwner)

HRESULT get_OwnerDefaulted(VARIANT_BOOL* retval)

HRESULT put_OwnerDefaulted(VARIANT_BOOL fOwnerDefaulted)

HRESULT get_Group(BSTR* retval)

HRESULT put_Group(BSTR bstrGroup)

HRESULT get_GroupDefaulted(VARIANT_BOOL* retval)

HRESULT put_GroupDefaulted(VARIANT_BOOL fGroupDefaulted)

HRESULT get_DiscretionaryAcl(IDispatch * retval)

HRESULT put_DiscretionaryAcl(IDispatch* pDiscretionaryAcl)

HRESULT get_DaclDefaulted(VARIANT_BOOL* retval)

HRESULT put_DaclDefaulted(VARIANT_BOOL fDaclDefaulted)

HRESULT get_SystemAcl(IDispatch* retval)

HRESULT put_SystemAcl(IDispatch* pSystemAcl)

HRESULT get_SaclDefaulted(VARIANT_BOOL* retval)

HRESULT put_SaclDefaulted(VARIANT_BOOL fSaclDefaulted)

HRESULT CopySecurityDescriptor(IDispatch * ppSecurityDescriptor)
```

IADsSyntax Interface

The IADsSyntax interface provides access to a syntax object in the abstract schema. Chapter 15 describes the IADsSyntax interface.

```
HRESULT get_OleAutoDataType(long* retval)

HRESULT put_OleAutoDataType(long lnOleAutoDataType)
```

IADsUser Interface

The IADsUser interface provides access to the attributes of Active Directory user object. Chapter 14 describes the IADsUser interface.

```
HRESULT get_BadLoginAddress(BSTR* retval)

HRESULT get_BadLoginCount(long* retval)

HRESULT get_LastLogin(DATE* retval)

HRESULT get_LastLogoff(DATE* retval)

HRESULT get_LastFailedLogin(DATE* retval)

HRESULT get_PasswordLastChanged(DATE* retval)

HRESULT get_Description(BSTR* retval)

HRESULT put_Description(BSTR bstrDescription)

HRESULT get_Division(BSTR* retval)

HRESULT put_Division(BSTR bstrDivision)

HRESULT get_Department(BSTR* retval)

HRESULT put_Department(BSTR bstrDepartment)

HRESULT get_EmployeeID(BSTR* retval)

HRESULT put_EmployeeID(BSTR bstrEmployeeID)

HRESULT get_FullName(BSTR* retval)

HRESULT put_FullName(BSTR bstrFullName)

HRESULT get_FirstName(BSTR* retval)

HRESULT put_FirstName(BSTR bstrFirstName)

HRESULT get_LastName(BSTR* retval)

HRESULT put_LastName(BSTR bstrLastName)

HRESULT get_OtherName(BSTR* retval)

HRESULT put_OtherName(BSTR bstrOtherName)

HRESULT get_NamePrefix(BSTR* retval)

HRESULT put_NamePrefix(BSTR bstrNamePrefix)

HRESULT get_NameSuffix(BSTR* retval)

HRESULT put_NameSuffix(BSTR bstrNameSuffix)

HRESULT get_Title(BSTR* retval)

HRESULT put_Title(BSTR bstrTitle)
```

```
HRESULT get_Manager(BSTR* retval)

HRESULT put_Manager(BSTR bstrManager)

HRESULT get_TelephoneHome(VARIANT* retval)

HRESULT put_TelephoneHome(VARIANT vTelephoneHome)

HRESULT get_TelephoneMobile(VARIANT* retval)

HRESULT put_TelephoneMobile(VARIANT vTelephoneMobile)

HRESULT get_TelephoneNumber(VARIANT* retval)

HRESULT put_TelephoneNumber(VARIANT vTelephoneNumber)

HRESULT get_TelephonePager(VARIANT* retval)

HRESULT put_TelephonePager(VARIANT vTelephonePager)

HRESULT get_FaxNumber(VARIANT* retval)

HRESULT put_FaxNumber(VARIANT vFaxNumber)

HRESULT get_OfficeLocations(VARIANT* retval)

HRESULT put_OfficeLocations(VARIANT vOfficeLocations)

HRESULT get_PostalAddresses(VARIANT* retval)

HRESULT put_PostalAddresses(VARIANT vPostalAddresses)

HRESULT get_PostalCodes(VARIANT* retval)

HRESULT put_PostalCodes(VARIANT vPostalCodes)

HRESULT get_SeeAlso(VARIANT* retval)

HRESULT put_SeeAlso(VARIANT vSeeAlso)

HRESULT get_AccountDisabled(VARIANT_BOOL* retval)

HRESULT put_AccountDisabled(VARIANT_BOOL fAccountDisabled)

HRESULT get_AccountExpirationDate(DATE* retval)

HRESULT put_AccountExpirationDate(DATE daAccountExpirationDate)

HRESULT get_GraceLoginsAllowed(long* retval)

HRESULT put_GraceLoginsAllowed(long lnGraceLoginsAllowed)

HRESULT get_GraceLoginsRemaining(long* retval)

HRESULT put_GraceLoginsRemaining(long lnGraceLoginsRemaining)

HRESULT get_IsAccountLocked(VARIANT_BOOL* retval)

HRESULT put_IsAccountLocked(VARIANT_BOOL fIsAccountLocked)

HRESULT get_LoginHours(VARIANT* retval)

HRESULT put_LoginHours(VARIANT vLoginHours)
```

```
HRESULT get_LoginWorkstations(VARIANT* retval)

HRESULT put_LoginWorkstations(VARIANT vLoginWorkstations)

HRESULT get_MaxLogins(long* retval)

HRESULT put_MaxLogins(long lnMaxLogins)

HRESULT get_MaxStorage(long* retval)

HRESULT put_MaxStorage(long lnMaxStorage)

HRESULT get_PasswordExpirationDate(DATE* retval)

HRESULT put_PasswordExpirationDate(DATE daPasswordExpirationDate)

HRESULT get_PasswordMinimumLength(long* retval)

HRESULT put_PasswordMinimumLength(long lnPasswordMinimumLength)

HRESULT get_PasswordRequired(VARIANT_BOOL* retval)

HRESULT put_PasswordRequired(VARIANT_BOOL fPasswordRequired)

HRESULT get_RequireUniquePassword(VARIANT_BOOL* retval)

HRESULT put_RequireUniquePassword(VARIANT_BOOL fRequireUniquePassword)

HRESULT put_EmailAddress(BSTR bstrEmailAddress)

HRESULT get_EmailAddress(BSTR* retval)

HRESULT get_HomeDirectory(BSTR* retval)

HRESULT put_HomeDirectory(BSTR bstrHomeDirectory)

HRESULT get_Languages(VARIANT* retval)

HRESULT put_Languages(VARIANT vLanguages)

HRESULT get_Profile(BSTR* retval)

HRESULT put_Profile(BSTR bstrProfile)

HRESULT get_LoginScript(BSTR* retval)

HRESULT put_LoginScript(BSTR bstrLoginScript)

HRESULT get_Picture(VARIANT* retval)

HRESULT put_Picture(VARIANT vPicture)

HRESULT get_HomePage(BSTR* retval)

HRESULT put_HomePage(BSTR bstrHomePage)

HRESULT Groups(IADsMembers * ppGroups)

HRESULT SetPassword(BSTR NewPassword)

HRESULT ChangePassword(BSTR bstrOldPassword, BSTR bstrNewPassword)
```

IDirectorySchemaMgmt Interface

The IDirectorySchemaMgmt interface provides a simplified interface to the "real" Active
Directory schema (as opposed to the abstract schema). This interface is not supported in
the current version of ADSI.

```
HRESULT EnumAttributes(LPWSTR* ppszAttrNames, DWORD dwNumAttributes,
➥PADS_ATTR_DEF* ppAttrDefinition, DWORD* pdwNumAttributes)
```

```
HRESULT CreateAttributeDefinition(LPWSTR pszAttributeName,
➥PADS_ATTR_DEF pAttributeDefinition)
```

```
HRESULT WriteAttributeDefinition(LPWSTR pszAttributeName,
➥PADS_ATTR_DEF pAttributeDefinition)
```

```
HRESULT DeleteAttributeDefinition(LPWSTR pszAttributeName)
```

```
HRESULT EnumClasses(LPWSTR* ppszClassNames, DWORD dwNumClasses,
➥PADS_CLASS_DEF* ppClassDefinition, DWORD* pdwNumClasses)
```

```
HRESULT WriteClassDefinition(LPWSTR pszClassName,
➥PADS_CLASS_DEF pClassDefinition)
```

```
HRESULT CreateClassDefinition(LPWSTR pszClassName,
➥PADS_CLASS_DEF pClassDefinition)
```

```
HRESULT DeleteClassDefinition(LPWSTR pszClassName)
```

IDirectorySearch Interface

The IDirectorySearch provides a relational table–like interface to an LDAP search.
Chapter 13, "Searching Active Directory with ADSI," describes the IDirectorySearch
interface.

```
HRESULT SetSearchPreference(PADS_SEARCHPREF_INFO pSearchPrefs,
➥DWORD dwNumPrefs)
```

```
HRESULT ExecuteSearch(LPWSTR pszSearchFilter, LPWSTR* pAttributeNames,
➥DWORD dwNumberAttributes, PADS_SEARCH_HANDLE phSearchResult)
```

```
HRESULT AbandonSearch(ADS_SEARCH_HANDLE phSearchResult)
```

```
HRESULT GetFirstRow(ADS_SEARCH_HANDLE hSearchResult)
```

```
HRESULT GetNextRow(ADS_SEARCH_HANDLE hSearchResult)
```

```
HRESULT GetPreviousRow(ADS_SEARCH_HANDLE hSearchResult)
```

```
HRESULT GetNextColumnName(ADS_SEARCH_HANDLE hSearchHandle,
➥LPWSTR* ppszColumnName)
```

```
HRESULT GetColumn(ADS_SEARCH_HANDLE hSearchResult, LPWSTR szColumnName,
➥PADS_SEARCH_COLUMN pSearchColumn)
```

```
HRESULT FreeColumn(PADS_SEARCH_COLUMN pSearchColumn)
```

```
HRESULT CloseSearchHandle(ADS_SEARCH_HANDLE hSearchResult)
```

IDirectoryObject Interface

The IDirectoryObject interface is another generic object interface (like IADs). It provides access to the attributes of a directory object using an array of ADS_ATTR_INFO structures, instead of through the property cache interface used by IADs. Chapter 12 describes the IDirectoryObject interface.

```
HRESULT GetObjectInformation(PADS_OBJECT_INFO* ppObjInfo)
➥HRESULT GetObjectAttributes(LPWSTR* pAttributeNames,
➥DWORD dwNumberAttributes, PADS_ATTR_INFO* ppAttributeEntries,
➥DWORD* pdwNumAttributesReturned)

HRESULT SetObjectAttributes(PADS_ATTR_INFO pAttributeEntries,
➥DWORD dwNumAttributes, DWORD* pdwNumAttributesModified)

HRESULT CreateDSObject(LPWSTR pszRDNName,
➥PADS_ATTR_INFO pAttributeEntries,
➥DWORD dwNumAttributes, IDispatch * ppObject)

HRESULT DeleteDSObject(LPWSTR pszRDNName)
```

Microsoft Windows 2000 LDAP Functions

LDAP Session Management Functions

```
LDAP* cldap_open( PCHAR HostName, ULONG PortNumber )

ULONG ldap_bind( LDAP* ld, const PCHAR dn, const PCHAR cred, ULONG method )

ULONG ldap_bind_s( LDAP* ld, const PCHAR dn, const PCHAR cred,
➥ULONG method )

ULONG ldap_cleanup( HANDLE hInstance )

LDAP* ldap_conn_from_msg( LDAP* PrimaryConn, LDAPMessage* res )

ULONG ldap_connect( LDAP* ld, struct l_timeval* timeout )

LDAP* ldap_init( const PCHAR HostName, ULONG PortNumber )

LDAP* ldap_open( const PCHAR HostName, ULONG PortNumber )

INT ldap_sasl_bind( LDAP* ExternalHandle, const PCHAR DistName,
➥const PCHAR AuthMechanism, const BERVAL* cred,
➥PLDAPControl* ServerCtrls, PLDAPControl* ClientCtrls,
➥int* MessageNumber )
```

```
INT ldap_sasl_bind_s( LDAP* ExternalHandle, const PCHAR DistName,
➥const PCHAR AuthMechanism, const BERVAL* cred,
➥PLDAPControl* ServerCtrls, PLDAPControl* ClientCtrls,
➥PBERVAL* ServerData )

ULONG ldap_simple_bind( LDAP* ld, const PCHAR dn, const PCHAR passwd )

ULONG ldap_simple_bind_s( LDAP* ld, const PCHAR dn, const PCHAR passwd )

LDAP* ldap_sslinit( PCHAR HostName, ULONG PortNumber, int secure )

ULONG ldap_startup( PLDAP_VERSION_INFO version, HANDLE* Instance )

ULONG ldap_unbind( LDAP* ld )

ULONG ldap_unbind_s( LDAP* ld )
```

LDAP Search and Compare Functions

```
ULONG ldap_check_filter( LDAP* ld, PCHAR SearchFilter )

ULONG ldap_compare( LDAP* ld, const PCHAR dn, const PCHAR attr,
➥PCHAR value )

ULONG ldap_compare_ext( LDAP* ld, const PCHAR dn, const PCHAR Attr,
➥const PCHAR Value, struct berval* Data,
➥PLDAPControl* ServerControls, PLDAPControl* ClientControls,
➥ULONG* MessageNumber )

ULONG ldap_compare_ext_s( LDAP* ld, const PCHAR dn, const PCHAR Attr,
➥const PCHAR Value, struct berval* Data,
➥PLDAPControl* ServerControls, PLDAPControl* ClientControls )

ULONG ldap_compare_s( LDAP* ld, const PCHAR dn, const PCHAR attr,
➥PCHAR value )

ULONG ldap_escape_filter_element( PCHAR sourceFilterElement,
➥ULONG sourceLength, PCHAR destFilterElement, ULONG destLength )

ULONG ldap_search( LDAP* ld, const PCHAR base, ULONG scope,
➥const PCHAR filter, PCHAR attrs[], ULONG attrsonly )

ULONG ldap_search_ext( LDAP* ld, const PCHAR base, ULONG scope,
➥const PCHAR filter, PCHAR attrs[], ULONG attrsonly,
➥PLDAPControl* ServerControls, PLDAPControl* ClientControls,
➥ULONG TimeLimit, ULONG SizeLimit, ULONG* MessageNumber )

ULONG ldap_search_ext_s( LDAP* ld, const PCHAR base, ULONG scope,
➥const PCHAR filter, PCHAR attrs[], ULONG attrsonly,
➥PLDAPControl* ServerControls, PLDAPControl* ClientControls,
➥struct l_timeval* timeout, ULONG SizeLimit, LDAPMessage** res )
```

```
ULONG ldap_search_s( LDAP* ld, const PCHAR base, ULONG scope,
➥const PCHAR filter, PCHAR attrs[], ULONG attrsonly,
➥LDAPMessage** res )

ULONG ldap_search_st( LDAP* ld, const PCHAR base, ULONG scope,
➥const PCHAR filter, PCHAR attrs[], ULONG attrsonly,
➥struct l_timeval* timeout, LDAPMessage** res )
```

LDAP Result Parsing Functions

```
VOID ber_bvfree( struct berval* bv )

ULONG ldap_abandon( LDAP* ld, ULONG msgid )

ULONG ldap_count_entries( LDAP* ld, LDAPMessage* res )

ULONG ldap_count_references( LDAP* ld, LDAPMessage* res )

ULONG ldap_count_values( PCHAR* vals )

ULONG ldap_count_values_len( struct berval** vals )

PCHAR ldap_first_attribute( LDAP* ld, LDAPMessage* entry,
➥BerElement** ptr )

LDAPMessage* ldap_first_entry( LDAP* ld, LDAPMessage* res )

LDAPMessage* ldap_first_reference( LDAP* ld, LDAPMessage* res )

PCHAR ldap_get_dn( LDAP* ld, LDAPMessage* entry )

PCHAR* ldap_get_values( LDAP* ld, LDAPMessage* entry, const PCHAR attr )

WINLDAPAPI struct berval **LDAPAPI ldap_get_values_len
➥( LDAP* ExternalHandle, LDAPMessage* Message, const PCHAR attr )

VOID ldap_memfree( PCHAR Block )

ULONG ldap_msgfree( LDAPMessage* res )

PCHAR ldap_next_attribute( LDAP* ld, LDAPMessage* entry, BerElement* ptr )

LDAPMessage* ldap_next_entry( LDAP* ld, LDAPMessage* entry )

LDAPMessage* ldap_next_reference( LDAP* ld, LDAPMessage* entry )

ULONG ldap_parse_reference( LDAP* Connection, LDAPMessage* ResultMessage,
➥PCHAR** Referrals )

ULONG ldap_parse_result( LDAP* Connection, LDAPMessage* ResultMessage,
➥ULONG* ReturnCode, PCHAR* MatchedDNs, PCHAR* ErrorMessage,
➥PCHAR** Referrals, PLDAPControl** ServerControls, BOOLEAN Freeit )
```

```
ULONG ldap_result( LDAP* ld, ULONG msgid, ULONG all,
➡struct l_timeval* timeout, LDAPMessage** res )

ULONG ldap_value_free( PCHAR* vals )

ULONG ldap_value_free_len( struct berval** vals )
```

LDAP Addition and Modification Functions

```
ULONG ldap_add( LDAP* ld, PCHAR dn, LDAPMod* attrs[] )

ULONG ldap_add_ext( LDAP* ld, const PCHAR dn, LDAPMod* attrs[],
➡PLDAPControl* ServerControls, PLDAPControl* ClientControls,
➡ULONG* MessageNumber )

ULONG ldap_add_ext_s( LDAP* ld, const PCHAR dn, LDAPMod* attrs[],
➡PLDAPControl* ServerControls, PLDAPControl* ClientControls )

ULONG ldap_add_s( LDAP* ld, PCHAR dn, LDAPMod* attrs[] )

ULONG ldap_delete( LDAP* ld, PCHAR dn )

ULONG ldap_delete_ext( LDAP* ld, const PCHAR dn,
➡PLDAPControl* ServerControls, PLDAPControl* ClientControls,
➡ULONG* MessageNumber )

ULONG ldap_delete_ext_s( LDAP* ld, const PCHAR dn,
➡PLDAPControl* ServerControls, PLDAPControl* ClientControls )

ULONG ldap_delete_s( LDAP* ld, PCHAR dn )

ULONG ldap_modify( LDAP* ld, PCHAR dn, LDAPMod* mods[] )

ULONG ldap_modify_ext( LDAP* ld, const PCHAR dn, LDAPMod* mods[],
➡PLDAPControl* ServerControls, PLDAPControl* ClientControls,
➡ULONG* MessageNumber )

ULONG ldap_modify_ext_s( LDAP* ld, const PCHAR dn, LDAPMod* mods[],
➡PLDAPControl* ServerControls, PLDAPControl* ClientControls )

ULONG ldap_modify_s( LDAP* ld, PCHAR dn, LDAPMod* mods[] )

ULONG ldap_modrdn( LDAP* ExternalHandle, const PCHAR DistinguishedName,
➡const PCHAR NewDistinguishedName )

ULONG ldap_modrdn_s( LDAP* ExternalHandle, const PCHAR DistinguishedName,
➡const PCHAR NewDistinguishedName )

ULONG ldap_modrdn2( LDAP* ExternalHandle, const PCHAR DistinguishedName,
➡const PCHAR NewDistinguishedName, INT DeleteOldRdn )

ULONG ldap_modrdn2_s( LDAP* ExternalHandle, const PCHAR DistinguishedName,
➡const PCHAR NewDistinguishedName, INT DeleteOldRdn )
```

```
ULONG ldap_rename_ext( LDAP* ld, const PCHAR dn, const PCHAR NewRDN,
➥const PCHAR NewParent, INT DeleteOldRdn,
➥PLDAPControl* ServerControls, PLDAPControl* ClientControls,
➥ULONG* MessageNumber )

ULONG ldap_rename_ext_s( LDAP* ld, const PCHAR dn, const PCHAR NewRDN,
➥const PCHAR NewParent, INT DeleteOldRdn,
➥PLDAPControl* ServerControls, PLDAPControl* ClientControls )
```

LDAP Extension Functions

```
ULONG ldap_close_extended_op( LDAP* ld, ULONG MessageNumber )

ULONG ldap_controls_free( LDAPControl** Control )

ULONG ldap_control_free( LDAPControl* Control )

ULONG ldap_create_page_control( PLDAP ExternalHandle, ULONG PageSize,
➥struct berval* Cookie, UCHAR IsCritical, PLDAPControl* Control )

ULONG ldap_create_sort_control( PLDAP ExternalHandle,
➥PLDAPSortKey* SortKeys, UCHAR IsCritical, PLDAPControl* Control )

ULONG ldap_encode_sort_control( PLDAP ExternalHandle,
➥PLDAPSortKey* SortKeys, PLDAPControl Control, BOOLEAN Criticality )

ULONG ldap_extended_operation( LDAP* ld, const PCHAR Oid,
➥struct berval* Data, PLDAPControl* ServerControls,
➥PLDAPControl* ClientControls, ULONG* MessageNumber )

ULONG ldap_get_next_page( PLDAP ExternalHandle, PLDAPSearch SearchHandle,
➥ULONG PageSize, ULONG* MessageNumber )

ULONG ldap_get_next_page_s( PLDAP ExternalHandle, PLDAPSearch
➥SearchHandle,struct l_timeval* timeout, ULONG PageSize,
➥ULONG* TotalCount, LDAPMessage** Results )

ULONG ldap_get_option( LDAP* ld, int option, void* outvalue )

ULONG ldap_get_paged_count( PLDAP ExternalHandle, PLDAPSearch SearchBlock,
➥ULONG* TotalCount, PLDAPMessage Results )

ULONG ldap_parse_extended_result( LDAP* Connection,
➥LDAPMessage* ResultMessage, PCHAR* ResultOID,
➥struct berval** ResultData, BOOLEAN Freeit )

ULONG ldap_parse_page_control( PLDAP ExternalHandle,
➥PLDAPControl* ServerControls, ULONG* TotalCount,
➥struct berval** Cookie )

ULONG ldap_parse_sort_control( PLDAP ExternalHandle,
➥PLDAPControl* Control, ULONG* Result, PCHAR* Attribute )
```

```
ULONG ldap_search_abandon_page( PLDAP ExternalHandle,
➥PLDAPSearch SearchBlock )
```

```
PLDAPSearch ldap_search_init_page( PLDAP ExternalHandle,
➥const PCHAR DistinguishedName, ULONG ScopeOfSearch,
➥const PCHAR SearchFilter, PCHAR AttributeList[],
➥ULONG AttributesOnly, PLDAPControl* ServerControls,
➥PLDAPControl* ClientControls, ULONG PageTimeLimit,
➥ULONG TotalSizeLimit, PLDAPSortKey* SortKeys )
```

```
ULONG ldap_set_option( LDAP* ld, int option, const void* invalue )
```

LDAP Error Functions

```
ULONG LdapGetLastError( VOID )
```

```
ULONG LdapMapErrorToWin32( ULONG LdapError )
```

```
PCHAR ldap_err2string( ULONG err )
```

```
void ldap_perror( LDAP* ld, const PCHAR msg )
```

```
ULONG ldap_result2error( LDAP* ld, LDAPMessage* res, ULONG freeit )
```

LDAP Distinguished Name and String Manipulation Functions

```
int LdapUTF8ToUnicode( LPCSTR lpSrcStr, int cchSrc, LPSTR lpDestStr,
➥int cchDest )
```

```
int LdapUnicodeToUTF8( LPCWSTR lpSrcStr, int cchSrc, LPSTR lpDestStr,
➥int cchDest )
```

```
PCHAR* ldap_explode_dn( const PCHAR dn, ULONG notypes )
```

```
PCHAR ldap_dn2ufn( const PCHAR dn )
```

```
ULONG ldap_ufn2dn( const PCHAR ufn, PCHAR* pDn )
```

INDEX

R

Other Related Titles

What's on the CD-ROM

The companion CD-ROM contains sample files, a demo version of Aelita software, which provides systems administrators with a central location for collecting, storing, and analyzing information contained in event logs. It offers a convenient method for event monitoring, automatic notification, and alerting..

Windows 95/98 or NT 4/Windows 2000 Installation Instructions

1. Insert the CD-ROM into your CD-ROM drive.
2. From the Windows 95 desktop, double-click the My Computer icon.
3. Double-click the icon representing your CD-ROM drive.
4. Double-click the icon titled START.EXE to run the CD-ROM interface.

NOTE

If Windows 95 is installed on your computer, and you have the AutoPlay feature enabled, the START.EXE program starts automatically whenever you insert the disc into your CD-ROM drive.